# AN INTRODUCTION TO PROGRAMMING USING MACINTOSH™ PASCAL

# AN INTRODUCTION TO PROGRAMMING USING MACINTOSH™ PASCAL


**PAUL PRITCHARD**
UNIVERSITY OF QUEENSLAND

**ADDISON-WESLEY PUBLISHING COMPANY**

Sydney • Wokingham, England • Reading, Massachusetts
Menlo Park, California • New York • Don Mills, Ontario
Amsterdam • Bonn • Singapore
Tokyo • Madrid • San Juan

The programs presented in this book have been included for their instructional value. They have been written and tested with care but are not guaranteed for any particular purpose. The publisher does not offer any warranties or representations, nor does it accept any liabilities with respect to the programs.

Cover design by 20/20 Graphics, Iver, Bucks.
Text design by Roger Walker/Linde Hardaker.
Typeset by Morton Computer Services Ltd, Scarborough.
Printed in Singapore by Times Printers.

First printed in 1988.

**British Library Cataloguing in Publication Data**

Pritchard, Paul
An introduction to programming using
Macintosh Pascal.
1. Macintosh (Computer) — Programming
2. PASCAL (Computer program language)
I. Title
005.2'65 QA76.8.M3

ISBN 0-201-17539-8

**Library of Congress Cataloguing in Publication Data**

Pritchard, Paul. 1951–
An introduction to programmming using Macintosh Pascal / Paul Pritchard
p. cm.
On t.p. the registered trademark symbol "TM" is superscript following "Macintosh" in the title.
Includes index.
ISBN 0-201-17539-8:
1. Macintosh (Computer) — Programming. 2. Pascal (Computer program language) I. Title.
QA76.8.M3P75 1988
005.265—dc 19

*To my mother and father*

# PREFACE

This book is aimed primarily at students taking an introductory course in computer programming, where the programming language is Pascal, and practical work is done using either Macintosh Pascal or Lightspeed Pascal.† It is intended to be suitable for both one-semester (half-year) and two-semester (full-year) university-level courses. It contains:

- A modern and thorough introduction to solving programming problems in a procedural language;
- A self-contained guide to the use of the Macintosh and the Macintosh Pascal programming environment;
- A complete description of ANSI Standard Pascal;
- A complete description of Macintosh Pascal's extensions to and deviations from Standard Pascal; and
- A thorough introduction to the use of Macintosh Pascal's libraries for graphics and numeric programming.

The reader is not assumed to have had any previous exposure to computers or programming, or any mathematical background beyond the level of simple high-school algebra. Nevertheless, the book should prove useful to those with prior programming experience.

The sections that follow elaborate on the book's objectives. It is left to the reader to judge how appropriate these are and how successfully they have been met. The proof is in the pudding, not in the preface.

## Philosophy

The emphasis is fairly and squarely on problem-solving in the domain of programming. Every opportunity is taken to expose the reader to new problems, and to increase the reader's problem-solving ability

†'Macintosh Pascal' will refer to both Macintosh Pascal and Lightspeed Pascal, unless otherwise indicated.

gradually. Particular emphasis is placed on stepwise refinement and program schemas. Each program is developed from its specifications, not presented as a *fait accompli*. Invariants are presented as of practical rather than theoretical interest. They are implicitly used from the start, and are explicitly identified first in Chapter 11, on one-dimensional arrays, in the guise of *general pictures*.

Learning a programming language is of secondary importance. Nevertheless, the student is entitled to a careful and complete description of the language he or she is using, and will find it in this book. Because programming to a recognized standard is important, Standard Pascal is defined as well as Macintosh Pascal, and the differences are described. And whenever one of Macintosh Pascal's predefined subprograms is introduced, it is properly specified.

## Case-studies

Few would dispute that it is very desirable for the beginner to be exposed to a variety of exemplary programs, but programming is the thought process that culminates in a program, not the finished product. Accordingly, a dozen case-studies are tackled and each results in a substantial, meticulously written program that illustrates the use of a particular feature of Pascal. All but one of these programs *is* (not *was*) developed from its specifications using stepwise refinement. Care has been taken to explain every significant design decision.

Most of the case-studies are much larger programming problems than are typically found in introductory texts, and lead to correspondingly larger programs. It is essential for students to be exposed to such problems as early as possible, lest they develop problem-solving habits that do not scale up. Although stepwise refinement reduces large problems to many small ones, it is the programmer who formulates these problems, using skills quite different from those used in solving small, given programming problems (exercises). The student is not asked to solve these large problems, only to follow the processes of their solutions.

## Programming style

This book treats the matter of programming style seriously. All programs and program fragments are written in a consistent and disciplined style, the main features of which are:

- Documentation of the process of stepwise refinement by means of comments representing high-level actions;

- Documentation of the meaning of each variable (unless it is clear from its name or obvious from the context of its use);
- Specification of all (sub)programs; and
- Eschewing global variables.

Every program or fragment of a program is written in accordance with these principles.

## Style of presentation

The philosophy is to expose the student early to a significant sub-language (the required simple types, basic control structures, textual input and output), and then to start solving problems. Further language constructs are introduced as needed, always in a problem-solving context.

Repetition accordingly precedes procedures and functions — no significant problem-solving can be done without it, and to do otherwise is to emphasize language issues when they are not important and cannot be appreciated. Subprograms are the next cab off the rank though, since they are needed as soon as programs get sufficiently complex.

Problems are chosen carefully to require only the language features at hand — problems that have significantly superior alternatives using unfamiliar features are avoided. In any case, the reader is informed whenever new features or concepts can be used to improve a solution, and the improvement appears either in the text or as an exercise.

Syntax is presented formally, in a highly simplified adaptation of Extended Backus Naur Formalism (EBNF), that uses typographic devices and familiar conventions in preference to special grammatical symbols, thereby achieving a written form that is as close as possible to that used in the display of Macintosh Pascal programs. Section A.3 of the Appendix presents the complete syntax of ANSI Standard Pascal in syntax diagrams, and Section A.4 gives a brief explanation of EBNF notation.

## Exercises

There are a great many exercises. Most have solutions at the end of the book. They are arranged to follow the order of material within each chapter, so that it is not necessary to complete a chapter before embarking on the early exercises. No indication of the difficulty of exercises is given. This is a deliberate policy — the difficulty of a programming problem depends on the programmer as much as the problem, and programmers are not normally given difficulty-ratings for their programming tasks. None of the exercises is meant to be beyond the ability of a beginner of average talent.

## Exploiting the Macintosh

This text was conceived to exploit the rich, predefined libraries of Macintosh Pascal to give more realistic and interesting examples than are possible in a generic Pascal text.

A thorough, self-contained introduction to the Macintosh, and to Macintosh Pascal as a programming environment, is given in Chapters 1, 2, and 4. The Macintosh's graphics capabilities are exploited in many case-studies, with an emphasis on getting meaningful and attractive results from a small body of graphics knowledge. Gimmicky programs that produce gee-whiz effects are conspicuously absent — programs are always written to specifications, not to see what interesting displays they might produce.

Macintosh Pascal's extensions for string-processing, which are very attractively done in the main, are exploited in Chapter 14. Chapter 15, on records, indicates how to implement Macintosh Pascal's string-types in Standard Pascal as an abstract data type.

Macintosh Pascal's facility to open random-access files permitting mixed reading and writing is explained in Chapter 16.

Situations in which Lightspeed Pascal differs from Macintosh Pascal are indicated by numbered icons in the margin. These refer the reader to Section A.5 in the Appendix. Although these icons officially represent bug spray cans, for our purposes they are better regarded as sources of light; candles are the obvious choice.

## About the chapters

- Chapters 1 and 2 introduce the Macintosh and Macintosh Pascal's editor. Their exercise sections lead the reader at a Macintosh systematically through all the important aspects.
- Chapter 3 previews Pascal, following the 'Reading Before Writing' school of language learning. It introduces the 'Macaveats' sections that inform the reader of the differences between Macintosh Pascal and ANSI Standard Pascal. Several have been discovered that are not documented by Apple.

- Chapter 4 documents the sophisticated execution features of Macintosh Pascal, and illustrates them using the programs presented in Chapter 3.
- Chapter 5 introduces our method of syntax definition, and presents a sublanguage that will enable the reader to embark on significant problem-solving.
- It is with Chapter 6 that problem-solving starts in earnest. It introduces stepwise refinement and program schemas, and exemplifies thoroughly the use of both in its two case-studies.
- Chapters 7 and 8 introduce functions and procedures, respectively. They are akin in style to Chapter 5, concentrating on explaining these new language features. The examples use subprograms to give improved solutions to previous problems.
- Chapter 9 presents two case-studies that exploit subprograms to solve new problems. It also introduces the fundamentals of Macintosh graphics that are heavily used thereafter.
- Chapter 10 gives the whole story on ordinal types and their associated control structures, in preparation for the following chapter on arrays. Nevertheless, it contains a substantial case-study that thoroughly exploits user-defined types, and provides notes for a further case-study involving graphics in its exercise section.
- Chapter 11, on one-dimensional arrays, is the most important chapter for an introductory course. Many interesting problems can be tackled and the opportunity arises to present invariants in a very natural way (through *general pictures*). Its case-study demonstrates the wisdom of writing general procedures — the graphics for *n*-processor scheduling use exactly the same procedures as for two-processor scheduling.
- Chapter 12 rounds out a most thorough introduction to programming with a discussion and illustration of two important aspects of programming methodology, namely, correctness and efficiency.

Ideally, a one-semester course would cover these first twelve chapters. The remaining chapters do not so much follow on from the ones mentioned as cover special topics. Instructors who, for example, like to introduce sets, records, recursion or string-processing in a first course, should have minimal difficulty selecting the chapters or sections of interest. These chapters contain exercises that do not rely on all the special topics covered previously. There are some dependencies in these chapters:

- Chapter 16 (on files) should be read after Chapter 15 (on records) as is natural;
- Case-study 11 in Chapter 18 makes use of sets (treated in Chapter 17) and Macintosh Pascal strings (treated in Chapter 14); and
- Chapter 20 (on dynamic data structures) assumes knowledge of the material in Chapter 15 (on records) as is inevitable.

## Software supplement

The dozen case-studies are substantial programs. Some of the exercises invite the reader to trace their execution, or to make certain modifications. A software supplement, available from the author, includes all the case-studies and complete subprograms in the book (together with test-drivers when necessary). Any of these programs may be copied freely for non-commercial purposes, provided that they are copied in full (with the source and copyright information retained).

For ordering information, write to 'Dr Paul Pritchard, Department of Computer Science, University of Queensland, St Lucia, Australia 4067'. Alternatively, e-mail may be sent to the author at one of the following addresses:

ACSnet: pap@uqcspe.oz
ARPA: pap%uqcspe.oz@uunet.uu.net
CSNET: pap@uqcspe.oz
UUCP: ...!uunet!munnari!uqcspe.oz!pap
JANET: uqcspe.oz!pap@ukc

Suggestions for improvements to the book are also most welcome, as are unsolicited testimonials.

Paul Pritchard
St Lucia, September 1987

# ACKNOWLEDGMENTS

The material in this book is based on courses given by the author in the Department of Computer Science at Cornell University, and later at the University of Queensland, Australia. Some of it has evolved from the rich store of material accumulated over the years by the professors who taught CS100 at Cornell: to my former colleagues Tim Teitelbaum (especially), Ken Birman, Alan Demers, John Gilbert, Dale 'Downhill' Skeen, and Kay Wagner, my thanks. John Gilbert kindly permitted me to adapt his notes on floating-point arithmetic. The neat sequence of three case-studies on job scheduling was suggested by Nava Aizikowitz. My antipodean colleague, Gordon Rose, generously allowed me to adapt his program for Case-study 12; Mike Henning did likewise for his notes on the Macintosh and Macintosh Pascal. And back in the USA, Chanderjit Bajaj graciously performed important cultural research on my behalf.

I am indebted to David Gries for giving me my chance in the Big Time, for serving as Master to my Apprentice in the art of programming and for his generosity in agreeing to review the manuscript. Andrew Lister gave me the flexitime needed to write the book, and together with other members of the Department of Computer Science at the University of Queensland, helped provide an environment conducive to writing and typesetting. Jim Welsh and John Elder produced syntax diagrams worth emulating. Niklaus Wirth, the Macintosh development team, and the Macintosh Pascal and Lightspeed Pascal development teams, respectively, created a language, a computer, and two programming environments worth writing about. Thanks to all of the above, to C.A.R. Hoare for his encouraging assessment of the book's quality, to Stephen Troth of Addison-Wesley for his support and professionalism, to the reviewers for their constructive suggestions, and to Cheryl Pritchard for proof-reading. Finally, my thanks go to Errol Martin and Özalp Babaoğlu for their friendship and encouragement, and with most gratitude, to Cheryl and Roxanne for their love and forbearance.

The author and publishers also wish to thank the following for permission to reproduce figures and quotations:

- Think Technologies, Inc., for permission to use Table 5.3 (the Macintosh Pascal character set), taken from Appendix E of the Macintosh Pascal Technical Appendix.
- Appleseed Music, Inc. for permission to use the quotation on page 383, taken from:

  ALICE'S RESTAURANT by Arlo Guthrie



Paul Pritchard
St Lucia, September 1987

**Trademark notice**
Macintosh is a trademark licensed to Apple Computer, Inc.; Apple and the Macintosh logo are trademarks of Apple Computer, Inc.; Ada is a trademark of the US Government – Ada Joint Program Office.

The publishers have made every attempt to supply trademark information about company names and products mentioned in this book. All designations used by manufacturers to distinguish their products are printed in initial caps or all caps, where Addison-Wesley was aware of a trademark claim.

# CONTENTS

# 1 ALGORITHMS AND THE MACINTOSH

'Okay,' said Lolita, 'here is where we start.'
— Vladimir Nabokov, *Lolita*

## 1.1 Algorithms

This book is mainly concerned with **algorithms**, which are also the major concern of computer science. Look up 'algorithm' in a dictionary. The second meaning listed in the *Concise Oxford Dictionary* reads 'Process or rules for (esp. machine) calculation etc.' This is close enough to the technical sense of the word, which is a precise, complete description of a course of action. The COD also tells us that the word entered Middle English from the Old French from the medieval Latin from the Arabicized Persian surname of a ninth century mathematician: alKuwarizmi, meaning man of Kuwarizm. The etymology is fascinating, but what interests the computer scientist more, even more than the meaning of the word, is the *process* or *rules* you used when you looked up the word. Because you used an algorithm!

Moreover, if you found the word reasonably quickly — the author took roughly ten seconds — you almost certainly used a quite sophisticated algorithm. (There are, after all, tens of thousands of words in the dictionary.) And it is apparent that you use many other algorithms in the course of your everyday life: when you drive a car, make your own World's Best Barbecue Sauce, knit a scarf. Some would even argue that *all* you do is follow an algorithm, but we shall avoid opening that philosophical can of worms.

Do you come to this book, then, as an expert on the subject? The answer, for most people, is no. The explanation for this seeming paradox is that although most of us may be quite competent at following algorithms, we have much less experience of the much more challenging task of creating them: it is much easier to follow a perfect recipe than to write one, to follow accurate directions than to give them, to follow precise knitting instructions than to write them. Furthermore, the algorithms created by programmers are often much more complex and sophisticated than the aforementioned everyday ones.

Algorithms are abstract. For example, the long-division algorithm (which was widely known before the advent of pocket calculators) is a precise method for calculating the quotient and remainder when one number is divided by another. It deals with numbers, not decimal numerals, and is known to many cultures with many different languages. But any explanation or presentation of the algorithm must involve a language, whether it be written, spoken, signed or whatever, and the resulting description we call a **program**. Algorithms are to programs what numbers are to numerals.

## 1.2 Computers

In this century algorithms have assumed unprecedented importance, because of the invention of man-made devices that are able to follow them with incomparably more speed and freedom from error than can people. These devices, which are currently based on electromagnetic technology, have come to play an indispensable role in modern industrialized society. They are called, as you know, **computers**; more properly, **digital computers**, to distinguish them from **analog computers** which do not follow algorithms but rather use physical models to solve problems. We shall henceforth confine ourselves to the former kind and drop the prefix 'digital'.

Algorithms written to be followed (we say **executed**) by computers are called **computer programs**, and the languages that they are expressed in are called **computer programming languages**. We henceforth limit these terms to computers and drop the prefix 'computer'.

A computer is, in essence, a simple device. It consists of a **central processing unit** (CPU), memory, and input and output devices, which are collectively called the **hardware**. Figure 1.1 represents a computer, with arrows indicating the main directions of flow of information.

The CPU is capable of performing a number of simple opera-

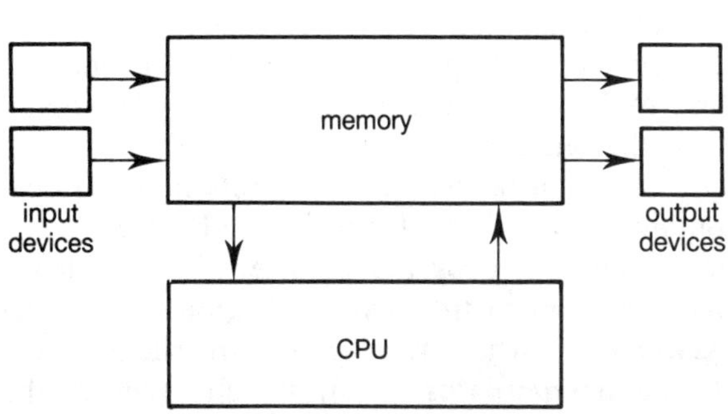


**Figure 1.1**
Information flow in a computer.

**Figure 1.2**
A one Megabyte main memory of 16-bit cells.

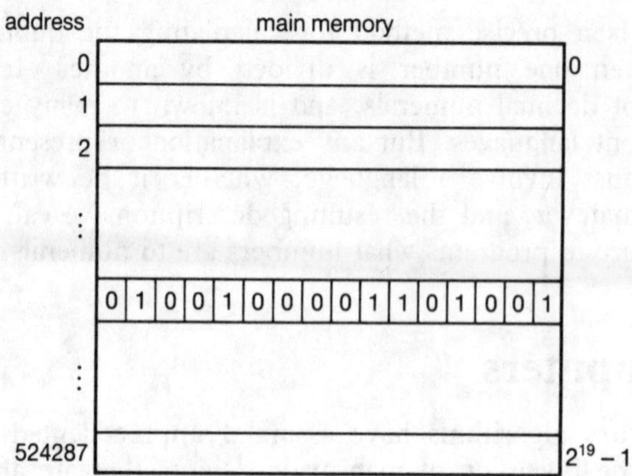


tions, called **machine instructions**. The number of different instructions is typically from 50 to 500. They are performed with essentially no error and at very high speeds, ranging from around 100 000 to 100 million per second (100 Mips). CPUs are currently made from miniature electronic circuits etched on small chips of silicon.

The other major component of a computer is its **memory**, which is divided for economic reasons into two parts: **primary memory** (or **main memory**) and **secondary memory**. The main memory consists of a sequence of identical **cells** (**locations**, **words**), with **addresses** running from zero onwards. A cell can store an instruction or data. It consists of a sequence of **bits** (the term comes from 'binary digit') each of which is zero or one. A minimal cell-size is 8 bits (called a **byte**); this is large enough to store a single character from an alphabet of 256 ($2^8$). Some machines have cells as large as 64 bits. Main memories typically have from 4096 to around 10 million bytes.

The letter 'k' is used to abbreviate the prefix 'kilo', which is ambiguously used to denote either 1000 or 1024 ($2^{10}$). The letter 'M' is used to abbreviate the prefix 'Mega', which denotes one million, but is likely to be an approximation to ($2^{20}$), which equals 1 048 576. These are used in conjunction with 'b' to abbreviate 'byte'. So the last sentence in the previous paragraph is written 'Main memories typically have from 4 kb to 10 Mb.' Figure 1.2 shows a 1 Mb main memory of 16-bit cells, and the bits comprising a typical cell.

The interpretation of the pattern of bits in a cell depends on the CPU. It contains a number of special high-speed cells, called **registers**. These include a **program counter** (PC), which contains the address in main memory of the next instruction to be executed, an **instruction register** (IR), which receives the instruction to be executed, and at least one **accumulator** (AC), which receives the results of

repeat indefinitely the following four steps:
*Fetch into IR the instruction whose address is in PC*;
*Increment PC*;
*Decode instruction in IR*;
*Execute instruction in IR*

**Figure 1.3**
The fetch–execute cycle.

arithmetic and logical operations (much like the display on a pocket calculator). The CPU obeys the simple algorithm shown in Figure 1.3, which is called the **fetch–execute cycle**.

Execution of an instruction might entail copying the contents of an AC into a specified cell of main memory, or copying in the other direction, or adding two ACs (i.e. interpreting them as representing numbers) and storing the result in another AC, or changing the address in the PC, or sending the contents of an AC to an output device (which might interpret it as text), and so on. On a Macintosh, the cell shown in Figure 1.2 represents the pair of characters `Hi` if interpreted as text, 18 537 if interpreted as a whole number, and who-knows-what instruction.

The great speed of computers arises from the technological fact that information can be transferred between the CPU and an arbitrary address in main memory very quickly. The term **RAM** is used to denote such a random-access memory. The CPU gets its instructions at a rate commensurate with its speed in executing them. If there has been a single Great Idea in the invention of computers, it was to store the instructions in the memory (which one more naturally thinks of as containing data).

Main memory is also realized in current technology with silicon chips. Because it is very expensive to provide main memories large enough for the massive amounts of information computers are expected to deal with, a secondary memory is used which is larger in capacity but slower in transferring information (to and from main memory). Secondary memory is most commonly in the form of spinning magnetic disks which record information by magnetizing tiny portions of their surfaces. Typical sizes are from 50 kb to 500 Mb; typical rates of transfer between main and secondary memory are from 10 kb to 1 Mb per second. Although the transfer rate can be high, there is a significant minimum access time before information can be transferred. This is typically from 10 to 100 milliseconds (thousandths of a second, written 'msecs').

**Input and output devices** (**I/O devices**) are used to transfer data between programs executing on the computer and the outside world. Examples are keyboards, card readers (a dying breed), paper tape readers (extinct?), printers, and visual display units (VDUs).

## 1.3 The Macintosh hardware

The members of the Macintosh family of personal computers are based on a Motorola 68 000 CPU chip which supports a cell-size of 32 bits. Standard issue for the original Macintosh was a RAM of 128 kb, a **ROM** (a read-only memory for storing permanent programs and data) of 64 kb, which together constitute the main memory, a 3.5 inch 400 kb single-sided internal microfloppy disk drive as secondary memory, a keyboard and mouse (a position-signaling device) as input devices, and a high resolution bit-mapped display screen, a sound generator, and an Imagewriter dot-matrix printer as output devices. Figure 1.4 presents a well-known still life of a Macintosh and an apple.

The term **bit-mapped** means that the screen is made up of thousands of spots (called **pixels**), each of which is on or off according to whether an associated bit of main memory is 1 or 0; the upshot is that the display can be changed very quickly. The **dot-matrix printer** can print arbitrary pages of black and white pictorial information, such as text or screen images, by printing immense numbers of suitably arranged small black dots.

The next-born was the better nourished Fat Mac, which differed mainly in having a 512 kb RAM. It was followed by the Macintosh Plus, with a 1 Mb RAM, 128 kb ROM, and 800 kb double-sided internal disk drive. More recently, the Macintosh II and the Macintosh SE have appeared, having 256 kb ROMs and various other enhancements. All the Macintoshs have provision for additional secondary memory in the form of external versions of the internal disk drives, and faster, more capacious (and more expensive) hard disk drives.

Your Macintosh will be one of the above (possibly enhanced), but for the purposes of learning to program with Macintosh Pascal, it does not much matter which.

## 1.4 Software

Programming is the process of creating and modifying programs. It is a difficult and challenging intellectual activity, and there seems to be a wide spectrum of levels of aptitude for it. Almost all programming is done by humans; computers are better at executing programs, but hopeless at programming, i.e. at creating programs that solve non-trivial problems. This is because humans have not been able to solve the programming problem of mimicking human intelligence — the Big Enchilada, as someone else said in another context. If you are intellectually ambitious, you need not worry about a shortage of hard programming problems!

A program in main memory for execution by a computer consists of a sequence of machine instructions, each of which is no more

**Figure 1.4**
An artist's impression of a Macintosh (and an apple).

than a pattern of bits. Creating the very long sequences of these very simple instructions needed to solve non-trivial programming problems is a boring, error-prone task, as a single wrong bit will probably cause the program to behave in wild and unpredictable ways. Fortunately, the computer itself can be exploited to relieve much of the burden.

What actually happens when a program is created is this. The underlying algorithm is expressed not in machine instructions but in a high-level programming language, such as Pascal, Modula-2, or Ada. By opening this book at almost any page after the introductory chapters you will see what programs written in Pascal look like. The details need not concern us now; the main point is that the level of expression is much higher than the computer's level of operation.

The program is prepared for execution by first typing it on a computer keyboard, as the input of an executing program called an **editor**. This will store the text as a **file**, that is, a package of information, on secondary memory. Editors allow text files to be prepared and maintained; they permit the insertion, deletion, replacement, and location of arbitrary text. This book was prepared with such an editor. Each computer system provides at least one editor; the best ones are **interactive** (i.e. request the user to enter input data during execution of the program, rather than preparing all input as a file beforehand) and display the text on a VDU as it changes.

Before a program written in a high-level language can be executed it must be translated to machine instructions. This task is accomplished by a program called a **translator**. At least one translator is needed for each high-level language used on a particular computer; all translate to the same machine language.

One of the great advantages of writing programs in high-level languages is that they can be run on any computer with a translator for that language, and should, of course, produce exactly the same results (as much as is possible; e.g. some computers represent real numbers more accurately than others — see Chapter 19). In order to permit such portability of programs, both programs and translators should conform to a recognized international standard.

There are two kinds of translators: **compilers** and **interpreters**. A compiler translates the entire program prior to execution, storing the resulting sequence of machine instructions as a file. That file can then be placed in main memory by another program called a **loader**, after which it can be executed.

An interpreter repeatedly translates and then immediately executes each high-level instruction as necessary. It will probably find it convenient to represent the program in symbolic rather than textual form, entailing a preliminary translation.

The two types of translators have contrasting properties. Interpreters hide the translation from the user of the program, give great flexibility in the execution process, provide more informative descriptions of errors during execution, and permit integrated editing, translation, and execution in a single consistent **programming environment**. These advantages make them perfectly suited to program development. Macintosh Pascal is based on an interpreter.

The price paid for the conveniences of interpretation is very slow execution speed, because high-level instructions have to be repeatedly translated before execution. When speed of execution is important — and it should not be in a learning context — a compiler should be used. A compiler-based version of Macintosh Pascal is available, called *Lightspeed Pascal*.

Needless to say, much goes on behind the scenes in the process of creating and executing programs. For example, a **file system** is needed that organizes files so that they may be quickly created, located, appended to, edited, combined, and moved. Such backstage work is handled by an integrated collection of **system programs** called the **operating system**. For details, consult the further reading list at the end of this chapter.

**Figure 1.5**
The software–hardware hierarchy.

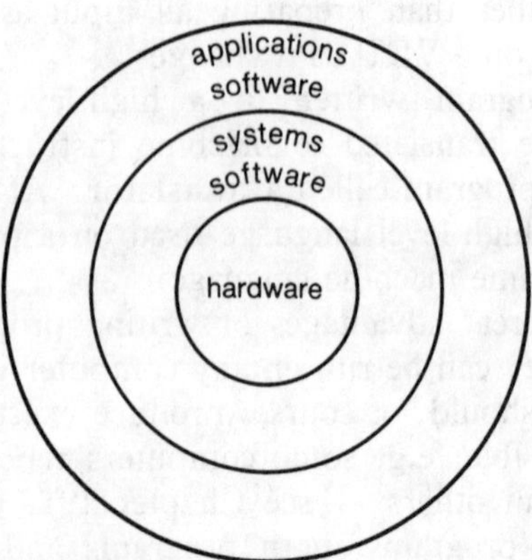

Programs written by or for the user for particular purposes (as distinct from general operating system tasks) are called **application programs**. An example is a spreadsheet program for managing financial data. Translators and editors are described as applications programs in Macintosh documents, though such programs that are used to prepare other programs are usually classified as systems programs. The programs used with a computer are called its **software**. The hardware and software together form a **computer system**, but the term is usually abbreviated to just 'computer'. Figure 1.5 shows the software–hardware hierarchy; this layered view makes sense at much finer levels of detail of both hardware and software.

## 1.5 An introduction to the Macintosh

We describe here the basic aspects of using the Macintosh. Those concerning Macintosh Pascal are left until Chapters 2 and 4. The last exercise (at the end of this chapter) invites the reader to try out the Macintosh; this is best done by following the text as you do so.

### 1.5.1 FLOPPY DISKS

You will need floppy disks to hold your program and data files. The type of disk used by the original and Fat Macintoshes is a 3.5-inch micro-floppy disk, single-sided, 135 tracks per inch; the later Macintoshes use double-sided versions. Although micro-floppies have their own protective plastic casing, they still require care in handling and transport.

Inside the protective cover is the actual disk itself, made of soft ('floppy') mylar plastic with a magnetic coating. This coating is extremely thin and fragile, and small particles of dirt or dust can damage its surface permanently. Special stiff cardboard envelopes with anti-static lining are available to protect your disks; the plastic covers that sometimes come with disks at least help keep out dust.

Never open a disk's metal dust-cover and touch the magnetic surface underneath; this will almost certainly render the disk useless. Do not leave your disk in a car parked in the sun, or near a source of high heat. The top of the Macintosh itself can get quite warm, so it is best not to leave disks there. Since a disk's information is magnetically recorded, any strong magnetic field can destroy it. You should therefore keep disks away from magnets (in speakers and telephones) and objects likely to generate magnetic fields (electric motors, TV sets, UFOs, etc.)

Disks are inserted into the drive with the metal end first and the label side up. Never use force when handling disks. In particular, never attempt to pull a disk out of its drive by hand; serious damage to both disk and drive could result — the Macintosh will eject the disk when operated correctly.

There is a movable plastic tab at the bottom right corner of the underside of a disk. This is normally away from the edge; if not, the disk is **locked**, meaning its information can be read but not altered.

### 1.5.2 STARTING A SESSION

The power-on switch of the Macintosh is at the rear, just above the socket for the power cord. The brightness control is at the front, underneath the protruding ledge just below the colored apple logo. Set the screen brightness to a comfortable level; an over bright or dull screen imposes unnecessary strain on the eyes.

After turning the power on you will see a small disk-symbol with a blinking question mark in the center of the screen. It indicates that the Macintosh is waiting for a startup disk (one containing the Macintosh's operating system). The Macintosh Pascal Program disk
1.1 will do. Insert it into a drive and push until the disk snaps into place with an audible click. The Macintosh displays the message 'Welcome to Macintosh'. After a few seconds, you will see the **desktop** (displayed in Figure 1.6).

There are three features of interest: a list of **menus** along the top, little pictures (called **icons**) of the disk and a trash can, and a little arrow (called a **cursor**). We shall deal with these in reverse order.

### 1.5.3 USING THE MOUSE

The cursor is controlled by the **mouse** — a small box on the end of a cord, with a rubber ball underneath and a button on top. Whenever you move the mouse, the pointer will duplicate the motion on the screen. You will use the mouse to move files around, select commands or text, and to otherwise communicate with the Macintosh.

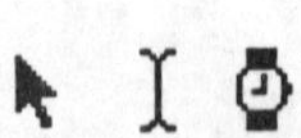

The cursor has different appearances in different situations. The most common shapes are an arrow for selecting items and an I-beam pointer for text editing. Another one looks like an (analog!) wrist watch, indicating that you have to wait for the Macintosh to finish something.

There are several ways to use the mouse:

- **Pointing**: moving the mouse until the cursor is positioned over the object to be pointed at.
- **Clicking**: pressing and releasing the mouse button once.

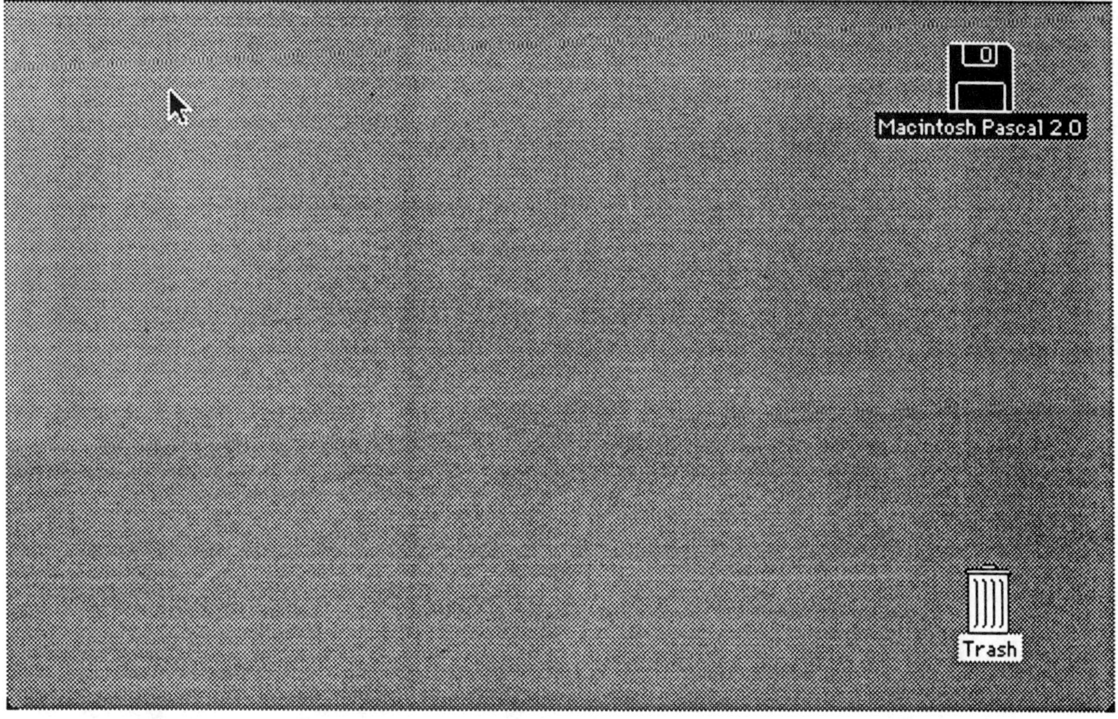


**Figure 1.6**
The desktop.

Double-clicking means clicking twice in quick succession. Advanced users sometimes even triple-click!

- **Pressing**: positioning the pointer on an object and then pressing the mouse button without moving the mouse until an action is complete.
- **Shift-clicking**: clicking while holding the Shift-key down.
- **Dragging** is used both for repositioning objects on the screen and for selecting text when editing. To drag an object, point at it, press and hold down the mouse button, move the mouse until the object has reached the desired place, and then release the button. Normally, while dragging an object, only an outline of the object follows the pointer on the screen; the object changes its position as soon as you release the button. If you are dragging across some text, the parts of the text you drag over are highlighted, meaning that they have been selected for some editing operation.

If you happen to run out of space on *your* desktop (as distinct from the Macintosh's) during a mouse operation, lift the mouse off the desk and place it where you can move it; the cursor follows the mouse only as long as the mouse slides over the surface of the desk.

### 1.5.4 ICONS

Icons are used to represent three things:

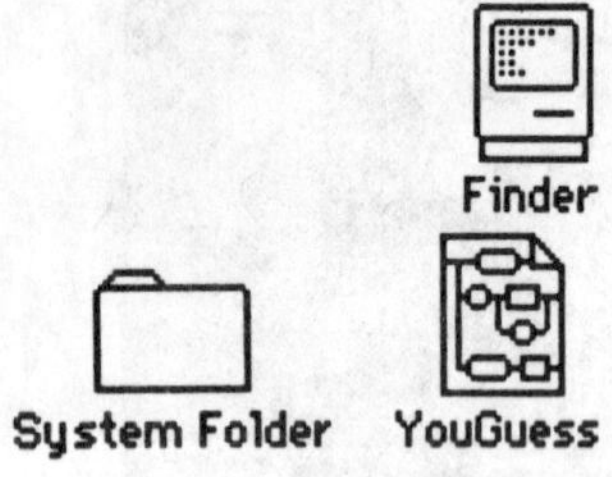


- **Applications**: what Macintosh manuals call compiled programs, whether they be systems programs (like the file system program Finder) or applications programs (like Macintosh Pascal);
- **Documents**: files of textual or pictorial information, such as Macintosh Pascal programs and data files;
- **Folders**: collections of applications, documents, and other folders.

There are two icons on the desktop shown in Figure 1.6, for the disk and trash can respectively; both are folders, albeit special ones. Icons can be dragged around as described above and **selected** for a future operation by clicking on them. A selected icon is indicated by color reversal.

### 1.5.5 WINDOWS

Double-clicking on a folder icon opens its **window**, a box on the screen representing its contents. Doing this to the Macintosh Pascal Program disk icon results in a screen like that shown in Figure 1.7.

Most of the information you deal with on a Macintosh is presented to you in windows. They are used to display and edit both text and pictures. Several windows can be present at once on the screen, but just one is distinguished as **active**. Its title bar is filled with horizontal stripes, and it will be on top of the desk (i.e. not under another window). Commands concerning windows always refer to this window.

Here is a summary of the main properties of windows:

- **Activating a window** is done by clicking anywhere inside it. If a window is completely obscured it can still be made active by choosing it from the Windows menu (see below).

- The **title bar** indicates the name of the window.
- **Repositioning a window** is done by pointing to the title bar and dragging it to its new position.

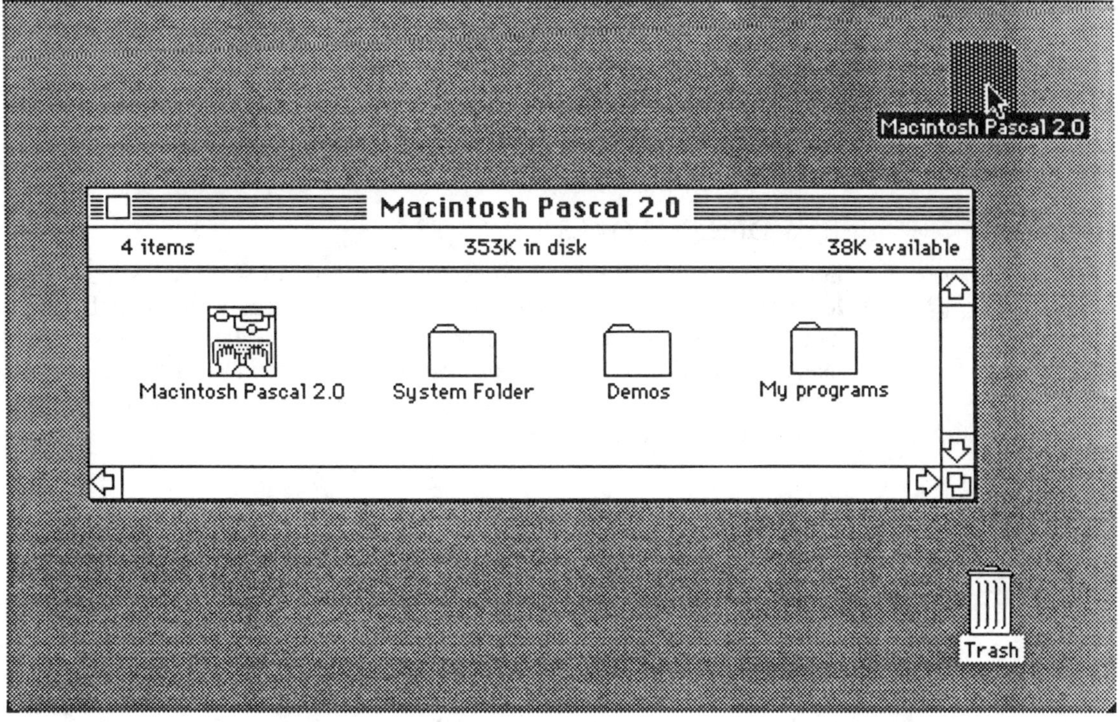


**Figure 1.7**
The desktop after opening the disk's window.

- **Changing a window's size** is done by pointing to the size box (bottom right corner) and dragging it to the desired place. The upper left corner of the window remains in its old position, so dragging the size box changes the window's size and/or shape.
- **Scrolling a window** enables you to examine hidden contents of a window, by moving the window relative to its contents. There are four ways to do so:
  - — Clicking on one of the scroll arrows scrolls the window by a small amount in the indicated direction. The physical location of the window on the screen doesn't change; rather, a different portion of the contents is shown inside the window.
  - — Pressing on one of the scroll arrows will scroll the window continuously until the mouse button is released.
  - — Clicking inside the scroll bar moves the window by almost one full window.

— Dragging the scroll box positions the window over a different part of the text. The position of the scroll box inside the scroll bar roughly indicates the current position of the window in relation to all its contents.

- **Closing a window** is done by clicking in the close box (in the upper left corner). The window is removed from the screen.

### 1.5.6 DIALOG BOXES

Sometimes you will come across a special type of window called a **dialog box**, which appears when the Macintosh needs a decision by you. You make your decision by clicking in one of the labeled buttons that usually appear in the box, or just by clicking in it if there are no buttons (in which case the box represents a message). The box disappears when you click.

### 1.5.7 THE MENU BAR

Along the top of the screen, you will find a white bar containing an apple symbol on the left followed by a few words. This is the **menu bar**. It is used to give commands, select files, edit text, and perform other operations. You **open a menu** by pressing on either the apple or one of the words (which function as headings); a menu appears underneath, presenting you with a number of choices. The menu disappears as soon as you release the mouse button.

To make a selection, open the menu and drag the cursor down the menu. As you drag, the line that the cursor is currently on is highlighted. As soon as you release the mouse button, the currently highlighted command is selected (i.e. the appropriate action is carried out) and the menu disappears. Figure 1.8 shows the Open command from the File menu being selected.

If you have dragged the cursor into the menu but have second thoughts, move the pointer out of the menu and release the mouse button; no selection is made.

Save

Sometimes some menu commands are dimmed (shown in gray print). This indicates that they are not currently applicable. When you drag across a dimmed command, it is not highlighted, and cannot be selected.

⌘

Some menu commands are followed by a clover symbol with a letter beside it. The symbol is called the **command symbol**. To the left of the space bar on the keyboard is a key labeled with this symbol. It is called the **Command-key** and is used as a shortcut for certain commands. It works like the Shift-key, in that it is held down while another key is pressed. For example, holding down the Command-key

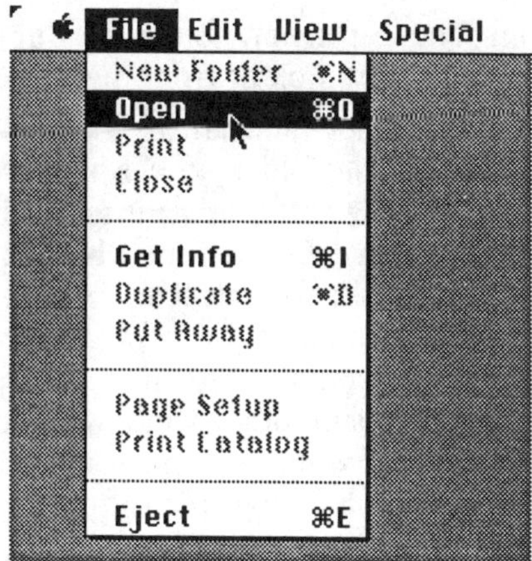


**Figure 1.8**
Selecting Open from the File menu.

while typing 'O' has exactly the same effect as using the mouse to choose Open from the File menu. Choosing a command in this way is described as 'using the keyboard equivalent' of the command.

Macintosh Pascal has its own menus, which are described in Chapters 2 and 4.

### 1.5.8 USING MACINTOSH PASCAL

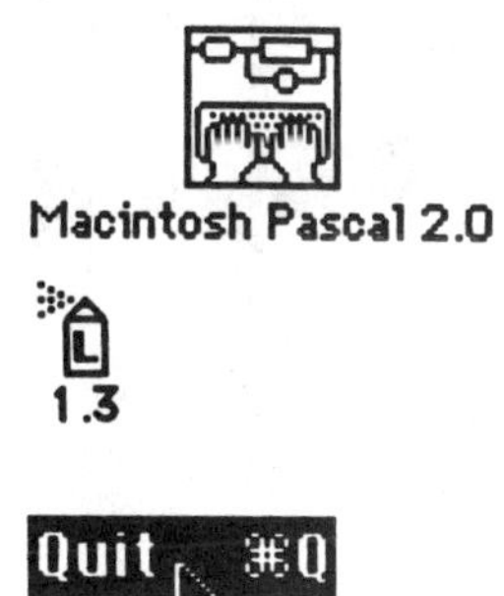


The Macintosh Pascal icon represents a program that enables you to prepare, edit, and run algorithms written in the programming language Macintosh Pascal, i.e. it implements a programming environment. You run this program by selecting the Macintosh Pascal icon, or the icon for a Macintosh Pascal program, and then opening it as just described. The desktop is replaced by a different one. Chapters 2 and 4 describe how to interact with the program. You end execution of Macintosh Pascal by choosing Quit from its File menu. This returns to the desktop.

### 1.5.9 MANAGING FILES

You will want to print, copy, move, and otherwise manipulate files created by Macintosh Pascal and other applications. Here is a summary of the important operations:

- To **rename** a file or folder, first select its icon and then either type the new name or edit it (in the same way that programs are edited in Macintosh Pascal — see Chapter 2).
- To **duplicate** a file or folder (including all its contents), select its icon, choose Duplicate from the File menu, and rename the

resulting icon. You get a new folder by duplicating the Empty Folder or choosing New Folder from the File menu.

- To **move** a file or folder (and all its contents) drag its icon. If you want to put it in a folder with a window on the desktop, move it into the window. If you want to put it in a folder which does not have an open window, but whose icon is visible, drag the object's icon onto the folder's icon (which will reverse color). If you want to put it in an invisible place, first move it onto the desktop (outside all windows); then make the folder's icon or window visible (by closing other windows or using the Windows menu), and finally move the icon from the desktop as described above. If you move something to a different disk it is copied — the original remains.

- To **delete** a file or folder (and all its contents) put it in the Trash folder. It has the special property that anything in it is removed when the disk that it belongs to is ejected, or when you choose Empty Trash from the Special menu, or when an application is opened. You can recover something in the Trash can by opening the Trash window and moving the file or folder out of it.

### 1.5.10 TERMINATING A SESSION

Once you have returned to the original desktop, you finish your session by choosing Shut Down from the Special menu. The Macintosh ejects all disks and returns to the same state as that following powering-up. If the Macintosh will not be used for several hours or more, power-down. Otherwise, leave the Macintosh on with the brightness turned down somewhat to prevent burning-in the image.

## 1.6 Further reading

(1) Anon. (1984). *Macintosh*. Apple product #M1500. USA and Canada: Apple Computer, Inc.
This is the manual that comes with each Macintosh. It is very simply and clearly written.

(2) Goldschlager, L. and Lister, A. (1987). *Computer Science: A Modern Introduction*. 2nd edition. Englewood Cliffs, New Jersey: Prentice-Hall.
This is a superb introduction to computer science, which anyone interested in the subject would profit from reading. Its Chapters 4 and 5 cover all the topics in the first part of this chapter.

(3) Lu, C. (1985). *The Apple Macintosh Book*. 2nd edition. Microsoft.
Another source of general information about the Macintosh, written in a similar style to the Macintosh manual.

## EXERCISES

**1.1** When you look up 'computer' in your dictionary you use the same algorithm as when you look up 'algorithm', yet you perform a different sequence of actions. How can this be?

**1.2** In the Victorian museum in Melbourne, Australia, there is a machine that has never been beaten at tic-tac-toe (which it calls noughts and crosses). The machine can play first or second. Assuming not all visitors to the museum are pushovers at tic-tac-toe, what does this suggest about algorithms for playing tic-tac-toe?

**1.3** Here is an extract from a program, but not a computer program:

```
sl 1, work 1, psso, * work in seed st to 2 sts before next marker,
work 2 tog, sl 1, work 1, psso, repeat from * 3 times more,
work in seed st to last 2 sts, work 2 tog.
```

What kind of algorithm is being described? *Hint*: If you do not know, ask your grandmother.

**1.4** Here are two algorithms, written in English, that indicate whether a given whole number is even or odd:

Algorithm (a):
1. Read the number.
2. Divide the number by 2 and get the remainder.
3. If it is 0, say 'even', otherwise say 'odd'.

Algorithm (b):
1. Read the number.
2. Get the number's rightmost digit.
3. If it is '0', '2', '4', '6' or '8' say 'even', otherwise say 'odd'.

Which algorithm is more abstract?

**1.5** How many words is a picture worth? *Hint*: Update a proverb.

**1.6** What is likely to be the biggest address in a computer with a main memory of 1 Mb and cells of 32 bits?

**1.7** How is it possible for a CPU to execute repeatedly a sequence of machine instructions?

**1.8** Obtain a Macintosh and a startup disk, and experiment by doing something like the following (in order):

- Power-up if necessary and insert the startup disk.
- Move the mouse around while observing the cursor. Pick up the mouse and reposition it a couple of times.

- Double-click on the icon for the disk. Close the window that results, then get it back again by choosing Open from the File menu.
- Move the disk's window around and change its size. Note that part but not all of a window can be off-screen.
- Open the window of the System Folder icon in the startup disk's window. Make it small and scroll both vertically and horizontally.
- Open up lots of windows — really mess up that desktop. Make various windows active by clicking and by choosing them in the Windows menu.
- Make a non-empty window active and wide, and choose various commands from the View menu (not mentioned in the text). Figure out what they do.
- Duplicate the Empty Folder and rename it 'Copies Folder'.
- Duplicate a file (any one will do), rename it if you like, and move it to the Copies Folder. Repeat using a different way of moving.
- Move the Copies Folder to the Trash can; open the latter's window and look inside. Choose Empty Trash from the Special menu.
- Otherwise experiment, being careful not to delete files unless you are sure they are unimportant. Think again even then.

# 2
# EDITING MACINTOSH PASCAL PROGRAMS

Give us the tools, and we will finish the job.
— Winston Churchill, *Radio Broadcast*,
9 February 1941, addressing President Roosevelt.

## 2.1 Introduction

This chapter explains how to use Macintosh Pascal's special-purpose editor to type and modify (i.e. edit) Macintosh Pascal programs. You need not know anything about Pascal to follow it. The material is written in such a way as to be useful as a reference when you eventually edit programs yourself. The exercises ask you to create and modify two of the three sample programs in Chapter 3; you may prefer to do them as you read that chapter.

## 2.2 The Macintosh Pascal environment

After entering Macintosh Pascal you will see a screen like that displayed in Figure 2.1. Macintosh Pascal initially shows three windows: the Program window, the Text window, and the Drawing window.

The Program window is used to enter and edit Pascal programs. If you entered Macintosh Pascal by opening its icon, a skeleton of a Pascal program is displayed (in white on a black rectangle, indicating that the skeleton has been selected — see below), and the name of the window is Untitled. This is the case in Figure 2.1. If, on the other hand, you opened the icon of a previously created program, a window full of that program will be displayed.

The Text window shows the text typed as input to, or written as output by, the program. The Drawing window shows graphics output. There are also special windows for editing the program and observing it during execution; these are opened as needed.

## 2.3 Editing

Macintosh Pascal has many editing features, and it is worthwhile to become familiar with them. Its editor is **special-purpose**: it is used only to edit Pascal programs, and takes advantage of this fact. Thus

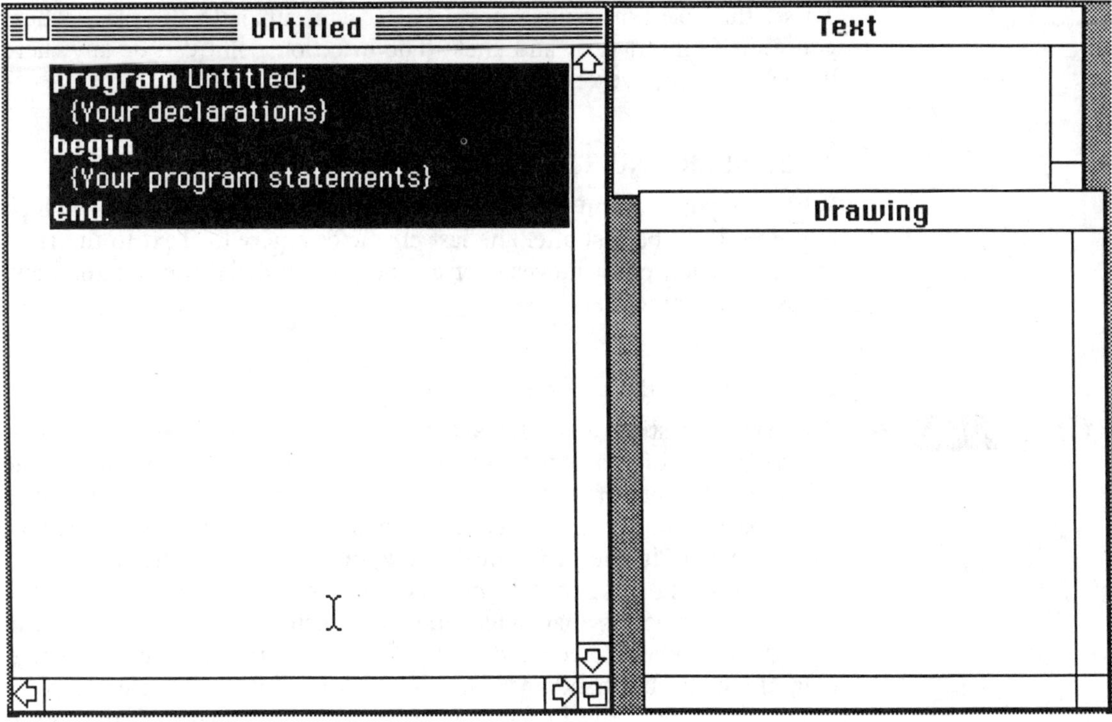
File
Edit
Search
Run
Windows
Untitled
program Untitled;
{Your declarations}
begin
{Your program statements}
end.
Text
Drawing

**Figure 2.1**
The Macintosh Pascal environment.

certain special words (called **reserved words**) are displayed in bold type, the syntax (grammatical form) of the program is checked, and the program is displayed using a consistent scheme of indentation. All of this happens automatically as you type. You need not even press the Return-key to get to a new line: the display is updated whenever you type a semicolon (;) or move the insertion point to a different part of the program.

Most editing takes place in the Program window, which always contains a blinking vertical bar. It marks the **insertion point** — the place where the text that you type on the keyboard appears. Whenever you move the cursor into the Program window, it changes into an I-beam. You use the I-beam cursor to change the insertion point and to select text for editing.

The main editing operations are as follows.

### 2.3.1 SETTING THE INSERTION POINT

To set the insertion point, move the I-beam cursor to the place where you want to insert text, and click. The insertion point can be anywhere in the program, even in the middle of a word.

### 2.3.2 INSERTING TEXT

Whatever you type on the keyboard starts at the insertion point, which moves so as to be just after the last character entered. Text to the right of the insertion point moves over as you type to make way for the newly inserted characters.

### 2.3.3 SELECTING TEXT

first select it

To change existing text first **select** it: position the I-beam cursor at the beginning of the text to be selected and drag it to the end of the selection. As you drag, the selected text is highlighted in white on a black background. If you have selected text but want to change it, click anywhere in the Program window, or select some other text.

Dragging to select text may be done in any direction — it is the start and end points that determine the selected text. A selection can extend over several lines and is not limited to line boundaries. Dragging along the left-hand margin selects entire lines. To select a piece of text larger than the Program window, drag the cursor off the top or bottom edge of the window without releasing the mouse button. The window will scroll, and the program text that moves into the window is included in the selection.

Select All ⌘A

Double-click to select a word; triple-click to select a whole line. To select the whole program, choose Select All from the Edit menu. A more convenient alternative for long selections is first to place the insertion point at the beginning of the text to be selected, then move (not drag) the cursor to the end and shift-click. The Program window can be scrolled during this operation.

### 2.3.4 EDITING SELECTED TEXT

To replace selected text, type the new text. To delete selected text, hit the Backspace-key. That is how to remove program Untitled in Figure 2.1.

To move selected text, first choose Cut from the Edit menu. The selected text disappears. Then set the insertion point as desired and choose Paste from the Edit menu. The cut text reappears starting at the insertion point.

To copy selected text, choose Copy instead of Cut and proceed as above. The selected text remains, but a copy is inserted after the insertion point when Paste is chosen.

Cut or copied text is placed in a file called the Clipboard, replacing whatever was there before. Choosing Paste simply inserts a copy of the Clipboard at the insertion point. It can be done as many times as desired. The Clipboard can be displayed by choosing Clipboard from the Windows menu.

### 2.3.5 DELETING TEXT WITHOUT SELECTING

Another way to delete text is to set the insertion point after the last character to be deleted, and then repeatedly hit the Backspace-key to remove the character just before the insertion point. This is the easiest way to delete one or two characters, or replace them, since you can insert afterwards.

### 2.3.6 SEARCHING AND REPLACING

It is common when editing to need to locate certain text. Often it is because you need to change it, possibly wherever it occurs. Such operations are done with the Search menu. If you choose What to find... , the dialog box shown in Figure 2.2 appears.

To search for occurrences of particular text, type it as the *Search for* text. Set the desired search conditions using the small buttons in the dialog box. Click OK to remove the dialog box. Now whenever you choose Find from the Search menu, the next occurrence of the text will be searched for and selected if found.

Find ⌘F

The *Replace with* text replaces the currently selected text (and itself remains selected) whenever you choose Replace from the Search

Replace ⌘R

Search for
Replace with
Separate Words
All Occurrences
Case Is Irrelevant
Cases Must Match
OK
Cancel

When this button is on, the *Search for* text must be surrounded by spaces or punctuation.

When this button is on, the context of the *Search for* text is irrelevant.

When this button is on, the case (upper or lower, i.e. capitalized or not) of letters in the *Search for* text is not significant.

When this button is on, the case of letters in the *Search for* text is significant.

**Figure 2.2**
The dialog box for What to find... .

menu. You can therefore replace multiple occurrences of the *Search for* text by repeatedly choosing first Find and then Replace if desired. To replace *every* occurrence automatically, choose Everywhere from the Search menu (just once). Always think twice before doing this, as you cannot halt the process once it is underway, and mistakes can be very painful.

Each search starts at the current insertion point and proceeds forwards through the program, as far as the end if necessary. If no occurrence of the *Search for* text is found, you get a message which misleadingly says that the text was not found in the active window. If a search is unexpectedly unsuccessful, check the settings in the What to find... box. If they are correct, move the insertion point to the start of the program and try again.

## 2.4 Controlling the environment

Two commands in the Windows menu allow you to control aspects of the programming environment.

Choosing Font Control... produces a dialog box that displays the font in use in the Program windows (the Program, Observe, and Instant windows) or the Text window, depending on which of two corresponding buttons is on. Font names are made up of a word and a number; thus 'Geneva-12' names the 12-point Geneva font. Buttons labeled Next and Prev enable you to cycle through the available fonts in either direction. Click OK when you have found the desired font. It is often best to choose a font with fixed-width characters for the Text window, to permit more control over the formatting of output. Suitable choices are Monaco-9 and Monaco-12.

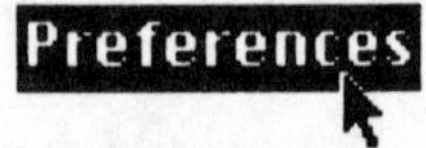


Choosing Preferences... produces a dialog box that displays certain current editing and output settings, and lets you change them. The Indent Width is the horizontal offset of an indented line. Tab Stops are the positions in a line associated with the Tab-key: pressing the Tab-key when typing text spaces to the next tab stop position. It is recommended that you set the Indent Width and Tab Stops values to the same value (12 seems about right); this enables you to use the Tab-key to line up comments with other lines of the program.

You can also control the maximum number of characters held in the Text window; if more are written by the program the extra ones written first are lost. Finally, you may specify that any output written to the Text window also be sent to a file (that you name) and/or the printer that is specified by choosing the Choose Printer desk accessory from the apple menu.

## 2.5 Error messages

To err is human. Macintosh Pascal knows this saw, and informs you whenever it detects an error. Certain types of error that occur when editing do not produce explicit messages; rather, the editor indicates them by displaying the offending part of the program text in outlined characters. This only happens when the editor finds something that cannot possibly be part of a Pascal program, e.g. when a right curly bracket to end a comment is missing, or when a semicolon is followed by the reserved word **else**. After such an error is corrected, the outlined characters do not immediately revert to normal type. But by moving the insertion point a few lines you can force the editor to re-check the program and update the screen.

else

Other errors are detected when you check (the syntax of ) your program or during execution, in which case an error message appears at the top of the screen. Figure 2.3 shows one such message. Usually the message states clearly what has gone wrong, but sometimes the best Macintosh Pascal can do is to issue a very general message such as 'This doesn't make sense.' There are over a hundred different error messages; try to get a copy of the file that comes with Macintosh Pascal which explains them.

Whenever you have an error, Macintosh Pascal refuses to respond to your commands until you acknowledge the error by clicking anywhere inside its box. Once you have done this, the box disappears and a hand in the left margin of the Program window points to the offending line. Usually the problem is in that line or at the end of the previous one, but sometimes, as with mistakes in the declarative part of the program, the symptom may be far removed from the cause.

It is hoped that you will not come across a type of error known as a **system error**. Messages like 'Sorry, a system error occurred' or 'Out of memory' mean that something has gone seriously wrong with the Macintosh's operating system. You will probably have no choice about how to proceed, but, if possible, get expert help.

## 2.6 Checking a program

If, when entering a program, you want to check whether you have made any mistakes so far, choose Check from the Run menu. This

A period (.) is required following the last END of the program but one has not been found.

**Figure 2.3**
An error message.

**Figure 2.4**
The dialog box for Save As... .

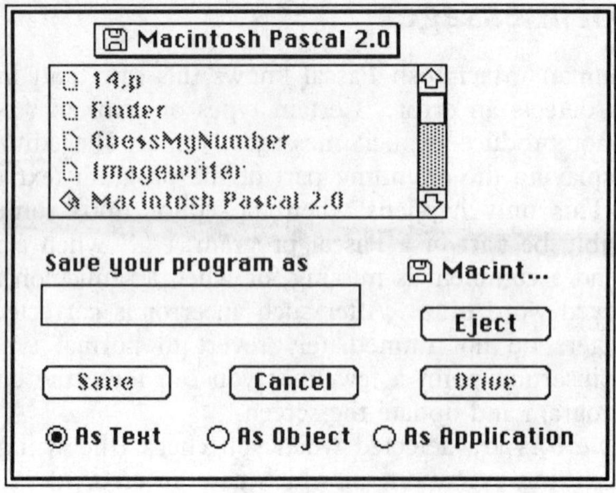


invokes the part of Macintosh Pascal that does the preliminary translation. It checks your program for syntactic errors. If none are reported you may run the program.

The many facilities provided for running Macintosh Pascal programs are described in Chapter 4.

## 2.7 Saving your program

In the File menu there are two commands for saving programs: Save As... and Save. When you create a new program the Program window has the name Untitled, and only the Save As... command is active. Choosing it produces a dialog box like that shown in Figure 2.4.

The topmost box shows the name of the disk currently chosen to receive the program, in this case 'Macintosh Pascal 2.0'. The biggest box is the contents window; scroll it to list all programs on this disk. The first part of the disk's name also appears just above the Eject button. If you want to save on a different disk, click the Eject button and insert the new disk; if you are using an external disk drive and want to save on the other disk, click the Drive button (which will not be dimmed if a disk is inserted).

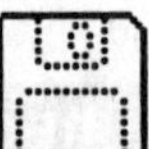

If you insert a virgin disk to receive the program, a dialog box will appear; it tells you that the disk is unreadable, and asks whether you want to initialize it. Sometimes this can happen with disks that have been initialized and contain files, in which case you should click Eject and try again. Clicking Initialize causes certain control information to be written on the disk. After a minute or so you will be asked to name the disk. Type any name you like as long as it does not contain a colon (:). Then click OK and resume saving your program.

Type the name under which you want to save your program in the box labeled 'Save your program as'. The name must not contain any colons. Click the Save button to save the program, or the Cancel button to avoid saving. The dialog box disappears in either case. You can save a copy by choosing Save As... again and using a different name or disk.

There are three forms in which to save a program, corresponding to the three buttons at the bottom of the box. The default and normal option is As Text, which saves the program as a text file. As Object saves it in Macintosh Pascal's translated form. Using this between editing sessions saves time by avoiding translation. Saving As Application is used to create an application, i.e. a program that does not involve the Macintosh Pascal editing and execution environment. *Never* save *only* in this form, as you will not be able to edit or even print your program. Consult the *Macintosh Pascal 2.0 Update* document on the Macintosh Pascal Utilities disk for details.

After saving with Save As... the title in the Program window changes to whatever name you specified. Also, the topmost item in the Windows menu gets that name, and choosing it displays the Program window. Choosing Save from the File menu automatically replaces the saved program with the current version, though Save As... is still available if you want to save with a different name (or disk).

It is a good idea to save your program at frequent intervals, say after adding or changing about twenty lines of code. You will be glad you did if there is a power failure, a system error, or, more likely, you inadvertently lose or change code when editing.

## 2.8 Reverting to the last version

When something goes terribly wrong (such as a substitution with Everywhere) and you feel that you have really messed up your program, choose Revert from the File menu. This will restore your program to the state it was in when you last saved it. A dialog box appears to double check with you before reverting.

## 2.9 Opening a saved program

After entering the desktop at the start of a session on a Macintosh, you can run Macintosh Pascal with an existing program by simply double-clicking on the icon of that program (providing Macintosh Pascal is present).

Alternatively, open Macintosh Pascal and choose Open... from the File menu. A dialog box is displayed that looks and functions in a similar way to the one for Save As... shown in Figure 2.4. Scroll the contents window until the name of the program appears, click on the name to select it (highlighting it), and click the Open button. A short-cut is just to double-click on the name.

If you finish with a program in a Macintosh Pascal session, and wish to work on another, save it, choose Close from the File menu, and then open the new program.

## 2.10 Copying between programs

To copy part of one program (such as a procedure or function) for use in another, open the program containing the text to be copied, select the text, and choose Copy from the Edit menu, putting it on the Clipboard. Then close the program and open the one to receive the text. Set the insertion point and choose Paste from the Edit menu. The text on the Clipboard is inserted.

The contents of the Clipboard can be copied into the Note Pad or Scrapbook **desk accessory** (if available) by choosing the accessory from the apple menu before choosing Paste from the Edit menu. Click in the bottom-left corner of the Note Pad to pick one of its eight pages, or scroll the Scrapbook to pick one of its areas. To copy from the Note Pad, select the desired text and Copy to the Clipboard. It is not possible to select part of a Scrapbook area — Copy copies all of the currently displayed area to the Clipboard.

To extract rather than copy part of a program proceed as above but choose Cut instead of Copy.

## 2.11 Printing

In the File menu there are two commands for printing: Page Setup... and Print... .

Choosing Page Setup... produces a dialog box that displays the current settings of various options that control printing, and allows you to change them by clicking the appropriate buttons. You do not normally need to choose this before printing.

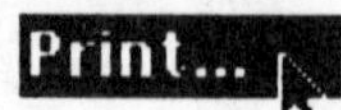


Choosing Print... produces a simple dialog box. The only option is to print all the program (the default) or to indicate a range of pages. To initiate printing, click OK.

You can print an image of the screen whenever your program is not running, by first engaging the Caps-Lock-key and then holding down both the Command-key and the Shift-key as you type '4'. If the Caps-Lock-key is disengaged, only the active window is printed.

## 2.12 Leaving Macintosh Pascal

To end a Macintosh Pascal session, choose Quit from the File menu. If you have not saved your program since the last change, a dialog box gives you the opportunity. The desktop will be restored to the state it was in when you left it, except that some additional program icons may be present.

## 2.13 Further reading

(1) Anon. (1986). *Macintosh Pascal 2.0 Update*.
This is a MacWrite document included on the *Macintosh Pascal Utilities* disk that comes with Macintosh Pascal 2.0. The section headed 'The Applications Shell' explains how to use programs Saved as Application. Much of the rest assumes familiarity with the Macintosh's operating system.

(2) Hueras, J. (1984). *Macintosh Pascal User's Guide*. Apple product #M1504. USA and Canada: Apple Computer, Inc.
This is one of the manuals that come with Macintosh Pascal. It covers much the same material as do this chapter and chapter 4, but is much richer in pictorial illustrations.

## EXERCISES

Open Macintosh Pascal by double-clicking on its icon, and put it through its paces by doing something like the following (in order):

**2.1** The Macintosh Pascal environment

Browse through the menus at the top of the screen.

Experiment with moving and changing the size of the windows on the screen.

Activate different windows on the screen. How do you activate a window that is completely hidden?

Make the Program window occupy the whole screen prior to entering a program.

2.10

**2.2** Editing; error messages

Type the Backspace-key to get rid of program Untitled, then enter program YouGuess2 from Chapter 3:

```
program YouGuess2 (Input, Output);
...
end.{ YouGuess2 }
```

If you make a mistake you can use the Backspace-key to erase character by character what you have typed so far. If you hold the Backspace-key down, it will auto-repeat, enabling you quickly to erase half a line or so.

It is sensible to save a newly entered program before checking or running it. Do so now.

Activate the Clipboard window, resize it to about three lines of half screen width, and reposition it at the bottom right corner of the screen.

Now edit the program into program YouGuess3 in Chapter 3. Do so by performing the following operations (which mostly proceed down through the program), observing the changing contents of the Clipboard:

- Insert and repeatedly before asks, by setting the insertion point before a, and typing the missing text.
- Select { and ... correct } and type the two lines that should replace it.
- Set the insertion point before **var** and type const ... number }. Notice that const is displayed in bold, viz. **const**.
- Replace the 10 after **mod** by MaxSecret.
- Update the line before the first Writeln, replacing it with two lines.
- Select 10 after and and replace it with ',MaxSecret, ', hitting the Return-key after the first comma to force a new line.
- Insert first after your .
- Copy the line if guess = secret then and replace the line before it with a copy. (You can Paste to replace selected text.)
- Select **if** in the first occurrence of the duplicated line by double-clicking, and type while to replace it; replace = by <>. Replace **then** by do begin.
- Insert end; Writeln('That''s correct!') after the second last line.
- Change = to > and update each of the two lines starting with Writeln.

- Copy the two lines before the line starting with **while**.
- After too low.'), add ; and then the two copied lines.
- Change first to next in the first added line, and remove the semicolon at the end of the second added line.

2.11

Use the Search menu to change the name of the program: Choose What to find... from the Search menu. Enter Guess2 as the *Search for* text and Guess3 as the *Replace with* text. Put the *All Occurrences* button on. Why? The setting of the other search option is unimportant here. Why? Click OK to both confirm your selection and close the dialog box.

Choose Everywhere from the Search menu. Is every occurrence of YouGuess2 changed to YouGuess3? (It should be.)

At this point your program should be identical to the one given in Chapter 3. Edit if necessary to make this the case.

Again choose What to find... and then Everywhere, this time to change all occurrences of secret to number. Make sure at least one of the *Cases Must Match* and the *Separate Words* buttons is on. Why?

Now try to reverse the previous change by repeating with the *Search for* and *Replace with* texts swapped. Note that some spurious occurrences of secret result.

| **Moral** Think carefully before you choose Everywhere. |
|---|

To restore the original occurrences of number, first choose What to find... from the search menu and exchange the *Search for* and *Replace with* texts. Then set the insertion point at the beginning of the program, and make the necessary changes with a sequence of Find or Replace commands. Use the keyboard equivalent each time.

Choose Replace again. What happens? Why?

If you saved the original program, also save this new one. How do you save a program once you have named it? What happens to the program that was stored previously under that name?

**2.3** Controlling the environment

2.12

Use Font Control from the Windows menu to peruse the available fonts, and change the fonts in both the Program windows and the Text window.

Choose Preferences from the Windows menu and change the indent width and the space between tab stops. Note how the first change affects the display of the program, and temporarily insert several tabs, noting their effects.

**2.4** Checking a program

Choose Check from the Run menu. Notice that the heading Run in the menu bar is highlighted during this operation. If Check does not find any errors, nothing further happens — you are not explicitly informed. Otherwise, an error message is displayed at the top of the screen informing you of the *first error* found.

In case Check did find an error, carefully check your program. The smallest deviations, such as an additional or missing comma (,), can invalidate the program.

If you did not get an error from Check, provoke one by simply removing any semicolon (;) in the program, and choose Check again. Fix the error before proceeding.

**2.5** Saving your program

Save the current program. If you have saved it before, save now under a different name. If you have not, and you have your own new disk, initialize it if necessary and save on it.

**2.6** Reverting to the last version

Select a substantial part of the program and hit Backspace. It disappears and, unlike the case with Cut, cannot be recovered with Paste. Choose Revert from the File menu to restore the last saved version.

**2.7** Opening a saved program

2.13 Close the current program and open a different one. It does not matter if you did not create it.

**2.8** Copying between programs

Put the Clipboard on the screen, and copy a section of the program. If the Note Pad or Scrapbook desk accessories are present, copy a different section into each of them.

2.14 Close the current program (without saving it) and open the one you worked on previously (**YouGuess3**). Insert the text in the Clipboard at a chosen place in the program. If you copied to the Note Pad or Scrapbook, insert the text you copied into the program.

Since you have just done something that makes no sense, revert to the last saved program!

**2.9** Printing

Obtain a printed listing of your program.

Send the current screen image to the printer, remembering to disengage the Caps-Lock-key afterwards.

Activate the Program window, set it to about half screen size, and print an image of it (but not the rest of the screen).

**2.10** Leaving Macintosh Pascal

First make sure that you have saved the current version of your program to disk, by opening the File menu and checking that the Save command is dimmed. If not, save the program.

Terminate the Macintosh Pascal session.

# 3
# A PREVIEW OF PASCAL

Language is the dress of thought.
— Dr Johnson, *Lives of the English Poets*

## 3.1 The history of Pascal

The programming language Pascal was created around 1970 by Niklaus Wirth, a professor of computer science at the Eidgenössische Technische Hochschule in Zürich, Switzerland. The period of its gestation was a heady one for computer science, in which great advances were made in understanding the programming process. Wirth set out to design a language that reflected the emerging fundamental structures and concepts of programming.

Despite having no corporate or government backing, Pascal achieved its present position as the virtual lingua franca of university-level teaching of programming, an important language for both systems and application programming, and the departing point for more modern languages such as Ada and Wirth's own Modula-2. Wirth succeeded because his goals were wisely chosen and by and large were met. He built a better bug-trap!

The final seals of approval were bestowed on Pascal when an international standard was approved by the International Organization for Standardization in 1982, and adopted (with one omission) by the American National Standards Institute in 1983. We shall call the language defined by ANSI, **Standard Pascal**, and the defining document, **the Standard**. The significance of the Standard is that a Pascal program that conforms to it is guaranteed to be treated in exactly the same way by each Pascal translator that itself conforms to the Standard, i.e. Standard Pascal programs are **transportable**.

This does not quite mean that an arbitrary Standard Pascal program will produce the same output, irrespective of the Standard Pascal translator that processed it, because certain properties of the Standard language may vary between implementations. Prime examples are the range and precision of real numbers (see Chapter 19). But in most realistic cases, the output will be identical, or nearly so for real numbers.

Except in a few relatively minor respects (all made explicit in the sequel) Macintosh Pascal is an **extension** of Standard Pascal, i.e.

Standard Pascal programs are accepted and behave as they should, but additional features are provided, most of which provide access to the built-in graphics and sound capabilities of the Macintosh, and, moreover, do little violence to the Standard.

Our attitude to the differences between Macintosh Pascal and Standard Pascal stems from the principle that language issues, and especially the fine points, should not detract from the overriding aim of learning how best to solve programming problems and how best to present the solutions. Our first priority is learning problem solving rather than learning Standard or Macintosh Pascal. Nevertheless, the ability to program to a Standard is a valuable one; indeed, it is essential to the professional programmer. Accordingly, usages at variance with the Standard are pointed out in end-of-chapter sections headed 'Macaveats', and kosher alternatives are outlined whenever possible.

## 3.2 Reading before writing

Although Pascal is a relatively modest language, and was designed with teaching in mind, its defining document runs to a hundred pages or so of very technical jargon-ridden English. One way to proceed in learning to program with Pascal is to start with its basic low-level constructs, learning all the details, and seeing examples of their application, and painstakingly working up to the higher levels of the language. Such a **bottom-up** approach is traditionally used in presenting mathematical theories, and it is the approach used in the formal definition.

Humans, of course, do not learn their own languages in that fashion. They are ambitious and impatient to use their language to communicate, before learning all the subtleties of grammar and vocabulary. Without wishing to push the analogy too hard, we take the view that it is desirable for the beginner to be exposed to a simple but non-trivial part of Pascal right from the start. This approach is consistent with our natural mode of language acquisition, provides a context that helps demystify the language constructs as they are explicated properly later, and shows those with prior experience of another programming language (Basic, perhaps) how Pascal compares with it.

So without further ado, let us launch with bold hearts and fearless spirits into an exciting voyage of discovery.

## 3.3 First program

Here is a complete Macintosh Pascal program:

```
program YouGuess (Input, Output);
{ Asks the user to guess a number, reads it, }
{ and announces that it is wrong! }
begin { YouGuess }
  Writeln('I''m thinking of a number between 1 and 10 inclusive.');
  Write('Please type your guess: ');
  Readln;
  Writeln('That''s wrong.')
end. { YouGuess }
```

3.1 Run this program by choosing Go from the Run menu. You will first see the text:

```
I'm thinking of a number between 1 and 10 inclusive.
```

appear at the top of the Text window. It will occupy one line, unless the window is too narrow, in which case it will take as many lines as necessary. Very soon after, a new line appears, and nothing further happens. The Text window is now as shown in Figure 3.1.

What has happened so far is this. The program basically consists of four **statements**, each of which specifies an action. Running the program amounts to executing the statements in turn, starting with:

```
Writeln('I''m thinking of a number between 1 and 10 inclusive.')
```

which printed the first line in the Text window. The next statement printed the second line, which **prompts** the user to enter input. The Macintosh is now executing the third statement, Readln, which reads one line of input. It cannot be completed until a line is entered. Do so by typing any text and then hitting the Return-key to finish the line. You will see the text appear in the Text window as it is typed, and then a third line appear very soon after you hit the Return-key. This is because the third statement was executed, reading your line of input, and then the fourth and last, writing the last line of output. Execution of the program has now finished, and the Text window is now as shown in Figure 3.2. (The input has been underlined to distinguish it from the program's output; it is not underlined on the Macintosh.)

Our first program plays a rather dirty trick on the user, reading but ignoring the input line: it's a tough program for tough times. If

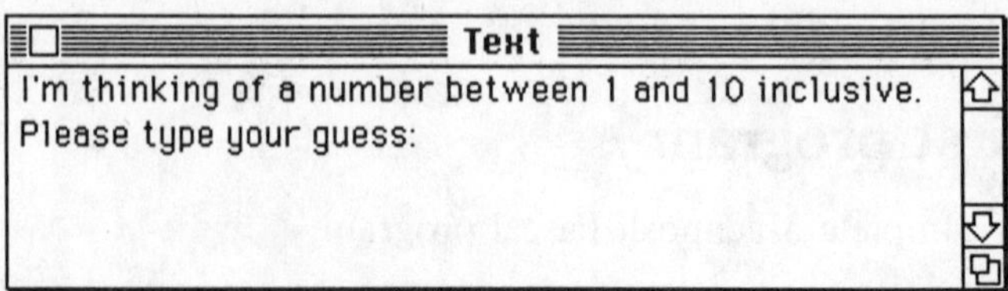
Text
I'm thinking of a number between 1 and 10 inclusive.
Please type your guess:

**Figure 3.1**
The Text window before input.

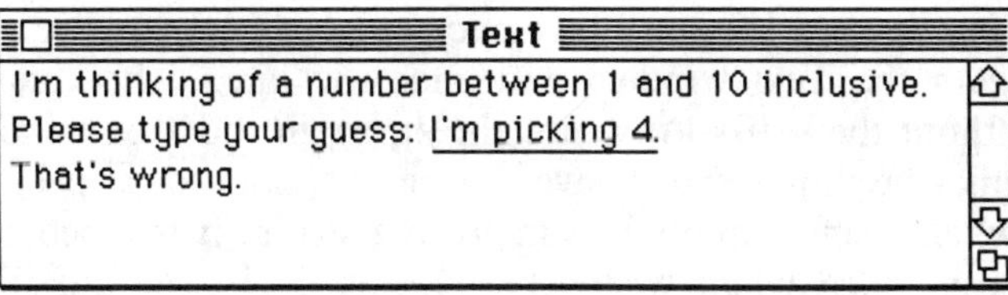
Text
I'm thinking of a number between 1 and 10 inclusive.
Please type your guess: I'm picking 4.
That's wrong.

**Figure 3.2**
The Text window after execution.

your style isn't so Nixonesque, you might change the last statement to print 'That's close.', or even 'That's correct.' if you can handle taunts of 'bleeding-heart liberal!'. Do so and rerun the program. You have successfully modified your first Pascal program!

3.2

Let us now examine the program and learn what we can about Pascal. We first notice some words in boldface; they are called **reserved words** and cannot be used for other purposes. We also notice that the other technical words, viz. Writeln, Write, and Readln, recognizably derive from English. The statements are *separated* by semicolons — there is no semicolon following the last statement because it is not followed by another statement. Macintosh Pascal has set out the statements one per line. (Basic programmers please note: statements are not numbered.) They appear in a context reminiscent of program Untitled (see Figure 2.1). Matching curly brackets and the text they enclose form a **comment**. Comments have no effect on execution; they are included for the human reader. We correctly deduce that a program may take the form:

```
program name (Input, Output);
comments
begin { name }
  statements
end. { name }
```

where italicized terms are not literally present, but act as **placeholders** for unspecified parts of the program. Each occurrence of *name* is the same here; commenting **begin** and **end** with the program's name is a convention we shall adhere to. Its utility will become apparent later. The first section of comments specifies what task the program performs, in terms of what input it expects and what output it produces. Do not worry about the presence of Input and Output in the first line; their significance is explained in Chapter 5.

So much for now for syntax. Let us turn to the meaning of the program: it is executed by executing each of the statements, in the order written. We have seen examples of two kinds of statements. The **output statement**:

```
Writeln(string)
```

where *string* denotes arbitrary text enclosed by single quotes ('), writes the string in the Text window and ends the line. The version using Write (without the suffix ln) writes the string in the Text window without ending the line. You have no doubt noticed a peculiarity of strings: when a single quote is wanted in a string, it is typed twice (but only appears once when written). This is so Pascal can distinguish single quotes in strings from those that delimit strings.
The **input statement**:

```
Readln
```

waits until a line of input is typed, and then ignores it! Actually, it reads the line without remembering it.

## 3.4 Second program

The output of our first program does not depend on the user's guess, and the user will either deduce its true nature or postulate some form of psychic (in)ability. The modified program below dispenses with the pretence, giving the user a chance. It introduces several new features which will shortly be explained, but you can probably figure out *how* it works by yourself. (*What* it does, at least in general terms, is stated in the comments.) Give it a try.

```
program YouGuess2 (Input, Output);
{ Picks a number, asks for and reads a guess, }
{ and announces whether or not it is correct. }
 var
  x, y, { (x, y) is the mouse's position }
  secret, { the number to be guessed }
  guess : integer;
begin { YouGuess2 }
{ Define the number to be guessed }
 GetMouse(x, y);
 secret := (x + y) mod 10 + 1;
{ Prompt for and read the guess }
 Writeln('I''m thinking of a number between 1 and 10 inclusive.');
 Write('Please type your guess: ');
 Readln(guess);
{ Announce the result of the guess }
 if guess = secret then
  Writeln('That''s correct.')
 else
  Writeln('That''s wrong.')
end. { YouGuess2 }
```

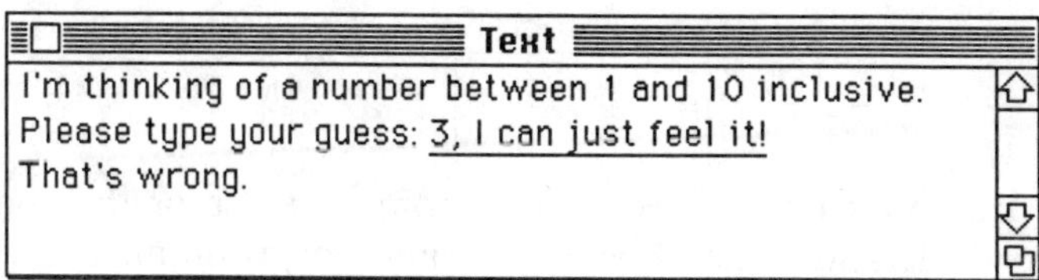

Text
I'm thinking of a number between 1 and 10 inclusive.
Please type your guess: 3, I can just feel it!
That's wrong.


**Figure 3.3**
The Text window after a run of YouGuess2.

Right! Execution of YouGuess2 proceeds as before up to the point where input is required. Now things ain't what they used to be. The input must start with a whole number (written with digits, not a word), although it may be preceded by spaces. After the Return-key is hit, a line is printed that announces the outcome. Furthermore, rerunning the program with the same guess does not usually produce the same output, as the secret number depends on the position of the mouse (and the user isn't told of that)! The Text window produced by a typical run is shown in Figure 3.3.

In reading YouGuess2 you surely noticed the three comments among the statements. These represent the high-level actions that were originally chosen to solve the problem. They remain in the program to describe what the Pascal statements do that follow (up to the next comment or blank line). Thus you understand the body of YouGuess2 at a high level as:

```
begin { YouGuess2 }
  Define the number to be guessed;
  Prompt for and read the guess;
  Announce the result of the guess
end. { YouGuess2 }
```

Some new kinds of statement and other new constructs are used. The most important new notion is that of a **variable**. It is a named container of a value; the name of the container is fixed, but its value may (and usually does) change during execution. The three lines following **var declare** four variables to be used in the program. Their names are x, y, secret, and guess, and they will all have integer values, i.e. whole numbers. There are many **types** of value in Pascal, and when each variable is declared, as it must be, its type is specified. Like its name, a variable's type is fixed.

All variables used by the program are declared in the **variable-declaration-part**, which starts with the reserved-word **var** and consists of one or more declarations each followed by a semicolon. Since comments may be ignored, we might correctly deduce from our program that a **declaration** consists of a list of one or more names separated by commas, then a colon (:), then a type (such as integer).

**Figure 3.4**
A picture of a variable.

secret

| 7 |
|---|

Unless a variable's purpose is obvious from its name or the context of its use, its declaration should be accompanied by a comment describing it.

We picture a variable as a named box containing its current value. Figure 3.4 illustrates the integer variable named secret, assuming its current value is 7. It would seem sensible to label the box with the variable's type, but we shall not do so since the type can be deduced from the value (together with the context, if necessary).

When execution of a program begins, the variables exist but have undefined values (which will be represented in pictures by question-marks (?)). There are two major ways in which a variable gets its initial value or a new value. One is by execution of an **assignment statement**, an example of which is:

```
secret := (x + y) mod 10 + 1
```

When executed, this computes the value of (**evaluates**) the expression on the right of the **assignment symbol** :=, and then makes this the new value of the variable on the left. The assignment symbol is read as 'gets'.

The expression above is a little complicated; let us see how it is evaluated. Suppose x and y have the values 205 and 137 respectively. The brackets around x + y force it to be evaluated first; the result is 342. The next value to be computed is 342 **mod** 10. The **operator** **mod** gives the remainder when the integer on its left is divided by the one on its right; in this case 10 into 342 goes 34 times with 2 remainder, so the result is 2. Finally, 2 + 1 is computed to get 3, which is the value of the entire expression. So the value of secret after execution of the assignment is 3.

The brackets around x + y are essential. Without them, Pascal's rules for expression evaluation require y **mod** 10 to be evaluated first. The result in the example above would be:

```
205 + (137 mod 10) + 1
```

which equals 213. The program would run, but the chances of the user guessing the secret would be unexpectedly remote! We shall see in Chapter 10 that variable secret (and variable guess) can be declared to have a value between 1 and 10, which if done (as it should be) would cause a run-time error when an attempt is made to assign an improper value.

The operators + and **mod** are not the only ones used in integer expressions. Also available are – (representing subtraction), * (representing multiplication), and **div** (representing integer division: 342 **div** 10 equals 34).

The other major way to give a variable a value is by reading a value from input. An example is the input statement:

```
Readln(guess)
```

which is an abbreviation of the sequence of two input statements:

```
Read(guess);
Readln
```

The first of these waits for and then reads the input, skipping over spaces and even new lines in search of a value for the integer variable guess. An optional sign and then digits are read until a non-digit character is encountered. The textual representation of the number read is converted to an integer value which then becomes the new value of the variable. We have met Readln before; it skips the rest of the line.

Another newly introduced statement is the **if-statement**, which has the form:

**if** *condition* **then**
  *statement*
**else**
  *statement*

A **condition** is a special kind of expression that when evaluated produces either the value true or the value false. The conditional statement is executed by first evaluating the condition. If it gives the value true, the statement following **then** is executed, otherwise the statement following **else** is executed. In our program, the condition is guess = secret. Since the names of variables always stand for their values in expressions, and = has its familiar mathematical meaning, this condition gives true just in case the values of variables guess and secret are equal.

It is not necessary to write variables either side of =; any two integer expressions can be compared. We shall see later that expressions of other types can also be compared. Neither is with = the only way to compare them; the full complement of **relational operators** is given in Table 3.1. The usual mathematical symbols in the last three cases are $\leqslant$, $\geqslant$ and $\neq$, respectively; these are not used since they are unavailable on most keyboards.

**Table 3.1** The relational operators.

| Relational operator | Meaning |
|---|---|
| = | equals |
| < | less than |
| > | greater than |
| <= | less than or equal to |
| >= | greater than or equal to |
| <> | not equal to |

A conditional statement is called a **structured statement** because it contains other statements as components. The part starting with **else** can be omitted, meaning 'else do nothing'.

YouGuess2 introduced one more new kind of statement:

```
GetMouse(x, y)
```

is a **procedure statement**. A procedure is a self-contained subprogram that does something in terms of **parameters**. Section 10.6.3.2 of the *Macintosh Pascal Reference Manual* (hereafter called *the Reference*) tells us that: GetMouse(x, y) ... returns in x and y the horizontal and vertical coordinates respectively of the ... cursor connected to the mouse ... at the time GetMouse is called. Coordinates are integer values; each position on the screen is defined by a horizontal coordinate and a vertical coordinate; the origin, i.e. the position with zero coordinates, is in the top-left corner of the Drawing window; horizontal coordinates increase to the right; vertical ones increase down (unlike the usual system in Cartesian geometry). The scale is 72 to the inch in each direction.

GetMouse is a **predefined procedure** of Macintosh Pascal. (Procedures can also be defined by the programmer; this facility is crucially important, and what we have to say now applies also to such procedures.) In the Reference the parameters x and y are used only to define the effect of calling GetMouse. As with calls of the **required** (by the Standard) **procedure** Read — yes, it is also a procedure, though a special one — the two integer variables supplied in the call to receive the values can have any names whatever. The same variable can even be supplied twice. So we could change the names x and y in YouGuess2 and the program would have the same effect. Of course, this applies also to the names of the other variables.

There is another kind of parameter used with procedures. Its role is to supply a value to the procedure, rather than, as happens with GetMouse, to supply a variable to receive a value from the procedure. The required procedure Write has such parameters.

## 3.5 Third program

YouGuess2 is hardly satisfactory even for its modest application. A respectable number-guessing game should let the user guess until he or she is successful. The modified program below does this, and also gives useful information about incorrect guesses.

```
program YouGuess3 (Input, Output);
{ Picks a number, and repeatedly asks for and reads a guess, }
{ indicating whether the guess is too high, too low, or correct }
{ (in which case it stops). }
  const
    MaxSecret = 10; { the biggest possible secret number }
  var
    x, y, { (x, y) is the mouse's position }
    secret, { the number to be guessed }
    guess : integer;
begin { YouGuess3 }
{ Define the number to be guessed }
  GetMouse(x, y);
  secret := (x + y) mod MaxSecret + 1;
{ Repeatedly prompt for, read, and describe }
{ guesses until the guess is correct }
  Writeln('I''m thinking of a number between 1 and',
           MaxSecret, ' inclusive.');
  Write('Please type your first guess: ');
  Readln(guess);
  while guess <> secret do
    begin
      if guess > secret then
        Writeln('That''s too high.')
      else
        Writeln('That''s too low.');
      Write('Please type your next guess: ');
      Readln(guess)
    end;
  Writeln('That''s correct!')
end. { YouGuess3 }
```

It is not so easy to guess what this program does, because a new type of statement is used that employs an English word, viz. 'while', in a way that differs from normal usage. The **while-statement** is written:

**while** *condition* **do**
  *statement*

It is executed by repeatedly executing the statement it contains (which is called its **body**), provided that before each successive repetition (including the first), the condition gives **true**. When the condition gives **false**, execution of the while-statement finishes.

It sometimes happens that the action that is to be repeatedly executed is expressed with several Pascal statements rather than one. For this reason, the while-statement is often used with a **compound statement**, which is a single statement formed by enclosing a sequence of statements between **begin** and **end**:

```
begin
  statements
end
```

It is executed by simply executing each of the statements in the sequence in the given order.

Another new feature is the **constant definition**:

```
MaxSecret = 10
```

which makes the name MaxSecret stand for the constant 10. Note that MaxSecret is not a variable — it makes as little sense to try to assign a value to it as it does to assign a value to 10. The **constant-definition-part** appears before the **variable-declaration-part**. It consists of the reserved word **const** followed by one or more constant definitions, each followed by a semicolon. It is good practice to use named constants to demystify various magic values in the program.

There is a new example of the Writeln-statement, hinting at the general form, where a list of expressions separated by commas may appear between the brackets. The effect is to evaluate and then print the value of each expression in turn, and then end the line. As with the Readln-statement,

```
Writeln(list-of-expressions)
```

is equivalent to:

```
Write(list-of-expressions);
Writeln
```

The first statement does the writing; the second ends the line. We have already seen that a string is written literally (and now know that strings, too, are expressions). An integer value is written in familiar decimal notation using a fixed number of characters. Enough leading spaces are written to ensure that the last character is the last digit. In Macintosh Pascal, eight characters are written; provided a fixed-width

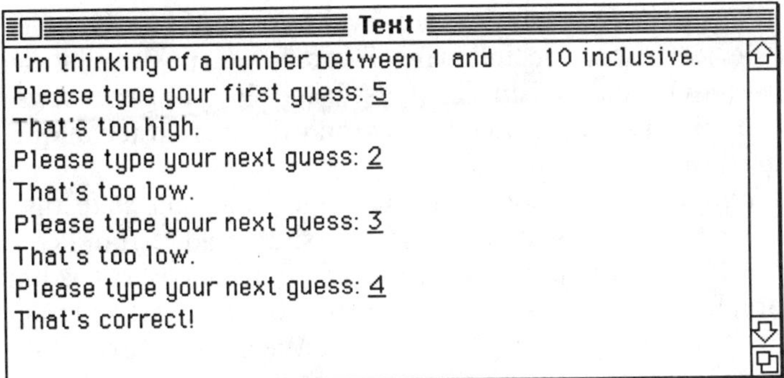

Text
I'm thinking of a number between 1 and 10 inclusive.
Please type your first guess: 5
That's too high.
Please type your next guess: 2
That's too low.
Please type your next guess: 3
That's too low.
Please type your next guess: 4
That's correct!


**Figure 3.5**
The Text window after a typical run of YouGuess3.

font is used in the Text window, the output width for an integer is constant.

Now we can understand YouGuess3, seeing that it does indeed do what its first group of comments claims. It starts by defining the secret number, and writing output as in YouGuess2, except that the *first* guess is requested. If it equals the secret, a new line announces that, and execution finishes. (Since the condition of a while-statement is checked before each potential execution of its body, the body will not be executed at all if the condition initially gives false.) If the guess is incorrect, the compound statement is executed that first announces whether the guess was high or low, and then prompts for and reads the next guess. Then that is compared to the secret, and so on until the correct value is guessed. The input and output for a typical run is shown in Figure 3.5.

The ability to describe repetition is one of the most important attributes of a programming language. The while-statement is the fundamental form of repetition in Pascal, although there are two other statements provided for expressing special forms of repetition.

This completes our preview of Pascal. It is important to appreciate that we have been reading programs, not writing them. You may now be able to execute a program that is composed of the features we have seen (although many details remain to be given). But it is a much bigger intellectual step to writing them. After all, even computers can do the former! And there are six-line while-statements whose understanding can tax even the most accomplished of programmers. We've only just begun ...

## 3.6 Macaveats

The scheme of interactive I/O illustrated in our example programs works very nicely on the Macintosh, but it need not according to the

Standard. Specifically, text output by **Write** need not be sent to the output device before the following **Read** is executed. The details of interactive I/O are given in Chapters 5 and 14. But the news is that the Standard cops out in this respect, and there is no technique that is guaranteed to be transportable.

Contrary to this book, the Reference does not state that an integer is written in a **field** of 8 characters. Instead, it implies (on pp. 9-16 to 9-18) that the minimum number of characters is used, so that, for example, 0 would be output as just `0`. This is contrary to the Standard and the observed behavior of Macintosh Pascal 2.0. Put it down to a bug in the Reference.

## 3.7 Further reading


(1) Anon. (1983). *Specification for Computer Programming Language Pascal*. Document ISO 7185:1983. International Organization for Standardization.
The international standard. Included for completeness only; there is little reason for a beginner to consult it.

(2) Anon. (1983). *American National Standard Pascal Computer Programming Language*. ANSI/IEEE770X3.97-1983. New York: IEEE/Wiley-Interscience.
The US standard — what this book calls *the Standard*. Differs from the ISO document in omitting conformant arrays.

(3) Cooper, D. (1983). *STANDARD PASCAL User Reference Manual*. New York: Norton.
Lives up to its self-description as 'a correct, comprehensive, and comprehensible reference for Pascal.' For the professional Pascal programmer or the stickler for detail.

3.3 (4) Hueras, J. (1984). *Macintosh Pascal Reference Manual*. Apple product #M1505. USA and Canada: Apple Computer, Inc.
*The Reference* — one of three manuals that come with Macintosh Pascal. Presumably intended to be definitive, but there are cases where the Macintosh Pascal software is at variance with it. Where the fault is an obvious bug in the software, this book sides with the Reference. But there are cases where the fault would appear to be in the Reference. An example is given in the last paragraph under 'Macaveats'. In such cases, this book sides with the software.

## EXERCISES

Exercises involving running the programs presented in this chapter are postponed until Chapter 4.

**3.1** The sample programs tell the user that a number has been chosen that is between 1 and 10 inclusive. Does the assignment to variable **secret** always give such a number? Why?

**3.2** What does the assignment statement

```
number := number + 1
```

do to the integer variable **number**?

The next three exercises actually involve writing and modifying Pascal programs. This may seem a little premature, but you did learn to speak English by imitation, the exercises are quite modest, and you have already written your own output statements. So why not give them a try?

**3.3** Modify program **YouGuess3** so that after the last (successful) guess it prints the number of guesses. You'll need a new integer variable which should be initialized to zero.

*Hint*: Use the answer to Exercise 3.2.

**3.4** Congratulations if you solved the previous question! (If not, don't worry, the technique you need is covered in Chapter 5.) If you just printed a bare number, spruce up the last output statement so that it prints something like:

```
You guessed    3 times.
```

**3.5** Write Algorithm (a) given in Exercise 1.4 in Pascal.

# 4
# RUNNING MACINTOSH PASCAL PROGRAMS

None of the programs in this monograph, needless to say, has been tested on a machine.
— Edsger W. Dijkstra, *A Discipline of Programming*

## 4.1 Introduction

Like Chapter 2, this chapter is designed to serve as a reference, so do not be worried if some of the material seems strange on first reading. The only way to learn how to exploit the features of the Macintosh Pascal programming environment properly is to experiment with them on a Macintosh. The exercises invite the reader to do just that. They are presented in the same order as the text, so that you can tackle them either after reading the whole chapter, or during the first reading as the appropriate material is covered.

## 4.2 Running a program

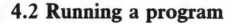

To run a program, choose Go from the Run menu. If changes have been made since the last Check or run, the translator is automatically invoked. If the translator detects no errors, execution begins. An error (such as an illegal operation) may occur during execution, in which case execution stops and a message is displayed. Or the program may run without error but never stop! If both these hurdles are passed, there is the further possibility — historically a probability for most new, non-trivial programs — that the output produced is incorrect. Then you need all the help you can get.

## 4.3 Controlling execution

Errors that are revealed by execution (called **bugs**) are the hardest to fix. Macintosh Pascal has sophisticated facilities for controlling and observing the execution of a program, which are very helpful for testing and **debugging** programs.

### 4.3.1 STOPPING EXECUTION

Whenever your program is running, the menu bar contains the Pause menu. Its only available command is Halt. If you press on Pause, execution is suspended until you release the mouse button. Choosing Halt stops execution of the program. To resume execution, choose Go from the Run menu; but if you want execution to start again from scratch, choose Reset and then Go from the Run menu.

### 4.3.2 STEPWISE EXECUTION

You can run your program one step at a time by choosing Step from the Run menu. A hand appears in the left margin of the Program window. Each time you choose Step, the line pointed to by the hand is executed, and the hand advances to the next line to be executed.

Choosing Step-Step from the Run menu causes execution to step continuously until it finishes, an error occurs, or you stop it. You can watch the hand trace through the program.

### 4.3.3 SETTING STOP MARKS

Stopping a program by choosing Halt from the Pause menu is a rather crude way of interrupting execution. A Pascal program executes many statements a second, and quite often you want a program to run normally until it reaches some critical statement and then stop precisely there. Unless you are a video games virtuoso, your chance of hitting that statement with Halt is small.

There is a much better way: choose Stops In from the Run menu. A white bar appears in the left margin of the Program window, with a small stop sign at the bottom. When you move the cursor into the bar, it changes into a stop sign. If you click when the stop sign cursor is before an executable statement, a stop sign is deposited there. You can deposit as many as you like. When the program is executed, it stops whenever the hand reaches a line marked with a stop sign (before executing it).

To restart the program, choose Go from the Run menu; the program resumes execution at the line where it stopped, and continues until the next stop mark is reached.

Choosing Go-Go from the Run menu causes the program to stop at each stop mark only long enough to update the Observe window (another testing aid, described below). Used in conjunction with a stop mark inside a loop, Go-Go enables you to observe the values of variables as they change after each iteration.

To remove a stop mark, point at it and click. To get rid of all stops, switch off the stop feature by choosing Stops Out from the Run menu.

## 4.4 Tracing execution

The Observe window allows you to observe the values of expressions (and therefore variables) as they change during execution. It is an invaluable aid to testing and debugging programs, particularly when used in conjunction with stepwise execution and stop marks.

When you choose Observe from the Windows menu, the Observe window becomes visible and active. It consists of a number of rows divided by a vertical line into two parts. In the right parts you can type (or Paste) expressions, using the Enter-key to skip to each new part. Whenever the program pauses or halts, the value of each expression is calculated and displayed to the left of the expression. Figure 4.1 shows the Observe window in use with program YouGuess3 from Chapter 3.

The best ways to use the Observe window are with Step-Step, when the values are updated after each step, or by leaving stop marks where the values of the expressions are of interest, and either to choose Go repeatedly to resume execution or to choose Go-Go just once.

A restriction should be noted: expressions that depend on keyboard input (such as eoln) cannot always be evaluated. In such cases you will get the error message ‘Can’t use keyboard’.

## 4.5 The Instant window

Any time that your program is not running, you can use the Instant window to execute any Pascal statement or statements immediately. You can even change the value of one or more of your program’s variables before resuming execution.

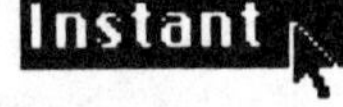


Choosing Instant from the Windows menu displays the Instant window and makes it active, as shown in Figure 4.2. You can enter and edit any Pascal statements there, using the Edit menu to copy and paste between the Program, Observe, and Instant windows. Clicking the Do It button executes the statements you have entered.

The Instant window is of limited and dubious use. It is limited because a call to a procedure that the interpreter has not yet encountered, for example, will not be executed. It is dubious because

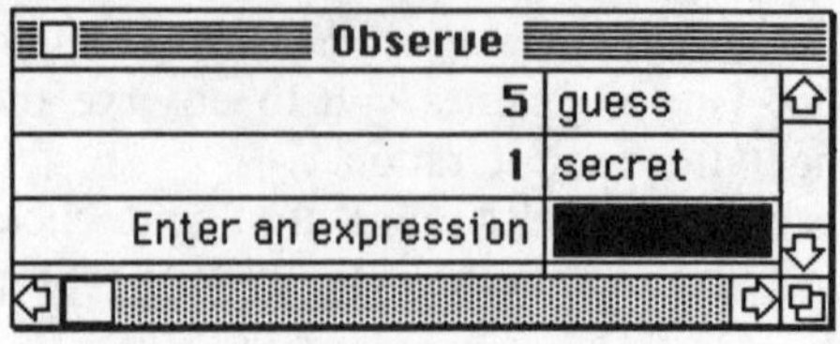


**Figure 4.1**
The Observe window.

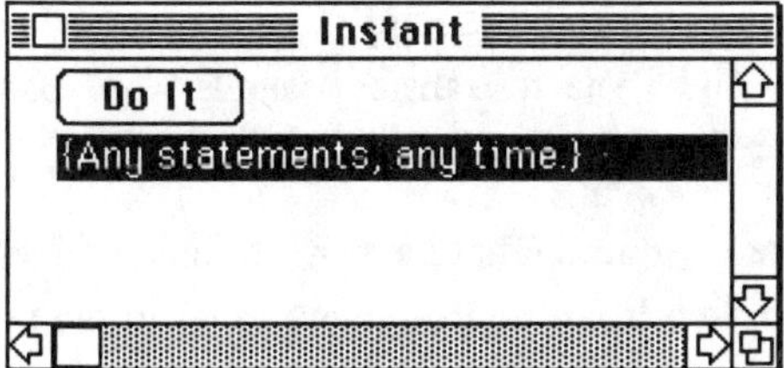


**Figure 4.2**
The Instant window.

there is little it does that cannot be done better with the Observe window or by editing the program, and because there is much it permits that is unwise (such as arbitrary assignments).

We shall use it mainly as an aid to learning low-level Pascal.

## EXERCISES

The first group of exercises assume that program **YouGuess3** from Chapter 3 is in the Program window, ready for execution.

4.9

**4.1** Running a program

Run the program. To be able to see its output you have to make the Text window visible. Whenever input is required the program will prompt you (with a message in the Text window) to enter input. To do so, type a number and press the Return-key. What happens?

**4.2** Controlling execution

Step through the program, observing the moving hand. Use the keyboard equivalent of Step from the Run menu.

Run the program again, but this time choose Step-Step from the Run menu instead of stepping manually.

Choose Stops In from the Run menu. Set a stop mark at the line that reads **while** guess <> secret **do**. Run the program by choosing Go from the Run menu. What is its keyboard equivalent?

What is the effect of the stop mark on execution? How do you restart the program?

Rerun the program, but this time choose Go-Go from the Run menu. How does this differ from using Go?

You can combine stop marks and stepwise execution. Choose Step-Step from the Run menu without removing the stop mark.

**4.3** Tracing execution

Activate the Observe window. Type guess in the first line.

Activate the Program window and select any of the occurrences of secret. Choose Copy from the Edit menu. Now activate the Observe window and set the insertion point to the second line. Choose Paste from the Edit menu to put **secret** there.

Using Copy and Paste to transfer a single word between the Program and the Observe window is hardly worth the effort in this case. When would it be?

Now run the program. What happens to the Observe window? Why?

Choose Step-Step from the Run menu to rerun the program.

Choose Go-Go from the Run menu to rerun the program.

Deactivate the stop feature.

**4.4** The Instant window

Activate the Instant window.

Enter **Writeln('Cogito Ergo Sum.')**. Make sure that the Text window is visible, then click Do It.

Make the Observe window active (with **guess** and **secret** entered), then run the program. Halt it when it prompts for input. What happens? Enter **secret := 2** in the Instant window (except if 2 appears to the left of **secret** in the Observe window, in which case use **3** instead of 2), then Do It. What happens? Resume execution of the program.

Use the Instant window to experiment with different output statements and different types of expressions. What output is produced by a condition?

**4.5** Change the value of **MaxSecret** to 100, then run the program. Note that it works as it should because every use of **MaxSecret** was explicitly identified. By the way, you should be able to guess the secret in at most 7 guesses!

The remaining exercises do not involve program **YouGuess3**.

**4.6** Use the Instant window to execute different Write- and Writeln-statements with string expressions only. Observe their effects in the Text window.

**4.7** Execute program **YouGuess2** by repeatedly using Step. Use the Observe window to track the values of the four variables. What happens if the same input is typed as for **YouGuess** in Figure 3.2?

**4.8** Investigate the coordinate system of the screen by writing a little program that just repeatedly gets the mouse position. It need never stop, so you can use **1 = 1** or just **true** for the condition of the while-statement. Use the Observe window to follow the changing values of the coordinate variables as you move the mouse around. Execute the program by repeatedly using Step.

# 5 BASIC PASCAL

Oh! *I* know their tricks and their manners.
— Charles Dickens, *Our Mutual Friend*

## 5.1 Introduction

This chapter presents the fine print for the part of Pascal previewed in Chapter 3. Several new features are introduced: the types real, char, and Boolean, required functions, the repeat-statement. With the exception of our method of specifying syntax, which is designed to be as natural and non-technical as possible, no major new concepts are introduced. The aim is to flesh out a modest sublanguage of Pascal, yet one that is sufficiently powerful to tackle interesting programming problems.

Much of the information in this chapter consists of relatively unimportant nitty-gritty details that are peculiar to Standard Pascal or Macintosh Pascal (if not outright peculiar). They are here because sooner, but most likely later, you will want to get the details right, or perhaps because something unexpected happens that involves some fine points. Be assured that the challenge in learning to program is not to memorize massive amounts of low-level knowledge, but rather to learn how to solve programming problems effectively. The tough get going in the next chapter.

## 5.2 Specifying syntax

Learning a new programming language necessarily involves learning its **syntax**, or written form. Your implicit working knowledge of the syntax of English was deduced from the set of examples of English that you were exposed to, and was perhaps augmented by an informal study of syntax at school ('a sentence is a subject followed by a verb followed by an object'). Such approaches will not do for a language that is to be translated by a computer: a formal method is needed. The Standard defines Pascal's syntax using a particular formal method called Extended Backus Naur Formalism, or EBNF for short. (It is briefly described in Section A.4 of the Appendix). We shall use a method that is loosely based on EBNF, but that strives closely to reflect the way programs are displayed by Macintosh Pascal. It tries to follow the principle that what you see is what you should get.

The Reference, as well as most texts on Pascal, presents syntax using graphical devices called **syntax diagrams**, sometimes called **syntax charts**. They were introduced by Wirth for his reports on Pascal, and have since become *de rigueur*. Accordingly, syntax diagrams for Pascal are presented in Section A.3 of the Appendix, after an explanation of their use in Section A.2.

Our method was broached in Chapter 3. The basic ideas are:

- To represent each important class of syntactic items by a technical term;

- To describe the typical member of each syntactic class by displaying it as does Macintosh Pascal, using *italicized* technical terms to stand for arbitrary members of their corresponding syntactic classes, and displaying literal text in the Helvetica font.

For example, we use the term 'identifier-list' for the class of comma-separated lists of legal Pascal names, 'type' for the class of types, and 'variable-declaration' for the class of (you guessed it) variable declarations. The syntactic form of a variable declaration is defined as follows:

variable-declaration: *identifier-list* : *type*

It says that a variable-declaration consists of an identifier-list followed by a colon followed by a type. Note that the colon, in Helvetica, appears literally. Spaces are not significant.

To express the notion of arbitrarily many, the time-honored device of three dots is used. When it appears on a line by itself, it represents arbitrarily many (possibly zero) appearances of the previous line, as in:

```
variable-declaration-part:
    var
     variable-declaration ;
     ...
```

This says that a variable-declaration-part starts with the reserved-word **var**, which is followed by one or more variable-declarations, each of which is followed by a semicolon. Moreover, it shows the layout used by Macintosh Pascal. Incidentally, this definition will be modified later to show that a variable-declaration-part may be empty.

When three dots occur within a line, the following part of the line may appear zero or more times, as in:

identifier-list: *identifier* ... , *identifier*

This says that an identifier-list consists of an identifier followed by zero or more groups, each consisting of a comma followed by an identifier. Note that, unlike in the other case, the repeated part might not appear at all.

Syntactic alternatives are separated by a vertical bar ('| ', read 'or'), as in:

input statement: *Read-statement* | *Readln-statement*

This says that an input statement is either a Read-statement or a Readln-statement.

A vertical line on the left indicates that the lines that it spans are optional. You may regard it as a vertical bar separating an empty alternative on its left from another on its right. For example:

statement-list:
| *statement* ;
| ...
*statement*

This says that a statement-list consists of a statement optionally preceded by one or more lines, each consisting of a statement followed by a semicolon.

Similarly, an underlined section of a line is optional. For example:

Readln-statement: **Readln** <u>(*variable-list*)</u>

It says that a Readln-statement consists of **Readln** optionally followed by a group consisting of a left-bracket followed by a variable-list followed by a right-bracket.

These techniques are all we need to specify Pascal's syntax. So now let us look at the language itself, working bottom-up from the simplest components.

## 5.3 Types of values

Each variable used in a Pascal program is declared to have a certain **type**. It determines the set of possible values of the variable, and what operations may be performed with it. Standard Pascal has four required simple types: integer, real, char, and Boolean. We shall look at each in turn.

### 5.3.1 INTEGER

As we saw in Chapter 3, type integer corresponds to the mathematical integers, i.e. all the whole numbers, whether positive, zero, or negative. For practical reasons, Pascal's integers are constrained to lie between minus and plus a machine-dependent limit, which is made available as a predefined constant:

```
const
  Maxint = 32767; { integers lie in the range –Maxint..Maxint }
```

Integer constants are written in familiar decimal notation. An integer constant is called a signed-integer. Its syntax is defined below, using some extra terms which are needed later.

signed-integer: *sign unsigned-integer*
sign: + | –
unsigned-integer: *digit-sequence*
digit-sequence: *digit* ... *digit*
digit: 0 | 1 | 2 | 3 | 4 | 5 | 6 | 7 | 8 | 9

Note that neither a decimal point nor the common convention of using commas to group digits into thousands is allowed. Here are some signed-integers:

```
2001   –65   0   007
```

Although leading zeros are permitted, it is not normal practice to use them. The plus sign is normally omitted; –0, +0, and 0 all represent the number of Beatles' singles that bombed.

Macintosh Pascal also provides a type longint that has a bigger range of values than integer. See Chapter 19.

Integer expressions are constructed from constants, variables, operators, and functions. The **operators** listed in Table 5.1 take two integer **operands** and return an integer result. Each of these operators is written between its two operands (but see below *re* + and –).

The value returned by **div** can be defined as the exact real quotient with its fractional part discarded. Division by zero is an error. For example:

31 **div** 7 gives 4, since $\frac{31}{7} = 4.428\,57\ldots$

Table 5.1 Integer operators.

| Operator | Operation |
|---|---|
| + | addition (or multiplication by +1) |
| – | subtraction (or multiplication by –1) |
| * | multiplication |
| **div** | integer division |
| **mod** | the modulo operation |

–21 **div** 5 gives –4, since $\frac{-21}{5} = -4.2$

2 **div** 9 gives 0, since $\frac{2}{9} = 0.222\,22\ldots$

The value of $x$ **mod** $y$ is defined only when $y > 0$ — it is an error otherwise. It is the smallest integer $\geqslant 0$ that leaves an integral multiple of $y$ when subtracted from $x$. It is thus in the range $0 .. y - 1$. When $x$ is non-negative, as it usually is in this context, $x$ **mod** $y$ is the remainder from $x$ **div** $y$. For example:

31 **mod** 7 gives 3, since $31 - 3 = 28 = 4 \times 7$
–21 **mod** 5 gives 4, since $-21 - 4 = -25 = -5 \times 5$
2 **mod** 9 gives 2, since $2 - 2 = 0 = 0 \times 9$

Operators + and – can also be placed in front of a single integer operand to denote multiplication by +1 or –1 respectively.

The remaining building-blocks for integer expressions are *functions*, which can either be predefined or defined by the programmer. A Pascal function returns a single value that depends upon given values called *arguments*, i.e. it is just like a mathematical function. There are two required (and therefore predefined) functions that take and return integers:

abs($x$): the absolute value of $x$, i.e. $x$ if $x \geqslant 0$ or $-x$ if $x < 0$.
sqr($x$): the square of $x$, i.e. $x^2$ ($x \times x$).

The rules for forming and evaluating expressions are dealt with in Section 5.4.

### 5.3.2 REAL

Type real corresponds to the mathematical real numbers. For practical reasons, Pascal's real numbers are constrained to lie between two limits, and also to have a limited number of significant digits. In

Macintosh Pascal, the range of real values is approximately $-3.4 \times 10^{38}$ to $3.4 \times 10^{38}$, that is, $-R$ to $+R$, where $R$ is approximately 340 000 000 000 000 000 000 000 000 000 000 000 000. The smallest positive non-zero real number is approximately $1.5 \times 10^{-45}$. The number of significant decimal digits is between 7 and 8. Unfortunately, none of these machine-dependent values is captured by a predefined constant.

Real constants may be written in familiar decimal notation, using a decimal point. But because they can be very large or small, they may also be written in **power notation**, i.e. using powers of 10 as above. Superscripts are avoided by writing E*n* instead of $\times 10^n$. The full syntax is specified as follows:

signed-real: *sign unsigned-real*
unsigned-real: *digit-sequence . digit-sequence* |
*digit-sequence . digit-sequence* E *scale-factor*
scale-factor: *sign unsigned-integer*

Note that if a decimal point appears it must have at least one digit on either side. Here are some signed-reals:

```
2001.0   -6.5E1   0.0   7E0
1E+9   1.0E+9   1E9   1000000000.0
1E-6   1.0E-6   0.000001
```

The numbers in the first line are real versions of the integers given previously, but they are not the same numbers. The numbers in the second line all represent the same real number: a (US) billion. The numbers in the third line all represent one millionth.

Macintosh Pascal also provides types double and extended that have bigger ranges of more precise real values. See Chapter 19.

The operators listed in Table 5.2 take two reals and return a real result. Again, each of these operators is written between its two real operands; also, + and – may be written in front of a single real operand. Real division is what you would expect:

| | | |
|---|---|---|
| 31 / 7 | gives | 4.42857 ... |
| -21 / 5 | gives | -4.2 |
| 2 / 9 | gives | 0.22222 ... |

Real operations rarely produce the exact result, and it is necessary to be very careful when doing calculations with real values. The topic is taken up in Chapter 19.

The functions abs and sqr may also be applied to a real argument, in which case a real value is returned. Several other required functions are provided that always produce real values:

**Table 5.2** Real operators.

| Operator | Operation |
|---|---|
| + | addition (or multiplication by +1) |
| – | subtraction (or multiplication by –1) |
| * | multiplication |
| / | real division |

sqrt($x$): the non-negative square root of $x$ ($x$ must be $\geqslant 0$)
sin($x$): the sine of $x$ ($x$ represents radians)
cos($x$): the cosine of $x$ ($x$ represents radians)
arctan($x$): the principal value, in radians, of the arctangent of $x$
exp($x$): $e$ to the power $x$
ln($x$): the natural logarithm of $x$ ($x$ must be $> 0$)

Because every integer value has a corresponding real value, integers may be used in expressions in place of reals. When only integers are used with +, –, *, **abs**, or **sqr**, the result is an integer, as stated previously. Otherwise, the result is real. Here are some examples:

```
1E2 * 0      gives    0.0
100.5 + 1    gives  101.5
9 / 5        gives    1.8 (not 1)
sqrt(9)      gives    3.0
```

Remember, the results may not be exactly those shown.

Real values do not have corresponding integers, but there are two required functions that convert real values to integer values, provided the results are in range:

trunc($x$): the integer part of $x$
round($x$): the nearest integer to $x$, rounding to a greater absolute value if there is a choice

Thus, for example:

```
trunc(19.95)     gives   19
trunc(–19.95)    gives  –19
round(19.95)     gives   20
round(–19.95)    gives  –20
round(1.5)       gives    2
round(–1.5)      gives   –2
```

They are called **transfer functions**, because they transfer between two types.

### 5.3.3 CHAR

Although digital computers were originally devoted mainly to numeric computation, number-crunching is no longer their most important task. The ubiquity of computers is due to their ability to perform all kinds of non-numeric computation. The most common form of non-numeric information is textual, and its basic unit is the character.

The Pascal type char has as its values the characters made available by a particular implementation. The set of these values, called the **character set**, is therefore implementation-dependent. Macintosh Pascal provides 256 characters, numbered 0 to 255. They are shown in Table 5.3, which is taken from Appendix E of the Macintosh Pascal Technical Appendix (see the 'Further reading' list at the end of Chapter 9). Not all of them are visible; those that are not are called **control characters**, because they are used to send control information

**Table 5.3** The Macintosh Pascal character set.

| | 0 | 1 | 2 | 3 | 4 | 5 | 6 | 7 | 8 | 9 | 10 | 11 | 12 | 13 | 14 | 15 |
|---|---|---|---|---|---|---|---|---|---|---|---|---|---|---|---|---|
| 0 | NUL | DLE | SP | 0 | @ | P | ` | p | Ä | ê | † | ∞ | ¿ | – | | |
| 1 | SOH | DC1 | ! | 1 | A | Q | a | q | Å | ë | ° | ± | ¡ | — | | |
| 2 | STX | DC2 | " | 2 | B | R | b | r | Ç | í | ¢ | ≤ | ¬ | “ | | |
| 3 | ETX Enter | DC3 | # | 3 | C | S | c | s | É | ì | £ | ≥ | √ | ” | | |
| 4 | EOT | DC4 | $ | 4 | D | T | d | t | Ñ | î | § | ¥ | ƒ | ‘ | | |
| 5 | ENQ | NAK | % | 5 | E | U | e | u | Ö | ï | • | µ | ≈ | ’ | | |
| 6 | ACK | SYN | & | 6 | F | V | f | v | Ü | ñ | ¶ | ∂ | ∆ | ÷ | | |
| 7 | BEL | ETB | ' | 7 | G | W | g | w | á | ó | ß | Σ | « | ◊ | | |
| 8 | BS | CAN | ( | 8 | H | X | h | x | à | ò | ® | Π | » | ÿ | | |
| 9 | HT | EM | ) | 9 | I | Y | i | y | â | ô | © | π | … | | | |
| 10 | LF | SUB | * | : | J | Z | j | z | ä | ö | ™ | ∫ | ␣ | | | |
| 11 | VT | ESC Clear | + | ; | K | [ | k | { | ã | õ | ´ | ª | À | | | |
| 12 | FF | FS ◀ | , | < | L | \ | l | \| | å | ú | ¨ | º | Ã | | | |
| 13 | CR | GS ▶ | - | = | M | ] | m | } | ç | ù | ≠ | Ω | Õ | | | |
| 14 | SO | RS ▲ | . | > | N | ^ | n | ~ | é | û | Æ | æ | Œ | | | |
| 15 | SI | US ▼ | / | ? | O | _ | o | DEL | è | ü | Ø | ø | œ | | | |

to various devices. The control characters are those in the first two columns.

Character constants are written by enclosing them in single quotes. As we saw previously, the single quote character is written twice, and enclosed in single quotes like the others, so that four single quotes represent the single quote character! Pascal does not have a special syntactic class for character constants, because they are the character-strings of one character. Their syntax is given by:

character-string: ' *string-element-sequence* '
string-element-sequence: *string-element* ... *string-element*
string-element: *string-character* | *apostrophe-image*
string-character: *one-of-the-visible-characters-in-Table-5.3-except-'*
apostrophe-image: ''

Here are seven different character constants:

```
'A'  'a'  '1'  '$'  '*'  ' '  ''''
```

The latter two are the space (or blank) and the single quote (or apostrophe).

There are no operators that give character values, but there are two required functions that do:

succ(*c*): the character after *c* in the character set
(it is an error if *c* is the last character)
pred(*c*): the character before *c* in the character set
(it is an error if *c* is the first character)

The ordering of the characters is captured by two required transfer functions:

ord(*c*): the position of *c* in the character set;
positions start with 0, and, in Macintosh Pascal, go to 255
chr(*i*): the character in position *i* in the character set
(it is an error if *i* is not in the range of positions)

Values returned by ord are called **ordinal values**. They may be read off Table 5.3 by multiplying the column number by 16 and adding the row number.

Here are some examples of the above functions:

| | | |
|---|---|---|
| succ('A') | gives | 'B' |
| pred('7') | gives | '6' |
| ord('a') | gives | 97 |
| chr(98) | gives | 'b' |

None of the above results is guaranteed by the Standard, which requires only that ordinal values increase when proceeding through both the upper-case (i.e. capital) letters and lower-case letters in alphabetic order, and that the digits form a contiguous group in numeric order. Thus, for example, ord('7') – ord('6') must give 1, but ord('c') – ord('b') need only give a value ⩾ 1 (although both groups of letters are contiguous in Macintosh Pascal, and in most other implementations).

### 5.3.4 BOOLEAN

The type Boolean is named after the nineteenth century English mathematician George Boole, because he first expounded the properties of its operators. It is a rare program that does not use Boolean values, since what were called **conditions** in Chapter 3 are Boolean expressions.

There are only two Boolean values, written:

```
false   true
```

The syntax of Boolean constants is subsumed in:

constant-identifier: *identifier*

The syntax of identifier is given later.

The three operators that take and return only Boolean values are listed in Table 5.4. They may be defined thus, letting *p* and *q* stand for Boolean values:

| | | |
|---|---|---|
| **not** *p* | gives | true if and only if *p* is false. |
| *p* **and** *q* | gives | true if and only if both *p* and *q* are true. |
| *p* **or** *q* | gives | true if and only if at least one of *p*, *q* is true. |

(We henceforth write 'iff' for 'if and only if'.) It is these technical definitions that you should keep in mind when you use these operators — everyday usage of the corresponding English words is less precise. Some examples:

| | | |
|---|---|---|
| **not** true | gives | false |
| true **and** false | gives | false |
| true **and** true | gives | true |
| false **or** true | gives | true |
| false **or** false | gives | false |

The operands of Boolean operators are typically produced by the relational operators that we met in Chapter 3:

**Table 5.4** Boolean operators.

| Operator | Operation |
|---|---|
| **not** | logical negation |
| **and** | logical and |
| **or** | logical inclusive or |

< > <= >= = <>

When used with numeric values they have their usual mathematical meanings. They may also be used with character values (and, as we shall see later, strings). In this case, the result is the same as that obtained by comparing the ordinal values of the two characters. For example:

'7' >= '0' gives true
'a' < 'b' gives true
'a' < 'B' gives false (in Macintosh Pascal)

Boolean values themselves can be compared: false < true gives true. This is not normally done, but it does allow other logical operators to be represented: <=, =, and <> correspond respectively to logical implication, equivalence, and exclusive or. (You need not worry if those terms are unfamiliar.)

Save for the fact that an integer may be compared with a real, the two operands of a relational operator must produce values of the same type. It makes no sense, for example, to compare a character to an integer.

Three required functions return Boolean values. Two of them, viz. eoln and eof, test certain input conditions, and are discussed later in this chapter. The other one is odd (so to speak):

odd($i$): true if and only if the integer value $i$ is odd,
i.e. iff $i$ **mod** 2 = 1.

## 5.4 Expressions

As stated previously, expressions are constructed from constants, variables (which stand for their current values), operators, and functions. One way to specify the legal expressions is as follows:

(1) A constant is an expression. Examples: 1, 1E2, '!', true, MaxSecret.

(2) A variable is an expression. Example: guess.

(3) An operator with arbitrary expressions as operand(s) is an expression, provided the number, order, and types of the operand(s) satisfy the appropriate requirements, and rules 6 and 7 are met. Examples: x + y, (x + y) **mod** 10, **not** odd(i).

(4) A function with arbitrary expressions as argument(s) is an expression, provided the number, order, and types of the argument(s) satisfy the appropriate requirements. Examples: sqr(x), sqrt(sqr(x) + sqr(y)).

(5) Any expression may be bracketed by ( and ). Example: (x + y).

(6) Two arithmetic operators may never be adjacent, ruling out, for example, 1 * –3.

(7) An operand of a relational operator may not be a relational expression, unless it is bracketed. For example, this rules out x < y < z (even if x, y, and z give Boolean values).

The meaning of an expression would not appear to be problematic, because we know the meaning of all the component parts. But there are potential ambiguities concerning operators which must be resolved. For example, does 3 – 2 – 1 mean (3 – 2) – 1, which gives 0, or 3 – (2 – 1), which gives 2? Similarly, what is the implied bracketing in x + y **mod** 10 + 1?

Such ambiguities in the order of evaluation are resolved by **precedence rules**, which come into play when there would otherwise be a choice:

(I) Operators are applied in order of decreasing precedence. Table 5.5 gives the precedence of each operator.

(II) Operators with equal precedence are performed from left to right.

We can now answer the questions about our examples. Rule II implies that 3 – 2 – 1 means (3 – 2) – 1, which gives 0. Regarding

```
x + y mod 10 + 1
```

rule I implies y **mod** 10 is a subexpression, because **mod** has pre-

**Table 5.5** Precedence of operators.

| Precedence | Operator(s) |
|---|---|
| 3 | **not** + (1 operand) – (1 operand) |
| 2 | * **div** **mod** / **and** |
| 1 | + – **or** |
| 0 | = < > <= >= <> |

cedence over +. Then rule II gets into the act, implying x and y **mod** 10 are added. The implicit bracketing is:

((x + (y **mod** 10)) + 1)

The effect of the rules is not to specify the precise order of evaluation of the operators and functions, but rather to specify completely the operand(s) of each operator and the argument(s) of each function. The distinction is illustrated by the expression:

(a <> 0) **and** (sqr(b) – 4 * a * c >= 0)

where a, b, and c are real variables. The implied bracketing is:

((a <> 0) **and** ((sqr(b) – ((4 * a) * c)) >= 0))

But there is still plenty of freedom in the evaluation, which can start with either a <> 0 or sqr(b) or 4 * a. Moreover, the left or right operand of **and** might not be evaluated at all, because if one gives false it is not necessary to evaluate the other. The Standard does not specify which of two operands of a single operator is evaluated first, or even that one or the other *is* evaluated first — they might be evaluated simultaneously — or not evaluated at all. The same goes for the arguments of a function. All this is hair-splitting rather than hair-raising, but there is at least one common hairy programming situation that is affected; see Subsection 11.4.2, 'Truncated safe linear search' for the bald facts.

The syntax rules for expressions are cleverly designed to imply their structure without needing the notion of operator precedence. We give them for completeness, but they need not keep you awake at night:

expression:
    *simple-expression relational-operator simple-expression*
simple-expression: *sign term ... adding-operator term*
term: *factor ... multiplying-operator factor*
factor: *variable* | *unsigned-constant* | *function-designator* |
    *(expression)* | **not** *factor*
unsigned-constant: *unsigned-integer* | *unsigned-real* |
    *character-string* | *constant-identifier*
relational-operator: = | < | > | <= | >= | <>
adding-operator: + | – | **or**
multiplying-operator: * | **div** | **mod** | / | **and**
function-designator: *function-identifier ( actual-parameter-list )*
function-identifier: *identifier*
actual-parameter-list: *actual-value ... , actual-value*
actual-value: *expression*

The writer of programs — as distinct from the reader prepared for anything — need not be fanatically concerned with the rules for expressions, since it is not necessary to rely on them when writing expressions. Stick to the following principles:

- Use extra brackets whenever they make it easier to understand an expression.
- Avoid very complex expressions by introducing variables for some of the subexpressions. Macintosh Pascal encourages this by insisting on placing long expressions on a single line!
- Always bracket relational subexpressions (since you have to).

A final piece of terminology relating to expressions: we say '(the value of) *e* is ... ' to mean 'evaluation of *e* gives the value ... '.

## 5.5 Constants and variables

Programs manipulate values; some values are fixed, others change. Simple values of the first kind may be represented by named constants; values of the second kind are represented by variables.

### 5.5.1 CONSTANT DEFINITIONS

A constant value used in a program may be given a name by means of a constant definition. Thereafter, the name may be used in place of the constant. Constant definitions are gathered in a possibly empty constant definition part. The syntax is as follows:

constant-definition-part:
  | **const**
  |   *constant-definition* ;
  |   ...

constant-definition: *identifier* = *constant*
constant: *character-string* | *sign* *unsigned-number* |
    *sign* *constant-identifier*
constant-identifier: *identifier*

We met an example in Chapter 3:

```
const
  MaxSecret = 10; { the biggest possible secret number }
```

Note that a constant may consist of a sign followed by a constant-identifier, allowing constructions such as:

```
Minint = –Maxint; { the minimum integer }
```

and that a string constant can be given a name, as in:

```
ChapterHeading = 'Basic Pascal';
```

The payoff from constant definitions is far greater than their simplicity might suggest:

- The name is usually more suggestive than the value.
- The value need only be written once, reducing the chance of error, especially when the value is modified.
- Different uses of the same value can be distinguished, by simply having two constant definitions with the same value. This allows one or both of the values to be changed without confusion.

Maxint is the only constant required to be predefined. Additionally, Macintosh Pascal provides:

```
pi = 3.14159265358979323 85; { an approximation to the ratio }
     { of a circle's circumference to its diameter }
```

as well as a host of other constants related to the Macintosh's operating system (for which see the Reference and the Technical Appendix).

### 5.5.2 VARIABLE DECLARATIONS

A variable, as we have seen, may be regarded as a named container of a value of a certain type. It is introduced by a variable declaration, which fixes its name and type. Initially its value is undefined, and may change arbitrarily often during execution of the program.

All variables used in a program must be declared. The variable declarations are collected in the variable declaration part, whose syntax is specified as follows:

variable-declaration-part:
| **var**
| *variable-declaration* ;
| ...

variable-declaration: *identifier-list* : *type*
identifier-list: *identifier* ... , *identifier*

Here is an example of a variable declaration part, contrived to involve each of the types we have seen so far:

```
var
  x, y : integer; { (x, y) is the mouse's position }
  declination : real; { angle in radians between line from (x, y) to }
                      { origin and line along top of Drawing window }
  FirstChar : char; { first character in current input line }
  IsCommand : Boolean; { true iff current input line is a command }
  NumberOfCommands : integer;
```

(For other examples, look at any of the programs throughout the book.)

The following stylistic guidelines are highly recommended, because they make for programs that are easier to read. They apply equally to constant definitions:

- Mnemonic names should be chosen, unless there is an established naming convention. Witness the names in the above example, which all suggest the roles of their variables (x and y are traditionally used for coordinates).
- A clear and concise comment should explain the role of each variable, unless its role is obvious from its name (as happens with NumberOfCommands).
- Related variables should be close to each other in the text, as illustrated by x, y, and declination. (It is not necessary for all variables of a certain type to appear in the same variable declaration.)

### 5.5.3 THE ASSIGNMENT STATEMENT

The assignment statement is the fundamental way of changing a variable's value. (The only other important way is by an input statement.) Its syntax is as follows:

assignment-statement:
  *variable-identifier* := *expression*
variable-identifier: *identifier*

An assignment statement is executed by first evaluating the expression, and then making the result the new value of the variable. The expression must produce a value that is **assignment-compatible** with the variable. This means that the value must belong to the declared type of the variable, unless that type is real, when the value may be an integer which will be converted to a real before the assignment.

When the assignment statement is used to **initialize** a variable, i.e. to give it its first defined value, the variable should not appear in the expression, lest the value of the expression be undefined. Here is a typical initializing assignment:

```
NumberOfCommands := 0
```

Once a variable has been initialized, however, it is perfectly natural and common for it to appear in the expression. The quintessential example occurs when an integer counter is increased by 1:

```
NumberOfCommands := NumberOfCommands + 1
```

Two typical assignment statements involving other types of variables are shown below:

```
declination := arctan(y / x)
IsCommand := FirstChar = '!'
```

The mathematics involved in the first does not concern us here; just note that y / x gives a real value as the argument of the predefined function arctan, which then gives a real value representing an angle in radians. In the second example, FirstChar = '!' is a Boolean expression which gives true if the value of the character variable FirstChar is the exclamation-mark, and false otherwise. Whatever the outcome, the result becomes the new value of the Boolean variable IsCommand.

We have now reached a milestone (but we hope not a millstone) because we are about to tackle our first programming problem. Solving programming problems is supposed to be the main concern of this book, so let us leap in.

The problem is to exchange the values of two variables a and b which have the same unspecified type. We assume that this problem occurs in a context where both variables have already been given values. For example, if the value of a is 5 and of b is 7, execution of our solution should result in b having the value 5 and a the value 7.

Let us examine the following attempt, which might cursorily be read as: give a the value of b and b the value of a.

```
{ Exchange values of a and b }
  a := b;
  b := a
```

We can test it by executing it by hand with the initial values as above, as shown in Figure 5.1.

Rats! Our mistake was to fail to take into account the consequences of sequential execution of a sequence of statements. An

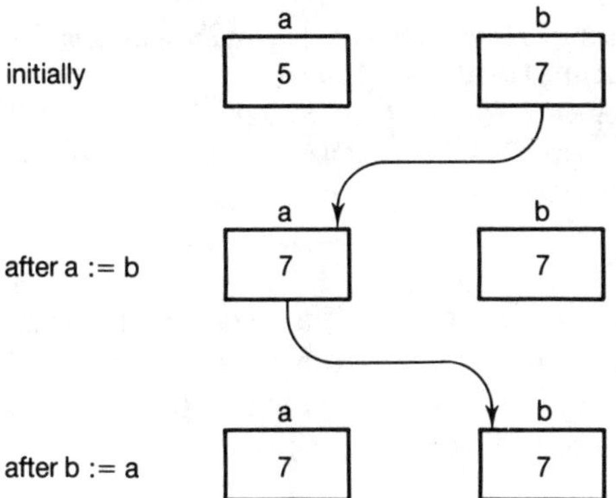


**Figure 5.1**
Execution of a := b;
b := a.

accurate reading of our attempted solution highlights the error: give a the current value of b *then* b the *current* value of a. We want to give b the *original* value of a; the solution is to remember it before it is lost.

```
{ Exchange values of a and b }
 temp := a;
 a := b;
 b := temp
```

The new variable temp must be declared to have the same type as a and b.

## 5.6 Input and output

Rather than try to second-guess the nature of I/O devices used by a Pascal program, which can vary greatly between implementations (and between runs on the same computer), the Standard takes an abstract approach. It decrees that textual input should come from an **input stream**, and textual output should form an **output stream**. Each of these streams of information has the same structure: it consists of a sequence of lines, each of which consists of a sequence of characters terminated by a special end-of-line marker. We represent the marker by □.

### 5.6.1 INPUT

The name of the input stream is Input (which is why that name appears in the heading at the start of a program). Two kinds of input statement are available; their syntax is as follows:

input-statement: *Read-statement* | *Readln-statement*
Read-statement: Read (*variable-list*)
Readln-statement: Readln (*variable-list*)
variable-list: *variable* ... , *variable*
variable: *identifier*

The effect of Pascal's input statements can most easily be defined by first breaking them down into sequences of the simplest versions. Let us write $a_1$, $a_2$, etc. for the first, second, etc. arguments of an input statement. Then:

```
Readln(a1 , a2 , ... )
```

is equivalent to:

```
begin
  Read(a1 , a2 , ... );
  Readln
end
```

and

```
Read(a1 , a2 , ... )
```

is equivalent to:

```
begin
  Read(a1);
  Read(a2);
  ...
end
```

Associated with the input stream is a unique **input position**. All characters or markers to its left have been read; those to its right remain to be read. The input position begins at the start of the input stream, and moves steadily to the right as information is read under control of the program. Once it reaches the end, it can go no farther, and we say that 'the end of the file has been reached.'

A required Boolean function is available to test for this condition:

eof: true if and only if the input position is at end-of-file.

Eof is actually a permitted abbreviation of eof(Input). It is an error to execute any input statement if the end of file has been reached.

Another required function indicates whether the end of a line has been reached:

eoln: true if and only if an end-of-line marker is immediately to the right of the input position.

It is similarly an abbreviation.

Executing

```
Readln
```

simply moves the input position to just past the next end-of-line marker, i.e. to the start of the next line. Eoln will give false afterwards unless this line is empty.

Executing

Read($a_1$)

moves the input position to the right and converts the character(s) and/or marker(s) read to a value which is then assigned to $a_1$. Any markers that are read are treated as blank characters. The details depend on the type of $a_1$.

- Integer: Spaces (and markers) are skipped until a character that can start a signed-integer is read. Starting with it, a maximal sequence of characters is read that form a signed-integer. It is an error if a complete signed-integer is not present. Any remaining characters are left over for the next input statement.
- Real: as for integer, except that a signed-integer or signed-real is acceptable.

An example of the effect of executing two input statements is given in Figure 5.2. The input position is represented by ↑. Each space is made explicit by representing it as ∧. Note that eoln would give false initially, true after execution of the Read-statement, and false after the Readln-statement.

- Char: A single character or marker is read; a marker is read as a space. In the example above, if the statement

  ```
  Read(ch)
  ```

  where ch is a character variable, was to be executed after the first input statement, it would move the input pointer past the marker and assign a space to ch.

**Figure 5.2**
Execution of two input statements.

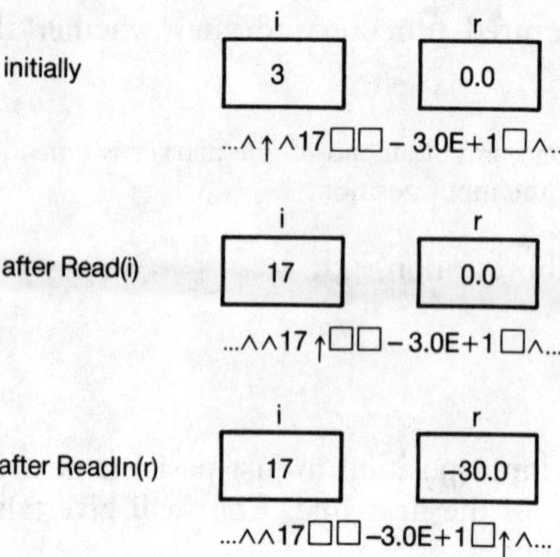


- **Boolean**: Standard Pascal does not provide for the input of Boolean values. Macintosh Pascal does — see Section 5.10, 'Macaveats'. There is, of course, nothing to stop a program from, say, reading a value into an integer or character variable and interpreting it as true (e.g. `1`, `T`) or false (e.g. `0`, `F`).

### 5.6.2 OUTPUT

The name of the output stream is **Output** (which is why that name appears in the heading at the start of a program). Two kinds of output statement are available; their syntax is as follows:

> output-statement: *Write-statement* | *Writeln-statement*
> Write-statement: **Write** (*output-value-list*)
> Writeln-statement: **Writeln** (*output-value-list*)
> output-value-list: *output-value* ... , *output-value*
> output-value: *expression*

As with input statements, we can break down a complex output statement into an equivalent sequence of simple ones:

Writeln($a_1$, $a_2$, ... )

is equivalent to:

**begin**
  Write($a_1$, $a_2$, ... );
  Writeln
**end**

and:

```
Write(a1 , a2 , ... )
```

is equivalent to:

```
begin
  Write(a1);
  Write(a2);
  ...
end
```

Executing

```
Writeln
```

appends an end-of-line marker to the end of the output stream. This will be interpreted by a VDU or a printer as a command to move the display position to the start of the next line. And, of course, if the output were presented later as the input to another Pascal program, eoln could be used to detect the marker.

Executing

```
Write(a1)
```

appends a character string indicating the value of $a_1$ to the end of the output stream. The expression must be a string, or have one of the types integer, real, char, Boolean. The length of the character string that is output is called its **field width**. Like the string itself, it depends on the type of $a_1$.

- Integer: A minimal length signed-integer is written, preceded by spaces if necessary to make up the field width. The field width is implementation-dependent; in Macintosh Pascal it is 8.
- Real: A signed-real in power notation is written, preceded by spaces if necessary. The details are implementation-dependent. In Macintosh Pascal, the field width is 10, and the number is written in the form *sd*.*d*e*scccc*, where the first *s* is either a space or minus, the second is plus or minus, each *d* is a decimal digit, the first *d* is not 0 unless the value is 0.0, and the four *c*s comprise a minimal decimal numeral followed by spaces if necessary (but see Section 5.10 'Macaveats').
- Char: The single character value is written (the field width is 1). For a string, as many characters as are in the string are written.

**Table 5.6** Output statements with default representations.

| Output statement | Appended to output stream |
|---|---|
| Write(10) | ∧∧∧∧∧∧10 |
| Write(–Maxint) | ∧∧–32767 |
| Write(0.0) | ∧0.0e+0∧∧∧ |
| Write(–pi) | –3.1e+0∧∧∧ |
| Write(98.6) | ∧9.9e+1∧∧∧ |
| Write(7E–11) | ∧7.0e–11∧∧ |
| Write('A') | A |
| Write(' ') | ∧ |
| Write(chr(38)) | & |
| Write('That''s All Folks.') | That's∧All∧Folks. |

- Boolean: If the value is true, the string 'True' is written (the field width is 4); otherwise, 'False' is written (the field width is 5).

Table 5.6 shows some Macintosh Pascal output statements with their effects. You can try others by using the Instant window. Note that the last significant digit of the string for a real value is rounded — the value displayed is only an approximation.

Pascal gives the programmer more control over the output for a value by allowing its field width to be specified. A field width must be greater than zero. Except in the case of reals, if it is greater than the length of the string representing the value, spaces are added on the left; for reals in power notation, the number of digits after the decimal point increases to make up the difference. If it is smaller, a field width is used that exactly accommodates the representation, unless the value is a string, in which case as many characters as specified are taken from the left. Additionally, for real values, further information in the form of a **fraction length** may be given. If present, the fraction length forces normal decimal notation with the fraction having the specified number of digits. A fraction length must be greater than zero.

The modified syntax for output values is:

output-value: *expression* : *field-width* : *fraction-length*
field-width: *integer-expression*
fraction-length: *integer-expression*

Table 5.7 gives some examples. Note that a real value in power notation always has either a space or a minus for its sign (see the second 98.6 example). Two useful tricks emerge:

- To write $n \geq 1$ spaces, use:

| Output statement | Appended to output stream |
|---|---|
| Write(10 : 8) | ∧∧∧∧∧∧10 |
| Write(10 : 1) | 10 |
| Write(–Maxint : 1) | −32767 |
| Write(pi : 15) | ∧3.141593e+0∧∧∧ |
| Write(pi : 10 : 7) | ∧3.1415927 |
| Write(pi : 1 : 7) | 3.1415927 |
| Write(–pi : 1 : 7) | −3.1415927 |
| Write(98.6 : 4 : 1) | 98.6 |
| Write(98.6 : 1) | ∧9.9e+1∧∧∧ |
| Write('A' : 2) | ∧A |
| Write(' ' : 6) | ∧∧∧∧∧∧ |
| Write('That''s All Folks.' : 10) | That's∧All |

**Table 5.7** Output statements with controlled representations.

Write(' ' : *n*)

- To include an integer *x* in text, with just a single space either side, use

  Write(' ... ', *x* : 1, ' ... ')

  See Exercise 5.15 if *x* is real. Also,

- It is a good idea to specify field widths explicitly (and fraction lengths if appropriate); output becomes more readable and attractive, and programs are less implementation-dependent.

The official syntax for I/O statements treats them as special procedure-statements.

### 5.6.3 INTERACTIVE I/O

The preceding abstract description of textual I/O in terms of separate input and output streams is all very well, coming as it does from the Standard horse's mouth. But the reader cannot fail to have noticed that it does not immediately jibe with our knowledge of Macintosh Pascal I/O that we gained by running the programs in Chapter 3, for the usual form of I/O in Macintosh Pascal is **interactive**. Input is typed on the keyboard in response to output from the program, and input and output text are intermixed in the Text window.

Fortunately, things are not as different as they seem. In fact, Macintosh Pascal's I/O does conform to the Standard's stream-based model. This is what happens. The input stream is associated with the keyboard, and the output stream with the Text window on the Macintosh's screen. The keyboard and the screen are separate devices. The main complication is that input is displayed as it is read.

Consider execution of program YouGuess3 from Chapter 3. The first Writeln-statement appends this to the output stream:

```
I'm∧thinking∧of∧a∧number∧between∧1∧and
∧∧∧∧∧∧10 ∧inclusive.□
```

Figure 3.5 shows how it is displayed. The cursor goes to the start of the next line. The Write-statement that follows appends this to the output stream:

```
Please∧type∧your∧first∧guess:∧
```

This time the cursor is positioned after the last character, a space, because no end-of-line marker was sent — see Figure 3.5 again. The next statement to be executed is:

```
Readln(guess)
```

It first expects to read a signed-integer, and then to skip past the next end-of-line marker. Since Input is associated with the keyboard, the Macintosh waits for you to create the input stream. You are permitted to type acceptable characters only — illegal ones cause a beep but are otherwise ignored. So first you may hit the space-bar and even the Return-key (which creates a marker) as often as you like, although there is no reason to do so in this context. Then you must type characters that form a signed-integer. As soon as you type a character that is not part of a signed-integer, the implicit statement:

```
Read(guess)
```

finishes executing and assigns the appropriate value to guess. Furthermore, the characters or markers that were read are displayed. (The effect is as if they were permanently appended to the output stream.) Up until this point you could remove them (back to a marker) by hitting the Backspace-key.

The other character or characters that you typed remain on the right of the input pointer for the next input statement, if any. In this case there is an implicit Readln-statement. If you have already hit the Return-key, it reads up to and over the marker created, whereafter execution of the program resumes. If you have not hit the Return-key, the Macintosh waits until you do, then reads over the marker. Since what is read is displayed, execution of the complete Readln-statement ends the second line.

This style of interactive I/O, where a Write-statement produces a prompt and a following Readln-statement reads the input and ends the line, works well. But suppose instead you wanted the prompt, the input, and the output in response to the input, to be on the same line. In the context of YouGuess3, this would mean producing a second line like:

```
Please type your first guess: 5 -- That's wrong.
```

You might expect to be able to do this by replacing both Readln-statements with a Read-statement, and inserting the characters ' -- ' at the front of the strings written in response. Try it. Depending on what you type as input, you will notice the problem, which is this. You must eventually type a character that is not part of a signed-integer, and that therefore is held over for the next input statement. In this case, if another input statement is executed, it expects an integer. So if you typed a comma, say, all you will get is a beep. That is not too bad. But if you typed, say, the Return-key, it will be read by the next Readln-statement, and therefore force a new line in the Text window, messing up your nice display.

In general, the effect of the extra character is to foul up the works.

**Moral** Use a Readln-statement to read prompted input, as in program YouGuess3.

There are some other traps for young players in interactive I/O. The main one is that evaluation of eoln or eof may require input information to be entered, even though it will not be read at that point. (You signal end-of-file by hitting the Enter-key.) But you should not become paranoid about interactive I/O: this information is supplied for reference only. As long as you stick to the schemes presented in this book, you can program in blissful ignorance of the fine points.

## 5.7 Conditional statements

Conditional actions are represented in Pascal by the **if-statement**, which comes in two forms:

if-statement:

```
if Boolean-expression then
  statement
| else
|   statement
```

Boolean-expression: *expression*

As we saw in Chapter 3, an if-statement is executed by evaluating the Boolean expression first. If it gives **true**, only the first component statement (the one following **then**) is executed; otherwise, the Boolean expression gives **false**, and only the second component statement (the one following **else**) is executed — provided it is present of course: if not, nothing is done. For examples of the full form, called an **if-then-else statement**, see programs YouGuess2 and YouGuess3 in Chapter 3. An example of the short form, called an **if-then statement**, will be given shortly.

The statement(s) occurring in the if-statement may, as usual, be any Pascal statement(s) whatsoever. It often happens that one or both of them should consist of a group of statements. In such cases, the **compound statement** is used.

compound-statement:

```
begin
  statement-list
end
```

statement-list:

```
| statement ;
| ...
  statement
```

Below is an example of an if-then statement with a compound component statement:

```
{ Arrange the values of a and b so that a <= b }
if a > b then
  begin { Exchange values of a and b }
    temp := a;
    a := b;
    b := temp
  end
```

There is a glitch in the syntax of Pascal concerning **nested** if-statements, i.e. if-statements containing other if-statements as components. Consider a statement of the form:

**if** $p$ **then if** $q$ **then** $S_1$ **else** $S_2$

where $p$, $q$ represent Boolean expressions, and $S_1$, $S_2$ represent statements. It has been set out on one line (which is legal) to illustrate the problem. It is ambiguous, i.e. there are two possible interpretations. One is:

```
if p then
   if q then
      S1
   else
      S2
```

In this case, the **else** belongs to the second **if**, $S_1$ is executed iff $p$ gives true and $q$ gives true, and $S_2$ is executed iff $p$ gives true and $q$ gives false.

The other possible interpretation is:

```
if p then
   if q then
      S1
else
   S2
```

In this case, the **else** belongs to the first **if**, $S_1$ is executed iff $p$ gives true and $q$ gives true, which is as before, but $S_2$ is executed iff $p$ gives false, which is different.

Will the real if-statement please stand up? *Drum roll.* It's the first one! As you would discover by the way it is laid out by Macintosh Pascal. If you do want the second form, put the inner if-then statement in a compound statement.

A common error with the if-then-else statement is to put a semicolon after the first component statement, as in:

```
...
if x > y then
  maximum := x; {XXXX ERROR XXXX}
else
  maximum := y;
...
```

Entering this provokes Macintosh Pascal to display the **else** in outlined characters, signaling that it may not appear in this context. The reason is that the semicolon after x is interpreted as separating an if-then statement from the next statement, which cannot start with **else**.

A common programming problem is to have a sequence $p_1$, $p_2$, ... , $p_n$ of conditions, a sequence $S_1$, $S_2$, ... , $S_n$ of corresponding statements, and to have to find the first true condition and then execute its corresponding statement. The statement to use is:

```
if p1 then
  S1
else if p2 then
  S2
...
else if pn then
  Sn
```

Notice that Macintosh Pascal does not indent when an if-statement follows an **else**: the **else**s do not march off to the right, despite the format of the if-statement in its syntactic definition.

A special case of the aforementioned situation occurs sufficiently often for Pascal to provide a special form of conditional statement called the **case-statement**. You can read about it in Chapter 10.

## 5.8 Repetitive statements

The fundamental form of repetition is **indefinite repetition**. It is sometimes called **condition-controlled repetition**, because the duration of the repetition is controlled by a condition that is repeatedly evaluated. Pascal caters for indefinite repetition with the while-statement:

while-statement:
 **while** *Boolean-expression* **do**
 *statement*

To execute a while-statement, simply follow the directions in step (1) below:

(1) Evaluate the Boolean expression. If it gives true, do step (2); otherwise, i.e. if it gives false, stop execution of the while-statement.

(2) Execute the statement (which is called the **body** of the while-statement). Then do step (1) again.

Here is a simple example involving integer variables x and PowerOf2:

```
{ Output the least non-negative power of 2 that is >= x }
 PowerOf2 := 1;
 while PowerOf2 < x do
  PowerOf2 := 2 * PowerOf2;
 Writeln ('The least non-negative power of 2 not less than ',
          x : 1, ' is ', PowerOf2 : 1)
```

The non-negative powers of 2 are $2^0 = 1$, $2^1 = 2$, $2^2 = 4$, $2^3 = 8$, etc. PowerOf2 takes on these values in increasing order, until PowerOf2 < x gives false, implying PowerOf2 >= x gives true.

To trace the execution of our example, first embed it in a complete program:

```
program WhileTest (Input, Output);
{ Executes a while-statement; run using Step-Step, }
{ and x and PowerOf2 in the Observe window. }
var
 x, { an arbitrary integer from Input }
 PowerOf2 : integer; { a non-negative power of 2 }
begin { WhileTest }
 Write('Pick an integer, any integer: ');
 Readln(x);
{ Output the least non-negative power of 2 that is >= x }
 ...
end. { WhileTest }
```

Now run WhileTest as its comment specifies. Follow the hand as it moves to indicate the next statement to be executed, and observe the changing value of PowerOf2. Try several different integers as input.

The while-statement is frequently used with a compound statement as its body, allowing a group of statements to be repeatedly executed. Here is one such instance:

```
{ Print all the squares between 1 and limit inclusive }
 Writeln('The squares between 1 and ', limit : 1, ' inclusive:');
 n := 1;
 while sqr(n) <= limit do
  begin
   Writeln (sqr(n) : 11);
   n := n + 1
  end;
 Writeln('===========')
```

If limit (which may be a variable or a constant) has the value 100, the output shown in Figure 5.3 will be produced.

**Figure 5.3**
Output produced by the loop that prints squares.

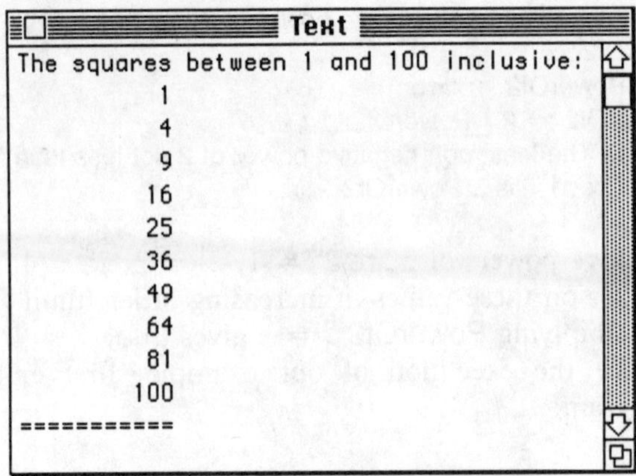


Some miscellaneous notes on the while-statement:

- The Boolean-expression is called the **condition** of the loop. When we say *the condition is true* (*false*), we mean that evaluation of the Boolean-expression gives **true** (**false**).
- The statement is called a **loop** because the flow of execution loops around and around the condition and body.
- The body of the loop will not be executed at all if the condition is initially false.
- The condition is tested *before* each potential repetition of the body, not *during* execution of the body: if the body is executed, it is completely executed.
- The body of a while-loop must contain some statement that can affect the value of its condition, such as an assignment or input statement. Otherwise, execution of the loop either does nothing (if the condition is initially false) or runs until the cows come home, and then some (if the condition is initially true).

There are occasions when the statement to be repeated must be executed at least once. The while-statement can handle such situations readily — it is only necessary to ensure that the condition is true initially (see Exercise 5.26). Sometimes this can be a little awkward, so Pascal provides another form of loop called the **repeat-statement**:

repeat-statement:
    **repeat**
        *statement-list*
    **until** *Boolean-expression*

Note that advantage is taken of the fact that **repeat** and **until** surround the body of the loop (like brackets) by allowing the body to be a statement-list.

To execute a repeat-loop, simply follow the directions shown in step (1):

(1) Execute the the body of the repeat-statement, i.e. the statement-list. Then do step (2).

(2) Evaluate the Boolean expression. If it is false, do step (1) again; otherwise, i.e. if it is true, stop execution of the repeat-statement.

Here is an example where a repeat-statement is marginally more suitable than a while-statement:

```
{ Read the next non-blank input character into ch }
 repeat
   Read(ch)
 until ch <> ' '
```

And here is an example with more than one statement in the body (all variables have type integer):

```
{ Set NrDigits = number of decimal digits in numeral of n }
 NrDigits := 0;
 RestOfn := n;
 repeat
   NrDigits := NrDigits + 1;
   RestOfn := RestOfn div 10
 until RestOfn = 0
```

Note that zero's numeral has one decimal digit, viz. 0. If you have trouble understanding the above, pick a value of n and follow the changing values of RestOfn and NrDigits.

A common special case of repetition is when a statement needs to be executed for each value between two limits which are known in advance. Pascal provides the **for-statement** for such occasions, although they can easily be handled by while-statements. While-statements capture the fundamental form of repetition, and it is essential that they be mastered. Since the for-statement tends to distract from their mastery, its introduction is delayed until Chapter 6, and its precise description delayed until Chapter 10, where it belongs naturally.

# 5.9 Programs

We need to describe both the high- and low-level syntactic structure of Pascal programs.

## 5.9.1 HIGH-LEVEL SYNTAX

The high-level syntax of programs is straightforward:

program:
    *program-heading*
    *program-block* .
program-heading:
    **program** *program-identifier* (*identifier-list*) ;
program-identifier: *identifier*
program-block: *block*
block:
    *constant-definition-part*
    *variable-declaration-part*
    *statement-part*
statement-part:
    *compound-statement*

Examples, naturally, occur throughout the book. The identifier list in the program heading names the external files used by the program. They will usually be Input and Output. Executing a program involves:

(1) Taking note of any constant definitions;
(2) Creating all declared variables and giving them undefined values;
(3) Executing the statement-part.

Now is a good time to recall the various kinds of statements we have met so far:

statement: *simple-statement* | *structured-statement*
simple-statement: *empty-statement* | *assignment-statement* |
    *input-statement* | *output-statement*
structured-statement: *compound-statement* | *if-statement* |
    *while-statement* | *repeat-statement*

A new statement sneaked in there; it is the simplest statement imaginable:

empty-statement:

That's right! The empty statement consists of precisely nothing. One of the consequences of having it is that you can sometimes get away with extra semicolons, as in:

```
begin
  Writeln(sqr(n) : 11);
  n := n + 1;
end
```

where the semicolon after the assignment to n separates it from the next statement, which is the empty-statement. But do not think you can let the semicolons take care of themselves. Consider this:

```
while PowerOf2 < x do; {XXXX ERROR XXXX}
PowerOf2 := 2 * PowerOf2;
...
```

It is also legal, but the way Macintosh Pascal displays it reveals that something is amiss: the first line is a while-statement with an empty body, which is separated from the next statement (the assignment to PowerOf2) by a semicolon. The offender is the semicolon after **do**, but the empty-statement is its accomplice.

A program can have other parts which we will meet in due course.

### 5.9.2 LOW-LEVEL SYNTAX

A Pascal program can be regarded as a sequence of symbols, called **tokens**, in the same way that an English paragraph can be regarded as a sequence of words and punctuation marks. Figure 5.4 shows program WhileTest above, when viewed at this low level. There is only one sequence of tokens — it is broken up into lines solely out of typographic necessity. Note that comments are treated just like spaces, tabs, and ends-of-lines: their only function as far as the translator is concerned is to act as **token separators** (so to speak). Their syntax is informally given by:

comment:
  { *any-characters-other-than-}* }

You may not have *) inside a comment, because it is treated as } (as required by the Standard).

We may note five kinds of tokens in Figure 5.4:

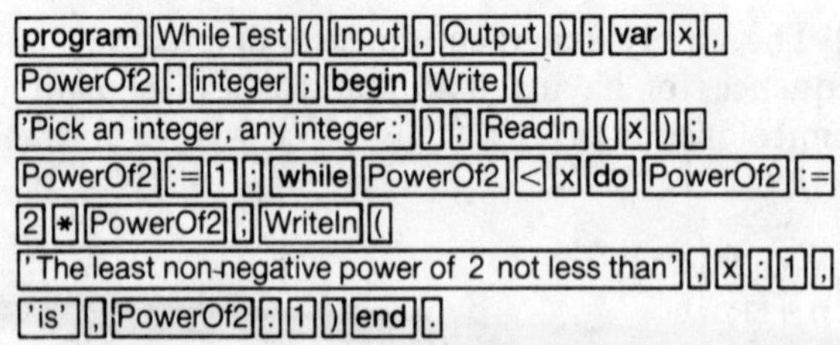


**Figure 5.4**
A program considered as a sequence of tokens.

(1) **special-symbols**, such as ( and := ;
(2) **word-symbols**, such as do and end ;
(3) **identifiers**, such as Write and PowerOf2 ;
(4) **numbers**, such as 1 and 2 ;
(5) **character-strings**, such as 'Pick an integer, any integer:' and 'is' .

Word symbols are classified as special symbols. The syntactic details for Standard Pascal are as follows:

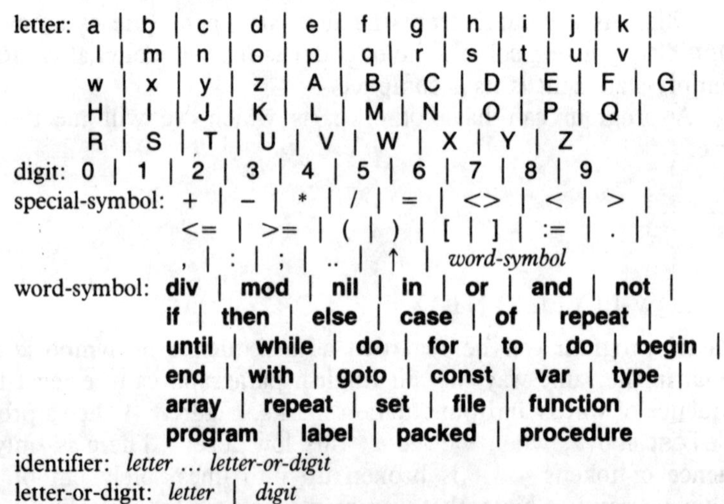
letter: a | b | c | d | e | f | g | h | i | j | k | l | m | n | o | p | q | r | s | t | u | v | w | x | y | z | A | B | C | D | E | F | G | H | I | J | K | L | M | N | O | P | Q | R | S | T | U | V | W | X | Y | Z
digit: 0 | 1 | 2 | 3 | 4 | 5 | 6 | 7 | 8 | 9
special-symbol: + | – | * | / | = | <> | < | > | <= | >= | ( | ) | [ | ] | := | . | , | : | ; | .. | ↑ | *word-symbol*
word-symbol: **div** | **mod** | **nil** | **in** | **or** | **and** | **not** | **if** | **then** | **else** | **case** | **of** | **repeat** | **until** | **while** | **do** | **for** | **to** | **do** | **begin** | **end** | **with** | **goto** | **const** | **var** | **type** | **array** | **repeat** | **set** | **file** | **function** | **program** | **label** | **packed** | **procedure**
identifier: *letter … letter-or-digit*
letter-or-digit: *letter* | *digit*

Square and curly brackets have alternative forms; see the Reference if you are interested. The word symbols are sometimes called **reserved words**, because they may not be used as identifiers. Macintosh Pascal displays them in bold face as shown. Character strings and numbers (signed integers and signed reals) have been dealt with previously.

Examples of identifiers:

PowerOf2 powerof2 x Route66 R2D2
AWopLopALooBopAWopBamBoom

The case of letters in identifiers is not significant, so the first two examples are regarded as the same. But you should give the reader a break and use exactly the same written form in each instance of an identifier. Every letter or digit in an identifier is supposed to be significant, but most implementations only go so far. In Macintosh Pascal, identifiers can have at most 255 characters, which is plenty.

Pascal requires tokens to be separated only when there would otherwise be confusion. The only requirement is that there be at least one token separator between two successive tokens, if each of them is an identifier or word-symbol or unsigned number. Note that a token separator cannot appear within a token; consequently, a character string must appear within a single line, and neither < > nor : =, for instance, is a token.

## 5.10 Macaveats

There are a number of minor ways in which Macintosh Pascal extends or deviates from the Standard:

- Boolean values can be read. Either `false` or `true` must appear, possibly preceded by blanks and end-of-line markers. The case of the letters is not significant.
- Output of real values in power notation is non-Standard. The Standard, and the Reference (!), specify that the exponent must consist of a sign and a fixed number of digits (4), and not be followed by any spaces.
- Although Macintosh Pascal 2.0 correctly outputs Boolean values as strings, the Reference implies that the complete identifier is always written, which violates the Standard.
- Hexadecimal numbers are permitted. They start with $ and use A, B, C, D, E, F for the extra base-16 digits. (It does not matter if you do not know what this means.)
- @ has a special meaning. It is not an alternative to ^, like ↑ is, although the Standard requires it to be.
- There are three extra reserved words: **otherwise**, **string**, and **uses**.

- The underscore (_) may be used in identifiers after the initial letter.
- Comments must be at the end of a line or on a separate line; a comment may not span more than 1 line.

## EXERCISES

**5.1** Consider the following syntactic definitions, with identifier defined as in Standard Pascal:

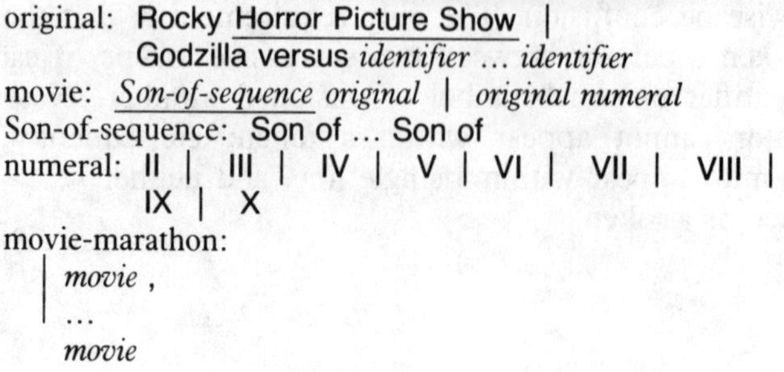

original: Rocky Horror Picture Show |
Godzilla versus *identifier* ... *identifier*
movie: *Son-of-sequence original* | *original numeral*
Son-of-sequence: Son of ... Son of
numeral: II | III | IV | V | VI | VII | VIII |
IX | X
movie-marathon:
*movie* ,
...
*movie*


(a) Which of the following is a movie?

(i) Rocky
(ii) Son of Son of Son of Godzilla versus The Three Stooges
(iii) Rocky versus Rambo
(iv) Rocky Horror Picture Show VIII
(v) Son of Rocky Horror Picture Show VIII
(vi) R2D2 versus Son of Son of Godzilla
(vii) Godzilla versus Son of Spartacus IV

(b) Give the shortest movie marathon.
(c) Give a movie marathon that demonstrates your complete mastery of these syntax rules.
(d) Can the same movie appear twice in a movie marathon?

**5.2** Give the value of each of the following expressions.

(a) 17 **div** (–7) (b) 13 **mod** 13
(c) abs(–Maxint) (d) sqr(–3)

**5.3** Suppose c = 20, d = 51 and e = 5. Give the value of:

(a) d **mod** c (b) d **div** c
(c) (e – d **mod** c) **mod** c (d) e + (d – e) **mod** c

**5.4** Suppose cigars come 20 to a box, and that a certain well-stocked cigar emporium only opens a box to get loose cigars. A customer asks for NrWanted cigars. Suppose NrLoose is the number of loose cigars (between 0 and 19 inclusive). Write a sequence of statements that:

- Sets NrSingles to the number of loose cigars given to the customer;
- Sets NrBoxes to the number of boxes given to the customer; and
- updates the value of NrLoose; if:

  (a) the attendant satisfies the order by first getting as many whole boxes as possible, then loose cigars if necessary;

  (b) the attendant first gets as many of the loose cigars as possible, then as many whole boxes as possible, and then more loose cigars from a new box if necessary.

**5.5** Give the value of each of the following expressions:

(a) 2.0 / 2E3 (b) 1.0 / 3.0
(c) 1 / 3 (d) sqrt(sqr(5) – sqr (3))
(e) round(5 / 9) (f) trunc(1.9E0 * 1E–1) – 1.0

**5.6** Give the value of each of the following expressions in Macintosh Pascal.

(a) succ('P') (b) pred('P')
(c) pred(succ('x')) (d) chr(ord('A') + 26 – 1)

Which expressions' values are guaranteed by the Standard?

**5.7** Suppose a, b, and c are real variables with current values 1.0, 8.0, and 15.0 respectively. Give the value of:

–b + sqrt(sqr(b) – 4 * a * c) / (2 * a)

**5.8** Suppose the cost of sending a letter first class is 22¢ for the first ounce and 17¢ for each additional ounce or part thereof.

(a) Write a constant definition part so that increased mail costs can be easily handled.

(b) Using the answer to (a), write a statement-sequence that assigns to integer variable cost the cost of sending a letter first class, given that its weight in ounces is the value of real variable weight.

*Hint*: Use function trunc.

**5.9** What is the value of the expression:

(a <> 0) **and** (sqr(b) – 4 * a * c >= 0)

(a) if a = 0.0, b = 10.0, c = 10.0?
(b) if a = 1.0, b = –5.0, c = 6.0?

**5.10** Suppose x and y are integer variables. Give a Boolean expression that gives true iff:

(a) x is between –y and +y inclusive.
(b) x is between 0 and 5 inclusive.
(c) x is not between 0 and 5 inclusive.
(d) x and y are not both negative.

**5.11** Modify the answers to Exercises 5.4(a),(b) so that they additionally set Boolean variable NewBoxOpened to true iff a new box is opened.

**5.12** Replace the statement:

```
if odd(n) then
  IsEven := false
else
  IsEven := true
```

with a simpler equivalent one.

**5.13** Suppose variables i, r, c, and p have types integer, real, char, and Boolean respectively. Give each of their values after execution of:

i := 9; r := i **div** 2; c := 'i'; p := c < 'r'

**5.14** Given the variables of the previous question, suppose that the input stream is currently in the state:

...∧↑∧215–1E2□–15□5∧...

Give the values of each of the variables, and the new input position, after execution of each of the following. Use the same initial state of the input stream, as shown above, for each part.

(a) Read(i, r, c)
(b) Readln(i, r); Readln(c)
(c) Read(i, c, r)

(d) Read(r, i, c)

(e) Readln(i); Readln (r); Readln (c)

**5.15** Suppose real variable LightSpeed contains an experimentally determined value for the speed of light, in miles per second, accurate to two decimal places. Give a statement that writes the value in decimal form, preceded by:

```
The speed of light is approximately
```

and followed by:

```
miles per second.
```

and an end-of-line marker.

**5.16** Show exactly what is appended to the output stream by execution of:

```
Writeln('I''m thinking of a number between 1 and',
        MaxSecret, ' inclusive.')
```

**5.17** Modify the statement in the previous question so that the value of MaxSecret has only one blank either side of it.

**5.18** Given that integer variable cost contains the cost of an item in cents, give an output statement that writes the cost in dollars. For example, if cost = 1795, the output should be `$17.95`.

**5.19** Change the scheme of interactive I/O in YouGuess3 as suggested in subsection 'Interactive I/O', and run it to observe the described behavior.

**5.20** What is the implication of the expression 'until the cows come home' used in our discussion of the while-statement?

**5.21** What integers cause program WhileTest to fail?

**5.22** How should the implementation of the action:

*Output the least non-negative power of 2 that is* $\geqslant$ x

in the text be modified if $\geqslant$ is changed to $>$?

**5.23** What happens when the implementation of the action:

*Print all the squares between 1 and* limit *inclusive*

in the text is executed if limit = 0?

**5.24** The body of a while-statement cannot be a statement-list rather than a single statement? Why?

**5.25** Show that a while-statement can be used to implement the action:
*Read the next non-blank input character into* ch
instead of a repeat-loop as used in the text.

**5.26** A typical repeat-statement has the form:

**repeat**
  $S_1$;
  ...
  $S_n$
**until** $p$

Show that it can be replaced by an equivalent statement that does not involve a repeat-statement.

**5.27** Suppose you are prepared to have the same prompt for each guess in program YouGuess3 in Chapter 3. (The first prompt in the given version is special.) Will the program behave properly if the while-statement and the two statements preceding it are replaced by the repeat-statement below?

```
repeat
  Write('Please type your guess: ');
  Readln(guess);
  if guess > secret then
    Writeln('That''s too high.')
  else
    Writeln('That''s too low.')
until guess = secret
```

**5.28** Which of the following are not legal Standard Pascal identifiers, and why not?

(a) TheCount (b) The_Count
(c) time-limit (d) H2O
(e) E235 (f) S.A.L.T.
(g) 'Dracula' (h) DownTo

**5.29** When you choose What to find... from the Search menu, you should normally ensure that the Case Is Irrelevant button is on. Why?

**5.30** Give a shortest Pascal program.

# 6

# SOLVING PROGRAMMING PROBLEMS

Each problem that I solved became a rule which served afterwards to solve other problems.
— René Descartes, *Discours de la Méthode*

## 6.1 Introduction

Programming is a creative act. It is not possible to specify in detail how to solve an arbitrary programming problem. To do so would amount to presenting an algorithm for writing algorithms, the existence of which would remove the need for programmers (and human intellectual workers of all kinds).

Programming is, however, a very special kind of creative act, because both the finished product and the tools with which to create it are rigidly specified. (We have nothing to say about writing programs *in the absence* of specifications: programs, that, for example, produce amusing graphics effects on the Macintosh. It may be fun, but it won't get you into the Programmers' Club.) Because of the enormous disparity in scale between our tools, which for us are the statements of Pascal, and the programs to be created, which can amount to literally millions of lines, a particular approach to programming has come to be seen as crucially important. It is called *stepwise refinement*, and we examine it in the next section.

Before we do, it is important to recall our goal, which should be kept firmly in mind throughout this chapter.

| **Goal** To learn how to write *correct* and *clear* programs as *easily* as possible. |
|---|

- **Correct**: Our programs must do precisely what they are supposed to do, *always*.
- **Clear**: Our programs must be as intelligible as possible, to *all* potential readers. Cleverness should be an ally of clarity, not an enemy.
- **Easily**: We must be able to solve a programming problem efficiently, with an amount of effort that is not out of proportion to its difficulty.

## 6.2 Stepwise refinement

The method of **stepwise refinement** is this. There is a given programming problem to be solved. A solution is formulated that is short enough to be easily understood: no more than several lines. This is done by employing sufficiently powerful actions and conditions in the solution. If the problem was a very simple one, these may be expressed directly in the programming language at hand, in which case we do so, and are done. If not, the high-level actions are regarded as subproblems, and stepwise refinement is applied to each of them. The process continues until all subproblems have solutions that are expressed in the programming language. Conditions are formulated in the programming language when the variables that they involve emerge.

All that sounds very abstract, because it is. Let us look at the method in action. We shall begin with a simple problem: the one for which program YouGuess2 in Chapter 3 is a solution. That problem can be deduced from the comments that immediately follow the program heading:

```
program YouGuess2 (Input, Output);
{ Picks a number, asks for and reads a guess, }
{ and announces whether or not it is correct. }
```

These comments are descriptive as well as prescriptive. They describe precisely what is achieved by running the program. Programming problems, recall, always involve doing something. Strictly speaking, it is the execution of the program that solves the problem. So the problem was:

*Pick a number, ask for and read a guess,*
*and announce whether or not it is correct.*

The way to write the comments is to complete the following:

Write a program that (when executed) ...

A short solution to the problem is apparent, and uses the simplest kind of solution: a sequence of actions. Since the problem at hand is the original problem, we write the sequence as the statement part of the program:

```
begin { YouGuess2 }
  Define the number to be guessed;
  Prompt for and read the guess;
```

```
Announce the result of the guess
end. { YouGuess2 }
```

You should not think of the above solution as a vague one; rather, it is a precise **high-level** solution, whose correctness is apparent.

We now need to solve three subproblems, and will do so by again using stepwise refinement. Let us start with the first, since it will influence the second. Now we discover that the specification of the original problem was incomplete, because it did not state anything about the secret number. Let us require it to be between 1 and 10 inclusive. It would be best to pick an unpredictable number, so let us base it on the position of the mouse. Our solution, which again uses a sequence of actions, is:

```
{ Define the number to be guessed }
Get the position of the mouse;
Compute a number between 1 and 10 that depends on the mouse's
position
```

Note that we retain the high-level action as a comment; what follows it is called its **refinement**.

In this case it happens that each of the actions employed in the solution can be directly formulated in Macintosh Pascal. We could elect to retain the comments, but it is rarely advantageous to do so for a single line solution. So we write:

```
var
  x, y, { (x, y) is the mouse's position }
  secret : integer; { the number to be guessed }

{ Define the number to be guessed }
  GetMouse(x, y);
  secret := (x + y) mod 10 + 1
```

The new variables x, y, and secret that are needed for the refinement are noted. Similarly, any newly defined constants should also be noted (such as MaxSecret = 10, if it were used here as it should be).

Having disposed of the first subproblem, we turn to the second. It is fairly straightforward to refine it directly into Pascal, yet again with a sequence of actions (statements):

```
var
  guess : integer;

{ Prompt for and read the guess }
  Writeln('I''m thinking of a number between 1 and 10 inclusive.');
```

```
Write('Please type your guess: ');
Readln(guess)
```

The name guess is sufficiently meaningful in this simple context as to not require elaboration with a comment.

Finally to the only remaining original subproblem. To *Announce the result of the guess* we need to write one of two messages, depending on whether or not the guess is correct. The apparent solution is to use the second fundamental form of action, viz. a choice. It can be directly formulated in Pascal using the if-then-else statement:

```
{ Announce the result of the guess }
 if guess = secret then
  Writeln('That''s correct.')
 else
  Writeln('That''s wrong.')
```

No new variables or constants are required here.

Our solution is complete. We say that the original problem or action has been **completely refined**, or **implemented in Pascal**. To save a few forests (would you believe *wood chips*?), please refer back to Chapter 3, where you will find the fully assembled solution in all its glory.

Besides a sequence of actions, and a conditional action, there is one other fundamental form of action used in solving subproblems: repetition.

## 6.3 Using repetition

Here is a new, more challenging problem. Instead of writing a complete program, we shall regard the problem as a subproblem from an unspecified program, and solve it with a **program segment**.

*Set* NextPrime = *the least prime number* ≥ n, *where* n ≥ 2.

Here n and NextPrime are given integer variables, and n already has a value ≥ 2. A prime number is a number ≥ 2 divisible by no number ≥ 2 except itself; the first five primes are 2, 3, 5, 7, 11.

This is not an easy problem. A sensible way to prepare for a high-level solution is to view the problem at a high level. We want to compute the smallest number ≥ n with a certain property (that of being prime), so we examine the numbers n, n + 1, n + 2, ... , in increasing order, until one is found with the required property. Clearly this is a repetitive action: the subaction that is repeated is adding one to the candidate answer, and the condition under which it should be done is that the candidate answer does not have the required property. Since the subaction may not need to be executed, a while-loop is appropriate, and we obtain:

```
var
  m : integer; { a number >= n to be tested for primality }

{ Set NextPrime = the least prime >= n }
  m := n;
  while m is not prime do
    m := m + 1;
  NextPrime := m
```

The variable m is introduced to represent candidate answers. NextPrime itself could be used, in which case the final assignment is unnecessary; we choose not to do so because the name NextPrime would then be misleading.

Think carefully about this solution: about why it is correct. Note that the loop continues executing only if the condition is true, i.e. it stops as soon as the condition is false, which is when m is prime.

To complete the solution, we need to refine the condition of the loop. From the definition of primality, we know that m is not prime just when it has a divisor $d$ satisfying $2 \leqslant d < \mathrm{m}$. Let us decide to search for such a divisor by examining the numbers $\geqslant 2$ in increasing order, which amounts to finding the *least* divisor $d \geqslant 2$ of m. If $d <$ m, the condition is true; otherwise the condition is false (and $d =$ m).

Finding the value $d$ is just like the original problem, since it is the least value $\geqslant 2$ with a certain property (that of dividing m). A variable d can be used to contain the candidate divisors. Its value is not a divisor just when m **mod** d <> 0 is true, leading to the following solution:

```
{ Set d = least divisor >= 2 of m }
  d := 2;
  while m mod d <> 0 do
    d := d + 1
```

Our reasoning has been essentially **language independent**, using only the concepts of assignment and condition-controlled repetition. And rightly so, because it is important to learn programming techniques that work for any language in Pascal's broad class (called **procedural languages**). But in attempting to formulate our solution in the sublanguage of Pascal defined in Chapter 5, the problem arises that the value of the *condition*:

m *is not prime*

must be computed with a Boolean expression — we may not use a statement-list.

There are several ways to overcome this. One is to use a richer sublanguage of Pascal, to define a function that tests for primality (just as the required function odd tests for oddness). This option becomes available after reading the next chapter, and Exercise 7.6 asks you to give such a solution.

Another technique involves using a Boolean variable to move the evaluation of the complex condition inside the loop, permitting a statement-list to be used. Our original high-level solution is therefore first transformed to:

```
var
  m : integer; { a number >= n to be tested for primality }
  continue : Boolean; { true if and only if m not known to be prime }
  d : integer; { a candidate for a divisor of m }

{ Set NextPrime = the least prime >= n }
  m := n;
  continue := true;
  while continue do
    begin
      Set d = least divisor ≥ 2 of m;
      if d < m then
        m := m + 1
      else
        continue := false
    end;
  NextPrime := m
```

You should examine this solution carefully, and satisfy yourself that it is equivalent to the original one.

We may now use our refinement of the remaining high-level action, giving the following solution:

```
var
  m : integer; { a number >= n to be tested for primality }
  continue : Boolean; { true if and only if m not known to be prime }
  d : integer; { a candidate for a divisor of m }

{ Set NextPrime = the least prime >= n }
  m := n;
  continue := true;
  while continue do
    begin
```

```
{ Set d = least divisor >= 2 of m }
  d := 2;
  while m mod d <> 0 do
    d := d + 1;

  if d < m then
    m := m + 1
  else
    continue := false
 end;
NextPrime := m
```

Note the empty line after the while-loop. This marks the end of the refinement of:

*Set* d = *least divisor* ≥ *2 of* m

If it were absent the reader might erroneously include the conditional statement that follows it in that refinement.

Note also that one loop is included in the body of another. This phenomenon is known as **nested loops**, but it is no Big Deal — nested loops arise naturally out of stepwise refinement, and should not cause the programmer any special concern.

Yet another approach arises out of the observation that repeat-loops with high-level conditions are very simply translated into Pascal, because the calculation of the condition can be done at the end of the body of the loop. So let us seek to use a repeat-loop in the present problem.

Variable m will now be increased before it is tested for primality. This slight problem can be overcome by the simple device of initializing m so that the first increase produces the first value to be tested. The rest of the development proceeds as before, and we obtain:

```
var
  m, { a number >= n to be tested for primality }
  d : integer; { a candidate for a divisor of m }

{ Set NextPrime = the least prime >= n }
  m := n – 1;
  repeat
    m := m + 1;
  { Set d = least divisor >= 2 of m }
    d := 2;
    while m mod d <> 0 do
      d := d + 1
  until d = m;
  NextPrime := m
```

This is preferable to the second solution, because it is easier to understand, i.e. clearer. The solution using a function is clearer still, because it directly represents the language-independent solution.

There is more than one way to skin a cat (or test for primality). But whatever insight your solution is based on, you must be able to express it as an algorithm. Learning to do that requires much thought and much practice.

## 6.4 Deriving loop conditions

Conditions for repeat-loops tend to give beginners less trouble than those for while-loops. The reason is that a repeat-loop's condition simply expresses the required state of affairs when the loop finishes, and this is foremost in the programmer's mind. Thus, in the above problem, a prime number is sought, and m is prime if and only if its least divisor $d \geqslant 2$ satisfies $d$ = m. So the condition for the repeat-loop is just d = m.

On the other hand, the condition for a while-loop describes a state of affairs that is opposite to the one required when the loop stops. However, since the relationship between a while-loop's condition and the required outcome of the loop is so clear cut, it is actually quite straightforward to formulate the condition: just negate the required condition with **not**. In the above problem, the inner loop searches for a divisor, i.e. a value of d satisfying m **mod** d = 0. Since it is formulated as a while-loop, its condition may be written **not** (m **mod** d = 0).

That is actually what we did above, only we did not stop there, because conditions involving **not** can often be simplified, in which case, in the name of clarity, they should be. We simplified **not** (m **mod** d = 0) by writing m **mod** d <> 0. This is an example of one of a general class of simplifications listed in Table 6.1, where $x$ and $y$ stand for arbitrary simple expressions.

It often happens that the condition to be negated is a Boolean expression formed with a Boolean operator. Consider, for example, the following refinement:

```
var
  ch : char; { last input character read }

{ Process next sentence }
  Read(ch);
  while not (ch is one of '.', '?', '!') do
    begin
      Process ch;
```

**Table 6.1** Simplifying negated relational expressions.

| Negated relational expression | Equivalent simpler form |
|---|---|
| **not** $(x = y)$ | $x <> y$ |
| **not** $(x < y)$ | $x >= y$ |
| **not** $(x > y)$ | $x <= y$ |
| **not** $(x <= y)$ | $x > y$ |
| **not** $(x >= y)$ | $x < y$ |
| **not** $(x <> y)$ | $x = y$ |

```
      Read(ch)
   end;
Process end-of-sentence mark ch
```

The loop should stop when ch is an end-of-sentence mark, i.e. when the following condition is true:

```
(ch = '.') or (ch = '?') or (ch = '!')
```

So the condition of the loop may be written:

```
not ((ch = '.') or (ch = '?') or (ch = '!'))
```

This can be written more simply as:

```
(ch <> '.') and (ch <> '?') and (ch <> '!')
```

Such simplifications can be derived using two logical equations due to Augustus De Morgan. They are given in Table 6.2, using *p* and *q* to stand for Boolean (sub)expressions. Note that the right-hand form is not advertised as simpler, only equivalent. In fact, Boolean expressions like those on the right can be simplified by using the corresponding form on the left! But when *p* and *q* are relational expressions, the right-hand forms can be simplified using Table 6.1. Thus, in our example, we start with:

```
not ((ch = '.') or (ch = '?') or (ch = '!'))
```

Using De Morgan's law for negated **or**s twice, we get:

```
not (ch = '.') and not (ch = '?') and not (ch = '!')
```

Finally, we use Table 6.1 to simplify each operand of **and**, obtaining:

| Negated Boolean expression | Equivalent form |
|---|---|
| **not** ($p$ **and** $q$) | **not** $p$ **or not** $q$ |
| **not** ($p$ **or** $q$) | **not** $p$ **and not** $q$ |

**Table 6.2** De Morgan's laws.

```
(ch <> '.') and (ch <> '?') and (ch <> '!')
```

There is always a choice when writing relational expressions, e.g. between ('.' = ch) and (ch = '.'), and it is best to stick to a consistent style. In such situations we prefer to mention the variable first. The only exception concerns a test involving an interval of values. The familiar mathematical notation:

$0 \leqslant n \leqslant 9$

is best mimicked in Pascal with

```
(0 <= n) and (n <= 9)
```

because the textual location of n is then between those of the expressions representing the limits of the interval.

## 6.5 Program schemas

Programming would be impossibly demanding if each new problem had to be solved from scratch. It is of the utmost importance, therefore, especially for beginners, to reflect carefully on each new solution, to abstract away from the details, uncover any general problem-solving principles, and file them away for later use. The principles that can be expressed as a high-level solution for stepwise refinement are called **program schemas**. Their level of abstraction is one up from programs. There are other, even higher-level, and therefore more vague principles called **paradigms**, but their further discussion now would be premature.

We have seen solutions to a few non-trivial problems, so now is a good time to reflect and begin stocking our problem-solving arsenal. Let us begin by focusing on the most recently solved problem (that of finding the next prime).

We obtained our original high-level solution, and the solution to the subproblem of finding the least divisor, using the same idea. It is applicable to any problem involving a sequence of values, where the first value with a specified property is wanted, and each successive value depends only on the previous one. We nail it down as schema

Sequential Search. The top part names the schema and defines the general problem situation to which it applies; the bottom part is the general solution, in a form ready for stepwise refinement. Variable $v$ is included in the first part here because it is part of the problem, not the solution. We use the notation $P(v)$ to imply that the property $P$ can be formulated as a Boolean expression.

```
Schema Sequential Search:
var
  v : the type of values in the sequence;
{ Given the first member of a sequence, a way of generating }
{ the next member from a given member, and a property P, }
{ set v = the first member having property P. }
-----------------------------------------------------------
  v := the first member of the sequence;
  while not P(v) do
    Set v = the next member of the sequence (after v)
```

Program schemas like this capture the knowledge that really matters: how to solve problems. Like Descartes, always be on the look-out for them — they are nuggets of pure programming gold. The more general they are the better, because then there are fewer to remember.

When using a schema to solve a particular problem, it is better to give problem-specific descriptions of the placeholders of the schema (the unrefined parts shown in italics), in order to define more precisely the subproblems to be solved.

The first example of a while-loop in Chapter 5 also employs this schema. There the problem was:

*Output the least non-negative power of 2 that is* ⩾ x

It was implicitly solved with:

```
Set PowerOf2 = the least non-negative power of 2 that is ⩾ x;
Writeln('The least non-negative power of 2 not less than ',
        x : 1, ' is ', PowerOf2 : 1)
```

The action to be refined fits the schema perfectly, with PowerOf2 for $v$. The sequence is the non-negative powers of 2, in increasing order; the first member is 1; the rule for generating successive members is to multiply by 2. $P(v)$ is $v \geqslant$ x. Refer back to Chapter 5 to see the solution provided by the schema.

What about the other while-loop in Chapter 5? There the problem was:

*Print all the squares between 1 and* limit *inclusive*

This does not quite fit the schema, because something must be done to each member of the sequence except the last. But it does not take much thought to modify the schema to accommodate this option, giving schema Sequential Search With Processing. Note that in this case $v$ is needed for the solution — it is not part of the problem. Even though this variation has been presented separately, you should not remember it that way. Instead, file the modifications to the original schema.

**Schema** Sequential Search With Processing:
{ Given the first member of a sequence, a way of generating }
{ the next member from a given member, and a property *P*, }
{ process all values up to but not including the first with }
{ property *P*. }

```
var
  v : the type of values in the sequence;

v := the first member of the sequence;
while not P(v) do
  begin
    Process v;
    Set v = the next member of the sequence (after v)
  end
```

Another generally applicable technique was used in the *next prime* problem: our implementation of a while-loop with a complex condition. By regarding the high-level loop as a high-level action to be refined, we can express the technique as schema Complex While Loop (see overleaf). Although programmer-defined functions can be used instead (see Chapter 7), this schema is useful when it would be unnatural to define a function.

'This emphasis on schemas is all very well,' you say. 'After all, why solve a problem from scratch, with the time and possibility of error involved, when I can use a canned solution with a written guarantee? But isn't it difficult to *recognize* the applicability of a schema in a given situation?' Good question. The answer is that the style of thinking involved here is exactly that used when you discover schemas: you try to characterize a problem abstractly. That means that your ability to discover schemas increases hand in hand with your ability to apply them. Both will come with practice, as long as you think about what you are doing.

**Schema** Complex While Loop:
{ while $C$ do $S$ }

```
var
  continue : Boolean;
  other variable declarations as needed;

continue := true;
while continue do
  begin
    Define variables so that C is equal to the expression p;
    if p then
      S
    else
      continue := false
  end
```

Program YouGuess3 in Chapter 3 is an instance of a the oft-used schema Interactive I/O. In this schema each instance of $v$ stands for the same variable. The condition of the loop does not require a single stopping-value; instead, it is only necessary to be able to recognize when the value of $v$ is not a regular value (and is therefore a stopping-value). If there is a single stopping-value, it is best defined as a named constant.

Read the schema carefully, to be sure you understand exactly how it works. Note that each input value (regular value or stopping-value) is prompted for, and must be followed by an end-of-line marker; i.e. the user types the input and then hits the Return-key. When all values are to be read before any output is produced, it may be appropriate to have a single initial prompt and omit the one in the body of the loop. See Exercise 6.9(a).

Each regular value is processed once, by the action inside the body of the loop. The stopping-value is not processed. There is provision for initialization (of counts, for example) and finalization; one or both might be dropped in a given instance of the schema. Occasionally it is convenient to initialize after the first Readln-statement, although this does *not* mean that the initialization processes the first input value, only that it sneaks a look at it — see Exercise 6.11 for an example.

We have already seen one instance of this schema: program YouGuess3. We will meet another in our first substantial complete program, which, like the others, is accorded the honorary title of 'case-study'. It should be coming along at the end of this sentence.

**Schema** Interactive I/O:
{ Repeatedly prompt for, read, and process input data }
{ until a stopping-value is read (which is not processed). }

```
var
  v : type of input data and stopping-value;

Initialize;
Write(prompt for input);
Readln(v);
while v is not a stopping-value do
  begin
    Process v;
    Write(prompt for input);
    Readln(v)
  end;
Finalize
```

## 6.6 Case-study 1: Scheduling

### 6.6.1 SETTING OF THE PROBLEM

A fundamental problem in the discipline of Operations Research is that of scheduling jobs on processors. The idea is very general: a *job* is some activity that takes a certain amount of time to process; a *processor* is something capable of performing the desired activity.

We shall assume the following situation applies. There is a sequence of jobs to be processed. The time needed to process each job is known in advance. Two processors are available, each capable of processing one job at a time, and starting a new job immediately the current one is finished. The jobs are to be assigned to the processors subject to two conditions.

(1) Jobs are assigned to processors in the order given.

(2) Each successive job is to be assigned to the first available processor, and then processed immediately. In case both processors become available at the same time, either may be chosen.

Many situations fit this model. One example is that of two craftspersons (restorers of old books, for instance) who work together, process jobs in the order received, and never catch up with their work.

### 6.6.2 SPECIFICATIONS

Our task is to write a Pascal program that meets the following specifications. Input is to be prompted by the program. Each prompt requests the time needed to process the next job, or an end-of-input signal; the latter, of course, does not correspond to a job. Times are assumed to be non-zero positive integers (representing hours, say). The prompt may specify a particular end-of-input signal (e.g. 0 or −1), but any number $\leqslant 0$ should be treated as the signal.

The processor assigned to a job must be indicated immediately, before prompting for more input. After all jobs have been assigned, the program should report:

(1) The number of jobs;

(2) The average of the times at which jobs complete; and

(3) The total time scheduled on each processor.

Note that (2) is *not* the average length of a job, but a statistic that measures how long on average a client must wait before a job is finished. Items (2) and (3) should only be reported if there is at least one job. (The program is expected to handle input of just `-1`, say, reasonably.)

For example, suppose the sequence of input values is:

```
4, 1, 2, 6, 2, -1
```

Then the jobs, numbered according to their position in the input sequence, are assigned to processors as shown in Figure 6.1. There are five jobs. The average job-completion time is:

$$\frac{4+1+3+9+6}{5} = 4.6.$$

The total time used on processor 1 is 6. The total time used on processor 2 is 9.

**Figure 6.1**
Jobs assigned chronologically to two processors.

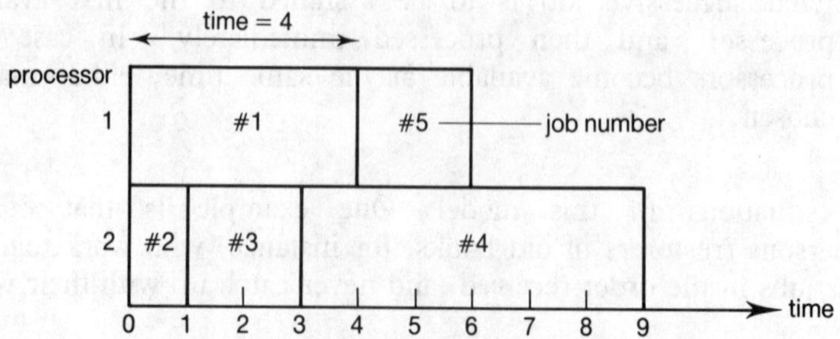

### 6.6.3 WRITING THE PROGRAM

We begin by writing the program heading, and precisely and concisely describing what the program is to do:

```
program JobScheduler1 (Input, Output);
{ Input: repeatedly prompts user to enter either a processing time }
{ for a job, which must be a positive integer, or -1 to end input. }
{ Jobs are assigned in input order to the first available of two }
{ processors. Output: for each job, the processor assigned to it; }
{ the average of the times at which jobs are completed; }
{ for each processor, the total time used. }
```

The comment follows a standard style: it first describes the expected input, then what is done with the input, and finally the output that is produced.

We now begin the process of stepwise refinement with a high-level solution:

```
begin { JobScheduler1 }
  Write heading;
  Prompt for, read, and process each job time, until a stopping-value
  is read;
  Write statistics
end. { JobScheduler1 }
```

It is usually most sensible to refine the last action in a sequence first, because it is the one that will establish the known goal. Then the immediately preceding action can be refined, and so on.

| **Principle** Refine the actions of a sequence in reverse order. |
|---|

So, bearing in mind that no jobs may be input, *Write statistics* is refined with:

```
var
  JobCount, { number of jobs processed }
  TotalTimeOn1, TotalTimeOn2, { total processing time on }
                              { each processor }
  SumOfCompletionTimes : integer; { sum of completion times of }
                                  { all jobs processed }

{ Write statistics }
  Writeln;
  Writeln(JobCount : 1, ' jobs processed.');
  if JobCount > 0 then
    begin
```

```
      Writeln('The total time used on processor 1 = ',
              TotalTimeOn1 : 1);
      Writeln('The total time used on processor 2 = ',
              TotalTimeOn2 : 1);
      Writeln('The average time at which jobs complete = ',
              SumOfCompletionTimes / JobCount : 1 : 1)
    end
```

Four variables have been introduced, and their required values specified by comments. Note that the required average is known implicitly in the form of a numerator (a sum) and a denominator (a count). The sum is an integer, since it is a sum of integer values — it matters not that the average will be a real value.

We next turn to the preceding action, which is the major one. We are in luck, since it fits schema Interactive I/O. We choose JobTime for $v$, and make the following simple refinements. Replace:

*prompt for input*

with:

'Enter processing time for job, or –1 to end input:

Replace:

JobTime *is not a stopping-value*

with:

JobTime > 0

Replace:

*Process* JobTime

with the high-level action:

*Assign job to processor and update statistics*

At this point, our refinement of this subproblem is:

```
var
  JobTime : integer; { processing time for current job, }
                     { or end-of-input signal }
{ Prompt for, read, and process each job time, until a }
{ stopping-value is read }
  Initialize;
  Write('Enter processing time for job, or –1 to end input: ');
  Readln(JobTime);
  while JobTime > 0 do
```

```
    begin
      Assign job to processor and update statistics;
      Write('Enter processing time for job, or -1 to end input: ');
      Readln(JobTime)
    end;
  Finalize
```

Three subproblems need to be refined. Again, it is most sensible to tackle them in reverse order. Action *Finalize* is not needed if the values required by *Write statistics* are updated by the body of the loop. So we first generalize the comments of the appropriate variables, by appending **so far** to them (see the complete solution). In refining:

```
Assign job to processor and update statistics
```

we know (thanks to the schema) that JobTime contains the processing time for the job. Since the job is assigned to the first available processor, we write:

```
{ Assign job to processor and update statistics }
 if TotalTimeOn1 <= TotalTimeOn2 then
   Assign to processor 1 and update statistics
 else
   Assign to processor 2 and update statistics
```

Refining deeper, we tackle the action *Assign to processor 1 and update statistics*. This involves updating the values of the variables used by *Write statistics*. We obtain:

```
begin { Assign to processor 1 and update statistics }
  Writeln('Job assigned to processor 1.');
  JobCount := JobCount + 1;
  TotalTimeOn1 := TotalTimeOn1 + JobTime;
  SumOfCompletionTimes := SumOfCompletionTimes +
                                   TotalTimeOn1
end
```

When a high-level action is refined with a compound statement, we document the action with a comment attached to **begin**. The refinement of the action for processor 2 is a trivial adaptation of the above refinement. In Chapter 8 we shall see how to capture this fact with a programmer-defined procedure.

Both actions in the conditional statement have refinements that include the same statement, viz.:

```
JobCount := JobCount + 1
```

and it is independent of the others. In such cases, the common statement can be removed and placed before or after the conditional statement, taking care to adjust any comments accordingly. See the fully assembled solution below.

After refining the body of a loop, only the initialization remains. Any new or previously introduced variables used in the body that are not involved in input statements need to be initialized. In our case we have:

```
{ Initialize statistics }
JobCount := 0;
TotalTimeOn1 := 0;
TotalTimeOn2 := 0;
SumOfCompletionTimes := 0
```

We have made the comment a little more problem-specific.

Finally, we consider the first highest-level action, viz. *Write heading*, and adhere to the following principle:

**Principle** Output should be intelligible on its own.

It is sound practice to head the output with the name of the program that produced it and the time and date of the run. We shall content ourselves for now with a simple heading:

```
{ Write heading }
Writeln('SCHEDULING JOBS ON TWO PROCESSORS IN
        CHRONOLOGICAL ORDER');
Writeln
```

Since strings cannot extend over more than one line, please consider the first output statement as being on one line. (We shall not mention this typographic problem in the sequel, so watch out.) The second output statement produces an empty line.

### 6.6.4 THE COMPLETE PROGRAM

After assembling all our refinements, we obtain the solution given below. Note that our style of laying out comments clearly documents that the initialization action is part of the action for the whole schema. Furthermore, the statements that refine the initialization action are delimited by the blank line that follows them. Macintosh Pascal can not always adequately handle the comments that emerge from a stepwise refinement. For example, three successive comments can not be indented without losing their relationship to their refinements.

There are styles of layout that better suit stepwise refinement.

Our preferred style is presented in 'Macaveats', Section 6.11, since it is important, but unfortunately inconsistent with Macintosh Pascal's automatic formatting.

```
program JobScheduler1 (Input, Output);
{ Input: repeatedly prompts user to enter either a processing time }
{ for a job, which must be a positive integer, or –1 to end input. }
{ Jobs are assigned in input order to the first available of two }
{ processors. Output: for each job, the processor assigned to it; }
{ the average of the times at which jobs are completed; }
{ for each processor, the total time used. }

    var
      JobCount, { number of jobs processed so far }
      JobTime,  { processing time for current job, }
                { or end-of-input signal }
      TotalTimeOn1, TotalTimeOn2, { total processing time on }
                                  { each processor so far }
      SumOfCompletionTimes { sum of completion times of }
                           { all jobs processed so far }
       : integer;

  begin { JobScheduler1 }
  { Write heading }
   Writeln('SCHEDULING JOBS ON TWO PROCESSORS IN
           CHRONOLOGICAL ORDER');
   Writeln;
  { Prompt for, read, and process each job time, until a }
  { stopping-value is read }
   { Initialize statistics }
   JobCount := 0;
   TotalTimeOn1 := 0;
   TotalTimeOn2 := 0;
   SumOfCompletionTimes := 0;

   Write('Enter processing time for job, or –1 to end input: ');
   Readln(JobTime);
   while JobTime > 0 do
     begin
     { Assign job to processor and update statistics }
       JobCount := JobCount + 1;
       if TotalTimeOn1 <= TotalTimeOn2 then
         begin { Assign to processor 1 and update sums }
           Writeln('Job assigned to processor 1.');
           TotalTimeOn1 := TotalTimeOn1 + JobTime;
           SumOfCompletionTimes := SumOfCompletionTimes +
                                   TotalTimeOn1
         end
       else
         begin { Assign to processor 2 and update sums }
```

```
                Writeln('Job assigned to processor 2.');
                TotalTimeOn2 := TotalTimeOn2 + JobTime;
                SumOfCompletionTimes := SumOfCompletionTimes +
                                                   TotalTimeOn2
              end;
          Write('Enter processing time for job, or -1 to end input: ');
          Readln(JobTime)
        end; { of while-loop }
      { Write statistics }
      Writeln;
      Writeln(JobCount : 1, ' jobs processed.');
      if JobCount > 0 then
      begin
        Writeln('The total time used on processor 1 = ',
                  TotalTimeOn1 : 1);
        Writeln('The total time used on processor 2 = ',
                  TotalTimeOn2 : 1);
        Writeln('The average time at which jobs complete = ',
                  SumOfCompletionTimes / JobCount : 1 : 1)
      end
    end. { JobScheduler1 }
```

Note that the end of the while-loop has been labeled with a comment, to make the program easier to read.

Figure 6.2 shows the output from a run of JobScheduler1. User input is underlined.

**Figure 6.2**
The Text window after a run of JobScheduler1.

```
Text
SCHEDULING JOBS ON TWO PROCESSORS IN CHRONOLOGICAL ORDER

Enter processing time for job, or -1 to end input: 4
Job assigned to processor 1.
Enter processing time for job, or -1 to end input: 1
Job assigned to processor 2.
Enter processing time for job, or -1 to end input: 2
Job assigned to processor 2.
Enter processing time for job, or -1 to end input: 6
Job assigned to processor 2.
Enter processing time for job, or -1 to end input: 2
Job assigned to processor 1.
Enter processing time for job, or -1 to end input: -1

5 jobs processed.
The total time used on processor 1 = 6
The total time used on processor 2 = 9
The average time at which jobs complete = 4.6
```

## 6.7 Some other schemas

Repeat-statements tend not to be used as often as while-statements. The reason is that it is prudent to test (the condition) before deciding to execute (the body). Even when a repeat-loop seems a good choice, a while-loop is often even better.

Here is a case in point concerning an important principle:

**Principle** Check input data as thoroughly as possible.

One way to do this with interactive input is repeatedly to prompt for, read, and check an input value until it is correct. It might seem that the natural way to do so is with:

```
repeat
  Write(Prompt for input);
  Readln(v)
until v is legal
```

Think again. The problem with this solution is that each prompt is the same: the user is not explicitly informed of a mistake, and may wrongly but understandably assume that a new prompt is a request for *more* input. The while-loop wins out once again, giving schema Check Interactive Input. The type of $v$ should be as large as possible so as to include illegal as well as legal input values; this will make more sense after Chapter 10. For an example of using this schema, see Exercise 6.10.

**Schema** Check Interactive Input:

```
var
  v : largest type that includes type of value requested;
{ Repeatedly prompt for, read into v, and check }
{ an input value, until it is legal }

  Write(Prompt for input);
  Readln(v);
  while v is not legal do
    begin
      Write(Error message & prompt for corrected input);
      Readln(v)
    end
```

Another common programming situation is to have to do something a given $n$ times, where $n \geqslant 0$. This can be regarded as a special case of the following action:

*For each value of v between first and last, in order, do A*

where, in general, the subaction $A$ depends on the value of $v$. This action can be refined with a while-statement, but Pascal provides a special statement precisely for this situation. The advantage of using it is that the schema is made explicit, informing the reader, for instance, that execution of this loop will definitely terminate (provided that of $A$ always does). The statement is called the **for-statement**, and it comes in two forms, depending on whether the values of $v$ are taken in increasing or decreasing order:

```
for-statement:
    for variable-identifier := initial-expression to-symbol
                               final-expression do
    statement
to-symbol: to | downto
initial-expression: expression
final-expression: expression
```

It would be premature to fully define the for-statement — we will wait until Chapter 10. In this sneak preview, we shall be content to use it in two schemas. The first, For Increasing Values In An Interval, is more common. Even though $v$ is mentioned in the definition of the problem, it is only as a notational convenience; it really belongs to the solution, and is shown as such. Note that if *lower* > *upper*, $A$ is never executed, because there are no values of $v$ in the specified interval. Like a while-loop, a for-loop looks before it leaps.

The other schema is For Decreasing Values In An Interval. Again, if *upper* < *lower*, $A$ is never executed.

The expressions *upper* and *lower* are evaluated once only, before the body of the loop is executed. They must be of the same type as the variable $v$, which can be integer, char, or even Boolean, but not real.

Here are three applications of these schemas. The first is the simplest case, where some action is to be repeated a given number of times.

```
Schema For Increasing Values In An Interval:
{ For each value v for which lower <= v <= upper, }
{ in increasing order, do A }
--------------------------------------------------
var
  v : type of lower and upper;

for v := lower to upper do
  A
```

| **Schema** For Decreasing Values In An Interval: { For each value *v* for which *upper* >= *v* >= *lower*, } { in decreasing order, do *A* } |
|---|
| **var**<br>  *v* : *type of upper and lower*;<br><br>**for** *v* := *upper* **downto** *lower* **do**<br>  *A* |

```
var
  count : integer;

{ Print a line of width LineWidth }
  for count := 1 to LineWidth do
    Write('-');
  Writeln
```

Variables used in for-loops must be declared like any others. The variable or constant LineWidth is assumed to exist already, since it is mentioned in the problem (in the comment).

In the second example, the action *A* depends on the value of the variable:

```
var
  ch : char; { ranges over entire character set }

{ Print the Macintosh Pascal character set in increasing order }
  for ch := chr(0) to chr(255) do
    Write(ch)
```

Macintosh Pascal will use as many lines of the Text window as necessary to display the long line that is produced. For a slight variation on this solution, see Exercise 6.12.

Our third example of the use of for-loops is a case-study.

## 6.8 Case-study 2: The character-set table

### 6.8.1 SPECIFICATIONS

The Macintosh Pascal character set is to be printed in the form used in Table 5.3, i.e. in a 16 × 16 grid, column by column from the left, with rows and columns numbered 0 to 15. The format for each row should be:

```
nn∧|∧CC∧CC∧ ∧c∧ ∧c∧ ∧c∧ ∧c∧ ∧c∧ ∧c∧ ∧c∧ ∧c∧ ∧c∧ ∧c∧ ∧c∧ ∧c∧ ∧c∧ ∧c∧ ∧c∧ ∧c∧|
```

where *nn* is a number between 0 and 15, CC is printed for each control character (to avoid chaos), ∧ represents a space, and *c* represents a visible character. The vertical bar (|) at each end will form the sides of a box. The top and bottom of the box, and column numbers, should also be printed.

### 6.8.2 WRITING THE PROGRAM

We begin with the program heading:

```
program CharacterSet (Input, Output);
{ Prints the Macintosh Pascal character set in a boxed 16 by 16 }
{ grid, column by column from the left, with rows and columns }
{ numbered 0 to 15, and a box around the grid. Each control }
{ character is represented by CC. }
```

Since all printing is done row by row, it will not do to take the characters in increasing order. Instead, we start our refinement with:

```
begin { CharacterSet }
  Print column numbers;
  Print top of box;
  Print rows 0 to 15, with row number & left & right sides of box;
  Print bottom of box
end. { CharacterSet }
```

The major part of each of these actions fits the schema For Increasing Values, leading directly to:

```
var
  row, col : integer; { number of row and column respectively }

{ Print column numbers }
  Write(' ' : 4);
  for col := 0 to 15 do
    Write(col : 3);
  Writeln;

{ Print top of box }
  Write('--' : 5);
  for col := 0 to 15 do
    Write('---');
  Writeln('-');

{ Print rows 0 to 15, with row number & left & right sides of box }
  for row := 0 to 15 do
```

*Print* row, *left side of box*, row'*th row of characters, and right side of box*;

```
{ Print bottom of box }
 Write('--' : 5);
 for col := 0 to 15 do
   Write('---');
 Writeln('-')
```

Note that the first and last actions are refined with the same code. We shall find out in Chapter 8 how to exploit this with a procedure.

For the last remaining refinement, we first print the row number, box side, and control characters in the first two columns, then the visible characters in columns 2 to 15, then print the other box side and end the line. The major action again fits the same schema, making five applications of it in all! For-loops, like cabs, tend to come in bunches.

```
{ Print row, left side of box, row'th row of characters, }
{ and right side of box }
begin
  Write(row : 2, ' | CC CC');
  for col := 2 to 15 do
    Write(chr(col * 16 + row) : 3);
  Writeln(' |')
end
```

### 6.8.3 THE COMPLETE PROGRAM

The task of assembling the program is left until Exercise 6.13. The output produced by the assembled program is shown in Figure 6.3. You will notice a glitch in the last row. It is caused by the fact that chr(127) is a control character that has strayed from its *compadres*. It prints as a zero-width space. Exercise 6.14 invites you to divert some of your intellectual funds to it and thereby fix the glitch.

## 6.9 Choosing the form of iteration

After you digest this book and become an expert on programming, you'll find that people who are aware of your guru status always ask the same question — at dinner parties, on talk shows, at celebrity get-togethers, at major product launches, anywhere you're likely to be invited — 'What sort of loop do I choose?' Here's what to answer.

First, most garden-variety programming can be done mainly with schemas, and this is increasingly so as you accumulate more of

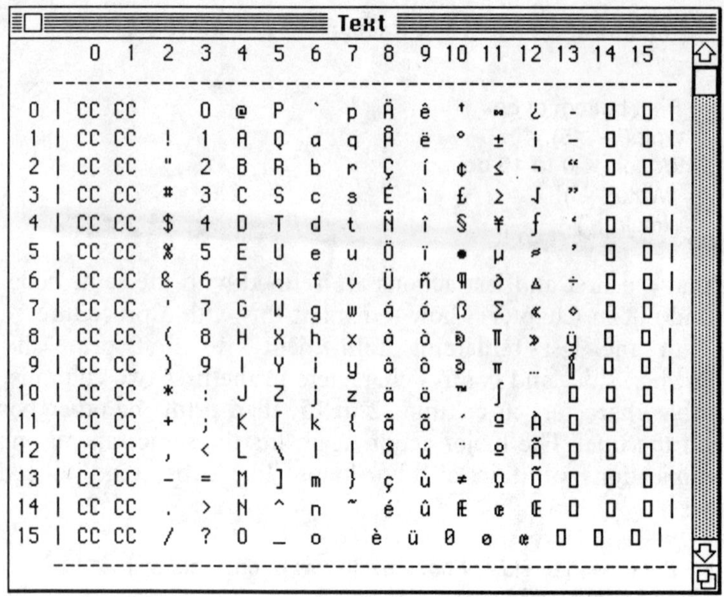

**Figure 6.3**
Output from program CharacterSet.

them with thoughtful experience. In such cases, the question should not arise, as the solution part of the schema will tell you which loop to use. (If more than one schema applies, choose the most specific.)

If you do not have a schema that fits, you can always use a while-loop. It can do anything the others can. Therefore, if you are after the neatest choice, as you should be, do not begin by asking 'Can I use a while-loop?' Instead, first check again to see if the problem can be cast in a form matching one of the two for-loop schemas. If it can, you are home. If not, the while-loop is usually your best bet. Only use a repeat-loop after carefully ensuring that you really do want to execute the action to be repeated at least once.

| **Principle** Favor while-loops over repeat-loops. |
|---|

In Chapters 11 and 12 you will find a valuable technique for solving hard problems with loops. It is based on a fundamental theorem about while-loops (which therefore applies also to the others). In the meantime we shall use the technique implicitly whenever we need it, so that the abstract technique will seem familiar by the time we formulate it explicitly.

For now, the exercises provide ample opportunity to practice solving problems that require loops for their solutions.

## 6.10 Testing, testing

### 6.10.1 THE ROLE OF TESTING

Testing is *not* an activity that should commence after writing a program, with the aim of discovering and correcting any mistakes made along the way. Implicit in such a view is a thoroughly discredited (but nevertheless still widely held) notion of how to program — that by some mysterious process the programmer assembles an 'almost correct' program, runs it with various sets of test data that reveal the 'bugs' that are present as a matter of course, and 'debugs' the program by modifying it until the results of the test runs are satisfactory. Bitter experience has shown that programs created in such a fashion take far too long to reach the point of usefulness (if they ever do), and require far too much maintenance to fix the bugs that inevitably continue to crop up.

Instead, correct programs are obtained by starting with precise specifications, and correctly managing the process of stepwise refinement. And the following principle is paramount:

| **Principle** Testing is no substitute for thinking. |
|---|

Nevertheless, testing does have an important role to play. It should be used right from the start, as a check on our reasoning (which may, despite all our care, occasionally be erroneous), and to help uncover any typographic errors. When the complete program is finally tested, we should be genuinely surprised if, typographical and other clerical mistakes aside, it does not perform properly. Our experience should be that testing is a process that confirms our confidence in the correctness of our creations, rather than one that shatters it.

### 6.10.2 WHAT AND WHEN TO TEST

The basic principle of testing is this:

| **Principle** Every refinement in the process of stepwise refinement should be tested. |
|---|

Testing implies comparing actual and required performance. There is simply no point in testing to see what a program-segment does, without knowing beforehand precisely what it should do. When testing the entire program, this information is provided by the program's specifications. When testing the refinement of a high-level action, this information is usually not formulated *precisely*, but the programmer must be *capable* of doing so.

### 6.10.3 DESK-CHECKING

How, then, is a refinement of a high-level action to be tested? Well, if it is the first refinement of a program, the specifications define the desired result, called the **postcondition**, and also the assumptions we may make about the input data, called the **precondition**. Otherwise, the postcondition is described by the action itself, and the precondition may be described either by the action or by the comments for the constants and variables involved. The rationale of our style of describing high-level actions is now apparent:

> **Principle** Describe a high-level action by specifying the desired result.

Let us consider our first refinement of the *next prime* problem:

```
{ Set NextPrime = the least prime >= n }
m := n;
while m is not prime do
  m := m + 1;
NextPrime := m
```

The postcondition is clear. It is that:

NextPrime = *the least prime* $\geqslant$ n.

and the precondition is that:

n $\geqslant$ 2.

The refinement is tested with pen and paper, by tracing its execution on selected values of the variables involved (provided they are consistent with the precondition). This process is known as **desk-checking**. There are two important guidelines:

(1) determine in advance what the outcome should be;

**Figure 6.4**
Desk-checking two cases.

| n | 3 | |
|---|---|---|
| m | ? | 3 |
| NextPrime | ? | 3 |

| n | 8 | | | | |
|---|---|---|---|---|---|
| m | ? | 8 | 9 | 10 | 11 |
| NextPrime | ? | 11 | | | |

| n | 3 | |
|---|---|---|
| m | ? | 3 |
| NextPrime | ? | 3 |

| n | 8 | 9 | 10 | 11 | 12 | ... |
|---|---|---|---|---|---|---|
| m | ? | 8 | | | | |
| NextPrime | ? | | | | | |

**Figure 6.5**
Desk-checking an erroneous refinement.

(2) act like a robot: execute each step mechanically, ignoring comments.

Adherence to these guidelines helps avoid the psychological problems of being predisposed to a correct outcome, and making the same assumptions in execution as were made in creation.

The more values that are checked the better, and it is a good idea to try extreme or pathological values, such as the smallest possible and the largest possible, as well as typical ones.

In the case at hand, only one variable changes in the loop, and it is sufficient to record its successive values, as shown in Figure 6.4.

Our refinement passes the tests, which should be no surprise. But suppose we accidentally wrote n := n + 1 for the body of the loop. We would obtain the traces shown in Figure 6.5. The first trace reveals nothing amiss, but not the second.

Do not think of an incorrect result as revealing a bug which needs to be fixed. No — an incorrect result simply means that our refinement is incorrect, and needs to be replaced by a correct one. It sometimes happens that the correct refinement can be obtained by making a minor adjustment to the incorrect one (as in the preceding example). If so, well and good. But in general, especially with novice programmers, the problem needs to be thought through again in the light of the test. After doing so, do not forget the following principle:

> **Principle** After replacing an erroneous refinement, desk-check the new one.

The new refinement should at least be tested with the sets of values used previously, and preferably some new ones as well. After all, we did get it wrong the first time.

Sometimes the value of more than one variable may be changed in the body of a loop, as in this example from Chapter 5:

```
{ Set NrDigits  = number of decimal digits in numeral of n }
  NrDigits := 0;
```

**Figure 6.6**
Desk-checking with two changing variables.

| NrDigits | ? | 0 | | 1 | | 2 | | 3 | | 4 | |
|---|---|---|---|---|---|---|---|---|---|---|---|
| RestOfn | ? | | 3709 | | 370 | | 37 | | 3 | | 0 |

```
RestOfn := n;
repeat
  NrDigits := NrDigits + 1;
  RestOfn := RestOfn div 10
until RestOfn = 0
```

It pays to be a little more careful in such cases. A sensible technique is to use a row for each variable, and a new column for each step, so that the trace shows the order in which changes occurred. Figure 6.6 gives an example with n = 3709.

### 6.10.4 TESTING BY EXECUTION

Whenever a program has been completely refined, i.e. when it is written entirely in the programming language, it should be tested by executing it. The first requirement of the test is this:

- Execution of the program terminates normally.

Assuming it is met, the output is then carefully checked to see that the second requirement is met.

- Output should be exactly as expected.

Whether or not all is well, the output should be saved for possible later reference. It should therefore be clearly labeled, preferably by the program itself.

### 6.10.5 COPING WITH ERRORS DETECTED BY TESTING

Errors revealed by desk-checking have already been discussed. In general, they are fixed by disposing of the incorrect refinement, and developing and testing a new one. So let us suppose that it is a test run that has revealed an error.

First, do not yell for help. Coping with your own errors is an important aspect of learning to program. Some beginners seem content to make an attempt at a solution, and get someone else to fix it when it does not work. If you are in that category, have some self-respect, and get out of it. Now is as good a time as any to learn how to cope with errors. If you are stumped, despite your best efforts, you have no recourse but to get help (or sleep on it, which often works); but ask your rescuer to show you *how* to find the problem, not just to find the problem. *End-of-homily.*

One's first thought, then, as a careful programmer, is that an error of transcription (a typo) has been made. So the first thing to do is carefully to check that the program has been faithfully typed. Look out for mistakes such as:

- Typing a similar character (e.g. O for 0, l for 1);
- Wrong identifiers of any kind (e.g. n for m);
- Wrong operations (e.g. + for *, **and** for **or**);
- Wrongly placed brackets in expressions;
- A semicolon or **begin** or **end** in the wrong place;
- Statements entered in the wrong place or wrong order;
- Missing statements or parts of conditions;

and so on, none of which need lead to a syntax error. Any such mistakes should be corrected and the program retested.

If an error remains, what you do next depends on its nature. If execution of the program does not terminate, observe the range of movement of the hand that indicates the statement being executed; use Step or Step-Step to slow it down if necessary. Observe the values of the variables appearing in the condition of the innermost loop that bounds the range of movement of the hand, and figure out why the value of its condition never changes.

> **Principle** When a while- or repeat-loop is written, confirm that its body is capable of changing the value of at least one variable appearing in its condition.

Check the reasoning that satisfied you that the loop would always terminate. Where did it go wrong?

If wrong output is produced, concentrate on the first discrepancy. At least one of the variables appearing in the printed expression must have been given the wrong value. Similarly for a run-time error: use the Observe window to find the variable(s) with incorrect values. Work backwards through the program, carefully checking each statement that affects any of these variables. Try desk-checking these statements. With luck, you will find the problem. Then retest, first with the same test data. (It is usually not worthwhile attempting to track down the cause of other incorrect output values, as it is too hard (and counterproductive) to take account of the error you discovered.)

If you are unable to find anything wrong with the program, you should check every precondition and postcondition, whether explicit or implicit. With the current test data, the final postcondition is not met. The problem is to find the point at which things first go wrong. Put STOP marks just before each high-level action, and rerun the program with the same test data. When a STOP mark is reached, check that the postcondition of the preceding high-level action (if any) and the precondition of the next one are true (they may be the same). If it is possible to formulate these conditions as Boolean expressions, use the Observe window to check their values. Remember, hitting the Enter-key will force the evaluation of an expression you have just typed. For more complex conditions, try to get all the information you need using the Observe window. It helps if you follow the following principle:

| **Principle** Begin testing with small, simple sets of test data. |
|---|

Alternatively, use the Instant window to print out the values of the variables involved, but be very careful not to change the values of any variables. (If you need a control-variable for a for-loop, remember its value and restore it afterwards.)

Sometimes another programmer will find the cause of your error with enviable speed, even though you may have unsuccessfully racked your brains until exhaustion. Put that down to a mental block — the error was obvious.

### 6.10.6 DEFENSIVE PROGRAMMING

It is not testing that is a drag, it is having to fix errors. A thorough test session that reveals no errors does not take an inordinate amount of time, increases one's confidence, and reinforces good programming practices. But test sessions that reveal errors are another matter. As you may well have discovered!

Much of the heartache can be avoided by being more disciplined and careful in the process of program development, and by performing a number of simple checks as soon as they are applicable — a stitch in time saves nine. One such check has already been mentioned:

- Check that each while- and repeat-loop has a chance of terminating. The body must affect the condition.

Here are some other worthwhile tests:

- Check for initialization before use. Each variable must get a value before being used in an expression.

- Check conditions carefully. English use of 'and' and 'or' is terribly imprecise. Many errors are caused by using **and** for **or** or vice versa.
- If you choose a repeat-loop, check that you really do want it to execute its body at least once.

### 6.10.7 FINAL WORDS ON TESTING

Do not expect to obtain a correct program by making random changes to an incorrect one. If your first few programming assignments are all small and simple, you might get away with such a policy, but it is hopeless for non-trivial programs. Programs do not evolve into correctness — almost all mutations are losers, and you do not have a million years. When it comes to programming, Creationism is the better theory.

When you have tried everything, and your program still says 1+1=3, consider the following two possibilities before you pull the trigger:

(1) The original specifications may have errors. A missile-monitoring system might be required only to report on missiles whose altitude over a country is decreasing, in the mistaken idea that only in that situation are the citizens in danger.

(2) Maybe the problem is in Macintosh Pascal. Even that cause can be tracked down by careful testing, after which the problem should be reproduced as simply as possible, and reported, as they say, to the authorities.

Chapter 12 presents a technique that helps the programmer to develop certifiably correct programs. If mastered, it will alleviate most of the burden of correcting errors revealed by testing.

## 6.11 Macaveats

When you next find yourself writing a Pascal program other than in Macintosh Pascal, chances are you will be worse off. You will probably even have to format your programs yourself. But along with this responsibility comes freedom, which permits you to use a formatting style that more clearly reflects the process of stepwise refinement. Our preferred style is based on just three simple principles:

(1) Each action in a sequence should be indented at the same level.

(2) The subactions that refine a high-level action should be indented with respect to a comment that describes it.

(3) In a multi-line Pascal statement, lines after the first line should be indented with respect to it. (This is sometimes bent for compound statements; see the example and commentary below.)

Actions here refer to both high-level actions and Pascal statements. The upshot of these rules is that the first-level refinement of each action can be read by simply collecting each sub-action at the next level of indentation. The same goes for the components of structured statements.

As an example, here is program JobScheduler1 laid out in this fashion. Some inessential detail has been suppressed with three dots.

```
program JobScheduler1 (Input, Output);
{ Input: repeatedly prompts user to enter either a processing time }
...
{ for each processor, the total time used. }
  var
    JobCount, { number of jobs processed so far }
    ...
        : integer;
  begin { JobScheduler1 }
    { Write heading }
      Writeln('SCHEDULING JOBS ON TWO PROCESSORS ... ');
      Writeln;
    { Prompt for, read, and process each job time, until a }
    { stopping-value is read }
      { Initialize statistics }
        JobCount := 0;
        ...
      Write('Enter processing time for job, or –1 to end input: ');
      Readln(JobTime);
      while JobTime > 0 do begin
        { Assign job to processor and update statistics }
          JobCount := JobCount + 1;
          if TotalTimeOn1 <= TotalTimeOn2
            then begin
              { Assign to processor 1 and update sums }
                Writeln('Job assigned to processor 1.');
                ...
                end
            else begin
              { Assign to processor 2 and update sums }
                Writeln('Job assigned to processor 2.');
                ...
                end;
```

```
      Write('Enter processing time for job, or -1 to end input: ');
      Readln(JobTime)
      end; { of while-loop }
  { Write statistics }
    Writeln;
    Writeln(JobCount : 1, ' jobs processed.');
    if JobCount > 0
      then begin
        Writeln('The total time used on processor 1 = ', ... );
        ...
        end
  end. { JobScheduler1 }
```

Note that when a compound statement is used as a component statement of a structured statement, its **begin** and **end** are kept out of the way. The effect is to focus on the statement sequence that they enclose.

## EXERCISES

There is no substitute for experience in learning to solve programming problems. If you are the programming equivalent of a gym rat, you will want to tackle all these exercises. If you can not find the time to do that, try giving a first refinement rather than a complete one, or just determining which schema or form of loop, if any, should be used. To keep you on your toes, a couple of problems have simpler solutions than might seem to be the case at first sight. Heh heh.

**6.1** What was the first refinement in the development of program YouGuess3?

**6.2** Use stepwise refinement to describe the following action in Pascal.

> *Given that integer variables* hours *and* minutes *represent the time on a 24-hour clock, print the time in 12-hour format. E.g., for 0,0 print* `12:00am`, *for 9,3 print* `9:03am`, *for 12,0 print* `12:00pm`, *for 17,5 print* `5:05pm`, *for 23,59 print* `11:59pm`

**6.3** Suppose value and limit are integer variables. Simplify each of the following expressions.

(a) value – 1 < limit

(b) **not** (value <= limit)

(c) **not**((–2 * limit <= value) **and** (value <= limit))

(d) **not**((–limit <= value) **and** (value <= limit))

**6.4** Suppose limit is non-negative. Use a required function to simplify part (d) of the previous question even further.

**6.5** Suppose temperature is a real variable (representing F) and sunny is a Boolean variable. Simplify the following expression that describes an atypical day in Ithaca, NY, to find out whether it is relatively pleasant or not.

**not**((temperature <= 32.0) **or not** sunny)

**6.6** A number $m >= 2$ is prime if and only if its greatest divisor $< m$ is 1. Use this fact to give a different solution to the *next prime* problem. Is the solution in the text preferable? Why?

**6.7** Here is the top part of a schema:

| **Schema** Sequential Search After First :<br>**var**<br>$v$ : *the type of values in the sequence*;<br>{ Given the first member $x_0$ of a sequence, a way of generating }<br>{ the next member from a given member, and a property $P$, }<br>{ set $v$ = the first member after $x_0$ with property $P$. } |
|---|

(a) Give the bottom part of the schema.

(b) Use the schema to solve the following problem:

*Set* NextPrime = *the least prime* > n

**6.8** Implement the following action, where x and Mult32 are integer variables, and x $\geqslant$ 0.

*Set* Mult32 = *the least multiple of 32* $\geqslant$ x

**6.9** The following problems all share a common context: the user is to be prompted, just once, to enter zero or more examination grades, each of which is an integer between 0 and 100 inclusive, and then a stopping-value of –1. After reading all the input, some information is to be printed.

(a) Give a high-level solution by adapting a schema.

(b) Write a program that prints the number of grades in the input data. Do so here, and in questions (c) and (d), by completely refining your answer to (a).

(c) Write a program that prints the average grade. If there are no grades, the average does not exist, so a suitable message should be printed instead.

(d) Write a program that prints the maximum grade. A suitable message should be printed if there are no grades. It would not do to print 0 in this case. Why?

(e) Suppose we decide to look out for illegal marks, and print how many were found, but otherwise ignore them. How should our general solution in (a) be modified? Note that schema Check Interactive Input is not applicable, because each grade is not individually prompted for.

**6.10** Suppose a user is to be prompted to enter a real number between lower and upper inclusive, to be read into variable measurement. Give a program segment that repeatedly does this until a legal number is entered.

**6.11** Write a program segment that prompts for and reads a sequence of positive integers followed by a stopping-value of –1, and sets max to the maximum value read (–1 if only a stopping-value is entered).

*Hint*: Initialize *after* the first input statement.

**6.12** Implement the action:

*Print the Macintosh Pascal character set in increasing order*

by using a for-loop with an integer variable.

**6.13** Assemble program CharacterSet. Run it with Step-Step and use the Observe window to follow the changing values of row and col.

**6.14** Implement this CC-rider to the specifications for Case-study 2: print CC instead of chr(127). Then run it to see what you have done.

**6.15** Modify program CharacterSet so that the characters appear in order when taken row by row from the top, rather than column by column from the left. Thus the first two rows will consist of CCs.

**6.16** Write another program to print the character set in the format of the previous question. This time, use a single for-loop to print all the characters.

*Hint*: After printing each character, have the program take special action if it is the last in a row.

**6.17** Implement the action:

*Set* sum = 1 + 2 + 3 + ... + n, *given* n $\geqslant$ 0.

**6.18** In Chapter 19 we shall learn that the most accurate way to implement the following action is by adding the values in increasing order. Implement it that way.

*Set* sum $= 1 + \frac{1}{2} + \frac{1}{3} + \cdots + \frac{1}{n}$, *given* n $\geqslant$ 0.

**6.19** Suppose part of an input line has been read. Write a program segment that reads the rest of the line and the end-of-line marker, and sets unused to the number of characters skipped (not including the marker).

**6.20** The Fibonacci sequence is 0, 1, 1, 2, 3, 5, 8, 13, ... ; the first member is 0, the second is 1, and each successive member is the sum of the two previous members. Implement the following actions.

(a) *Print the Fibonacci numbers* $\leqslant$ limit.

(b) *Print the first* n *Fibonacci numbers, given* n $\geqslant$ *0.*

*Hint*: Consider the sequence of successive pairs, i.e. (0,1), (1,1), (1,2), (2,3), (3,5), (5,8), (8,13), ... . Since each successive member of *this* sequence can be computed from the previous member, our Sequential Search schemas are applicable.

**6.21** Consider the action:

*Set* d = *least divisor* $\geqslant$ *2 of* m

(a) What is its postcondition?

(b) What is its precondition?

(c) Desk-check the given refinement.

**6.22** Ask a friend to make a minor change to one of your programs, preferably one you have not thought about for a while. Suggested changes are altering a variable, deleting a statement, deleting part of a condition; the change should not introduce syntax errors. First try to find the error by checking the points listed in the section 'Defensive programming.' Then, if necessary, test by execution.

# 7 FUNCTIONS

The Form remains, the Function never dies.
— William Wordsworth, *The River Duncton*

## 7.1 Predefined functions: A review

In Chapter 5 we met some of Pascal's required functions. Examples are abs, exp, ln, chr, and odd. Each one of these is a function in the mathematical sense; i.e. when supplied with a value (called an argument), it gives back a value (said to be the result of applying the function to the argument). For example, abs(–3.8) gives 3.8, odd(1987) gives true.

Each of the required functions happens to have one argument (even eof and eoln, whose file argument may be implicit). But the concept of a function allows for an arbitrary list of arguments, and there is nothing to stop an implementation supplying a predefined function that takes more than one argument, or even no arguments. (Macintosh Pascal has several; see, for example, the functions associated with strings given in Chapter 14.)

The Standard's term for the application of a function to an argument list is a **function-designator**. A function-designator is an expression which belongs to the syntactic category **factor**. Its argument list is called an **actual-parameter-list**. We recall the relevant definitions from Chapter 5:

> factor: *variable* | *unsigned-constant* | *function-designator* |
> *(expression)* | **not** *factor*
> function-designator: *function-identifier* <u>*( actual-parameter-list )*</u>
> function-identifier: *identifier*
> actual-parameter-list: *actual-parameter* ... , *actual-parameter*
> actual-parameter: *actual-value*
> actual-value: *expression*

Predefined functions play a useful role in programs even when the service that they perform is a very simple one. We could, for example, replace every application of odd by an equivalent expression: odd(x * y) could be replaced by x * y **mod** 2 = 1, odd(a + b) by (a + b) **mod** 2 = 1, and, in general, odd(*i*) by (*i*) **mod** 2 = 1.

Similarly, but with more trouble, every use of abs could be avoided by using extra variables and conditional statements.

But the effect would be deleterious even in these very simple cases, let alone those where non-trivial algorithms are needed to compute the result (of an application of arctan, for example). It is apparent that predefined functions make an important contribution to the clarity of our programs. Because applications of predefined functions do not have to be refined, programs are shorter and, more importantly, higher-level than they would otherwise be, and **localization** is increased, meaning that closely related parts of a program are textually closer.

There are many occasions in programming when what we do abstractly is to apply a function. If it is predefined, we are in luck. But chances are it will not be. Nevertheless, the advantages mentioned above can still be obtained in Pascal, because we can define our own functions, and thereafter use them in just the same way as predefined functions. With user-defined functions, of course, it is necessary to specify how to compute the result. But this is done in a separate section of the program, and is only done once, no matter how many times the function is used. The idea is to specify the result in terms of named parameters, much like we did above with odd, where we denoted its argument by $i$.

## 7.2 User-defined functions

Here is an example of a simple but useful user-defined function.

```
function IsDigit (ch : char) : Boolean;
{ Returns true if ch is a digit, otherwise false. }
begin { IsDigit }
  IsDigit := ('0' <= ch) and (ch <= '9')
end; { IsDigit }
```

The first line contains the **function heading**, which states that:

- The name of the function is IsDigit;
- It is used with a single argument of type char;
- In the definition of the function, the value of the argument is represented by the name ch; it is called a **formal parameter**;
- The function gives a Boolean value.

Next comes a comment that defines the value of the function in terms of its formal parameter. Together with the heading, it is all that needs to be known to use the function. Finally comes the statement-part of the function. Its job is to compute the value of the function, which is specified by assigning it to the name of the function. We need to update the definition of assignment-statement to allow this:

assignment-statement: *variable-identifier* := *expression* |
*function-identifier* := *expression*

The statement-part of **IsDigit** is minimal, as a single assignment statement suffices to compute and specify the result.

The definition of a function is called a **function-declaration**. Function declarations come just before the statement-part of a program, i.e. after the variable-declarations. Our syntax definition for *block* needs updating to reflect this:

block:
*constant-definition-part*
*variable-declaration-part*
*function-declaration-part*
*statement-part*

function-declaration-part:
| *function-declaration* ;
| ...

Here is a simple program that tests function **IsDigit**:

```
program TestIsDigit (Input, Output);
{ Interactively tests function IsDigit. Run for instructions. }
 var
   c : char; { latest character read }
 function IsDigit (ch : char) : Boolean;
 { Returns true if ch is a digit, otherwise false. }
 begin { IsDigit }
   IsDigit := ('0' <= ch) and (ch <= '9')
 end; { IsDigit }
begin { TestIsDigit }
  Writeln('Type characters one at a time, waiting for a response
          before typing another. Finish by typing a period (.).');
  repeat
   Read(c);
   if IsDigit(c) then
     Writeln(' is a digit.')
   else
     Writeln(' is NOT a digit.')
  until c = '.'
end. { TestIsDigit }
```

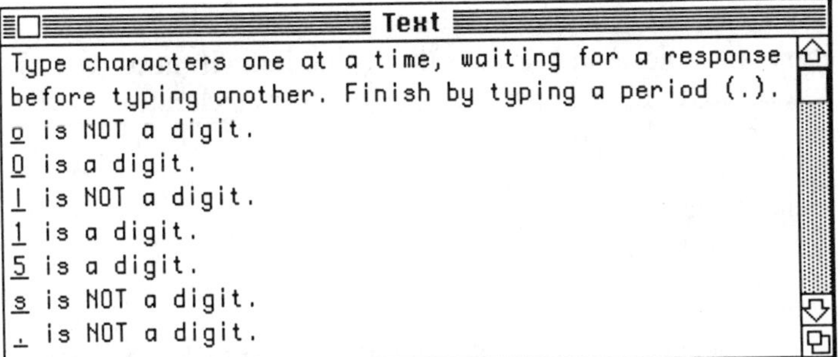

Text
Type characters one at a time, waiting for a response
before typing another. Finish by typing a period (.).
o is NOT a digit.
0 is a digit.
l is NOT a digit.
1 is a digit.
5 is a digit.
s is NOT a digit.
. is NOT a digit.


**Figure 7.1**
The text window after a run of TestIsDigit.

Typical output is shown in Figure 7.1, with input underlined.

Two points should be noted now. First, the function is used to form a Boolean expression. It takes exactly one argument, which may be any expression of type char. Thus, for example, we may write **not** IsDigit(chr(100)). Second, a function-declaration is always followed by a semicolon. Because our practice is to follow that with a comment giving the name of the function, whenever we present a function-declaration we add the semicolon at the end, in order not to mislead the reader.

Here is a declaration of another function; it has two formal parameters.

```
function power (a, b : real) : real;
{ Assumes a > 0; }
{ returns a to the power b. }
begin { power }
  power := exp(b * ln(a))
end; { power }
```

Exercise 7.4 explains how to test this function with minimal programming effort. Note that you need not understand how it computes its result — to test or otherwise use it, you need know only its heading and associated comment, which define how to use it and what value it returns. Testing it will reveal that both real and integer arguments are acceptable, just as with predefined functions that expect real arguments, such as sin. The result, though, is always real. Also, of course, you will observe that the order of the arguments is important.

# 7.3 Functions as subprograms

## 7.3.1 SYNTAX OF FUNCTION-DECLARATIONS

The value to be returned by a function may require a complex algorithm for its calculation. Pascal therefore allows all its resources to be brought to bear, and decrees that the body of a function should be a block. That means that a function-declaration can introduce its own constants, variables, and even other functions if need be, since we now know that blocks may have function-declarations. Function-declarations are called **subprograms**, for obvious reasons.

function-declaration:
  *function-heading* ;
  *function-body*
function-heading:
  **function** *function-identifier* (*formal-parameter-list*) : *result-type*
result-type: *type-identifier*
type-identifier: *identifier*
function-body: *block*
formal-parameter-list:
  *formal-parameter-section* ... ; *formal-parameter-section*
formal-parameter-section: *value-parameter-section*
value-parameter-section: *identifier-list* : *parameter-type*
parameter-type: *type-identifier*

All examples but the next in this chapter have a formal-parameter-list consisting of a single formal-parameter-section. You will need more than one if there is more than one type of formal parameter. For example:

```
function ForceUpper (ch : char; upper : Boolean) : char;
{ If ch is a lower-case letter and upper is true, }
{ returns the upper-case version of ch, otherwise ch. }
```

Thus, for example:

```
ForceUpper('a', false)   gives   'a'
ForceUpper('x', true)    gives   'X'
ForceUpper('&', true)    gives   '&'
```

There are some requirements that are not captured by the above rules:

- The result-type of a function must be an **unstructured type**; for now, just note that all the types we have met so far are unstructured.
- The statement-part of the function-body must include at least one assignment to the function-identifier.
- Although the function-identifier may appear on the left of an assignment statement, it may not be used in an expression as if it were a variable. (But see Chapter 18 on recursion.)

A function-declaration limits the class of legal function-designators in two ways:

(1) The number of arguments must equal the number of formal parameters.

(2) Each argument expression must be assignment-compatible with a variable of the corresponding formal parameter's type. Parameter/argument correspondence is by position; i.e. they are paired off from left to right.

Here is an example of a function with a more complex body:

```
function lpf (n : integer) : integer;
{ Assumes n > 1; }
{ returns the least prime factor of n. }
  var
    d : integer; { candidate for a divisor of n }
begin { lpf }
{ Set d = least divisor > 1 of n }
  d := 2;
  while n mod d <> 0 do
    d := d + 1;

  lpf := d
end; { lpf }
```

It will doubtless seem familiar, because it incorporates the solution to a subproblem of the *next prime* problem in Chapter 6. Note that we cannot dispense with d and work directly with lpf instead, because lpf := lpf + 1 is illegal.

### 7.3.2 INVOKING A FUNCTION

A function is **invoked** during the evaluation of an expression that includes one of its function-designators. The following sequence of events then occurs:

(1) Each argument (actual parameter) is evaluated.

(2) For each formal parameter, a quasi-variable is created and assigned the value of the corresponding argument (which is why it must be assignment-compatible). The quasi-variable henceforth behaves as if it was a variable.

(3) For each variable declaration in the variable-declaration-part of the function-declaration's block, a variable is created with an undefined value.

(4) The statement-part of the function-declaration's block is executed. It may refer to the parameters, which denote their corresponding quasi-variables, and the variables created in step (3). Any constants or functions introduced by the function-declaration's block are also available. Values of the function's type may be assigned to the function-identifier.

(5) When execution of the previous step terminates, the last value assigned to the function-identifier becomes the value of the function-designator. It is an error for this value to be undefined. Furthermore, all quasi-variables introduced for parameters in step (2) are exterminated, and all variables created in step (3) are annihilated.

In summary, the function's block is treated just the same as the program's (or any other block).

Let us trace the evaluation of the function-designator lpf(m), where m is an integer variable declared in the same block as the function.

(1) The argument (actual parameter) m is evaluated, giving, say, 9.

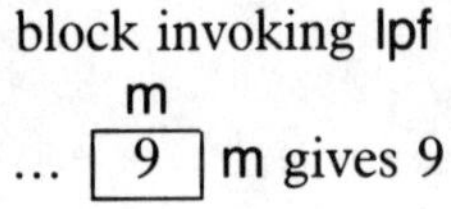

block invoking lpf

m

... [9] m gives 9

(2) A quasi-variable is created for the formal parameter n of lpf, and initialized to 9.

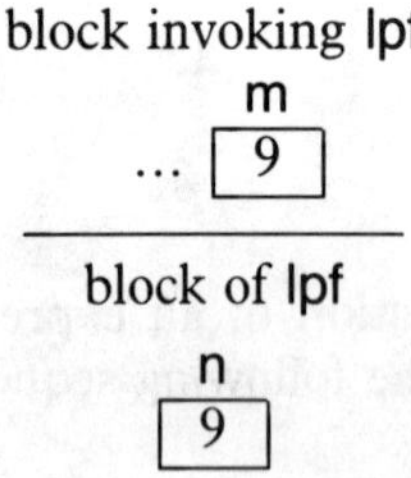

block invoking lpf

m

... [9]

---

block of lpf

n

[9]

(3) The variable d of lpf is created with an undefined value.

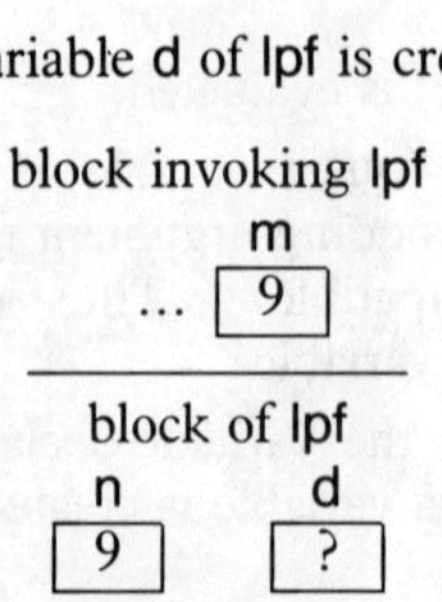

block invoking lpf

m

... [9]

---

block of lpf

n d

[9] [?]

(4) The statement-part of lpf is executed. On completion we have:

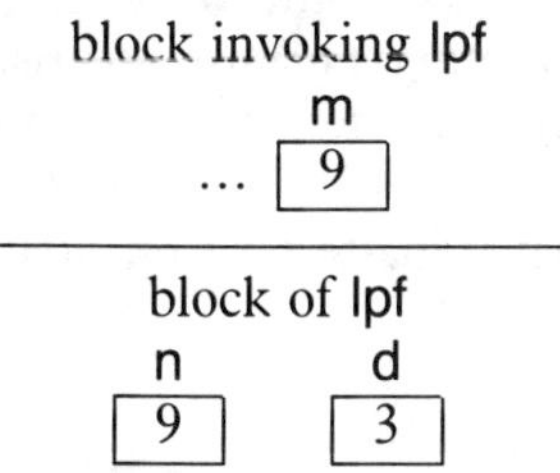


last value assigned to lpf: 3

(5) Execution terminates: 3 is the value of the function-designator; all quasi-variables and variables introduced in steps (2) and (3) are destroyed. Execution continues in the context of the expression that included lpf(m).

block invoking lpf

m

... [9] lpf(m) gives 3

## 7.4 Writing functions

When writing a function it is very important that you do not try to think in terms of the previous pictorial illustration of a function invocation. That is strictly behind-the-scenes stuff, to clarify and illustrate the discussion prior to it. No, you write a function-declaration by solving a programming problem in the usual way — with stepwise refinement. The problem is to assign the result of the function to the function-identifier, and you may treat the formal parameters as variables which have already been given values.

The description of step (4) of invoking a function is not the *whole* truth, though it *is* the truth and nothing but the truth, because a function-declaration's statement-part may refer to additional parameters, constants, variables, and functions. For example, it may refer to any of these that are predefined, such as the constant pi and the function succ. The issue here is what is available in a given part of a program. It is dealt with fully in the next chapter, under the rubric of *Scope rules*. OK?

For the present, let us restrict our interest to function-declarations. A function-declaration makes the function available throughout the block in whose function-declaration-part it is declared. There are two riders to this stipulation, however. One is that Pascal follows the principle of **declaration before use**, which means what it says: in particular, if a function *G* makes use of another function $F$ declared in the same function-declaration-part, then the declaration of $F$ must come first. The other rider is that a function-identifier may be reused for some other purpose, decreasing the region of availability of the function. Again, refer to the next chapter for the full story.

An example should clarify matters. Consider the following program:

```
program Primes (Input, Output);
{ Prompts for and reads an integer, and prints all the prime }
{ numbers not exceeding it, in increasing order. }
 var
  limit, { bound on size of prime numbers }
  n, { a number to be tested for primality }
  i { n = i'th odd number }
   : integer;

 { (A) FUNCTION lpf CAN BE DECLARED HERE }

 function IsPrime (n : integer) : Boolean;
 { Returns true if n is prime, i.e. a number > 1 whose only }
 { divisor > 1 is itself; otherwise returns false. }

   { (B) OR FUNCTION lpf CAN BE DECLARED HERE }

 begin { IsPrime }
  if n < 2 then
   IsPrime := false
  else
   IsPrime := lpf(n) = n
 end; { IsPrime }

   { (C) BUT FUNCTION lpf CANNOT BE DECLARED HERE }

begin { Primes }
 Write('Enter bound on size of prime numbers: ');
 Readln(limit);
 Writeln('The primes not exceeding ', limit : 1, ' are as follows:');
 if limit >= 2 then
  begin
  { Print the only even prime }
   Write(2);
  { Print in order the odd primes <= limit }
   for i := 2 to (limit + 1) div 2 do
    begin
     n := 2 * i - 1;
     if IsPrime(n) then
```

```
        Write(n)
      end { for-loop }
    end { limit >= 2 }
  end. { Primes }
```

### 7.4.1 MODULARITY

Position (B) is the most natural one for the declaration of lpf. For then we read program Primes as declaring three variables and the function IsPrime, which are all that it uses in its statement-part. And reading deeper, we see that IsPrime declares a function lpf, which is then used in *its* statement-part. Function IsPrime is completely self-contained: its only interaction with its environment is per medium of its formal parameter. We say it is **modular**. So also is function lpf, wherever it is declared.

Modularity is a Good Thing: a modular function can be read and completely understood without any knowledge of the program that uses it. It can be tested independently, and incorporated in any program with complete confidence. It can also be included in a **library** of functions to be made available to any program.

> **Principle** A subprogram should be modular: it should interact with its environment solely through its formal parameter(s).

A function that performs input or output is not a function in the mathematical sense. One may debate whether Real Men eat quiche, but certainly Real Functions do not change anything — they only compute a value. It makes no sense for evaluation of an expression to affect the input or output streams, except where output is necessary to signal an error condition.

> **Principle** Functions should not move the input position, and should only produce output to signal an error condition.

Note that this principle permits functions with file parameters, such as eoln, as long as they do not affect them.

If lpf is declared in position (A), we read program Primes as declaring two functions, each of which is therefore available throughout the program (i.e., throughout the program's block). So lpf may be used by IsPrime, as the requirement of declaration-before-use is met. In this version, IsPrime is not completely independent of its environment: it can only be used by a program that makes function lpf available to it. A comment should indicate this.

> **Principle** If a subprogram makes an assumption about its environment, the comment accompanying its heading should say so.

Modularity is not an absolute thing; there are degrees of it. With **lpf** declared in position (A), function **IsPrime** fails to be completely modular in a relatively minor way; a way, moreover, that is often unavoidable in practice without going to ridiculous extremes. For example, consider a program that needs to make use of both **lpf** and **IsPrime**. It makes sense to declare them as above with **lpf** in position (A); the alternative is to make **IsPrime** fully modular by redeclaring **lpf** in it, and that is ridiculous. A similar situation is where a program needs to use two functions, each of which needs to use another. In that case, all three should be declared at the same level, with the latter first. The upshot is that declaring **lpf** at (A) is so familiar that some would not consider it at all stylistically inferior. You pay your money and you take your choice. Position (C) is illegal for declaring **lpf** because it is used beforehand.

Another advantage of modularity is that the body of a function can be replaced by another with no change to the results of any program that uses it (except if results depend on timing considerations). It is only necessary that the new body implements the comment accompanying the function-heading. A reason, by the way, why such comments should be as precise as possible. Thus improvements in the efficiency of the calculation of the function's value can be made independently of its use.

Here is an example of this possibility. The calculation for function **lpf** can be sped up considerably by exploiting the fact that if the smallest divisor of a number $n > 1$ exceeds $\sqrt{n}$ then it must be $n$ itself. Accordingly, we might like to replace the original **lpf** by the following version, and can do so with impunity.

```
function lpf (n : integer) : integer;
{ Assumes n > 1; }
{ returns the least prime factor of n. }
  var
    d : integer; { candidate for a divisor of n }
begin { lpf }
  { Set d = minimum of: (a) least divisor > 1 of n, and }
  { (b) least integer >= sqrt(n) }
  d := 2;
  while (n mod d <> 0) and (sqr(d) < n) do
    d := d + 1;
  if n mod d = 0 then
    lpf := d
  else
    lpf := n
end; { lpf }
```

Exercise 7.12 invites you to make yet another improvement to the efficiency of **lpf**.

## 7.5 Macaveats

Macintosh Pascal allows the result-type of a function to be a string-type, even though it is a structured type. See Chapter 14.

## EXERCISES

**7.1** Complete the following partial function-declaration:

```
function IsLetter (ch : char) : Boolean;
{ Returns true if ch is a letter, otherwise false. }
{ N.B. Assumes both upper- & lower-case letters contiguous. }
```

**7.2** Complete the following partial function-declaration:
(a) using the required function odd,
(b) without using odd.

```
function even (i : integer) : Boolean;
{ Returns true if i is even, otherwise false. }
```

**7.3** Write a function that returns the maximum of two integers.

**7.4** Test function power by first declaring it in a skeletal program, such as Program Untitled. Then choose Step from the Run menu to process the declaration. Finally, use the Observe window to evaluate the function with various argument lists.

**7.5** Package the solution to Exercise 6.7(b) as a function.

**7.6** Use function IsPrime to implement the original high-level solution to the *next prime* problem in Chapter 6.

**7.7** Solve Exercise 6.18 by declaring and using a suitable function.

**7.8** Write a function that returns the cost of mailing a letter when given its weight. Use the information in Exercise 5.8.

**7.9** Write function ForceUpper. It may assume that both the lower- and upper-case letters are contiguous.

**7.10** Test your function ForceUpper by writing a program along the lines of program TestIsDigit.

**7.11** Modify program Primes to print the primes 10 to a line. *Hint*: Count up to 10 and start again.

**Table 7.1** Bizarro multiplication of 109 by 57. (Exercise 7.13)

| First | Second | Sum |
|---|---|---|
| 57 | 109 | 109 |
| 28 | 218 | 109 |
| 14 | 436 | 109 |
| 7 | 872 | 981 |
| 3 | 1744 | 2725 |
| 1 | 3488 | 6213 |

**7.12** Speed up function **lpf** even further by exploiting the fact that the smallest divisor $> 1$ of a number $> 1$ is either 2 or odd.

**7.13** The denizens of the planet Bizarro multiply two integers $> 0$ as follows. Call the smaller the first number, and the larger the second. The first is repeatedly halved as the second is doubled, until the first becomes 1. But whenever the first is odd, the second is added to a cumulative sum. The answer is the final sum. The Bizarro-calculation of $109 \times 57 = 6213$ is shown in Table 7.1.

Write a function that multiplies two integers $> 0$ by this method. It should not use any multiplications, and should avoid an unnecessary doubling at the end. If that was too easy, modify your solution to handle any integers.

**7.14** One of the earliest recorded algorithms is Euclid's beautiful method for calculating gcd($x$, $y$), the greatest common divisor of two non-negative integers $x$, $y$, which is defined as long as both integers are not zero. It is based on three facts:

(1) gcd(0, $y$) = $y$, if $y \neq 0$,

(2) gcd($x$, $y$) = gcd($x$, $y$ **mod** $x$), if $x \neq 0$,

(3) gcd($x$, $y$) = gcd($y$, $x$).

Table 7.2 illustrates the method applied to calculating gcd (5460, 294). In each line, gcd ($x$, $y$) is the same, by (2) and (3). In the last line, it is 42, by (1), which is therefore the answer.

Write Euclid's algorithm as a function.

**Table 7.2** Computing gcd(5460,294) by Euclid's algorithm.

| $x$ | $y$ | $y$ **mod** $x$ |
|---|---|---|
| 5460 | 294 | 294 |
| 294 | 5460 | 168 |
| 168 | 294 | 126 |
| 126 | 168 | 42 |
| 42 | 126 | 0 |
| 0 | 42 | (illegal) |

# 8
# PROCEDURES

'In such cases,' said the Owl, 'the customary procedure is as follows.'
'What does Crustimoney Proceedcake mean?,' said Pooh. 'For I am a bear of very little brain, and long words bother me.'
'It means the thing to do.'
— A. A. Milne, *Winnie the Pooh*

## 8.1 Introduction

Suppose you look up a recipe in a well-organized cook book. You will notice that the recipes are quite short — most in *The Joy of Cooking*, for instance, occupy only half a column or so — because they frequently refer the reader to other recipes that explain how to prepare certain ingredients, or perform certain stock techniques (so to speak). And these subrecipes are presented in exactly the same way.

The benefits are great. Each recipe is read easily and quickly, because details do not get in the way. There is no loss of precision, though, because the details can be pursued elsewhere. Furthermore, much space is saved, because the preparation of a common ingredient or the way to perform an important technique needs to be explained once only.

With stepwise refinement, we create programs by giving high-level descriptions and then refining their component parts. But, with our present knowledge, the details can be removed only when subproblems are solved with predefined procedures. Imagine how much worse off we would be if, for instance, *each* read of a real value had to be spelled out in detail, *on the spot*, with all the complications of reading a character at a time, processing a sign, a decimal point, an exponent, and so on.

Well, have we got good news for you! Because all the advantages of predefined procedures are available to you in the privacy of your own programming environment. All you need is Pascal's facility to define your very own procedures. Once you have tried them, you'll never know how you did without.

## 8.2 Parameterless procedures

Recall our first refinement of program CharacterSet:

*Print column numbers*;
*Print top of box*;
*Print rows 0 to 15, with row number & left & right sides of box*;
*Print bottom of box*

Two of the high-level actions have exactly the same refinement, viz. *Print top of box* and *Print bottom of box*. Instead of refining each as in Chapter 6, we can define a procedure and use it twice. The definition is called a **procedure-declaration**. The one we need is as follows. (As with function-declarations, we always present procedure-declarations with the following semicolon.)

```
procedure PrintBoxSide;
{ Prints line representing top or bottom of box. }
 var
   col : integer; { column number }
begin { PrintBoxSide }
 Write('--' : 5);
 for col := 0 to 15 do
   Write('---');
 Writeln('-')
end; { PrintBoxSide }
```

This should be reminiscent of a function-declaration, because it is also a subprogram. The first line is the heading, which in this case simply names the procedure, which is **parameterless**, i.e. has no formal parameters. The accompanying comment describes what the procedure does, and the block that follows specifies how it does it. All we have done is incorporate the statement-list used as the original refinement in the statement-part, and declare that it uses variable col. Like variables declared in a function-declaration, col is said to be **local** to the procedure.

Procedure-declarations appear in the same part of a block as function-declarations. We update the syntactic description of a block to reflect this.

block:
    *constant-definition-part*;
    *variable-declaration-part*;
    *procedure-and-function-declaration-part*;
    *statement-part*

procedure-and-function-declaration-part:
    | *procedure-or-function-declaration*;
    | ...

procedure-or-function-declaration:
    *procedure-declaration* | *function-declaration*

Having declared a procedure, a new statement, called a **procedure-statement**, becomes available. The act of executing it is called a **procedure call**. We also take the opportunity to treat input-statements and output-statements syntactically as procedure-statements with special actual-parameter-lists.

simple-statement: *empty-statement* | *assignment-statement* |
*procedure-statement*

A parameterless procedure's procedure-statement consists solely of its name. So, in program CharacterSet, the two high-level actions are refined as follows:

```
{ Print top of box }
  PrintBoxSide

{ Print bottom of box }
  PrintBoxSide
```

The effect of each of these procedure-statements is to execute the block of the procedure-declaration. The variable col is created with an undefined value, and then the statement-part is executed, which uses col to print a horizontal side of the box. On completion, variable col disappears.

A great advantage of this solution over the original is that the refinement for printing a side is specified just once, saving space and reducing the opportunity for error. But also, because details are removed, the program is more readable and the high-level solution is more apparent. This latter property is sufficiently important to justify implementing a high-level action with a procedure-statement, even when it is the procedure's only use.

We can do this for one of the two remaining high-level actions of program CharacterSet with a parameterless procedure:

```
procedure NumberColumns;
{ Prints column numbers. }
  var
    col : integer; { column number }
begin { NumberColumns }
  Write(' ' : 4);
  for col := 0 to 15 do
    Write(col : 3);
  Writeln
end; { NumberColumns }
```

The refinement becomes just:

NumberColumns

Retaining the original description of the high-level action as a comment is hardly worthwhile here. The comments for the refinements using PrintBoxSide were retained because they add information, although it is so slight as to make the decision a finicky one.

# 8.3 Parameters

## 8.3.1 VALUE PARAMETERS

The remaining high-level action in the original refinement of program CharacterSet exactly matches a schema, giving the refinement:

```
{ Print rows 0 to 15, with row number & left & right sides of box }
 for row := 0 to 15 do
   Print row of table numbered with row
```

There is no reason to use a procedure-statement for this refinement, both because there is hardly any detail worth hiding, and because printing a line of the table is the appropriate level of abstraction, since that is what each of the other high-level actions does.

But the component action is another matter. Here the computation to be performed depends on a value, namely that of row, so we declare a procedure with a single parameter:

```
procedure PrintRow (RowNumber : integer);
{ Prints row of table, consisting of row number, left side of box, }
{ characters in row, and right side of box. }
 const
   OrdOfSpecialCC = 127; { ord value of isolated control
                           character }
 var
   col, { column number }
   OrdValue { ordinal value of character to be printed }
     : integer;
begin { PrintRow }
{ Print start of row, with control characters in cols 1,2 }
 Write(RowNumber : 2, ' | CC CC');
{ Print remaining characters in row }
 for col := 2 to 15 do
   begin
     OrdValue := col * 16 + RowNumber;
     if OrdValue = OrdOfSpecialCC then { indicate control
                                         character }
       Write(' CC')
```

```
      else
        Write(chr(OrdValue) : 3)
    end;
  { Print end of row }
  Writeln(' |')
end; { PrintRow }
```

We have used the modification requested in Exercise 6.14 that indicates that chr(127) is a control-character, and added comments because of the extra complication.

The formal parameter RowNumber is called a **value-parameter**. It is the kind of parameter used for functions in the previous chapter. The procedure statement:

```
PrintRow(row)
```

that refines the body of the loop is executed in much the same way as a function-invocation, i.e. the actual-parameter row is evaluated, the resulting value is assigned to the quasi-variable created for RowNumber, the local variables col and OrdValue are created, and the statement-part of the procedure-declaration is executed. The only difference is that there is no notion of a result, so that it is illegal to assign a value to the procedure-identifier, and that the invocation is from a statement rather than an expression.

The three procedures that were introduced for program CharacterSet are all modular, in the sense of depending only on their parameters (if any). But they are nevertheless not **independent**, because they each make common assumptions about how the character-set table is to be formatted. The best way to document their mutual dependence is to make them procedures that are declared by a master procedure that prints the character-set. This done, the program to print the character-set is as follows. The blocks for each of the low-level procedures have been omitted.

```
program CharacterSet (Output);
{ Prints the Macintosh Pascal character-set. }

  procedure PrintCharacterSet;
  { Prints character set column by column from the left, }
  { as in Macintosh Pascal Technical Appendix. }
   var
    row : integer; { number of row }

   procedure PrintBoxSide;
   { Prints line representing top or bottom of box. }
   ...
```

```
    procedure NumberColumns;
    { Prints column numbers. }
    ...

    procedure PrintRow (RowNumber : integer);
    { Prints row of table, consisting of row number, left side of box, }
    { characters in row, and right side of box. }
    ...

  begin { PrintCharacterSet }
    NumberColumns;
  { Print top of box }
    PrintBoxSide;
  { Print rows 0 to 15, with row number & left & right sides of box }
    for row := 0 to 15 do
      PrintRow(row);
  { Print bottom of box }
    PrintBoxSide
  end; { PrintCharacterSet }

begin { CharacterSet }
  PrintCharacterSet
end. { CharacterSet }
```

Notice that procedure PrintCharacterSet declares only a single variable, viz. row, since that is all it uses. The program itself uses no variables. The important thing to appreciate is how much more readable this version of the program is than the procedureless original (with the modification to handle chr(127)). Each subprogram has a short and easily understood statement-part, either because it is simple (NumberColumns, PrintBoxSide, PrintRow), or because the details are handled by calls of other procedures (PrintCharacterSet, CharacterSet).

### 8.3.2 VARIABLE PARAMETERS

It often happens that a program segment which we would like to encapsulate as a subprogram changes the value of one or more variables that belong to the environment of its use. If only one variable is affected, and there is no input or output, a function is the appropriate form of subprogram: the variable can simply be assigned the value of the function.

But suppose more than one variable is affected, or that input or output is performed. Then a procedure is called for (if you'll pardon the expression). Since the procedure should be modular, any variables that it affects should be actual parameters of the call. But they cannot be the kind of parameters we have used so far, because value parameters are only capable of *sending* information (in the form of values) *to* a procedure, not *receiving* information (in the form of changed values of variables) *from* it.

Pascal provides another kind of parameter for such occasions, called a **variable parameter**. Variable parameters are signaled by the appearance of **var** at the front of their formal-parameter-section of the formal-parameter-list. A variable formal parameter acts as a temporary name for the variable which must be supplied as the corresponding actual parameter in the procedure-statement.

Here is an example. In program JobScheduler1 from Chapter 6 the following refinement occurs.

```
{ Assign job to processor and update statistics }
 if TotalTimeOn1 <= TotalTimeOn2 then
   Assign to processor 1 and update statistics
 else
   Assign to processor 2 and update statistics
```

Each of the two component high-level actions involves the same computation, except that some of the variables involved depend on the action.

The best way to refine these actions is with the help of a single procedure:

```
procedure schedule (duration, processor : integer;
                            var StartTime, sum : integer);
{ Schedules job of length duration on given processor, starting at }
{ time StartTime: outputs scheduling decision; updates StartTime }
{ to the starting time for the next job on this processor; updates }
{ the sum of completion times (sum) of all jobs. }
begin { schedule }
  Writeln('Job assigned to processor ', processor : 1, '.');
  StartTime := StartTime + duration;
  sum := sum + StartTime
end; { schedule }
```

The refinement becomes:

```
begin { Assign job to processor and update statistics }
  JobCount := JobCount + 1;
  if TotalTimeOn1 <= TotalTimeOn2 then
    schedule(JobTime, 1, TotalTimeOn1, SumOfCompletionTimes)
  else
    schedule(JobTime, 2, TotalTimeOn2, SumOfCompletionTimes)
end
```

This example shows that the role of formal parameters is not just to capture the variation in effects between different calls of a procedure, but also to make procedures modular. Some of the actual parameters may, in practice, be the same in all uses of a procedure, as happens with the first and fourth parameters above.

An actual variable parameter must be a variable of the same type as the formal parameter. When a procedure-statement is executed, a variable formal parameter becomes a temporary name for the actual parameter variable; any operation on the formal parameter is an operation on that variable. The temporary name is rescinded when execution of the procedure's statement-part is completed.

Let us trace the execution of the procedure-statement:

```
schedule(JobTime, 1, TotalTimeOn1, SumOfCompletionTimes)
```

after input of 4, 1, 2, has been processed, and the next input value 6 has been read into variable JobTime. This is part of the run illustrated in Figure 6.1.

(1) The actual value parameters JobTime and 1 are evaluated.

block of JobScheduler1

JobTime gives 6 1 gives 1

TotalTimeOn1 SumOfCompletionTimes

4 8

(2) The quasi-variables for the value formal parameters duration and processor are created and initialized, and the variable formal parameters StartTime and sum are made temporary names of their corresponding actual variable parameters.

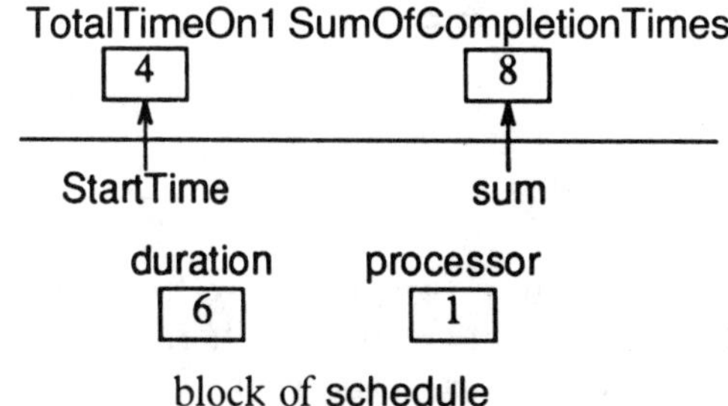


(3) (Procedure schedule has no local variables.)

(4) The statement-part is executed. On completion, the situation is as shown below. (That the output stream has been appended to is not shown.)

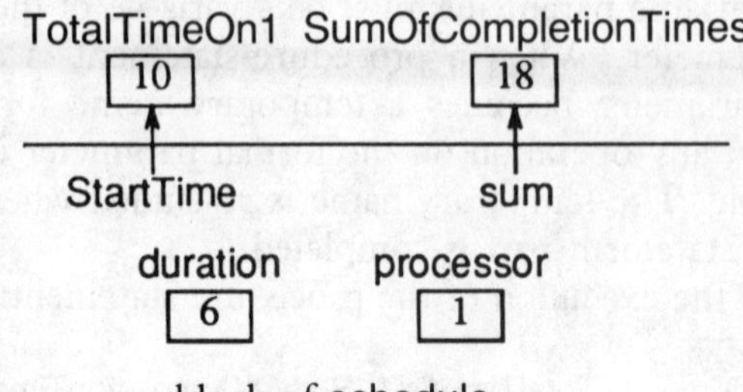


block of schedule

(5) All the information introduced for the execution of the procedure-statement vanishes. Execution resumes in JobScheduler1.

block of JobScheduler1

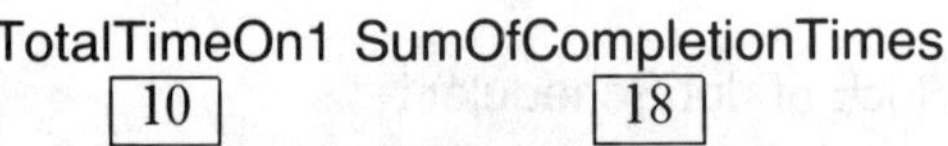


The action *Write statistics* in JobScheduler1 is also ripe for implementation with a procedure-statement; see Exercise 8.6.

### 8.3.3 ALIASING

Suppose two actual variable parameters are the same. When the procedure-call is executed, two formal variable parameters will each act as a temporary name of the actual parameter. This phenomenon is known as **aliasing**, and it is Bad News. For example, suppose x and y are two formal variable parameters aliased to the same integer actual variable parameter. Then, after execution of:

```
y := 0;
x := x + 1
```

the value of y is 1!

We almost always solve programming problems under the assumption that different identifiers name different variables. When this is violated, anything can happen, and probably will.

> **Principle** Avoid procedure-calls with identical actual variable parameters.

### 8.3.4 SYNTAX OF PROCEDURE-DECLARATIONS

Except for minor differences in their headings, procedure-declarations have the same syntax as function-declarations.

> procedure-declaration:
>     *procedure-heading* ;
>     *procedure-body*
> procedure-heading:
>     **procedure** *procedure-identifier* *(formal-parameter-list)*
> procedure-body: *block*

## 8.4 Pascal's parameter mechanism: A summary

### 8.4.1 SYNTAX

We need to update our syntax descriptions to accommodate variable parameters. First come formal-parameter-sections of formal-parameter-lists:

> formal-parameter-section: *value-parameter-section* | *variable-parameter-section*
> variable-parameter-section: **var** *identifier-list* : *parameter-type*

Note that a **var** at the head of a formal-parameter-section affects only the identifiers in that section; each section of variable formal parameters must be headed by **var**.

Next come actual-parameters of function-designators and procedure-statements:

> actual-parameter: *actual-value* | *actual-variable*
> actual-variable: *variable*

Note that the last definition does not state that an actual-variable must *be* a variable, only that it has the same syntax as a variable. It is perfectly normal for actual-variables to be formal parameters of the procedure whose statement-part contains the procedure-statement.

The syntax definitions do not distinguish between the formal- or actual-parameter-lists of functions and procedures. That is to say, functions may have variable parameters. But except for reasons of efficiency concerned with large structured variables (which we have yet to meet), it is not a good idea to exploit this loophole, because functions should not change their environment. A function that sins against this principle by moving the input position, producing output, or changing the value of a variable (via a variable parameter, for instance), is said to have **side-effects**. This is a pejorative term.

| **Principle** Functions should not have side-effects. |
|---|

### 8.4.2 FUNCTION-DECLARATIONS

A function-declaration associates a name with a parameterized subprogram that computes a value of a specified type. A comment should specify what value is returned, in terms of the parameters, if any. In the statement-part of a function-declaration, the name of the function may be assigned values of the result-type of the function. Function declarations come after the variable-declaration-part of a block.

### 8.4.3 PROCEDURE-DECLARATIONS

A procedure-declaration associates a name with a parameterized subprogram that performs some clearly defined action. A comment should specify what the procedure does, in terms of its parameters, if any. Procedure declarations come after the variable-declaration-part of a block.

### 8.4.4 VALUE PARAMETERS

A value formal parameter acts like a local variable that is initialized to the value of its corresponding actual parameter (argument), which must be an expression that is assignment-compatible with the type of the parameter. An assignment to a value formal parameter has no effect on its corresponding actual parameter, even if it happens to be a variable.

### 8.4.5 VARIABLE PARAMETERS

A variable formal parameter (also called a **var-parameter**) acts as a temporary local name for its corresponding actual parameter, which must be either a variable or a formal parameter of the same type. An assignment to a variable parameter changes the value of its corresponding actual parameter.

### 8.4.6 WHICH KIND OF PARAMETER?

Functions should use only value parameters. The only exception to this rule concerns large structured types (see Chapter 11). When a procedure only *needs a value*, use a value parameter. Such a parameter is sometimes called an **input parameter**, because it transmits input to the procedure; e.g. formal parameter RowNumber of procedure PrintRow. When a procedure only *returns a value*, use a variable parameter. Such a parameter is called an **output parameter**, because it receives output from a procedure; e.g. both parameters of the pre-defined procedure GetMouse. When a procedure *updates a value*, use a variable parameter. Such a parameter is both an input and output parameter; e.g. formal parameter sum of procedure schedule. These terms are not entirely happy choices: the parameters of the predefined input procedure Read are output parameters, and those of the pre-defined output procedure Write are input parameters!

Exercise 8.4 highlights the difference between value and variable parameters.

### 8.4.7 FORMAL AND ACTUAL PARAMETER CORRESPONDENCE

Formal and actual parameters are matched by position, i.e. they are paired off according to their positions in their respective sections. There must be the same number of parameters of each kind. Actual value parameters are expressions; actual variable parameters are variables or formal parameters.

### 8.4.8 LOCAL VARIABLES

Local variables are created, with undefined values, when a subprogram is invoked. They are used during execution of the subprogram's statement-part, and are disposed of when that execution is completed.

### 8.4.9 FUNCTION INVOCATION

A function is invoked when one of its function-designators is evaluated as part (or all) of the evaluation of an expression. Execution of the statement-part of the function-declaration should assign a value to the function-identifier. The last value so assigned becomes the value of the function-designator.

### 8.4.10 PROCEDURE INVOCATION

Procedure invocation occurs when a procedure-statement is executed. Execution of the statement-part of the procedure-declaration may either change the values of actual variable parameters, or produce output, or cause input to be read, or a combination of these actions.

## 8.5 Scope

### 8.5.1 THE ISSUE OF SCOPE

Predefined constants, functions, and procedures may be used anywhere in a program — as long as they are not used by the programmer for another purpose. Because it is perfectly acceptable to reuse a predefined identifier for our own purposes, in which case our definition or declaration takes precedence — predefined identifiers are not, after all, reserved words. And it is just as well, because the number of such identifiers in Macintosh Pascal is quite large. We, too, would sometimes like to make constants, functions, or procedures available throughout a program, or, in general, in particular parts of a program.

The issue here is that of **scope**. The scope of a definition or declaration is the textual part of the program in which it is in effect. It is accepted practice to refer to the scope of an identifier to mean that of its definition or declaration, and we shall occasionally do so. In Pascal, scope is defined in terms of blocks. A block, we recall, is all but the heading of a program, function-declaration, or procedure-declaration. A block may contain other blocks, since it may contain function- and procedure-declarations. We say that blocks may be **nested**, but blocks never overlap. Because blocks are the carriers of definitions and declarations, and the mediators of the scopes of their associated identifiers, Pascal is said to be a **block-structured language**.

### 8.5.2 SCOPE RULES

Pascal's scope rules are simple and uniform. The first two define the **region** of an identifier, which is its largest possible scope:

(1) The region of a definition or declaration is the smallest block in which it occurs.

(2) The region of a formal parameter is its formal-parameter-list together with the block that starts immediately after the heading in which this list occurs.

A region is either a block, or a block and a little extra for a parameter. All the blocks contained in this block are included in the region. The third rule defines all scopes.

(3) The scope of an identifier is its region minus all other regions for the same identifier that are contained within it.

The region of a predefined identifier is a notional block that contains the entire program; this is a different region from the program's block. Pascal has two requirements for definitions and declarations.

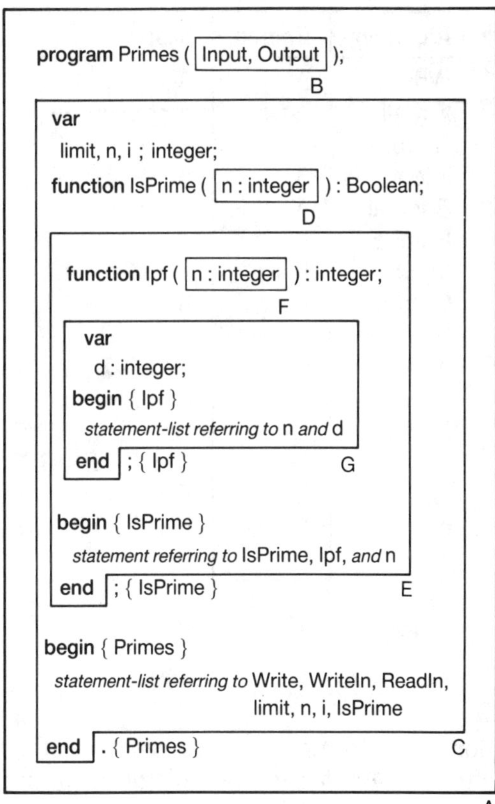


**Figure 8.1**
The regions of program Primes.

(4) There cannot be more than one definition or declaration of an identifier with the same region.

(5) An identifier may not be used before its defining point.

Let us look at these rules as they relate to program Primes from Chapter 7, with function lpf declared in position (B), i.e. local to function IsPrimes. The various regions of identifiers are shown in Figure 8.1.

It is straightforward to check that rule (4) is obeyed. This allows us unambiguously to specify a particular definition or declaration of an identifier by also giving its region. Thus, for example, identifier n whose region is D + E is the formal parameter of function IsPrime. Similarly, we can check that rule (5) is obeyed.

Table 8.1 gives the region and scope of each identifier that appears in program Primes. Region A is the notional block that encloses the program. These regions and scopes are found using scope rules (1) to (3) above. Let us consider three examples.

**Table 8.1** Scopes of all identifiers in program Primes.

| Identifier | Region | Scope |
|---|---|---|
| Write | A | A |
| Writeln | A | A |
| Readln | A | A |
| integer | A | A |
| Boolean | A | A |
| Primes | A | A |
| Input | B + C | B + C |
| Output | B + C | B + C |
| limit | C | C |
| n | C | C – D – E |
| i | C | C |
| IsPrime | C | C |
| n | D + E | D + E – F – G |
| lpf | E | E |
| n | F + G | F + G |
| d | G | G |

(a) The region for IsPrime is C, by rule (1). Since there are no other definitions or declarations of the identifier IsPrime in C, its scope is also C by rule (3). It follows that function IsPrime can be invoked in any statement-part of C, although it is used only in the program's statement-part.

(b) The region for variable n of Primes is also C, by rule (1), since, as with IsPrime, that is the smallest block containing its declaration. But it is reused twice within C, the first time as a formal parameter of IsPrime, with the region D + E by rule (2). So D + E is not within the scope of variable n. The second is within D + E so it does not further reduce the scope. It follows that variable n may only be used in the statement-part of Primes.

(c) The region of local variable d of lpf is G, by rule (1). Its identifier is not reused in G, so its scope is G, by rule (3). A reference to d in the statement-part of IsPrime, for example, would be detected as illegal, because there is no instance of d whose scope includes that part of the program.

Figure 8.1 and Table 8.1 may be used to check that every use of an identifier in Primes is legal, and, moreover, refers to the appropriate definition or declaration.

### 8.5.3 SCOPE RULES AND THE PROGRAMMER

The recommended attitude for the reader who has scrupulously slogged through all this scope scrap is that it is reassuring that Pascal gets everything right. It would be a big mistake to think that a programmer needs to draw complex diagrams, and perform tedious calculations for each identifier. We certainly did no such thing when we wrote program Primes. No, it is sufficient to choose the right kinds of parameters, and then to refine subprograms in the usual way. Modular subprograms can be written independently with safety; the details take care of themselves, because local definitions and declarations take precedence, but only have a local scope.

Occasionally, however, we need to take advantage of the rules. For example as mentioned previously, it is easy to imagine a program that makes use of functions lpf and IsPrime in, say, a statement-part of a single block $B$. The scope rules tell us that if lpf and IsPrime are declared by $B$, in that order, all is well, because the scope of lpf will include $B$'s statement-part and also the statement-part of the function-declaration for IsPrime:

```
    function lpf (n : integer) : integer;
    ...
    end; { lpf }
    function IsPrime (n : integer) : Boolean;
    begin { IsPrime }
      statement-list referring to lpf
    end; { IsPrime }
  begin { B }
    statement-list referring to lpf and IsPrime
  end { B }
```

The occurrence of lpf in IsPrime is said to be **non-local** or **relatively global**. Incidentally, identifiers introduced in the program-block are called **global**, because potentially they are available everywhere. Warning: it is common practice to say that an identifier is global to a block when it is non-local, and we shall do so when documenting subprograms.

Another example where we need to exploit the scope rules is when constants are used to document the common assumptions of related subprograms. This practice is very common with graphics; see, for example, the two case-studies in the next chapter.

Using non-local subprograms and constants is a common and relatively safe practice, but using non-local variables or formal parameters is another matter. It is much more dangerous, because variables change, unlike subprograms and constants. A subprogram that relies on a non-local constant or subprogram only requires its environment to provide a definition or declaration, which is easily checked. But one that uses a non-local variable requires its environment to maintain its value appropriately. This is a matter of faith, and when it comes to programming, it pays to be sceptical. Not only that, but if a non-local variable of a procedure is used as an actual-variable in one of its calls, the dreaded specter of aliasing arises.

> **Principle** A procedure should not use relatively global variables or formal parameters unless it is specific to the subprogram that introduces them.

Be reassured that the details of scope do not intrude much in the programming process. The fundamental principle concerning scope is one that maximizes modularity:

> **Principle** In the absence of a reason to the contrary, give each identifier the minimum possible scope.

Much of the information in this chapter is about the programming language Pascal, rather than programming per se. As such it is of secondary importance. Other programming languages may differ from Pascal in their parameter mechanisms and how they handle the issue of scope. In particular, Wirth's successor to Pascal, Modula-2, differs mainly in how it treats the latter issue.

Subprograms are such an important aid to programming that the next chapter is devoted to their use. It includes two substantial case-studies.

## EXERCISES

**8.1** Check out *The Joy of Cooking*, and bake yourself a Pumpkin Gelatin Chiffon Pie. While you're enjoying the pie, meditate on the usefulness of procedures.

**8.2** Trace the execution of program CharacterSet. First put stop signs at the start of each local procedure of PrintCharacterSet. Then run the program. Whenever it stops at a stop sign, enter any formal parameters or local variables in the Observe window, and resume execution with Step-Step. Note especially the initial values displayed.

**8.3** Suppose a block has the following variable-declaration-section:

```
var
  a, b, c, d : integer;
  sum : real;
  ch : char;
```

Suppose further that the procedure **schedule** given earlier in this chapter is declared in the same block. Say whether each of the following calls of **schedule** is legal or not, and in the latter case, say why. Never mind that the calls may not make any sense — be legalistic.

(a) schedule(a, '1', c, d)
(b) schedule(a + b, a – b, c, d)
(c) schedule(trunc(sum), a, b, sum)
(d) schedule(sum, ord(ch) – ord('A') + 1, b, c)
(e) schedule(a, 3, c, round(sum))
(f) schedule(a, b, c, 0)

**8.4** Consider the partial program below; parts in italics remain to be filled in.

```
program test (Output);
{ Demonstration of missing1 parameters }
  var
    x, y : integer;

  procedure ParameterTest (missing2 x, y : integer);
  begin { ParameterTest }
    x := y;
    y := 0;
    Writeln(x, y)
  end; { ParameterTest }

begin { test }
  x := 1;
  y := 2;
  Writeln(x, y);
  ParameterTest(x, y);
  Writeln(x, y)
end. { test }
```

(a) Suppose x and y are value-parameters, i.e. *missing1* is replaced by **value**, and *missing2* is replaced by nothing. What output does execution of **test** produce?

(b) Suppose **x** and **y** are variable parameters, i.e. *missing1* is replaced by **variable**, and *missing2* is replaced by **var**. What output does execution of **test** produce?

**8.5** Suppose a procedure is written to solve the cigar problem presented in Exercises 5.4(a) and 5.11. Its formal parameters should be **NrWanted, NrLoose, NrSingles, NrBoxes, and NewBoxOpened.**

(a) What are the input parameters?
(b) What are the output parameters?
(c) What are the input and output parameters?
(d) What are the value formal parameters?
(e) What are the variable formal parameters?

**8.6** Declare and call a procedure **WriteStats** to refine the action *Write statistics* in program **JobScheduler1**.

**8.7** Write a procedure **swap** that exchanges the values of two real variables.

**8.8** Write a procedure **order** that arranges the values of two real variables so that the second is at least as big as the first. It may use the non-local procedure **swap**.

**8.9** Solve Exercise 6.10 by declaring and using a suitable procedure.

**8.10** What is wrong with this procedure?

```
procedure getmax (var a, b, max : integer);
{ Sets max = bigger of a and b. }
{XXXX NOT RECOMMENDED XXXX}
begin { getmax }
  max := a;
  if b > max then
    max := b
end; { getmax }
```

**8.11** Suppose procedure **getmax** is as declared above, and **big** and **x** are integer variables. What is printed as a result of executing the statement-list below? Why?

```
big := 100;
x := 1;
getmax(x, big, big);
Writeln(big)
```

**8.12** Produce the equivalents of Figure 8.1 and Table 8.1 for the version of program **Primes** in Chapter 7 that declares function **lpf** in position (A). Convince yourself that all is well.

**8.13** The following situation violates Pascal's scope rules. In what way?

```
const
  base = 10;
procedure p;
  const
    pbase = base;
  var
    base : integer;
begin { p }
...
```

**8.14** Show by example how aliasing arises if a non-local variable of a procedure is supplied as an actual-variable in one of its calls.

# 9
# PROGRAMMING WITH PROCEDURES

Good things come in small packages.
— Proverb

## 9.1 Introduction

Programming with procedures is in no sense a special topic — from now on, all our programming will exploit the many advantages of procedures, and the other kind of subprogram, viz. functions. The opportunity to use procedures arises continually in stepwise refinement, because unrefined actions are prime candidates for implementation with procedure-statements.

There are usually more procedure-statements than declarations. There are two major reasons for this, other than the obvious one that we need not write any of Pascal's required procedures. One is that several actions may be refined with a single procedure, as with *Print top of box* and *Print bottom of box* in program CharacterSet. The other reason is that much programming is done with predefined libraries of subprograms which may be provided by Pascal systems for special kinds of applications. Macintosh Pascal provides two major libraries: one for graphics, called QuickDraw, and one for numeric computing, called SANE (Standard Apple Numeric Environment). Both are models of their kind, and are comprehensively described in the Technical Appendix (one of the three Macintosh Pascal manuals). SANE is dealt with in Chapter 19.

Both case-studies in this chapter use the part of QuickDraw, called QuickDraw1, that is automatically available to Macintosh Pascal programs. Note that incorporating a library (such as QuickDraw1) in a program effectively introduces its constants, types, variables, and subprograms in the program-block. Consequently, the identifiers so introduced may be reused only in enclosed regions.

One of the advantages of using procedures is highlighted by Case-study 3: writing a program in terms of modular subprograms makes it much more amenable to modification to meet extended specifications, which is a task that programmers are very often asked to perform.

# 9.2 Macintosh graphics

## 9.2.1 THE COORDINATE PLANE

QuickDraw graphics take place in a coordinate plane, which is a square grid. There are two notional, infinitely thin grid lines associated with each integer value: a vertical line and a horizontal line. Every pair of a vertical and horizontal grid line defines a point at their intersection. A point is represented as an ordered pair of coordinates: the horizontal coordinate corresponds to the vertical grid line, and vice versa. It is customary to use x (or h) for the horizontal coordinate, and y (or v) for the vertical coordinate, and to write the point as (x, y) (or (h, v)). Horizontal coordinates increase to the right; vertical coordinates increase downwards (which is contrary to the convention in Cartesian geometry). The coordinate plane is illustrated in Figure 9.1.

Mathematical objects such as lines and rectangles are always defined in terms of points in the coordinate plane. The Drawing window is superimposed on the coordinate plane by regarding each pixel in the window as a square bounded by successive vertical and horizontal grid lines, and by fixing the top-left corner of the window at some point in the plane. By default that point is the **origin** (0, 0). The Macintosh's screen is 512 pixels across and 342 down, which limits the dimensions of the Drawing window. The scale is 72 pixels per inch (approximately 28.35 per centimeter).

## 9.2.2 THE PEN

A unique pen is associated with the Drawing window. It has four characteristics, all of which can be changed: a size, a location, a pattern, and a mode. The shape of the pen is rectangular. The **pen size** is 1×1

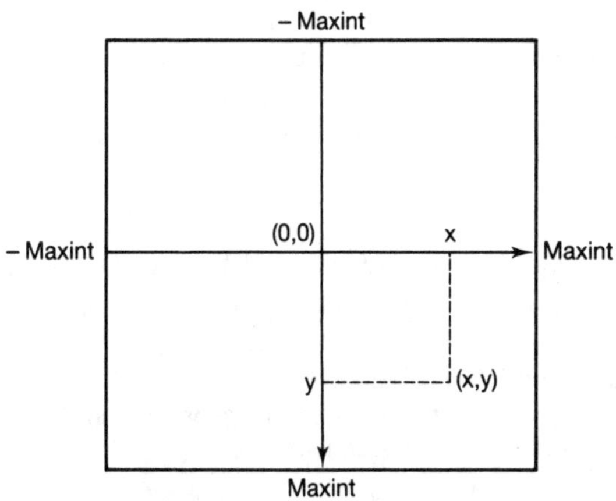


**Figure 9.1**
The coordinate plane.

by default; it can be changed by calling the predefined procedure PenSize.

```
procedure PenSize (width, height : integer);
{ Sets the width and height of the pen to the given values }
{ (if either is negative, both are set to zero). }
```

The **pen location** corresponds to the top-left corner of its rectangle. Two procedures are provided to set and change its coordinates respectively:

```
procedure MoveTo (h, v : integer);
{ Moves the pen location to the point (h, v). }

procedure Move (dh, dv : integer);
{ Moves the pen by adding dh to its current horizontal }
{ coordinate and dv to its current vertical coordinate. }
```

We say that Move adds (dh,dv) to the current pen location. It is permitted for the pen to be outside the Drawing window. Procedures that either depend on or affect the pen's position or do both will have comments to that effect in their headings.

The **pen pattern** is the pattern drawn by the pen. Five predefined patterns are provided: white, ltGray, gray, dkGray, and black, in order of increasing darkness. These are predeclared global variables of the predefined structured type Pattern (see Case-study 7 in Chapter 13). The default pen pattern is black. A procedure is provided to set it:

```
procedure PenPat (pat : Pattern);
{ Sets the pen pattern to pat. }
```

Although we have yet to meet structured types, it should be no surprise, for instance, that PenPat(dkGray) is a legal statement which does the expected.

To find out about the **pen mode**, see the Technical Appendix.

### 9.2.3 DRAWING LINES, RECTANGLES, AND OVALS

There are three procedures to draw lines:

```
procedure LineTo (h, v : integer);
{ Draws a line from the current pen location to point (h, v), }
{ which becomes the new pen location. }
```

```
procedure Line (dh, dv : integer);
{ Adds (dh, dv) to the current pen location, and draws a line }
{ from the old pen location to the new one. }

procedure DrawLine (x1, y1, x2, y2 : integer);
{ Draws a line from point (x1, y1) to point (x2, y2). }
```

Remember that the pen hangs down from and to the right of its location. The region of the Drawing window that is traversed by the pen as it moves between the end points of the line is filled with the pen's pattern. The result need not look like a line at all.

There are several related procedures for drawing rectangles and ovals (and therefore circles). For rectangles:

```
procedure FrameRect (t, l, b, r : integer);
{ Draws a rectangle inside the rectangular section }
{ with top left corner at (l, t) and bottom right corner at (r, b), }
{ keeping the pen's outer edge(s) against the rectangle's. }

procedure PaintRect (t, l, b, r : integer);
{ Paints the rectangular section with top left corner at (l, t) }
{ and bottom right corner at (r, b). }

procedure EraseRect (t, l, b, r : integer);
{ Paints the rectangular section with top left corner at (l, t) }
{ and bottom right cornor at (r, b) with the background pattern, }
{ which by default is white. }

procedure InvertRect (t, l, b, r : integer);
{ Changes each pixel in the rectangular section with top left }
{ corner at (l, t) and bottom right corner at (r, b). }
```

There are four similar procedures for ovals. Their names are obtained by replacing Rect with Oval. The formal parameters define the corners of a rectangle with all four sides tangential to the oval, which is inside the rectangle. Therefore if the rectangle is square, the oval is circular.

Two special procedures are provided for drawing circles:

```
procedure PaintCircle (x, y, r : integer);
{ Paints the circle with center (x, y) and radius r. }

procedure InvertCircle (x, y, r : integer);
{ Inverts the circle with center (x, y) and radius r. }
```

### 9.2.4 DRAWING TEXT

Textual information may be drawn in the Drawing window. It has four characteristics, all of which can be changed: a font, a size, a style, and a mode.

The **font** is specified by a number; the default is 0, representing the system font (Chicago — it's a wonderful font). There is a procedure to set it:

```
procedure TextFont (font : integer);
{ Sets the current font to the given one. }
```

Common fonts and their numbers are Chicago: 0, Geneva: 1,3, New York: 2, Monaco: 4, Venice: 5, London: 6, Athens: 7, San Francisco: 8, Toronto: 9. The available fonts and their sizes can be inspected by choosing Font Control ... from the Windows menu.

The **type size** is specified in points, which correspond in size to pixels. It may be set by the following procedure:

```
procedure TextSize (size : integer);
{ Sets the current type size to the given number of points. }
```

The default is 12, which is unaltered if a size $< 1$ is specified. If the current font is not available in the specified size, an existing size will be scaled, which can look unattractive, especially if the scaling factor is not integral.

**Text style** (italic, bold, outlined, etc., and combinations thereof) is specified by sets — see Chapter 17. **Text mode** need not concern us.

A single procedure called WriteDraw suffices for all drawing of text. It takes an actual-parameter-list identical to that for Write, i.e. an output-value-list. (It is therefore not possible to give its heading, since it has a variable number of parameters.) The string that results from its output-value-list is written starting at the current pen position. Specifically, the first character begins just to the right of its horizontal coordinate, and the base line is at its vertical coordinate.

## 9.3 Case-study 3: Scheduling II

### 9.3.1 SETTING OF THE PROBLEM

The setting of the problem is exactly the same as for Case-study 1 in Chapter 6: jobs have to be scheduled chronologically on two identical processors.

### 9.3.2 SPECIFICATIONS

A program is to be written that accepts exactly the same input as specified in Case-study 1. It should maintain a diagram showing all the scheduling decisions, which must be updated immediately after reading each processing time. Jobs are to be identified in the diagram by their position in the input (1,2,3, ... ). It must be possible to read off quickly the number of the job assigned to each processor at any point on a time axis, and the total time allocated to each processor. The output in the Text window need only announce the number of jobs processed and, if that is not zero, the average of the times at which jobs complete.

### 9.3.3 WRITING THE PROGRAM

The program should obviously be obtained by modifying our program for Case-study 1, viz. **JobScheduler1**. We will work with the version from Chapter 8 that uses procedure **schedule**, but will not need procedure **WriteStats** (requested in Exercise 8.6). Making the minor modifications that reduce the Text output is a cinch, leaving the graphics output to be dealt with. The specification allows plenty of freedom, so we need to decide the details ourselves. Let us settle on a diagram as shown in Figure 9.2, where the sequence of input values 2, 1, 1, 3, 7, 1, 4 has been processed.

This diagram satisfies all the specifications. Writing job numbers in the top-left corner of their rectangles rather than their centers is partly a matter of expediency — until we learn about strings in Chapter 14, it is difficult to position text precisely in the Drawing window. More importantly, though, this approach enjoys the property that it is easy to see that jobs have been scheduled chronologically, as their numbers should then appear in ascending order from left to right!

It is essential to get graphics details exactly right. The safest way to do so is to draw a blown-up picture labeled with the important coordinates, such as the one given in Figure 9.3, which shows the diagram after input of 2, 1, 1 has been processed.

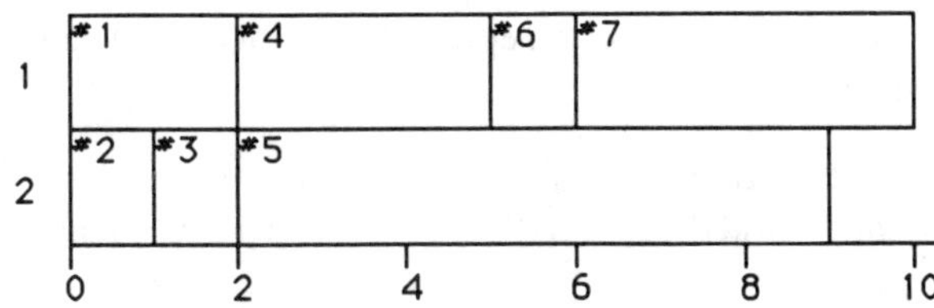


**Figure 9.2**
A scheduling diagram.

**Figure 9.3**
A blow-up of the diagram.

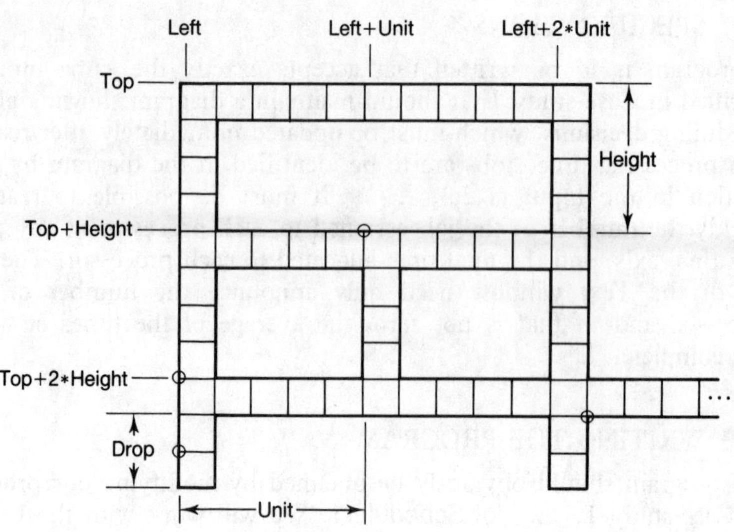


The individual squares represent the black pixels that make up the lines in the diagram. Textual information, such as job numbers, is not shown. Below we note the constants that determine the size or location of parts of the diagram. They need not all appear in the same constant-definition-part, and their values in Figure 9.3 are certainly unrealistic.

```
const
  Top = ...;  { top-left corner of drawing is ... }
  Left = ...; { ... at (Left,Top). }
  Height = ...; { height of rectangle for job }
  Unit = ...;  { size of time-unit }
  Drop = ...; { depth of marker on time axis }
  NrProcessors = 2; { number of processors }
```

NrProcessors is not shown in Figure 9.3; it corresponds to the occurrence of 2 in the vertical coordinate Top + 2 * Height.

It is important to appreciate why the indicated values of Height and Unit are the appropriate ones — they lead to simple and regular formulas for the crucial vertical and horizontal coordinates respectively.

> **Principle** Always measure a repeated distance between the same relative positions.

In this case, we read off Height between the top edges of horizontal screen lines, and Unit between the left edges of vertical screen lines.

The two circled points near the middle and bottom-right respectively of Figure 9.3 define the top-left and bottom-right corners of the rectangle drawn for job number 3. The two circled points near the bottom-left define the line drawn for the marker for time 0; remember, the pen hangs below and to the right of its location.

There are two distinct parts of our scheduling diagram. The first consists of the axes, i.e. the processor numbers, and the time axis and its labeled markers. The other consists of the rectangles for the scheduled jobs. We decide to create the first by calling a procedure DrawAxes before processing the input, and the second as jobs are scheduled by procedure schedule.

We begin with DrawAxes, and first specify it:

```
procedure DrawAxes;
{ Draws time axis with labeled markers, and labels processors. }
```

For the first refinement, we use a sequence of actions:

```
begin { DrawAxes }
  Label processors;
  Draw time axis;
  Draw and label markers for time axis
end; { DrawAxes }
```

The first action fits schema For Increasing Values, giving;

```
var
  p : integer; { number of a processor }
{ Label processors }
  for p := 1 to NrProcessors do
    Label processor p
```

The body of the loop is implemented with a sequence of two statements; the first moves to the appropriate place, the second writes the label.

```
const
  PointSize = 12; { size of text }
begin { Label processor p }
  MoveTo(Left – 2 * PointSize, Top + p * Height –
                                (Height – PointSize) div 2);
  WriteDraw(p : 2)
end
```

The chosen coordinates of **MoveTo** will cause the text to be roughly centered in, and to the left of, the row for the processor. The text size needs to be initialized at the start of the program with:

```
TextSize(PointSize)
```

The second high-level action of **DrawAxes** is simply implemented. We decide to draw a line that extends to the end of the widest possible Drawing window, and introduce a constant accordingly. We also introduce a variable to avoid repeating an expression.

```
const
 MaxWidth = 512;  { maximum width of Drawing window }

var
 base : integer; { vertical coordinate of top of time axis }

{ Draw time axis }
 base := Top + NrProcessors * Height;
 DrawLine(Left, base, MaxWidth, base)
```

Any drawing outside the boundaries of the Drawing window is lost, but does no harm.

We now tackle the last high-level action of **DrawAxes**. To compute the number of markers, we reason as follows. One marker is drawn at horizontal coordinate **Left**. There are at most **MaxWidth – Left – 1** pixels to the right of this marker, and a marker is drawn every **2 * Unit** pixels. So the total number of markers is at most:

```
1 + (MaxWidth – Left – 1) div (2 * Unit)
```

Now schema For Increasing Values applies, and we get:

```
var
  i : integer; { number of marker: 1,2, ... }
{ Draw and label markers for time axis }
 for i := 1 to 1 + (MaxWidth – Left – 1) div (2 * Unit) do
   Draw and label i'th marker
```

If the above sort of calculation gives you the heebie-jeebies, you will be pleased to know that it can be avoided by using a while-loop; see Exercise 9.6.

To refine the body of the loop we use a sequence of simple actions, introducing a variable:

```
var
 time : integer; { label of marker on time-axis }
```

```
begin { Draw and label i'th marker }
  time := 2 * (i – 1);
  MoveTo(Left + time * Unit, base);
  Line(0, Drop);
  Move(–PointSize div 2, PointSize);
  WriteDraw(time : 2)
end
```

Since variable base is used also in this refinement, it should strictly be defined prior to the first refinement that uses it.

We have now completed our implementation of procedure DrawAxes. See the complete program below for the assembled procedure. It can and should be tested now, by embedding it in a program that simply calls it. It should be tried out with many different values for the constants that it depends on.

Let us turn now to the drawing of the job-rectangles, which, since it is part of the scheduling of jobs, will come under the umbrella of procedure schedule. We first add the following formal parameter, so that the diagram can include job numbers:

```
NrJob : integer;
```

After updating the description of the procedure, we proceed to modify its body, making one change: adding an action to draw the job-rectangle.

```
begin { schedule }
  Draw and label a rectangle for this job;
{ Update StartTime and sum }
  StartTime := StartTime + duration;
  sum := sum + StartTime
end; { schedule }
```

The unrefined action is implemented with a procedure-statement, after first determining its formal parameters and writing its heading.

```
procedure DrawRect (from, length, row, ID : integer);
{ Draws rectangle of given length in given row, starting at }
{ time from; draws ID in rectangle. }

{ Draw and label a rectangle for this job }
  DrawRect(StartTime, duration, processor, NrJob)
```

DrawRect is typical of procedures that only produce output: all its parameters are value-parameters. Note how it is defined in general rather than problem-specific terms: the procedure draws rectangles, and should be written and understood in those terms. Although it will be used only to display job allocations, when writing DrawRect it helps to be unencumbered by all the notions associated with scheduling, which are irrelevant to the task at hand.

| **Principle** When writing subprograms, be general. |
|---|

We refine the body of DrawRect with a sequence of three actions:

```
begin { DrawRect }
  Set corners of rectangle;
  Draw rectangle;
  Draw ID in rectangle
end; { DrawRect }
```

The first action is not subsumed in the second because the information it creates is used also in the third action.

To refine the first action, we introduce four variables to define the corners of the rectangle, and assign the appropriate values to them, with the help of Figure 9.3:

```
var
  t, l, b, r : integer; { top, left, bottom, & right of rectangle }

{ Set corners of rectangle }
  l := Left + from * Unit;
  r := l + length * Unit + 1;
  t := Top + (row – 1) * Height;
  b := t + Height + 1
```

The second action can now be implemented with the procedure-statement:

```
{ Draw rectangle }
  FrameRect(t, l, b, r)
```

There is no great need to retain the original description of the action as a comment, but we may as well, because otherwise a blank line is needed to mark the end of the previous refinement.

It is straightforward to implement the final action with a sequence of two statements:

```
{ Draw ID in rectangle }
  MoveTo(l, t + PointSize);
  WriteDraw('#', ID : 1)
```

### 9.3.4 THE COMPLETE PROGRAM

This completes the implementation of procedure **DrawRect**. Several constants are used in both **DrawRect** and **DrawAxes**; they must therefore be declared in the same block as **DrawRect** and **schedule**, which happens to be the program-block. The complete program is as shown below:

```
program JobScheduler2 (Input, Output);
{ Input: repeatedly prompts user to enter either a processing }
{ time for a job, which must be a positive integer, or -1 to end }
{ input. Jobs are assigned in input order to the 1st available of 2 }
{ processors. Output: a diagram is maintained showing the jobs }
{ assigned to each processor; each job is specified by its position }
{ in the input. On completion, the number of jobs processed, }
{ and the average of the times at which jobs are completed are }
{ printed. }
 const
  NrProcessors = 2;
  Top = 12; { top-left corner of drawing is ... }
  Left = 24; { ... at (Left,Top). }
  Height = 40; { height of rectangle }
  Unit = 30; { size of time-unit in pixels }
  PointSize = 12; { size of text }
 var
  JobTime, { processing time for current job, or end-of-input }
              { signal }
  TotalTimeOn1, TotalTimeOn2, { total processing time on }
                                 { each processor so far }
  JobCount, { number of jobs processed so far }
  SumOfCompletionTimes { of all jobs processed }
   : integer;


procedure DrawAxes;
{ Draws time axis with labeled markers, and labels processors. }
{ Global constants: NrProcessors, Top, Left, Height, Unit,
                       PointSize. }
 const
  Drop = 8; { depth of marker on time axis }
  MaxWidth = 512; { maximum width of Drawing window }
 var
  base, { vertical coordinate of top of time axis }
  time, { label of marker on time-axis }
  p, { number of a processor }
  i : integer; { number of marker: 1,2, ... }
begin { DrawAxes }
{ Label processors }
 for p := 1 to NrProcessors do
```

```
    begin { Label processor p }
      MoveTo(Left - 2 * PointSize, Top + p * Height -
                                          (Height - PointSize) div 2);
      WriteDraw(p : 2)
    end;

  base := Top + NrProcessors * Height;
{ Draw time axis }
  DrawLine(Left, base, MaxWidth, base);
{ Draw and label markers for time axis }
  for i := 1 to 1 + (MaxWidth - Left - 1) div (2 * Unit) do
    begin { Draw and label i'th marker }
      time := 2 * (i - 1);
      MoveTo(Left + time * Unit, base);
      Line(0, Drop);
      Move(-PointSize div 2, PointSize);
      WriteDraw(time : 2)
    end
end; { DrawAxes }

procedure schedule (duration, processor : integer;
                          var StartTime : integer;
                          NrJob : integer;
                          var sum : integer);
{ Schedules job of length duration on given processor, starting }
{ at time StartTime: updates diagram of scheduling decisions, }
{ identifying job with NrJob; updates StartTime to the starting }
{ time for the next job on this processor; updates sum of }
{ completion times (sum) of all jobs. }

  procedure DrawRect (from, length, row, ID : integer);
  { Draws rectangle of given length in given row, starting at }
  { time from; draws ID in rectangle. }
  { Global constants: Top, Left, Height, Unit, PointSize. }
  var
    t, l, b, r : integer; { top, left, bottom, & right of rectangle }
  begin { DrawRect }
  { Set corners of rectangle }
    l := Left + from * Unit;
    r := l + length * Unit + 1;
    t := Top + (row - 1) * Height;
    b := t + Height + 1;
  { Draw rectangle }
    FrameRect(t, l, b, r);
  { Draw ID in rectangle }
    MoveTo(l, t + PointSize);
    WriteDraw('#', ID : 1)
  end; { DrawRect }
```

```
begin { schedule }
{ Draw and label a rectangle for this job }
  DrawRect(StartTime, duration, processor, NrJob);
{ Update StartTime and sum }
  StartTime := StartTime + duration;
  sum := sum + StartTime
end; { schedule }

begin { JobScheduler2 }
{ Write heading }
  Writeln('SCHEDULING JOBS ON TWO PROCESSORS IN
          CHRONOLOGICAL ORDER');
  Writeln;

  TextSize(PointSize);
  DrawAxes;
{ Prompt for, read and process each job time, until a }
{ stopping-value is read }
  { Initialize sums and counts }
  JobCount := 0;
  TotalTimeOn1 := 0;
  TotalTimeOn2 := 0;
  SumOfCompletionTimes := 0;

  Write('Enter processing time for job, or -1 to end input: ');
  Readln(JobTime);
  while JobTime > 0 do
    begin
      JobCount := JobCount + 1;
      if TotalTimeOn1 <= TotalTimeOn2 then
        schedule(JobTime, 1, TotalTimeOn1, JobCount,
                 SumOfCompletionTimes)
      else
        schedule(JobTime, 2, TotalTimeOn2, JobCount,
                 SumOfCompletionTimes);
      Write('Enter processing time for job, or -1 to end input: ');
      Readln(JobTime)
    end; { of while loop }

  Writeln;
  Writeln(JobCount : 1, ' jobs processed.');
  if JobCount > 0 then
    Writeln('The average time at which jobs complete = ',
            SumOfCompletionTimes / JobCount : 1 : 1)
end. { JobScheduler2 }
```

The components of program JobScheduler2 have been arranged according to the principle of minimizing scopes. So the constants that

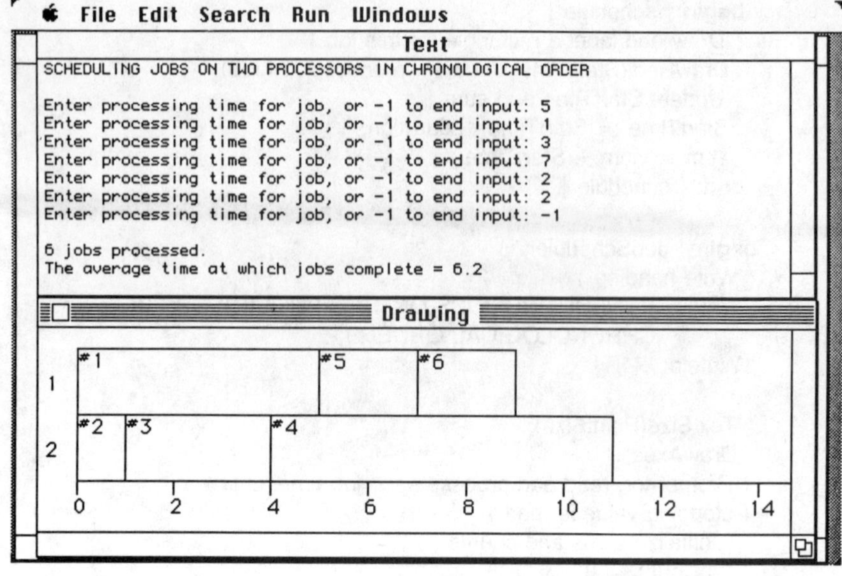
File Edit Search Run Windows
Text
SCHEDULING JOBS ON TWO PROCESSORS IN CHRONOLOGICAL ORDER
Enter processing time for job, or -1 to end input: 5
Enter processing time for job, or -1 to end input: 1
Enter processing time for job, or -1 to end input: 3
Enter processing time for job, or -1 to end input: 7
Enter processing time for job, or -1 to end input: 2
Enter processing time for job, or -1 to end input: 2
Enter processing time for job, or -1 to end input: -1
6 jobs processed.
The average time at which jobs complete = 6.2
Drawing
#1
#5
#6
1
#2
#3
#4
2
0
2
4
6
8
10
12
14

**Figure 9.4**
The screen after a run of **JobScheduler2**.

are used only in **DrawAxes** are made local to it, and **DrawRect** is declared local to **schedule** (although it could be declared in the program-block, because it depends only on the global constants which are explicitly documented in its heading-comment). We think that there is a better way to organize the program. The overriding principle involved is announced at the end of the next case-study. Exercise 9.13 asks you to give the alternative arrangement of **JobScheduler2**.

The resulting state of the screen after running **JobScheduler2** with input 4, 1, 2, 6, 2, −1 is shown in Figure 9.4. This is the same input as used in Figure 6.1.

## 9.4 Case-study 4: MiniNim

### 9.4.1 SETTING OF THE PROBLEM

A simple version of the game of Nim is played as follows. Two players each take turns removing matches from a single pile. On each turn, the number of matches taken can be any number between 1 and a predetermined limit. The player who takes the last match wins the game. For example, suppose there are 12 matches and a limit of 4 per move. Players Alonzo and Brigit might make the following moves, in which case Alonzo wins: $A$:2, $B$:1, $A$:4, $B$:3, $A$:2.

A little thought reveals the best strategy. Consider the case where the limit is 2, for example. If $A$ is to move and has 1 or 2 matches left, he can win by taking them all. But with 3 left, both choices leave *B* in a situation from which she can win. With 4 or 5 left, *A* can win by removing 1 or 2 respectively; and so on. It is not difficult to see that if:

*number of matches left* **mod** 3 > 0

then the player to move can win by taking that many matches and playing similarly thereafter; otherwise, any move will leave the opponent in a situation from which she can win. The strategy readily generalizes to an arbitrary limit $n$ on the number of matches that may be taken per move: 3 is replaced by $n + 1$ in the above condition.

### 9.4.2 SPECIFICATIONS

A Macintosh Pascal program is to be written that plays MiniNim with the user. The program should explain the game first, and then ask if it can make the first move. If the reply starts with the letter 'Y' (in upper- or lower-case) the program should (re-)move first, otherwise it should ask the user to move. The number of matches taken on each move is to be indicated in the Text window, along with the number of matches remaining. Also, the program should maintain in the Drawing window a picture of the remaining matches, and erase matches from the right after each move. The program must use the strategy outlined previously; if it cannot force a win in the current situation, it should take 1 match.

### 9.4.3 WRITING THE PROGRAM

Our first refinement uses a sequence of four actions:

```
begin { MiniNim }
  Introduce the game;
  Determine whether Macintosh or user should move first;
  Process moves until game is over & determine who moved last;
  Announce winner
end. { MiniNim }
```

The first action is refined with a procedure-statement:

```
procedure introduce;
{ Explains the game and draws the matches. }

introduce
```

There is no need to retain the comment. We refine the second action with another procedure-statement, after deciding to use a Boolean variable to record which player moves next:

```
var
  MacNext : Boolean; { true iff Macintosh moves next }

procedure FindOut (var IsYes : Boolean { true iff 'Y' or 'y' typed
                  );                      first }
{ Asks for & reads a yes/no response, & sets IsYes accordingly. }

Findout(MacNext)
```

There is again no need to retain the original action as a comment. Note that the formal parameter of **FindOut** is described with its own comment, rather than in the header-comment. Either way is acceptable, as long as the following principle is followed:

> **Principle** The heading of a procedure should specify what it does, in terms of its parameters. It should provide sufficient information to employ the procedure.

The third action involves processing moves repeatedly until the game is over. Since the number of moves cannot be known in advance, a for-loop is unsuitable. We choose a repeat-loop because at least one move will be made. A procedure is declared to handle moves; it will be told which player is to move, and update the number of matches remaining. After each move, the value of **MacNext** is changed; its final value therefore determines who moved last (and therefore who won). The initial number of matches is given by a constant.

```
const
  StartMatches = ...; { initial number of matches }

var
  MatchesLeft : integer; { number of matches left }

procedure move (var LeftOver : integer; { number of
                                          matches remaining }
       MacToMove : Boolean { true iff Macintosh is to move }
       );
{ Makes move, updating LeftOver. }

{ Process moves until game is over & determine who moved last }
 MatchesLeft := StartMatches;
 repeat
   move(MatchesLeft, MacNext);
```

```
  MacNext := not MacNext
until MatchesLeft = 0
```

Note that it is more logical for the program to record whose turn it is to move than it is for **move** — the program decides who moves; the procedure carries out the move on its behalf.

Now is the time to dispose of the last highest-level action, because it follows readily from the previous refinement: **MacNext** will be true if the user made the last move, and false if the program did.

```
{ Announce winner }
 if MacNext then
  Writeln('Congratulations, you won!')
 else
  Writeln('I won!')
```

It remains to refine three procedures. The first procedure, **introduce**, writes a description of the game and draws the matches. The former action can be implemented directly, after defining a new constant. For the latter, we decide to number matches 1,2,3, ... from the left, and to draw the required number of matches with a for-loop. A procedure is introduced to draw a specified match.

```
const
  MaxTake = ...; { maximum number of matches that can be taken
                   in 1 move }

var
  MatchIndex : integer; { number of match }

procedure DrawMatch (MatchNr : integer);
{ Draws match number MatchNr. }

begin { introduce }
  Writeln('This is the game of MiniNim, in which we take turns
          removing matches from a pile of ', StartMatches : 1, '.');
  Writeln('On each move at least 1 but at most ', MaxTake : 1,
          ' matches must be taken.');
  Writeln('The player who takes the last match wins.');
  for MatchIndex := 1 to StartMatches do
   DrawMatch(MatchIndex)
end; { introduce }
```

We also note (in its heading-comment) that **introduce** uses the global constants **StartMatches** and **MaxTake**.

We postpone refining **DrawMatch** until all the graphics actions are specified, and instead turn to procedure **FindOut**.

```
var
  response : char; { answer to yes/no question }

begin { FindOut }
  Write('May I move first? ');
  Readln(response);
  IsYes := (response = 'y') or (response = 'Y')
end; { FindOut }
```

The next cab off the rank is move. This is the heart of the program, so we decide to proceed slowly and carefully.

```
begin { move }
  if MacToMove then
    Determine & print Macintosh's move
  else
    Read user's move;
  Remove matches;
  Writeln('There are ', LeftOver : 1, ' remaining.')
end; { move }
```

The first unrefined action is refined with a sequence of actions, which is formulated as a compound statement because of its context.

```
var
  taken : integer; { number of matches to take }

begin { Determine & print Macintosh's move }
  Write('Hit Return to see my move.');
  Readln;
  Set taken = number of matches Macintosh will remove;
  Writeln('I take ', taken : 1, '.')
end
```

The idea of using the I/O statements might occur only after testing a version without them, which would respond too quickly to the player's moves. Such niceties of the **user-interface** should not be pooh-poohed — perhaps they are why you are learning to program on a Macintosh.

Refining deeper, we implement the action that determines the strategy.

```
{ Set taken = number of matches Macintosh will remove }
taken := LeftOver mod (MaxTake + 1);
if taken = 0 then
  taken := 1
```

Reading the user's move is straightforward:

```
begin { Read user's move }
 Write('How many matches do you take? ');
 Readln(taken)
end
```

Exercise 9.9 asks you to fix a problem with the above — it does not check that the value read is permissible.

There are two parts to the action *Remove matches*: decreasing the count of matches and erasing the drawings of those removed. It is convenient to do the latter first, because it uses the count before it is reduced. The numbers (i.e. positions) of the matches removed are easily calculated, so a for-loop is appropriate. The decreasing form is used so that matches are taken individually from the right. It employs a procedure EraseMatch that is the inverse of DrawMatch. Again, thinking from the user's point of view, a procedure wait is used so that the removals occur at human rather than computer speed, and each removal is signaled with a beep.

```
var
 MatchIndex : integer; { index of match }

procedure EraseMatch (MatchNr : integer);
{ Erases drawing of match number MatchNr. }

procedure wait (n : integer);
{ Pauses for n 60ths of a second (ticks). }

{ Remove matches }
 for MatchIndex := LeftOver downto LeftOver – taken + 1 do
  begin
   EraseMatch(MatchIndex);
   SysBeep(11);
   wait(15)
  end;
 LeftOver := LeftOver – taken
```

The unit of time in wait happens to be the natural one on the Macintosh, as you can see from its implementation:

```
var
 time : longint; { TickCount when procedure called. }
begin { wait }
 time := TickCount;
 repeat
 until TickCount >= time + n
end; { wait }
```

The predefined, parameterless function **TickCount** is specified as:

```
function TickCount : longint;
{ Returns the elapsed time since startup in 60ths of a second. }
```

The predefined procedure **SysBeep**, whose effect you have doubtless heard if you have used a Macintosh, is specified as follows:

```
procedure SysBeep (duration : integer);
{ Sounds a square-wave tone lasting approx. duration * 0.022 s. }
```

The actual-value 11 in the call of SysBeep thus represents about a quarter-second, as does the actual-value 15 in the call of wait. These figures might be arrived at after testing with various values to get the most pleasing effect.

Only the graphics details remain. Again, we begin by carefully planning the drawing and noting the constants that determine its placement and size. We decide to draw each match about a vertical line of symmetry whose distance from the left side of the Drawing window is a multiple of a certain constant. The complete specifications are shown in Figure 9.5.

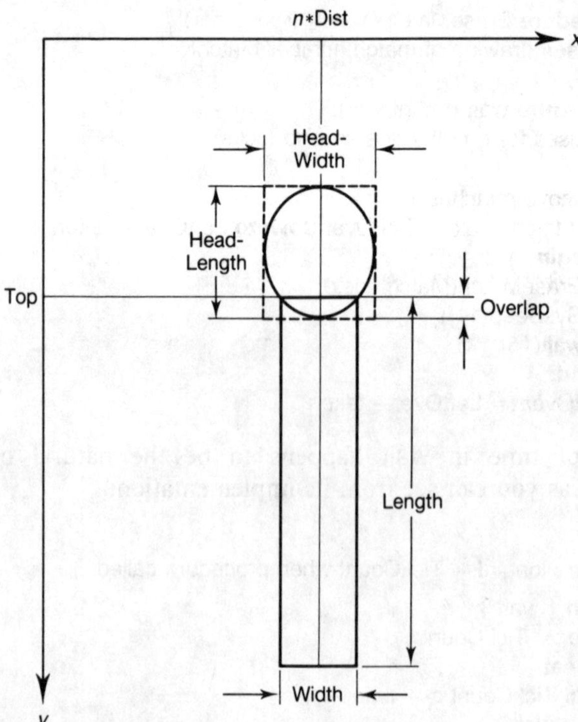


**Figure 9.5**
The *n*th match.

Because QuickDraw draws *inside* mathematical rectangles, we take coordinates according to the following principle:

| **Principle** Read coordinates from the outer edges of rectangles. |
|---|

The constants that we have introduced are defined as follows; all have integer values.

```
const
  Top = ...; { vertical coordinate of top of matchstick }
  Length = ...;  { length of matchstick }
  Dist = ...; { space between matches }
  Width = ...; { width of matchstick; must be even }
  HeadLength = ...; { length of match head }
  HeadWidth = ...; { width of match head; must be even }
  Overlap = ...; { overlap of head on stick }
```

Both widths must be even for the match to be symmetrical about the central vertical line.

It is now a simple matter to refine our two graphics procedures. A match is drawn by framing a rectangle for the stick and painting an oval for the head. The appropriate coordinates are read off Figure 9.5:

```
begin { DrawMatch }
  FrameRect(Top, MatchNr * Dist – Width div 2, Top + Length,
                MatchNr * Dist + Width div 2);
  PaintOval(Top – HeadLength + Overlap, MatchNr * Dist –
                                            HeadWidth div 2,
              Top + Overlap, MatchNr * Dist + HeadWidth div 2)
end; { DrawMatch }
```

There is no need to erase the rectangle and oval separately; it suffices to erase a rectangle containing both:

```
begin { EraseMatch }
  EraseRect(Top – HeadLength + Overlap, MatchNr * Dist –
                                            HeadWidth div 2,
              Top + Length, MatchNr * Dist + HeadWidth div 2)
end; { EraseMatch }
```

We record the assumption HeadWidth >= Width in the header-comment.

### 9.4.4 THE COMPLETE PROGRAM

Finally, we write the program heading and assemble the program. Since the game explains itself, the heading need only say how to run the program. Assembling the program amounts to choosing values for constants (which can be fine-tuned by testing), and deciding where the various definitions and declarations should be placed. In this instance the general principle of minimizing scope is too crude. It is more natural, for example, to assemble all the graphics-related definitions and declarations in one place, viz. at the start of the program block, because the two graphics procedures are so strongly related (one is the inverse of the other). There is an overriding principle at work here:

**Principle** Try to keep strongly related definitions and declarations together.

Similarly, **StartMatches** could be local to **introduce**, but it is more sensible to declare it with **MaxTake** at the start of the program, so that they can easily be changed to give different games. Finally, **wait** is also made global according to the following principle:

**Principle** Declare low-level modular utility procedures at the start of the program.

These procedures are then available throughout the program, if needed, and you know where to look for them in other programs.

The procedures that use global constants say so in their headings, to guard against the possibility of inadvertently accessing a non-local variable or the wrong non-local constant. Reliance on global subprograms is also documented (as an aid to testing).

```
program MiniNim (Input, Output);
{ Plays a game of MiniNim with the user. Run with Text and }
{ Drawing windows each half screen size and stacked vertically. }
 const
  StartMatches = 23; { initial number of matches }
  MaxTake = 4; { maximum number of matches that can be
                 taken in 1 move }
  Top = 20; { vertical coordinate of top of matchstick }
  Length = 90;  { length of matchstick }
  Dist = 20; { space between matches }
  Width = 6; { width of matchstick; must be even }
  HeadLength = 10; { length of match head }
  HeadWidth = 8; { width of match head; must be even }
  Overlap = 3; { overlap of head on stick }
 var
  MatchesLeft : integer; { number of matches left }
  MacNext : Boolean; { true iff Macintosh moves next  }


 procedure DrawMatch (MatchNr : integer);
 { Draws match number MatchNr. }
```

```
{ Global constants: Top, Dist, Width, Length, HeadWidth,
                    HeadLength, Overlap. }
begin { DrawMatch }
  FrameRect(Top, MatchNr * Dist - Width div 2, Top + Length,
            MatchNr * Dist + Width div 2);
  PaintOval(Top - HeadLength + Overlap, MatchNr * Dist -
                                        HeadWidth div 2,
            Top + Overlap, MatchNr * Dist + HeadWidth div 2)
end; { DrawMatch }

procedure EraseMatch (MatchNr : integer);
{ Erases drawing of match number MatchNr; }
{ assumes HeadWidth >= Width. }
{ Global constants: Top, Dist, Length, HeadLength, HeadWidth,
  Overlap. }
begin { EraseMatch }
  EraseRect(Top - HeadLength + Overlap, MatchNr * Dist -
                                        HeadWidth div 2,
            Top + Length, MatchNr * Dist + HeadWidth div 2)
end; { EraseMatch }

procedure wait (n : integer);
{ Pauses for n 60ths of a second (ticks). }
 var
   time : longint; { TickCount when procedure called. }
 begin { wait }
  time := TickCount;
  repeat
  until TickCount >= time + n
 end; { wait }

procedure introduce;
{ Explains the game and draws the matches. }
{ Global constants: StartMatches, MaxTake. }
{ Global subprogram: DrawMatch. }
 var
   MatchIndex : integer; { number of match }

begin { introduce }
  Writeln('This is the game of MiniNim, in which we take turns
          removing matches from a pile of ', StartMatches : 1, '.');
  Writeln('On each move at least 1 but at most ', MaxTake : 1,
          ' matches must be taken.');
  Writeln('The player who takes the last match wins.');
  for MatchIndex := 1 to StartMatches do
    DrawMatch(MatchIndex)
 end; { introduce }
```

```
procedure FindOut (var IsYes : Boolean { true iff 'Y' or 'y' typed
                                            first }
                              );
{ Asks for & reads a yes/no response, & sets IsYes accordingly. }
 var
   response : char; { answer to yes/no question }
 begin { FindOut }
  Write('May I move first? ');
  Readln(response);
  IsYes := (response = 'y') or (response = 'Y')
 end; { FindOut }

procedure move (var LeftOver : integer; { number of
                                           matches remaining }
      MacToMove : Boolean { true iff Macintosh to move }
      );
{ Makes move, updating LeftOver. }
{ Global constant: MaxTake. }
{ Global subprograms: EraseMatch, wait. }
 var
   taken, { number of matches to take }
   MatchIndex { index of match }
     : integer;


begin { move }
 if MacToMove then
   begin { Determine & print Macintosh's move }
     Write('Hit Return to see my move.');
     Readln;
   { Set taken = number of matches Macintosh will remove }
     taken := LeftOver mod (MaxTake + 1);
     if taken = 0 then
       taken := 1;

     Writeln('I take ', taken : 1, '.')
   end
 else
   begin { Read user's move }
     Write('How many matches do you take? ');
     Readln(taken)
   end;
{ Remove matches }
 for MatchIndex := LeftOver downto LeftOver - taken + 1 do
   begin
     EraseMatch(MatchIndex);
     SysBeep(11);
     wait(15)
   end;
 LeftOver := LeftOver - taken;
```

```
    Writeln('There are ', LeftOver : 1, ' remaining.')
  end; { move }

begin { MiniNim }
  introduce;
  FindOut(MacNext);
{ Process moves until game is over & determine who moved last }
  MatchesLeft := StartMatches;
  repeat
    move(MatchesLeft, MacNext);
    MacNext := not MacNext
  until MatchesLeft = 0;
{ Announce winner }
  if MacNext then
    Writeln('Congratulations, you won!')
  else
    Writeln('I won!')
end. { MiniNim }
```

Figure 9.6 shows the screen after the first two moves in a game with StartMatches = 23 and MaxTake = 4. Unfortunately, no figure can do justice to the visual and sonic fireworks of the program.

A couple of improvements to MiniNim should be made. One is that user input should be checked, to make sure that the number of matches taken is permissible. See Exercise 9.9. The other is that there are many instances where variables may take only a restricted range of integers as their values; we shall see in the next chapter how to declare such information explicitly, and why it is useful to do so.

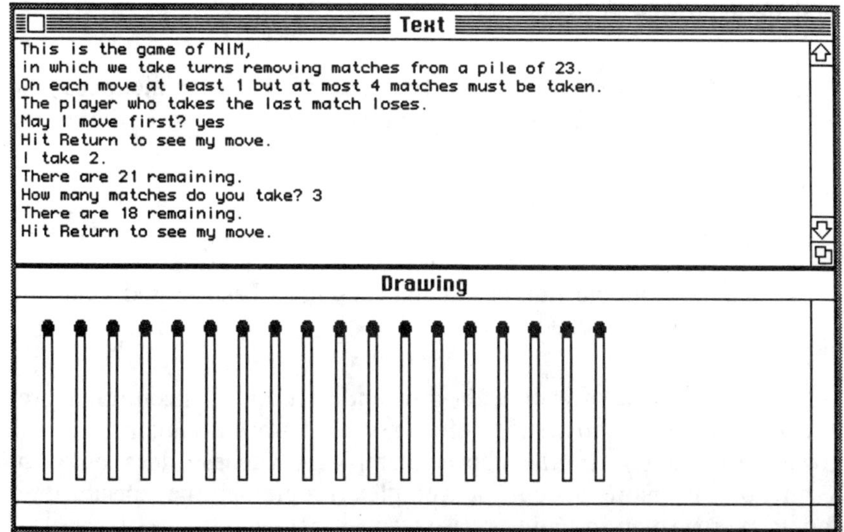


**Figure 9.6**
The screen after two moves.

## 9.5 Testing procedures

For the sake of specificity, this section focuses attention on the role of *procedures* in testing programs. The methods advanced need only minor alterations to be applicable to functions. The topic is treated under the same subheadings as used in Section 6.10, 'Testing, testing'.

### 9.5.1 PRECONDITIONS AND POSTCONDITIONS

Procedures are a great help in the task of testing every refinement. One reason is that the precondition and postcondition of a procedure are documented in its specifications. The precondition is that input parameters (value formal parameters and variable formal parameters that are updated) and global constants have appropriate values; sometimes this is explicitly formulated, as when the comment includes a clause assumes ... , but often it is implicit. The postcondition should always be explicitly documented (even if the details are left implicit). It should state that the output parameters (var-parameters) receive the appropriate values, and that appropriate output is produced and/or input read (if applicable).

Consider procedure move from program MiniNim, for example. From its specification we obtain the following precondition:

> LeftOver is the number of matches remaining (it is therefore > 0, and there should be that many matches in the display).

And the following postcondition:

> If MacToMove was true, the Macintosh has announced the move defined by the specified strategy, otherwise the user's move has been read.
>
> LeftOver = its value on entry minus the number of matches taken.
>
> The appropriate number of matches have been erased from the right of the display.

The exercise of stating the precondition and postcondition precisely, as a prelude to testing, often reveals flaws or vagueness in the given specification. In the above example, vagueness does no great harm, but in more serious or complex programs, the specification should be rewritten in more precise terms.

### 9.5.2 DESK-CHECKING

Desk-checking the refinement of a procedure reduces to the same exercise as desk-checking the refinement of a high-level action. Value formal parameters are treated as variables already initialized in accordance with the precondition; variable formal parameters are treated as variables which are initialized only if the parameter is an input parameter (i.e. is updated). Local variables are initially undefined. After tracing the execution of the body with selected values for the input parameters, we check that the output parameters have the appropriate values.

### 9.5.3 TESTING BY EXECUTION

Whenever a procedure has been completely refined, i.e. when it is written entirely in the programming language, it should be tested by executing it. A program called a **test-driver** is created that consists of a sequence of three actions: the first initializes; the second calls the procedure; and the third prints out appropriate values.

The initialization action needs to give values to all variables used as actual input parameters; these values must be consistent with the precondition of the procedure. One way to do this is to prompt for and read the values from the programmer as user (the values will then be conveniently displayed). The third action should print the value of all actual output parameters (and other selected variables if you are very suspicious).

The first requirement of the test is that:

(1) Execution of the procedure terminates normally.

Assuming it is met, the output is then carefully checked, to see that the following requirements are met.

(2) If the procedure produces output, it should be as expected.
(3) The values of all actual output parameters should be as expected.
(4) The values of all variables that are not used as actual output parameters are unchanged.

Whether or not all is well, the output should be saved for possible later reference. It should therefore be clearly labeled, preferably by the test-driver.

There is a problem with the above scenario: the procedure to be tested may call other subprograms which have yet to be written. This

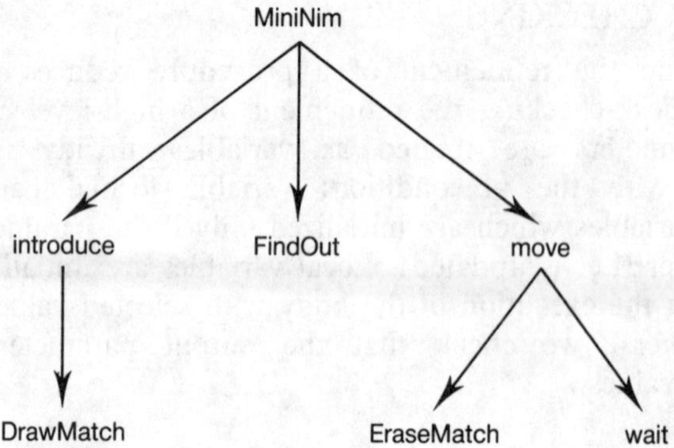


**Figure 9.7**
The calling diagram for program MiniNim.

sort of situation occurs frequently with stepwise refinement. One response is simply to postpone testing until all the required subprograms, and all the subprograms that they call, and so on, have been implemented and tested. This style of testing is called **bottom-up testing**, because the first subprograms to be tested are those that depend on no others, and others are tested after all the subprograms that they call have been tested, until finally the complete program is tested.

Consider program MiniNim for Case-study 4. The dependencies among the programmer-defined subprograms are captured by Figure 9.7, which is called a **calling-diagram**. An arrow from subprogram *A* to subprogram *B* signifies that *A* calls *B*.

We can see that DrawMatch, FindOut, EraseMatch, and wait can be tested as soon as they are implemented, in any order; introduce can be tested after DrawMatch is implemented and tested; move after both EraseMatch and wait; MiniNim after all of introduce, FindOut, and move (and the subprograms they call).

There is another style of testing, called **top-down testing**, which allows subprograms to be partially tested as soon as they are implemented. The idea is to give very simple special implementations for all the as-yet-unwritten subprograms that might be called as a result of calling the subprogram at hand. These special implementations are called **stubs**, or **dummy subprograms**. Common forms are procedures that do nothing, functions that prompt for and read the value to be returned, and procedures that do likewise for output parameters. Consider procedure move in program MiniNim, for example. It calls procedure EraseMatch, but can be tested perfectly satisfactorily by writing a stub for EraseMatch that simply writes the number of the match whose drawing it was supposed to erase (which does not exist).

These two kinds of testing have compensating advantages and disadvantages. The attraction of top-down testing is that it can be done as early as possible, allowing mistakes and misconceptions to be corrected before they do too much damage. The problem is that the testing is done in an incomplete context. Sometimes it is simply not feasible to write a stub — e.g. for a subprogram producing values that can only be found by extensive computation. And stubs are inherently error-prone. They are untested and untestable, and it is all too easy for them to give erroneous results.

The obvious attraction of bottom-up testing is that there is no need to use stubs, and that the testing is not incomplete. The problem with relying exclusively on bottom-up testing is that it comes too late in the programming process. What is the poor programmer to do? The answer is as obvious as it is onerous: both types of testing.

A temptation with both ways of testing subprograms is to test in the context of the program at hand. With bottom-up testing, this might mean testing everything just by running the entire program; with top-down, testing a subprogram by using an existing procedure as the test-driver. This is almost always a mistake, and does not make for genuine modularity. For example, it is all too easy to omit the declaration of a local variable or constant, and accidentally operate on a global one. And even if the program is correct as a whole, it may well contain incorrect subprograms which will fail when used in another context. With testing, as in programming in general, you get out of it what you put into it. Does that sound familiar?

### 9.5.4 COPING WITH ERRORS DETECTED BY TESTING

In checking for errors of transcription (typos), look out for mistakes such as:

- Declaring a value parameter where a variable parameter is needed. Remember that **var** lasts only up to the next semicolon (or right-bracket);
- Vice versa;
- Using the wrong actual parameters.

If the procedure calls other subprograms, carefully check the actual-parameters of each call; make sure that they match the corresponding formal parameters. If you are calling stubs, check that their formal parameters are value- or var-parameters as appropriate.

If an actual output parameter receives an incorrect value, work backwards through the procedure, carefully checking each statement that affects this variable.

If you are unable to find anything wrong with the procedure, you should check every precondition and postcondition contained within it: the precondition of the procedure itself (Garbage in, Garbage Out), the precondition and postcondition of each high-level action not refined with a procedure-statement, the preconditions required for calls of subprograms (in terms of the actual parameters), and the postconditions just after those calls (again, in terms of the parameters).

If the precondition for a call of a subprogram is true, but the corresponding postcondition is false, turn your attention to the subprogram called. But first carefully recheck the actual parameters; since you previously tested the subprogram, and it passed, the problem is quite likely to concern the parameters.

Once you have found the first false condition, you know that the statements which are supposed to make it true are faulty. This does not mean that it is a bug that is responsible; i.e. a small isolated error or oversight. It simply means, as in desk-checking, that the relevant refinements are incorrect, and need to be rethought. If you are a careful and correctness-oriented programmer, chances are the problem is a bug. Otherwise, it is quite possible that much of the subprogram is just completely wrong.

If all else fails, rewrite the erroneous subprogram from scratch, and test it. This is not as drastic a measure as it may sound. If the subprogram is yours, it is short. Otherwise, you are trying to correct someone else's subprogram, and there is nothing worse (unless it is short and precisely specified, or the error is obvious). If that is your job, ask for a raise — you are underpaid.

### 9.5.5 DEFENSIVE PROGRAMMING

The following simple checks have already been mentioned. They should always be performed prior to testing by execution:

- Check that all formal parameters are var- or value-parameters as appropriate, and that all actual parameters are appropriate.

Another worthwhile test is to:

- Check that all variables are declared. Because of Pascal's scope rules, missing declarations need not lead to syntax errors.

## 9.6 Using procedures: A summary

It should now be apparent *why* procedures should be used:

- Procedures help in the writing and reading of large programs, because the messy details are postponed and removed from the text, respectively.

- Procedures permit modularity: parts of a program can be developed and tested independently, and the program can more easily be adapted to meet new requirements.
- A procedure can be called many times in many different parts of a program.
- Procedures developed for one program can be reused in others. Procedure wait, for example, is reused in program Nim for Case-study 10 in Chapter 17.

*How* procedures should be used is best learned by example and practice. They should be used to encapsulate high-level actions. The heading of a procedure should include a comment that specifies what the procedure does, in terms of its parameters, if any, and what assumptions it makes about its parameters. The meaning of each formal parameter should either be apparent from this comment or be given by a comment immediately following its declaration. A procedure should not use non-local variables unless it is local to an enclosing subprogram that declares them.

## 9.7 Further reading

(1) Hueras, J. (1984). *Macintosh Pascal Technical Appendix*. Apple Product #M1507. USA and Canada: Apple Computer, Inc. 9.3
*The Technical Appendix* — one of the three manuals that come with Macintosh Pascal. Describes the QuickDraw libraries for graphics applications, and the SANE library for numeric computing.

## EXERCISES

**9.1** How many different points are there in QuickDraw's coordinate plane?

**9.2** How many pixels will be set to black as a result of executing Line(0,2)

(a) if the pen size is 1 × 1?
(b) if the pen size is 3 × 3?

**9.3** How many pixels are set to black by executing the following statement-list?

```
PenSize(2, 1);
FrameRect(0, 0, 5, 5)
```

**9.4** Write a procedure that draws a horizontal arrow a specified distance to the right from the current pen location, and moves the pen to the end. Use formal parameters to specify the length (along the shaft) and the width (across the shaft) of the arrow-head.

**9.5** Write a procedure that draws a given number of dots in a horizontal line, as follows. The first dot should be at the current pen location, and each successive dot should be a given distance (possibly negative) from the previous one. The final pen location should be the top-left corner of the last dot. You may assume that the pen size is 1 × 1.
*Hint*: Line(0,0) draws a dot.

**9.6** Here is an alternative way to draw and label markers in procedure DrawAxes:

```
var
  MarkerAt, { horizontal coordinate of next marker }
  time : integer;

{ Draw and label markers for time axis }
  time := 0;
  MarkerAt := Left;
  while MarkerAt <= MaxWidth do
    begin
      Draw and label next marker;
      Update time and MarkerAt
    end
```

Complete the implementation of this action.

**9.7** Write a procedure that draws a horizontal axis. The formal parameters should specify the position of the origin of the axis, the size of its unit, its length in units, and the gap in units between its markers.

**9.8** Suppose the player who takes the last match *loses* the game of Mini-Nim. Modify the program accordingly.

**9.9** Use schema Check Interactive Input from Chapter 6 to ensure that the opponent of program MiniNim always takes a permissible number of matches.

**9.10** How big must constant Dist of program MiniNim be to guarantee that matches do not overlap?

**9.11** What is the statement-list for the body of the repeat-loop in procedure wait?

**9.12** A general way to highlight the removal of a graphical object is to make it repeatedly disappear and reappear before erasing it for good. Modify MiniNim to use this flash method of removing matches.

**9.13** Reorganize program JobScheduler2 according to the principles used for program MiniNim.

**9.14** Use a test-driver to test procedure move from program MiniNim. Write a stub for procedure EraseMatch.

**9.15** Here is a substantial programming assignment involving graphics. Write an interactive program that creates a histogram. First it should request the user to type the number of columns to be displayed and the maximum column value, after which vertical and horizontal axes are drawn. The vertical axis should span almost the entire height of the Drawing window; the horizontal axis should do likewise provided there are sufficiently many columns. The vertical axis should have suitable labeled markers. Next the program should ask for all column values to be entered; it may assume that none are negative. After each value is read, a column of the appropriate height should be drawn, and labeled at the center of its base with its number (1,2,3, ... ). You might like to paint alternate columns with contrasting patterns, but they will look best with outlines as well.

# 10 ORDINAL TYPES

How can anyone govern a country that has 246 different kinds of cheese?
— Charles de Gaulle

## 10.1 Required ordinal types

In Chapter 5 we met Pascal's four required, simple types: integer, real, char, and Boolean. The values in each of these types are ordered, which is to say that, given any two values $x$ and $y$, precisely one of the conditions $x < y$, $x = y$, and $x > y$ is true.

The three types other than real share a stronger property: it is possible to list their values in order from the minimum to the maximum. Any value other than the last has a successor, and any value other than the first has a predecessor. Such types are called **ordinal types**. We already know that the functions succ and pred give the successor and predecessor respectively of a character value. They perform the same function for every other ordinal type. In particular, if $i$ is an integer value:

| | | |
|---|---|---|
| succ($i$) | gives | $i + 1$ |
| pred($i$) | gives | $i - 1$ |

and, for what it is worth,

| | | |
|---|---|---|
| succ(false) | gives | true |
| pred(true) | gives | false |

Similarly, the function ord can be applied to a value $x$ of any ordinal type, and satisfies the following properties:

ord(succ($x$)) equals ord($x$) + 1, provided $x$ is not the last value,
ord(pred($x$)) equals ord($x$) – 1, provided $x$ is not the first value.

It should be no surprise that:

| | | |
|---|---|---|
| ord($i$) | gives | $i$ |
| ord(false) | gives | 0 |
| ord(true) | gives | 1 |

Except for integer values, ord($x$) gives the position of $x$ in the ordered list of all values of its type, starting with position 0.

Pascal programs may introduce their own ordinal types. There are two ways to do so, and we proceed to examine each in turn.

## 10.2 Enumerated types

An **enumerated type** is specified by listing its values in order. Here are three typical examples:

```
(Sunday, Monday, Tuesday, Wednesday, Thursday, Friday, Saturday)
(Bad, Indifferent, Good)
(Male, Female)
```

Each value is represented by an identifier, whose appearance constitutes an implicit constant definition. It follows from the scope rules that no value may appear in more than one enumerated type introduced in a particular block.

The syntax of enumerated types is as follows:

enumerated-type: ( *identifier-list* )

Relatively little can be done with values of an enumerated type. Since enumerated types are ordinal types, the functions succ, pred, and ord are available. The successor of a value is the next one in the list, the predecessor is the previous one in the list; the ordinal values start with 0. Thus, for example:

| | | |
|---|---|---|
| succ(Friday) | gives | Saturday |
| succ(Saturday) | gives | *an error* |
| pred(Female) | gives | Male |
| ord(Indifferent) | gives | 1 |

Moreover, two values from the same enumerated type may be compared with a relational operator; the result is the same as if their ordinal values were compared. For example:

| | | |
|---|---|---|
| Monday >= Friday | gives | false |
| Indifferent < Good | gives | true |

The existence of an ordering does not imply that it need be used — only the operators = and <> are likely to be used with values of the type (Male, Female), for example.

A variable with an enumerated type may be assigned a value, but there is no provision in Standard Pascal for input or output of values of an enumerated type, though there is in Macintosh Pascal (see 'Macaveats', Section 10.8). Neither is there a function like chr that gives the value in an enumerated type with a specified ordinal value (but see Exercise 11.3).

Despite the lack of operations available with them, enumerated types can make a great contribution to the readability of programs, as we shall see in Case-study 5.

## 10.3 Subrange types

The other kind of programmer-defined ordinal type is a **subrange type**. It is defined by giving its first and last values, which must both be in the same ordinal type, with the last being greater than or equal to the first. The values of the type are just those in the specified range. Here are three examples:

```
1..10
'a'..'z'
Monday..Friday
```

The syntax is as follows:

subrange-type: *constant* .. *constant*

A subrange type has an associated **host type**, which is the largest (ordinal) type that contains its values. A variable of a subrange type inherits all the properties of a variable of the host type, except that its values must lie in the specified range. Suppose we are given the variable declarations in:

```
var
  value : integer;
  grade : 0..100;
```

Then the statement:

```
value := grade { OK }
```

is legal (provided grade is defined), but each of the statements:

```
Read(grade) { needs run-time check }
grade := value { needs run-time check }
```

will be legal only if the next input value is an integer between 0 and 100 inclusive, and the value of value is between 0 and 100 inclusive, respectively. Macintosh Pascal, like all respectable Pascal systems, will check such statements during execution.

Subrange types also can make a substantial contribution to the readability of programs, and to their correctness too, because out-of-range errors will be detected as soon as they occur, rather than when their consequences become apparent (if ever). They should be exploited as much as possible.

## 10.4 Type definitions

It is convenient to be able to give a name to a user-defined type, just as the name Boolean is given to the enumerated type (false, true). It is actually essential to be able to do this, because the types of formal parameters are specified by type-identifiers. Pascal makes provision for a section of **type definitions** just after the constant-definition-part of a block:

block:
*constant-definition-part*
*type-definition-part*
*variable-declaration-part*
*procedure-and-function-declaration-part*

Here is an example of a type-definition-part:

```
type
  day = (Sunday, Monday, Tuesday, Wednesday, Thursday, Friday,
            Saturday);
  weekday = Monday..Friday;
  digit = '0'..'9';
  counter = 0..Bound;
  gear = (Reverse, First, Second, Third, Fourth, Fifth);
```

Bound must be an integer constant. The identifiers on the left denote their corresponding types on the right throughout their scope (which is defined in the usual way).

The syntax is specified as follows:

type-definition-part:
**type**
*type-definition* ;
...

type-definition: *identifier* = *type*

type: *simple-type* | *type-identifier*
simple-type: *enumerated-type* | *subrange-type*

Note that it is permitted to define a new name with a previously defined one, as in:

```
cost = integer; { values represent numbers of cents }
```

When this happens, the new identifier (cost) is said to denote the **same type** as the other one (integer) and all its other same types. The main application of this definition is with var-parameters, where the actual-variable must be of the same type as the formal parameter.

## 10.5 Two simple examples

Here are two easily digested examples of the use of user-defined types.

### 10.5.1 EXAMPLE ONE

An extract from a customized word-processing program for lawyers:

```
type
  sex = (Male, Female);
  ...
var
  SexOfClient : sex;
  ...
procedure ReadSex (var s : sex);
{ Reads one character and sets s to Male if it is 'M' or 'm', or }
{ Female if it is 'F' or 'f'. Writes error-message if other }
{ character. }
  var
    ch : char; { next character from input }
begin { ReadSex }
  Read(ch);
  if (ch = 'M') or (ch = 'm') then
    s := Male
  else if (ch = 'F') or (ch = 'f') then
    s := Female
  else
    Writeln('ERROR in procedure ReadSex: next character ', ch,
            ' unexpected.')
end; { ReadSex }

procedure WritePersonalPronoun (s : sex);
```

```
{ Writes personal pronoun for s. }
begin { WritePersonalPronoun }
  if s = Female then
    Write('she')
  else
    Write('he')
end; { WritePersonalPronoun }
```

Thus if the next character in the input data is `S` and:

```
ReadSex(SexOfClient)
```

is executed, variable SexOfClient will receive the value Female. Then execution of the statement-list:

```
WritePersonalPronoun(SexOfClient);
Write(' emphatically denies all the allegations')
```

will produce the output:

```
she emphatically denies all the allegations
```

### 10.5.2 EXAMPLE TWO

An extract from a program that gives feedback, albeit minimal, on the performance of students in an examination:

```
type
  GradeRange = 0..100;
  CategoryType = (Bad, Indifferent, Good);
var
  category : CategoryType;
  grade : GradeRange;
...
function CategoryOf (grade : GradeRange) : CategoryType;
{ Returns category of performance represented by grade. }
begin { CategoryOf }
  if grade < 25 then
    CategoryOf := Bad
  else if grade > 75 then
    CategoryOf := Good
  else
    CategoryOf := Indifferent
end; { CategoryOf }
```

Thus if the statement-list:

```
Read(grade);
category := CategoryOf(grade)
```

were executed, and the remaining input data starts with 65 , **grade** would receive the value 65 and **category** the value **Indifferent**.

## 10.6 Statements associated with ordinal types

Pascal has two statements that may be used with arbitrary ordinal types.

### 10.6.1 THE CASE-STATEMENT

The first of these statements is a generalized form of conditional statement called the **case-statement**. It specifies a statement to be executed for each possible value (at run-time) of an expression of an ordinal type. Its syntax is as follows:

case-statement:
  **case** *expression* **of**
   *case-list-element*;
   ...
   *case-list-element* ;
  **end**
case-list-element:
  *case-label-list* :
   *statement*
case-label-list: *constant* ... , *constant*

The expression and the constants that label the alternative statements must have the same ordinal type. No constant may appear more than once in the statement; the order of constants in a case-label-list is immaterial.

A case-statement is executed by first evaluating the expression, and then executing the (single) statement that is prefixed by the value of the expression. It is an error if the value is not present. If no statement should be executed for some possible values of the expression, they should label an empty statement (which is best placed last). Macintosh Pascal allows an extended form of case-statement — see 'Macaveats', Section 10.8.

Here is an example:

```
type
  Months = (January, February, March, April, May, June, July,
            August, September, October, November, December);
  Years = 1753..9999;
  MonthLengths = 28..31;
...
function LengthOfMonth (month : Months; year : Years) :
                                    MonthLengths;
{ Returns number of days in given month for given year. }
begin { LengthOfMonth }
  case month of
    January, March, May, July, August, October, December :
      LengthOfMonth := 31;
    April, June, September, November :
      LengthOfMonth := 30;
    February :
      if ((year mod 4 = 0) and (year mod 100 <> 0)) or
         (year mod 400 = 0) then
        LengthOfMonth := 29
      else
        LengthOfMonth := 28
  end { case }
end; { LengthOfMonth }
```

Case-statements are often used in Standard Pascal to implement a procedure that prints a string representing a given value of an enumerated type — see Exercise 10.6. This is unnecessary in Macintosh Pascal (see 'Macaveats').

### 10.6.2 THE FOR-STATEMENT

The other statement involving values from an ordinal type is the **for-statement**, which we previewed in two schemas in Chapter 6. We recall its syntax:

for-statement:
    **for** *variable-identifier* := *initial-expression to-symbol*
                *final-expression* **do**
      *statement*
to-symbol: **to** | **downto**

The variable-identifier is called a **control variable**. It must be declared, in the block whose statement-part contains the for-statement, to have an ordinal type. The values of the initial- and final-expression must be **assignment-compatible** with the variable-identifier's type if the body is executed, but only **compatible** if it is not. This means, for example, that the loop shown below is always legal, *even if* count *gives 0*.

```
const
  Limit = 100;
var
  count : 0..Limit;
  position : 1..Limit;
...
  for position := 1 to count do
    ...
```

Unfortunately, Macintosh Pascal treats this statement as erroneous (see 'Macaveats').

When the to-symbol is **to**, the control-variable is assigned each value $v$ in the range $v1 \leqslant v \leqslant v2$ in increasing order, where $v1$ is the value of the initial-expression, and $v2$ is the value of the final-expression, evaluation taking place before execution of the statement. For each such value (there may be none) the component statement is executed. On termination, the value of the control-variable is undefined. The same applies when the to-symbol is **downto**, except that the range of values $v$ is $v1 \geqslant v \geqslant v2$, and they are taken on in decreasing order.

The initial values of the initial- and final-expression determine the sequence of values taken on by the control-variable. To ensure this, it is illegal to **threaten** the value of the control-variable in the body of the loop or any subprogram which *could* be called in it. Assignment statements, input statements, uses as an actual variable parameter, and uses as a control-variable of another for-loop are all threats.

Every use of a for-loop conforms to one of the two schemas given in Chapter 6.

## 10.7 Case-study 5: An arithmetic tutor

This case-study is an exercise in program reading rather than writing. Other than simple uses of the case-statement, no new schemas or statements are used. However the program makes extensive use of enumerated and subrange types, and it is these aspects we should concentrate on.

Program Arithmetic is a very modest but nevertheless illustrative contribution to the **application-area** called **computer-assisted teaching**, or CAT. It is expected to be of more use (from the *user's* point of view) to the reader's kid brother or sister than it is to the reader.

The specifications of the program are given in the comments following the program-heading. Figure 10.1 gives the state of the Text window after a particular run of Arithmetic; input is underlined.

The program sets, corrects, and assesses performance on simple arithmetic exercises (which it calls *tests*). Effort has been expended to

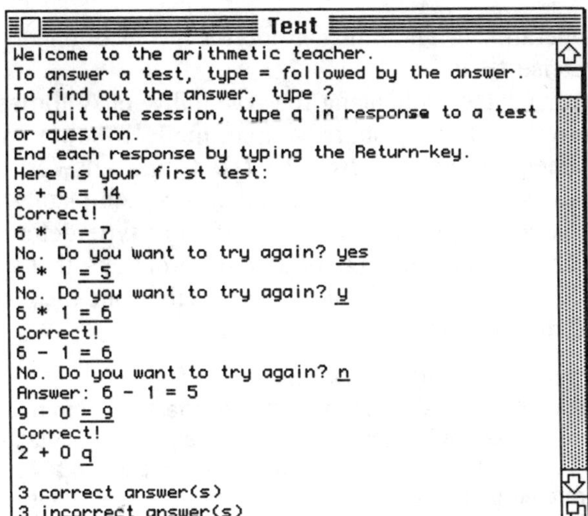

Text
Welcome to the arithmetic teacher.
To answer a test, type = followed by the answer.
To find out the answer, type ?
To quit the session, type q in response to a test
or question.
End each response by typing the Return-key.
Here is your first test:
8 + 6 = 14
Correct!
6 * 1 = 7
No. Do you want to try again? yes
6 * 1 = 5
No. Do you want to try again? y
6 * 1 = 6
Correct!
6 - 1 = 6
No. Do you want to try again? n
Answer: 6 - 1 = 5
9 - 0 = 9
Correct!
2 + 0 q
3 correct answer(s)
3 incorrect answer(s)


**Figure 10.1**
The Text window after a run of Arithmetic.

give a polished and realistic program for its limited domain. The polish shows in one main respect: the program accepts any single line of input in response to a test or question, and imposes a reasonable interpretation. In the former case, a line starting with = is treated as an attempt, one starting with Q or q as a request to quit, and any other line as a query. In the latter case, a line starting with N or n is treated as 'no', one starting with Q or q as 'quit', and any other line, including the empty one (when only the Return-key is hit), as 'yes'

The realistic aspects of the program are as follows:

(1) All three components of the tests are randomly generated. Rerunning the program will produce a different sequence of tests.

(2) Whenever the user queries a test, i.e. asks for the answer, or declines to reattempt an unsuccessfully answered test, a new test is generated that has the same operation.

(3) The user is given the opportunity to quit the session whenever input is required.

Despite its complications and length, program Arithmetic is not especially difficult to understand. Two factors take most of the credit for this. One is its use of enumerated types, which tend to produce plain and suggestive code (an unlikely sounding combination), often described as **transparent**. It is especially important to appreciate why the enumerated type operation best represents the arithmetic operations: it is because the values are both mnemonic and abstract. The values '+', '–', and '*' of type char are, for example, much inferior alternatives. Although mnemonic, they are not abstract, and there is no way to indicate that only these values may be taken by variables representing operations. The clincher for the prosecution of these characters is Exercise 10.10.

The other factor enhancing the readability of Arithmetic is that it is written in terms of many short, simple, modular subprograms, some of which, namely ReadYesOrNo, PrintTest, and answer, are used in more than one block. Each subprogram can be completely understood in a context consisting only of the constant and type definitions in the program-block and the headings of any subprograms that it calls. The stepwise refinement can be deduced, as usual, from the structure and comments of the program.

```
program Arithmetic (Input, Output);
{ Repeatedly generates random arithmetic tests of form n1 op n2, }
{ where n1, n2 are integers, and op is an arithmetic operation. }
{ If '=' and then an integer n3 is typed in response, n3 is }
{ interpreted as the user's answer; if correct, a new test is created; }
{ if incorrect, the user is given the opportunity to try again. If it is }
{ declined, the answer is revealed and a new test with the same }
{ operation is generated. A response of 'Q' or 'q' to a test or }
{ question quits the session after printing a summary of the user's }
{ performance. Any other response to a test is taken as a query; }
{ again, the answer is revealed and a new test with the same }
{ operation is generated. }
 const
   lower = 0; { lower limit to values of operands }
   upper = 10; { upper limit to values of operands }
   OrdOfLastOp = 2; { ordinal value of last operation (see below) }
 type
   count = 0..Maxint;
   operand = lower..upper;
   response = (correct, incorrect, query, QuitSession);
   ReplyType = (Yes, No, Quit);
   operation = (plus, minus, times);
 var
   NrCorrect, { number of correct answers }
   NrIncorrect { number of incorrect answers }
     : count;
   a, b : operand; { operands of a test }
   op : operation; { operation of a test }
   outcome : response; { outcome of a test }
   reply : ReplyType;

 function ran (lower, upper : integer) : integer;
 { Returns a random value uniformly distributed in lower..upper; }
 { assumes lower <= upper. }
 begin { ran }
   ran := lower + trunc((Random + Maxint + 1) / (2 * (Maxint + 1)) *
                          (upper - lower + 1))
 end; { ran }
```

10.1

```
procedure ReadReply (var reply : ReplyType);
{ Reads rest of line and sets reply according to first character: }
{ if 'N', 'n': no; 'Q', 'q': quit; anything else: yes. }
 var
   ch : char; { first character of response }
begin { ReadReply }
 if eoln then
   Read(ch) { space for end-of-line marker }
 else
   Readln(ch);
 if (ch = 'N') or (ch = 'n') then
   reply := no
 else if (ch = 'Q') or (ch = 'q') then
   reply := quit
 else
   reply := yes
end; { ReadReply }


procedure introduce;
{ Explains to user how to interact with this program. }
begin { introduce }
 Writeln('Welcome to the arithmetic teacher.');
 Writeln('To answer a test, type = followed by the answer.');
 Writeln('To find out the answer, type ?');
 Writeln('To quit the session, type q in response to a test
          or question.');
 Writeln('End each response by typing the Return-key.');
 Writeln('Here is your first test:')
end; { introduce }


procedure NewTest (var n1 : operand;
                   var op : operation;
                   var n2 : operand);
{ Gives a new random value to each parameter. }
{ Global const: lower, upper, OrdOfLastOp. }
{ Global subprogram: ran. }
 var
   i : 0..OrdOfLastOp; { N.B. 0 can be 1 in Standard Pascal }
begin { NewTest }
 n1 := ran(lower, upper);
 n2 := ran(lower, upper);
{ Set op to a random operation }
 op := plus;
 for i := 1 to ran(0, OrdOfLastOp) do
   op := succ(op)
end; { NewTest }
```

```
procedure PrintTest (n1 : operand; op : operation; n2 : operand);
{ Prints test n1 op n2. }
begin { PrintTest }
  Write(n1 : 1, ' ');
  case op of
    plus :
      Write('+');
    minus :
      Write('-');
    times :
      Write('*')
  end;
  Write(' ', n2 : 1, ' ')
end; { PrintTest }

function answer ( n1 : operand; op : operation; n2 : operand) :
                  integer;
{ Returns the answer to the test n1 op n2. }
begin { answer }
  case op of
    plus :
      answer := n1 + n2;
    minus :
      answer := n1 - n2;
    times :
      answer := n1 * n2
  end
end; { answer }

procedure PrintAnswer (n1 : operand; op : operation; n2 : operand);
{ Prints test n1 op n2 and its answer. }
{ Global subprograms: PrintTest, answer. }
begin { PrintAnswer }
  Write('Answer: ');
  PrintTest(n1, op, n2);
  Writeln('= ', answer(n1, op, n2) : 1)
end; { PrintAnswer }

procedure test (n1 : operand; op : operation; n2 : operand;
                var outcome : response);
{ Presents test n1 op n2, reads response, and sets }
{ outcome accordingly. }
{ Global subprograms: PrintTest, answer. }
  var
    ch : char; { first character of response }
    n3 : integer; { number typed after '=' }
begin { test }
  PrintTest(n1, op, n2);
```

```
    if eoln then { treat as query }
      ch := '?'
    else
      Read(ch);
    if (ch = 'q') or (ch = 'Q') then
      outcome := QuitSession
    else if ch = '=' then
      begin { Read answer and set outcome accordingly }
        Read(n3);
        if n3 = answer(n1, op, n2) then
          outcome := correct
        else
          outcome := incorrect
        end
      else { ch is none of 'q', 'Q', '=' }
        outcome := query;
    Readln
  end; { test }

  procedure EndTest (var n1 : operand;
                     op : operation;
                     var n2 : operand);
  { Reveals answer to test n1 op n2, and gets new random values }
  { for n1 and n2 (but NOT op). }
  { Global subprograms: PrintAnswer, NewTest. }
  begin { EndTest }
    PrintAnswer(n1, op, n2);
    NewTest(a, op, b) { leaves actual-parameter for op unchanged }
  end; { EndTest }

begin { Arithmetic }
{ initialize counts }
  NrCorrect := 0;
  NrIncorrect := 0;

  introduce;
  NewTest(a, op, b);
  repeat
  { Give test and process response }
    test(a, op, b, outcome);
    case outcome of
      correct :
        begin
          NrCorrect := NrCorrect + 1;
          Writeln('Correct!');
          NewTest(a, op, b)
        end;
      incorrect :
```

```
          begin
            NrIncorrect := NrIncorrect + 1;
            Write('No. Do you want to try again? ');
            ReadReply(reply);
            case reply of
              no :
                EndTest(a, op, b);
              yes :
                ; { will repeat same test }
              quit :
                outcome := QuitSession
            end
          end;
        query :
          EndTest(a, op, b);
        QuitSession :
      end { case }
    until outcome = QuitSession;

  { Summarize user's performance }
    Writeln;
    Writeln(NrCorrect : 1, ' correct answer(s)');
    Writeln(NrIncorrect : 1, ' incorrect answer(s)')
  end. { Arithmetic }
```

## Notes

(1) Function ran uses the predefined QuickDraw function Random, which returns a value in the range –Maxint–1..Maxint. (The value depends on a global variable randSeed, which is initialized to 1 when Macintosh Pascal is entered, and changed by the function-call.)

(2) The condition eoln in procedure ReadYesOrNo cannot be evaluated until some input is typed, because the next character or marker in the input stream must be available. It is OK in this context because input is expected in response to a question.

(3) Since there is no function that gives the value in a particular enumerated type with a given ordinal value, procedure NewTest picks a random operation by first picking a random ordinal value of an operation, and then using a for-loop to find the corresponding operation. Alternatively, a case-statement can be used; see Exercise 10.9. For a more efficient method for large enumerated types, see Exercise 11.3.

(4) The implementation of EndTest is a little tricky, but does highlight the difference between value and variable parameters. You might prefer to rewrite it more plainly.

> **Principle** Avoid tricks; but if you can not resist the temptation, at least explain the trick very clearly.

(5) The case-statement that processes variable **reply** in the statement with case-label **incorrect** could be written as a conditional statement:

```
if reply = no then
  EndTest(a, op, b)
else if reply = quit then
  outcome := QuitSession
```

The given code is preferable since it explicitly shows how each possible value is treated.

(6) The loop in the statement-part of **Arithmetic** is representative of an attractive style, where the body assigns a value to a variable of an enumerated type, and the loop stops when the variable gets a special value. This variable is called a **state-variable**.

## 10.8 Macaveats

Macintosh Pascal provides for input and output of values of any enumerated type. If $v$ is a variable of an enumerated type $T$, then Read($v$) will skip any leading spaces or end-of-line markers, and then read characters as long as they form part of an identifier. If a value of type $T$ has the identifier that is read (ignoring the case of letters), that value is given to $v$; otherwise an error occurs. Macintosh Pascal 2.0 also allows $T$ to be a subrange of an enumerated type (although the Reference does not mention this).

This extension is less useful than it might seem, since the names chosen for the values of an enumerated type should be as natural as possible, for the sake of readability. When preparing input, though, these values are likely to be represented more economically, and may not be separated as required.

The extension to permit output of enumerated type values is more natural and more useful. If an expression gives a value of an enumerated type, it is treated as if it were the string corresponding to the identifier for that value. Thus:

```
Write(succ(Monday) : n)
```

is equivalent to:

```
Write('Tuesday' : n)
```

The Reference states that the complete identifier is always printed, but Macintosh Pascal 2.0 prints only *n* characters (as for strings), which is consistent with Standard Pascal's treatment of Boolean values. The best way to print enumerated type values in Standard Pascal is with a procedure built around a case-statement; see Exercise 10.6.

There is a significant problem with the Macintosh Pascal 2.0 for-statement. Its initial- and final-expression must be **assignment-compatible** with the control variable. This sometimes forces us to declare the control variable with a larger ordinal type than necessary; such instances will be pointed out in the sequel.

Macintosh Pascal has an extended form of case-statement, which can specify a statement to be executed when the value of the expression does not equal one of the listed constants. The appendage is called an **otherwise-clause**. It is described in the Reference.

## EXERCISES

**10.1** What kind of Pascal type is best suited to represent the 246 *fromages français*?

**10.2** Given the type definition:

```
Days = (Su, Mo, Tu, We, Th, Fr, Sa)
```

implement the following function:

```
function NextDay (ThisDay : Days) : Days;
{ Returns day in week following ThisDay. }
```

**10.3** What are the best types for variables secret and guess in programs YouGuess2 and YouGuess3?

**10.4** Define a type for the variables and formal parameters in program CharacterSet (in Chapter 8) that represent rows or columns of the character set table.

**10.5** Modify program MiniNim in Chapter 9 by adding and exploiting the following type-definition section.

```
type
  MatchRange = 0..StartMatches;
                    { possible numbers of matches left }
  TakeRange = 1..MaxTake;
                    { possible numbers of matches to remove }
```

Introduce a variable to help compute the value for taken in procedure move, so that the type of taken can be TakeRange (as it naturally should be).

**10.6** Implement the following procedure in Standard Pascal. *Hint*: Use a case-statement.

```
procedure PrintMonth (m : Months);
{ Prints the string corresponding to the identifier of m. }
```

**10.7** Give two reasons why the type of the local variable n3 of procedure test is integer rather than operand.

**10.8** Implement the following procedure and use it to avoid the three uses of (s) at the end of program Arithmetic.

```
procedure Pluralize (n : count);
{ Appends 's' to output if n <> 1. }
```

For a better but non-Standard approach, see function plural in Chapter 14.

**10.9** Complete the following partial implementation of an action in procedure NewTest:

```
{ Set op to a random operation }
 case ran(0, OrdOfLastOp) of
 ...
```

**10.10** Modify program Arithmetic to include the operations **div** and **mod** as defined by Pascal. Ensure that the value of n2 is legal.

**10.11** Here is a substantial programming exercise involving enumerated and subrange types, and QuickDraw graphics. Write a program to draw a calendar month by month, after the style of Figure 10.2. Here are some suggestions.

- Use the type definition in Exercise 10.2, and a similar one for months (use three-character identifiers for the months to simplify the task of centering them).
- Use functions LengthOfMonth and NextDay from earlier in this chapter and Exercise 10.2 respectively.

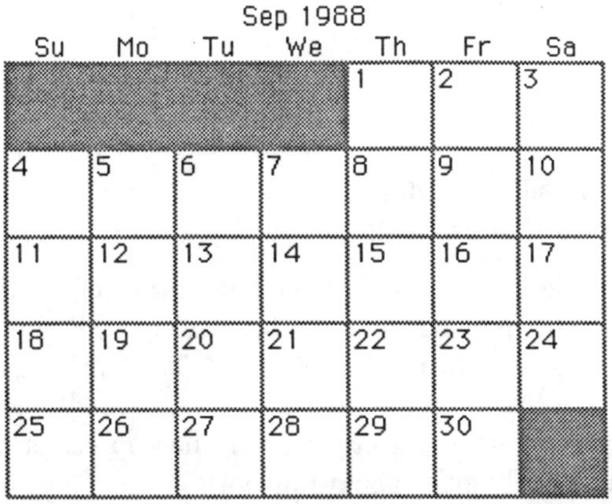

Sep 1988

| Su | Mo | Tu | We | Th | Fr | Sa |
|---|---|---|---|---|---|---|
| | | | | 1 | 2 | 3 |
| 4 | 5 | 6 | 7 | 8 | 9 | 10 |
| 11 | 12 | 13 | 14 | 15 | 16 | 17 |
| 18 | 19 | 20 | 21 | 22 | 23 | 24 |
| 25 | 26 | 27 | 28 | 29 | 30 | |

**Figure 10.2**
A calendar for a particular month.

- Draw the entire calendar with:

```
procedure DrawCal (year : Years;
                   Jan1 : days);
{ Draws a month by month calendar for given year, with }
{ January 1st on day Jan1; waits for user to hit Return-key }
{ before printing new month. }

DrawCal(1988, Fr)
```

- Use the following local procedure in DrawCal.

```
procedure DrawMonth (month : Months;
                     NrDays : MonthLengths;
                     var FirstDay : Days);
{ Draws calendar for given month having NrDays days and }
{ first day on FirstDay; updates FirstDay to first day }
{ of next month. }
```

- Here is a partial implementation of DrawMonth:

```
var
  NrRows : 1..6; { number of rows in month's calendar }
  day : Days; { current day }
  DayNumber: 1..31; { number of current day }

begin { DrawMonth }
  NrRows := (NrDays + ord(FirstDay) + 6) div 7;
  Clear Drawing window;
  Paint gray background for calendar;
  Draw headings (month and days);
  Set coordinates of box for first day;
  day := FirstDay;
  for DayNumber := 1 to NrDays do
    begin
      Erase box for day;
      Draw DayNumber in box;
      Advance day and set coordinates of its box
    end;
  FirstDay := day
end; { DrawMonth }
```

  The main idea is to calculate the coordinates of the next box from those of the previous one. Alternatively, you might prefer to calculate box coordinates directly from DayNumber and day.

- In Chapter 14 we will learn properly how to center strings, so do not worry overly much about this now.

# 11 ARRAYS

A place for everything, and everything in its place.
— Samuel Smiles, *Thrift*

## 11.1 Introduction

Consider the problem of reading a number of examination scores, each of which is between 0 and 100 inclusive, and displaying them as a histogram, i.e. a table or diagram that shows the frequency of each score. Let us decide for the moment to produce output like the following in the Text window, which shows that there were no scores of 0 or 1, 1 score of 2, no scores of 3, ... , 2 scores of 99, and no scores of 100.

```
Score      Frequency
  0            0
  1            0
  2            1
  3            0
    ...          ...
 99            2
100            0
```

Since the number of scores is unspecified, we might decide to prompt for all the scores to be entered followed by a stopping-value of, say, –1. The high-level solution to our problem is obtained from the variant of schema Interactive I/O that uses a single, initial prompt and Read- rather than Readln-statements. We write:

```
const
  MaxScore = 100;
var
  score : –1..MaxScore; { exam score or stopping-value of –1 }
Initialize;
Writeln('Enter exam scores, separated by spaces, then –1 to end
        input: ');
Read(score);
```

```
while score >= 0 do
  begin
    Process score;
    Read(score)
  end;
Readln;
Finalize
```

Since the purpose of the solution is to print the table, we proceed first by asking which part should accomplish this. Although printing the table may well involve repetition, it cannot be accomplished by the while-loop, because no frequencies are known until all the data has been processed. The printing must be the province of the action *Finalize*, but attempting to refine it reveals a major difficulty: 101 different variables are needed, one for each of the possible scores. We could call these:

```
freq0, freq1, ... , freq99, freq100,
```

and go on to refine *Process* score with a gigantic (well, very large) case-statement, *Initialize* with a sequence of 101 assignments, *Finalize* with a sequence of 102 Writeln-statements, and declare all these variables. But there must be a better way!

All the variables we have used thus far have had simple types, i.e. have been capable of containing only a single value. But Pascal also has **structured-types**; variables of these types may contain a collection of values. The kind of structured-type we need for our problem is called an **array-type**. Specifically, consider the variable-declaration below (which is preceded by some type-definitions):

```
type
  count = 0..Maxint;
  ScoreRange = 0..MaxScore;
  histogram = array[ScoreRange] of count;
var
  freq : histogram;
```

Variable freq has an array-type, and we say that it is an **array**. It consists of 101 component variables, one for each value of type ScoreRange; each has the type count. Their names are:

```
freq[0], freq[1], ... , freq[99], freq[100]
```

The component variables are called the **elements** of the array; the value of type ScoreRange that identifies a particular element is called its **index**. Except for their unusual names, the elements of array freq have the same properties as a simple variable of type count (but for some minor restrictions mentioned later). The entire array is pictured below; each box represents an element, and its index is shown on top.

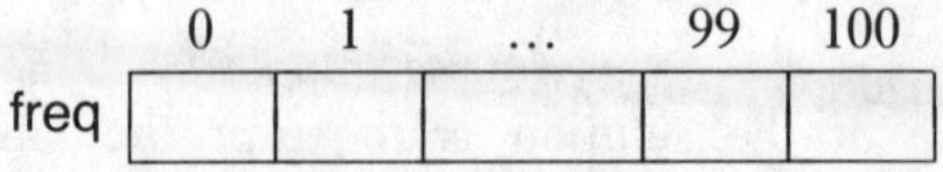

|  | 0 | 1 | ... | 99 | 100 |
|---|---|---|---|---|---|
| freq |  |  |  |  |  |

So far, so good — we have certainly saved a lot of declarations. But the real power of arrays stems from the ability to specify an element during execution by evaluating an expression to get its index. Such a name for an element is called an **indexed-variable**. A typical example is:

```
freq[score]
```

where score must have a value between 0 and 100 inclusive.

We now know enough to complete our solution. *Initialize* is replaced by:

```
{ Zero all frequencies }
 for score := 0 to MaxScore do
  freq[score] := 0
```

The body of this loop is executed with score taking the successive values 0, 1, ... , 99, 100. On the first iteration, score has the value 0. So the indexed-variable freq[score] represents freq[0], which gets the value 0. (Like all variables, its value was initially undefined.) On the next iteration, score has the value 1, so freq[1] gets 0, and so on, until freq[100] gets 0 on the last iteration.

To *Process* score means adding 1 to the appropriate element: the one whose index is the value of score. We need only write:

```
freq[score] := freq[score] + 1
```

For example, if the most recently read input value was 56, score will have that value, and each instance of freq[score] in the above assignment statement will represent freq[56]. The value of the expression on the right is thus 1 more than the number of scores of 56 previously processed, and this becomes the new value of freq[56].

Finally, *Finalize* is replaced by:

```
{ Print histogram }
 Writeln('Score   Frequency');
```

```
for score := 0 to MaxScore do
  Writeln(score : 4, freq[score] : 10)
```

The Writeln-statement will be executed with **score** taking the successive values 0, 1, ... , 100. Each such index is printed together with the corresponding element of array **freq**.

## 11.2 Array-types

The syntax of array-types is as follows:

type: *simple-type* | *structured-type* | *type-identifier*
structured-type: *array-type*
array-type: **array** [ *index-type* ] **of** *component-type*
index-type: *ordinal-type*
component-type: *type*

Note that the index-type of an array can be any ordinal-type, and the component-type any type at all (including, as we shall see in Chapter 13, another array-type). An array-type can be given a name with a type-definition, as with type **histogram** above, or directly used as the type of a variable, as in:

```
var
  freq : array[ScoreRange] of count;
```

The virtue of using a type definition is that it permits formal parameters to have the same type as the array, so that the array can be used as a corresponding actual parameter.

The syntax of indexed-variables is as follows:

indexed-variable: *array-variable* [ *expression* ]
array-variable: *variable*
variable: *entire-variable* | *component-variable*
entire-variable: *variable-identifier*
component-variable: *indexed-variable*

The index of an indexed-variable is sometimes called a **subscript**, because the mathematical notation for Pascal's **freq[0]** is $freq_0$, where 0 is called the subscript of *freq*. The subscript must give a value that is assignment-compatible with the array-variable's index-type. Macintosh Pascal will check this during execution. Suppose, for example, that two input values in the histogram example were accidentally run together, giving 5674. If **score** was declared to have type **integer**, the error message shown in Figure 11.1 would appear when the statement:

**Figure 11.1**
The error message for an illegal subscript.

**The value of a variable or subexpression is out of range for its intended use.**

```
freq[score] := freq[score] + 1
```

was executed for this value of score.

> **Principle** If a variable is used only as a subscript, declare it to have the indexed-type of the array. (See Section 11.4, 'Linear search', for a caveat.)

Our solution to the histogram problem does not violate this principle, since score is not used only as a subscript. But the deviation is minor and perfectly safe in its context.

Note that the syntax rules treat indexed-variables as variables, permitting them to be used, e.g. in input-statements, as actual variable parameters, as subscripts (exploited later in Case-study 6), and even, as we shall see in Chapter 13, as the array-variable part of an indexed-variable.

One should not confuse the subscript of an element with its value. Subscripts and elements may not even have the same type, as in the following example.

### 11.2.1 ANOTHER PROGRAM USING AN ARRAY

The problem here is to print the number of occurrences of each letter that appears in the input data. The problem essentially is the same as that of printing the histogram of scores, so its solution will take the same form. Here a count is maintained for every lower-case letter, so the index-type of the array will be 'a'..'z'.

```
program Letters (Input, Output);
{ Prompts user to enter a sentence using only lower-case letters, }
{ and prints the letters employed together with their frequencies. }
{ N.B. assumes lower-case letters are contiguous. }
  type
    count = 0..Maxint;
    letter = 'a'..'z';
    LetterCounts = array[letter] of count;
  var
    freq : LetterCounts; { freq[l] is number of letter l's read so far,
                                  l = 'a', ... , 'z'. }
    ch : char; { last character read, or control-variable }
begin { Letters }
{ Zero all letter frequencies }
```

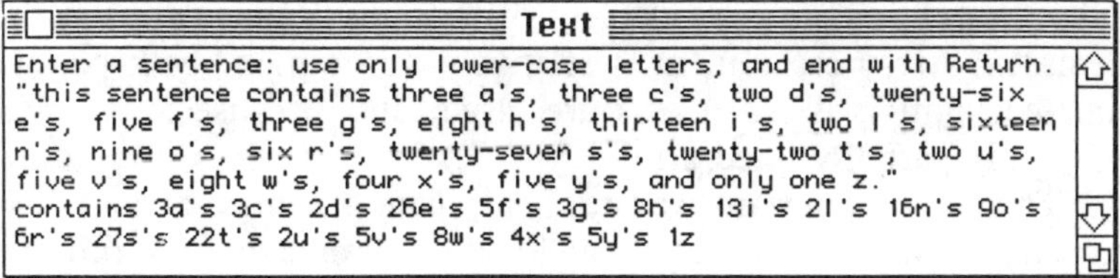

Text
Enter a sentence: use only lower-case letters, and end with Return.
"this sentence contains three a's, three c's, two d's, twenty-six
e's, five f's, three g's, eight h's, thirteen i's, two l's, sixteen
n's, nine o's, six r's, twenty-seven s's, twenty-two t's, two u's,
five v's, eight w's, four x's, five y's, and only one z."
contains 3a's 3c's 2d's 26e's 5f's 3g's 8h's 13i's 2l's 16n's 9o's
6r's 27s's 22t's 2u's 5v's 8w's 4x's 5y's 1z


**Figure 11.2**
The Text window after a run of Letters.

```
  for ch := 'a' to 'z' do
    freq[ch] := 0;
{ Prompt for input after quote }
  Writeln('Enter a sentence: use only lower-case letters, and end
            with Return.');
  Write('"');
{ Read input, count letters, and append quote }
  while not eoln do
    begin
      Read(ch);
      if ('a' <= ch) and (ch <= 'z') then
        freq[ch] := freq[ch] + 1
    end;
  Writeln('"');
{ Announce non-zero letter frequencies }
  Write('contains');
  for ch := 'a' to 'z' do
    if freq[ch] > 0 then
      begin
        Write(' ', freq[ch] : 1, ch);
        if freq[ch] > 1 then
          Write('''s')
      end
end. { Letters }
```

The Text window after an atypical run of program Letters is shown in Figure 11.2.

## 11.3 Operations on an entire array

Arrays generally are manipulated through their components. However, there are ways to work with an entire array variable. One of these is with an assignment statement:

```
A := B
```

Provided array B has the same type as array A, the assignment is permitted, and assigns each element of B to the element of A with the same index. Array assignment is relatively uncommon, both because it is time-consuming if the arrays are large, and because it is usual to employ only partially filled arrays.

The most important way to manipulate an entire array is to use it as an actual parameter of a function-designator or procedure-statement. Even though within the subprogram the array may be used element-by-element, in the context of the call it is used as a unit. Pascal's parameter mechanism treats arrays according to exactly the same rules as for parameters of other types:

- **Value array parameters** A formal value parameter of an array-type is treated as a local variable of that type which is assigned the value of its corresponding actual parameter before execution of the subprogram's block. (This is why array-assignment is permitted!) Except in the case of strings, which we discuss later in this chapter, the actual parameter must be an array of the same type.
- **Variable array parameters** A formal variable parameter of an array-type is treated as a local renaming of its corresponding actual parameter, which must be an array of the same type. Since no array-assignment is involved in this case, input parameters of an array type are often made variable parameters, even though conceptually a value parameter is preferable. Note that since there are no array expressions, the range of potential actual parameters is not diminished. Care, however, must be taken not to change any element of such an input array parameter.

## 11.4 Linear search

### 11.4.1 OPTIMISTIC LINEAR SEARCH

Suppose that the histogram of scores is to be printed starting with the lowest score attained. We might decide to compute this value with the following function:

```
function FirstNonZero (var h : histogram) : ScoreRange;
{ Returns the least index of a non-zero element of h; }
{ assumes at least one element is non-zero. }
```

Here it is sensible to make h a var-parameter, lest the function begin by copying 101 variables of type count into a local array. We note our obligation not to change any element of h.

The problem fits schema Sequential Search from Chapter 6: the sequence is that of the values in ScoreRange, in increasing order; the property $P(v)$ is h[$v$] <> 0. Using low for $v$, we obtain:

```
var
  low : ScoreRange; { low <= index of first non-zero element }
begin { FirstNonZero }
 low := 0;
 while h[low] = 0 do
  low := low + 1;
 FirstNonZero := low
end; { FirstNonZero }
```

Note how informative and yet concise is the comment for low — such comments are the most helpful to the reader.

A specialization of schema Sequential Search to the case where each new value is the successor (or predecessor) of the previous one, is known as **linear search**. Specifically, the one above is the *optimistic* version, where a solution is assumed (i.e. known) to exist. In the context of our histogram of examination scores the assumption is justified. But consider the next problem.

### 11.4.2 TRUNCATED SAFE LINEAR SEARCH

The sentence in Figure 11.2 has the appealing property (if you like that sort of thing) of being self-describing — it is called an *autogram*. Autogramophiles are also interested in *pangrams*, which are sentences that contain every letter of the alphabet. After reading a sentence as in program Letters, therefore, a program might execute the following assignment:

```
var
  IsPangram : Boolean; { true iff the input sentence is a pangram }
...
function AllNonZero (var instances : LetterCounts) : Boolean;
{ Returns true iff all elements of instances are non-zero. }
...
  IsPangram := AllNonZero(freq)
```

Our problem is to implement function AllNonZero.

> **Principle** To evaluate functions such as AllNonZero that are true iff *all* values in some range have a certain property, search for a value that does *not* have the property; the result is true iff the search is unsuccessful.

For our problem, therefore, we might decide to use a variable aLetter to range over the letters, and have the loop terminate when the following condition is true:

```
(aLetter > 'z') or (instances[aLetter] = 0)
```

The first operand of **or** should be true iff the search is unsuccessful (in finding a letter with a zero frequency); the second iff it is successful (and aLetter is the first letter with a zero frequency). So, after negating the stopping-condition to get the condition of the while-loop, we might write:

```
var
  aLetter : char; { BEWARE }
begin { AllNonZero }
 aLetter := 'a';
 while (aLetter <= 'z') and (instances[aLetter] <> 0) do
 { BEWARE }
  aLetter := succ(aLetter);
 AllNonZero := aLetter > 'z'
end; { AllNonZero }
```

Note that we have declared aLetter to have the type char rather than letter, because it might be assigned the value succ('z'). Unfortunately, the existence of such a value is not guaranteed by the Standard. It does exist in Macintosh Pascal and all the important character sets, so we might be inclined to document our assumption and leave it at that. But then a second problem emerges, because the condition of the loop might be evaluated by first evaluating the indexed-variable, and instances[succ('z')] does not exist.

| **Principle** Rather than patch a flawed solution, think again. |
|---|

There is a neat solution to our problem. (One school of thought holds that there is a neat solution to *every* programming problem, a proposition that is not as Panglossian as it may seem.) The idea is to limit the search to the letters < 'z'. If it stops because instances[aLetter] = 0, the function should return false. Otherwise, it stops because aLetter = 'z', and the function should return false iff instances['z'] = 0. In either case, the result of the function is the value of instances[aLetter] <> 0. Our solution is therefore:

```
var
  aLetter : letter;
begin { AllNonZero }
 aLetter := 'a';
 while (aLetter < 'z') and (instances[aLetter] <> 0) do
```

```
      aLetter := succ(aLetter);
    AllNonZero := instances[aLetter] <> 0
  end; { AllNonZero }
```

This is the simplest solution to our problem. Note that it allows aLetter to have type letter. The underlying schema is called Truncated Safe Linear Search ('Safe' because it makes no assumption that the search will be successful). In a given application, only the value of *NoneHaveP* or of $v$ might be of interest.

**Schema** Truncated Safe Linear Search:

```
var
  NoneHaveP : Boolean;
  v : a..b;
{ If no values in a..b have property P, set NoneHaveP = true; else }
{ set NoneHaveP = false and v = least value in a..b with property P; }
{ assume a <= b. }
-----------------------------------------------------------------
  v := a;
  while (v < b) and not P(v) do
    v := succ(v);
  NoneHaveP := not P(v)
```

For another approach to testing for pangrams, see Exercise 17.7.

### 11.4.3 SENTINEL SEARCH

Our next problem has the following context:

```
const
  MaxIndex = ... ;
type
  index = 1..MaxIndex;
  count = 0..MaxIndex;
  values = array[index] of ElementType;
var
  A : values;
  n : count;
```

Suppose the elements of A with indexes from 1 up to n have been given values.

**Notation** A[$a..b$] denotes the section of array A consisting of the elements A[$i$] with $a \leqslant i \leqslant b$. If $b < a$, this collection is empty.

Our problem is to remove any duplicated values from A[1..n], decreasing n if necessary, so that on completion A[1..n] contains just the distinct values originally present. For example, suppose *ElementType* is integer, MaxIndex = 10, n = 8, and A is as shown below:

| | 1 | 2 | 3 | 4 | 5 | 6 | 7 | 8 | 9 | 10 |
|---|---|---|---|---|---|---|---|---|---|---|
| A | 6 | 5 | 5 | –1 | 6 | 4 | 0 | 6 | ? | ? |

Then after execution of our solution, n must be 5, and a suitable configuration for A is:

| | 1 | 2 | 3 | 4 | 5 | 6 | 7 | 8 | 9 | 10 |
|---|---|---|---|---|---|---|---|---|---|---|
| A | 6 | 5 | –1 | 4 | 0 | ? | ? | ? | ? | ? |

Let us decide to process the elements from left to right, accumulating the distinct values on the left. Before writing, though, we must be completely specific. A very useful technique for any array problem is to draw a picture that is sufficiently general to represent the situation at any point in the computation. We employ the following variables:

```
var
  m : count; { number of distinct values accumulated }
  r : index; { index of next remaining original element }
```

The general picture is shown in Figure 11.3. Some of the sections shown may be empty, e.g. if m = 0 or m = r – 1.

The general picture is called an **invariant** because it invariantly is true before each iteration of the loop that is based on it. Invariants need not have anything to do with arrays. They are invaluable for writing correct programs and solving hard problems, and are treated in more detail in Chapter 12. To exploit our general picture, we use a loop preceded by initialization statements.

- The initialization must make the depicted situation apply.
- The loop should terminate when the picture represents the goal.
- The body of the loop must make progress toward the goal, taking care that the picture still applies afterward.

**Figure 11.3**
The general picture for the distinct-values problem.

| | 1 … m | | r … n | |
|---|---|---|---|---|
| A | distinct values in original A[1..r – 1] | ? | original values | ? |

The first requirement is met by setting m = 0 and r = 1. Our goal is to have r = n + 1, whence all distinct values have been accumulated, and we only need set n = m. So if we use a while-loop, its condition will be r <= n, and r could not be declared to have type index. A for-loop is more appropriate, though, and permits our declaration of r to stand; however, for consistency with the invariant, we need to regard r as equal to n + 1 on termination. Finally, we make progress in the body of the loop by increasing r. In order to maintain the general picture, we must add A[r] to the distinct values if necessary. We have arrived at:

```
m := 0;
for r := 1 to n do
  Add A[r] to the distinct values if it does not occur in A[1..m];
n := m
```

The major task for the body of the loop is to search A[1..m] for A[r]. A safe linear search is needed, because it may not occur. In this situation, there is a very neat way to avoid the complications of a safe search and write a simple, optimistic search. It is to guarantee success by storing A[r] in A[m + 1] and searching A[1..m + 1]! Since r > m, it is perfectly safe to do this — even if r = m + 1, the assignment does no harm. The search is successful (meaning A[r] is a duplicated value) iff it terminates before reaching A[m + 1]. In that case, nothing more need be done. Otherwise, we need only increment m, because the new value is already in the correct place. We have:

```
var
  first : index; { least index with A[first] = A[r] }

{ Add A[r] to the distinct values if it does not occur in A[1..m] }
 begin
   A[m + 1] := A[r];
 { Set first = least index with A[first] = A[r] }
   first := 1;
   while A[first] <> A[r] do
     first := first + 1;

   if first = m + 1 then
     m := m + 1
 end
```

This technique is known as **sentinel search**, because the value appended to ensure success is called a **sentinel**. The schema is simply that of optimistic linear search preceded by the appending of the sentinel.

### 11.4.4 BOOLEAN SAFE LINEAR SEARCH

In the context of the previous problem, suppose now that the values of *ElementType* are ordered, and the problem is to test whether or not the values in A[1..n] are non-decreasing, i.e. if:

A[$i$] ≤ A[$i$ + 1], for $i$ = 1, 2, ... , n–1.

If so, the array-section is said to be **sorted** in non-decreasing (or, loo. ly speaking, increasing) order. We formulate the problem as a fu.. tion:

```
function sorted (var A : values; n : count) : Boolean;
{ Returns true iff A[1..n] is sorted in non-decreasing order. }
```

Note again the use of a var-parameter for efficiency, even though this is a function.

According to our principle given earlier, we introduce a variable i and search for a value such that A[i] > A[i + 1] gives true. The result of sorted is true iff the search is unsuccessful.

Using a sentinel would require setting A[n + 1] to a value < A[n]. There are two problems with this: A[n + 1] may not exist, and there may not be a value < A[n]. There is a problem also with using a truncated search: the condition of the while-loop would be:

```
(i < n – 1) and (A[i] <= A[i + 1])
```

but it could give a subscript error at the outset if n = 0 or 1. So we instead use a new form of safe linear search, that employs a Boolean variable:

```
var
  i : index;
  SortedSoFar : Boolean; { true iff A[1..i] is sorted }
begin { sorted }
 i := 1;
 SortedSoFar := true;
 while SortedSoFar and (i < n) do
  if A[i] <= A[i + 1] then
   i := i + 1
  else
   SortedSoFar := false;
 sorted := SortedSoFar
end; { sorted }
```

If an out-of-order pair is found, SortedSoFar becomes false, the loop stops, and the function returns false; otherwise, the loop stops when i = n, with SortedSoFar still true, and the function returns true.

The underlying schema is formulated as schema Boolean Safe Linear Search (which is really just a specialization of a variant of schema Complex While Loop). This method requires succ($b$) to exist. The requirement was met in our problem because $b$ was n − 1. In practice, only a single Boolean variable might be used.

```
Schema Boolean Safe Linear Search:
var
  NoneHaveP : Boolean;
  v : a type containing a..succ(b);
{ If no values in a..b have property P, set NoneHaveP = true; else }
{ set NoneHaveP = false and v = least value in a..b with property P; }
{ assume succ(b) exists. }
--------------------------------------------------------------------
 var
  NoneHavePSoFar : Boolean; { true iff no values < v have property P }

 v := a;
 NoneHavePSoFar := true;
 while NoneHavePSoFar and (v <= b) do
  if v has property P then
    NoneHavePSoFar := false
  else
    v := succ(v);
 NoneHaveP := NoneHavePSoFar
```

### 11.4.5 THE RIGHT SEARCH FOR THE RIGHT OCCASION

Assuming a linear search is indicated, we have four versions to choose from. Each has its advantages and disadvantages. We consider them in order of increasing complexity.

(1) **Optimistic linear search** should be used if the search is guaranteed to be successful.

(2) **Sentinel search** is also a simple method, and should be used whenever it is possible to use a sentinel without undue trickery. Some advocate declaring arrays with an extra element to make this style of search possible.

(3) **Truncated safe linear search** is the method for potentially unsuccessful searches where the maximum value that can be examined has no successor, and where the desired property can be written as a Boolean expression.

(4) **Boolean safe linear search** should be used for potentially unsuccessful searches over potentially empty ranges of values, provided the maximum value that can be examined has a successor.

None of these searches is limited to arrays, as is apparent from the schemas. Also, each has a variation that searches a sequence of decreasing rather than increasing values.

# 11.5 Sorting

## 11.5.1 THE PROBLEM

The most important problem involving arrays is that of sorting, because arranging information in some order enables it to be searched more efficiently. This should be no surprise to anyone who has used a dictionary or a telephone directory. A fast and simple method for searching in a sorted array, called **binary search**, is presented in Chapter 12.

We shall work in the context of the previous type-definitions, assuming *ElementType* is an ordered type. But our algorithms can easily be generalized to apply to arbitrary types of element, as long as a Boolean function of two arguments is provided that defines an ordering of the values.

The problem, then, is to implement the following procedure:

```
procedure sort (var A : values; n : count);
{ Sorts A[1..n] into non-decreasing order. }
```

More precisely, the values A[1..n] are to be rearranged so that sorted(A,n) gives true. This is known as sorting **in place**, or **in situ**: by changing A rather than returning the result in another array, we halve our space requirement, and maximize the size of the arrays that can be handled. There is an understanding, therefore, that no local arrays be used in procedure sort.

## 11.5.2 SELECTION SORT

Perhaps the most straightforward approach is to find (the index of) the largest element and swap that element with the last, then find the next-to-largest and swap it with the next-to-last, and so on. Before starting to write, we need to be precise, and begin by drawing the general picture shown in Figure 11.4.

**Figure 11.4**
The general picture for our sorting algorithm.

```
   1                 NrLeft                        n
  +-------------------+----------------------------+
A |     unsorted      |    in final positions      |
  +-------------------+----------------------------+
```

We have introduced:

```
var
  NrLeft : count; { only A[1..NrLeft] remains to be sorted }
```

Now, following our principle for exploiting invariants, we:

- make the invariant apply initially by setting NrLeft = n;
- note that the loop should stop when NrLeft = 1, because then all of A[1..n] must be sorted;
- make progress in the body of the loop by finding the maximum value in A[1..NrLeft], swapping it with A[NrLeft], and then decreasing NrLeft by 1.

All of this can be done with a for-loop:

```
var
  MaxAt : index; { A[MaxAt] is maximum value in A[1..NrLeft] }

begin { sort }
  for NrLeft := n downto 2 do
    begin
      Set MaxAt so that A[MaxAt] = maximum value in A[1..NrLeft];
      swap(A[MaxAt], A[NrLeft])
    end
end; { sort }
```

Note that the loop stops *after* processing NrLeft = 2, which for the purposes of the invariant, is equivalent to stopping *when* NrLeft = 1 with a while-loop.

Procedure swap is familiar, though the type of its two var-parameters must be *ElementType*. Note that swap has nothing to do with arrays: it is perfectly capable of swapping array-elements as is. The abstract action in the body of the loop may be implemented with a function:

```
function IndexOfMax (var A : values; left, right : index) : index;
{ Returns the index of the maximum element in A[left..right]; }
{ assumes left <= right. }

MaxAt := IndexOfMax(A,1, NrLeft)
```

The function may as well be made more general than necessary. We have documented the assumption that ensures its value is well defined.

To implement the function, all elements with subscripts in the range left..right need to be examined. The method is to remember the index of the maximum value seen so far, which can be initialized to left. The remaining indexes are processed with a for-loop:

```
var
  i : 1..Maxint; { can have type index in Standard Pascal }
  ind : index; { A[ind] is maximum value in A[left..i – 1] }
begin { IndexOfMax }
 ind := left;
 for i := left + 1 to right do
   if A[i] > A[ind] then
     ind := i;
 IndexOfMax := ind
end; { IndexOfMax }
```

Procedure sort is now complete. Function IndexOfMax and procedure swap are both modular, so each can be declared either prior to sort or as local subprograms. Also, each can and should be tested separately. Procedure sort can be tested by a simple test-driver like the following:

```
program TestSort (Input, Output);
{ Tests sort procedure: Reads integers into an array, sorts them, }
{ and then prints them in sorted order. }
 constants, types & subprograms (ElementType is integer)
 var
   list : values;
   ListSize : count; { list[1..ListSize] contains values read }
   i : count; { ranges over 1..ListSize }
             { N.B. can have type index in Standard Pascal }
begin { TestSort }
{ Prompt for and read list of integers }
 Writeln('Enter a list of integers; hit Return immediately after last
          value.');
 Writeln('Integers after the ', MaxIndex : 1, '''th will be ignored.');
 ListSize := 0;
 while not eoln and (ListSize < MaxIndex) do
   begin
     ListSize := ListSize + 1;
     Read(list[ListSize])
   end;
 Writeln;

 sort(list, ListSize);
 Writeln('The input values in non-decreasing order:');
 for i := 1 to ListSize do
   Write(list[i])
end. { TestSort }
```

The test should work if no values are input, i.e. just the Return-key is typed.

The algorithm we have employed, which repeatedly selects the maximum remaining value and puts it in its correct position, is called **selection sort**.

### 11.5.3 BUBBLE SORT

Selection sort is not the only algorithm that uses the invariant in Figure 11.4: there are other ways to move the largest value in A[1..NrLeft] to the end, permitting NrLeft to be decreased by 1, and thereby making progress in the body of the loop. One of these is to compare A[1] & A[2], A[2] & A[3], ... , A[NrLeft – 1] & A[NrLeft], swapping each pair if it is out of order. The effect is that large values bubble up, i.e. move to the right, and the largest will bubble all the way up to the end. Desk-check it with a small array-section.

Let us use variable k for the lesser index of the two elements to be compared. The bubbling step involves processing the values k = 1, 2, ... , NrLeft – 1, so is best implemented as a for-loop. The complete procedure is as follows:

```
procedure sort (var A : values; n : count);
{ Sorts A[1..n] into non-decreasing order. }
{ Global subprogram: swap. }
  var
    NrLeft : count; { only A[1..NrLeft] remains to be sorted }
      { N.B. can have type index in Standard Pascal }
    k : index; { A[k] & A[k + 1] are compared }
begin { sort }
  for NrLeft := n downto 2 do
    for k := 1 to NrLeft – 1 do
      if A[k] > A[k + 1] then
        swap(A[k], A[k + 1])
end; { sort }
```

This algorithm is called **bubble sort**. Procedure sort can, of course, be tested with program TestSort above, since only its implementation has changed, not its specification.

Trace the above version of bubble sort using the technique suggested in Exercise 11.12. You will discover that except in unusual cases, the array-section will be sorted well before the outer for-loop is finished. *Very interesting*. A little thought reveals the explanation: much more progress is made on each iteration than simply putting the maximum remaining value in its correct place.

We can take advantage of this by making the outer loop

terminate if it is known that the array is already sorted. And a sufficient and easily-tested condition is that no swaps are performed in the bubbling step! Thus the sortedness of the array will be discovered on the iteration after the one that does the last swap. In fact, we can make this our only termination condition, because in the unlikely event that NrLeft reaches 1, no swaps will be performed. Since at least one iteration will now be performed, we use a repeat-loop. Our New Improved Bubble Sort with Early Termination is as follows:

```
procedure sort (var A : values; n : count);
{ Sorts A[1..n] into non-decreasing order. }
{ Global subprogram: swap. }
 var
  NrLeft : -1..MaxIndex; { only A[1..NrLeft] remains to be sorted }
  k : -1..MaxIndex; { A[k] & A[k + 1] are compared }
     { N.B. can have type index in Standard Pascal }
  KnownSorted : Boolean; { true iff (outer loop:) A[1..n] known to }
    { be sorted; (inner loop:) A[1..k] known to be sorted }
begin { sort }
 NrLeft := n;
 repeat
  KnownSorted := true;
  for k := 1 to NrLeft - 1 do
   if A[k] > A[k + 1] then
    begin
     swap(A[k], A[k + 1]);
     KnownSorted := false
    end;
  NrLeft := NrLeft - 1
 until KnownSorted
end; { sort }
```

Note how KnownSorted is used. For the inner loop, it starts out true and only becomes false if a swap is performed. So when the condition of the outer loop is evaluated, it is true iff A[1..n] is known to be sorted.

## 11.6 Strings in standard Pascal

### 11.6.1 PACKED ARRAYS

Variables of structured types can have values that require large amounts of main memory. An array with *n* elements would usually be expected to use *n* times as much memory as a variable of its element-type. Thus, for example, arrays with Boolean or char elements might be allocated one cell per element.

Sometimes the size of main memory constrains the size of problems that can be solved. To help in such cases, Pascal permits arrays (and other structured types) to be **packed**. This is indicated by giving the word-symbol **packed** before **array** in a type definition or variable declaration:

structured-type: **packed** *unpacked-structured-type*
unpacked-structured-type: *array-type*

The effect depends on the implementation. For example, a packed array of 1000 Boolean elements might only use 1000 bits rather than cells. In Macintosh Pascal 2.0, only arrays with the following element-types are affected by packing:

```
char      0..255      –128..127
```

Each such element uses one byte rather than two.

Only implementations with significant main memory limitations are likely automatically to pack arrays. The reason is that packing will increase the time needed to handle an indexed-variable, and this is a much more common operation than array assignment which will be faster.

A packed array type is not the same type as its unpacked version. A packed array therefore cannot be used where an unpacked array is expected, and vice versa. There is another restriction: an
element of a packed array may not be used as an actual variable 11.1
parameter.

A good compromise in some situations is to use packed arrays, unpack them into local arrays before processing them element-by-element, and repack them afterwards if necessary. Pascal has two required procedures to facilitate this approach. Suppose the following variables are given:

**var**
  pA : **packed array**[$p_1..p_2$] **of** *T*;
  uA : **array**[*uIndexType*] **of** *T*;

Let *uindex* represent an expression whose value is assignment-compatible with *uIndexType*. Then the procedure call:

unpack(pA, uA, *uindex*)

copies pA[$p_1..p_2$] into uA starting at uA[*uindex*], taking elements in order of increasing subscripts. It is an error if there are insufficient elements in uA.

Similarly, the procedure call:

```
pack(uA, uindex, pA)
```

copies values from uA into pA[$p_1..p_2$], starting with uA[*uindex*]. It is an error if there are insufficient elements to fill pA. The index-type of the packed array need not be a subrange type — the above formulation used one only as a convenient way of indicating the range of indexes.

### 11.6.2 STRINGS

A type of the form:

```
packed array[1..n] of char
```

where *n* is an integer constant ≥ 2, is called a **string-type**, and a variable of that type is called a **string variable**. String-variables have special status in Pascal: they are used in a half-hearted attempt to provide text processing operations. Unlike for any other arrays, whether packed or not, the following provisions are made (illustrated in the following context):

```
type
  string10 = packed array[1..10] of char;
var
  s1, s2 : string10;
  s3 : packed array[1..10] of char;
```

- Each string type has constant values: the character strings of its length *n*. Thus the following assignments are permitted:

  ```
  s1 := 'Dear Sir  ';
  s3 := 'Dear Madam'
  ```

  Note the two spaces at the end of the first string constant, which must have length 10. Similarly, a string constant may be used as an actual value parameter for a formal parameter of a string type. However, a string constant may not be given for pA in a procedure-statement for unpack.

- The assignment compatibility rules for string variables are relaxed: a string variable is assignment compatible with any string type of the same length. Thus the following assignments are permitted:

```
s2 := s1; { ordinary array-assignment }
s2 := s3  { only permitted with string variables }
```

The second assignment is special because s2 and s3 do not have the same type. Similarly, s3 may be used as an actual value parameter for a formal parameter of type string10.

- String variables may appear in output statements; for example:

```
Write(s1 : 8, ', drop dead.')
```

prints:

```
Dear Sir, drop dead.
```

Input, however, has to be done character by character.

- Two string values *of the same length* may be compared with a relational operator. They are equal if all corresponding characters are equal; otherwise, the result is determined by the first index at which the characters differ, and is obtained simply by comparing the two characters. Thus, for example:

s1 < s3 gives false, since 'S' < 'M' gives false

'96' > '69' gives true, since '9' > '6' gives true

'new ' < 'news' is implementation-dependent

The last example shows that Pascal's ordering of strings may not be the same as that in a dictionary.

Many implementations of Pascal provide extensions in this area. Macintosh Pascal's extensions are covered in Chapter 14.

## 11.7 Case-study 6: Scheduling III

### 11.7.1 SETTING OF THE PROBLEM

The problem setting is as for Case-study 3 in Chapter 9, but with two changes:

- The number of available processors is given in advance, but it is not necessarily two.
- Jobs are not necessarily scheduled in the order they are given on input. Instead, the jobs are to be scheduled so as to minimize the average time at which jobs complete.

## 11.7.2 SPECIFICATIONS

The input will be as for Case-study 3: a list of processing times followed by a stopping-value ≤ 0. The output should have the same format, except that the scheduling diagram will have as many rows as there are processors. The jobs are to be scheduled by taking them in order of non-decreasing processing times, and assigning them cyclically to processors, i.e. in the order 1, 2, 3, ... , *n*, 1, 2, 3, ... , *n*, ... , where *n* is the number of processors. Our friendly neighborhood operations researcher has informed us that this minimizes the average time at which jobs complete.

The number of processors is at least one. The program may limit the number of jobs that it can handle, in which case the limit must be announced to the user prior to input. If it is exceeded, the extra jobs should be ignored.

## 11.7.3 WRITING THE PROGRAM

Realizing that all the processing times (and the associated job numbers) must be stored before they can be processed, we write our first refinement:

```
begin { JobScheduler3 }
  Write heading;
  Prompt for, read, count, & store job times;
  Create the job numbers corresponding to the job times;
  Sort job information into scheduling order;
  Schedule all jobs, create diagram, & print statistics
end. { JobScheduler3 }
```

The first action is easily disposed of:

```
const
  NrProcessors = ... ; { >= 1; number of processors }

{ Write heading }
  Writeln('SCHEDULING JOBS ON ', NrProcessors : 1,
           ' PROCESSORS TO MINIMIZE AVERAGE
           JOB-COMPLETION TIME');
  Writeln
```

The next action we should consider is the last, since it will determine what job information is needed and how it should be stored and sorted. To do the scheduling, each processing time and associated job number must be obtained in non-decreasing order of processing times. There are several alternatives (some of which we are not yet aware of), but let us decide on the following. The job numbers should be obtained from an array in order of increasing subscripts; the processing times are held in another array in the original input order, enabling the processing time for a given job number to be obtained by using the job number as an index. The attraction of this technique in general is that only indexes rather than large elements need be sorted; the pedagogical attraction in the current context is that it forces us to distinguish carefully between elements and their subscripts.

We introduce, therefore, the following definitions and declarations:

```
const
  MaxNrJobs = ... ; { maximum number of jobs that can be
                      scheduled }
type
  JobNumber = 1..MaxNrJobs;
  JobCount = 0..MaxNrJobs;
  time = 0..Maxint;
  JobTimes = array[JobNumber] of time;
  JobNumbers = array[JobNumber] of JobNumber;
var
  JobTime : JobTimes;  { JobTime[i] = the processing time of }
                       { the i'th job in the input order. }
  JobNr : JobNumbers; { the i'th job in the current order was }
                       { JobNr[i]'th in the input order. }
  NrJobs : JobCount; { number of jobs to be processed }
                     { (1 <= i <= NrJobs, above) }
```

As an example, suppose the following processing times were entered in the order shown:

3, 5, 1, 2, 7, 5, 4, 2

Then before executing the final action (scheduling all jobs), NrJobs = 8, and the arrays might look as shown in Figure 11.5. The information needed to schedule the first job is the job number JobNr[1] = 3, and the processing time JobTime[JobNr[1]] = JobTime[3] = 1. And so on for the remaining jobs.

| | 1 | 2 | 3 | 4 | 5 | 6 | 7 | 8 | 9 | 10 | ... |
|---|---|---|---|---|---|---|---|---|---|---|---|
| JobNr | 3 | 4 | 8 | 1 | 7 | 2 | 6 | 5 | ? | ? | |

| | 1 | 2 | 3 | 4 | 5 | 6 | 7 | 8 | 9 | 10 | ... |
|---|---|---|---|---|---|---|---|---|---|---|---|
| JobTime | 3 | 5 | 1 | 2 | 7 | 5 | 4 | 2 | ? | ? | |

**Figure 11.5**
The arrays just before scheduling.

We decide to implement the scheduling with a procedure-statement:

```
procedure ScheduleAll (var JobNr : JobNumbers;
                       var JobTime : JobTimes;
                       count : JobCount);
{ Schedules the job with job-number JobNr[i] and processing }
{ time JobTime[JobNr[i]], for i = 1, 2, ... , count, cyclically }
{ assigning jobs to processors 1, 2, ... , NrProcessors, 1, 2, ... ; }
{ produces scheduling diagram and prints statistics. }
{ Global const: NrProcessors. }

ScheduleAll(JobNr, JobTime, NrJobs)
```

There is no need to retain the original description of the action as a comment.

Now we can tackle the three remaining highest-level actions, and decide to use a procedure-statement for each. For reading:

```
procedure ReadTimes (var JobTime : JobTimes;
                     var count : JobCount);
{ Prompts for, reads, and counts job times, storing in }
{ JobTime[1..count]. }

ReadTimes(JobTime, NrJobs)
```

For creating the job numbers:

```
procedure NumberJobs (var JobNr : JobNumbers;
                      count : JobCount);
{ Sets JobNr[1..count] = (1,2, ... , count). }

NumberJobs(JobNr, NrJobs)
```

For sorting:

```
procedure SortIndexes (var index : JobNumbers;
                       var A : JobTimes;
                       n : JobCount);
{ Sorts index[1..n] so that for 1 <= k <= n: }
{ A[index[k]] <= A[index[k + 1]]. }

SortIndexes(JobNr, JobTime, NrJobs)
```

A is a var-parameter for efficiency.

Procedure ReadTimes is obtained from our familiar schema Interactive I/O, prompting once rather than repeatedly. The schema needs a slight modification to handle the possibility that too many processing times are input. This amounts to stopping the loop when the following condition gives true:

(*v is a stopping value*) **or** (*number of jobs read* = MaxNrJobs)

Negating this, we obtain for the condition of the while-loop:

(*v is not a stopping value*) **and** (*number of jobs read* <> MaxNrJobs)

The implementation of ReadTimes can be seen below in the listing of the complete program. It should be tested with a program that calls it and then prints the stored values.

Procedure NumberJobs is implemented using schema For Increasing Values; see the complete program.

Procedure SortIndexes can be obtained by modifying any of our sort procedures, or, indeed, anyone else's (if you trust them). Let us decide to work with our most efficient version: New Improved Bubble Sort etc. The main modification concerns swaps. The condition under which a swap is performed is the opposite of the condition that is to be established, which is given in the specification of the procedure. It is therefore:

```
A[index[k]] > A[index[k + 1]]
```

When this condition gives true, it is not the *elements* of A that are to be swapped, but rather their *indexes* held in the array index, which implicitly define the ordering of A[1..n]. The other modifications simply concern the types of the local variables, and the types of the formal parameters and local variable of swap.

The implementation of SortIndexes is given below in the listing of the complete program. Since it is modular, it is a simple matter to test it with a small main program, which may as well take advantage of what we have written and tested thus far, especially procedure ReadTimes. This practice is not generally recommended — see the discussion on testing procedures in Chapter 9. After sorting, it makes most sense to print with:

```
for k := 1 to NrJobs do
  Write('#', JobNr[k] : 1, ': ', JobTime[JobNr[k]] : 1, ' ')
```

to check that the processing times are in order, and that the values are consistent with the input data.

It remains to write procedure ScheduleAll, which has to print the number of jobs, and also if that is greater than zero, to compute and print the average job completion-time and draw the scheduling diagram. Two levels of uncomplicated refinements lead to:

```
const
  PointSize = 12; { size of text }
var
  SumOfCompletionTimes : time; { of all jobs }

begin { ScheduleAll }
  Writeln('There are ', count : 1, ' jobs to be scheduled.');
  if count > 0 then
    begin
      TextSize(PointSize);
      Draw axes;
      Schedule all jobs;
      Writeln('The average time at which jobs complete = ',
                 SumOfCompletionTimes / count : 1 : 1)
    end
end; { ScheduleAll }
```

The main step is *Schedule all jobs*, so we now tackle it. It amounts to scheduling the job with job number JobNr[$i$] and processing time JobTime[JobNr[$i$]], for $i = 1, 2, \ldots$, count. The natural refinement is with a for-loop, and we use a variable JobNrIndex in place of $i$ above. The body of the for-loop need only call a procedure with the same specifications as procedure schedule from Case-study 3 in Chapter 9 (except for the changes in the types of its formal parameters). However, we precede the call with an assignment to simplify some actual parameters, and follow it with one that gets the next processor, since computing the processor directly from JobNrIndex is less transparent. As in JobScheduler2, variables are needed to keep track of the total time used on each processor and the sum of completion times. For the former purpose, an array is ideal.

```
type
  ProcessorType = 1..NrProcessors;
  TotalTimes = array[ProcessorType] of time;
var
  TotalTimeOn : TotalTimes; { total processing time on each
                               processor so far }
  JobNrIndex : JobNumber; { Index of current job, in 1..NrJobs }
  NrJob : JobNumber;
  processor : ProcessorType; { Processor number }

  function next (p : ProcessorType) : ProcessorType;
  { Returns processor after processor p in cyclic order. }
```

```
{ Schedule all jobs }
 Initialize;
 for JobNrIndex := 1 to count do
   begin
     NrJob := JobNr[JobNrIndex];
     schedule(JobTime[NrJob], processor, TotalTimeOn[processor],
              NrJob, SumOfCompletionTimes);
     processor := next(processor)
   end
```

The initialization is straightforward:

```
{ Initialize }
 for processor := 1 to NrProcessors do
   TotalTimeOn[Processor] := 0;
 SumOfCompletionTimes := 0;
 processor := 1
```

So, too, is the implementation of function **next**, which may be found in the complete program below.

Since procedure **schedule** has exactly the same specifications as in program **JobScheduler2**, exactly the same implementation will do. This is a very telling illustration of the benefits of the following principle:

> **Principle** Take the little trouble required to make procedures as general as possible.

The remaining action, *Draw axes*, can be implemented by the procedure-statement **DrawAxes**. Again, even though the present problem is more general, our original procedure works perfectly.

## 11.7.4 THE COMPLETE PROGRAM

```
program JobScheduler3 (Input, Output);
{ Input: prompts user to enter a sequence of processing times }
{ for jobs, which must be positive integers, followed by a –1 }
{ to end input. Jobs after the first MaxNrJobs will be ignored. }
{ Jobs are assigned to processors to minimize the average of }
{ the times at which jobs are completed. }
{ Output: the number of jobs processed; the average of the times }
{ at which jobs are completed; a diagram showing the jobs }
{ assigned to each processor. In the diagram, each job is }
{ specified by its position in the input sequence. }
  const
```

```
  MaxNrJobs = 20; { maximum number of jobs that can be
                      scheduled }
  NrProcessors = 4; { >= 1; number of processors }
type
  JobNumber = 1..MaxNrJobs;
  JobCount = 0..MaxNrJobs;
  time = 0..Maxint;
  JobTimes = array[JobNumber] of time;
  JobNumbers = array[JobNumber] of JobNumber;
var
  JobTime : JobTimes;  { JobTime[i] = the processing time of }
                       { the i'th job in the input order. }
  JobNr : JobNumbers; { the i'th job in the current order was }
                      { JobNr[i]'th in the input order. }
  NrJobs : JobCount; { number of jobs to be processed }
                     { (1 <= i <= NrJobs, above) }

procedure ReadTimes (var JobTime : JobTimes;
                     var count : JobCount);
{ Prompts for, reads, and counts job times, storing in }
{ JobTime[1..count]. Global const: MaxNrJobs. }
  var
  InValue : integer; { last input value read }
begin { ReadTimes }
  Writeln('Enter processing times for jobs to be scheduled.');
  Writeln('Enter 0 to terminate the list.');
  Writeln('Jobs after the ', MaxNrJobs : 1, '''th will be ignored.');
  Write('>>');
  count := 0;
  Read(InValue);
  while (InValue > 0) and (count <> MaxNrJobs) do
    begin
      count := count + 1;
      JobTime[count] := InValue;
      Read(InValue)
    end;
  Writeln
end; { ReadTimes}

procedure NumberJobs (var JobNr : JobNumbers;
                      count : JobCount);
{ Sets JobNr[1..count] = (1,2, ... , count). }
  var
  i : JobCount; { ranges over 1..count }
begin { NumberJobs }
  for i := 1 to count do
    JobNr[i] := i
end; { NumberJobs }
```

```
procedure SortIndexes (var index : JobNumbers;
                        var A : JobTimes;
                        n : JobCount);
{ Permutes index[1..n] so that for 1 <= k <= n: }
{ A[index[k]] <= A[index[k + 1]]. }
 var
   NrLeft : -1..MaxNrJobs; { only index[1..NrLeft] remains to be
                                 permuted }
   k : -1..MaxNrJobs; { A[index[k]] & A[index[k + 1]] are compared }
     { N.B. can have type JobNumber in Standard Pascal }
   KnownSorted : Boolean;
     { true iff (outer loop:) index[1..n] known to be properly }
     { permuted; (inner loop:) A[index[1]] <= ... <= A[index[k]] }

 procedure swap (var x, y : JobNumber);
 { Exchanges values of x and y. }
 as in Exercise 8.7 except temp : JobNumber

begin { SortIndexes }
  NrLeft := n;
  repeat
    KnownSorted := true;
    for k := 1 to NrLeft - 1 do
      if A[index[k]] > A[index[k + 1]] then
        begin
          swap(index[k], index[k + 1]);
          KnownSorted := false
        end;
    NrLeft := NrLeft - 1
  until KnownSorted
end; { SortIndexes }

procedure ScheduleAll (var JobNr : JobNumbers;
                        var JobTime : JobTimes;
                        count : JobCount);
{ Schedules the job with job-number JobNr[i] and processing }
{ time JobTime[JobNr[i]], for i = 1, 2, ... , count, cyclically }
{ assigning jobs to processors 1, 2, ... , NrProcessors, 1, 2, ... ; }
{ produces scheduling diagram and prints statistics. }
{ Global const: NrProcessors. }
  const
    Top = 12; { top-left corner of drawing is ... }
    Left = 24; { ... at (Left,Top) }
    Height = 40; { height of rectangle }
    Unit = 30; { size of time unit in pixels }
    PointSize = 12; { size of text }                          11.2
  type
    ProcessorType = 1..NrProcessors;
    TotalTimes = array[ProcessorType] of time;
```

```
var
  TotalTimeOn : TotalTimes; { total processing time on each
                              processor so far }
  JobNrIndex : JobNumber; { Index of current job, in 1..JobCount }
  NrJob : JobNumber;
  processor : ProcessorType; { Processor number }
  SumOfCompletionTimes : time; { of all jobs }

procedure DrawAxes;
{ Draws time axis and labels processors. }
{ Global constants: NrProcessors, Top, Left, Height, Unit,
                    PointSize. }
as in JobScheduler2, except t : time replaces time : integer
(and t replaces time throughout) and p : ProcessorType

procedure schedule (duration : time; processor : ProcessorType;
                    var StartTime : time;
                    NrJob : JobCount;
                    var Sum : time);
{ Schedules job of length duration on given processor, starting }
{ at time StartTime: updates diagram of scheduling decisions, }
{ identifying job with NrJob; updates StartTime to the starting }
{ time for the next job on this processor; updates sum of }
{ completion times (sum) of all jobs. }
same as in JobScheduler2

function next (p : ProcessorType) : ProcessorType;
{ Returns processor after processor p in cyclic order. }
{ Global const: NrProcessors. }
begin { next }
  if p = NrProcessors then
    next := 1
  else
    next := p + 1
end; { next }

begin { ScheduleAll }
  Writeln('There are ', count : 1, ' jobs to be scheduled.');
  if count > 0 then
    begin
      TextSize(PointSize);
      DrawAxes;
    { Schedule all jobs }
      { Initialize }
      for processor := 1 to NrProcessors do
        TotalTimeOn[processor] := 0;
      SumOfCompletionTimes := 0;
      processor := 1;

      for JobNrIndex := 1 to count do
```

```
        begin
          NrJob := JobNr[JobNrIndex];
          schedule(JobTime[NrJob], processor,
                   TotalTimeOn[processor],
                   NrJob, SumOfCompletionTimes);
          processor := next(processor)
        end;

      Writeln('The average time at which jobs complete = ',
              SumOfCompletionTimes / count : 1 : 1)
    end
  end; { ScheduleAll }

begin { JobScheduler3 }
{ Write heading }
  Writeln('SCHEDULING JOBS ON ', NrProcessors : 1,
          ' PROCESSORS TO MINIMIZE AVERAGE JOB-
          COMPLETION TIME');
  Writeln;

  ReadTimes(JobTime, NrJobs);
  NumberJobs(JobNr, NrJobs);
  SortIndexes(JobNr, JobTime, NrJobs);
  ScheduleAll(JobNr, JobTime, NrJobs)
end. { JobScheduler3 }
```

Figure 11.6 shows the screen after a test run of JobScheduler3 with NrProcessors = 4 and MaxNrJobs = 20. A good test to include

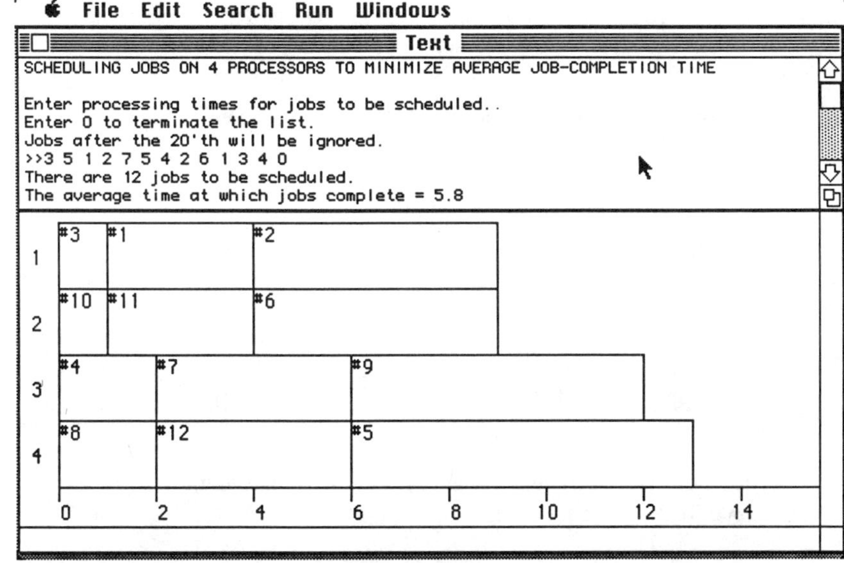


**Figure 11.6**
The screen after a run of JobScheduler3.

is one where the processing times are entered in non-decreasing order, and NrProcessors = 2, because then the output can be compared with that from JobScheduler2.

## 11.8 Macaveats

The Reference uses the term *packed-string-type* for the Standard's *string-type*, and *string-type* for Macintosh Pascal's own string types. The latter are much more convenient and sophisticated, and should be used for all programs designed solely for the Macintosh.

## 11.9 Further reading

(1) Sallows, L. C. F. (1985). 'In quest of a pangram' *Abacus* 2, 22–40.
The self-describing sentence in Figure 11.2 comes from this article. See also the follow-up article by John R. Letaw in the same issue. For lettermen and women only.

## EXERCISES

**11.1** Assemble the program that prints a histogram of scores, and trace its execution as follows. Redefine MaxScore to be 3, and enter the expressions freq[0], freq[1], freq[2], freq[3], and score in the Observe window. Make sure it is large enough to display all of them. Then execute the program by choosing Step-Step from the Run menu.

**11.2** Suppose the variables C and D are declared as follows:

```
var
  C, D : array[1..5] of integer;
```

and have been given values as shown below:

| | 1 | 2 | 3 | 4 | 5 |
|---|---|---|---|---|---|
| C | 3 | 4 | 2 | 5 | 1 |

| | 1 | 2 | 3 | 4 | 5 |
|---|---|---|---|---|---|
| D | 12 | 8 | 9 | 2 | 5 |

Also assume that integer variable i = 2. Evaluate the following expressions, looking out for errors.

(a) C[2 * i – 1]

(b) D[(i – 1) **div** 2]

(c) D[C[i]]

(d) C[2 * D[2 * i]]

**11.3** The simplest way to mimic a function that returns a value of an enumerated type when given its ordinal value is to use an array. Implement the action below that creates such an array for the type operation from program Arithmetic in Chapter 10.

```
const
  OrdOfLastOp = 2; { ordinal value of last operation (see below) }
type
  operation = (plus, minus, times);
  OrdOfOperation = 0..OrdOfLastOp;
var
  OpWithOrd : array[OrdOfOperation] of operation;
                { OpWithOrd[i] = operation with ordinal value i }

Define OpWithOrd
```

The way to use an array like OpWithOrd is to regard it as a globally defined function (which, conceptually, it is).

**11.4** In the context of the problem of the histogram of examination scores, implement the following procedure.

```
procedure PrintFrom (LowScore : ScoreRange;
                              var h : histogram);
{ Prints each score s and its frequency h[s], }
{ for s = LowScore, ... , MaxScore, in two headed columns. }
{ Global const: MaxScore. }
```

**11.5** Rewrite the program for the histogram of examination scores by using procedure PrintFrom from the previous question, and by implementing and using the following procedures:

```
procedure zero (var h : histogram);
{ Sets every element of h to zero. }

procedure ReadAndCompute (var h : histogram);
{ Prompts for and reads exam scores, and computes their }
{ histogram h. }
```

**11.6** Using function FirstNonZero from the text, modify the program for the previous question to print the histogram from the lowest score obtained. You may assume that at least one examination score is input.

**11.7** What is the best way to modify your program for the previous question to allow for the possibility of no examination scores?

**11.8** Formulate schema Sentinel Search.

**11.9** What modifications are necessary to use sentinel search to implement function AllNonZero? Are there any problems with this approach?

**11.10** Does our solution to the distinct values problem properly handle the case n = 0?

**11.11** Implement the following function in the given context, in two different ways. Which is best?

```
const
  Length = ... ; { >= 2 }
type
  index = 1..Length;
  ExtendedIndex = 0..Length;
  message = packed array[index] of char;
function DifferAt (var m1, m2 : message) : ExtendedIndex;
{ Returns 0 if m1 and m2 are identical, otherwise the least }
{ index at which they differ. Global const: Length. }
```

For example, if Length = 7, DifferAt('Dolly  ', 'Dolores') gives 4 and DifferAt('Humbert', 'Humbert') gives 0.

**11.12** Here is a nifty way to trace the execution of any sort procedure based on swaps. First choose a small value of n — no more than 10. Choose Stops In from the Run menu and place a STOP sign just after the call of procedure swap. It may be necessary to enclose the call in **begin** and **end** and place the STOP to the left of the **end**. Open the Observe window, and enter all the elements of the array, in order. Also enter the subscripts of the two indexed-variables appearing in the call of swap. Run the test program by choosing Go-Go from the Run menu. If it runs too quickly, run by repeatedly using the keyboard equivalent of Go.

Do this for each of our three implementations of procedure sort, using TestSort as the test-driver. For sorts that base a swap on a comparison of the elements, such as both versions of bubble sort, you might also like to put a STOP at the left of the comparison, so that the values of the subscripts are updated.

**11.13** Why not use one of our four versions of linear search to implement function IndexOfMax?

**11.14** Does our selection sort always give arguments for function IndexOfMax for which left ≤ right?

**11.15** Modify selection sort to avoid a swap if MaxAt = NrLeft.

**11.16** Given the same context as for procedure sort (except count = 0.. Maxint) implement the following function.

```
function NumberOfInversions (var A : values;
                             n : count) : count;
{ Returns the number of out-of-order pairs of elements }
{ in A[1..n]. }
```

For example, if n = 4 and A[1..4] contains (4, 3, 7, 1), the collection of all pairs of element values is **(4, 3)**, (4, 7), **(4, 1)**, (3, 7), **(3, 1)**, **(7, 1)**; the number of inversions is 4, corresponding to the bold pairs.

**11.17** Another sorting algorithm can be based on the general picture shown in Figure 11.7. Progress is made by inserting A[next] into A[1..next −1] so that the non-decreasing order is preserved, moving larger elements one position to the right to make room.

The first two refinements might lead to:

```
var
  next : count; { A[1..next – 1] is in non-decreasing order }
  pos : index; { position to insert A[next]; in 1..next }
  temp : ElementType; { holds A[next] }

for next := 2 to n do
  begin { Insert A[next] so that A[1..next] is sorted }
    Set pos = 1 if A[next] < A[1], otherwise set pos = maximum
    index in 2..next such that A[pos – 1] ≤ A[next];
    temp := A[next];
    Move A[pos..next – 1] to A[pos + 1..next];
    A[pos] := temp
  end
```

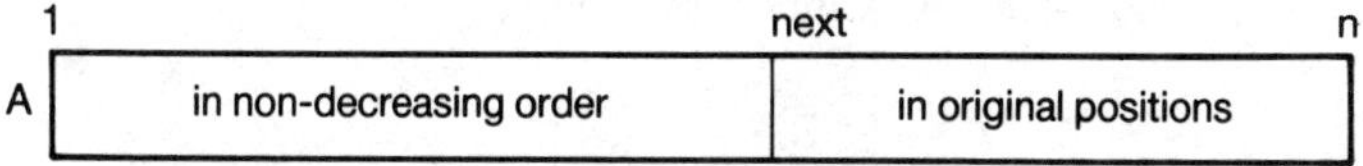


**Figure 11.7** The general picture for insertion sort.

(a) Use a version of linear search (with decreasing rather than increasing values) to implement the first unrefined action. *Hint*: Sentinel search can be used if the case **pos** = 1 is handled separately.

(b) Implement the other unrefined action.

*Note*: A very neat version of this method is possible if A[0] exists, because it can be used in place of **temp**, allowing a sentinel search to be used even if **pos** = 1.

**11.18** Implement the following procedure.

```
procedure reverse (var A : values;
                   left, right : index);
{ Reverses the order of the values in A[left..right]. }
```

*Hint*: Swap elements at equal distances from the ends; draw a general picture before writing.

**11.19** Implement the following procedure.

```
procedure ArraySwap (var V : values;
                     a, b, c : index);
{ Swaps the array sections V[a..b – 1] and V[b..c]. E.g. if }
{ a = 4, b = 7, c = 11, V[4..11] = (2, 4, 6, 8, 10, 12, 14, 16), }
{ then after the swap V[4..11] = (8, 10, 12, 14, 16, 2, 4, 6); }
{ assumes 1 <= a < b <= c <= MaxIndex. }
```

*Hint*: The problem can be solved with just three statements, each a call of procedure **reverse** from the previous question. (The problem occurs in editing, when a block of text is moved from one place to another.)

**11.20** Implement the following procedure in the given context.

```
const
  NumberOfCards = 52; { must be even }
type
  card = ... ;
  number = 1..NumberOfCards;
  deck = array[number] of card;
```

```
procedure PerfectShuffle (var OldDeck, NewDeck : deck);
{ Sets NewDeck by splitting OldDeck exactly in half and }
{ merging the cards, alternating between one half and the }
{ other; the first card should come from the second half. }
{ E.g. if NumberOfCards = 8 and OldDeck contains }
{ (c1, c2, c3, c4, c5, c6, c7, c8), then NewDeck should be }
{ set to (c5, c1, c6, c2, c7, c3, c8, c4). }
```

**11.21** Use the **mod** operation to implement function next in JobScheduler3 with a single assignment statement.

**11.22** What happens if a **dummy** procedure SortIndexes is used in program JobScheduler3, i.e. a stub that does nothing. When might it make sense to do this?

Several challenging exercises involving arrays can be found in the exercises in Chapter 12. The following exercises are substantial programming tasks.

**11.23** Since all the input data is known before JobScheduler3 draws the scheduling diagram, it is possible to adjust the time axis to suit the data. Do so by making Unit a variable and determining its value, and by changing DrawAxes to draw suitably spaced markers.

**11.24** Add graphics output to the histogram of the examination scores program, by drawing a **bar chart**. For each score, draw a rectangle (bar) whose height is proportional to the frequency of that score. Arrange the rectangles along a horizontal axis in order of increasing scores, with regularly spaced labels (i.e. scores) centered beneath the bottom sides of their corresponding rectangles. Draw a vertical axis with markers at the left.

**11.25** Extend program MiniNim in Chapter 9 to play the full game of Nim, in which there are several piles of matches, and on each turn the player may take arbitrarily many (but at least one) from a single pile. Have the program play a woeful game by taking a random number of matches from a random non-empty pile. Enjoy beating it, because in Chapter 17 we shall develop a program that plays perfectly.

# 12 ON CORRECTNESS AND EFFICIENCY

He who has nothing to assert has no style and can have none.
— George Bernard Shaw, *Man and Superman*

## 12.1 Programming methodology

**Programming methodology** means the body of methods used in the programming process; this process can be categorized as follows:

- Formulation of specifications;
- Stepwise refinement, including the choice of types for variables and the decomposition of the program into subprograms;
- Testing;
- Program modification, to repair errors detected in the testing stage (a process which is misleadingly known as *debugging*), to improve the efficiency of the program, or to meet modified specifications (a process which is known as **program maintenance**).

The progression through these stages is by no means strictly sequential. Testing, as we have seen, need not wait until the program is complete, and, moreover, may reveal the need for alterations to the original specifications.

Stepwise refinement, the use of modular subprograms for program decomposition, and the role of testing, have already been examined in some depth, and will continue to be illustrated in the case-studies.

This chapter discusses two other aspects of programming methodology, viz. correctness and efficiency. It commences with a discussion of the use of assertions in program documentation, development, and testing, emphasizing their role in the development of loops, an appreciation of which is a *sine qua non* for the serious programmer. It closes with a brief introduction to the measurement and achievement of efficiency of programs.

# 12.2 Assertions and invariants

## 12.2.1 ASSERTIONS

Our programming style has exploited comments for four purposes:

(1) To stand for high-level actions, thereby documenting the stepwise refinements which led to the solution of a programming problem.

(2) To describe the purpose of each variable, unless this is clear from its name or its use.

(3) To describe the assumptions and effect of each subprogram, including the program itself, in terms of its parameters. (The parameters of the program are its external files.)

(4) To comment about a Pascal statement, as in these two examples from program Arithmetic for Case-study 5. The first, from procedure EndTest, explains a subtlety:

```
NewTest(a, op, b); { leaves actual-parameter for op unchanged }
```

The second, from procedure test, illustrates a more common situation, where the remaining case to be treated by a nest of conditional statements is described:

```
else { ch is none of 'q', 'Q', '=' }
  outcome := query
```

Uses (3) and (4) are examples of an important notion, that of an **assertion**. (We shall see later that the other uses can also be treated as being in this category.) An assertion is a claim about the variables and the parameters of a (sub)program at the point where the assertion is made. Consider the example immediately above. The assertion:

```
{ ch is none of 'q', 'Q', '=' }
```

claims that whenever the hand that traces the execution of the program reaches the line:

```
else { ch is none of 'q', 'Q', '=' }
```

then the value of ch is not any of the three values shown. This is always the case, and we say that the assertion is **valid**.

### 12.2.2 SPECIFICATIONS

As we saw in Chapter 9, comments of type (3), i.e. specifications, have two parts: a precondition, stating the assumptions made by the subprogram, and a postcondition, stating the effect of its execution (provided the assumptions hold). Here is an example from Chapter 11:

```
function FirstNonZero (var h : histogram) : ScoreRange;
{ Returns the least index of a non-zero element of h; }
{ assumes at least one element is non-zero. }
```

The precondition is an assertion at the start of the subprogram. In the above case, the claim is that before executing the statement-part of FirstNonZero, at least one element of h is non-zero. The postcondition is an assertion at the end of the subprogram. In the above case, the claim is that after execution of the statement-part, the pseudo-variable FirstNonZero is the least index of a non-zero element of h.

### 12.2.3 EXPRESSING ASSERTIONS

Simple assertions may be written as Boolean expressions. For example, the assertion about the value of ch may be written:

```
{ (ch <> 'q') and (ch <> 'Q') and (ch <> '=') }
```

For this assertion to be valid means that, if its value is observed whenever execution reaches the line containing it, the result is always **true**.

More complex assertions, particularly specifications, need a more powerful language. Later on in your study of programming you should be introduced to suitable **specification-languages**, which derive from mathematical logic. The reference at the end of this chapter is a good starting point. We shall content ourselves with precise and concise technical English.

The ability to write and reason about assertions is important, which is why formal, i.e. mathematical, methods are attractive. An example concerning the operators **mod** and **div** is given in the next section.

When assertions are included in the statement part of a subprogram, they should be distinguished from comments describing high-level actions. In the style advocated in this book, every high-level action is distinguished by starting with a verb (in the imperative mood, written with an upper-case first letter). Moreover, the refinement of a high-level action is indented with respect to its comment whenever possible (in Macintosh Pascal).

### 12.2.4 PROVING A PROGRAM CORRECT

The main concern of a programmer should be to write *correct* programs. The importance of assertions is that they are the best way to reason, i.e. think, about programs, whether that be done by formal means or not. And a programmer must be able to do so if he or she is confidently to create correct programs. Testing is not enough. As pointed out by one of the most insightful thinkers about programming, E. W. Dijkstra:

> Program testing can be used to show the presence of bugs, but never to show their absence.

Assertions are used to reason about a program as follows. Every subprogram, including the main program, is provided with specifications. The precondition of the program itself states the assumptions made about the input data. The postcondition states what output is produced on its external files. The programmer must write a statement-part that produces the desired output given the expected form of input. Wherever a subprogram is called, its precondition must be shown to be valid just before the call (with actual parameters replacing formal parameters). Provided the subprogram is correct, its post-condition will be valid just after the call. Knowing the effect of each statement, the programmer reasons that the desired postcondition of the program must be valid.

The correctness of subprograms is shown in exactly the same way. If the subprogram is modular, its correctness will not depend on assertions about non-local objects such as global variables, which is a great advantage, because it can then be reasoned about in isolation.

Reasoning about the effect of a simple statement is usually fairly straightforward. And for a conditional statement, one just reasons about each of the two possible outcomes. However, loops cause Big Problems. It is much harder to feel confident about the effect of a statement that may execute a component statement a great and often unknown number of times.

Fortunately, a powerful and completely adequate technique is known for reasoning about loops. It is based on special assertions called *invariants*, which made an appearance in the previous chapter under the guise of *general pictures*.

### 12.2.5 INVARIANTS

The while-loop is the fundamental form of repetition; it can be used to express every other form of loop. So let us consider the generic while-loop:

```
while C do
  S
```

Suppose the following two properties of a particular while-loop can be demonstrated to hold:

(1) An assertion $I$ just before the loop is valid, i.e. always true when execution reaches that point.

(2) If both $I$ and $C$ are true before $S$ is executed, then $I$ must be true afterwards. Then no matter how many times $S$ is executed, the assertion $I$ placed just before evaluation of the condition $C$ is valid, i.e. $I$ is true prior to each evaluation of $C$. $I$ is called an **invariant assertion** (or just **invariant**) of the loop.

Suppose that execution of the loop terminates. Then $I$ must be true, since it is always true before evaluation of $C$, and execution of $C$ cannot change any values, because we never write functions that have side-effects. But $C$ must be false for the loop to terminate. We therefore know a valid assertion for just after the loop, namely:

{ $I$ and not $C$ }

So provided we can demonstrate that the loop terminates, we have determined something about the effect of executing it. Let us call our result the **Invariance Theorem**.

Here is a simple example of its application. Suppose the operations **div** and **mod** are not provided, so we write the following procedure that implements both together.

```
procedure divide (x, y : count;
                       var q, r : count);
{ Sets q = x div y and r = x mod y; assumes y > 0. }
begin { divide }
  r := x;
  q := 0;
  { Invariant: (x = q * y + r) and (r >= 0) }
  while r >= y do
    begin
      r := r - y;
      q := q + 1
    end
end; { divide }
```

Note that an invariant assertion is not indented with respect to the loop that follows it.

Proving that divide is correct means showing the validity of the postcondition:

{ (q = x div y) and (r = x mod y) }

assuming the validity of the precondition:

{ (x >= 0) and (y > 0) }

The assumption about x is implicit in its type.

A purported invariant has been provided, so we begin by establishing its validity by showing that the two conditions of the Invariance Theorem do indeed hold. The first is easy: after the assignments to r and q, the invariant is indeed true, since:

(x = 0 * y + x) and (x ⩾ 0)

Now for the second condition. We may suppose that $I$ and $C$ are true before executing $S$, i.e. that:

(x = q * y + r) and (r ⩾ 0) and (r ⩾ y)

With a smidgen of algebra we obtain:

(x = (q + 1) * y + (r – y)) and ((r – y) ⩾ 0)

Executing the body of the loop, $S$, stores q + 1 in q and r – y in r. So afterwards,

(x = q * y + r) and (r ⩾ 0)

i.e. $I$ is still true as required. So by the Invariance Theorem, when the loop stops we have:

(x = q * y + r) and (0 ⩽ r < y)

But this is equivalent to the desired postcondition (it is the *definition* of **div** and **mod**). Hence procedure divide is correct, provided the loop always terminates.

### 12.2.6 PROVING TERMINATION

In practice, it is usually much easier to demonstrate that a loop terminates than it is to discover an invariant for it. In particular, the rules of Pascal are such that for-loops always terminate, provided that execution of the body of the loop always terminates. This is the main contribution of for-loops, and it is a very worthwhile one.

In the above example, $r \geqslant 0$ is invariantly true before evaluation of the condition. Also, r is strictly decreased by execution of the body of the loop, because $y > 0$. So the loop cannot execute forever.

This suggests a general technique for showing termination. We find an integer expression that is always non-negative before evaluation of the condition of the loop, and that is strictly decreased by execution of the body of the loop. The initial value of that expression is then a bound on the number of executions of the body of the loop. We have seen that r is one such expression for the above example. One that gives a tighter bound is r **div** y.

### 12.2.7 SOLVING PROBLEMS WITH INVARIANTS

Proving the correctness of programs, whether it is carried out as formally as in the above example or not, boils down to having appropriate specifications and an invariant for each loop. For a substantial program, it might seem like an enormous task to come up with all these assertions as, indeed, it would be if the assertions had to be added after the fact.

But that is no way to obtain correct programs. Correct programs are obtained by carefully reasoning about each stage in the programming process. In particular, by reasoning about each refinement made in the process of stepwise refinement. Specifications emerge naturally when we introduce procedures and functions to carry out certain computations. We have already developed the habit of carefully specifying each subprogram, yielding its precondition and postcondition.

What about invariants? Well, it turns out that the Invariance Theorem is by far the most important tool that we have for developing loops, which is the hardest single aspect of solving programming problems.

| **Principle** Writing a loop amounts to finding an invariant. |
|---|

Because once the invariant *I* is known, the three-step process presented in Chapter 11 can be used to develop the loop, which is guaranteed to be correct. We recapitulate:

(1) Write initialization actions that make the invariant *I* true. This corresponds to the first requirement of the Invariance Theorem.

(2) Obtain a termination condition **not** *C* that together with the invariant *I* establishes the desired result. Negate it to obtain the condition *C* of the while-loop.

(3) Write the body of the loop to make progress without disturbing the invariant. This corresponds to the second requirement of the Invariance Theorem. Making progress corresponds to decreasing the non-negative integer-valued expression used to prove termination.

If the loop is more naturally expressed as a repeat- or for-loop, we do so. However, with repeat-loops, we must check that the original while-loop would have executed at least once.

All right. But how are invariants found? There are several useful techniques, but they all share the property of being **goal-directed**.

> **Principle** Programming is a goal-directed activity. Create invariants by generalizing the desired assertions.

One specific technique was presented in Chapter 11 — the general picture. Many others will emerge with thoughtful experience. A very good source is the book by David Gries mentioned at the end of this chapter.

So the issue of correctness is not something that need raise its ugly head after writing a (probably incorrect) program, but something that should guide the programming process. Correct programs can be obtained as a matter of course. We proceed to illustrate this style — the thinking person's style! — of programming.

### 12.2.8 AN EXAMPLE OF CORRECTNESS-ORIENTED PROGRAMMING

Given is an array-section L[1..n] of non-decreasing values. Our problem is to find the index of a given value x, if it is present. The problem is presented in a deliberately (and typically) vague manner. It is up to the programmer to decide what should be done if x is not present, or present in more than one element, and how best to package the solution.

We decide to write a subprogram, and begin by seeking a sensible postcondition. Let us decide to find the greatest index $i$ just after which x can be inserted to preserve the ordering, defining $i = 0$ if x < L[1]. This appeals because it finesses the question of what to do if x is not present: x is present iff $i \neq 0$ and x = L[$i$].

It is much more convenient to work with a more formal postcondition. We might try to characterize $i$ as follows:

$$L[i] \leqslant x < L[i+1]$$

This does not quite work, because when $i = 0$ it requires L[0] ⩽ x, and when $i$ = n it requires x < L[n + 1]. Rather than complicate the formal postcondition, let us just pretend that:

$$L[0] = -\infty < x < +\infty = L[n + 1]$$

This is harmless provided L[0] and L[n + 1] are not referenced by our subprogram. We have arrived at the specifications for a subprogram, and choose a function because a single value is being returned. It is natural to allow the case n = 0.

```
const
  MaxIndex = ... ; { >= 1 }
type
  index = 1..MaxIndex;
  ExtendedIndex = 0..MaxIndex;
  values = array[index] of ItemType;

function IndexOf (x : ItemType;
                  var L : values;
                  n : ExtendedIndex) : ExtendedIndex;
{ Assumes L[1..n] is non-decreasing; returns i such that }
{ L[i] <= x < L[i + 1], pretending L[0] < x and x < L[n + 1]. }
```

*ItemType* must be an ordinal type, real, or a Pascal- or Mac-string-type, in order for elements to be ordered and compared.

The precondition implies, by fiat, that:

$$L[0] < x < L[n + 1]$$

Using a local variable i to compute the result, the postcondition is:

$$(L[i] \leq x < L[i + 1]) \text{ and } (0 \leq i \leq n)$$

A suitable invariant will generalize both of these, like a general picture. Let us decide on the following, which, roughly speaking, says that at a general point in the computation, we know the limits of the interval containing x:

$$(L[i] \leq x < L[j]) \text{ and } (0 \leq i < j \leq n + 1)$$

A new local variable j has been introduced.

Writing the loop amounts to following the three steps given previously. First, the initialization. This is obtained by matching the precondition to the invariant:

```
i := 0;
j := n + 1
```

Second, the termination condition. This is obtained by matching the postcondition to the invariant. The termination condition clearly is j = i + 1. We negate the termination condition to obtain the condition of the while-loop: j <> i + 1.

Finally, the body of the loop must make progress without disturbing the invariant. Progress is made by decreasing j – i. We could do this by examining L[i] or L[j], but after our experience with the dictionary in the first chapter, and program YouGuess3 in Chapter 3, we decide that we should look half-way between i and j, thereby exploiting the ordering of the array-section to speed up the search.

The index (i + j) **div** 2 will do, because the condition of the loop guarantees that i + 1 < j, so this value will be strictly between i and j. So let us set a local variable mid to this value, and examine L[mid]. If L[mid] ≤ x, then i can be set to mid without disturbing the invariant. Otherwise, x < L[mid], so j can be set to mid. In either case progress is made, so we have completed the body of the loop.

The body of the function is as follows:

```
  var
    i : ExtendedIndex;
    j : 1..Maxint; { in 1..n + 1 }
    mid : index; { = (i + j) div 2 }
begin { IndexOf }
  i := 0;
  j := n + 1;
  { Invariant: (0 <= i < j <= n + 1) and (L[i] <= x < L[j]) }
  while i + 1 <> j do
    begin
      mid := (i + j) div 2; { i < mid < j }
      if L[mid] <= x then
        i := mid
      else
        j := mid
    end;
  IndexOf := i
end; { IndexOf }
```

There is no need to prove IndexOf is correct — it was *born* to be correct. Notice that the invariant is left as documentation. An assertion to the right of a statement, such as the one about mid above, is to be taken as applying after execution of that statement.

> **Principle** Assertions, especially invariants, are the best form of documentation.

It is a mechanical task for the reader familiar with the use of assertions and invariants to check the correctness of function IndexOf.

The algorithm that we have used is called **binary search**. Our version is due to E. W. Dijkstra; the idea of using the phantom values L[0] and L[n + 1] is due to David Gries.

### 12.2.9 OTHER EXAMPLES OF INVARIANTS

General pictures, as introduced in Chapter 11, are a helpful but imprecise example of invariants. Pictures are incapable of representing every possibility, especially pathological ones such as empty array-sections. Furthermore, they are difficult to use as documentation. For these reasons it is best to learn to express invariants in a more precise form. For example, the general picture that describes the idea behind both insertion sort and bubble sort may be expressed as an invariant as follows:

```
{ Invariant: A[1..n] contains a permutation of its initial values, }
{ A[NrLeft + 1..n] are in their final sorted positions, }
{ and 1 <= NrLeft <= n. }
```

When a for-loop is equipped with an invariant, as in this case, it should be thought of as being placed just before the implicit check that the tentative next value of the control variable is within the given limit.

It is possible to be more precise. For example, the second clause in the invariant, viz.:

> A[NrLeft + 1..n] are in their final sorted positions

can be expressed more formally as:

> A[NrLeft + 1..n] is in non-decreasing order, and
> no value in A[1..NrLeft] exceeds any value in A[NrLeft + 1..n].

The best level of expression for invariants is a matter of taste and judgment.

Invariants for loops in program segments given earlier in this book have often been implicit in the comments following the declaration of the variables involved. (This is how comments of type (1) can be regarded as assertions.) It is more helpful, especially in subtle cases, to present the invariant explicitly just before the loop. Consider, for example, function sorted from Chapter 11. The variable SortedSoFar was declared with:

```
var
  SortedSoFar : Boolean; { true iff A[1..i] is sorted }
```

The condition of the while-loop is:

SortedSoFar **and** (i < n)

The loop can be documented with the following invariant:

{ Invariant: SortedSoFar is true iff A[1..i] is sorted, and i <= n }

The Invariance Theorem tells us that when the loop stops we have:

SortedSoFar is true iff A[1..i] is sorted, and i ≤ n, and
**not** (SortedSoFar **and** (i < n))

This implies:

(**not** SortedSoFar **and** A[1..i] is not sorted) **or**
(SortedSoFar **and** A[1..n] is sorted)

Therefore A[1..n] is sorted iff SortedSoFar is true, as required.

### 12.2.10 HOW INVARIANTS EXPEDITE TESTING

The short answer to the question of how invariants expedite testing is that, in the hands of a master at least, they rule out all but typographical errors. (See the provocative quote introducing Chapter 4.) More realistically, they help in catching the most elusive errors, the bane of every debugger. For suppose that extensive execution testing shows that, at a certain stage in execution, a certain variable has an incorrect value. Suppose further that it received that value as a result of executing a loop. If the loop is not obviously incorrect, and the programmer cannot formulate an invariant, the tester has no way of discovering *why* the final value is incorrect, because there is no way of recognizing an incorrect intermediate value.

On the other hand, if an invariant is present as documentation, the tester has an assertion which may be checked before each iteration of the body of the loop, permitting the first incorrect intermediate value to be detected.

**Principle** Take the trouble to give invariants for loops. Not only will you greatly reduce the likelihood of errors, but if an error should occur, you will have the information you need to discover its cause. *If you do not know how the loop* should *be working, you can not fix it.*

Some languages or implementations permit **executable asser-**

**tions**; the idea is to evaluate each assertion when it is encountered, and to stop the program if the result is false. The computer thus relieves much of the burden of testing. A particularly useful feature of Pascal is subrange types. Use them fanatically — they are a form of executable assertion! It is much better for an error to be detected early, rather than later when its consequences eventually become apparent or, even worse, go undetected.

## 12.3 Efficiency

### 12.3.1 INTRODUCTION

This book concentrates on efficiency of programming rather than efficiency of programs. Correctness and clarity must be the programmer's primary concerns. It does not matter how efficient an incorrect program is — the minimal program is useless, but it is certainly efficient.

Efficiency is not an important issue in many contexts. Consider an interactive program that runs only on a single-user system such as a Macintosh; the programs MiniNim and Arithmetic from Chapters 9 and 10 respectively are two examples. The user will be happy as long as the dialog flows smoothly *on a human time-scale*. It matters not whether it takes a millisecond or half a second to process input, although the respective processing speeds differ by a factor of 500.

Inefficiency is tolerable for programs that do not consume many resources in their lifetime, such as programs that are run only once or twice, or very infrequently. It is not worth spending an extra five hours on a program to decrease its total running time by 15 minutes. Computer time and memory are becoming cheaper; programmer time is becoming more expensive.

Nevertheless, efficiency is sometimes quite important. Programs that simulate and predict natural phenomena such as weather had better run appreciably faster than Father Time. Programs that run frequently or for long periods, especially on computers which support many users, should preferably use as few resources as possible. Speed is critical for programs that process events in real-time; memory-space is critical for heavily used systems programs.

We proceed to discuss the two basic aspects of efficiency, viz. how it is measured and how it is achieved.

### 12.3.2 PERFORMANCE EVALUATION

The two major resources of a computer are main memory and CPU-time. The demands of a program or subprogram on each of these resources will generally vary with the input data or input parameters respectively, the computer on which it is run, and the translator (and hence the programming language).

Let us concentrate for now on CPU-time, since it is normally the more important factor when efficiency is important. Consider procedure **sort** as implemented with the first version of bubble sort in Chapter 11:

```
procedure sort (var A : values; n : count);
{ Sorts A[1..n] into non-decreasing order. }
{ Global subprogram: swap. }
  var
    NrLeft : count; { only A[1..NrLeft] remains to be sorted }
    k : index; { A[k] & A[k + 1] are compared }
begin { sort }
  for NrLeft := n downto 2 do
    for k := 1 to NrLeft – 1 do
      if A[k] > A[k + 1] then
        swap(A[k], A[k + 1])
end; { sort }
```

Its running-time is a function of n. The precise function varies with the computer and translator, but it is nevertheless possible usefully to characterize it, because what is of interest is the running-time for *large* values of n. Almost any algorithm will do to sort five items, but not so for 100 000 items.

Consider an execution of a particular machine-language version of this procedure. The running time is dominated by the executions of the if-statement (and the accompanying implicit incrementing and comparison of k with NrLeft – 1). For a given value of NrLeft, this happens NrLeft – 1 times. Since NrLeft takes on the values n, n – 1, ... , 2, the total number of executions of the if-statement is given by:

$$(n-1) + (n-2) + \cdots + 1 = \frac{n^2 - n}{2}$$

The time taken to execute an instance of the if-statement depends on whether or not a swap is done; but, for a particular machine-language version, the time is between two (small) positive values. The total running-time therefore grows as does $n^2$. This characterizes the efficiency of the algorithm with respect to time; we say that its **time-complexity** is **order** $n^2$, or **quadratic** in the **problem size** n.

Now consider New Improved Bubble Sort With Early Termination (see Chapter 11). It sometimes executes in time proportional to n, e.g. when A[1..n] is initially in sorted order. Yet there are cases in which it takes time proportional to $n^2$, e.g. when A[1..n] is initially in the reverse of sorted order. For this reason, two measures of complexity are distinguished: **worst-case** and **average-case**. The worst-case time-complexity of New Improved Bubble Sort is order $n^2$. In general, average-case complexity is much more difficult to define and compute, because it depends on statistical distributions of the input values. If all possible orderings of A[1..n] are assumed to be equally likely, it can be shown that the average-case time-complexity of New Improved Bubble Sort is also order $n^2$.

An algorithm called *heapsort* has a worst-case time-complexity of order nlogn; another called *quicksort* has an average-case time-complexity of order nlogn, but a worst-case time-complexity of $n^2$. These are regarded as more efficient with respect to time than either version of bubble sort. To see why, suppose bubble sort executes about $5n^2$ machine instructions in the worst-case, compared to $15\log_2 n$ for heapsort. (Here $\log_2$ denotes log to the base 2, a commonly occurring function in computing.) The ratio of these numbers is:

$$\frac{\text{instructions executed for bubble sort}}{\text{instructions executed for heapsort}} = \frac{n}{3\log n}$$

This grows without limit with n. So even though bubble sort actually may be slightly faster for small values of n, it is much slower for large values. For example, with $n = 2^{15} = 32768$, bubble sort would take over 700 times longer!

Reductions to the order of complexity are overwhelmingly more important than reductions to the constant factor. Table 12.1 ranks some commonly occurring orders of complexity and gives their English terms. Complexity increases going down.

A very broad distinction can be made. Algorithms whose time-complexity is bounded by a constant power of n are called **polynomial-time** algorithms. They are regarded as useful, in that

**Table 12.1** Increasing orders of complexity.

| Order | Description |
|---|---|
| 1 | constant |
| $\log n$ | logarithmic |
| $n$ | linear |
| $n \log n$ | |
| $n\sqrt{n}$ | |
| $n^2$ | quadratic |
| $n^3$ | cubic |
| $c^n$ | exponential |

significantly bigger problems can be solved if significantly more time is allocated, particularly as powers larger than 3 are uncommon in practice. Algorithms that are not polynomial-time are regarded as useless in practice, in that the running-time grows far too quickly for problems of significant size to be solved. The distinction is not absolutely clear-cut. For example an algorithm whose time complexity is $n^{\log(\log n)}$ is 'almost polynomial', since $\log(\log n)$ grows very slowly with $n$. But the broad division is an important one, particularly for the theoretical study of the complexity of algorithms.

Here are the worst-case time-complexities of some algorithms that we have encountered:

- Naive computation of lpf($n$), the least prime factor of $n$ (Chapter 6): order lpf($n$)
- Improved computation of lpf($n$) (Chapter 7): order minimum of lpf($n$) and $\sqrt{n}$
- Linear search in an array-section of $n$ elements (Chapter 11): order $n$ (hence the name)
- Binary search in an ordered array-section of $n$ elements (Chapter 12): order $\log n$
- Selection sort with an array-section of $n$ elements (Chapter 11): order $n^2$

Let us now consider the resource of main memory. The amount of space consumed by a subprogram is that occupied by the machine-language instructions, plus the maximum amount of space needed for variables that come into existence when it is executed. Note that only the formal parameters and local variables of active subprograms actually consume space (and that a variable-formal-parameter consumes only constant space). The amount of space for the code and for simple variables does not vary with the input values (in the absence of recursion — see Chapter 18). It is the space for arrays that dominates for large problem sizes. Again the same principles apply. We say that the **space-complexity** of an algorithm is order $f(n)$ if the maximum amount of space created by execution of the algorithm is proportional to $f(n)$. The unit may be cells or bits. The space needed for the input values is not normally counted, being regarded as part of the problem rather than the algorithm that solves it. Thus the space-complexity (in cells) of each of the sorting algorithms presented in Chapter 11 is constant. However, if function IndexOfMax declared array A as a value-parameter, its space-complexity, and therefore that of selection sort also, would be linear.

Many, er, complexities, have been swept under the rug in the above account. For example, the running-time or space-consumption might vary with two or more independent quantities, which jointly constitute the problem size. Also, special mathematical notation is used to reason more precisely about complexities. The most important is the notation:

$$f(n) = O(g(n))$$

which means that there is an integer $n_0 \geqslant 0$ and a real number $c > 0$ such that $f(n) \leqslant c\, g(n)$ for all $n \geqslant n_0$, i.e. that $f(n)$ is bounded above by a constant multiple of $g(n)$ for all sufficiently large values of $n$. Typically, $f(n)$ is the time- or space-complexity for a problem of size $n$, and $g(n)$ a familiar function. We should read this as:

$f(n)$ is of order at most $g(n)$

Thus, for example, we can say that the time-complexity of the naive version of function lpf is $O(n)$.

### 12.3.3 CREATING EFFICIENT PROGRAMS

There are two basic ways of improving the efficiency of a solution to a programming problem. One is to find a new solution with a lower order of complexity. This offers by far the best chance of big gains in efficiency, but typically demands cleverness and insight. The other is to transform the current solution to increase its efficiency. This is usually easier, but can decrease the clarity of the solution, making it harder to maintain; also, the gain is usually a reduction in the constant factor, which is much less significant than a reduction in order.

Before embarking on either approach, you should discover which part of the solution dominates the complexity. Usually only a small part of a program dominates its execution time — the body of the innermost loop — and it is not worthwhile seeking improvements elsewhere.

Various techniques can help to improve the efficiency of an algorithm. Some are a matter of habit. For instance, we always use while- rather than for-loops for linear searches, so that they might terminate as soon as possible; and we avoid using local arrays, even though solutions employing them are often much easier to find. A good example of the latter policy is procedure RotateAnti in the next chapter. A very general technique is to make maximal use of previously computed values. An example of this is the exploitation of the mathematical notion of a *recurrence*. For example, in refining the action:

*Set* A[i] = 1 + 2 + ... + i, *for* i = 1, 2, ... , n,

A[i + 1] should be computed by adding i + 1 to A[i]. Recurrences occur frequently in numeric computation. Another instance of this class of techniques is to avoid recomputing subexpressions, especially if they contain function designators.

A typical transformation that improves efficiency concerns an expression that is computed in a loop. If the value of the expression is not changed by the body of the loop, it can safely be computed prior to the loop. An example occurs in procedure FillCell in Case-study 7 in the next chapter.

This is not the place to give general advice about discovering efficient algorithms; instead the reader is referred to the further reading list at the end of this chapter. We will confine ourselves to one observation and one example. The observation is that efficient algorithms are usually based on properties of the abstract objects being manipulated. These *may* be deep mathematical results, but it is surprising how often simple insights pay big dividends. Sometimes just expressing the specifications formally is enough. Here is an example. Our problem is to complete the following function in the given context:

```
const
  MaxIndex = ... ; { >= 1 }
type
  index = 1..MaxIndex;
  values = array[index] of ElementType;

function WrongPos (var A : values; n : index) : index;
{ Returns index of first element of A[1..n] that would have a }
{ different value if A[1..n] were sorted into non-decreasing }
{ order, or n if A[1..n] is in non-decreasing order. }
```

For example, if B[1..4] contains (5, 6, 8, 7), WrongPos(B, 4) should return 3, since if B[1..4] were sorted it would contain (5, 6, 7, 8), and the first discrepancy is in the third position. Since this is a function, it must not sort the array. Also, it should not use local array variables unless absolutely necessary.

The naive solution is to check each position 1,2,3, ... in turn:

```
var
  i : index;
  InPosition : Boolean;
begin { WrongPos }
 i := 1;
 InPosition := true;
 { Invariant: InPosition is true iff A[1..i – 1] are in sorted positions,
              and i <= n }
 while InPosition and (i < n) do
```

```
  If A[i] is not in its sorted position, set InPosition = false,
      otherwise increment i;
  WrongPos := i
end; { WrongPos }
```

This uses a variant of schema Complex While Loop in which only the part of the condition that cannot be written as a Boolean expression is moved inside the loop.

The unrefined action amounts to searching A[i + 1..n] for a value < A[i]. Searching backwards from A[n] avoids the need for a Boolean variable:

```
var
  j : index;

{ If A[i] is not in its sorted position, set InPosition = false, }
{ otherwise increment i }
begin
  j := n;
  { Invariant: A[i] <= all of A[j + 1..n] }
  while (j > i) and (A[j] >= A[i]) do
    j := j – 1;
  if j > i then
    InPosition := false
  else
    i := i + 1
end
```

formally." You might like to compare this solution with one that uses a forward search.

The worst-case time-complexity of this solution occurs when A[1..n] is in sorted order; it is not difficult to see that it is order $n^2$.

Our intuition tells us that we should be able to do better. Let us start by expressing the postcondition more formally, i.e. by formally characterizing the value of WrongPos. If inspiration is lacking, it is a good idea to try some test cases. Figure 12.1 shows one such case, with

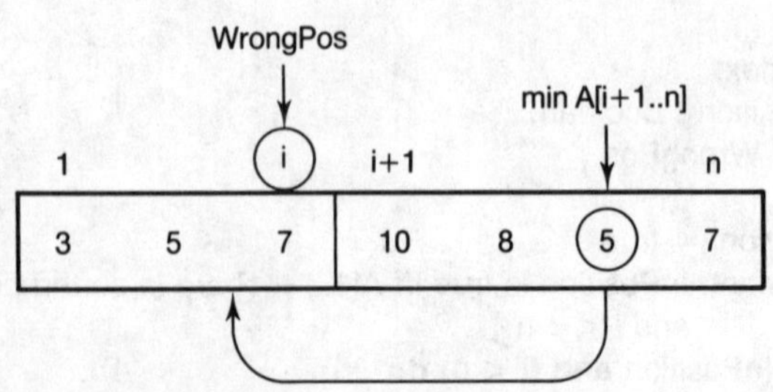


**Figure 12.1**
Defining WrongPos formally.

n = 7 and WrongPos = 3. After considering this and other cases, we arrive at the following specification:

```
{ If A[1..n] is in non-decreasing order, returns n; otherwise }
{ returns the unique value i such that A[1..i] is in non-decreasing }
{ order and A[i – 1] <= minimum of A[i + 1..n] < A[i], }
{ regarding A[0] as –∞. }
```

It is preferable to deduce the specification by mathematical reasoning; the ability to do so will grow with thoughtful experience. However, it is still prudent to test the specification on some examples.

| **Principle** Specifications should also be desk-checked. |
|---|

It is not possible to compute the required value i directly. But we soon realize that we need only find the maximum sorted section starting at A[1]; let this be A[1..k]. For then if k = n, the result is n; otherwise the minimum of A[i + 1..n] is just the minimum of A[k + 1..n]. Comparing Figure 12.2 to Figure 12.1 makes this point clear.

It is apparent that when k < n, the result is just:

```
IndexOf(minimum of A[k + 1..n], A, k) + 1.
```

We have arrived at the following solution:

```
  var
    k : index; { max index such that A[1..k] is in sorted order }
    min : ElementType; { = minimum of A[k + 1..n] }
begin { WrongPos }
  Set k = maximum value such that A[1..k] is in non-decreasing order;
  if k = n then
    WrongPos := n
  else
    begin
      Set min = minimum of A[k + 1..n];
      WrongPos := IndexOf(min, A, k) + 1
    end
end; { WrongPos }
```

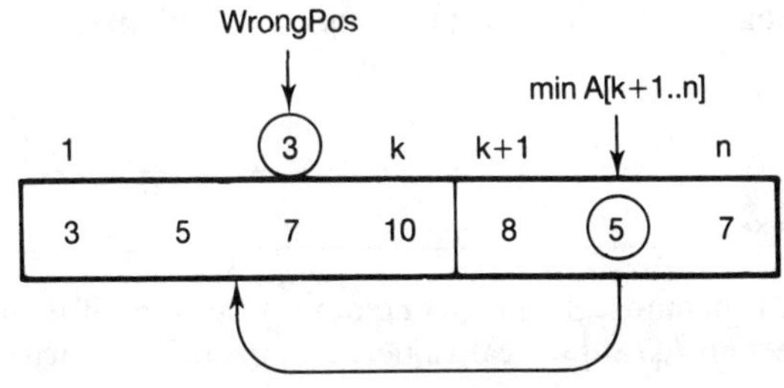


**Figure 12.2** An example of computing WrongPos.

Exercises 12.14 and 12.15 ask you to implement the two unrefined actions. It is clear that the worst-case time-complexity of the resulting function WrongPos is order n, which is a big improvement on the naive solution.

Before embarking on a quest for increased efficiency, it is worthwhile asking whether or not our measure is appropriate. For example, if all orderings of A[1..n] are equally likely, the average-case time-complexity of the original version of WrongPos is constant! This is because it is highly probable that a smaller value than A[1] will be quickly found. A function like WrongPos might very well be used where this assumption is unrealistic; but if it *is* justified, the original algorithm is faster on average, because the average-case time-complexity of the 'improved' version is order n.

It is not difficult to transform the second version of WrongPos so that it has the best of both worlds: a time-complexity that is linear in the worst-case and constant in the average-case (under the above assumption). Exercise 12.16 gives the idea behind the transformation, but leaves the details to the reader.

## 12.4 Further reading


(1) Aho, A. V., Hopcroft, J. E. and Ullman, J. D. (1974). *The Design and Analysis of Computer Algorithms*. Reading, Mass: Addison-Wesley.
A classic advanced text on the design of efficient algorithms.

(2) Bentley, J. L. (1982). *Writing Efficient Programs*. Englewood Cliffs, NJ: Prentice-Hall.
Written by the oyster of the 'Programming Pearls' column in *Communications of the ACM*, which is to programming columns in hobbyist magazines as pearls are to plastic beads.

(3) Gries, D. (1981). *The Science of Programming*. New York: Springer-Verlag.
Develops the basic logical apparatus needed for writing formal assertions, and convincingly shows how to exploit invariants in developing solutions to programming problems. Chock-a-block with elegant solutions to challenging problems.


## EXERCISES

**12.1** Write a program-segment that computes the sum of the elements in the array-section A[1..n] of real values, and document it with an invariant.

**12.2** Pick one of the Linear Search schemas given in Chapter 11 and use the Invariance Theorem to prove that it is correct. After that, you really can use the schema with confidence.

**12.3** Find another introductory programming textbook that uses Pascal — if you haven't done so already! — and see if it presents a version of binary search. If it doesn't, trash it. Otherwise give the invariant and use it to prove that the version is correct (or otherwise). Demonstrate that the loop terminates (or otherwise). Which version was easier to understand?

**12.4** Complete the following function in the given context.

```
const
  MaxIndex = ... ; { >= 1 }
type
  index = 1..MaxIndex;
  values = array[index] of integer;

procedure split (var A : values;
                     n : index);
{ Rearranges A[1..n] so that the negative values precede the }
{ rest. }
```

Use the following invariant:

```
{ Invariant: A[1..left – 1] are negative, A[right + 1..n] are }
{ non-negative, 1 <= left, and right <= n. }
```

Make progress by decreasing right–left.

**12.5** Define a *plateau* to be an array-section of equal values. Complete the following function:

```
function LongestPlateau (var A : values;
                              n : index) : index;
{ Returns the length of the longest plateau in A[1..n]. }
```

For example, if n = 10 and A[1..10] contains (2, 9, 2, 2, 1, 2, 1, 1, 1, – 1), the longest plateau is 1, 1, 1 which has length 3. Base your solution on the following invariant:

```
{ Invariant: length = length of longest plateau ending at }
{ A[pos – 1], and MaxLength = length of longest plateau in }
{ A[1..pos – 1] }
```

Make progress by increasing pos.

**12.6** Express the following assertions more formally:

(a) A[NrLeft + 1..n] is in non-decreasing order;
(b) no value in A[1..NrLeft] exceeds any value in A[NrLeft + 1..n]

**12.7** Desk-check each of the refinements used in creating each version of function WrongPos at the end of this chapter.

**12.8** What is the time-complexity of the algorithm for computing the number of decimal digits of n? (The algorithm was given in Chapter 5 to illustrate a repeat-loop.)

**12.9** What is the time-complexity of function IsDigit in Chapter 7?

**12.10** What is the time-complexity of computing the first n Fibonacci numbers using your solution to Exercise 6.20(b)?

**12.11** Specify the time-complexity of:

(a) program JobScheduler1 in Chapter 6;
(b) program JobScheduler3 in Chapter 11 (without the graphics).

**12.12** What is the best way to improve the time-complexity of program JobScheduler3 in Chapter 11?

**12.13** Consider procedure ArraySwap implemented as requested in Exercise 11.19.

(a) What is its worst-case time-complexity?
(b) Suppose ArraySwap were implemented by repeatedly shifting all the elements in A[a..c] one position to the left, with A[a] moving to A[c]. What is the time-complexity of this version?

The specification for ArraySwap might have formulated the problem as shifting an array-section a given number of places to the left, with the leftmost element regarded as adjacent to the rightmost. This is called a **circular shift**. If this were the case, it is all too easy to think of solution (b) rather than the much more efficient original solution.

> **Moral** Be wary of reading algorithmic information into a specification, and thereby prejudicing its implementation. Specifications say *what* to do, not *how* to do it.

**12.14** Implement the following action from function WrongPos in the text:

*Set* k = *maximum value such that* A[1..k] *is in non-decreasing order*

Use the following invariant:

```
{ Invariant: increasing = true iff A[1..k] are in non-decreasing }
{ order, and k <= n }
```

**12.15** Implement the following action from function WrongPos:

*Set* min = *minimum of* A[k + 1..n]

Use a familiar schema. What is the invariant in this example?

**12.16** Consider the computation of min in the previous question. If and as soon as min is discovered to be < A[1], the search can stop because WrongPos must be 1. Implement this transformation.

**12.17** Here is a clever attempt at improving the efficiency of WrongPos:

```
  var
    k : index; { max index such that A[1..k] is in sorted order }
    i : 1..Maxint; { in 1..n + 1 }
    minpos : 0..MaxIndex; { in 0..k – 1 }
begin { WrongPos }
  Set k = maximum value such that A[1..k] are in non-decreasing
  order;
  if k = n then
    WrongPos := n
  else
    begin
      i := k + 2;
      minpos := IndexOf(A[k + 1], A, k);
      { Invariant: A[minpos] <= min A[k + 1..i – 1] < }
      { A[minpos + 1], pretending A[0] = –∞ }
      while (i <= n) and (minpos <> 0) do
        begin
          if A[i] < A[minpos] then
            minpos := IndexOf(A[i], A, minpos);
          i := i + 1
        end;
      WrongPos := minpos + 1
    end
end; { WrongPos }
```

(a) May the third actual parameter in each call of **IndexOf** be reduced by 1?

(b) Desk-check the above implementation with **n** = 11 and **A[1..11]** containing (1, 2, 3, 4, 5, 6, 5, 4, 3, 2, 1).

(c) By considering the trace obtained above, deduce the worst-case time-complexity of this version.

| **Moral** One can be too clever. |
|---|

# 13 MULTIDIMENSIONAL ARRAYS

I am thinking that all these tables might be calculated by machinery.
— Charles Babbage, *Passages from the Life of a Philosopher*

## 13.1 Two-dimensional arrays

### 13.1.1 INTRODUCTION

What do the following have in common: tic-tac-toe (noughts and crosses), chess, Scrabble, crossword puzzles, the Macintosh screen, the bits in the Macintosh's main memory, a giant screen at a sports stadium, a page printed by a laser printer, the seats on an airliner, a train timetable, a spreadsheet, the game-by-game record of turnovers by everyone who played for the New York Knicks last season, the characters in *Dallas*? Right. They are all two-dimensional. More precisely, with a single forgettable exception, they all involve two-dimensional aggregates of things of the same kind.

Two-dimensional information is ubiquitous, and a general-purpose programming language such as Pascal must provide for its manipulation. Pascal does so by allowing arrays to have two (or more) dimensions, i.e. index-types. We begin our examination of them by looking at two typical examples of their use.

### 13.1.2 TWO EXAMPLES

Here are two examples of two-dimensional information:

**Figure 13.1**
Inventory for *Bob and Marge's Gift and Gun.*

| | store 1 | store 2 | store 3 |
|---|---|---|---|
| Barbie doll | 800 | 375 | 25 |
| Rubik's cube | 415 | 77 | 68 |
| Smith and Wesson revolver | 0 | 56 | 13 |
| AK-47 assault rifle | 51 | 109 | 0 |
| Uzi submachine-gun | 5 | 22 | 0 |

| O | | X |
|---|---|---|
| | O | O |
| X | X | X |

**Figure 13.2**
During a game of tic-tac-toe.

(1) Suppose business booms for *Bob and Marge's Gift and Gun* in downtown Lafayette, Indiana, and they decide to open stores in The Village and The Mall, and, naturally, to computerize. Their inventory is shown in Figure 13.1. There are 375 Barbie dolls in store 2, and store 3 has sold out of Uzis.

(2) A tic-tac-toe board, as shown in Figure 13.2. An 'O' has been written in the third column of the second row.

In Pascal, we can represent this information as follows:

(1)

```
const
  NrStores = 3;
type
  count = 0..Maxint;
  StoreNumber = 1..NrStores;
  ItemType = (Barbie, cube, SandW, AK47, Uzi);
  inventory = array[ItemType, StoreNumber] of count;
var
  store : StoreNumber;
  item : ItemType;
  stock : inventory;
```

An element of this 2-dimensional array can be accessed with the indexed-variable:

```
stock[item, store]
```

For example, stock[AK47, 2] is a variable of type count whose current value is 109.

(2)

```
type
  mark = (Empty, O, X);
  index = 1..3;
  board = array[index, index] of mark;
var
  square : board;
  row, col : index;
```

An element of this 2-dimensional array can be accessed with the indexed-variable:

```
square[row, col]
```

For example, **square[3, 1]** is a variable of type **mark** whose current value is X.

It is traditional to diagram a two-dimensional array by associating its first index-type with the rows of a table, and its second index-type with the columns. We shall stick with this convention.

## 13.2 General arrays

### 13.2.1 SYNTAX

The full syntax of Pascal's array-types is as follows:

array-type: **array** [ *index-type-list* ] **of** *component-type*
index-type-list: *index-type* … , *index-type*
index-type: *ordinal-type*
component-type: *type*

And of indexed-variables:

indexed-variable: *array-variable* [ *expression-list* ]
array-variable: *variable*
expression-list: *expression* … , *expression*
variable: *entire-variable* | *component-variable*
entire-variable: *variable-identifier*
component-variable: *indexed-variable*

### 13.2.2 ARRAYS OF ARRAYS

A careful reading of the above syntax rules reveals that the array-variable part of an indexed-variable can itself be an indexed-variable. The reason is that Pascal treats an $n$-dimensional array, $n > 1$, as a 1-dimensional array, each of whose elements is an $(n - 1)$-dimensional array (and so on for the elements if applicable). For example:

```
inventory = array[ItemType, StoreNumber] of count
```

is treated exactly the same as:

```
inventory = array[ItemType] of array [StoreNumber] of count
```

Similarly, instead of:

```
stock[item, store]
```

we may write:

```
stock[item][store]
```

These are not the only consequences. For example, the following is a perfectly legal way of initializing each element of **stock** to zero. It is also probably the quickest, but too unnatural to be recommended.

```
stock[Barbie, 1] := 0;
stock[Barbie, 2] := 0;
stock[Barbie, 3] := 0;
for item := cube to Uzi do
  stock[item] := stock[Barbie]
```

The first three statements are assignments to variables of type count. The body of the for-loop is an array-assignment. Each side is a variable of the same type, viz.:

```
array [StoreNumber] of count
```

The scheme generalizes to higher-dimensional arrays: an $n$-dimensional array A may have between 0 and $n$ subscripts.

Another complication concerns the effect of packing a high-dimensional array. The rule is that putting **packed** in front of an array-type affects the types all the way down the line, even the component-type if it is an unpacked-structured-type. For example, writing:

```
packed array[ItemType, StoreNumber] of count
```

is equivalent to writing:

```
packed array[ItemType] of packed array [StoreNumber] of count
```

## 13.3 Two inventory problems

Suppose Bob and Marge have made us an offer we can not refuse, and we agree to write some stock-control software for them. Consider the following two problems that arise. The first is to implement the action:

*Print the total number of each item*

(assuming the inventory is already defined).

**Figure 13.3**
Output for first inventory problem.

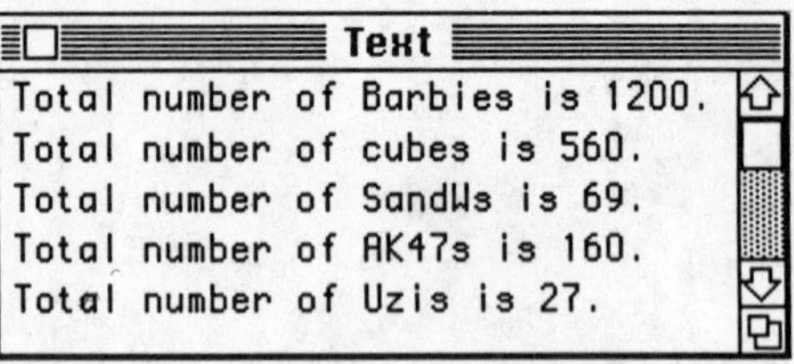

Text
Total number of Barbies is 1200.
Total number of cubes is 560.
Total number of SandWs is 69.
Total number of AK47s is 160.
Total number of Uzis is 27.


This fits the familiar for-loop schema, and we write:

```
var
  TotalItems : count; { total number of item }

{ Print the total number of each item }
  for item := Barbie to Uzi do
    begin
      Set TotalItems = number of item;
      Writeln('Total number of ', item, 's is ', TotalItems : 1, '.')
    end
```

We have exploited Macintosh Pascal's ability to print a string for a value of an enumerated type.

The remaining action can also be refined with a for-loop:

```
{ Set TotalItems = number of item }
  TotalItems := 0;
  for store := 1 to NrStores do
    TotalItems := TotalItems + stock[item, store]
```

The output with the inventory in Figure 13.1 is shown in Figure 13.3.

The other problem is similar; it is to print the total number of items of all kinds held by each store. Exactly the same kind of reasoning leads to the following solution:

```
{ Print total number of items at each store }
  for store := 1 to NrStores do
    begin
    { Set TotalItems = total number of items in store }
      TotalItems := 0;
      for item := Barbie to Uzi do
        TotalItems := TotalItems + stock[item, store];

      Writeln('Total number of items in store ', store : 1, ' is ',
                TotalItems : 1, '.')
    end
```

The output with the inventory in Figure 13.1 is shown in Figure 13.4.

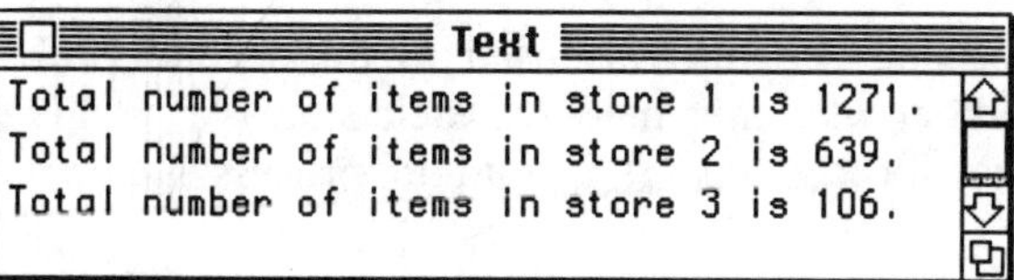
Text
Total number of items in store 1 is 1271.
Total number of items in store 2 is 639.
Total number of items in store 3 is 106.

**Figure 13.4**
Output for second inventory problem.

## 13.4 Two schemas for rectangular array-sections

Our notation for a possibly empty array-section readily generalizes to the multidimensional case. In particular, we use the following notation:

> **Notation** $A[a..b,\ c..d]$ denotes the rectangular section of the two-dimensional array $A$ consisting of the elements $A[i, j]$ with $a \leqslant i \leqslant b$ and $c \leqslant j \leqslant d$.

The solutions to the two inventory problems are typical of a large class of algorithms for two-dimensional arrays. We generalize them to two schemas. The first was used in the first problem (printing totals of each item). It is given as schema Row-Major Processing, which is said to process elements in **row-major order**. Sometimes there will be no need for the initialization or finalization for each row; if neither is needed, the compound statement can be dispensed with.

```
Schema Row-Major Processing:
var
  A : array[IndexType1, IndexType2 ] of ElementType;
          { IndexType1 contains row1..row2 }
          { IndexType2 contains col1..col2 }
{ Process each element of A[row1..row2 , col1..col2], }
{ taking rows in increasing order, and processing each }
{ row from left to right. }
--------------------------------------------------------
  var
    r : a type containing row1..row2 ;
    c : a type containing col1..col2 ;

  for r := row1 to row2 do
    begin
      Initialize for row r;
      for c := col1 to col2 do
        Process A[r, c];
      Finalize for row r
    end
```

The second schema was used in the second problem (printing the total number of items held by each store). It is given as schema Column-Major Processing. It is said to process elements in **column-major order**.

```
Schema Column-Major Processing:
var
  A : array[IndexType1, IndexType2 ] of ElementType;
          { IndexType1 contains row1..row2 }
          { IndexType2 contains col1..col2 }
{ Process each element of A[row1..row2 , col1..col2], }
{ taking columns in increasing order, and processing }
{ each column from top to bottom. }
--------------------------------------------------------
 var
   r : a type containing row1..row2 ;
   c : a type containing col1..col2 ;

 for c := col1 to col2 do
  begin
   Initialize for column c;
   for r := row1 to row2 do
    Process A[r, c];
   Finalize for column c
  end
```

# 13.5 Geometric problems

Another important class of operations on two-dimensional arrays can be categorized as *geometric*. This is not intended to suggest that such algorithms occur only in explicitly geometric application areas, such as computer-aided design, but rather that the operations they perform can be visualized in geometric terms. A notable feature of this class of algorithms is subscript manipulation.

## 13.5.1 PROBLEM ONE

The first problem, stated geometrically, is to revolve a square array-section 180° on its minor diagonal. The *minor diagonal* is the diagonal between the top-right and bottom-left corners. As usual, we shall aim for a solution that rearranges the original array rather than involving another array. Figure 13.5 gives before-and-after diagrams that illustrate the effect of the operation on an array-section A[1..5, 1..5] of

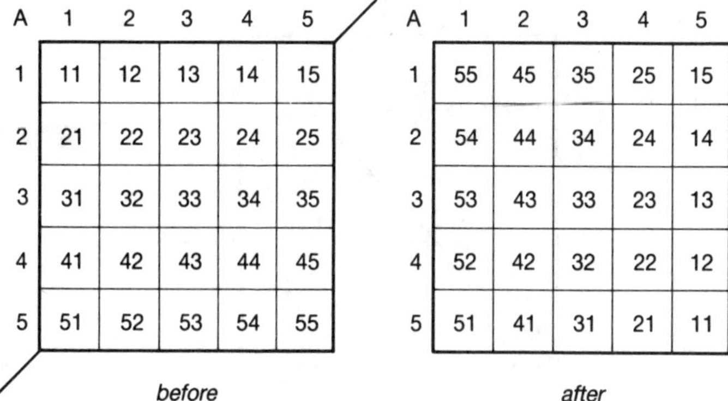


**Figure 13.5**
Revolving A[1..5, 1..5] 180° around its minor diagonal.

integer elements, whose initial values encode their subscripts in an obvious way.

We formulate the problem as a procedure that operates on a square section of a square array:

```
const
  MaxIndex = ... ; { >= 1 }
type
  index = 1..MaxIndex;
  matrix = array[index, index] of ElementType;

procedure MinorFlip (var A : matrix; n : index);
{ Revolves (flips) A[1..n, 1..n] 180 degrees on its minor diagonal. }
```

In trying to understand how the values are rearranged, we start by focusing on a typical element A[i, j]. Its value is exchanged with its mirror-image on the other side of the minor diagonal, as shown in Figure 13.6. The row of the mirror-image is the j'th counting back from the last, i.e. n + 1 – j. Similarly, its column is the i'th counting back from the last, i.e. n + 1 – i. The element is therefore A[n + 1 – j, n + 1 – i]. As a check, we find that *its* mirror-image is A[n + 1 – (n + 1 – i), n + 1 – (n + 1 – j)], which is A[i, j] as expected.

We now need only arrange to find a representative A[i, j] of each pair to be swapped. Let us choose the elements on the same side of the minor diagonal as A[1, 1]. Since there is no point in swapping the elements on the diagonal with themselves, we see that the required elements lie in rows 1 to n – 1; and in row i, the elements we want are in columns 1 to n – i. For example, the representatives for the 5 × 5 case in Figure 13.5 are:

```
A[1, 1]   A[1, 2]   A[1, 3]   A[1, 4]
A[2, 1]   A[2, 2]   A[2, 3]
A[3, 1]   A[3, 2]
A[4, 1]
```

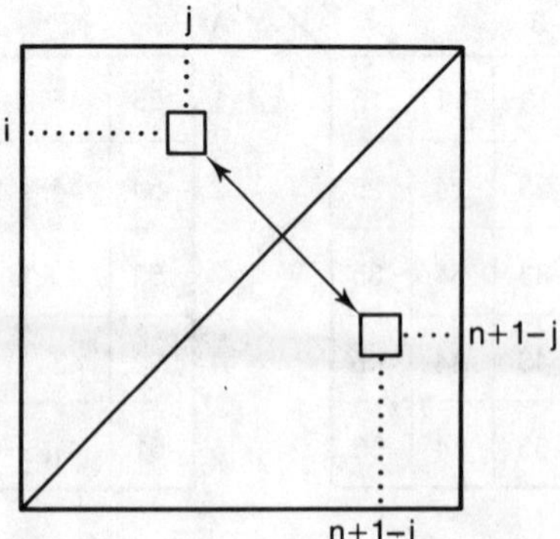


**Figure 13.6**
The typical pair of elements to be swapped.

A solution is now immediate; it processes representatives row-by-row:

```
var
  i, j : index; { A[i, j] is to be swapped with its mirror-image }

begin { MinorFlip }
  for i := 1 to n – 1 do
    for j := 1 to n – i do
      swap(A[i, j], A[n + 1 – j, n + 1 – i])
end; { MinorFlip }
```

### 13.5.2 PROBLEM TWO

The second problem is to rotate a square array-section 90° anticlockwise round its center. Figure 13.7 illustrates the effect of this operation on an array-section A[1..4, 1..4].

We again formulate the problem as a procedure that operates on a square section of a square array:

```
procedure RotateAnti (var A : matrix; n : index);
{ Rotates A[1..n, 1..n] 90 degrees anticlockwise round its center. }
```

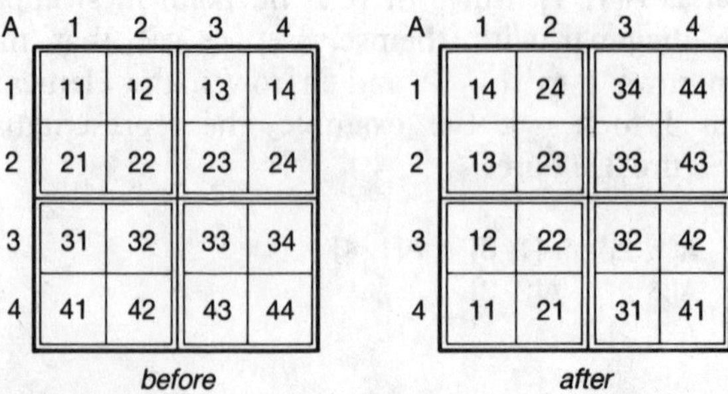

| A | 1 | 2 | 3 | 4 |
|---|---|---|---|---|
| 1 | 11 | 12 | 13 | 14 |
| 2 | 21 | 22 | 23 | 24 |
| 3 | 31 | 32 | 33 | 34 |
| 4 | 41 | 42 | 43 | 44 |

*before*

| A | 1 | 2 | 3 | 4 |
|---|---|---|---|---|
| 1 | 14 | 24 | 34 | 44 |
| 2 | 13 | 23 | 33 | 43 |
| 3 | 12 | 22 | 32 | 42 |
| 4 | 11 | 21 | 31 | 41 |

*after*

**Figure 13.7**
Rotating A[1..4, 1..4] 90° around its center.

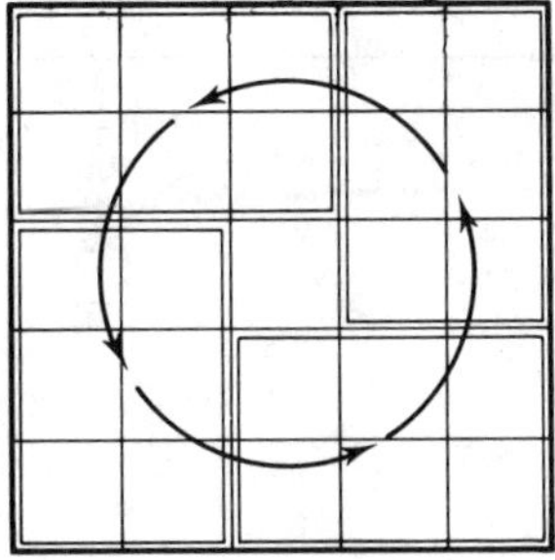

**Figure 13.8**
Rotating A[1..5, 1..5] 90° around its center.

We notice that the effect in Figure 13.7 is to rotate each of the four 2 × 2 subsections shown; i.e. the elements in the entire array-section can be arranged into a number of circular groups of four, containing one element from each subsection, such that each value simply shifts one position. For example:

| | | |
|---|---|---|
| A[1, 1] | is replaced by | A[1, 4], |
| A[1, 4] | is replaced by | A[4, 4], |
| A[4, 4] | is replaced by | A[4, 1], |
| A[4, 1] | is replaced by | A[1, 1]. |

This circular shifting operation is a generalization of a swap, and can be implemented in the same way.

Pictures can be very helpful, but they can be misleading because they are inherently unable to represent every possibility.

> **Principle** When using pictures as an aid to problem-solving, be very careful not to make unjustified assumptions.

In the present context, we should consider an example with n odd, because the previous one assumed n was even. Figure 13.8 shows what happens in the case n = 5.

We realize that our previous analysis was correct: there are still four subsections. However, we have discovered that the subsections are not necessarily square. A little thought shows that the top-left subsection can be taken to be A[1..n **div** 2, 1..(n + 1) **div** 2]. Our first refinement is therefore:

```
var
  i, j : index; { A[i, j] is a member of the group of 4 to be
                  circularly shifted }

begin { RotateAnti }
  for i := 1 to n div 2 do
    for j := 1 to (n + 1) div 2 do
      Circularly shift the 4 members of A[i, j]'s group
end; { RotateAnti }
```

**Figure 13.9**
The element that shifts to A[i, j].

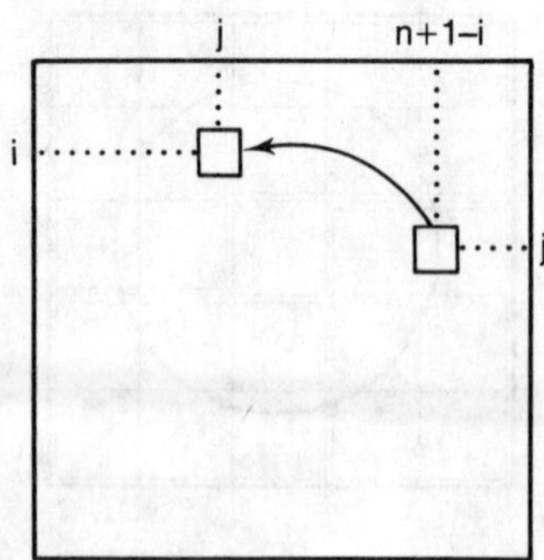


It remains to determine the rest of A[i, j]'s group. We determine the element that replaces A[i, j] with the aid of Figure 13.9. It shows that A[i, j] is replaced by A[j, n + 1 – i].

There is no need to repeat the above sort of calculation to find the remaining members of A[i, j]'s group. Our analysis did not assume that A[i, j] was in the top-left subsection — it applies to any element. We therefore immediately find that:

A[j, n + 1 – i] is replaced by A[n + 1 – i, n + 1 – j],

A[n + 1 – i, n + 1 – j] is replaced by A[n + 1 – j,
  n + 1 – (n + 1 – i)], i.e. A[n + 1 – j, i]

Exercise 13.8 invites you to check that this last member is replaced by A[i, j].

Using a generalization of our code for swapping two elements, we implement the body of the inner loop as follows:

```
var
  temp : ElementType;

begin { Circularly shift the 4 members of A[i, j]'s group }
  temp := A[i, j];
  A[i, j] :=  A[j, n + 1 – i];
  A[j, n + 1 – i] :=  A[n + 1 – i, n + 1 – j];
  A[n +1 – i, n + 1 – j] := A[n + 1 – j, i];
  A[n + 1 – j, i] := temp
end
```

## 13.6 Case-study 7: A random walk

### 13.6.1 SETTING OF THE PROBLEM

Random walks are used in the study of certain physical phenomena, most notably those that involve Brownian motion. They also provide models of various statistical distributions. The idea is that a particle starts off at a known location in some space, and makes a succession of moves. Each move involves choosing one of a number of possible directions, which have certain associated probabilities that are independent of the particle's location, and taking a single step in the chosen direction.

### 13.6.2 SPECIFICATIONS

A program is to be written that simulates random walks on a rectangular grid of cells. It should begin by displaying the grid, and prompting the user to specify the number of steps and the starting location. Then the walk should be simulated, with the changing location of the particle displayed.

The frequency of visits to each cell is to be recorded. On completion of the walk, the program should display the relative frequencies on the grid. Each cell that was visited should be filled with a gray pattern whose darkness is proportional to the relative frequency of its visits; only cells which were not visited should be displayed as white. With white included, the **gray-scale** should range in uniform steps from white to black.

The possible directions for a step are to be those leading to a neighboring cell. They are shown in Figure 13.10(a). There will be fewer than the eight shown if the particle is on the border of the grid. All directions are equiprobable. It must be as simple as possible to modify the program to experiment with different sets of directions, such as the set shown in Figure 13.10(b).

### 13.6.3 WRITING THE PROGRAM

Our highest-level solution consists of a sequence of three actions. First, the necessary information is prompted for and read. Second, the simulation is performed and the frequencies accumulated. Third, the information is displayed. We decide to formulate each of these actions with a procedure-statement. Already it is apparent that a two-dimensional array should be used to contain the frequencies. We have obtained:

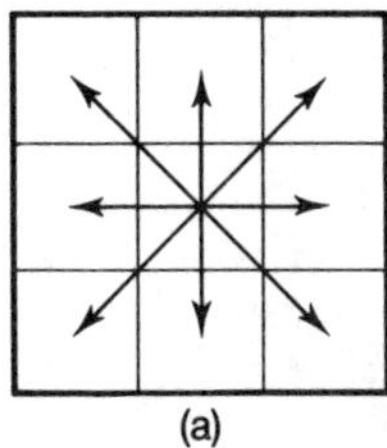
(a)

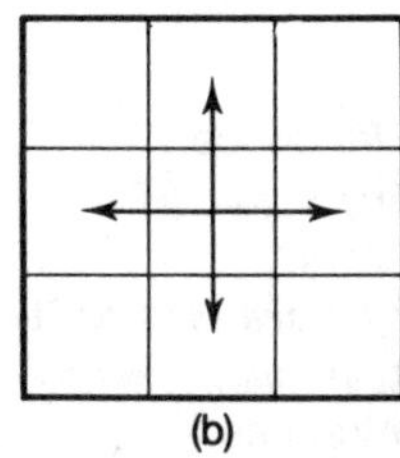
(b)

**Figure 13.10**
Two sets of directions for a step.

```
const
  MaxIndex1 = 25; { number of rows in grid }
  MaxIndex2 = 25; { number of columns in grid }
type
  count = 0..Maxint;
  index1 = 1..MaxIndex1;
  index2 = 1..MaxIndex2;
  VisitCounts = array[index1, index2] of count;
var
  RequiredSteps : count; { number of steps in walk }
  VisitsTo : VisitCounts; { VisitsTo[r,c] is number of times cell }
                          { in row r and column c was visited }
  StartRow : index1; { random walk starts in row StartRow ... }
  StartCol : index2; { ... and column StartCol }

procedure introduce (var row : index1;
                     var col : index2;
                     var NrSteps : count);
{ Draws empty grid, explains its purpose, prompts user to click }
{ in starting cell, sets row and col of starting cell, marks it, }
{ and prompts for and sets number of steps NrSteps. }

procedure simulate (StartRow : index1;
                    StartCol : index2;
                    var freq : VisitCounts;
                    RequiredSteps : count);
{ Simulates and displays a random walk of RequiredSteps }
{ steps, starting in cell in row StartRow and column StartCol, }
{ and records number of visits to each cell in freq. }

procedure display (var freq : VisitCounts);
{ Displays relative frequency of each element of freq, using }
{ a gray-scale; display is preceded by a description. }

begin { RandomWalk }
 introduce(StartRow, StartCol, RequiredSteps);
 simulate(StartRow, StartCol, VisitsTo, RequiredSteps);
 display(VisitsTo)
end. { RandomWalk }
```

We begin the implementation of introduce with a sequence of four actions:

```
begin { introduce }
  Draw empty grid;
  Describe grid;
  Prompt for and read NrSteps;
  Prompt for and process click in starting cell
end; { introduce }
```

We refine the first action with the procedure-statement DrawEmptyGrid, but will implement the procedure later, together with the other graphics operations that emerge. The fourth action involves graphics, so its implementation is also postponed. The other two actions are easily disposed of, and we turn next to procedure simulate, and start its implementation with a sequence of three actions:

```
begin { simulate }
  Zero every element of freq;
  Simulate and display walk and accumulate frequencies;
  Erase last mark
end; { simulate }
```

The first action fits each of the schemas for processing each element of a rectangular array-section. In this case the array-section is the entire array, and each element is processed by assigning zero to it. When the order of processing is unimportant, as in this case, it is conventional to use *row-major processing* (at least in cultures whose written language is displayed in that order). The implementation is given in the complete program. We note that simulate uses the global constants MaxIndex1 and MaxIndex2.

We choose a for-loop for the second action, because the number of steps is known in advance. The body of the loop first determines the new cell to move to, and then makes the move. We provide for initialization, to be determined later.

```
var
  NrSteps : count; { number of steps in walk so far }

{ Simulate and display walk and accumulate frequencies }
  Initialize;
  for NrSteps := 1 to RequiredSteps do
    begin
      Determine location of neighboring cell in random possible direction;
      Erase previous mark, move to and mark new cell, and record visit
    end
```

The body of the loop is tackled next, since it determines the initialization. For the first action, we repeatedly (and at least once) choose a random direction until the neighboring cell in that direction is in the grid:

```
{ Determine location of neighboring cell in random possible direction }
  repeat
    Pick a random direction;
    Determine location of the neighboring cell in this direction
  until the neighboring cell is in grid
```

To refine deeper, we must first decide how to represent directions. One possibility is to use an enumerated type, perhaps with compass points as identifiers, and to use a case-statement to determine the new location. However, it is easier to choose a random integer value, so we decide instead to use a subrange of **integer**. Variables are also introduced to represent the current position and the position of the neighboring cell (which can be outside the grid). The body of the repeat-loop becomes:

```
const
  NrDirections = 8; { number of directions }
type
  direction = 1..NrDirections;
var
  row : index1;
  col : index2; { (row, col) is current position }
  NewRow, NewCol : integer; { tentative next position }
  dir : direction; { tentative direction to move in }

function ran (lower, upper : integer) : integer;
{ Returns a random value uniformly distributed in lower..upper; }
{ assumes lower <= upper. }

dir := ran(1, NrDirections);
case dir of
  1: { North }
    begin NewRow := row - 1;
    NewCol := col end;
  2: { North-East }
    begin NewRow := row - 1;
    NewCol := col + 1 end;
  ...
end { case }
```

To modularize the information concerning directions, the computation of the neighboring cell in a given direction is better expressed as a procedure.

But there is an even better way. We observe that the value of NewRow is that of row plus 0 or 1 or –1, depending only on the direction; and similarly for NewCol. So we introduce two arrays which give the change to the row and column respectively for a move in each possible direction. Abstractly, they are functions, because their values never change.

> **Moral** Sometimes functions may be better implemented with arrays than with Pascal functions.

```
type
  DiffTable = array[direction] of -1..1;
var
  diff1, diff2 : DiffTable; { coordinate changes for a move in each
                              direction }
```

The body of the repeat-loop becomes:

```
dir := ran(1, NrDirections);
NewRow := row + diff1[dir];
NewCol := col + diff2[dir]
```

The arrays diff1 and diff2 are initialized by a call of a special procedure, making it easy to change to another set of directions. The rest of the initialization is straightforward:

```
procedure SetUp (var diff1, diff2 : DiffTable);
{ For each direction d, sets diff1[d] (diff2[d]) = change to }
{ row (column) to move in direction d. }

{ Initialize }
  SetUp(diff1, diff2);
  freq[StartRow, StartCol] := 1;
  row := StartRow;
  col := StartCol
```

Procedure SetUp is trivial, consisting of two assignment statements for each direction. It is given later in the complete program.

Returning to a higher-level now, we refine the other action in the body of the for-loop.

```
{ Erase previous mark, move to and mark new cell, and record visit }
  Erase mark in cell (row, col);
  row := NewRow;
  col := NewCol;
  Draw mark in cell (row, col);
  freq[row, col] := freq[row, col] + 1
```

We postpone implementation of the two graphics actions. The graphics-free part of simulate is now complete, so we tackle the final highest-level procedure, viz. display.

Our first refinement consists of a sequence of three actions. The first describes the display; the second computes the maximum frequency, because it must be known if relative frequencies are to be determined; the third does the drawing. In practice, the need for the second action might become apparent only during the refinement of the third.

```
var
  MaxFreq : count; { maximum element of freq }

begin { display }
  Describe the forthcoming display;
  Set MaxFreq = maximum element of freq;
  Fill each cell whose corresponding frequency is non-zero
end; { display }
```

The maximum frequency is computed with a function call.

```
function max (var freq : PairCounts) : count;
{ Returns maximum element of freq. }

MaxFreq := max(freq)
```

Function max fits each of our schemas for processing each element in a rectangular array-section, so its implementation is quite straightforward.

All the remaining unrefined actions are concerned with graphics, so we prepare the way, as usual, by defining the displays in terms of constants. The displays of both the moving particle and the final relative frequencies of visits are based on the same rectangular grid. Figure 13.11 determines its form.

The top edge of the last horizontal line will be at vertical coordinate Offset1 + MaxIndex1 * Gap. The left edge of the last horizontal line will be at horizontal coordinate Offset2 + MaxIndex2 * Gap. The constants used are:

```
const
  Offset1 = ... ; { top-left corner of grid is ... }
  Offset2 = ... ; { ... at (Offset2, Offset1) }
  Gap = ... ; { gap between successive grid lines }
```

Their values can be determined later.

DrawEmptyGrid presents no new problems; it is implemented with a sequence of two for-loops — one to draw the horizontal grid lines, and the other to draw the vertical grid lines. We return now to procedure introduce. Its main display-related action is refined as follows:

```
var
  x, y : integer; { (x, y) is a mouse position }

{ Prompt for and process click in starting cell }
  Writeln('Click in starting cell to commence random walk.');
  repeat
```

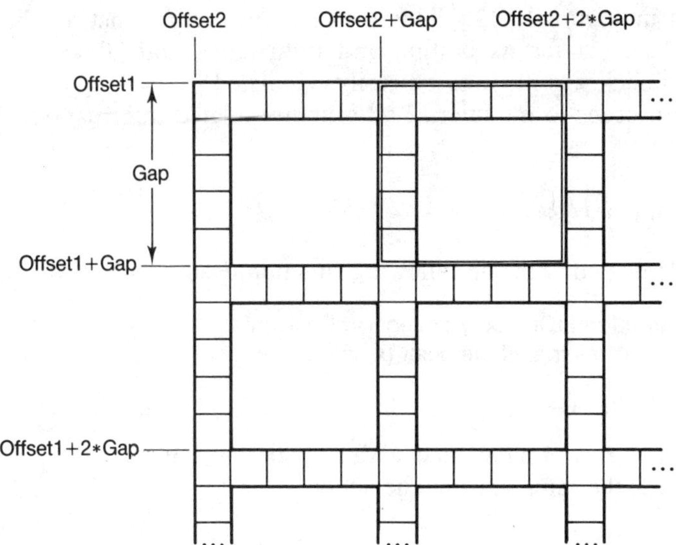


**Figure 13.11**
A blow-up of the top-left corner of the grid.

```
      Set (x, y) to position of next click
    until (x, y) is in the grid;
    Set (row, col) to the cell containing point (x, y);
    Draw mark in cell (row, col)
```

A loop is used in case the user clicks outside the grid. If so, nothing happens until the mouse is clicked in the grid; no extra prompt is necessary as the original suffices.

To implement the first action in the loop, the program waits until a click is made, and then gets the mouse's position. It does the former by repeatedly calling the predefined function **Button**:

```
function Button : Boolean;
{ Returns true iff the mouse button is being held down when }
{ Button is called. }
```

The body of the loop is an empty-statement. A repeat-loop reads more naturally than a while-loop.

```
{ Set (x, y) to position of next click }
  repeat
  until Button;
  GetMouse(x, y)
```

To determine which cell is indicated, we decide that the point (x, y) is in a cell if the pixel below and to the right is in the interior of the cell or in its left or top border. The region for cell (1, 2) is indicated in Figure 13.11. This prescription ensures that all the grid is covered except for its bottom and right edge, and allows the cell in which a click was made to be easily calculated.

In order to modularize all graphics-related information, the condition

(x, y) *is in the grid*

is implemented with the following function-designator:

```
function InGrid (x, y : integer) : Boolean;
{ Returns true iff the point (x, y) is in the grid. }

InGrid(x, y)
```

The function is implemented with a single assignment.

For the same reason, the action:

*Set* (row, col) *to the cell containing point* (x, y)

is implemented with:

```
procedure ScreenToGrid (x, y : integer;
                        var row : index1;
                        var col : index2);
{ Sets (row, col) to cell containing screen position (x, y); }
{ assumes (x, y) is in grid. }

ScreenToGrid(x, y, row, col)
```

The procedure is implemented with a sequence of two assignments.

The action *Draw mark in cell* (row, col) occurs in both introduce and simulate. Actions that undo its effect occur twice in simulate. All these actions can be regarded as painting part of a specified cell with a particular pattern: black to make a mark, white to erase one. They are therefore implemented with a single procedure:

```
procedure FillCell (row : index1;
                    col : index2;
                    pat : Pattern);
{ Fills all but outer border of interior of cell in given row and }
{ column with pat; changes pen pattern to pat. }
```

The type Pattern is predefined in Macintosh Pascal:

```
type
  Pattern = packed array[0..7] of 0..255;
```

The two types of action are implemented as follows, using the pre-declared and predefined global variables black and white:

```
{ Draw mark in cell (row, col) }
  FillCell(row, col, black)

{ Erase mark in cell (row, col) }
  FillCell(row, col, white)
```

The implementation of FillCell consists of a procedure-statement for PenPat followed by one for PaintRect. The relevant coordinates are determined with the help of Figure 13.11.

We turn finally to the major graphics action in procedure display. It amounts to displaying each cell, which fits our schema for rectangular array-sections. Again preferring row-major order, we write:

```
var
  row : index1; { row of element of freq }
  col : index2; { col of element of freq }

{ Fill each cell whose corresponding frequency is non-zero }
  for row := 1 to MaxIndex1 do
    for col := 1 to MaxIndex2 do
      if freq[row, col] > 0 then
        Fill cell corresponding to freq[row, col]
```

The body of the inner loop is refined with a sequence of three actions:

```
var
  t, l, b, r : integer; { top, left, bottom, right coordinates of inside
                          of cell }

begin { Fill cell corresponding to freq[row, col] }
  Set t, l, b, r to coordinates of cell (row, col);
  PenPat(the appropriate shade from the gray-scale);
  PaintRect(t, l, b, r)
end
```

The coordinates are determined from Figure 13.11. Since the values of t and b depend only on row, their calculation is moved into the outer loop.

Determining the appropriate pattern is tricky, so we proceed very carefully. We consider first a manageable example, where there

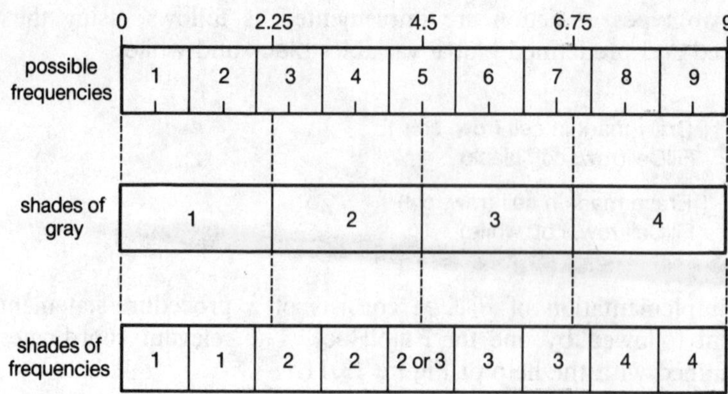


**Figure 13.12**
Matching the frequency- and gray-scales.

are four shades in the gray-scale and the maximum frequency of visits to a cell is nine. Our first task is to assign the appropriate shade to each possible non-zero frequency. After deciding that it makes more sense to work with intervals rather than integers, we produce the diagram shown in Figure 13.12.

Frequencies of 1 and 2 should get the first (lightest) shade of gray; frequency 3 should get the next shade because more of its interval overlaps the interval of shade 2 than shade 1; and so on. It is apparent that it is the coordinate of the midpoint of a frequency interval (on the scale 0.0 to 9.0) that determines which shade it should get. If $f$ is the frequency, this value is $f - 0.5$. The number of the shade is 1 more than the whole number of times 2.25 goes into this value. Generalizing, with *mf* for the maximum frequency, and *ns* for the number of shades of gray, the shade-number *s* for frequency *f* is given by:

```
trunc((f - 0.5) / (mf / ns)) + 1
```

To define the shade of gray associated with each shade-number, again we use an array as a function:

```
const
  NrShades = 4; { number of shades of gray in gray-scale }
type
  ShadeNumber = 1..NrShades;
  ShadeTable = array[ShadeNumber] of Pattern;
var
  shade : ShadeTable; { shades in order of increasing darkness; }
  { if white were added, the steps are uniform from white to black }
```

Variable **shade** is an array of arrays. A procedure is defined to initialize it:

```
procedure SetUp (var shade : ShadeTable);
{ Stores patterns in shade in order of increasing darkness; if }
{ white were added, the steps are uniform from white to black. }
```

The Technical Appendix describes how to interpret a pattern. We can make our own, but shall content ourselves with using the four pre-declared and initialized pattern variables (other than white). SetUp is thus implemented with a sequence of four array-assignments.

Meanwhile, back at the program, the action:

PenPat(*the appropriate shade from the gray-scale*)

is implemented with:

```
PenPat(shade[trunc((freq[row, col] – 0.5) * NrShades / MaxFreq) + 1])
```

The remaining unrefined actions are very easy going compared to the above!

### 13.6.4 THE COMPLETE PROGRAM

The complete program is given below. The general-purpose function ran is declared in the program-block. So too is function max, because it has nothing to do with the graphical display *per se*, and it is designed only for use with the main program variable freq. The constants and subprograms concerned with the graphics display are gathered together in the program-block.

```
program RandomWalk (Input, Output);
{ Simulates and displays a random walk in a rectangular grid, }
{ then displays the relative frequency of visits to each cell, }
{ using a gray scale. }
  const
    MaxIndex1 = 25; { number of rows in grid }
    MaxIndex2 = 25; { number of columns in grid }
    Offset1 = 20; { top-left corner of grid is ... }
    Offset2 = 20; { ... at (Offset2, Offset1) }
    Gap = 10; { gap between successive grid lines }
  type
    count = 0..Maxint;
    index1 = 1..MaxIndex1;
    index2 = 1..MaxIndex2;
    VisitCounts = array[index1, index2] of count;
  var
    RequiredSteps : count; { number of steps in walk }
    VisitsTo : VisitCounts; { VisitsTo[r, c] is number of times cell }
                            { in row r and column c was visited }
```

```
  StartRow : index1; { random walk starts in row StartRow ... }
  StartCol : index2; { ... and column StartCol }

function ran (lower, upper : integer) : integer;
{ Returns a random value uniformly distributed in lower..upper; }
{ assumes lower <= upper. }
see program Arithmetic in Chapter 10

function max (var freq : VisitCounts) : count;
{ Returns maximum element of freq. }
{ Global consts: MaxIndex1, MaxIndex2. }
 var
   row : index1;
   col : index2;
   big : count; { maximum element so far }
begin { max }
  big := 0;
  for row := 1 to MaxIndex1 do
    for col := 1 to MaxIndex2 do
      if freq[row, col] > big then
        big := freq[row, col];
  max := big
end; { max }

procedure DrawEmptyGrid;
{ Draws empty grid of cells. }
{ Global consts: Gap, Offset1, Offset2, MaxIndex1, MaxIndex2. }
 var
   n : 0..Maxint; { number of a grid-line }
   dist : integer; { constant coordinate of grid-line }
begin { DrawEmptyGrid }
{ Draw horizontal grid lines }
 for n := 0 to MaxIndex1 do
   begin
     dist := Offset1 + n * Gap;
     DrawLine(Offset2, dist, Offset2 + MaxIndex2 * Gap, dist)
   end;
{ Draw vertical grid lines }
 for n := 0 to MaxIndex2 do
   begin
     dist := Offset2 + n * Gap;
     DrawLine(dist, Offset1, dist, Offset1 + MaxIndex1 * Gap);
   end
end; { DrawEmptyGrid }

function InGrid (x, y : integer) : Boolean;
{ Returns true iff the point (x, y) is in the grid. }
{ Global consts: Offset1, Offset2, Gap, MaxIndex1, MaxIndex2. }
```

```
begin { InGrid }
  InGrid := (Offset2 <= x) and (x < Offset2 + MaxIndex2 * Gap)
            and (Offset1 <= y) and (y < Offset1
            + MaxIndex1 * Gap)
end; { InGrid }

procedure ScreenToGrid (x, y : integer;
                        var row : index1;
                        var col : index2);
{ Sets (row, col) to cell containing screen position (x, y); }
{ assumes (x, y) is in grid. }
{ Global consts: Offset1, Offset2, Gap. }
begin { ScreenToGrid }
  row := (y - Offset1) div Gap + 1;
  col := (x - Offset2) div Gap + 1;
end; { ScreenToGrid }

procedure FillCell (row : index1;
                    col : index2;
                    pat : Pattern);
{ Fills all but outer border of interior of cell in given row and }
{ column with pat; changes pen pattern to pat. }
begin { FillCell }
  PenPat(pat);
  PaintRect(Offset1 + (row - 1) * Gap + 2, Offset2 + (col - 1) * Gap
            + 2, Offset1 + row * Gap - 1, Offset2 + col * Gap - 1)
end; { FillCell }

procedure display (var freq : VisitCounts);
{ Displays relative frequency of each element of freq, using }
{ a gray-scale; display is preceded by a description. }
{ Global consts: Offset1, Offset2, Gap, MaxIndex1, MaxIndex2. }
{ Global subprogram: max. }
  const
    NrShades = 4; { number of shades of gray in gray-scale }
  type
    ShadeNumber = 1..NrShades;
    ShadeTable = array[ShadeNumber] of Pattern;
  var
    shade : ShadeTable; { shades in order of increasing darkness; }
    { if white were added, the steps are uniform from white to black }
    MaxFreq : count; { maximum element of freq }
    row : index1; { row of element of freq }
    col : index2; { col of element of freq }
    t, l, b, r : integer; { top, left, bottom, right coordinates of inside
                          of cell }

  procedure SetUp (var shade : ShadeTable);
  { Stores patterns in shade in order of increasing darkness; if }
  { white were added, the steps are uniform from white to black. }
```

```
begin { SetUp }
  shade[1] := ltGray;
  shade[2] := Gray;
  shade[3] := dkGray;
  shade[4] := black
end; { SetUp }

begin { display }
  Write('In the display, the darkness of a cell is proportional ');
  Writeln('to the relative frequency of its visits.');
  Writeln('The gray-scale has ', NrShades : 1, ' shades of gray.');
  SetUp(shade);
  MaxFreq := max(freq);
{ Fill each cell whose corresponding frequency is non-zero }
  for row := 1 to MaxIndex1 do
    begin
    { Set t, b to top and bottom coordinates of cells in row }
      b := Offset1 + row * Gap;
      t := b - Gap + 1;

      for col := 1 to MaxIndex2 do
        if freq[row, col] > 0 then
          begin { Fill cell corresponding to freq[row, col] }
          { Set l, r to left and right coordinates of cell in column }
            r := Offset2 + col * Gap;
            l := r - Gap + 1;

            PenPat(shade[trunc((freq[row, col] - 0.5) * NrShades /
                                  MaxFreq) + 1]);
            PaintRect(t, l, b, r)
          end
    end
end; { display }

procedure introduce (var row : index1;
                     var col : index2;
                     var NrSteps : count);
{ Draws empty grid, explains its purpose, prompts user to click }
{ in starting cell, sets row and col of starting cell, marks it, }
{ and prompts for and sets number of steps NrSteps. }
{ Global consts: MaxIndex1, MaxIndex2. }
{ Global subprograms: DrawEmptyGrid, InGrid, ScreenToGrid,
                      FillCell. }
  var
    x, y : integer; { (x, y) is a mouse position }
begin { introduce }
  DrawEmptyGrid;
{ Describe grid }
  Write('This program simulates a random walk in a grid of ');
```

```
  Writeln(MaxIndex1 : 1, ' rows and ', MaxIndex2 : 1, ' columns.');
{ Prompt for and read NrSteps }
  Write('Enter number of steps in walk: ');
  Readln(NrSteps);
{ Prompt for and process click in starting cell }
  Writeln('Click in starting cell to commence random walk.');
  repeat { set (x, y) to position of next click }
    repeat
    until Button;
    GetMouse(x, y)
  until InGrid(x, y);
  ScreenToGrid(x, y, row, col);
  FillCell(row, col, black)
end; { introduce }

procedure simulate (StartRow : index1;
                    StartCol : index2;
                    var freq : VisitCounts;
                    RequiredSteps : count);
{ Simulates and displays a random walk of RequiredSteps steps, }
{ starting in cell in row StartRow and column StartCol, and }
{ records number of visits to each cell in freq. }
{ Global consts: MaxIndex1, MaxIndex2. }
{ Global subprograms: ran, FillCell. }
  const
    NrDirections = 8; { number of directions }
  type
    direction = 1..NrDirections;
    DiffTable = array[direction] of -1..1;
  var
    row : index1;
    col : index2; { (row, col) is current position }
    dir : direction; { tentative direction to move in }
    NewRow, NewCol : integer; { (NewRow, NewCol) is tentative
                                  next position }
    NrSteps : count; { number of steps in walk so far }
    diff1, diff2 : DiffTable; { coordinate changes for a move in
                                 each direction }

  procedure SetUp (var diff1, diff2 : DiffTable);
  { For each direction d, sets diff1[d] (diff2[d]) = change to }
  { row (column) to move in direction d. }
  begin { SetUp }
    diff1[1] := -1;
    diff1[2] := -1;
    diff1[3] := 0;
    diff1[4] := 1;
    diff1[5] := 1;
    diff1[6] := 1;
```

```
      diff1[7] := 0;
      diff1[8] := −1;
      diff2[1] := 0;
      diff2[2] := 1;
      diff2[3] := 1;
      diff2[4] := 1;
      diff2[5] := 0;
      diff2[6] := −1;
      diff2[7] := −1;
      diff2[8] := −1
    end; { SetUp }
  begin { simulate }
  { Zero every element of freq }
    for row := 1 to MaxIndex1 do
      for col := 1 to MaxIndex2 do
        freq[row, col] := 0;
  { Simulate and display walk and accumulate frequencies }
    { Initialize }
    SetUp(diff1, diff2);
    freq[StartRow, StartCol] := 1;
    row := StartRow;
    col := StartCol;
    for NrSteps := 1 to RequiredSteps do
      begin
      { Determine location of neighboring cell in random
        possible direction }
        repeat
          dir := ran(1, NrDirections);
          NewRow := row + diff1[dir];
          NewCol := col + diff2[dir]
        until (1 <= NewRow) and (NewRow <= MaxIndex1) and
              (1 <= NewCol) and (NewCol <= MaxIndex2);
      { Erase previous mark, move to and mark new cell, and
        record visit }
        FillCell(row, col, white);
        row := NewRow;
        col := NewCol;
        FillCell(row, col, black);
        freq[row, col] := freq[row, col] + 1
      end;
  { Erase last mark }
    FillCell(row, col, white)
  end; { simulate }
begin { RandomWalk }
  introduce(StartRow, StartCol, RequiredSteps);
  simulate(StartRow, StartCol, VisitsTo, RequiredSteps);
  display(VisitsTo)
end. { RandomWalk }
```

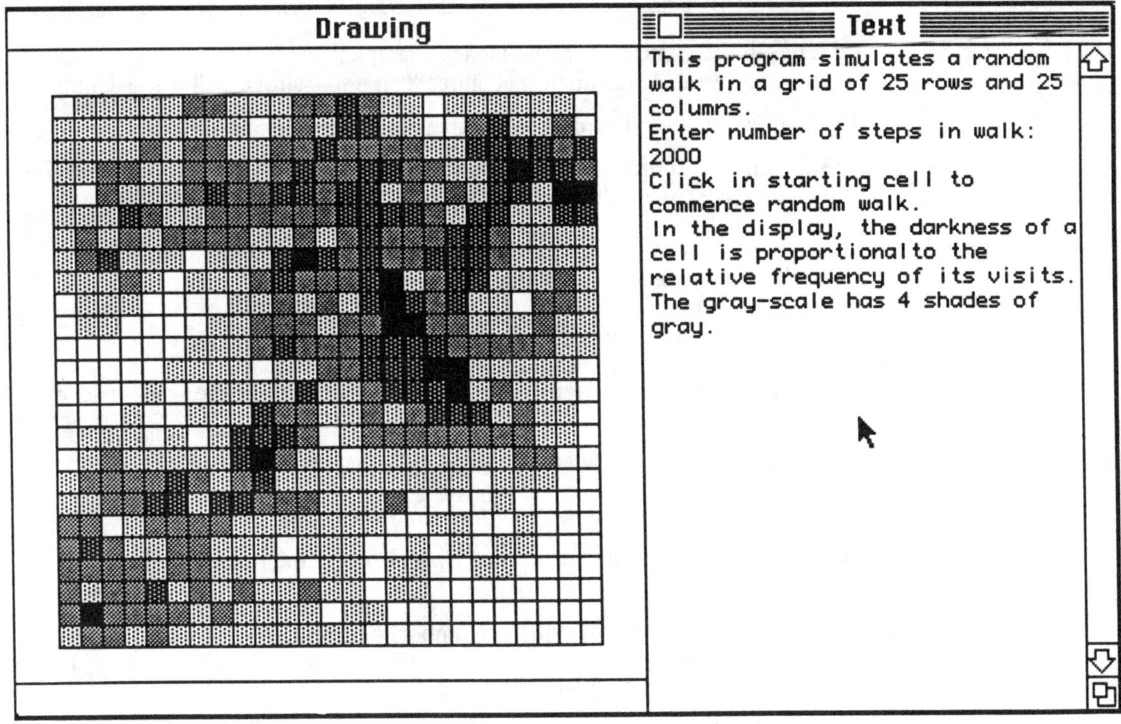
File Edit Search Run Windows
Drawing
Text
This program simulates a random walk in a grid of 25 rows and 25 columns.
Enter number of steps in walk:
2000
Click in starting cell to commence random walk.
In the display, the darkness of a cell is proportionalto the relative frequency of its visits.
The gray-scale has 4 shades of gray.

**Figure 13.13**
The screen after a run of RandomWalk.

Figure 13.13 shows the results of a run consisting of 2000 steps on a 25 × 25 grid, with the starting point in the center, and the directions as shown in Figure 13.10(a).

See the exercises for some suggested modifications to or experiments with RandomWalk.

## 13.7 Further reading

(1) Tufte, E. R. (1983). *The Visual Display of Quantitative Information.* Connecticut: Graphics Press.
A marvelous book. Should be required reading for anyone planning to display quantitative information using the Macintosh's graphics capabilities.

## EXERCISES

**13.1** In the context of the tic-tac-toe example,

(a) Write a statement that stores X in square[row, col] if it is empty.

(b) Write a statement that initializes every position to Empty.

**13.2** In the context of the inventory for *Bob and Marge's Gift and Gun*, suppose the following variable is declared:

```
type
  costs = array[ItemType] of count;
var
  cost : costs; { cost[i] = cost of item i in cents }
```

(a) Write a function that returns the total cost of the stock held by a given store.

(b) Using your answer to (a), implement the following action:

*Print the total cost of the stock held by each store*

**13.3** In the context of the inventory problems, is the following legal?

```
var
  temp : array[StoreNumber] of count;

temp := stock[cube]
```

If not (what a give-away!), change the type definitions to permit it.

**13.4** How many elements does the rectangular array-section A[*a*..*b*, *c*..*d*] contain?

**13.5** On an 8 × 8 chess-board, a king *protects* the 9 squares in the 3 × 3 region centered on his square. (This region is reduced if the king is on an edge.) Write a program that prompts for and reads the positions of an arbitrary number of kings, and prints the total number of squares protected by them.

*Hint*: Use extra *phantom* rows and columns to avoid special treatment for kings on edges.

**13.6** Implement the following procedure:

```
procedure transpose (var A : matrix;
                         n : index);
{ Revolves A[1..n, 1..n] 180 degrees on its major diagonal; }
{ i.e. the i'th row becomes the i'th column, and vice versa. }
```

The major diagonal runs from A[1, 1] to A[n, n].

**13.7** An array section A[1..n, 1..n] is said to be *symmetric* iff transpose(A, n) leaves it unchanged. Write a function that tests for this property. Ensure that it does not do unnecessary testing if the section is found not to be symmetric.

**13.8** With respect to procedure RotateAnti, show that the last member of A[i, j]'s group is replaced by A[i, j].

**13.9** Implement the following procedure:

```
procedure rotate (var A : matrix;
                  n : index);
{ Rotates A[1..n, 1..n] 90 degrees clockwise round its center. }
```

**13.10** Complete the following procedure in the given context:

```
const
  MaxRow = ... ;
  MaxCol = ... ;
type
  RowIndex = 1..MaxRow;
  ColIndex = 1..MaxCol;
  matrix = array[RowIndex, ColIndex] of real;

procedure VFlip (var A : matrix;
                 rows : RowIndex;
                 cols : ColIndex);
{ Revolves A[1..rows, 1..cols] 180 degrees round its central }
{ vertical axis, i.e., A[r, 1] is swapped with A[r, cols], }
{ A[r, 2] is swapped with A[r, cols – 1], etc. }
```

**13.11** The fact that procedure ScreenToGrid assumes that its input parameters x and y represent a point in the grid is hardly satisfactory. It could check this first by calling function InGrid, but it would not then be self-contained, and the problem remains as to what to do if the result of the call is false. A much better idea is for ScreenToGrid to absorb the role of InGrid, by changing its specifications as follows.

```
type
  ExtendedIndex1 = 0..MaxIndex1;
  ExtendedIndex2 = 0..MaxIndex2;

procedure ScreenToGrid (x, y : integer;
                        var row : ExtendedIndex1;
                        var col : ExtendedIndex2);
{ If screen position (x, y) is in grid, sets (row,col) to cell }
{ containing (x, y); otherwise sets row and col to 0. }
```

Implement this new version of ScreenToGrid, and modify the program accordingly.

**13.12** Modify program RandomWalk to use the set of directions in Figure 13.10(b). This should be an easy exercise, because the constant NrDirections and the procedure SetUp (local to simulate) encapsulate all the information concerning directions.

**13.13** Modify RandomWalk so that the walk terminates as soon as a randomly selected direction would cause the particle to leave the grid.

**13.14** Modify RandomWalk so that white is included in the gray-scale. This is the natural way to use a gray-scale to plot the relative values of a statistic according to (often geographic) location. It will no longer be true that a visited cell is never displayed as white, but it will remain true that every unvisited cell is displayed as white (provided the number of possible frequencies is not smaller than the number of gray tones).

**13.15** As it stands, procedure display mixes graphics details with high-level actions. Use a procedure like FillCell to fix this problem.

**13.16** A desk accessory called *Puzzle* comes with the Macintosh System Disk. Selecting it from the apple menu produces a picture like those shown in Figure 13.14. There are 15 squares and one free space in a 4 × 4 regular grid. Clicking on a square vertically or horizontally adjacent to the space causes it to move into the space, leaving a space where it was. For example, clicking on square 13 changes each of the states of the puzzle in Figure 13.14 to the other.

This is the famous 15-puzzle — the Rubik's cube of the nineteenth century — created by the incomparable American puzzle-maker Sam Loyd. The idea is to make a sequence of moves that rearranges the squares so that the numbers increase in row-major order, with the space in the bottom-right.

Implement the 15-puzzle in Macintosh Pascal — the puzzle, not an algorithm that solves it. This is a substantial programming exercise, but all the important techniques occur in program RandomWalk.

*Warning*: Only half the possible arrangements permit a solution, so you might want to start by displaying the desired arrangement, then having the program mess it up by making a sequence of random moves. Displaying these moves might add to the puzzle's appeal!

**Figure 13.14**
Two states of the 15-puzzle.

# 14 TEXT PROCESSING

Amend my statements last night and insert the word 'lose' where I had the word 'win'.

— Morris Udall, referring to a premature victory speech at the Wisconsin primary, 1976

## 14.1 Introduction

Computers were originally applied to large-scale scientific and engineering calculations. The view of computers as exclusively or even mainly number-crunchers is no longer appropriate. Even computers that are devoted to numeric applications spend considerable time processing text rather than numbers: the input to a programming language translator, for example, is textual data. More generally, almost all input data prepared directly by people is textual, no matter what its interpretation.

Many applications do little other than process text. The text that you are now reading, for example, was processed by an interactive editor, and later processed by a spelling-checker and a typesetter. Such programs spend most of their time reading, expanding, changing, rearranging, writing, and otherwise manipulating text. With the advent of the automated-office and the personal computer, text processing has become arguably the most common form of computation.

Standard Pascal provides a predefined type to represent files of textual information, and special procedures to handle their input and output. These are the subject of the first major section of this chapter. However, Pascal's facilities for lower-level processing of text, called **string-processing**, are rather primitive — there are fixed-length strings in the guise of packed arrays of characters, but very few operations or required procedures and functions to process them. Macintosh Pascal, like many other implementations of Pascal, extends the Standard in this area. Its facilities for string-processing are described in Section 14.3. The chapter concludes with a case-study that illustrates text-processing in Macintosh Pascal.

## 14.2 Text files

### 14.2.1 INPUT AND OUTPUT AS TEXT FILES

It is time to reveal the identity of the identifiers Input and Output (which have appeared in the program-heading of the programs we have seen thus far) — they are variables of the required structured type **text**, and are implicitly declared in the program-block. Like all variables of type **text**, they are called **text files**, and are used to perform input and output.

A text file is normally associated with secondary memory, that is, with files on a Macintosh Pascal disk, but may be associated with input/output devices such as printers and modems. The text file **Input** is associated with the standard input stream (see Chapter 5), which in Macintosh Pascal is produced by the keyboard. **Output** is associated with the standard output stream, which in Macintosh Pascal goes to the Text window.

### 14.2.2 INTERNAL AND EXTERNAL TEXT FILES

Text files that exist only during execution of a program are called **internal files**. A text file that exists prior to or after the execution of a program is called an **external file**; it will be represented on a Macintosh by an icon. The Standard requires external files that are used or created by a program to be identified by listing them as the program parameters. If either **Input** or **Output** is used, implicitly or explicitly, it must appear in the list of program parameters. Macintosh Pascal uses a non-Standard method that is described below — it does not permit other program parameters.

### 14.2.3 USING A TEXT FILE

The value of a text file is a sequence of zero or more lines, each of which consists of zero or more characters followed by an end-of-line marker. A text file can be created only by appending characters or end-of-line markers to an initially empty file. Assignment to an entire text file is not permitted; neither is it possible directly to change a character part way through a text file. A text file may be examined only by reading successive characters and markers starting from the first one. Because their components can only be accessed sequentially, Pascal text files are called **sequential files**. Macintosh Pascal is more flexible, allowing access to an arbitrary position, and permiting mixed reading and writing; i.e. it supports **random-access** files — see Chapter 16.

### 14.2.4 THE FILE POSITION AND THE FILE BUFFER

Each text file has a unique **file position**. When a file is being read, its file position separates the characters and markers that have been read from those that have yet to be read. When a file is being written, its file position is after its last character or marker.

The declaration of a text file $f$ automatically creates a variable $f$^ of type char called the **file-buffer** of $f$. It is used to transmit characters to and from $f$, as explained below. It is classified as a new kind of component-variable:

component-variable: *indexed-variable* | *file-buffer*
file-buffer: *file-variable*^
file-variable: *variable*

### 14.2.5 WRITING A TEXT FILE

The first operation on a text file $f$ indicates whether it is to be written or read. The procedure call:

```
Rewrite(f)
```

makes $f$ available for writing. The file becomes empty, and the file position is at end-of-file. Accordingly, eof($f$) gives true. Rewrite is implicitly applied to Output at the outset of a program, and should not be reapplied. The functions eof and eoln may be applied to any text file; if the file parameter is omitted, Input is assumed. (More accurately, the standard input stream is assumed, as the identifier Input may be redefined.)

The output statements Write and Writeln may be used with any text file $f$, simply by giving $f$ as the first parameter in the list. If it is omitted, Output (i.e. the standard output stream) is assumed. The effects are as described in Chapter 5, except that it is $f$ that is affected. The file position remains at the end-of-file throughout the writing process, and eof($f$) continues to give true.

A Write-statement is actually implemented in terms of a primitive output operation. The procedure call:

```
put(f)
```

appends the value of the file-buffer $f$^ to $f$, moves the file position to the end, and makes $f$^ undefined. The file-buffer may be given a value by any means permitted for a non-simple variable of type char. If OutFile is a variable of type text, then the output statement:

```
Write(OutFile, '!')
```

is equivalent to:

```
begin
  OutFile^ := '!';
  put(OutFile)
end
```

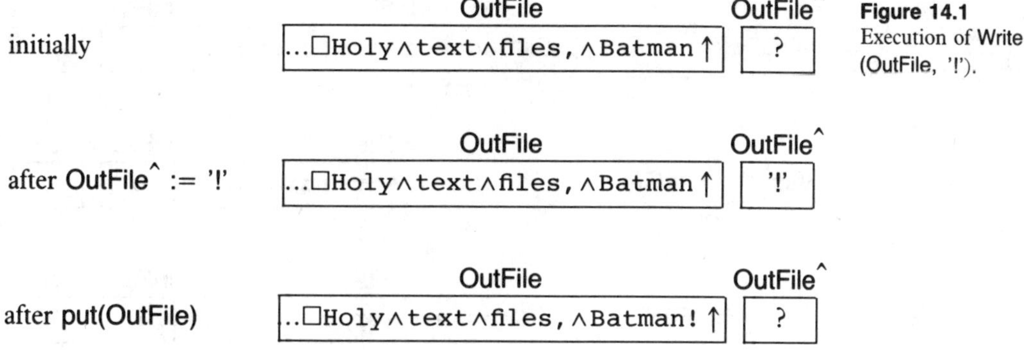


**Figure 14.1**
Execution of Write (OutFile, '!').

Its effect is illustrated in Figure 14.1. As in Chapter 5, □ denotes an end-of-line marker, ∧ denotes a space character, and ↑ denotes the file-position.

### 14.2.6 READING A TEXT FILE

The procedure call:

```
Reset(f)
```

makes *f* available for reading. The file position moves to the start and **eof**(*f*) gives **true** iff the file is empty. Moreover, **eoln**(*f*) gives **true** iff the file starts with an end-of-line marker. **Reset** is implicitly applied to **Input** at the outset of a program, and should not be reapplied.

The file buffer *f*^ is defined throughout the reading process provided only that **eof**(*f*) gives **false**. It contains the character immediately following the file position, unless it is followed immediately by an end-of-line marker, in which case it contains the space character.

The input statements **Read** and **Readln** may be used with any text file *f*^, simply by giving *f* as the first parameter in the list. If it is omitted, **Input** (i.e. the standard input stream) is assumed. The effects are as described in Chapter 5, except that it is *f* that is affected.

A Read-statement is actually implemented in terms of a primitive input operation. The procedure call:

```
get(f)
```

advances the file position past the current character or marker, and

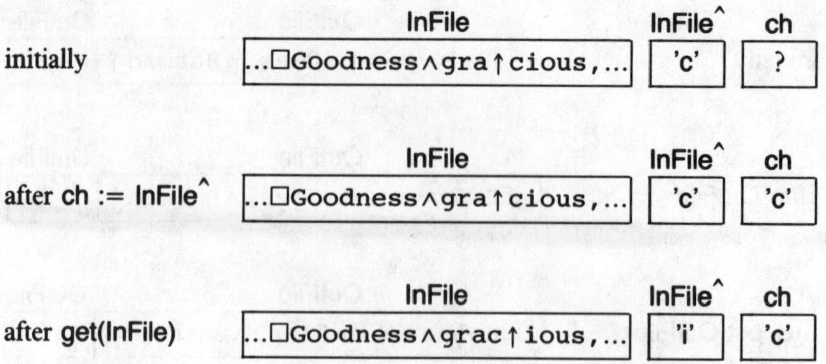


**Figure 14.2**
Execution of Read (InFile, ch).

updates the value of the file-buffer $f\hat{}$. It is an error if the file position is at end-of-file before the call. If **InFile** is a variable of type **text**, and **ch** is a variable of type **char**, then the input statement:

```
Read(InFile, ch)
```

is equivalent to:

```
begin
  ch := InFile^;
  get(InFile)
end
```

Its effect is illustrated in Figure 14.2.

In Macintosh Pascal, execution of **get(Input)** does not cause the character or marker skipped over to be echoed in the Text window, unlike the situation with **Read** and **Readln**.

## 14.2.7 EXTERNAL TEXT FILES IN MACINTOSH PASCAL

In Macintosh Pascal, a text file is associated with an external file by naming the external file with an optional second parameter of **Reset** or **Rewrite**, the first time one of these procedures is applied to the file. Later calls of **Reset** or **Rewrite** should not have this second parameter.

The optional parameter is an expression that gives a string value. A text file on a Macintosh disk is denoted by the string consisting of the name of the disk, followed by a colon (:) and then the external name of the file. For example, to prepare to read the file named *Errors.Text* on the *Macintosh Pascal Utilities* disk, we might write:

```
var
  errors : text;
...
  Reset(errors, 'Macintosh Pascal Utilities:Errors.Text')
```

It is necessary for the required disk's icon to be on the desktop.

Two very useful functions are provided for interactive programs. The function-call:

```
OldFileName(prompt)
```

in which the expression *prompt* gives a string value, produces a dialog box that displays *prompt* and allows the user to select an existing file on an arbitrary disk. The result of the call is a string that names the file in the form required by Reset and Rewrite. A typical application of it is shown below.

```
var
  data : text;
...
  Reset(data, OldFileName('Please select the data file.'))
```

For technical reasons, do not end *prompt* with an asterisk (*) lest irrelevant files be listed.

Similarly, the function call:

```
NewFileName(prompt)
```

allows the user to create and name a new empty file, and returns its name.

### 14.2.8 TWO EXAMPLES

The predefined input and output procedures are normally used in preference to low-level operations with file-buffers, but there is one situation where a file-buffer is very useful. Suppose, in the context of program Arithmetic in Chapter 10, that exercises are presented with an equality symbol. So in response to the exercise:

```
8 + 7 =
```

the user might type a number (such as 15) that represents an attempt, or ? to get the answer, or q or Q to quit, or just hit Return (which is interpreted as ?). We would like to sneak a look at the next character in the input stream to determine whether or not to read an integer and can do so as follows:

```
if eoln or (Input^ = '?') then
  outcome := query
```

```
else if (Input^ = 'q') or (Input^ = 'Q') then
  outcome := QuitSession
else
  Read answer and set outcome accordingly;
Readln
```

Without using the file-buffer, we would have no alternative but to read a character, which is most inconvenient for processing attempted answers. We shall see later in this chapter that Macintosh Pascal provides a more powerful method (using procedure ReadString).

Our second example is a utility-procedure.

```
procedure append (var extra, f : text);
{ Appends extra to f; assumes f is being written and extra has }
{ already been associated with an external file if necessary. }
begin { append }
  Reset(extra);
  while not eof(extra) do
    begin { append next line from extra to f }
      while not eoln(extra) do
        begin
          Read(extra, f^);
          put(f)
        end;
      Writeln(f)
    end
end; { append }
```

Since assignment to a text file is not permitted, text file parameters must be var-parameters.

## 14.3 Strings in Macintosh Pascal

### 14.3.1 SYNTAX

Macintosh Pascal provides special string-types that permit more elaborate string-processing than do Pascal's. Mac-string-types have some of the properties of a simple-type (such as being permitted as the result-type of a function), and some of those of a structured-type (such as having a component-type). Their syntax is as follows:

type: *simple-type* | *structured-type* | *Mac-string-type*
Mac-string-type: **string** [ *size-attribute* ]
size-attribute: *unsigned-integer*

The optional size-attribute must be between 1 and 255 inclusive.

A value of a Mac-string-type is a sequence of characters. The number of characters in the sequence, called its **length**, is constrained to lie inclusively between 0 and the declared size-attribute, which defaults to 255 if not given. Mac-string-types provide variable-length strings, as compared to Pascal's fixed-length strings.

An extra constant is introduced to denote the **empty string** — the unique string whose length is 0. It is written ''.

Mac-character-string: *character-string* | *empty-string*
empty-string: ''

The syntactic term Mac-character-string replaces character-string in Pascal's syntax rules.

As already mentioned, a function can return a value of a Mac-string-type, but the result-type must be specified by a type-identifier or **string**. The same goes for formal parameters of functions and procedures.

result-type: *type-identifier* | **string**
parameter-type: *type-identifier* | **string**

The rules concerning parameters are relaxed for var-parameters of type **string**: a variable of *any* Mac-string-type is accepted as an actual-parameter. The size-attribute of the actual parameter becomes that of the formal parameter. This makes it possible to write perfectly general string-processing procedures.

## 14.3.2 ASSIGNMENT

A variable of a Mac-string-type *T* may be assigned any value of type char, any value of a Pascal string-type whose (fixed) length does not exceed the size-attribute of *T*, or any value of a Mac-string-type whose length does not exceed the size-attribute of *T*. The other direction is more strict: a variable of a Pascal string-type may be assigned a value of a Mac-string-type provided the lengths agree, and a variable of type char may be assigned a value of a Mac-string-type provided its length is 1. These rules simply codify the philosophy of permitting any assignment that makes sense, so there is little need to worry about them.

One consequence is that a value formal parameter of a Mac-string-type can handle any string or character value, provided only that the value's length does not exceed the parameter's size-attribute.

Here are two simple but convenient string-processing functions. The first can be used to avoid the three ugly uses of (s) in the output statements at the end of program Arithmetic in Chapter 10.

```
type
  string1 = string[1];

function plural (n : integer) : string1;
{ Returns 's' if n <> 1, else the empty string. }
begin { plural }
  if n <> 1 then
    plural := 's'
  else
    plural := ''
end; { plural }
```

For example, the first of these output statements becomes:

```
Writeln(NrCorrect : 1, ' correct answer', plural(NrCorrect))
```

If NrCorrect = 3, it prints:

```
3 correct answers
```

If NrCorrect = 1, it prints:

```
1 correct answer
```

This is a much neater solution than using the procedure Pluralize suggested in Exercise 10.8. Function plural could have been given the result-type **string**, but the chosen type is more precise and economical.

A more general function can easily be written that takes care of more complex situations involving plural forms:

```
function choose (SingularStr, PluralStr : string;
                 n : count) : string;
{ Returns SingularStr if n = 1, otherwise PluralStr. }
begin { choose }
  if n = 1 then
    choose := SingularStr
  else
    choose := PluralStr
end; { choose }
```

The expression plural($n$) is equivalent to choose('', 's', $n$). Program MiniNim from Chapter 9 might use the following statement to announce the number of matches remaining:

```
Writeln('There ', choose('is ', 'are ', LeftOver), LeftOver : 1,
        ' match', choose('', 'es', LeftOver), ' remaining.')
```

If LeftOver = 12, it prints:

```
There are 3 matches remaining.
```

If LeftOver = 1, it prints:

```
There is 1 match remaining.
```

It is possible to access a component of a variable of a Mac-string-type with an indexed-variable, which has type char. The subscript must be between 1 and the current length of the string, inclusive. Accessing components in this manner is recommended only in a couple of situations (described later), because there are higher-level alternatives that are more general. It is not possible, for instance, to extend a string as attempted below:

```
var
  s : string;

  s := 'Greatest Hits Vol. I'; { now length of s = 20 }
  s[21] := 'I' {XXXX ERROR XXXX}
```

### 14.3.3 STRING INPUT/OUTPUT

Output of a value of a Mac-string-type works as for a corresponding value of a Pascal string-type. We have seen two examples above, and there are plenty more in the sequel. The details are given in Chapter 5.

The same does not hold for input. Variables of Pascal string-types must be read character by character, but those of Mac-string-types need not and should not be read that way. Instead, a value may be read directly by including the variable in an input statement. If *s* is a variable of a Mac-string-type, the statement:

```
Read(s)
```

reads the sequence of characters up to but not including the next end-of-line marker, and gives the corresponding string to *s*. The length of *s* becomes the number of characters read; it must not exceed its size-attribute.

Consider the following program segment:

```
type
  index = 1..3;
var
  line : array[index] of string[80];
  i : index;
```

```
for i := 1 to 3 do
  Readln(line[i])
```

If before execution of the loop the input stream contains:

```
... ↑ I've∧got□plenty∧of□□...
```

then after execution

| | | |
|---|---|---|
| line[1] | contains | 'I''ve got' |
| line[2] | contains | 'plenty of' |
| line[3] | contains | '' |

and the input position is after the last marker shown.

Because characters past a marker will not be read, strings are invariably read with **Readln** rather than **Read**. Schema Process Lines is commonly used.

Another useful schema reads and processes one or more lines until an empty line is read; it uses a repeat loop with the stopping condition *line* = ''.

**Schema** Process Lines:

```
var
  f : text; { file to be processed }
{ Read and process f a line at a time up to end-of-file; }
{ assume file f is ready for reading, }
{ and has no line with more than 255 characters. }
--------------------------------------------------
  var
    line : string;

  while not eof(f) do
    begin
      Readln(f, line);
      Process line
    end
```

### 14.3.4 QUASI-I/O

We saw earlier that we can look one character ahead in the input by accessing the file-buffer, and use this information to determine what kind of value to read. A much more powerful method is possible in Macintosh Pascal. It is to read a line into a variable of a Mac-string-type, inspect the string (using the operators and functions described below), and then read *from the string* using the predefined procedure ReadString.

ReadString is like Read, but with two main differences. First, its first parameter is a value of a Mac-string-type rather than a text file, and is not optional. The other parameters are as for Read. Second, information is read and converted as necessary from the string rather than from a text file. If a string is read, an implicit end-of-line marker is assumed after the last character. It is an error if an attempt is made to read beyond the last character.

For example, if n is an integer variable, and s has type **string**, then after execution of:

```
ReadString('96 tears', n, s)
```

n = 96 and s = ' tears'.

When processing information that is mainly textual, it is easiest to use the above schema, and, if necessary, apply ReadString to the line read to convert embedded numeric or otherwise non-textual information. This technique is used later in this chapter in Case-study 9, in procedure SkipRestOfMessage.

There is a similar facility for output. This time a *function*, called StringOf, is provided. It takes exactly the same arguments as does Write with Output implicit, field widths included, and returns the string that Write would have appended to Output. It is an error if that string has more than 255 characters.

For example, if NrCorrect = 3, then:

```
StringOf(NrCorrect : 1, ' correct answer', plural(NrCorrect))
```

gives the value '3 correct answers'.

StringOf is most useful for assembling textual information to be displayed in the Drawing window, because its size can then be calculated, allowing it to be placed precisely. See the discussion following procedure DrawStringC later in this chapter.

### 14.3.5 COMPARING STRINGS

The only operators that may be used with values of Mac-string-types are the relational operators. Any two values of Mac-string-types or Pascal string-types or character-types may be compared — they do not need to have the same length. The outcome for equal-length strings is as specified by the Standard, and described in Chapter 11; otherwise, it is as if the shorter string were padded out with copies of an imaginary character that precedes the first one in the ordering. This scheme is consistent with dictionary ordering for words comprised of letters of the same case. Only identical strings are equal.

Here are some examples:

| | | |
|---|---|---|
| 'Blues' < 'Blues Brothers' | gives | true |
| 'Pascal strings are' < 'Perfect' | gives | true |
| '' < 'anything else' | gives | true |
| '99' < '100' | gives | false |
| 'Zulu' < 'aardvark' | gives | true *on the Mac* |

As the last example shows, the ordering is partly implementation-dependent.

### 14.3.6 PREDEFINED FUNCTIONS FOR STRINGS

A number of predefined functions are provided for string-processing. They can only be applied to values of Mac-string-types, but single characters and character strings are treated as constants of such types. Note that the string parameters of these functions act like neither var- nor value-parameters.

The function-call:

length(*s*)

returns the length of the string *s*. With array line as defined earlier (line[1] = 'I''ve got', line[2] = 'plenty of', line[3] = '') we find:

| | | |
|---|---|---|
| length(line[1]) | gives | 8 |
| length(line[2]) | gives | 9 |
| length(line[3]) | gives | 0 |
| length('line[3]') | gives | 7 |
| length('?') | gives | 1 |

Note that, despite the last two examples, length cannot be applied to a variable of a Pascal string-type, or a variable of type char.

A fundamental operation on strings is to join two strings together; it is called **concatenation**. It is provided in Macintosh Pascal by a function that can concatenate one or more string values. The function-call:

concat($s_1$, … , $s_n$)

returns the string obtained by concatenating the arguments in the given order. The length of the result is the sum of the lengths of the arguments. Here are some examples:

```
concat(line[1], line[2])            gives   'I''ve got plenty of'
concat(line[1], line[2], line[3])   gives   'I''ve got plenty of'
concat('Joliet', ' ', 'Jake')       gives   'Joliet Jake'
concat(' ', 'Joliet', 'Jake')       gives   ' JolietJake'
```

Consider the following program segment:

```
var
  phrase : string;
  i : 1..3;

  phrase := 'A rose';
  for i := 1 to 3 do
    phrase := concat(phrase, ' is a rose');
  phrase := concat(phrase, '.');
  Write(phrase)
```

It prints:

```
A rose is a rose is a rose is a rose.
```

Another fundamental operation, that of extracting a contiguous part of a string, called a **substring**, is provided by function copy. The function call:

copy(*s*, *index*, *count*)

where *index* and *count* are integer expressions, returns the substring of *s* containing *count* characters starting at character *s*[*index*], provided this substring exists. Otherwise, as much of the specified substring as exists is returned. No error ever occurs. Here are some examples:

```
copy('abcde', 2, 3)   gives   'bcd'
copy('abcde', 2, 0)   gives   ''
copy('abcde', 0, 3)   gives   'ab'
copy('abc', 2, 3)     gives   'bc'
copy('abc', 4, 1)     gives   ''
```

When *index* is between 1 and the length of *s*, copy(*s*, *index*, 1) can and should be replaced by *s*[*index*]. The latter form documents the assumption about *index*, and causes an error if it is not met. This is much more helpful to the programmer than continued execution.

Here is a function that uses the three string-processing functions we have met so far:

```
type
  StringIndex = 0..255;
```

```
function reverse (s : string) : string;
{ Returns the reverse of s. }
 var
   rev : string; { reverse of copy(s, 1, i – 1) }
   i : StringIndex;
begin { reverse }
 rev := '';
 for i := 1 to length(s) do
   rev := concat(copy(s, i, 1), rev);
 reverse := rev
end; { reverse }
```

In this case, copy(s, i, 1) can safely be replaced by s[i].

Execution of:

```
Writeln(reverse('A man, a plan, a canal: Panama'))
```

prints:

```
amanaP :lanac a ,nalp a ,nam A
```

A function is provided for searching a string for a given substring. The function-call:

pos(*sub*, *s*)

returns the least $i \geqslant 1$ such that:

copy(*s*, *i*, length(*sub*)) = *sub*

unless *s* is empty or no such *i* exists, in which case it returns 0. Here are some examples:

| | | |
|---|---|---|
| pos('yeah', 'yeah, yeah, yeah') | gives | 1 |
| pos('yeah', 'Yeah, yeah, yeah') | gives | 7 |
| pos('he', 'shenanigans') | gives | 2 |
| pos('.', 'Help!') | gives | 0 |
| pos('', 'not empty') | gives | 1 |

Here is a typical example of the use of pos:

```
var
 i : StringIndex; { position of first comma in name }
 name : string;

{ Assuming name has the form 'lastname, firstname', }
{ print 'firstname lastname' }
```

```
i := pos(',', name);
Write (copy(name, i + 2, length(name)), ' ', copy(name, 1, i – 1))
```

For example, if name = 'Blues, Elwood', then `Elwood Blues` is printed. The natural third argument of the first application of copy is length(name) – i – 1 — function copy allows us to be a little lazy.

Two other string-processing functions are provided. Function omit takes the same arguments as copy, and returns the string obtained by omitting the copied string. For example:

```
omit('abcde', 2, 3)  gives  'ae'
```

Function include does the opposite. It inserts a substring into a string at a specified position. The function call:

include(*s*, *sub*, *i*)

is equivalent to:

concat(copy(*s*, 1, *i* – 1), *sub*, copy(*s*, *i* + 1, length(*s*))

For example,

```
include(' ('Fatha")', 'Earl Hines', 5)  gives  'Earl ('Fatha") Hines',
```

The only possible error is an attempt to create a string with more than 255 characters.

### 14.3.7 PREDEFINED STRING PROCEDURES

Functions omit and include have corresponding procedures which are likely to be used more often. In each case the actual parameter *s* must be a variable of a Mac-string-type, and is changed by the procedure call. Its new value is the value returned by the corresponding function.

Procedure delete corresponds to function omit. For example, if variable s has the value 'abcde', then after execution of:  14.1

```
delete(s, 2, 3)
```

the new value of s is 'ae'.

Procedure insert corresponds to function include. For example, if variable s has the value 'Earl Hines', then after execution of:

```
insert(' ('Fatha")', s, 5)
```

the new value of s is 'Earl ('Fatha") Hines'.

Here is a procedure that employs these two predefined procedures.

```
procedure replace (old, new : string;
                   var s : string);
{ Replaces first occurrence of old in s by new. }
 var
  i : StringIndex;
begin { replace }
 i := pos(old, s);
 if i <> 0 then
  begin
   delete(s, i, length(old));
   insert(new, s, i)
  end
end; { replace }
```

For example, if word = 'mipselling', then after execution of:

```
replace('ps', 'ssp', word)
```

the new value of word is 'misspelling'.

Suppose now that we are asked (by Morris Udall's press secretary perhaps) to write a procedure that replaces *each* occurrence of a substring. It will not do simply to apply replace repeatedly to the entire string, because a replacement may cause new instances of the substring to appear. Attempting to replace each 's' with 'ss' in this way, for instance, would hiss until an error occurs.

Our algorithm instead repeatedly peels off the replaced part of s and appends it to an initially empty string t, so that t grows as s shrinks. This is an efficient approach to many string-processing problems, as it avoids repeated searches through a long string. It is difficult to *draw* a general picture, but easy enough to describe the general situation in technical English, as does the comment accompanying the declaration of t.

```
procedure ReplaceAll (old, new : string;
                      var s : string);
{ Replaces all occurrences of old in s by new; assumes old <> ''. }
 var
  t : string; { final value of s = concat(t, s-with-new-for-each-old) }
  i : StringIndex; { = pos(old, s) }
begin { ReplaceAll }
 t := '';
 i := pos(old, s);
 while i <> 0 do
  begin { suppose s = ... old----- }
```

```
      t := concat(t, copy(s, 1, i – 1), new); { t := t ... new }
      delete(s, 1, i + length(old) – 1); { s := ----- }
      i := pos(old, s)
    end;
  s := concat(t, s)
end; { ReplaceAll }
```

The comments help the reader understand the effect of the body of the loop.

Suppose the procedure call ReplaceAll(s, 'ch', 'ch ch') is executed, with s = 'ch changes'. The following table shows the values of the crucial variables before each evaluation of the loop's condition. Note that the comment for t is effectively an invariant.

| t | s | i |
|---:|---|---:|
| '' | 'ch changes' | 1 |
| 'ch ch' | ' changes' | 2 |
| 'ch ch ch ch' | 'anges' | 2 |

On termination of the loop, s receives the value 'ch ch ch changes', as required.

### 14.3.8 DRAWING STRINGS

Subsection 9.2.4, 'Drawing text', introduced the predefined procedure WriteDraw, which is sufficient for all displaying of text in the Drawing window. Macintosh Pascal also provides procedures DrawChar and DrawString, which live up to their names but do nothing that WriteDraw can not.

WriteDraw draws to the right of the current pen position. Since it is the left edge of the text that is precisely positioned, the text is said to be **left-aligned**. Often text should be centered, or perhaps right-aligned. The predefined procedure StringWidth comes to the rescue. It returns the width, in pixels, of a given string if it is drawn with the current options in effect.

This procedure centers a string at the current pen position:

```
procedure DrawStringC (s : string);
{ Draws s with the center of its base line at the current pen }
{ position; leaves the pen position at the end of the string. }
begin { DrawStringC }
  Move(–StringWidth(s) div 2, 0);
  DrawString(s)
end; { DrawStringC }
```

A procedure like WriteDraw cannot be written, because it takes the same list of arguments as does Write (with Output implicit). But the desired effect can easily be obtained. To center the string resulting from an output-value-list $a_1, \ldots, a_n$, use:

```
DrawStringC(StringOf(a1, ... , an))
```

For example, to center an appropriate heading for the display produced by program JobScheduler3 in Chapter 11, we might use:

```
const
  ScreenWidth = 512; { width of Macintosh's screen in pixels }

MoveTo(ScreenWidth div 2, Top – (PointSize div 2));
DrawStringC(StringOf('Job-scheduling on ', NrProcessors : 1,
                     ' processors.'))
```

## 14.4 Case-study 8: A mail minder

### 14.4.1 SETTING OF THE PROBLEM

Electronic mail can be sent between users whose computers belong to the same network. Mail is transmitted from computer to computer in the network, using telephone lines or other connections, along a path that starts with the sender's computer and ends with the receiver's. The computers are called the nodes of the network. Although messages may be encoded for transmission, as far as the sender and receiver are concerned, electronic mail consists entirely of textual information.

A networked computer automatically delivers mail for a given user in a particular file. We will write a program that reads newly arrived messages, and creates a file of replies to those messages which have urgent priority. The file will be in the form required by the system program that sends mail. The content of each reply is to be read from a file prepared by the user. Before leaving for an extended period, the user will arrange for the program to be run each night, so that senders of urgent messages can be informed of how to contact the user, or of whatever information the user chooses.

### 14.4.2 SPECIFICATIONS

Incoming mail appears in a particular external file. The file contains zero or more messages, each consisting of a number of header lines followed by lines containing the content of the message. No line has more than 80 characters. Each message has the form shown in Figure 14.3. Note that the header lines of interest appear in a known order, but may have other header lines interspersed. None of the string values in a header line may be empty. A path consists of 1 or more node names separated by exclamation marks. For example:

```
...
From: sender
...
Date: date message was sent
...
Path: path from sender to receiver
...
Priority: priority of message
...
Lines(n1):
n1 lines containing content of message
```

**Figure 14.3**
The form of a message.

doc!grumpy!happy!bashful!sneezy!dopey!sleepy

An external file is to be created that contains a reply to each message in the incoming mail that has *priority of message* = URGENT. Each reply is to have the form shown in Figure 14.4.

The system mailer program will convert this information into the appropriate form for transmission. The addressee of each reply is to be recorded on file Output.

### 14.4.3 WRITING THE PROGRAM

At the highest level, the program just processes each message, but before doing so, it must ready the three external files:

```
begin { MailMinder }
  Prepare external files for reading or writing;
  while there are more received messages to process do
    Process next received message
end. { MailMinder }
```

The first action is implemented with Macintosh Pascal's extended form of Reset and Rewrite. String constants are used prominently to display the names of the three external files, which in this case reside on the disk named 'pp'.

```
const
  MailboxFile = 'pp:mbox';
  MailToSendFile = 'pp:mdeliver';
  InfoFile = 'pp:info';
var
  mailbox, { messages received }
  MailToSend, { replies to URGENT priority messages }
  info { message to send in reply }
```

**Figure 14.4**
The form of a reply.

`To:` *sender of urgent received message*
`Path:` *path to sender of urgent received message*
`Re: your mail of` *date urgent received message was sent*
*copy of the external file containing the reply*

```
    : text;
  Reset(mailbox, MailboxFile);
  Rewrite(MailToSend, MailToSendFile);
  Reset(info, InfoFile)
```

The condition of the loop can now be formulated as **not** eof(mailbox). To *Process next received message*, the relevant information is extracted, a reply appended to file MailToSend if the message has urgent priority, and the rest of the message skipped:

```
const
  MaxLineLength = 80;
type
  str = string[MaxLineLength];
var
  sender, { sender of received message }
  DateSent, { date of received message }
  PathToMe, { path from sender to me }
  priority { of received message }
    : str;

begin { Process next received message }
  Set sender = sender of message;
  Set DateSent = date message was sent;
  Set PathToMe = path from sender to me;
  Set priority = priority of message;
  if priority = 'URGENT' then
    Append a reply to MailToSend;
  Skip rest of message
end
```

The four actions that assign to variables of Mac-string-types are understood to involve reading mailbox; they are refined with a single procedure. The remaining actions are refined with appropriate procedures:

```
procedure FindField (header : str;
      var value : str);
{ Repeatedly reads lines from file mailbox until one starting }
{ with header is found, then sets value to rest of line; }
{ assumes such a line will be found. Global var: mailbox. }
```

```
procedure SendInfo (addressee : str;
      path : string; { path to addressee }
      date : str); { date of message from addressee }
{ Sends reply consisting of header lines giving the addressee, }
{ path, and a reference to date, followed by contents }
{ of global text file info; records addressee on Output. }
{ Global vars: MailToSend, info. }

procedure SkipRestOfMessage;
{ Reads remaining lines of current message; }
{ assumes line beginning 'Lines(' not yet read. }
{ Global var: mailbox. }

begin { Process next received message }
  FindField('From: ', sender);
  FindField('Date: ', DateSent);
  FindField('Path: ', PathToMe);
  FindField('Priority: ', priority);
    if priority = 'URGENT' then
      SendInfo(sender, reverse of path PathToMe, DateSent);
  SkipRestOfMessage
end
```

Note the use of global file variables. In this problem there is little to be gained by avoiding their use, because the procedures involved share the same context. Also, there is a convention of doing so, albeit implicitly, with the external text file variables Input and Output.

FindField is short and simple, though note that it relies on the fact that the string values in header lines are non-empty. The other procedures are also straightforward. All the procedures are given below in the complete program.

The most interesting problem is that of computing the string argument

```
reverse of path PathToMe
```

of procedure SendInfo. We decide to do so with a function:

```
function ReversePath (path : str) : str;
{ Returns reverse of path: If path = 'node1!node2! ... !noden', }
{ then result = 'noden! ... !node2!node1'. }

ReversePath(PathToMe)
```

The solution uses the same schema as employed in procedure ReplaceAll earlier in the chapter, viz. accumulating the result in an initially empty string variable (rev) as the parameter (path) is reduced.

Specifically, each iteration peels off a node and the following '!', and adds the '!' followed by the node to the front of **rev**. So the invariant is that after $k$ iterations,

$$\text{rev} = \text{'}!node_k! \ldots !node_1\text{'},$$

and

$$\text{path} = \text{'}node_{k+1}! \ldots !node_n\text{'}.$$

So the loop should stop when only a single node remains, i.e. when **pos('!', path) = 0** gives true. Negating this condition gives the condition for the while-loop. A while-loop is used in preference to a repeat-loop, because a path might consist of a single node; this would happen if an urgent message is sent by a user of the same computer. On termination, the result is obtained by concatenating **path** and **rev**. See the complete program for the details.

### 14.4.4 THE COMPLETE PROGRAM

Once again the program consists of a number of short subprograms. Procedures **append** and **field** could be declared by the single respective procedures that call them, but are declared at the start of the program-block, following our policy for subprograms of general utility.

```
program MailMinder (Output);
{ Reads all messages in file mailbox, and creates replies to }
{ those of urgent priority in file MailToSend; the content of }
{ each reply is read from file info. }
 const
  MaxLineLength = 80;
  MailboxFile = 'pp:mbox';
  MailToSendFile = 'pp:mdeliver';
  InfoFile = 'pp:info';
 type
  str = string[MaxLineLength];
  count = 0..Maxint;
 var
  mailbox, { messages received }
  MailToSend, { replies to URGENT priority messages }
  info { message to send in reply }
   : text;
  sender, { sender of received message }
  DateSent, { date of received message }
```

```
  PathToMe, { path from sender to me }
  priority { of received message }
    : str;
```

```
procedure append (var extra, f : text);
{ Appends extra to f; assumes f is being written and extra has }
{ already been associated with an external file if necessary. }
```
*given earlier in Section 14.2.8*

```
function field (header : str;
      line : str) : str;
{ If line = concat(header, s), returns s, else empty string. }
{ Global const: MaxLineLength. }
begin { field }
  if copy(line, 1, length(header)) = header then
    field := copy(line, length(header) + 1, MaxLineLength)
  else
    field := ''
end; { field }
```

```
procedure FindField (header : str;
      var value : str);
{ Repeatedly reads lines from file mailbox until one starting }
{ with header is found, then sets value to rest of line; }
{ assumes such a line will be found. Global var: mailbox. }
{ Global subprogram: field. }
  var
    line : str; { line of received message }
begin { FindField }
  value := '';
  repeat
    Readln(mailbox, line);
    value := field(header, line)
  until value <> ''
end; { FindField }
```

```
function ReversePath (path : str) : str;
{ Returns reverse of path: If path = 'node1!node2! ... !noden', }
{ then result = 'noden! ... !node2!node1'. }
  var
    rev : str; { result = concat(reverse of path, rev) }
    i : 0..255; { = pos('!', path); N.B. path is changed }
begin { ReversePath }
  i := pos('!', path);
  rev := '';
  while i > 0 do
```

```
    begin
      rev := concat('!', copy(path, 1, i – 1), rev);
      delete(path, 1, i);
      i := pos('!', path)
    end;
  ReversePath := concat(path, rev)
end; { ReversePath }


procedure SkipRestOfMessage;
{ Reads remaining lines of current message; }
{ assumes line beginning 'Lines(' not yet read. }
{ Global var: mailbox. }
{ Global subprogram: field. }
 var
  line : str; { rest of or complete line of received message }
  NrLines, { number of lines remaining in received message }
  i : count;
begin { SkipRestOfMessage }
  FindField('Lines(', line);
  ReadString(line, NrLines);
  for i := 1 to NrLines do
    Readln(mailbox, line)
end; { SkipRestOfMessage }


procedure SendInfo (addressee : str;
      path : string; { path to addressee }
      date : str); { date of message from addressee }
{ Sends reply consisting of header lines giving the addressee, }
{ path, and a reference to date, followed by contents }
{ of global text file info; records addressee on Output. }
{ Global vars: MailToSend, info. }
{ Global subprogram: append. }
begin { SendInfo }
  Writeln(MailToSend, 'To: ', addressee);
  Writeln(MailToSend, 'Path: ', path);
  Writeln(MailToSend, 'Re: your mail of ', date);
  append(info, MailToSend);
  Writeln('Notice sent to ', addressee)
end; { SendInfo }

begin { MailMinder }
  Reset(mailbox, MailboxFile);
  Rewrite(MailToSend, MailToSendFile);
  Reset(info, InfoFile);
  while not eof(mailbox) do
    begin { process next received message }
      FindField('From: ', sender);
```

```
    FindField('Date: ', DateSent);
    FindField('Path: ', PathToMe);
    FindField('Priority: ', priority);
    if priority = 'URGENT' then
      SendInfo(sender, ReversePath(PathToMe), DateSent);
    SkipRestOfMessage
  end
end. { MailMinder }
```

## 14.5 Macaveats

Macintosh Pascal allows only **Input** and **Output** as program parameters; its method of associating text file variables with external files is non-Standard (though common).

Although string values of different lengths may be compared, this is an extension rather than a violation, because the comparisons permitted by the Standard are properly carried out.

## EXERCISES

**14.1** Suppose the rest of the input stream contains:

↑□the∧last∧line.□

(a) What is the value of Input^?

(b) What is the value of Input^ after execution of get(Input)?

(c) What is the value of Input^ after the further execution of Readln?

**14.2** What is the value of Output^ after execution of:

(a) Output^ := '#'    (b) Write('h')

**14.3** Write a program that prompts the user to select an external text file, and prints the number of lines in the file selected. It should use OldFileName to select the file, and read the file using get rather than Read or Readln.

**14.4** Show what is printed by:

Writeln('I came ', n : 1, ' time', choose('.', 's!', n))

(a) when n = 1    (b) when n = 3    (c) when n = 0

**14.5** With line and i as defined in the text, describe the effect of executing:

```
for i := 1 to 3 do
  Readln(line[i])
```

**14.6** Procedure append can be implemented by using a local variable of a Mac-string-type to read and write a line at a time. Give such an implementation.

**14.7** What schema did you use to solve the previous question?

**14.8** A string $s_1$ is a *cyclic permutation* of another string $s_2$ iff $s_2$ is not empty and there are strings $x$ and $y$ such that $s_1$ = concat($x$, $y$) and $s_2$ = concat($y$, $x$). For example, the cyclic permutations of 'abc' are 'abc', 'bca', and 'cab'.

(a) Implement the following procedure:

```
type
  str100 = string[100];

procedure PrintCycle (s : str100);
{ Prints each of the length(s) cyclic permutations of s, }
{ one per line. }
```

(b) Implement the following function:

```
function CyclicPermutation (s1, s2 : str100) : Boolean;
{ Returns true iff s1 is a cyclic permutation of s2. }
```

**14.9** Implement the following action:

*Assuming* name *has the form 'firstname lastname',*
*print 'lastname, firstname'*

**14.10** Implement the following function:

```
function ShortForm (name : string) : string;
{ Assumes that name consists of 1 or more first names }
{ followed by a surname, with successive names separated }
{ by one space. Returns a name consisting of the initial }
```

{ letters of the first names, in order, each followed by }
{ a period, then a space and the surname; e.g. if name = }
'Martin Luther King', then 'M.L. King' should be returned. }

**14.11** Implement the following function:

```
function anagram (s1, s2 : string) : Boolean;
{ Returns true iff s1 and s2 are anagrams, i.e. both contain }
{ the same characters with the same frequencies, as with }
{ 'slow' and 'owls', but not 'oops' and 'pops'. }
```

*Hint*: First check the lengths; if they are equal, attempt to take each character in s1, locate it in s2, and remove it from s2.

**14.12** Implement the following procedure:

```
procedure substitute (sub : string;
                      var s : string;
                      i : integer);
{ Replaces the substring of s of length length(sub) starting }
{ at position i with sub; as much of the substring as exists is }
{ replaced with an initial substring of sub of the same length, }
{ so length(s) is unchanged. }
```

**14.13** Implement the following procedure:

```
procedure compress (var s : string);
{ Assumes s is a string of words separated by 1 or }
{ more blanks; removes blanks so that successive words }
{ are separated by one space. }
```

Base the solution on the following invariant:

t = '$part_1 \wedge part_2 \wedge \ldots \wedge part_k \wedge$',
s = '$part_{k+1} \wedge \ldots \wedge part_{k+2} \wedge \ldots \wedge \ldots \wedge \ldots \wedge\ part_n$', and
i = pos('$\wedge\wedge$', s)

for some $k \geqslant 0$, where a part is a string of words separated by single spaces, $\wedge$ denotes a space, and initially:

s = '$part_1\ \wedge \ldots \wedge part_2 \wedge \ldots \wedge \ldots \wedge \ldots \wedge part_n$'.

The idea is to process a part at a time, rather than a word at a time.

**14.14** Implement the following procedure:

```
procedure DrawStringR (s : string);
{ Draws s with the right of its base line at the current }
{ pen position; leaves the pen position unchanged. }
```

**14.15** Use your answer to the previous question, and procedure DrawStringC from the text, to place all textual information correctly in the diagram drawn by program JobScheduler3 in Chapter 11.

**14.16** What changes would be needed in program MailMinder if a header line could have no characters following its first colon (`:`)?

**14.17** Suppose, in the context of Case-study 8, that a second form of message can occur that accommodates long paths. It differs from the form given in Figure 14.3 in that the line beginning `Path:` is replaced by:

`Path(`$n_p$`)` : *first part of path*
$n_p - 1$ *lines containing the rest of the path*

Suppose further that no path requires more than three lines (so it may be represented by a single variable of type **string**), and that the system mailer program will accept a long path in a return message (whose form remains that given in Figure 14.4).

Modify program MailMinder so that it can handle both types of message.

# 15 RECORDS

Life is a great bundle of little things.
— Oliver Wendell Holmes Sen., *The Professor at the Breakfast Table*

## 15.1 Introduction

Often an object to be manipulated by a program has several attributes, and is therefore represented by several variables of appropriate types. For example, program Arithmetic for Case-study 5 in Chapter 10 deals mainly with arithmetic tests, which consist of a left and right operand and an operation. So it defines the appropriate types:

```
const
  lower = 0; { lower limit to values of operands }
  upper = 10; { upper limit to values of operands }
type
  operand = lower..upper;
  operation = (plus, minus, times);
```

The program-block uses a single test at a time, which it represents with three variables:

```
var
  a, b : operand; { operands of a test }
  op : operation; { operation of a test }
```

Similarly, the subprograms that manipulate tests declare suitable formal parameters. Here is one example:

```
procedure NewTest (var n1 : operand;
                   var op : operation;
                   var n2 : operand);
{ Gives a new random value to each parameter. }
```

There is something unsatisfactory here. There is nothing other than context that documents the important fact that the two operands and the operation are aspects of a single object. That fact is unclear particularly in the program-block, where the three variables concerned appear together with several others.

Fortunately, Pascal provides a means of gathering a collection of values of possibly different types into a single, structured value called a **record**. In the example at hand, we might define a type to represent tests as follows:

```
type
  test = record
      n1, n2 : operand;
      op : operation
    end;
```

test is called a **record type**. A value of type test is a record consisting of three named components, or **fields**, which are values of the declared types. The field-names n1, n2, and op distinguish the components.

The program can now represent a test with a single variable:

```
var
  t : test; { the next test to be given }
```

Similarly, procedure NewTest now needs only a single formal parameter:

```
procedure NewTest (var t : test);
{ Sets each component of t to a random value. }
```

The components of a variable of type test are themselves variables. They are named using **dot notation**. For example, the three components of variable t are:

t.n1, a variable of type operand,

t.n2, a variable of type operand,

t.op, a variable of type operation.

The entire record-variable may be pictured as shown in Figure 15.1, which shows a typical value after execution of:

```
NewTest(t)
```

We see that:

t.n1 contains 5,

t.n2 contains 7,

t.op contains times.

There are two ways to give a value to a record-variable. One is

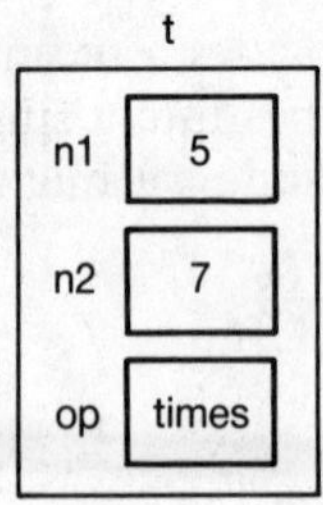


**Figure 15.1**
The record-variable t of type test.

by operating on the individual components, as exemplified by the body of procedure **NewTest**:

```
var
  i : 0..OrdOfLastOp;
begin { NewTest }
  t.n1 := ran(lower, upper);
  t.n2 := ran(lower, upper);
{ Set t.op to a random operation }
  t.op := plus;
  for i := 1 to ran(0, OrdOfLastOp) do
    t.op := succ(t.op)
end; { NewTest }
```

Components of a record variable are just like other variables of their respective types; they may be given values by assignment, as above, or by execution of an input-statement. Of course, there is no compunction to give new values to *all* components — a record may be **selectively updated** by giving a single component a new value; the values of the other components are unchanged.

The other way is to give a value to the entire record-variable, by **record-assignment**, or, as we shall see in the next chapter, by reading a value from a file of records. If t1 and t2 are variables of type test, then the assignment:

```
t1 := t2
```

is equivalent to:

```
begin
  t1.n1 := t2.n1;
  t1.n2 := t2.n2;
  t1.op := t2.op
end
```

Clearly the first formulation is preferable. It is higher-level, more concise, and likely to be implemented more efficiently. Naturally, all components of t2 must be defined.

## 15.2 Syntax

A record-type is a new unpacked-structured-type. The record-types that we have met have only a fixed-part. There is provision for another part, called a variant-part, which we will meet later.

> unpacked-structured-type: *array-type* | *file-type* | *record-type*
> record-type: **record**
> *field-list*
> **end**
> field-list: | *fixed-part* ; | *variant-part* ; |
> *fixed-part* ;
> *variant-part* ;
> fixed-part: | *record-section* ;
> ...
> *record-section*
> record-section: *identifier-list* : *type*

Note that the field-list may be followed by an optional semicolon, and may even be empty (a possibility required for variant-parts). The field-identifiers appearing in a particular record-type must be distinct. Technically, the scopes of other identifiers do not include the field-list, so the field-identifiers need not differ from other identifiers. However, it is usually clearer if new names are chosen.

Record-components are a new kind of component-variable. They have a very simple syntax:

> component-variable: *indexed-variable* | *file-buffer* | *field-designator*
> field-designator: *record-variable* . *field-identifier*
> record-variable: *variable*
> field-identifier: *identifier*

Some other syntactic points should be noted:

- Record-assignment is permitted only when both record-types are the same.
- A record-type is a structured-type, and therefore cannot be the result-type of a function.
- A component of a packed record may not be used as an actual variable parameter.

## 15.3 Some predefined record-types

QuickDraw defines several record-types. The simplest is the type for points on the coordinate plane:

```
type
  Point = record
      v, h : integer
    end
```

A point is a record of two integer components, representing a vertical and a horizontal coordinate. Their field-names are v and h respectively.

In this example all components of the record have the same type.

> **Moral** There are occasions where a record-type should be used even though an array-type is applicable.

For instance, it can happen that the attributes of an object accidentally have the same type, even though conceptually they are of different kinds. In such cases, it is extremely unlikely that the ability to compute the index of a subscripted-variable will be exploited. A record is then the better choice because of the increased readability afforded by field names.

The pen-position is a value of type Point. It can be ascertained by calling the following predefined procedure:

```
procedure GetPen (var pt : Point);
{ Sets pt to the current pen-position. }
```

For an example of the use of this procedure, see program TextStyles in Chapter 18.

A position is not the only attribute of the pen. It also has a size, a mode, and a pattern. So the following predefined type is used to describe the state of the pen:

```
type
  PenState = record
        pnLoc, pnSize : Point;
        pnMode : integer;
        pnPat : Pattern
      end
```

It is somewhat of a pun to use the type Point for the size of the pen —

perhaps it is a ball-point pen. But the size does consist of a pair of integers, one a vertical dimension and the other a horizontal one. The significance of the pnMode field is described in the Technical Appendix.

There are predefined procedures to get and set the state of the pen:

```
procedure GetPenState (var pnState : PenState);
{ Sets pnState to the state of the pen. }

procedure SetPenState (pnState : PenState);
{ Sets the state of the pen to pnState. }
```

These can be used to write truly independent graphics procedures, by having them save and restore the state of the pen. For example, a procedure that uses a square pen having a certain size, but otherwise with the current settings, could have a body like the following:

```
  const
    SideOfPen = ...; { length of each side of pen }
  var
    OldPenState : PenState;
begin
  GetPenState(OldPenState);
  PenSize(SideOfPen, SideOfPen);
  ...
{ Restore previous state of pen }
  PenSize(OldPenState.pnSize.h, OldPenState.pnSize.v)
end
```

The PenSize procedure is used to restore the previous state because it documents the fact that only the size was changed. Also, it needs to do less work than procedure SetPenState.

Arguments like those in the second call of PenSize can occur when record-types contain other record-types.

OldPenState is a variable of type PenState;

OldPenState.pnSize is a variable of type Point;

OldPenState.pnSize.h is a variable of type integer.

Component-variables can get quite complex, especially when array- and record-types are used together. They are always read from left to right. See Exercise 15.6 for an example.

## 15.4 The with-statement

A localized part of a program often has several field-designators with the same record-variable. The body of procedure **NewTest**, as given earlier in this chapter, is a good example. Pascal provides a special statement for such situations, called the **with-statement**. It enables the record-variable to be specified at the outset, after which its components need be named only by their field-names. For example, the statement-part of **NewTest** may be written:

```
begin { NewTest }
  with t do
    begin
      n1 := ran(lower, upper);
      n2 := ran(lower, upper);
      { Set t.op to a random operation }
      op := plus;
      for i := 1 to ran(0, OrdOfLastOp) do
        op := succ(op)
    end { with t }
end; { NewTest }
```

The syntax of this new structured-statement is as follows:

structured-statement: *compound-statement* | *repetitive-statement* | *conditional-statement* | *with-statement*

with-statement: **with** *record-variable-list* **do** *statement*

record-variable-list: *record-variable* ... , *record-variable*

With a single record-variable in the list, as in the example above, a new scope is created in which the field-names of the variable's record-type stand for the corresponding fields of the variable. There is no confusion with variables, constants, etc. with the same names; in the body of the with-statement, the new meanings override the old.

The full form of the with-statement permits more than one record-variable to be specified. A with-statement of the form:

**with** $v_1$ , $v_2$ , ..., $v_n$ **do**
  $S$

is defined to be equivalent to:

**with** $v_1$ **do**
  **with** $v_2$ **do**
    ...
      **with** $v_n$ **do**
        $S$

It follows that if two or more of the record-variables $v_i$ have a field with the same name, then the field is taken to belong to the rightmost of these record-variables in the list. Such fields of the other record-variables can still be accessed by giving their complete field-designators, but bear in mind the following principle:

> **Principle** Avoid multiple record-variables in a field-list if they are the least bit confusing.

As another example of a with-statement, the last statement in the exemplary graphics procedure given previously can be written:

```
with OldPenState.pnSize do
  PenSize(h, v)
```

Note that it could have been written:

```
with OldPenState, pnSize do
  PenSize(h, v)
```

because this is equivalent to:

```
with OldPenState do
  with pnSize do
    PenSize(h, v)
```

which in turn is equivalent to:

```
with OldPenState do
  PenSize(pnSize.h, pnSize.v)
```

There is no point in doing this in the example at hand, but occasionally the technique can be usefully applied to abbreviate all the lowest-level components of a nested record variable. Connoisseurs of the curious will note that it is one of the few occasions where a significant character may be mistyped with impunity!

## 15.5 Implementing variable-length strings

Truly natural string-processing demands variable-length strings and at least the fundamental operations of creation, comparison, determination of length, concatenation, extraction of substrings, assignment, and input and output. Other operations can be expressed if needed in terms of these fundamental ones. For example, deleting part of a string amounts to concatenating the two remaining substrings. All of these operations are provided in Macintosh Pascal by Mac-string-types, as shown in Chapter 14.

However, these types are an extension to Standard Pascal, and are not available in many, perhaps most, implementations. A programmer who wishes to do Macintosh-style string processing in Standard Pascal should take the view that the objects to be manipulated, viz. variable-length strings, need to be implemented with structured types, and that a sufficient set of operations on them needs to be implemented with subprograms. Record-types are the natural implementation in this and the majority of like situations.

A type of variable-length strings of a specified maximum length can be represented as follows:

```
const
  MaxStringLength = ... ;
type
  StringLength = 0..MaxStringLength;
  StringIndex = 1..MaxStringLength;
  string = record
      ch : packed array[StringIndex] of char;
      length : StringLength
    end;
    { represents the string ch[1], ch[2], ... , ch[length] }
```

The length of a string may be computed with a function:

```
function length (var s : string) : StringLength;
{ Returns the length of s. }
begin { length }
  length := s.length
end; { length }
```

It is safe to use a var-parameter here.

And here is a procedure that implements concatenation:

```
procedure concat (s1, s2 : string;
                           var result : string);
{ Sets result to s1 concatenated with s2; }
{ assumes length(s1) + length(s2) <= MaxStringLength. }
  var
    i : StringIndex;
begin { concat }
  if s1.length + s2.length > MaxStringLength then
```

```
      Writeln('ERROR in concat: result too long')
    else
      with result do
        begin
          for i := 1 to s1.length do
            ch[i] := s1.ch[i];
          for i := 1 to s2.length do
            ch[s1.length + i] := s2.ch[i];
          length := s1.length + s2.length
        end { with result }
  end; { concat }
```

Here the input parameters must be value-parameters to permit calls such as concat(t, s, s), which is used in the example below.

The following example shows how the procedure ReplaceAll from Chapter 14 would look when adapted to use this new type of variable-length strings. It assumes that equivalents of Macintosh Pascal's function pos and procedures insert and delete have been implemented; also a procedure that mimics the function copy, and a procedure that creates an empty string. Writing these subprograms is left to Exercise 15.8; see Chapter 14 for their specifications.

```
  procedure ReplaceAll (old, new : string;
                                  var s : string);
  { Replaces all occurrences of old in s by new; }
  { assumes the result is not too long. }
    var
      t : string; { final value of s = t concatenated with
                  s-with-new-for-each-old }
      i : StringLength; { = pos(old, s) }
      temp : string;
  begin { ReplaceAll }
    MakeEmptyString(t);
    i := pos(old, s);
    while i <> 0 do
      begin { suppose s = ... old--- }
      { Set t to t ... new }
        copy(s, 1, i – 1, temp);
        insert(temp, t, length(t) + 1);
        insert(new, t, length(t) + 1);

        delete(s, 1, i + length(old) – 1); { s := --- }
        i := pos(old, s)
      end;
    concat(t, s, s)
  end; { ReplaceAll }
```

This version is certainly more awkward than the original, mainly because Pascal does not permit functions to have structured result-types, but the fit is not too bad.

Besides the inability to have functions of the new type string, the other major source of awkwardness is the inability to have constants of this type.

## 15.6 Abstract data types

The ideas behind our implementation of variable-length strings in Standard Pascal are very important. Increasingly, as you tackle more complex programming problems, it will happen that the conceptual objects of a high-level solution cannot be represented with simple Pascal types. By far the best approach in such situations is to represent the values of an abstract type of object with a structured type, and to represent the abstract operations on these values with subprograms. The benefit is that solutions to programming problems can then be formulated in a language that reflects the conceptual language of the high-level solution.

A new type implemented in this fashion, such as the type string of variable-length strings, is called an **abstract data type**.

> **Principle** The set of operations provided for an abstract data type should be sufficiently rich that the new type can be used *without ever knowing how it is implemented*.

For example, consider procedure ReplaceAll above. It is formulated entirely in terms of abstract types (StringLength, string) and abstract operations (MakeEmptyString, pos, copy, length, insert, delete, concat). Even if the implementation of type string were radically changed, this procedure would need no changes.

Mac-string-types can be regarded as predefined abstract data types. They fail in only one way in hiding the details of their implementation from the user: in allowing individual characters in a string to be accessed as if they were components of an array. Using s[i] as an abbreviation for copy(s, i ,1) when $1 \leqslant$ i $\leqslant$ length(s) does no great violence to the principle of abstraction, but permitting a character to be assigned to s[i] under the same conditions is way out of line. The proper approach would have been to provide procedure substitute from Exercise 14.12.

Abstract data types are easiest to employ when there is a natural, well-defined concept of the abstract objects that a solution should be expressed in. Not surprisingly, many useful abstract data types are borrowed from mathematics; examples are sets with arbitrary base-types, relations (which are fundamental to data-base software), and sequences.

Records play an indispensable role in implementing abstract data types. Further examples occur in Exercises 15.10 and 15.11, and in Chapter 20. The topic is a large one, and the reader is referred to the further reading at the end of this chapter and also in Chapter 20. In Chapter 20 it is noted that Macintosh Pascal permits the order of definitions and declarations to be arranged to document better an abstract data type.

15.1

## 15.7 Variant records

Suppose a program has to work with a simple English vocabulary. The following information is to be kept about each word:

- spelling;
- a concise definition;
- syntactic category: noun, verb, adverb, or adjective;
- for a noun, its plural form;
- for a verb, its type (transitive or intransitive or both) and past participle.

A record is the natural choice in Pascal for such a description. There is little trouble in choosing an appropriate type for each piece of information, but it would be wasteful and unclear to include a field for every possibility. This is where variant-fields come to the fore, as Pascal provides for the latter part of a record to contain a collection of fields that depends on the value of a field in the fixed-part. For example, a suitable type in Macintosh Pascal for words would be:

```
type
  category = (noun, verb, adverb, adjective);
  VerbType = (transitive, intransitive);
  VerbTypes = set of VerbType;
  word = record
        spelling : string[20];
        definition : string;
        case kind : category of
          noun : (
            plural : string[20]
            );
          verb : (
            VerbKinds : VerbTypes;
```

```
PastPart : string[20]
);
adverb, adjective : ()
end
```

(The meaning of **VerbTypes** will become clear after reading Chapter 17.) In Standard Pascal, fixed-length strings with either blank padding or an accompanying length indicator (in a record!) could be used in place of the Mac-strings.

The fields named spelling, definition, and kind belong to every value of type word. However, field kind is special; it is called the **tag-field**, and its value determines the remaining fields of the record. If its value is noun, there is one more field, named plural; if verb, two more fields named VerbTypes and VerbKinds; otherwise there are no more fields. Figure 15.2 gives diagrammatic examples of four variables of type word:

```
var
  aNoun, aVerb, anAdverb, anAdjective : word;
```

The boxes for the entire records are the same size, to reflect the fact that the usual implementation reserves as much memory as needed for the largest possible variant-part. The definitions, by the way, are from Ambrose Bierce's *The Devil's Dictionary*.

Another example of a record-type with a variant-part is type FormatItem in program IdiotSheet for Case-study 9 in Section 16.4.

### 15.7.1 SYNTAX

Type word illustrates the general form of the variant-part. The syntax rules are:

variant-part: **case** *tag-field type-identifier* **of**
  | *variant* ;
  | ...
  *variant*
tag-field: *identifier* :
variant: *case-label-list* : (
  *field-list*
  )

It can be seen that Macintosh Pascal is lavish with space when displaying record-types.

The syntax of a variant-part tends to give trouble because it is not as similar to that for a case-statement as one might expect. Traps for young players are:

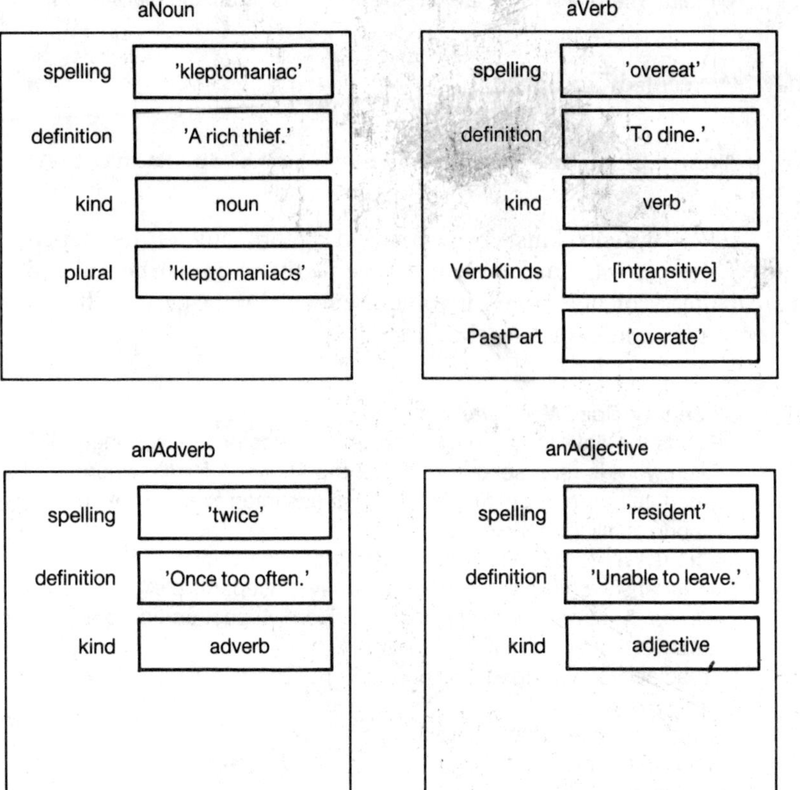


**Figure 15.2**
Four variables of type **word**.

- There is no matching **end** for the reserved-word **case**;
- Every value of the tag-field's type, which must be an ordinal type, must appear exactly once as a case-label;
- An empty variant is explicitly denoted by ( ).

Note also that the field-list of a variant may itself contain a variant-part, making nested variants possible.

### 15.7.2 USING VARIANT-RECORDS

The fields in a variant-part may be accessed just like the fields in a fixed-part, provided they exist by virtue of the tag-field having the appropriate value. For example, since **aNoun.category** contains **noun**, the field **aNoun.plural** may be used in any way permitted for a variable of type **string**[20]. The output-statement:

```
Writeln('The plural of '', aNoun.spelling, ''' is '', aNoun.plural, '''.')
```

may be executed, and prints:

```
The plural of 'kleptomaniac' is 'kleptomaniacs'.
```

The tag-field must be initialized before any of its dependent fields. The case-statement is suited perfectly to initialization and the great majority of operations involving entire variant-parts. The following example should suggest the idea:

```
procedure ReadWord (var w : word);
{ Reads the data for a word and sets the fields of w accordingly. }
{ Each word is represented in one of the following forms, where }
{ $ denotes an end-of-line. The input is assumed to be error-free. }
{ a noun:spelling$definition$n plural$, }
{ a transitive verb:spelling$definition$vt past-participle$, }
{ an intransitive verb:spelling$definition$vi past-participle$, }
{ a trans. & intrans. verb:spelling$definition$vti past-participle$, }
{ an adverb:spelling$definition$adv$, }
{ an adjective:spelling$definition$adj$. }
 var
   ch : char; { an input character }
begin { ReadWord }
 with w do
   begin
     Readln(spelling);
     Readln(definition);
     Read(ch);
     case ch of
       'n' :
         begin { noun }
           kind := noun;
           get(input); { skips space }
           Readln(plural)
         end; { noun }
       'v' :
         begin { verb }
           kind := verb;
           Read(ch);
           case ch of
             'i' : VerbKinds := [intransitive];
             't' :
               begin { transitive }
                 VerbKinds := [transitive];
                 if input^ = 'i' then
```

```
                begin { also intransitive }
                  VerbKinds := VerbKinds + [intransitive];
                  get(input) { skips 'i' }
                end { also intransitive }
              end { transitive }
            end; { case ch }
            get(input); { skips space }
            Readln(PastPart)
          end; { verb }
        'a' :
          begin { adverb or adjective }
            get(input); { skips 'd' }
            Read(ch);
            case ch of
              'v' : kind := verb;
              'j' : kind := adjective
            end
          end { adverb or adjective }
        end { case ch }
      end { with w }
    end; { ReadWord }
```

In the above example the determination of the value of the tag-field itself used a case-statement, which also processed the dependent variants. In many cases the tag-field is determined separately (like the fields spelling and definition), *after* which a case-statement takes care of the rest of the fields.

It is perfectly possible, indeed usual, for a record-variable to have more than one variant in its lifetime. The variant changes whenever the tag-field is assigned a different value, after which the previous variant fields cease to exist, and the new ones come into existence (with undefined values).

### 15.7.3 UNDISCRIMINATED VARIANTS

The syntax rules for a variant-part permit the tag-field, but not the associated type-identifier, to be omitted. The intention is that either context or the combined values of the fields in the fixed-part or both are sufficient to determine which variant is in effect, and therefore which other fields may be used. These variants are called **undiscriminated**.

This is very tricky business, and best avoided. The official rules of Standard Pascal are that a change of variant occurs when a field of a different variant is accessed, at which time the new variant fields come into existence with undefined values, and the previous ones disappear. However, it is well known that very few implementations take the considerable trouble necessary to enforce this rule.

Consider, for example, the predefined **QuickDraw** type for rectangles:

```
type
  Rect = record
      case integer of
        0 : (
          top, left, bottom, right : integer
          );
        1 : (
          topLeft, botRight : Point
          )
    end
```

This violates the Standard in that not every value of type **integer** appears as a case-label. It can easily be repaired by defining a type 0..1. More serious is the stated intention in the Technical Appendix of being conveniently able to view a variable of type **Rect** in either of two ways, for example executing:

```
var
  rec : Rect;
  t, l, b, r : integer;
  p : Point;
...
{ Initialize rec }
  with rec do
    begin
      top := t;
      left := l;
      bottom := b;
      right := r
    end;
...
{ Set bottom-right corner of rec to p }
  rec.botRight := p;
FrameRect(rec)
```

All this is very well, at least up until the last statement. It is syntactically legal, by the way — all the procedures involving rectangles really have a single parameter of type **Rect** rather than the four integer parameters we have used thus far; that form is provided impurely as a convenience. The trouble is that after the penultimate statement the second variant is in effect, but its field **topLeft** is officially undefined. So the call of **FrameRect** officially has an undefined parameter.

The above solution works perfectly well in Macintosh Pascal, and one suspects that undiscriminated variants were provided with just this sort of thing in mind, even though officially it is illegal, because it relies on implementation knowledge. The semantic pitfalls are well-illustrated by the following predefined procedure:

```
procedure SetRect (var r : Rect;
                   left, top, right, bottom : integer);
{ Sets r to the rectangle with the given coordinates. }
```

Since the implementation is not given, it is impossible to know which of the two variants it creates!

### 15.7.4 RESTRICTIONS CONCERNING VARIANT-RECORDS

There are two further rules concerning the use of variant records, whether they have tag-fields or not.

(1) If a variant field is being used as an actual variable parameter, or as the record-variable of a with-statement, its record may not undergo a change of variant.

(2) A tag-field may not be used as an actual variable parameter.

These and the other rules concerning variants are very difficult or inefficient to police, so most implementations do not bother. Thus when mistakes are made, the results can be very baffling.

| **Moral** One cannot be too careful when using variant records. |
|---|

## 15.8 Case-studies involving records

Unlike arrays, records do not introduce the need for new problem-solving techniques; at least, not until they are used in conjunction with pointers in Chapter 20. They are a very valuable descriptive technique, however, and it is well worth exploiting them to recast some of the case-studies.

Program Arithmetic for Case-study 5 in Chapter 10 can be improved by using the record-type test, as discussed earlier in this chapter. The new version of procedure NewTest has already been given; Exercises 15.1 and 15.2 ask you similarly to recast the rest of the program.

Program Scheduling3 for Case-study 6 in Chapter 11 used an algorithm that obviated the need for records. Specifically, the processing time and the job number for each job were stored in separate arrays, because only the job numbers were sorted. An alternative solution is to store all the job information in a single array of records:

```
type
  JobNumber = 1..MaxNrJobs;
  JobCount = 0..MaxNrJobs;
  job = record
      JobTime : time;
      JobNr : JobNumber
    end;
  JobInformation = array[JobNumber] of job;
var
  JobInfo : JobInformation; { JobInfo[i] describes the i'th job in the
                                current order }
  NrJobs : JobCount; { number of jobs to be processed }
                        { (1 <= i <= NrJobs, above) }
```

Jobs are stored in array JobInfo as they are read, with the JobNr field set to the position of the job in the input data. Then the array is sorted so that the JobTime fields are in non-decreasing order. This is said to be the **key** field for the sort. The sort procedure will use a procedure swap that exchanges values of type job. Exercise 15.13 invites you to modify the program along these lines. The new solution will be more natural.

If JobScheduler3 were written using an algorithm that sorted all the information about a job, but without using records, the phenomenon of **parallel arrays** would be observed. This is where two or more arrays with the same index-type are used, such that elements with the same indexes represent different aspects of a single object.

**Principle** Use a single array of records in preference to parallel arrays.

Program RandomWalk for Case-study 7 in Chapter 13 can benefit in a number of relatively minor ways by using records. A screen location is better represented by a value of type Point than by two separate integer variables. Similarly, the variables row and col which together represent a position in the grid are better represented with a record. The moving particle can then be represented with a record having two fields: a position in the grid, and a direction. Finally, diff1 and diff2 are parallel arrays, and come under the jurisdiction of the above principle. Exercise 15.14 invites you to carry out these improvements.

Program MailMinder for Case-study 8 in Chapter 14 would not benefit significantly from the use of records. Most file-processing problems that are not concerned exclusively with text files deal with files of records. Much data-processing activity falls into this category.

Program IdiotSheet for Case-study 9 in the next chapter processes a file of records.

Program Nim for Case-study 11 in Chapter 17 is an exercise in using sets. Although it appears after this chapter, Chapter 17 was written to be independent of it. Accordingly, program Nim does not use records. Variables size and BinarySize are parallel arrays, and therefore can be replaced by an array of records. But the program is best formulated by using an abstract data-type representing a collection of piles of matches. The operations that are needed are initializing the collection of piles, determining the number of piles, determining the number of empty piles, determining the size of a given pile, removing a given number of matches from a given pile, and determining the parity of the collection of piles. The operations that create or change the collection should be automatically reflected in the display.

Program ShowTree for Case-study 12 in Chapter 20 is an example of the use of pointers, which are almost always used in conjunction with records. For the record, this program is no exception.

## 15.9 Macaveats

Macintosh Pascal does not support packed records.

As mentioned in the text, the intended use of undiscriminated variants in QuickDraw type Rect is a violation of the Standard. Type Point is also an undiscriminated variant: 15.2

```
type
  VHSelect = (v, h);
  Point = record
      case integer of { should be a type-identifier for 0..1 }
        0 : (
          v, h : integer
          );
        1 : (
          vh : array[VHSelect] of integer
          )
      end
```

## 15.10 Further reading


(1) Stubbs, D. F. and Webre, N. W. (1985). *Data Structures and Abstract Data-Types with Pascal.* Monterey, California: Brooks/Cole.
A second-level programming text, emphasizing abstract data-types, and using Pascal.

## EXERCISES

**15.1** Rewrite subprograms **PrintTest**, **answer**, **PrintAnswer** and **EndTest** from program **Arithmetic**, along the lines of procedure **NewTest** in the text.

*Hint*: In **EndTest**, save and restore the operation.

**15.2** Rewrite the rest of program **Arithmetic** to use the subprograms given in the text and the previous question.

**15.3** A digital 24-hour clock displays the current hour (00 to 23), minute, and second.

(a) Define a type for the time on such a clock.

(b) Write a procedure that advances a given time by 1 second.

(c) Write a function that returns a string representing the given time in the format '*hh*:*mm*:*ssx*m', where each *h*, *m*, and *s* is a decimal digit, and *x* is either a or p. For example, if the current hour, minute, and second are 23, 5, and 33 respectively, the result should be '11:05:33pm'. If you have not read about the type **string**, write a procedure that prints the time instead.

**15.4** A date consists of a day, a month, and a year. Assume enumerated types day and month are defined.

(a) Define a type for dates.

(b) Write a procedure that changes a date to the following date.

(c) Write a function that returns a string representing the given date in a suitable format. If you have not read about the type **string**, write a procedure that prints the date instead.

**15.5** Implement the following procedure:

```
procedure GetMousePt (var pt : Point);
{ Sets pt to the position of the mouse. }
```

*Hint*: Use procedure **GetMouse**.

**15.6** Give type-definitions and variable-declarations that make the following statements legal.

```
x := y;
...
x.a[y.d].b[y.c] := 0
```

**15.7** Rework each previous exercise for which a with-statement was appropriate but was not used.

**15.8** Implement subprograms MakeEmptyString, pos, insert, delete, and copy, as used in procedure ReplaceAll in the text.

**15.9** Implement the following function, where type string is as defined in the text.

```
type
  relation = (LessThan, Equal, GreaterThan);

function relationship (var s1, s2 : string) : relation;
{ If s1 and s2 are identical, returns Equal; otherwise returns }
{ LessThan if s1 precedes s2 in dictionary order, or }
{ GreaterThan if vice versa. }
```

*Note*: Any comparison can be neatly formulated with this function, using sets where necessary (see Chapter 17). For example, for s1 <= s2 we write

```
relationship(s1, s2) in [LessThan, Equal]
```

**15.10** A *complex number* can be regarded as an ordered pair of real numbers $(x, y)$ subject to the following operations (among others):

$$(x_1, y_1) + (x_2, y_2) = (x_1 + x_2, y_1 + y_2)$$
$$(x_1, y_1) \times (x_2, y_2) = (x_1 x_2 - y_1 y_2, x_1 y_2 + y_1 x_2)$$

Begin the implementation of an abstract data-type for complex numbers by doing each of the following.

(a) Define a type to represent complex numbers. Choose field-names to reflect that $x$ is called the *real-part* and $y$ the *imaginary part*.

(b) Write procedures to implement the operations of addition and multiplication.

(c) Write procedures to read and write complex numbers, using the representation $x$ + `yi` when $y$ is non-negative, and $x$ − `yi` when $y$ is negative. Skip leading spaces on input. For example, input of `∧∧1.0 − 1.5i` should be treated as (1.0, – 1.5).

**15.11** Implement an abstract data-type for fractions, i.e. rational numbers of the form $x / y$, where both the *numerator* $x$ and the *denominator* $y$ are integers, and $y > 0$.

*Hint*: Use the gcd function as implemented in Exercise 7.14 to divide out gcd($x$, $y$).

**15.12** Implement the following procedure:

```
procedure DragARect (DownAt : Point
                     var r : Rect);
{ Assumes mouse button was pressed at location DownAt, and }
{ is still down; repeatedly draws and erases the frame of the }
{ rectangle with top-left corner at DownAt and bottom-right }
{ corner at current mouse position, until the mouse button is }
{ released. Only the last rectangle's frame remains; }
{ its coordinates are returned in r. }
```

*Hint*: Use the variant of type **Rect** that consists of two points.

**15.13** Modify program **JobScheduler3** as suggested in the text.

**15.14** In the context of program **RandomWalk** for Case-study 7 in Chapter 13:

(a) Define a record-type that represents a position in the grid.

(b) Define a record-type that represents the grid-position and direction of the moving particle.

(c) Define a type to represent the change to a position when moving in each direction.

(d) Modify the program to use the types given in parts (a)–(c).

# 16 FILES

And friend, somewhere in Washington, enshrined in some little folder, is a study, in black and white, of my fingerprints.
— Arlo Guthrie, *Alice's Restaurant*

## 16.1 Introduction

Files address two needs:

(1) to access and/or create information that exists prior to and/or after execution of a program;

(2) to store temporary information that may be too copious to fit into main memory.

As we know from Chapter 14, files in the first category are called **external files**, and those in the second **internal files**. Both are stored in secondary memory.

A file is an arbitrarily long sequence of component values. Text files have already been discussed in Chapter 14. Each of their components is either a character or an end-of-line marker, and there are special procedures to convert their information to and from values of simple Pascal types.

Pascal permits files to have components of any type that is not itself a file-type and does not contain a component of a file-type. Of course, all components of a particular file have the same type. Processing a general file is like processing a text file character by character. All the relevant properties and subprograms were described in Chapter 14; the following section is content mainly to summarize them.

## 16.2 Sequential files

### 16.2.1 SYNTAX

The syntax of a file-type is as follows:

unpacked-structured-type: *array-type* | *record-type* | *file-type*
file-type: **file of** *component-type*

The component-type may not involve a file-type.

File-variables and formal parameters of file-types are declared in the usual way, but the latter must be var-parameters. Associated with each file-variable *f* is a file-buffer *f*^, which is an implicitly declared variable of *f*'s component-type. Its role is described in the sequel.

### 16.2.2 WRITING A FILE

A file *f* is made available for writing by executing:

```
Rewrite(f)
```

The file becomes empty, and its file-position is at end-of-file. In Standard Pascal *f* is an external file if it appears in the program-parameters of the program-heading, otherwise it is an internal file.

Macintosh Pascal uses a different system. It distinguishes the first call of either Rewrite or Reset (the equivalent for reading) from any later calls. It is said to **open** the file. An external file can be opened only by giving a second actual parameter in the call — a string-value giving the external name of the file. The user may be prompted to select the external name by calling the function NewFileName (or OldFileName if an existing file is to be rewritten). See Chapter 14 for examples. If the optional second string-parameter is not given when the file is opened, the file is internal.

Standard Pascal files are sequential files. Their components can be processed only in strict left-to-right order. A file is written by repeatedly appending a value to the end. The basic way to do so is to execute:

```
put(f)
```

This appends the value of *f*^ to file *f*, advances the file-position to the new end-of-file, and makes *f*^ undefined. The file-buffer may have obtained its value in any way permissible for a component-variable of its type: by execution of an assignment, an input-statement, or a procedure-statement with the file-buffer as an actual var-parameter.

Figure 16.1 shows the effect of an execution of put(intfile), where intfile is declared as follows:

```
type
  IntegerFile = file of integer;
var
  intfile : IntegerFile;
```

The file-position is indicated with an arrow.

It is very common to assign a value to the file-buffer and then

**Figure 16.1**
Execution of put(intfile).

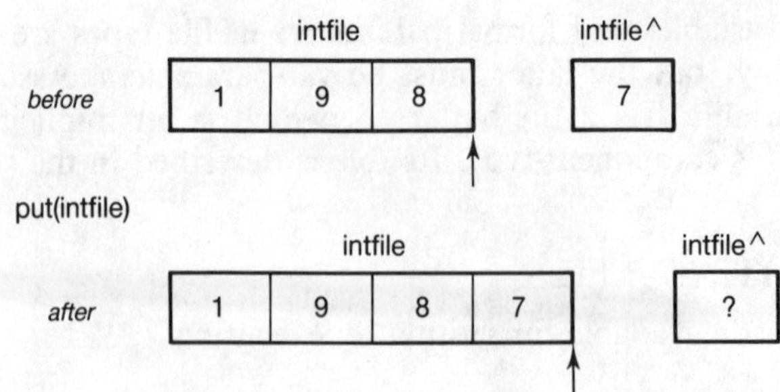


immediately call put to append it. Pascal accordingly provides an abbreviation. The procedure-statement:

Write($f$, $a_1$, ... , $a_n$)

where $n \geqslant 1$, is equivalent (except possibly when $f$ is a text-file) to:

```
begin
  f^ := a1;
  put(f);
  ...
  f^ := an;
  put(f)
end
```

i.e. it appends the values in the listed order. Each value $a_i$ must be assignment-compatible with the component-type of $f$.

### 16.2.3 READING A FILE

A file $f$ is made available for reading by executing:

Reset($f$)

The file-position moves to the start of the file, before the first component if there is one. In Standard Pascal $f$ is an external file if it appears in the program-parameters of the program-heading, and otherwise is an internal file.

As we have seen, in Macintosh Pascal $f$ in the above statement is an external file only if it has already been opened as one. If an external file $f$ is to be opened for reading, its external name must be given with a string-value as the second actual parameter of **Reset**. Whenever a file is to be read after it has been written, the simple form of the **Reset** statement is used, because the file has already been opened.

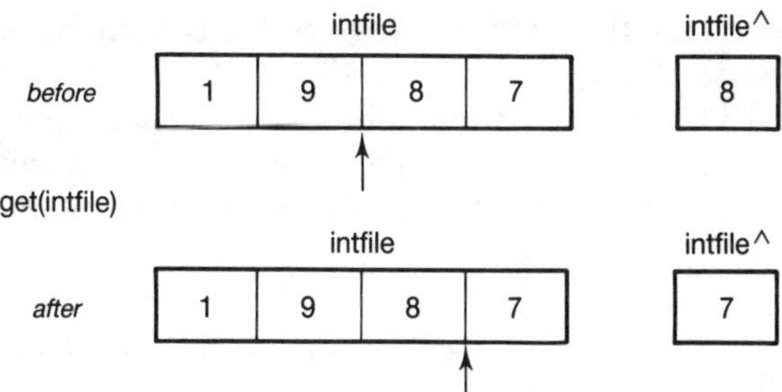


**Figure 16.2**
Execution of **get(intfile)**.

A file is read by repeatedly advancing the file-position, making successive components available in the file-buffer. The basic way to do so is to execute:

```
get(f)
```

This advances the file position past the next component, and sets the value of $f\hat{}$ to the component just after the new file-position. It is an error if the file-position was at end-of-file before the call. The new value of the file-buffer may be used in any way appropriate to a value of its type.

Figure 16.2 shows the effect of an execution of **get(intfile)**, where **intfile** is as declared previously.

It is very common to assign the value of the file-buffer to a variable immediately after the call of **get**. Pascal accordingly provides an abbreviation. The procedure-statement:

```
Read(f, v1, ... , vn)
```

where $n \geq 1$, is equivalent (except possibly when $f$ is a text-file) to:

```
begin
  v1 := f^;
  get(f);
  ...
  vn := f^;
  get(f)
end
```

i.e. it reads successive values into the variables in the listed order. Each component of $f$ must be assignment-compatible with the type of the variable it is assigned to.

The required function **eof** may be applied to any file $f$. If $f$ is being written, **eof(*f*)** gives **true**. If $f$ is being read, **eof(*f*)** gives **true** if and only if the file-position is after the last component, in which case $f\hat{}$

is undefined. Note that **eof(intfile)** gives **false** both before and after the call in Figure 16.2.

Schema Process File is typically used to process the components of a file *f* in the order in which they appear. The action *Process v* often involves writing *v* to another file, such as when file *f* is being updated.

```
Schema Process File:
var
  f : a file-type T;
{ Process the components of f in order. }
--------------------------------------------------
 var
   v : the component-type of T;

 Reset(f); { add 2nd parameter if this is to open an external f }
 while not eof(f) do
  begin
    Read(v);
    Process v
  end
```

### 16.2.4 A SIMPLE EXAMPLE: MERGING

A common operation involving files is that of **merging** two ordered files, i.e. creating a single ordered file containing all the components of each file (each value occurring as many times as in the two files combined). Here is a Macintosh Pascal program that merges two files of integers in non-decreasing order:

```
program MergeIntFiles (Output);
{ Merges two files of integers in non-decreasing order; the user }
{ is prompted to select the two input files and the output file. }
 type
   IntegerFile = file of integer;
 var
   infile1, infile2, MergedFile : IntegerFile;

begin { MergeIntFiles }
{ Select and open the three files }
 Reset(infile1, OldFileName('Select first file to be merged.'));
 Reset(infile2, OldFileName('Select second file to be merged.'));
 Rewrite(MergedFile, NewFileName('Select merged file.'));
{ Merge until all components of one file have been taken }
 while not (eof(infile1) or eof(infile2)) do
```

```
    if infile1^ <= infile2^ then
      begin { Take from infile1 }
        Write(MergedFile, infile1^);
        get(infile1)
      end
    else
      begin { Take from infile2 }
        Write(MergedFile, infile2^);
        get(infile2)
      end;
  { Append any remaining components of infile1 }
  while not eof(infile1) do
    begin
      Write(MergedFile, infile1^);
      get(infile1)
    end;
  { Append any remaining components of infile2 }
  while not eof(infile2) do
    begin
      Write(MergedFile, infile2^);
      get(infile2)
    end;
  Writeln('Merge complete.')
end. { MergeIntFiles }
```

Note that if both input files are non-empty then exactly one of the last two while-loops will execute its body.

### 16.2.5 AVOIDING TEXT FILES

It is by no means unrealistic to choose a file of integers instead of a text file to represent a potentially long sequence of integers. The former choice enjoys three advantages.

(1) A conversion is avoided between the internal (probably binary) form of integers and their textual representations, during both input and output.

(2) In Macintosh Pascal an integer occupies two bytes; but a field-width of at least six is needed to separate arbitrary integers written to a text file, and each character consumes a byte.

(3) The purpose of the file is clearly documented; on the other hand, there is no guarantee that a text file contains a sequence of integer representations.

Both space and time are conserved by sticking to the following principle:

**Principle** Use text files only for information that is to be read by humans.

## 16.3 Random-access files

Pascal's notion of a file reflects the long tradition of using magnetic tape as a secondary storage medium. The only way to find the *n*'th component of a tape-file is to search from the start, skipping the first $n - 1$ components. Similarly recording normally proceeds sequentially from the start.

Macintosh Pascal takes advantage of the capabilities of the Macintosh's disk-based file-system, and provides **random-access files**:

- The *n*'th component can be directly accessed.
- An arbitrary component can be changed without affecting other components.
- Mixed reading and writing is possible.

This facility applies only to external files.

An external file is opened for random-access with the predefined procedure open. The call:

```
open(f, s)
```

opens file-variable *f* for random read/write access. The external name of *f* is given by the string *s*, which must be present. If no file of that name exists, an empty one is created. The file-position is at the start, and the file-buffer is assigned the first component if any.

File *f* may now be written or read as in Standard Pascal, but mixed reading and writing is also permitted. Whenever the file-position is not at end-of-file, get(*f*) may be executed, and has its usual effect. And put(*f*) is *always* permitted. If *f* is at end-of-file, the effect is as usual. Otherwise, the value of *f*^ replaces the component just after the file-position, the file-position advances past the changed component, and *f*^ is set to the component just after the new file-position (it is undefined if the file-position is at end-of-file). As with files opened with Reset or Rewrite, eof(*f*) returns true if there is no component following the file-position, and false otherwise.

Random access is provided by the predefined procedure seek. The call:

```
seek(f, n)
```

where $n \geqslant 0$ is a value of type longint, places the file-position of *f* just after the *n*'th component, or after the last component if *n* exceeds the number of components. File *f* must have been opened with **open**. Note that:

- **Seek(*f*, 0)** is equivalent to **Reset(*f*)**;
- No file may have more than **Maxlongint** components, so **seek(*f*, Maxlongint)** puts the file-position at end-of-file;
- To put the *n*'th component in the file-buffer, use **seek(*f*, *n* – 1)**.

Mixed reading and writing, and the procedure **seek**, apply only to a file opened with **open**; but it does not matter how the file was created.

A couple of extra, predefined subprograms are provided in Macintosh Pascal. The function-call:

```
filepos(f)
```

returns the number of components of *f* to the left of its file-position, as a value of type **longint**; *f* may be any open file. The procedure-call:

```
close(f)
```

returns the open external file *f* to its unopened state. This is done automatically at the end of *f*'s lifetime, but the explicit form permits *f* to be reopened as another file.

### 16.3.1 A SIMPLE EXAMPLE: ERROR MESSAGES

Large programs that process large amounts of complex data may find it necessary to have a substantial number of error messages. One example is the Macintosh Pascal interpreter. The messages are best kept in secondary memory. A good data structure is as follows. The messages are numbered from 1 onwards, and stored in an external text file, as in this example:

```
1:∧No∧way!□2:∧This∧is∧a∧joke,∧right?□3:∧...
```

To enable a particular message to be quickly found, the file-position at the start of the *n*'th message is recorded as the *n*'th component of an external file of integers. Note that the error numbers need not now be part of the messages, but the extra space is worthwhile for the increased human readability. The auxiliary file, called **ErrorPosFile**, will be as follows for the above example:

**ErrorPosFile**

| 0 | 11 | 37 | ... |
|---|---|---|---|

Here are the relevant sections of the program:

```
program Major (Input, Output);
...
 const
  MaxErrorNumber = ... ;
 type
  IntegerFile = file of integer;
  ErrorNumber = 1..MaxErrorNumber;
 var
  ErrorFile : text; { error messages, in order }
  ErrorPosFile : IntegerFile; { the i'th component is the file- }
   { position at the start of the i'th error message in ErrorFile. }
...
 procedure PrintErrorMessage (n : ErrorNumber);
 { Prints error message number n; assumes both files have been }
 { opened with open. Global vars: ErrorsFile, ErrorPosFile. }
  var
   StartPos : integer; { file-position at start of message }
   MessageLength, i : 1..Maxint;
 begin { PrintErrorMessage }
 { Define StartPos }
  seek(ErrorPosFile, n – 1);
  StartPos := ErrorPosFile^;
 { Define MessageLength }
  get(ErrorPosFile);
  if not eof(ErrorPosFile) then
   MessageLength := ErrorPosFile^ – StartPos
  else
   begin
    seek(ErrorFile, Maxlongint);
    MessageLength := filepos(ErrorFile) – StartPos
   end;
 { Print message }
  Write('ERROR ');
  seek(ErrorFile, StartPos);
  for i := 1 to MessageLength do
   begin
    if eoln(ErrorFile) then
     Writeln
    else
     Write(ErrorFile^);
    get(ErrorFile)
   end
 end; { PrintErrorMessage }
 ...
 open(ErrorFile, 'MajorDisk:ErrorText');
 open(ErrorPosFile, 'MajorDisk:ErrorPositions');
```

```
...
  PrintErrorMessage(99);
...
end. { Major }
```

## 16.4 Case-study 9: An idiot sheet

### 16.4.1 SETTING OF THE PROBLEM

The televised fireside chat has become an institution in this age of media politics. In order for the politician confidently to fix his or her gaze at the viewer, and still avoid the risks attending spontaneous speeches, he or she reads from what is called in the trade an *idiot sheet* (a more colorful term than the alternative: *autocue*). The term comes from film production where an off-camera stooge would hold up large cardboard sheets of 'lines'. Nowadays the politician is likely to have a Macintosh on the desk to promote a modern, technologically aware image. Accordingly, the Macintosh can function as a high-tech idiot sheet, by continuously scrolling the text of the talk, at a suitably slow rate.

### 16.4.2 SPECIFICATIONS

A program is to be written that displays a nominated, external text file line-by-line. The displayed text is to be continuously scrolled upwards, with new lines being introduced at the bottom of the display.

Furthermore, a second external file is to be read that controls the formatting of the text proper. This file should contain a sequence of formatting changes. Each change should specify the line number and character position just before which the change should take place, the kind of change, and the parameters determining the change. The associated file-positions of the changes must be in non-decreasing order.

Two kinds of formatting changes are to be provided in the preliminary version: to the size and style of the text. Auxiliary programs are needed to prepare the files for a talk, but they need not be written now.

### 16.4.3 WRITING THE PROGRAM

The most natural form for the statement-part of the program-block is a loop that processes one line of the text file in each iteration. To permit format changes, the text must be displayed in the Drawing window. We soon arrive at the following first refinement:

```
const
  InitialSizeOfText = ... ;
var
  TheText : text; { text to be displayed line by line }
begin { IdiotSheet }
  Reset the text and formatting files;
  Make Drawing window active and occupying entire screen;
  TextSize(InitialSizeOfText);
  while not eof(TheText) do
    Display new line of text and scroll screen up for next line
end. { IdiotSheet }
```

The first action is implemented by using Reset twice in conjunction with function OldFileName to prompt the user for the names of the files. Although there is no need to decide on the file-type for the format changes at this early stage, we do so since the best choice is clear. We use the following variables:

```
const
  MaxLineLength = ... ; { maximum number of characters in a line
                          of TheText }
type
  LinePos = 1..MaxLineLength;
  LineNumber = 1..Maxint;
  ChangeType = (InStyle, InSize);
  FormatItem = record
      LineNr : LineNumber; { change takes effect at this line
                              before ... }
      pos : LinePos; { ... printing character in this position }
      case change : ChangeType of
        InStyle : (
          NewStyle : Style
          );
        InSize : (
          NewSize : 1..Maxint
          )
    end;
  FormatFile = file of FormatItem;
var
  format : FormatFile; { formatting changes in order }
```

The second action is implemented with the help of two new, predefined procedures:

```
procedure SetDrawingRect (r : Rect);
{ Makes the Drawing window occupy the rectangle r in the }
{ screen's coordinate system (origin in top-left corner). }
```

```
procedure ShowDrawing;
{ Makes Drawing window active (placing it on top of desktop). }
```

The implementation is trivial, and may be found below in the complete solution.

Finally, to the body of the loop. It is apparent that lines must be counted, so a counter must be initialized before the loop. We decide to read each line into a Mac-string variable, and to call appropriate procedures to display the line and scroll the screen:

```
const
  Spacing = ... ; { gap between base-lines of displayed lines }
type
  str = string[MaxLineLength];
var
  NrLines : 0..Maxint; { number of lines read from TheText }
  line : str; { line number NrLines of TheText }

procedure ShowLine (line : str;
                    LineNr : LineNumber;
                    var format : FormatFile);
{ Displays given line at bottom of Drawing window, reading and }
{ processing any associated format changes from format; ass- }
{ umes file position of format is after last item for an earlier line. }

procedure ScrollUp (section : Rect;
                    distance : integer);
{ Scrolls given section of Drawing window up given vertical }
{ distance, one unit at a time. }

NrLines := 0;
while not eof(TheText) do
  begin { Display new line of text and scroll screen up for next }
    Readln(TheText, line);
    NrLines := NrLines + 1;
    ShowLine(line, NrLines, format);
    ScrollUp(screen, Spacing)
  end
```

Variable screen is the rectangle corresponding to the full Macintosh screen; it was introduced for the second high-level action.

It remains to implement procedures ScrollUp and ShowLine. The former is easily implemented using a couple of sophisticated features of Macintosh Pascal. The implementation is given in the complete solution. Here is a brief explanation for the incurably curious. The call:

ScrollRect($r$, $h$, $v$, $RH$)

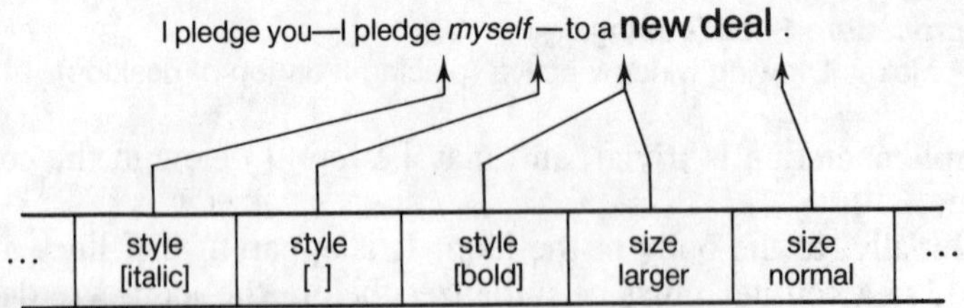


**Figure 16.3**
A line and its associated format changes.

scrolls the contents of rectangle *r* by *h* units to the right and *v* units down. The vacated area is filled with the background pattern, which by default is white. A description of the vacated region is returned in the *dynamic variable RH* of type RgnHandle, which is created by the function call NewRgn and eventually disposed of by calling procedure DisposeRgn. Details may be found in the Technical Appendix.

Let us now consider procedure ShowLine. Figure 16.3 shows a reasonably complex line: one subject to five format changes.

We decide to process a line by reading each associated format change, printing the remaining text to the left of that change, and making the change. This is done with a while-loop, and any remaining text is printed afterwards. First we write:

```
const
  BaseLine = ... ; { base line for displaying a new line }
  Indent = ... ; { indent for each displayed line }

begin { ShowLine }
  MoveTo(Indent, BaseLine);
  Process each format change, by printing the remaining text to its left,
  making the change, and advancing past the change;
  Display the rest of the line
end; { ShowLine }
```

A while-loop is chosen for the main action, because there may be no format changes for a line:

```
{ Process each format change, by printing the remaining text to }
{ its left, making the change, and advancing past the change }
while there is another change for this line do
  Process this format change
```

The loop should stop if file format is at end-of-file, or if the next change (which is in the file-buffer) is for a later line. Because Pascal's conditions may be evaluated in any order, and the file-buffer is undefined at end-of-file, the loop is recast by using a Boolean variable:

```
var
 done : Boolean; { true iff all changes for line have been done }

{ Process each format change, by printing the remaining text to }
{ its left, making the change, and advancing past the change }
 done := false;
 while not (eof(format) or done) do
  if format^.LineNr = LineNr then
   Process this format change
  else
   done := true
```

This is an oft-used technique in file-processing in Pascal.

We end our discussion of the stepwise-refinement of program IdiotSheet at this point, because the remaining refinements are unproblematic. You may reconstruct them from the complete solution.

### 16.4.4 THE COMPLETE PROGRAM

The complete program utilizes a new feature of Macintosh Pascal, called the **uses-clause**. It appears after the program heading, and names those libraries whose definitions and declarations are to be included in the declaration-section of the program-block. It is necessary in this instance because the type RgnHandle, the function NewRgn, and the procedures DisposeRgn and ScrollRect belong to the QuickDraw2 library. The QuickDraw1 library is mentioned for completeness, it is automatically included in every Macintosh Pascal program. 16.1

The syntax of a uses-clause is as follows:

program: *program-heading* ;
*uses-clause*
*program-block* .
uses-clause: **uses** *identifier-list* ;

One other available library, called SANE, is described in Chapter 19.

Here is the complete program.

```
program IdiotSheet;
{ Acts as idiot sheet for user, by displaying the text in file TheText }
{ according to the formatting information in file format; old lines }
{ scroll off the top as new lines appear at the bottom. }
{ External files: TheText, format. }

 uses
  QuickDraw1, QuickDraw2;
```

```
const
  MaxLineLength = 80; { maximum number of characters in a line
                        of TheText }
  Spacing = 40; { gap between base-lines of displayed lines }
  BaseLine = 300; { base line for displaying a new line }
  Indent = 10; { indent for each displayed line }
  ScreenWidth = 512; { full width of Mac's screen }
  ScreenDepth = 342; { full depth of Mac's screen }
  InitialSizeOfText = 18;

type
  str = string[MaxLineLength];
  LinePos = 1..MaxLineLength;
  LineNumber = 1..Maxint;
  ChangeType = (InStyle, InSize);
  FormatItem = record
      LineNr : LineNumber; { change takes effect at this line
                             before ... }
      pos : LinePos; { ... printing character in this position }
      case change : ChangeType of
        InStyle : (
          NewStyle : Style
          );
        InSize : (
          NewSize : 1..Maxint
          )
    end;
  FormatFile = file of FormatItem;

var
  TheText : text; { text to be displayed line by line }
  NrLines : 0..Maxint; { number of lines read from TheText }
  line : str; { line number NrLines of TheText }
  format : FormatFile; { formatting changes in order }
  screen : Rect; { location of Drawing window }

procedure ScrollUp (section : Rect;
                    distance : integer);
{ Scrolls given section of Drawing window given vertical }
{ distance, one unit at a time. }
  var
    i : integer; { number of unit scrolls so far }
    dummy : RgnHandle; { used as dummy output parameter }
begin { ScrollUp }
  dummy := NewRgn;
  for i := 1 to distance do
    ScrollRect(section, 0, -1, dummy);
  DisposeRgn(dummy)
end; { ScrollUp }
```

```
procedure ShowLine (line : str;
                    LineNr : LineNumber;
                    var format : FormatFile);
{ Displays given line at bottom of Drawing window, reading and }
{ processing any associated format changes from format; ass- }
{ umes file position of format is after last item for an earlier line. }
{ Global consts: MaxLineLength, BaseLine, Indent. }
 var
  done : Boolean; { true iff all changes for line have been done }
  left : LinePos; { position of leftmost character in line not yet
                    printed }

 procedure ChangeFormat (ChangeInfo : FormatItem);
 { Changes display format according to ChangeInfo. }
 begin { ChangeFormat }
  with ChangeInfo do
   case change of
    InStyle :
     TextFace(NewStyle);
    InSize :
     TextSize(NewSize)
   end { case }
 end; { ChangeFormat }

begin { ShowLine }
 MoveTo(Indent, BaseLine);
{ Process each format change, by printing the remaining text to }
{ its left, making the change, and advancing past the change }
 left := 1;
 done := false;
 while not (eof(format) or done) do
  if format^.LineNr = LineNr then
   begin { Process this format change }
    DrawString(copy(line, left, format^.pos – left));
    left := format^.pos;
    ChangeFormat(format^);
    get(format)
   end
  else
   done := true;
{ Display the rest of the line }
 DrawString(copy(line, left, MaxLineLength))
end; { ShowLine }

begin { IdiotSheet }
 Reset(TheText, OldFileName('Open the text file.'));
 Reset(format, OldFileName('Open the format file.') );
{ Make Drawing window active and occupying entire screen }
```

**Figure 16.4**
Two states of the display during a run of IdiotSheet.

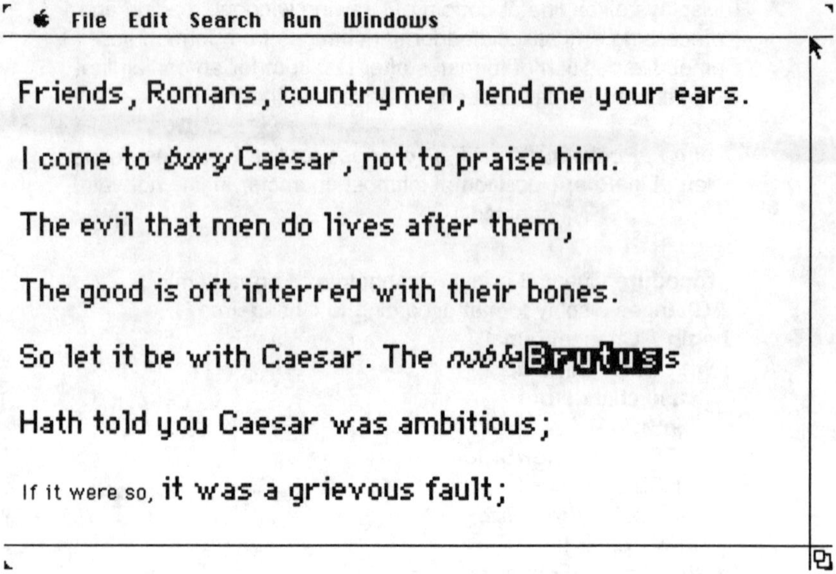

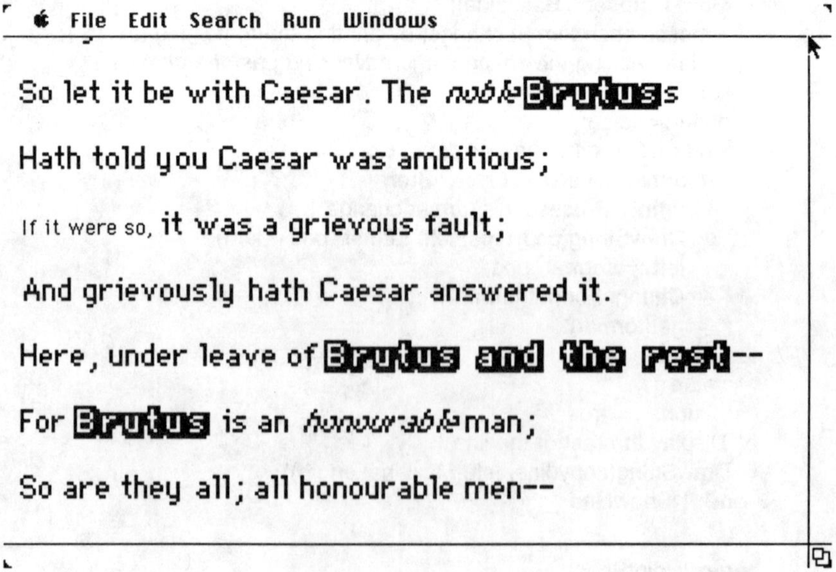

File Edit Search Run Windows
Friends, Romans, countrymen, lend me your ears.
I come to bury Caesar, not to praise him.
The evil that men do lives after them,
The good is oft interred with their bones.
So let it be with Caesar. The noble Brutus
Hath told you Caesar was ambitious;
If it were so, it was a grievous fault;

File Edit Search Run Windows
So let it be with Caesar. The noble Brutus
Hath told you Caesar was ambitious;
If it were so, it was a grievous fault;
And grievously hath Caesar answered it.
Here, under leave of Brutus and the rest--
For Brutus is an honourable man;
So are they all; all honourable men--

```
  SetRect(screen, 0, 0, ScreenWidth, ScreenDepth);
  SetDrawingRect(screen);
  ShowDrawing;

  TextSize(InitialSizeOfText);
  NrLines := 0;
  while not eof(TheText) do

 begin { Display new line of text and scroll screen up for next }
  Readln(TheText, line);
  NrLines := NrLines + 1;
  ShowLine(line, NrLines, format);
  ScrollUp(screen, Spacing)
 end
end. { IdiotSheet }
```

Program IdiotSheet maintains a continuously changing display, but Figure 16.4 gives some idea of its effect. The unwanted 's' after 'Brutus' at the end of a line is due to an error in Macintosh Pascal 2.0's implementation of the copy function.

## 16.5 Macaveats

16.2

Macintosh Pascal does not permit packed file-types.

16.3

Macintosh Pascal 2.0 has a couple of annoying bugs concerning files. The first is that Read(*f*), where *f* is a file, is not detected as an error. So be very careful not to write this inadvertently instead of get(*f*).

The other bug occurs because Macintosh Pascal is overly diligent in checking accesses to file-buffers. It will complain about the statement:

Read($f_1$, $f_2$^)

where $f_1$ and $f_2$ are files of the same type, if $f_2$^ is not defined. However, the express purpose of this statement is to define it!

## EXERCISES

**16.1** In Figure 16.2, how many *more* executions of get(intfile) can be done before eof(intfile) gives true?

**16.2** Implement the following procedure in the given context:

```
const
  MaxValue = ... ;
  MaxGap = ... ; { much smaller than MaxValue }

type
  FileOfValues = file of 0..MaxValue;
  FileOfGaps = file of 0..MaxGap;

procedure CreateDiffFile (var ValuesFile : FileOfValues;
                          var GapsFile : FileOfGaps);

{ Sets the i'th component of GapsFile to the difference }
{ between the (i + 1)'th and i'th components of ValuesFile; }
{ assumes values in ValuesFile are non-decreasing. }
```

*Hint*: Use a slight modification of schema Process File.

*Note*: If the original file is always processed sequentially from the start, the file of gaps can be used instead, provided the first component of the original file is remembered. And the file of gaps may occupy much less storage in many situations. For example, the maximum gap between successive prime numbers less than 2 614 941 711 251 is only 602.

**16.3** Desk-check program **MergeIntFiles**. Use two small input files, and keep track of their file-positions with an arrow as used in Figures 16.1 and 16.2.

**16.4** An inventory of a large number of different items is represented by a master file of records. There is one record for each item, containing a number identifying the item, the quantity in stock, a reorder-point, and a desired level. When the quantity in stock falls to or below the reorder-point, an order needs to be placed to bring the quantity up to the desired level. The records are kept in increasing order of their IDs. As ordered items are received and outgoing orders are filled, a file of transactions is prepared. Each transaction specifies the item concerned and the change to its quantity. Periodically, the file of transactions is sorted to put the item IDs in increasing order, and is used to update the master file.

(a) Give a suitable type for the master file.

(b) Give a suitable type for the transaction file.

(c) Write a program that reads the master file and a sorted transaction file, and prepares a new master file.

(d) Write a program that reads a master file and places the appropriate orders to bring items in insufficient quantities up to their desired levels.

**16.5** Suppose intfile is currently in the second state shown in Figure 16.2, and was opened with open. Show the state of intfile and its file-buffer, as in Figure 16.2, after executing each of the statements in the following sequence; i is an integer variable.

```
Read(intfile, i);
Write(intfile, i – 1);
seek(intfile, 1);
Read(intfile, i);
Write(intfile, i + 1)
```

**16.6** Implement the following action, where n is an variable of type longint, and intfile is a file of integers opened with open.

*Add 1 to the* n*'th component of* intfile

**16.7** What is the maximum total length assumed by program Major of all error messages but the last?

**16.8** Consider the conditional statement used in implementing the action

*Define* MessageLength

in program Major.

(a) Why can't it be replaced by:

```
MessageLength := ErrorPosFile^ – StartPos
```

(b) What simple change to ErrorPosFile permits this replacement?

**16.9** Write a program that creates ErrorPosFile given ErrorFile. It may assume that only the first line of an error message may start with a digit.

**16.10** Modify your solution to the previous question to use the modified scheme requested in Exercise 16.8(b).

**16.11** Desk-check the execution of the first refinement of ShowLine on the line shown in Figure 16.3. Six separate sections of the line should be printed, the first five of which should be followed by a format change.

**16.12** Write an interactive program that creates a file of format changes to be used in conjunction with a given text file by program IdiotSheet. It should display each new line of the text file, with each character position clearly indicated, and then prompt for changes. The LineNr field of the FormatItem for each change should be set automatically.

**16.13** Modify program IdiotSheet to allow a vertical increment to be specified, thereby permitting superscripts and subscripts as well as variable spacing between lines.

# 17
# SETS

I don't want to belong to any club that will accept me as a member.
— Groucho Marx, *attributed telegram*

## 17.1 Introduction

QuickDraw has the ability to display text of a given size and from a given font in many different styles. For instance, it can be displayed as normal, or **bold**, or *italic,* or ***bold and italic***, etc. The different options of a style, such as bold, italic, underlined, and so on, are constants of a predefined enumerated type:

```
type
  StyleItem = (bold, italic, underline, outline, shadow, condense,
              extend);
```

A style is any selection of these constants. The style for text which is both bold and italic may be written:

```
[bold, italic]
```

The ordering is of no consequence — the above style could just as well have been written:

```
[italic, bold]
```

Here are four more styles:

```
[italic, shadow, extend]
[underline]
[bold, italic, underline, outline, shadow, condense, extend]
[]
```

The first has three options active, the second just one, the third all seven, and the fourth none — you have grown accustomed to that typeface.

There are $2^7 = 128$ different styles, since each of the seven options may be present or not independently. Figure 17.1 gives a

File Edit Search Run Windows

[] [b] [i] [bi] [u] [bu] [iu] [biu] [o] [bo] [io] [bio] [uo] [buo]
[iuo] [biuo] [s] [bs] [is] [bis] [us] [bus] [ius] [bius]
[os] [bos] [ios] [bios] [uos] [buos] [iuos] [biuos]
[c] [bc] [ic] [bic] [uc] [buc] [iuc] [biuc] [oc] [boc] [ioc] [bioc] [uoc]
[buoc] [iuoc] [biuoc] [sc] [bsc] [isc] [bisc] [usc] [busc] [iusc]
[biusc] [osc] [bosc] [iosc] [biosc] [uosc] [buosc]
[iuosc] [biuosc] [e] [be] [ie] [bie] [ue] [bue] [iue] [biue]
[oe] [boe] [ioe] [bioe] [uoe] [buoe] [iuoe] [biuoe] [se]
[bse] [ise] [bise] [use] [buse] [iuse] [biuse]
[ose] [bose] [iose] [biose] [uose] [buose]
[iuose] [biuose] [ce] [bce] [ice] [bice] [uce] [buce] [iuce]
[biuce] [oce] [boce] [ioce] [bioce] [uoce] [buoce] [iuoce]
[biuoce] [sce] [bsce] [isce] [bisce] [usce] [busce]
[iusce] [biusce] [osce] [bosce] [iosce] [biosce]
[uosce] [buosce] [iuosce] [biuosce]

**Figure 17.1** The 128 different styles of text.

sample of text for each style, consisting of an abbreviated representation of the style. The abbreviation is obtained by omitting commas and giving only the first letter of each option.

A style is an example of what mathematicians call a **set**, i.e. an unordered collection of different values. Pascal has set-types. The 128 different styles of text are the values of the following predefined type:

```
type
  Style = set of StyleItem;
```

## 17.2 Syntax of set types

In the example above, StyleItem is called the **base-type** of the **set-type** Style. A set-type is a structured-type. The syntax is as follows:

unpacked-structured-type: *array-type* | *record-type* | *file-type* | *set-type*
set-type: **set of** *base-type*
base-type: *type*

The base-type must be an ordinal-type. Implementations of Pascal almost always either restrict the base-type to have ordinal values between two limits, or restrict the number of values in the base-type. Some do not even permit the type:

```
set of char
```

which is a minimal requirement for respectability. Macintosh Pascal is near the top of the class; its restriction is that the ordinal values of the base-type must lie in the range –8192..8191. So **set of** integer is not permitted, but almost everything else is.

A set-type is an unpacked-structured-type. It may therefore be packed, but there are few implementations in which this will save any storage. You are recommended against using packed set-types; they are not compatible with unpacked ones.

The rules for declaring variables or formal parameters of set-types are the same as for any other types. Here are two declarations of set-variables:

```
var
  TextStyle : Style;
  digits : set of 0..9;
```

Because set-types are structured-types, their constants cannot be named in constant-definitions, and they cannot be used as result-types of functions.

# 17.3 Constructing sets

## 17.3.1 SET CONSTRUCTORS

The basic way to construct a set is by specifying all its members by means of a **set-constructor**, which is syntactically classified as a factor of an expression:

factor: *variable* | *unsigned-constant* | *function-designator* |
*set-constructor* | ( *expression* ) | **not** *factor*
set-constructor: [ *element-list* ]
element-list: *element ... , element*
element: *expression .. expression*

[] denotes a set with no members, called the **empty set**. A non-empty set is constructed by enclosing a list of one or more elements, separated by commas, in square brackets. Elements come in two forms. One is simply an expression, in which case its value is made a member of the set. In all the examples given above, this form was used with a constant for the expression. The other form is two expressions separated by ..; in this case all values that are greater than or equal to the value of the first expression and less than or equal to the value of the second are made members of the set. There may be no such values.

All expressions in the elements of a given set-constructor must be of the same ordinal type. The type of a set-constructor is taken to be **set of** *T*, where *T* is the largest ordinal type containing the members. The type of [ ] is determined by context. Thus, for example:

| | |
|---|---|
| [bold, shadow..extend] | denotes the same set as [bold, shadow, condense, extend]; its type is **set of** StyleItem. |
| [bold, extend..shadow] | denotes the same set as [bold]; its type is **set of** StyleItem. |
| ['r', 'o', 'u', 't', 'e', '6', '6'] | denotes the same set as ['6', 'e', 'o', 'r', 't', 'u']; its type is **set of** char. |
| [0..9] | denotes the same set as [0, 1, 2, 3, 4, 5, 6, 7, 8, 9]; its type is **set of** integer. |
| [0..–1] | denotes the empty set of type **set of** integer. |

Packing aside, a value *s* of set-type $T_1$ is assignment-compatible with a set-type $T_2$ if the base-types have the same host-type and every member of *s* is a value of type $T_2$. For example, each of these assignment statements is legal:

```
TextStyle := [bold, shadow..extend]
TextStyle := [ ]
digits := [0..9]
digits := [0..–1]
```

However, the following two lines are not legal assignment statements:

```
TextStyle := [1..0] {XXXX ERROR XXXX}
digits := [1..10] {XXXX ERROR XXXX}
```

Note that in the first case the type of the set-constructor is **set of integer**.

### 17.3.2 SET-VALUED OPERATIONS

The operators +, *, and –, when applied to sets, represent the mathematical operations of **union**, **intersection**, and **set difference** respectively. In each case the base-types of the two sets involved must have the same host-type. Let *s* and *t* represent such sets. Then:

$s + t$ is the union of $s$ and $t$: the set of all values that are in $s$, or $t$, or both;

$s * t$ is the intersection of $s$ and $t$: the set of all values that are in both $s$ and $t$;

$s - t$ is the difference of $s$ and $t$: the set of all values that are in $s$ but not $t$.

Here are some examples:

| | | |
|---|---|---|
| [bold, italic] + [underline] | gives | [bold, italic, underline] |
| [bold, italic] + [bold] | gives | [bold, italic] |
| [2, 3, 5, 7] * [1, 3, 5, 7, 9] | gives | [3, 5, 7] |
| [0..9] * [9..10] | gives | [9] |
| ['c', 'a', 't'] – ['a'..'z'] | gives | [] |
| ['6', 'e', 'o', 'r', 't', 'u'] – ['0'..'9'] | gives | ['e', 'o', 'r', 't', 'u'] |

Since the precedence of operators is a syntactic matter in Pascal, these operators have the same precedence as their arithmetic counterparts.

## 17.4 Boolean operations on sets

Four of the relational operators are applicable to sets, namely:

= <> <= >=

They denote the mathematical notions of **set equality**, **set inequality**, the **subset** relation, and the **superset** relation respectively. The base-type of the two compared sets must have the same host-type. Let $s$ and $t$ be such sets. Then:

| | | |
|---|---|---|
| $s = t$ | gives | true iff $s$ and $t$ have exactly the same members. |
| $s <> t$ | gives | true iff $s = t$ gives false. |
| $s <= t$ | gives | true iff every member of $s$ is a member of $t$. |
| $s >= t$ | gives | true iff every member of $t$ is a member of $s$. |

Here are some examples:

| | | |
|---|---|---|
| ['A'..'Z'] = ['a'..'z'] | gives | false |
| [0..9] = [0, 1, 2, 3, 4, 5, 6, 7, 8, 9] | gives | true |
| [0] <> [] | gives | true |
| [italic] <= [bold..extend] | gives | true |
| [] <= [0] | gives | true |
| [0..9] <= [9, 10] | gives | false |
| [9,10] >= [0..9] | gives | false |
| [bold..extend] >= [italic, shadow] | gives | true |

Bear in mind the following:

- Only the relational operators associated with equality are available. The symbols < and > do not represent operations on sets in Pascal.
- [] <= *s* gives **true** for any set *s*, even [] itself.
- *s* <= *t* and *t* <= *s* may both give **false**, unlike the situation with any other type of values.

Pascal provides one more Boolean operation involving sets, corresponding to what mathematicians call the **membership** relation (usually written ∈). Let *s* be a set whose base-type is *T*, and *x* be a value of the host-type of *T*. Then:

*x* **in** *s* gives **true** iff *x* is a member of *s*.

For example:

```
italic in [bold..extend]   gives   true
's' in ['a'..'z']          gives   true
10 in [0..9]               gives   false
```

Remember that the left-operand is not a set

Boolean expressions can often be written most neatly using sets. For example, here is a condition from program RandomWalk for Case-study 7:

```
(1 <= NewRow) and (NewRow <= MaxIndex1) and
(1 <= NewCol) and (NewCol <= MaxIndex2)
```

It can be written more simply as:

```
(NewRow in [1..MaxIndex1]) and (NewCol in [1..MaxIndex2])
```

The condition:

```
(1 <= NewRow) and (NewRow <= MaxIndex) and
(1 <= NewCol) and (NewCol <= MaxIndex)
```

which would occur if the grid was always square, can be written as:

```
[NewRow, NewCol] <= [1..MaxIndex]
```

## 17.5 Subprograms involving sets

Parameters of subprograms can have set-types. For example, the procedure that sets the style for text displayed in the Drawing window is predefined as follows:

```
procedure TextFace (face : Style);
{ Sets the style for text displayed in Drawing window to face. }
```

The reader might like to think now about how to produce the output shown in Figure 17.1. A neat solution is presented in Chapter 18. It exploits the technique of recursion that is introduced in Chapter 18 (and also uses Macintosh Pascal strings as described in Chapter 14).

As another example, suppose we need to find the **symmetric difference** of two sets, which is the set of values that belong to exactly one of the sets. This is abstractly a function, but must be implemented in Pascal as a procedure, because functions cannot return values of structured-types.

```
procedure SymmetricDifference (s, t : SetType;
                                        var result : SetType);
{ Sets result = symmetric difference of s and t. }
begin { SymmetricDifference }
  result := s + t - s * t
end; { SymmetricDifference }
```

Suppose, for example, that *SetType* is DigitSet, which is defined as follows:

```
type
  digit = 0..9;
  DigitSet = set of digit;
var
  digits : DigitSet;
```

Then after execution of:

```
SymmetricDifference([2, 3, 5, 7], [1, 3, 5, 7, 9], digits)
```

digits contains [1, 2, 9]. This procedure is employed in Case-study 10 in Section 17.7.

## 17.6 Binary numbers as sets

### 17.6.1 BINARY REPRESENTATIONS

Consider a non-negative integer $x$ less than a limit $10^n$, where $n \geqslant 1$. It has a unique decimal representation $d_{n-1}d_{n-2} \ldots d_1d_0$, where $0 \leqslant d_i \leqslant 9$

for $i = 0, 1, \ldots, n-1$. It is defined by:

$$x = d_{n-1} \times 10^{n-1} + d_{n-2} \times 10^{n-2} + \ldots + d_1 \times 10^1 + d_0 \times 10^0$$

Thus, for example, with $x = 38$ and $n = 4$, the decimal representation is 0038, because

$$38 = 0 \times 10^3 + 0 \times 10^2 + 3 \times 10^1 + 8 \times 10^0$$

Now consider a non-negative integer $x$ less than a limit $2^n$, where $n \geqslant 1$. It has a unique **binary representation** $d_{n-1}d_{n-2} \ldots d_1d_0$, where $0 \leqslant d_i \leqslant 1$ for $i = 0, 1, \ldots, n-1$. It is defined by:

$$x = d_{n-1} \times 2^{n-1} + d_{n-2} \times 2^{n-2} + \ldots + d_1 \times 2^1 + d_0 \times 2^0$$

For example, with $x = 13$ and $n = 4$, the binary representation is 1101, because

$$13 = 1 \times 2^3 + 1 \times 2^2 + 0 \times 2^1 + 1 \times 2^0$$

Suppose that a program needs to work with such binary representations. A suitable data structure is needed to represent them. Perhaps the most obvious possibility is an array of binary digits. Two others are a string of '0' or '1' characters, and an array of Boolean values — see Exercise 17.13. But there is yet another possible data structure: the set of bit positions which are 1. For the above example, this would be [3, 2, 0], because $13 = 2^3 + 2^2 + 2^0$. This is likely to be the best representation, because sets are more easily manipulated than arrays, and because the operations on sets are more useful in this context than those on strings.

Suitable type-definitions would be:

```
const
  MaxExponent = 14; { exponent of maximum power of 2
                        <= Maxint }
type
  count = 0..Maxint;
  exponent = 0..MaxExponent;
  BinaryNumber = set of exponent;
```

Here MaxExponent is playing the role of $n$ above. Each value of type count has a characteristic corresponding value of type BinaryNumber.

Operations on binary numbers would be represented in Pascal by subprograms. We shall give two that handle conversions between integers and their binary representations.

The first converts a binary representation to the corresponding number. The idea is to compute the successive powers of 2, and add those exponents in the given set to a cumulative sum. The comments for the local variables amount to an invariant.

```
function number (bnum : BinaryNumber) : count;
{ Returns number whose binary representation is bnum. }
{ Global const: MaxExponent. }
  var
    i : exponent;
    num : count; { sum of powers of 2 with exponents < i and in
                   bnum }
    power : count; { = 2 to the power i }
begin { number }
  num := 0;
  power := 1;
  for i := 0 to MaxExponent – 1 do
    begin
      if i in bnum then
        num := num + power;
      power := power * 2
    end;
  if MaxExponent in bnum then
    number := num + power
  else
    number := num
end; { number }
```

A couple of points should be noted. One is that the powers are computed with a recurrence; it would be needlessly inefficient, and more complicated (which is worse), to compute each from scratch. The other is more subtle. The limit for the for-loop is one less than the natural limit, forcing extra computation after the loop. This avoids computing a value for **power** that exceeds **Maxint**.

The second subprogram converts in the other direction; it has to be a procedure. The idea is explained by an explicit invariant.

```
procedure binary (n : count;
                  var BinaryOfn : BinaryNumber);
{ Sets BinaryOfn = binary representation of n. }
  var
    i : 0..Maxint; { in 0..MaxExponent + 1 }
begin { binary }
  BinaryOfn := [];
  i := 0;
  { Invariant: BinaryOfn = set of dj with j < i and dj = 1, and }
  { n = dm * 2-to-the-power-(m – i) + ... + di * 2-to-the-power-0, }
  { where originally n = dm * 2-to-the-power-m + ... + }
  { d0 * 2-to-the-power-0 }
```

```
    while n <> 0 do
      begin
        if odd(n) then
          BinaryOfn := BinaryOfn + [i];
        i := i + 1;
        n := n div 2
      end
  end; { binary }
```

In this case the loop has not been halted prematurely, but at the minor cost of being unable to declare i as of type **exponent**. This procedure exemplifies a commonly used schema for constructing a set: to start with the empty set and iteratively add a single member. Note that this member must be enclosed in square brackets.

## 17.7 Case-study 10: Nim

### 17.7.1 SETTING OF THE PROBLEM

A simple version of the game of Nim was introduced in Case-study 4. The full game of Nim differs in having several piles of matches, rather than just one. On each move, one or more matches must be taken from a single pile; there is no limit on the number that may be taken. The player who takes the last match wins the game.

The optimal strategy for Nim is more complicated than that for MiniNim, but it is also based on a kind of invariant. Suppose there is an assertion (about the state of the game) with the following properties.

- If the assertion is false before a player's move, he or she or it can always move so that it is true afterwards.
- If the assertion is true before a player's move, it cannot be true after the move.
- In the winning state the assertion is true.

Then the perfect strategy is to move so as to make the assertion true (as soon as this is possible) and thereafter restore the invariant after each move by the opponent.

The *winning invariant* for the game of MiniNim was:

*number of matches left* **mod** $(max + 1) = 0$

where *max* is the agreed maximum number of matches that may be taken on a move. It is easy to verify that it has the three required properties.

The winning invariant for Nim is much harder to find; we shall

**Table 17.1** Parity of each bit-position.

| Number | Binary digit | | | |
|---|---|---|---|---|
| | $d_3$ | $d_2$ | $d_1$ | $d_0$ |
| 1 | 0 | 0 | 0 | 1 |
| 5 | 0 | 1 | 0 | 1 |
| 9 | 1 | 0 | 0 | 1 |
| 2 | 0 | 0 | 1 | 0 |
| 4 | 0 | 1 | 0 | 0 |
| 7 | 0 | 1 | 1 | 1 |
| Parity | odd | odd | even | even |

be content to pull it out of a hat and show that it works. It is this: consider the binary representations of the number of matches left in each pile. For each bit-position, add up the number of digits = 1. Then each of these numbers is even. We say that the **parity** of each bit-position must be even. For example, suppose there are six piles and their sizes are 1, 5, 9, 2, 0, 7. Table 17.1 displays the parity of each bit-position. It is apparent that the winning invariant is not true in this state.

Let us check that the above assertion has the three required properties. The third holds because if all numbers are zero then all parities are even. The second is only slightly harder to see. For suppose all parities are even. The next move will change at least one binary digit of the number for the pile involved, but will not affect any other numbers. So the parity of at least one position will become odd.

Finally, consider the first requirement. Suppose at least one parity is odd. There must be a pile whose binary representation has a 1-digit in the highest position with odd parity. In the example above, this is the pile with 9 matches. Change the bits which are in positions of odd parity. In our example, these are positions 3 and 2, and the resulting binary representation is 0101. This represents a smaller number. In the example, it is 5. By moving to leave this many matches, all parities become even. So there is only one move to make in the state shown in the example. Take 4 matches from the pile with 9. Table 17.2 shows the resulting state.

### 17.7.2 SPECIFICATIONS

A Macintosh Pascal program is to be written that plays Nim with the user. The specifications are as in Case-study 4 for the game of Mini-Nim, but adapted to the full game. Unlike before, the number of matches remaining after a move need not be indicated in the Text window (because there will be several piles with small numbers of

| Number | Binary digit | | | |
|---|---|---|---|---|
| | $d_3$ | $d_2$ | $d_1$ | $d_0$ |
| 1 | 0 | 0 | 0 | 1 |
| 5 | 0 | 1 | 0 | 1 |
| 5 | 0 | 1 | 0 | 1 |
| 2 | 0 | 0 | 1 | 0 |
| 4 | 0 | 1 | 0 | 0 |
| 7 | 0 | 1 | 1 | 1 |
| Parity | even | even | even | even |

**Table 17.2** Parities after the perfect move.

matches). Also, if the program is not in a winning position, it should take a random number of matches from some pile. The diagram should label the piles so that the user can specify which pile to take from.

### 17.7.3 WRITING THE PROGRAM

At a high-level, this program will differ little from program MiniNim in Chapter 9. So we will confine our attention here to procedure move, which is where the important differences will emerge.

Move needs to have the size of each pile as both an input and output parameter, and an input parameter that tells it whether the program or the user is to move next. Furthermore, since the game ends when all piles are empty, we shall provide the number of empty piles as an input and output parameter; this is redundant, but convenient and efficient. We choose appropriate types, and obtain the provisional heading shown below.

```
const
  MaxMatches = ... ; { maximum number of matches in a pile }
  NrPiles = ... ; { number of piles of matches }
type
  MatchCount = 0..MaxMatches; { possible numbers of matches
                                 left in a pile }
  PileCount = 0..NrPiles;
  PileIndex = 1..NrPiles;
  PileCounts = array[PileIndex] of MatchCount;

procedure move (var size : PileCounts; { size of each pile }
        var NrEmpty : PileCount; { number of empty piles }
        MacToMove : Boolean); { true iff Macintosh to move }
{ Makes move, updating size and NrEmpty; }
{ assumes NrEmpty < NrPiles. }
```

The first couple of refinements of the statement-part lead to:

```
begin { move }
  if MacToMove then
    begin { Determine and report Macintosh's move }
      Write('Hit Return to see my move.');
      if the winning invariant is already true then
        Take a random number from a non-empty pile
      else
        Choose a move that makes the winning invariant true;
      Readln;
      Report Macintosh's move
    end
  else
    Prompt for and read user's move;
  Remove the matches, updating the appropriate variables and the display
end; { move }
```

The Readln has been positioned to allow the Macintosh to use the period before the user responds to calculate its move.

A move is characterized by two values: the number of matches to remove and the pile to take them from. Two local variables are therefore introduced:

```
var
  taken : MatchCount; { number of matches to take }
  FromPile : PileIndex; { pile matches are taken from }
```

Most of the remaining refinements are straightforward. The exceptions are the condition:

*the winning invariant is already true*

and the action:

*Choose a move that makes the winning invariant true*

which both involve the winning strategy.

The additional information needed to implement this condition and action is the binary representation of the size of each pile and the parity of each bit-position. All of this information can be computed by move from the sizes of the piles, but it is simpler and more efficient to update it after a move (by either the Macintosh or the user), because only one pile's binary representation is affected by a move. We therefore provide the information through parameters, and hand the obligation to update them after a move to the action:

*Remove the matches, updating the appropriate variables and the display*

The binary versions of the pile sizes are represented with sets, as described previously. The parity information also is represented by a single set of the same kind; its members are the bit positions with odd parity. The new parameters and their context are:

```
const
  MaxExponent = 3; { exponent of maximum power of 2
                     <= MaxMatches }
type
  exponent = 0..MaxExponent;
  BinaryNumber = set of exponent; { binary form of a MatchCount }
  BinaryPileCounts = array[PileIndex] of BinaryNumber;

procedure move (...
    var BinarySize : BinaryPileCounts; { binary version of size }
    var parity : BinaryNumber); { bit-positions of BinarySize with
                                  odd parity }
```

The condition is implemented very simply, with:

```
parity = []
```

The first refinement of the action to choose a best move expresses the method given previously:

```
var
  BigExponent : exponent; { biggest member of parity }
  NewBinary : BinaryNumber; { new value of BinarySize[FromPile] }

begin { Choose a move that makes the winning invariant true }
  Set BigExponent = biggest member of parity;
  Set FromPile such that BigExponent in BinarySize[FromPile];
  Set NewBinary to the symmetric difference of parity and
  BinarySize[FromPile];
  taken := size[FromPile] – the number whose binary representation
  is NewBinary
end
```

Let us desk-check this on the example presented in Tables 17.1 and 17.2. The state before the move is as shown in Table 17.3. We calculate that:

```
BigExponent = 3
FromPile = 3
NewBinary = the symmetric difference of [3, 2] and [3, 0] = [2, 0]
taken = 9 – 5 = 4
```

**Table 17.3** The Pascal version of Table 17.1.

| i | size[i] | BinarySize[i] |
|---|---|---|
| 1 | 1 | [0] |
| 2 | 5 | [2, 0] |
| 3 | 9 | [3, 0] |
| 4 | 2 | [1, 0] |
| 5 | 4 | [2, 0] |
| 6 | 7 | [2, 1, 0] |

parity = [3, 2]

All is as it should be, and we proceed with the refinements. Th[illegible] fir[illegible] two actions are standard linear searches; the others simply employ procedure SymmetricDifference and function number developed previously. All may be found in the complete solution given later.

Finally, we turn to the part of the action:

*Remove the matches, updating the appropriate variables and the display*

that updates the extra parameters BinarySize and parity. Note that if the program moved *from a state with* parity ≠ [], then the new value of BinarySize[FromPile] is NewBinary and the new value of parity is []. We choose to recalculate since the code reads better and the calculation is simple. Exercise 17.19 invites you to avoid the recalculation.

Updating BinarySize[FromPile] is trivial: procedure binary is simply applied to the new size. Now consider parity. The symmetric difference *d* of the old and new values of BinarySize[FromPile] gives the changed bit positions. So the new value of parity is just the symmetric difference of the old value and *d*. The translation into Pascal twice employs procedure SymmetricDifference.

Variables used as the actual parameters corresponding to parity and BinarySize are declared in the program-block. The same names are used. These variables need to be initialized before moves are made. The initialization is quite straightforward.

### 17.7.4 THE COMPLETE PROGRAM

Here is an almost complete program. Exercise 17.20 asks you to complete it by modifying it to check the user's input.

```
program Nim (Input, Output);
{ Plays a game of Nim with the user; run for instructions. }

  const
    MaxMatches = 10; { maximum number of matches in a pile }
```

```
  MaxExponent = 3; { exponent of maximum power of 2
                       <= MaxMatches }
  NrPiles = 6; { number of piles of matches }
  Length = 37;  { length of matchstick }
  Dist = 20; { space between matches }
  Width = 6; { width of matchstick }
  HeadLength = 9; { length of match head }
  HeadWidth = 8; { width of match head }
  Overlap = 4; { overlap of head on stick }
  LabelWidth = 45; { width allocated for a label for each pile }
  Pointsize = 12;

type
  MatchCount = 0..MaxMatches; { possible numbers of matches
                                  left in a pile }
  exponent = 0..MaxExponent;
  BinaryNumber = set of exponent; { binary form of a
                                      MatchCount }
  PileIndex = 1..NrPiles;
  PileCount = 0..NrPiles;
  PileCounts = array[PileIndex] of MatchCount;
  BinaryPileCounts = array[PileIndex] of BinaryNumber;

var
  size : PileCounts; { size[i] = number of matches in pile i }
  BinarySize : BinaryPileCounts;
    { BinarySize[i] = binary representation of size[i] }
  parity : BinaryNumber; { e in parity is true iff number of times }
    { e in BinarySize[i] is true is odd (i = 1, ... , NrPiles) }
  EmptyPiles : PileCount; { number of empty piles }
  NrPile : PileIndex;
  MacNext : Boolean; { true iff Macintosh moves next }

procedure LabelRow (row : PileIndex);
{ Draws label for given row of display; }
{ N.B. must have width of label < LabelWidth. }
{ Global consts: Length, HeadLength, PointSize, LabelWidth. }
begin { LabelRow }
  MoveTo(0, row * (Length + HeadLength) –
           (Length + HeadLength – Pointsize) div 2);
  DrawString(StringOf(' pile ', row : 1))
end; { LabelRow }

procedure DrawMatch (MatchNr : MatchCount;
                     row : PileIndex);
{ Draws match number MatchNr in given row. }
{ Global consts: Length, Dist, Width, HeadLength, HeadWidth,
               Overlap, LabelWidth. }
  var
    base : integer;
```

```
begin { DrawMatch }
 base := row * (Length + HeadLength);
 FrameRect(base – Length,
              LabelWidth + MatchNr * Dist – Width div 2,
              base, LabelWidth + MatchNr * Dist + Width div 2);
 PaintOval(base – Length – HeadLength + Overlap,
             LabelWidth + MatchNr * Dist – HeadWidth div 2,
             base – Length + Overlap,
             LabelWidth + MatchNr * Dist + HeadWidth div 2)
end; { DrawMatch }

procedure EraseMatch (MatchNr : MatchCount;
                          row : PileIndex);
{ Erases drawing of match number MatchNr in given row. }
{ Global consts: Length, Dist, HeadLength, Overlap, LabelWidth. }
 var
  base : integer;
begin { EraseMatch }
 base := row * (Length + HeadLength);
 EraseRect(base – Length – HeadLength + Overlap,
             LabelWidth + MatchNr * Dist – Dist div 2, base,
             LabelWidth + MatchNr * Dist + Dist div 2)
end; { EraseMatch }

function ran (lower, upper : integer) : integer;
{ Returns a random value uniformly distributed in lower..upper; }
{ assumes lower <= upper. }
as in program Arithmetic in Chapter 10

procedure SymmetricDifference (s, t : BinaryNumber;
                                      var result : BinaryNumber);
{ Sets result = symmetric difference of s and t. }
as for procedure SymmetricDifference in text

function number (bnum : BinaryNumber) : MatchCount;
{ Returns number whose binary representation is bnum. }
as for procedure number in text, but with MatchCount
instead of count

procedure binary (n : MatchCount;
                    var BinaryOfn : BinaryNumber);
{ Sets BinaryOfn = binary representation of n. }
as for function binary in text

procedure introduce (var size : PileCounts); { size of each pile }
{ Explains game, and creates and draws the piles of matches. }
{ Global consts: PointSize, NrPiles, MaxMatches. }
{ Global subprograms: DrawMatch, LabelRow, ran. }
```

```
  var
    MatchIndex : MatchCount; { number of match }
    row : PileIndex;
begin { introduce }
{ Explain the game }
  Writeln('This is the game of NIM, in which we take turn
            removing matches.');
  Writeln('On each move a number of matches must be taken
            from a single pile.');
  Writeln('The pile is arbitrary provided at least one match is
            taken from it.');
  Writeln('The player who takes the last match wins.');
{ Create, draw, and label each pile of matches }
  TextSize(Pointsize);
  for row := 1 to NrPiles do
    begin { Create, label, and draw the pile in this row }
      size[row] := ran(1, MaxMatches);
      LabelRow(row);
      for MatchIndex := 1 to size[row] do
        DrawMatch(MatchIndex, row)
    end
end; { introduce }

procedure FindOut (var IsYes : Boolean
                                          { true iff 'Y' or 'y' typed first }
      );
{ Asks for & reads a yes/no response, & sets IsYes accordingly. }
as in program MiniNim in Chapter 9

procedure move (var size : PileCounts; { size of each pile }
          var NrEmpty : PileCount; { number of empty piles }
          MacToMove : Boolean; { true iff Macintosh to move }
          var BinarySize : BinaryPileCounts; { binary version of size }
          var parity : BinaryNumber); { bit-positions of BinarySize
                                          with odd parity }
{ Makes next move, updating size, BinarySize, parity, & NrEmpty; }
{ assumes NrEmpty < NrPiles. }
{ Global const: MaxExponent. }
{ Global subprograms: ran, SymmetricDifference, number, binary,
                        EraseMatch. }
  var
    taken : MatchCount; { number of matches to take }
    OldBinary, NewBinary : BinaryNumber; { old and new values of
                                              BinarySize[FromPile] }
    BigExponent : exponent; { biggest member of parity }
    FromPile, { pile matches are taken from }
    pile : PileIndex;
    MatchIndex : MatchCount;
    BinaryDiff : BinaryNumber;
```

```
begin { move }
  if MacToMove then
    begin { Determine and report Macintosh's move }
      Write('Hit Return to see my move.');
      if parity = [] then
        begin { Take a random number from a non-empty pile }
          { Set FromPile = index of a non-empty pile }
          FromPile := 1;
          while size[FromPile] = 0 do
            FromPile := FromPile + 1;

          taken := ran(1, size[FromPile])
        end
      else
        begin { Choose a move that makes parity = [] }
          { Set BigExponent = biggest member of parity }
          BigExponent := MaxExponent;
          while not (BigExponent in parity) do
            BigExponent := BigExponent - 1;
         { Set FromPile s.t. BigExponent in BinarySize[FromPile] }
          FromPile := 1;
          while not (BigExponent in BinarySize[FromPile]) do
            FromPile := FromPile + 1;

          SymmetricDifference(parity, BinarySize[FromPile],
                               NewBinary);
          taken := size[FromPile] - number(NewBinary)
        end;
      Readln;
      Writeln('I take ', taken : 1, ' matches from pile ', FromPile
               : 1, '.')
    end
  else
    begin { Prompt for and read user's move }
      Write('What pile do you take from? ');
      Readln(FromPile);
      Write('How many matches do you take? ');
      Readln(taken)
    end;
{ Remove the matches, updating the appropriate variables and
  the display }
  for MatchIndex := size[FromPile] downto
                    size[FromPile] - taken + 1 do
    EraseMatch(MatchIndex, FromPile);
  size[FromPile] := size[FromPile] - taken;
  if size[FromPile] = 0 then
    NrEmpty := NrEmpty + 1;
{ Update BinarySize and parity }
```

```
      OldBinary := BinarySize[FromPile];
      binary(size[FromPile], BinarySize[FromPile]);
      SymmetricDifference(BinarySize[FromPile], OldBinary,
                                BinaryDiff);
      SymmetricDifference(BinaryDiff, parity, parity)
    end; { move }

  begin { Nim }
    introduce(size);
  { Initialize BinarySize and parity }
    parity := [];
    for NrPile := 1 to NrPiles do
      begin
        binary(size[NrPile], BinarySize[NrPile]);
        SymmetricDifference(parity, BinarySize[NrPile], parity)
      end;
  { Make moves until all piles are empty, remembering last player }
  { to move }
    FindOut(MacNext);
    EmptyPiles := 0;
    while EmptyPiles < NrPiles do
      begin
        move(size, EmptyPiles, MacNext, BinarySize, parity);
        MacNext := not MacNext
      end;
  { Announce winner }
    if MacNext then
      Writeln('Congratulations, you won !')
    else
      Writeln('I won!')
  end. { Nim }
```

Figure 17.2 shows the screen at an early stage in a typical game. The original state was as in our example, i.e. as in Tables 17.1 and 17.3. The user blew the opportunity to win.

Most Pascal implementations would implement values of the types MatchCount and BinaryNumber from program Nim in the same way, i.e. as an array of bits in a byte or cell. Subprograms number and binary simply return the same values as their arguments on such systems! This point is elaborated briefly in Chapter 19, where it is noted that these functions can be avoided in a lower-level Macintosh Pascal version of Nim. The great advantage of the given version is that it is written in Standard Pascal and is therefore portable (aside from the graphics).

Situations where the calling (sub)program declares variables that logically belong to the called subprogram, as with parity and Binary-

Figure 17.2
The screen during a run of program Nim.

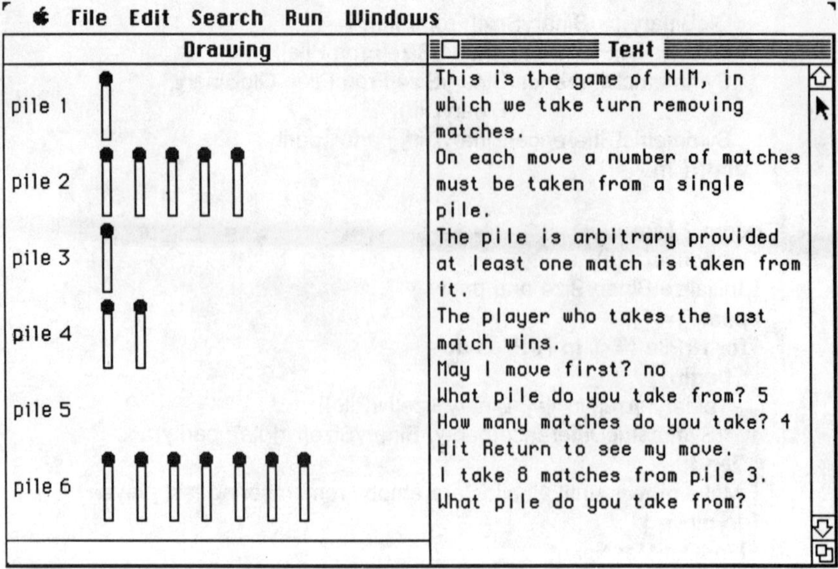

File Edit Search Run Windows
Drawing
Text
pile 1
pile 2
pile 3
pile 4
pile 5
pile 6
This is the game of NIM, in which we take turn removing matches.
On each move a number of matches must be taken from a single pile.
The pile is arbitrary provided at least one match is taken from it.
The player who takes the last match wins.
May I move first? no
What pile do you take from? 5
How many matches do you take? 4
Hit Return to see my move.
I take 8 matches from pile 3.
What pile do you take from?


Size in this program, are often symptomatic of the need to use an *abstract data type*. See the discussions in Chapters 15 and 20.

## 17.8 Macaveats

17.1 Macintosh Pascal does not permit packed sets. However this is no great loss.

## EXERCISES

**17.1** How many values of type Style:

(a) contain bold?

(b) contain italic but not underline?

(c) represent different styles of text? Assume that extend cancels the effect of condense.

**17.2** Given that i = 2 and j = 4, evaluate each of the following expressions:

(a) [i..j] (b) [j..i]

(c) [i – j..j – i] (d) [i, i + 2, j, j+2]

(e) ['0'..chr(ord('0') + i)] (f) ['i'..'j']

You may assume that the lower-case letters are contiguous.

**17.3** Show how to use a set-constructor to ensure that a case-statement is not executed if the value of the expression is not one of the case-labels. That is, show how to get the effect of Macintosh Pascal's **otherwise** clause in Standard Pascal.

**17.4** Evaluate each of the following expressions:

(a) [2, 5, 8] + [0, 2, 4, 6, 8] (b) [2, 5, 8] – [0, 2, 4, 6, 8]
(c) [0, 2, 4, 6, 8] – [2, 5, 8] (d) [2, 5, 8] * [0, 2, 4, 6, 8]

**17.5** Evaluate each of the following expressions:

(a) [0, 9] <= [0..9] (b) [9..0] <= [0, 9]
(c) [1, 3, 5] >= [3..5] (d) [] <> ['9'..'0']
(e) [bold, bold] = [bold] (f) shadow **in** [bold..extend]

**17.6** Assume the following context:

```
var
  TypeFace : Style;

procedure GetTextStyle (var face : Style);
{ Sets face to the current text style (for the Drawing window). }
```

Implement each of the following actions:

(a) *Set* TypeFace *to the current text style*
(b) *Add* underline *to the current text style if it is not already present*
(c) *Remove* extend *and* condense *from the current text style if both are present in it.*

**17.7** Implement the following action in the given context:

```
var
  letters : set of 'a'..'z';
  IsPangram : Boolean;
```

*Set* IsPangram = true *if every lower-case letter is present in* letters, *otherwise* false

You may assume that the lower-case letters are contiguous.

**17.8** Use sets to implement each of the following expressions, where ch and b are variables of types char and 2..10 respectively.

(a) ch *is either* 'Y' *or* 'y'

(b) ch *is a decimal digit*

(c) ch *is a digit in base* b

(d) ch *is a control-character in Macintosh Pascal*.

**17.9** Write a function that returns the number of members in a given set of characters.

**17.10** Write a program that reports each of the characters that appear in the input data.

**17.11** Suppose that the seating on an airplane consists of rows numbered from 1 onwards, and that each row consists of six seats labeled 'A' to 'F'. Give a suitable data structure for representing whether or not each seat has been assigned.

**17.12** Suppose you are writing a program that colors each country on a map so that two countries which share a border have different colors. The available colors are red, blue, green and yellow. It is known that these suffice. Give a data structure that enables the following actions to be neatly implemented.

*Initialize so that no country has a color*
*Assign a given color to a given country*
*Deassign a given color from a given country*
*Check whether a country sharing a border with a given country has a given color*

*Hint*: Record the countries adjacent to each country and the countries that have been assigned each color.

**17.13** Give a comment that explains this alternative implementation of a binary number:

```
type
  BinaryNumber = array[0..MaxExponent] of Boolean;
```

**17.14** Subprogram binary cannot be written as a function. Why?

**17.15** Verify that the winning invariant for the game of MiniNim has the three required properties.

**17.16** In the game of Nim, is it usually better to move first or second? Why?

**17.17** Assuming that at least one bit-position has odd parity, can there ever be more than one best move? If so, give an example.

**17.18** What is the best move if the non-empty piles have sizes 8, 6, and 5?

**17.19** Modify procedure `move` to avoid the recalculation of `parity` and `BinarySize[FromPile]` when the program has moved to a state in which the winning invariant is true. The argument for doing so is that the strategy is thereby made more apparent.

**17.20** Complete program `Nim` by having it check the user's input.

# 18 ADVANCED USE OF SUBPROGRAMS

(Stories inside stories, movies inside movies, paintings inside paintings, Russian dolls inside Russian dolls, (even parenthetical comments inside parenthetical comments!) — these are just a few of the charms of recursion.)
— Douglas R. Hofstadter, *Gödel, Escher, Bach: An Eternal Golden Braid*

## 18.1 Recursion

### 18.1.1 A RECURSIVE FUNCTION

Exercise 6.20 was concerned with computing the Fibonacci numbers, which were defined informally in English. The definition can be formalized by writing $F_n$ for the $n$'th Fibonacci number, $n \geqslant 0$, and defining it as follows:

$$F_n = \begin{cases} 0, & \text{if } n = 0, \\ 1, & \text{if } n = 1, \\ F_{n-1} + F_{n-2}, & \text{if } n > 1. \end{cases}$$

Such a definition is familiar to the mathematician. It defines the *sequence* of Fibonacci numbers: the first two members are 0 and 1, and each successive term is the sum of the two previous ones. Exercise 6.20 required the computation of an initial segment of the sequence.

The above definition is easily recast to define the corresponding Fibonacci *function* $F$:

$$F(n) = \begin{cases} 0, & \text{if } n = 0, \\ 1, & \text{if } n = 1, \\ F(n-1) + F(n-2), & \text{if } n > 1. \end{cases}$$

This is called a **recursive** definition, meaning that the function is defined in terms of itself. And it suggests a way of computing any particular value of the function. For example, $F(4)$ can be computed as follows:

$$\begin{aligned} F(4) &= F(3) + F(2) \\ &= (F(2) + F(1)) + (F(1) + F(0)) \\ &= ((F(1) + F(0)) + 1) + (1 + 0) \\ &= ((1 + 0) + 1) + 1 \end{aligned}$$

```
= (1 + 1) + 1
= 2 + 1
= 3
```

One might wonder whether the above definition of the Fibonacci function can be translated into a Pascal function. The answer is yes. The scope of a function identifier includes its own body, implying that the function may be called in that body. The translation into Pascal is very straightforward, yielding the following **recursive function**:

```
function Fibonacci (n : count) : count;
{ Returns the n'th Fibonacci number. }
begin { Fibonacci }
  if n = 0 then
    Fibonacci := 0
  else if n = 1 then
    Fibonacci := 1
  else
    Fibonacci := Fibonacci(n – 1) + Fibonacci(n – 2)
end; { Fibonacci }
```

The computation of a particular value of the function proceeds just as in the example of $F(4)$ above.

Now we can appreciate the reason for Pascal's restriction that the name of a function acts like a variable that may only be assigned to — it cannot be used *as a variable* in an expression in the function body because such uses are reserved for recursive applications of the function, such as Fibonacci(n – 1).

### 18.1.2 A RECURSIVE PROCEDURE

Pascal also permits **recursive procedures**. Suppose a procedure is desired that prints out the reverse of the rest of the current input line. A neat way to describe the process is:

- if the input position is at end-of-line, do nothing;
- otherwise, read a character, print the reverse of the rest of the line, then print the character read.

In Pascal:

```
procedure PrintReverseOfLine;
{ Reads rest of input line and prints it in reverse, }
{ preceded by a label. }
```

**Figure 18.1**
The Text window after a run of program **test**.

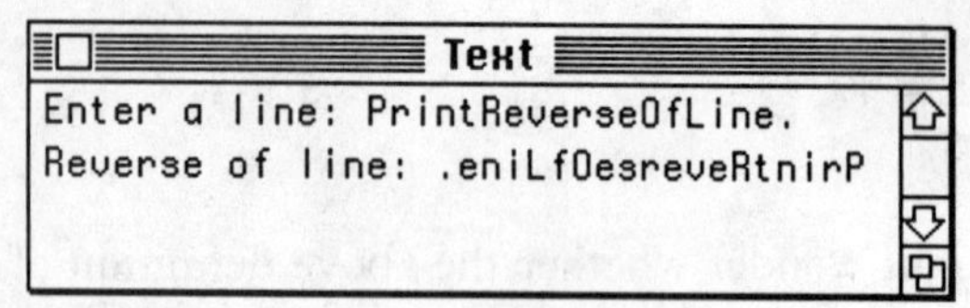
Text
Enter a line: PrintReverseOfLine.
Reverse of line: .eniLfOesreveRtnirP

```
  var
    ch : char; { next character of input line }
begin { PrintReverseOfLine }
  if eoln then
    begin
      Readln;
      Write('Reverse of line: ')
    end
  else
    begin
      Read(ch);
      PrintReverseOfLine;
      Write(ch)
    end
end; { PrintReverseOfLine }
```

A test reveals that this really does work (did you ever doubt it?): Figure 18.1 shows the result of a run of the following test-driver.

```
program test (Input, Output);
{ Tests procedure PrintReverseOfLine. }
  declaration of PrintReverseOfLine
begin { test }
  Write('Enter a line: ');
  PrintReverseOfLine
end. { test }
```

### 18.1.3 EXPLOITING RECURSION: AN EXAMPLE

Although recursion tends to strike the novice as magical, that is not to decry its value in problem-solving — to the contrary, magic is an excellent way to solve problems. Recursion very often permits simpler and clearer solutions than are possible without it. We shall demonstrate with two examples. One is given as Case-study 11 later in the chapter.

The other example concerns the legend of the towers of Hanoi. An order of monks was given a task, the completion of which would signal the end of the world. The task involved three pegs. On one there was a pile of 64 disks whose diameter strictly increased from top to bottom; the other two had no disks. The task was to move the disks so that they end up in their original order on one of the two empty

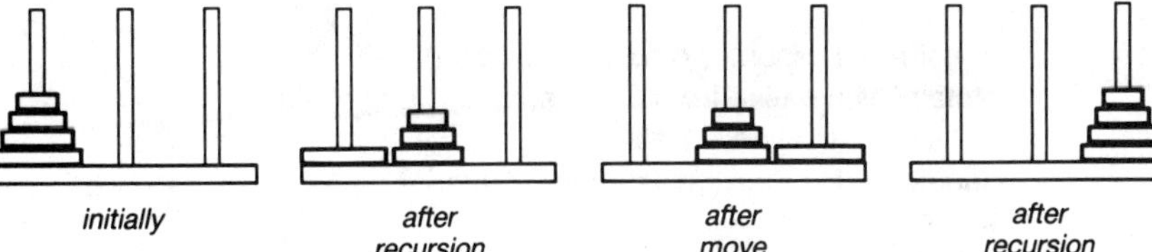


**Figure 18.2**
A recursive solution to the Towers of Hanoi.

pegs. Only one disk could be moved at a time, from one peg to another, provided it was not thereby placed on a smaller disk. The monks were no fools — they sold the rights to a US toy company, bought a Macintosh with the proceeds, and wrote a program to print out the solution.

Let us emulate them, by writing a procedure that prints a sequence of moves that solves the problem for an arbitrary number of disks. We make the following definitions and declaration:

```
const
  MaxDisks = 64;
type
  DiskCount = 0..MaxDisks;
  peg = (left, middle, right);

procedure Hanoi (n : DiskCount); { TENTATIVE }
{ Prints a sequence of moves that move n disks from peg left to }
{ peg right, according to the rules for the towers of Hanoi. }
```

Already we have made progress: using a procedure with parameter n opens the possibility of recursive uses with arguments smaller than n. Let us think. If n = 0, there is nothing to do. Otherwise, if we can solve the problem for n – 1 disks, we can adapt it to move the top n – 1 disks to the *middle* peg, then move the largest disk from the left to the right peg, then re-adapt the solution for n – 1 disks to move the disks from the *middle* to the right peg. At no stage is a larger disk placed on a smaller one. Figure 18.2 illustrates the three-step recursive solution for the 4-disk version.

We need to generalize our procedure so that the source and destination pegs are parameters. Rather than compute the other peg, it too is provided as a parameter. The solution is now easily written:

```
procedure Hanoi (n : DiskCount;
                    source, destination, other : peg);
{ Prints a sequence of moves that move n disks from the }
{ source to the destination, according to the rules for the towers }
{ of Hanoi; other is the other peg. }
begin { Hanoi }
  if n > 0 then
```

```
    begin
      Hanoi(n – 1, source, other, destination);
      Writeln('Move disk from the ', source, ' peg to the ',
              destination, ' peg.');
      Hanoi(n – 1, other, destination, source)
    end
  end; { Hanoi }
```

We have taken advantage of Macintosh Pascal's ability to print values of enumerated types directly. Figure 18.3 shows the output produced by the procedure-call:

```
Hanoi(4, left, right, middle)
```

### 18.1.4 EXPLOITING RECURSION: THE FUNDAMENTAL PRINCIPLES

The previous example illustrates the four fundamental principles of using recursion:

(1) The specifications must be sufficiently general to permit the use of recursive calls. Generalization is usually done by adding additional parameters (as with the three extra formal parameters of Hanoi).

(2) There must be at least one **base-case** where execution of the body of the subprogram does not involve any recursive calls. With Hanoi, this is when n = 0.

**Figure 18.3**
The solution to the four-disk version of Towers of Hanoi.

```
Text
Move disk from the left peg to the middle peg.
Move disk from the left peg to the right peg.
Move disk from the middle peg to the right peg.
Move disk from the left peg to the middle peg.
Move disk from the right peg to the left peg.
Move disk from the right peg to the middle peg.
Move disk from the left peg to the middle peg.
Move disk from the left peg to the right peg.
Move disk from the middle peg to the right peg.
Move disk from the middle peg to the left peg.
Move disk from the right peg to the left peg.
Move disk from the middle peg to the right peg.
Move disk from the left peg to the middle peg.
Move disk from the left peg to the right peg.
Move disk from the middle peg to the right peg.
```

(3) The values of the actual parameters of each recursive call in the body of the subprogram must be closer to a base-case than those of the formal parameters. With Hanoi, n – 1 is closer to 0 than n if n > 0.

(4) The body of the subprogram must meet the specifications, assuming each recursive call in the body obeys the specifications. We reasoned that the body of Hanoi is correct assuming that each recursive call acts as specified.

The first requirement permits a recursive solution; the second and third ensure that the recursion terminates (provided the non-recursive parts do so); the last requirement ensures that the subprogram is correct, a fact which may be proved by mathematical induction.

### 18.1.5 MUTUAL RECURSION

A Pascal subprogram is said to be recursive if it can call itself. Recursion can manifest itself indirectly. If a subprogram *A* calls another subprogram *B*, which in turn calls *A*, either directly or by a chain of calls ending in a call of *A*, *A* and *B* are said to be **mutually recursive**.

This is a common phenomenon in certain application areas, notably that of programming language translators. A natural way to write a translator involves having a procedure for each grammatical category. The procedure that handles a for-statement processes the body of the for-statement by calling the procedure that handles a statement, which in turn calls the former if the body of the for-statement is itself a for-statement. The syntax of Pascal is inherently recursive, so this phenomenon can arise in many different ways, some quite indirect.

The main reason for singling out mutual recursion is that it can cause syntactic complications. If *A* and *B* are mutually recursive, then the rule of declaration before use requires that *B* be declared before *A* uses it, and vice versa. This is no problem if one subprogram is declared inside the body of the other, because then both headings (which give the necessary information) appear before any uses of the subprograms. But if *A* and *B* are declared at the same level, there is a problem.

The solution adopted in Pascal is to allow the heading of a subprogram to be separated from its body. So the heading of *A*, say, can be given first, then all of *B*, and the body of *A* can be given later in the same declaration-section. A body to be given later is signaled by **forward**, which is called a **directive**. Here is a very artificial example; the mutually recursive subprograms are the functions gcd1 and gcd2.

```
function gcd (x, y : count) : count;
{ Returns the greatest common divisor of x and y; }
{ assumes x and y are not both zero. }

  function gcd2 (x, y : count) : count; forward;
  { Returns the greatest common divisor of x and y; }
  { assumes 0 <= x < y. }

  function gcd1 (x, y : count) : count;
  { Returns the greatest common divisor of x and y; }
  { assumes 0 <= y <= x and x > 0. }
  begin { gcd1 }
    if y = 0 then
      gcd1 := x
    else
      gcd1:= gcd2(x mod y, y)
  end; { gcd1 }

  function gcd2; { see above for heading }
  begin { gcd2 }
    if x = 0 then
      gcd2 := y
    else
      gcd2 := gcd1(x, y mod x)
  end; { gcd2 }

begin { gcd }
  if x >= y then
    gcd := gcd1(x, y)
  else
    gcd := gcd2(x, y)
end; { gcd }
```

Notice that only the name of the subprogram is given in the heading accompanying its body, if it has already been declared with **forward**.

The necessary changes to the syntax rules are as follows:

function-declaration:
 *function-heading* ; *function-body* |
 *function-heading* ; *directive* |
 *function-identification* ; *function-body*
directive: **forward**
function-identification: **function** *function-identifier*
function-identifier: *identifier*
procedure-declaration:
 *procedure-heading* ; *procedure-body* |
 *procedure-heading* ; *directive* |

*procedure-identification* ; *procedure-body*
procedure-identification: **procedure** *procedure-identifier*
procedure-identifier: *identifier*

### 18.1.6 EXECUTING RECURSIVE SUBPROGRAMS

There are only five possible reasons for wanting to know *how* recursive subprograms are executed. And none of them has much to do with writing recursive subprograms:

> **Principle** You need not understand how recursive subprograms are executed in order to use them to solve programming problems. In fact, it is best to avoid thinking about their execution.

Recursive solutions are obtained instead by following the four principles outlined previously.

These are the five legitimate reasons:

(1) to desk-check recursive subprograms;

(2) to understand some error-messages concerned with recursion;

(3) to determine the (time- and/or space-) complexity of a recursive subprogram;

(4) to satisfy your intellectual curiosity;

(5) none of the above.

So, the answer is that recursive subprograms are executed in exactly the same way as non-recursive ones. To wit: when a subprogram is called, its formal value parameters act like local variables initialized to the values of their corresponding expressions, its formal var-parameters act as local names for their corresponding variables, and its local variables are created with undefined values. Then the body of the subprogram is executed. All information concerning parameters and local variables is lost when execution of the body terminates. The crucial fact concerning recursion is that each call creates a new set of information.

For example, procedure PrintReverseOfLine stores the characters in the rest of the current input line as the values of the local variable ch for each of its calls. The number of calls is 1 more than the number of characters initially in the rest of the input line, so the space-complexity is of that order, which is the best possible. A non-recursive solution using a string or an array needs space proportional to the longest possible input line.

To desk-check a recursive subprogram, you must create new information for each call. For a var-parameter, use an arrow pointing to the row of successive values of the corresponding actual variable; for a value parameter, create a new row and enter the value of the corresponding expression; for a local variable, create a new row and enter a ? for an undefined value. Then trace the execution of the body as usual, repeating the process for recursive calls. On completion of execution of the body, erase all the (ar)rows you created for the call.

The information needed to execute calls of subprograms, whether recursive or not, is kept in an area of memory called the **run-time stack**. If you get an error-message that announces that the stack has overflowed or run out of space, it may be because too many recursive calls have been executed. Perhaps you have not ensured that each recursive call eventually leads to a non-recursive base-case; i.e. you may have created **infinite recursion**.

To compute the time-complexity of a recursive subprogram, you must work out how much time is needed to execute the statements of the body other than the recursive calls, and how many recursive calls will occur. Unless there are large value parameters, the overhead for each recursive call is constant (i.e. independent of the problem-size). To compute the space-complexity of a recursive subprogram, you must compute the space needed for each instance, and the maximum length of a chain of recursive calls, i.e. the maximum number of uncompleted calls at any one time. This is called the **depth of recursion**.

Consider function Fibonacci, for instance. Let $c_n$ be the total number of function calls to evaluate $F_n$. We see that:

$$c_n = \begin{cases} 1, & \text{if } n = 0, \\ 1, & \text{if } n = 1, \\ 1 + c_{n-1} + c_{n-2}, & \text{if } n > 1. \end{cases}$$

It follows that $c_n = 2F_{n+1} - 1$, and, more importantly, that $c_n$ is exponential in $n$. Function Fibonacci therefore takes time exponential in $n$, although the iterative solution based on a recurrence takes time linear in $n$. In this case, the natural recursive solution is *very* inefficient. The reason is that it calculates the same function-values over and over again.

| **Principle** Check that a recursive solution is not needlessly inefficient. |
|---|

A similar technique can be used to compute the total number of calls when Hanoi($n$, ... ) is executed. Including the first, $2^{n+1} - 1$ calls of Hanoi are made, producing a sequence of $2^n - 1$ moves. So the recursive solution, although exponential in $n$, is optimal (up to a constant factor), because the solution is unique. With $n = 64$, $2^{64} - 1$ moves are made, a *very* large number. So now the punch line of the story can be given (with apologies to Chuck Berry): if you are asked to join an obscure religious sect with headquarters in Hanoi, answer 'Too much monky business for me to be involved in.'

## 18.2 Case-study 11: Illustrating all text styles

### 18.2.1 SETTING OF THE PROBLEM

Macintosh Pascal enables the style of text in the Drawing window to be specified by calling the predefined procedure TextFace with the desired style as the actual value parameter. A style is a set of style items, which are values of the predefined enumerated type StyleItem. There are seven values of this type, and therefore $2^7 = 128$ different sets of style items. See the introduction to Chapter 17 for more details.

### 18.2.2 SPECIFICATIONS

A program is to be written that displays a sample of text in each possible style. The samples are to be arranged in a systematic order. The sample of text for a given style is to be an abbreviated representation of the set of style items. Specifically, it should consist of the first letters of each of the style items present in the set, arranged in increasing order of the items, and enclosed in square brackets. For example, the style:

```
[underline, shadow, condense]
```

should be represented by the text `[usc]`, in the appropriate style of course. Each piece of sample text is to be separated from the next on the same line by a fixed gap; a sample of text may not be broken at a line boundary.

### 18.2.3 WRITING THE PROGRAM

The direct approach to the problem is to write seven nested loops, one for each style item. Each loop will have two iterations, the first without the corresponding style item in the current style, the second with it. With just three style items, we would write something like the following:

```
var
  s : Style; { the style for the next sample text }
  items : string[3]; { string of first letters of members of s }
  i0, i1, i2 : 0..1;
```

```
s := [];
items := '';
for i0 := 0 to 1 do
  begin { i0 }
    if i0 = 1 then
      begin { add item 0 to current style }
        s := [bold];
        items := 'b'
      end;
    for i1 := 0 to 1 do
      begin { i1 }
        if i1 = 1 then
          begin { add item 1 to current style }
            s := s + [italic];
            items := concat(items, 'i')
          end;
        for i2 := 0 to 1 do
          begin { i2 }
            if i2 = 1 then
              begin { add item 2 to current style }
                s := s + [underline];
                items := concat(items, 'u')
              end;
            Display items in square brackets in style s;
            if i2 = 1 then { subtract item 2 from current style }
              begin
                s := s – [underline];
                delete(items, length(items), 1)
              end
          end; { i2 }
        if i1 = 1 then { subtract item 1 from current style }
          begin
            s := s – [italic];
            delete(items, length(items), 1)
          end
      end { i1 }
  end { i0 }
```

That is hard enough to understand, but its extension to handle all seven style items is much worse. We're talking *ugly* here, as people say who talk ugly. We might try to tidy up the solution by writing a separate procedure for each loop, in which case we would notice that each procedure was very similar (except the first, and only because it has been optimized). That suggests the possibility of a recursive solution.

> **Principle** Rather than trying to simplify a complex solution, start over and find the simple solution directly.

If recursion is to be exploited, we need a more general procedure than a parameterless one that simply prints a sample of all styles. Suppose we have a procedure that is given a set made up of style items no greater than a given item. It can print samples of all styles obtainable by adding items greater than the given one, by simply printing with the given style if the given item is the last, or by making two recursive calls otherwise: one without the next item in the set, the other with, each with the next item as the new limit. And such a procedure can be used to print all styles by calling it twice with the first item as the limit, once without and once with that item in the set.

That about concludes the hard thinking. The rest is simply a matter of translating the idea into Pascal, and tidying up loose ends. Our solution is a minor variation that works with a lower limit rather than an upper one, to achieve a more natural ordering of the styles: one where all styles containing only the first $n$ style items are printed before any styles containing the $(n + 1)$'th item.

### 18.2.4 THE COMPLETE PROGRAM

Here is the complete program. The recursive procedure ShowStyles should be understood according to the previously enunciated principles; i.e. you should check that its body meets its specifications assuming that the recursive calls obey them, and show that the values of the actual parameters of each recursive call bring it closer to a base-case than those of the formal parameters. You should *not* attempt to understand ShowStyles by mentally executing it.

```
program TextStyles;
{ Displays each of the 128 styles of text in the Drawing window; }
{ the sample text for each style is a shorthand form of its set. }

 const
  BarSize = 15; { thickness of right & bottom bars of window }
  MenuBarSize = 20; { depth of Menu bar at top of screen }
  ScreenWidth = 512; { full width of Mac's screen }
  ScreenDepth = 342; { full depth of Mac's screen }
  LineGap = 20; { vertical distance between successive lines }
  TextGap = 12; { horizontal distance between 2 sample texts }

 type
  str7 = string[7];

 var
  screen : Rect; { location of Drawing window }
```

```
procedure ShowStyles (s : Style;
    FirstItem : StyleItem; { s is a set of FirstItem..extend }
    items : str7); { string of first letters of members of s }
  { Displays a sample of each style of text obtainable by adding }
  { to s a set of style-items < FirstItem ; the sample text for }
  { each style is a shorthand form of its set. }
  { Global consts: ScreenWidth, LineGap, TextGap. }
  var
    PenPos : Point; { pen position }
    description : string[9]; { shorthand form of set for s }
  begin { ShowStyles }
   if FirstItem = bold then
    begin { display text for s (on new line if necessary) }
     TextFace(s);
     description := concat('[', items, ']');
     GetPen(PenPos);
     if PenPos.h + StringWidth(description) >
       ScreenWidth - TextGap div 2 then
      MoveTo(TextGap div 2, PenPos.v + LineGap);
     WriteDraw(description);
     Move(TextGap, 0)
    end
   else
    begin
    { Display all required styles not containing pred(FirstItem) }
     ShowStyles(s, pred(FirstItem), items);
    { Display all required styles containing pred(FirstItem) }
     ShowStyles(s + [pred(FirstItem)], pred(FirstItem),
                concat(copy(StringOf(pred(FirstItem)), 1, 1),
                items))
    end
  end; { ShowStyles }

begin { TextStyles }
  SetRect(screen, 0, 0, ScreenWidth + BarSize,
        ScreenDepth + BarSize);
  SetDrawingRect(screen);
  ShowDrawing;
  MoveTo(TextGap div 2, MenuBarSize + LineGap);
  ShowStyles([ ], extend, '');
  ShowStyles([extend], extend, 'e')
end. { TextStyles }
```

Figure 17.1 (not 18.1) shows the Drawing window after running this program.

Notice how ShowStyles differs from a general loop of the non-recursive solution. It does not need to subtract a style item after adding it, because the style information is carried by a value-parameter instead of a global variable. The latter alternative is possible, but is clumsier and less modular than the given version, although it does decrease the overhead for parameters.

There is a schema lurking in this program. It applies to any problem which could in principle be solved by a bunch of nested loops of the same form. The number of loops can be variable. Exercise 18.11 presents one such problem. The only reason that TextStyles uses two calls of ShowStyles, which are suspiciously like the recursive calls in the latter's body, is that StyleItem is an enumerated type, and therefore its biggest value has no successor. This situation usually does not occur with subrange types, in which case this minor inelegance can be avoided. See also Exercise 18.15 for an alternative.

Program TextStyles exploits Macintosh Pascal's predefined subprograms to the fullest. It chooses a Drawing window that is just large enough for the right and bottom bars to be off-screen, thereby maximizing the visible area; it determines whether or not the next sample text to be displayed will fit on the current line, by getting the pen position and the length of the text to be displayed; and it uses Mac-strings to manage the sample text conveniently.

> **Moral** A comprehensive library of predefined subprograms effectively increases the level of the programming language, because stepwise refinement terminates at a higher level than it otherwise would.

Program ShowTree for Case study 12 in Chapter 20 contains another example of a recursive procedure. Recursion is a very important technique for advanced data-types, many of which are inherently recursive. Also, it seems likely that recursion will play a fundamental role in programming languages of the near future, especially in the manner used in program TextStyles, where value-parameters are used in preference to global variables. The serious programmer will study it (recursion!) thoroughly. Besides, it's fun.

## 18.3 Subprograms as parameters

### 18.3.1 EXAMPLES

Suppose a program needs to sort an array several times, using different criteria for ordering the elements. The ordering relation between two elements could be computed by the sort procedure, perhaps by using an extra parameter as the expression controlling a case-statement. But the resulting procedure would be clumsy and messy to modify if the ordering criteria were changed.

Pascal permits a neater solution, because it permits functions (and procedures) to be used as parameters. Using the simple version of bubble sort as the sorting algorithm, the procedure is written as follows:

```
const
  MaxIndex = ... ;
type
  index = 1..MaxIndex;
  count = 0..MaxIndex;
  item = ... ;
  values = array[index] of item;
...
procedure sort (var A : values;
               n : count;
               function GreaterThan (x, y : item) : Boolean);
{ Sorts A[1..n] into non-decreasing order; }
{ item x > item y iff GreaterThan(x, y) is true. }
{ Global subprogram: swap. }
  var
    NrLeft : count; { only A[1..NrLeft] remains to be sorted }
    k : index; { A[k] & A[k + 1] are compared }
begin { sort }
  for NrLeft := n downto 2 do
    for k := 1 to NrLeft – 1 do
      if GreaterThan(A[k], A[k + 1]) then
        swap(A[k], A[k + 1])
end; { sort }
```

GreaterThan is a formal **function parameter** of procedure sort. It may be used in the body of sort just like a locally defined function with the same heading.

In a procedure-statement for sort, the third actual parameter must be the identifier of a function of the same kind as GreaterThan. This means that the supplied function's heading may differ only in its name and the names of its formal parameters. The rest of its heading must be identical to that of GreaterThan.

For example, suppose the following definitions and declarations are made:

```
type
  item = record
     name : string[30]; { last name, other names }
     SocSecNr : longint; { social security number }
     ...
    end;
```

```
var
  employee : values; { employee[1..NrEmployees] are... }
  NrEmployees : count; { ...the employees }

function GreaterName (item1, item2 : item) : Boolean;
{ Returns true iff the name of item1 comes after that of item2. }
begin { GreaterName }
  GreaterName := item1.name > item2.name
end; { GreaterName }

function GreaterSSN (item1, item2 : item) : Boolean;
{ Returns true iff the social security number of item1 exceeds }
{ that of item2. }
begin { GreaterSSN }
  GreaterSSN := item1.SocSecNr > item2.SocSecNr
end; { GreaterSSN }
```

The call:

```
sort(employee, NrEmployees, GreaterName)
```

will rearrange the elements of the array-section employee [1..NrEmployees] into non-decreasing order of their names (roughly speaking, into alphabetical order). And the call:

```
sort(employee, NrEmployees, GreaterSSN)
```

will rearrange the employees into increasing order of their social security numbers (assuming no two have the same number).

The ability to pass functions and procedures as parameters enables very high-level subprograms to be written. For example, here is a function which forms what mathematicians call the *iterated-composition* of a given function:

```
function compose (function f (x : real) : real;
                  n : count;
                  x : real) : real;
{ Returns the n-fold composition of f applied to x; }
{ i.e., f(f( ... f(x) ... )), where there are n f's; }
{ the 0-fold composition is defined to be x. }
  var
    result : real;
    i : 0..Maxint; { in 1..n }
begin { compose }
  result := x;
  for i := 1 to n do
    result := f(result);
  compose := result
end; { compose }
```

Pascal does not permit predefined functions and procedures to be passed as actual function and procedure parameters, respectively. So to supply the natural logarithm function ln, for example, we must first define an equivalent function:

```
function loge (x : real) : real;
{ Returns the natural logarithm of x; assumes x > 0. }
begin { loge }
  loge := ln(x)
end; { loge }
```

Then the following statement is legal:

```
Writeln('log log log (Maxint) = ', compose(loge, 3, Maxint) : 1 : 6)
```

It prints:

```
log log log (Maxint) = 0.850806
```

Another situation where a function parameter would be used is in a function to compute the integral of a given function over a given interval. Procedure parameters are used in an analogous way to function parameters. Although there are occasions where function and procedure parameters are undoubtedly useful, they should never be used for their own sake, because their effects can be hard to understand, especially when the actual parameter subprograms access nonlocal variables.

### 18.3.2 SYNTAX

The syntax rules for function and procedure parameters are as follows:

formal-parameter-section: *value-parameter-section* |
*variable-parameter-section* |
*function-parameter-section* |
*procedure-parameter-section*
function-parameter-section: *function-heading*
procedure-parameter-section: *procedure-heading*

The names of the formal parameters of a formal function or procedure parameter are required simply to avoid complicating the syntax.

Next come actual-parameters of function-designators and procedure-statements:

actual-parameter: *actual-value* | *actual-variable* |
*actual-function* *actual-procedure*
actual-function: *function-identifier*
actual-procedure: *procedure-identifier*

## 18.4 Conformant arrays

The ISO definition of Pascal distinguishes two levels of the language: level 0 and level 1. Level 1 differs in having an extra kind of parameter, called a **conformant array parameter**. Such a parameter does not declare the precise index-type(s) of the array; rather, it declares type(s) which will *contain* the corresponding actual parameter's index-type(s). Thus, for example, by using the type integer in this role, a subprogram is created that can operate on any array of elements of the appropriate type, provided only that its index-type is a subrange of integer. Formal names are declared to enable the subprogram to refer to the least and greatest values of the index-type of the actual array supplied in the call.

There are many complications and restrictions pertaining to this feature. Since it is not part of (ANSI) Standard Pascal, not provided in Macintosh Pascal (and many other implementations), and has no place in an introduction to programming, we are content to refer the interested reader to 'Further reading', Section 18.5.

## 18.5 Further reading

(1) Pritchard, P. (1988). *An Introduction to Programming using Macintosh Pascal.* Reading, Mass: Addison-Wesley.
An incomparable but immodest text. Its chapter on recursion contains an amusing example.

(2) Rohl, J. (1984). *Recursion via Pascal.* Cambridge: Cambridge University Press.
The Joy of Recursion.

(3) Welsh, J. and Elder, J. (1988). *Introduction to Pascal.* 3rd edition. London: Prentice-Hall.
Has a comprehensive discussion of conformant array parameters.

## EXERCISES

**18.1** Function Fibonacci can be slightly simplified by combining the cases n = 0,1. Do so.

**18.2** The factorial function can be defined as follows, where $n!$ denotes the value of factorial $n$:

$$n! = \begin{cases} 1, & \text{if } n = 0, \\ n \times (n-1)!, & \text{if } n > 0. \end{cases}$$

(a) Translate this definition into a recursive Pascal function.

(b) Give an iterative (i.e. non-recursive) version.

(c) Compare the time- and space-complexity of the two solutions.

**18.3** Give a recursive implementation of function reverse in Chapter 14.

**18.4** Powers of a number can be computed by a function taking two arguments: the number and the integer exponent of the desired power. The $n$th power of $x$ is usually written $x^n$, and may be defined as follows for $n \geqslant 0$:

$$x^n = \begin{cases} 1, & \text{if } n = 0, \\ x \times x^{n-1}, & \text{if } n \textit{ is odd}, \\ (x^{n \,\textbf{div}\, 2})^2, & \text{if } n > 0 \text{ and } n \textit{ is even}. \end{cases}$$

Write a recursive function to compute a non-negative integer power of a real number.

*Hint*: Use the predefined function sqr.

**18.5** Give a version of Hanoi for n $\geqslant$ 1 which makes exactly one move per procedure call.

**18.6** Give a simple, directly recursive implementation of the greatest common divisor function.

**18.7** Desk-check the procedure-call Hanoi(2, left, right, middle).

**18.8** Give a recursive implementation (but still using binary search) of function IndexOf in Chapter 12.

**18.9** Suppose a program deals with possibly nested boxes. The boxes are numbered from 1 onwards, and an array around records the arrangement of the boxes as follows:

```
const
  MaxBoxNr = ... ;
type
  BoxNr = 1..MaxBoxNr;
var
  around : array[BoxNr] of 0..MaxBoxNr;
  NrBoxes : BoxNr;
    { around[i] = 0 if no box contains box i, or j if box i is }
    { immediately contained in box j, 1 <= i <= NrBoxes. }
```

For example, suppose there are seven boxes, in the following arrangement:

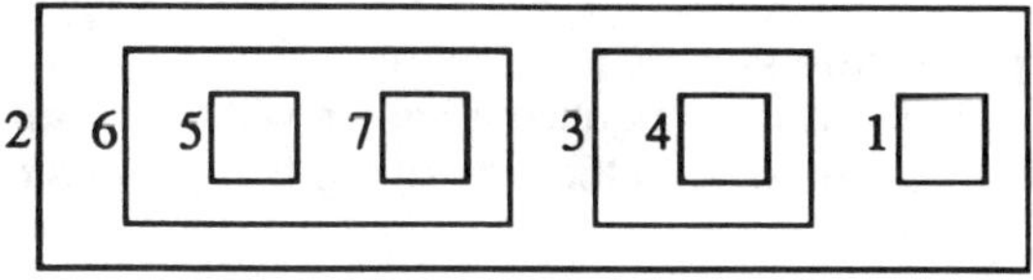


Then NrBoxes = 7, and around = (2, 0, 2, 3, 6, 2, 6).

Give a recursive implementation of the following function:

```
function surrounds (x, y : BoxNr) : Boolean;
{ Returns true iff box x contains box y, not necessarily }
{ directly; Global vars: NrBoxes, around. }
```

For example, surrounds(2, 7) gives true and surrounds(5, 3) gives false.

**18.10** A neat recursive implementation can be given for procedure ArraySwap specified in Exercise 11.19, which swaps two adjacent array-sections. The idea is first to write a procedure EqualSwap that swaps two array-sections that are of equal size but are not necessarily adjacent. ArraySwap then works as follows. If both sections are of the same size, it simply calls EqualSwap. Otherwise, it first calls EqualSwap to swap the smaller section with an equal-sized section at the opposite end of the larger section, then makes a recursive call to complete its task. Here is what happens in the example given in Exercise 11.19:

A[4..6] and A[7..11] are to be swapped:

| | 4 | 5 | 6 | 7 | 8 | 9 | 10 | 11 |
|---|---|---|---|---|---|---|---|---|
| A | 2 | 4 | 6 | 8 | 10 | 12 | 14 | 16 |

after the call of EqualSwap to swap A[4..6] and A[9..11]:

| | 4 | 5 | 6 | 7 | 8 | 9 | 10 | 11 |
|---|---|---|---|---|---|---|---|---|
| A | 12 | 14 | 16 | 8 | 10 | 2 | 4 | 6 |

after the recursive call to swap A[4..6] and A[7..8]:

| | 4 | 5 | 6 | 7 | 8 | 9 | 10 | 11 |
|---|---|---|---|---|---|---|---|---|
| A | 8 | 10 | 12 | 14 | 16 | 2 | 4 | 6 |

Write the recursive version of procedure ArraySwap.

**18.11** Implement the following procedure:

```
procedure powers (n : count);
{ Prints all non-negative numbers with n decimal digits }
{ that are equal to the sum of the n'th powers of their decimal }
{ digits. }
```

You may assume the existence of the following function:

```
function power (a, n : count) : count;
{ Returns a to the power n. }
```

*Hint*: If n were fixed at 2, the following would do:

```
 var
   d1, d0 : 0..9; { tens digit, units digit }
begin { powers }
 for d1 := 0 to 9 do
   for d0 := 0 to 9 do
     if sqr(d1) + sqr(d0) = 10 * d1 + d0 then
       Writeln(10 * d1 + d0)
end; { powers }
```

**18.12** Write a function that returns the sum of the values of a given function between two given limits. Assume the given function takes a single integer argument.

**18.13** Around the turn of the century there was some interest in producing space-filling curves. Perhaps the simplest is due to the great German mathematician David Hilbert. Hilbert's curve is the limit of an infinite sequence of curves, suitably scaled and placed to fit in a 1 × 1 square. An arbitrary member of this sequence may be described very simply using recursion (ignoring size and placement).

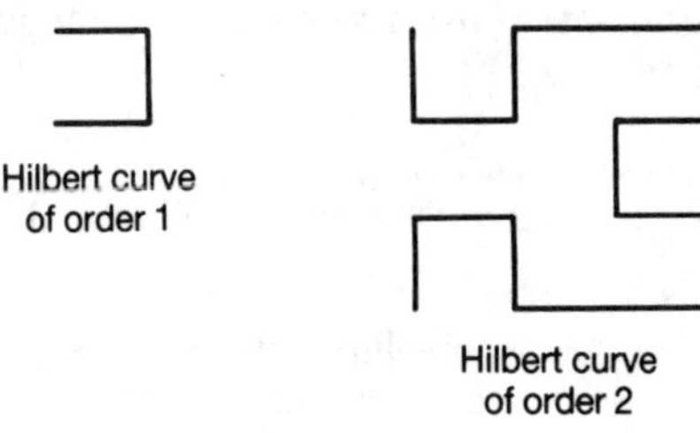


**Figure 18.4**
The Hilbert curves of orders 1 and 2.

The first curve, called the *Hilbert curve of order 1*, consists of three sides of a square, as shown in Figure 18.4. The second is made by connecting four Hilbert curves of order 1, suitably rotated, by three lines of the same length as the sides of the four Hilbert squares, which by themselves would form a Hilbert-curve of order 1. It is also shown in Figure 18.4.

Since the second-order curve lies on or within the boundary of a square, and starts and ends in the top-left and bottom-left corners, just like the first-order curve, a third-order curve may be obtained by connecting four Hilbert curves of order 2 in exactly the same way. Moreover, by positing an empty Hilbert curve of order 0, we may use the same general recursive construction for all the Hilbert curves. A rotated fourth-order curve is incorporated in Figure A.3.8 (in Appendix Section A.3).

Implement the following procedure in the given context.

```
type
  direction = (up, down, right, left); { directions relative to
                                          screen }
  UnitMoves = array[direction] of Point;
var
  vector : UnitMoves; { vector[d] is change to position to move
                          1 unit in direction d }

procedure Hilbert (d1, d2, d3, dOther : direction;
                        i : integer);
{ Draws i'th order Hilbert curve starting at current position; }
{ leaves pen at end of curve; d1 is direction of 1st connect- }
{ ing move; sim. for d2, d3; dOther is direction other than }
{ d1-3; i.e. 1st order curve is drawn with: move d1, move d2, }
{ move d3. }
```

*Hints*: Define vector (which represents a function) using the following predefined procedure of Macintosh Pascal:

```
procedure SetPt (var p : Point; x, y : integer);
{ Sets p to (x, y). }
```

Use **vector** in conjunction with procedure **Line** to do the drawing.

**18.14** Another class of curves whose limit fills a square is due to Sierpinski. One quarter of a Sierpinski curve of order 4 is also incorporated in Figure A.3.8. If you are a glutton for punishment, see if you can write a procedure to draw such a segment of a Sierpinski curve of given order and given orientation. (A sequence of four suitable calls of the procedure, with four connecting lines, produces a closed curve which fits in a square.)
*Hints*: Characterize each move by two elements of **vector**, whose net effect defines the endpoints of the line drawn; use the following predefined Macintosh Pascal procedure to help implement such a move:

```
procedure AddPt (ChangeToP : Point; var P : Point);
{ Adds the coordinates of ChangeToP to those of P. }
```

**18.15** Change the specification of procedure **ShowStyles** by replacing **< FirstItem** by **<= FirstItem**, implement the new procedure and use it to print all text styles with a single call.

# 19 NUMERIC COMPUTING

I do not mind lying, but I hate inaccuracy.
— Samuel Butler, *Truth and Convenience*

## 19.1 Representing integer values

An integer is represented in Macintosh Pascal by a fixed number of bytes. Type integer uses 2 bytes, type longint uses 4. Each of these types represents a finite range of the mathematical integers:

```
const
  Maxint = 32767; { = 2 to the power 15 – 1 }
  Maxlongint = 2147483647; { = 2 to the power 31 – 1 }
type
  integer = –Maxint..Maxint; { 2 bytes = 16 bits }
  longint = –Maxlongint..Maxlongint; { 4 bytes = 32 bits }
```

Only type integer is required by the Standard.

In Pascal, it is an error if an operation gives an integer result outside the required range. This applies to each of the intermediate operations in an expression, not just the final result. In Macintosh Pascal, all integer-valued operators (such as +) and predefined ar-

ithmetic functions (such as sqr) return results of type longint when
19.1 applied to integer values. Only when an attempt is made to assign an out-of-range longint value to a variable of type integer does an error occur. The error message is shown in Figure 19.1.

The finite range of Pascal's integers should be kept in mind. For example, here is a refinement given in Chapter 5 as an example of a repeat-loop. All variables are of type integer.

```
{ Set NrDigits = number of decimal digits in numeral of n }
 NrDigits := 0;
 RestOfn := n;
 repeat
   NrDigits := NrDigits + 1;
   RestOfn := RestOfn div 10
 until RestOfn = 0
```

Compare it with the following solution, taken from one of the better textbooks on Pascal:

**The value of a variable or subexpression is out of range for its intended use.**

**Figure 19.1**
The error-message for an out-of-range integer value.

```
NrDigits := 1;
PowerOf10 := 10;
while PowerOf10 <= n do
  begin
    NrDigits := NrDigits + 1;
    PowerOf10 := PowerOf10 * 10
  end
```

This latter solution, which is meant to work only for non-negative values of n, will fail for all values of n that have as many decimal digits as Maxint; on the Macintosh, for 9999 < n ⩽ 32 767, i.e. *most* values of n!

The type longint is used for systems-programming on the Macintosh, and for this reason is treated differently from type integer. Two important differences are:

(1) The value –Maxlongint – 1 is permissible;

(2) Results outside the range –Maxlongint–1..Maxlongint are *not* detected as errors; the effect is as if the values are arranged in a circle by defining succ(Maxlongint) = –Maxlongint – 1. For example, Maxlongint + 4 gives the same value as does –Maxlongint + 2, viz. –2 147 483 645. 19.2

**Principle** Because out-of-range errors in longint arithmetic are not detected, large integers are best represented as values of the type computational (which is described in the next section).

Unfortunately, because longint arithmetic is not secure, neither is arithmetic with integer values; see 'Macaveats', Section 19.5.  19.3

Several predefined functions work with the binary representations of longint values. They make it possible to rewrite program Nim for Case-study 10 in Chapter 17 to dispense with several of the variables and subprograms. Procedure SymmetricDifference, for instance, corresponds to the predefined function BitXor, which is defined along with the others in Section 10.6.4.1 of the Reference. The resulting version of Nim is much shorter, but also much lower-level and far less portable, than the original.

## 19.2 Representing real numbers

More concessions have to be made to represent the real numbers, because in any range there are infinitely many. The solution is to restrict both the range and the **precision** (the number of significant digits).

Consider the real number $\pi$, the ratio of a circle's circumference to its diameter. We can write it as:

$$+31\,415.926\ldots \times 10^{-4}, \text{ or}$$
$$+0.314\,159\,26\ldots \times 10^{1}, \text{ or}$$
$$+3.141\,592\,6\ldots \times 10^{0},$$

and so forth, where the three dots stand for an infinite string of decimal digits. In this representation, the string of digits is called the **significand** (or the **mantissa**), and the power of 10 is called the **exponent**. We do not have to use base 10; if we use base 2, with digits 0 and 1, $\pi$ can be written as:

$$+11.001001000011\ldots \times 2^{0}, \text{ or}$$
$$+1.1001001000011\ldots \times 2^{1}, \text{ etc.}$$

For example, the first representation means:

$$1 \times 2^{1} + 1 \times 2^{0} + 0 \times 2^{-1} + 0 \times 2^{-2} + 1 \times 2^{-3} + \ldots =$$
$$1 \times 2 + 1 \times 1 + 0 \times 0.5 + 0 \times 0.25 + 1 \times 0.125 + \ldots =$$
$$2 + 1 + 0.125 + \ldots =$$
$$3.125 + \ldots$$

The last member of each of the two groups of representations above is called the **normalized** representation. Once we choose a base $b$, we can write any real number except 0.0 as:

$$sign\ d_1 \,.\, d_2 d_3 \ldots \times b^{exponent}$$

Here *sign* is + or –, each $d_i$ is a digit, and $d_1 \neq 0$. This normalized representation is unique (if we exclude significands ending in an infinite string of $(b - 1)$-digits). By convention, the normalized representation of 0 is:

$$+0.000\ldots \times b^{0}.$$

A real number is represented in Macintosh Pascal by a fixed-length significand and an exponent in a fixed range of the integers. The

| Type | real | double | extended |
|---|---|---|---|
| size (bytes:bits) | 4:32 | 8:64 | 10:80 |
| minimum exponent | –126 | –1022 | –16383 |
| maximum exponent | 127 | 1023 | 16384 |
| bits in significand | 24 | 53 | 64 |
| significant decimal digits | 7–8 | 15–16 | 19–20 |
| range | $\pm 3.4 \times 10^{38}$ | $\pm 1.7 \times 10^{308}$ | $\pm 1.1 \times 10^{4932}$ |
| smallest (positive) | $1.5 \times 10^{-45}$ | $5.0 \times 10^{-324}$ | $1.9 \times 10^{-4951}$ |
| smallest normalized (+ve) | $1.2 \times 10^{-38}$ | $2.3 \times 10^{-308}$ | $1.7 \times 10^{-4932}$ |

**Table 19.1** Three types of real numbers in Macintosh Pascal.

base $b = 2$. The normalized form is used unless the number is too small, because this maximizes the number of significant digits. This scheme for representing real numbers is called a **floating point** system; 'point' refers to the decimal point. Three types of real-numbers are provided in Macintosh Pascal; their properties are summarized in Table 19.1. The decimal values in Table 19.1 are only approximate. The smallest positive and negative numbers have only one significant binary digit.

A special type called computational is provided in Macintosh Pascal. Its values are the integers in the range $-2^{63} - 1..2^{63} - 1$, but they are treated in some respects as real values. For example, a value of type computational can be given a fraction-length when printed. The effect is to move the implicit decimal point so many places to the left. For example, execution of:

```
var
  price : computational;

price := 19999;
Writeln('and it''s yours for a mere $', price : 1 : 2)
```

prints:

```
and it's yours for a mere $199.99
```

 19.4

The intended use of this type is to represent so-called **fixed-point** real numbers, which are regarded by the program as having an implicit decimal point in a fixed position. Such usages are error-prone, because it is up to the program to treat the numbers properly. The type is more usefully applied to representing large integers, because out-of-range errors are detected. There is a problem with output, however; see 'Macaveats', Section 19.5.

### 19.2.1 REPRESENTATION ROUNDOFF ERROR

An important property of real numbers in Pascal is already apparent: *almost all real numbers are not represented exactly*. For example, the predefined Macintosh Pascal **extended** constant pi is *not* equal to the real number $\pi$ (which has an infinite significand in *any* base); pi exceeds $\pi$ by about $5 \times 10^{-20}$. Even numbers that have simple decimal representations may have infinite binary ones; if the base for the internal representation is a power of 2, they will not be represented exactly. For example, 0.1 has the infinite binary representation 0.0001100110011 ...; execution of:

```
var
  r : real;

r := 0.1;
Write(r : 1 : 25)
```

will print:

```
0.1000000014901161194000000
```

The errors introduced by using approximate representations for real constants and input values are called **representation roundoff errors**.

Macintosh Pascal 2.0 does not print more than 19 significant decimal digits; extra ones are printed as 0. The reason is presumably that the 20th decimal digit is not accurate. But there is an unfortunate consequence: there are unequal numbers which cannot be distinguished by printing them. More importantly, the above example highlights the following principle:

> **Principle** Do not print more significant digits than are present in the data; extra digits are at best meaningless and at worse misleading.

## 19.3 Problems with real arithmetic

There are no physical constants known with anywhere near the precision of **extended** numbers (not by *earthlings*, at least). But nevertheless there is good reason for the high precision of type **extended**: as we shall see later in this section, it helps overcome the loss of precision inherent in real arithmetic in Pascal.

In Macintosh Pascal, all real-valued operations and predefined arithmetic functions produce results of type **extended**. All values of types real, double, and computational are converted to extended values before either arithmetic and relational operators or arithmetic functions are applied. There are some unintuitive consequences. For example, execution of the following program-segment prints `False`:

```
var
  x : real;

x := 1 / 3;
Write(x = 1 / 3)
```

The reason is that the real-number 1/3 has an infinite binary significand. Each of the expressions 1 / 3 produces an extended approximation to 1/3, but only the nearest value of type real is stored in x. It is converted to an equal extended value before the comparison, but the extra bits appended to the significand are 0, so it is not equal to the extended approximation to 1/3.

### 19.3.1 OVERFLOW

As with integer-arithmetic, real-arithmetic may produce a value that is out of range. This happens whenever the exponent of the result exceeds the maximum permitted for extended values, e.g. when evaluating 1E2500 * 1E2500. This is a serious error, and is most likely to result from either a multiplication, division or function-call. The error-condition is called **overflow**; the default action is to halt the program with the error-message shown in Figure 19.2.

The same error-condition occurs when a real-value is assigned to a variable of a real-type with a maximum exponent that is too small, as in:

```
var
  r : real;

r := exp(100); { approx. 2.7E43 }
```

A floating-point error-message, rather than that in Figure 19.1, occurs when an attempt is made to assign an out-of-range value to a variable of type computational.

**Floating point arithmetic exception: Overflow occurred.**

**Figure 19.2**
The error-message for an out-of-range real value.

### 19.3.2 UNDERFLOW

Real-arithmetic may produce a non-zero result with an exponent that is less than the least permitted for **extended** values, as when evaluating **1E–2500 / 1E2500**. Similarly, an attempt may be made to assign a real-value to a variable of a real-type with a minimum exponent that is too large. In some cases, a non-zero approximation can be obtained by using an unnormalized representation (at the cost of losing significant digits). If this is not possible, we say that **underflow** occurs. As with overflow, it is most likely owing to either a multiplication, division or function-call.

Underflow is usually not regarded as a serious error, because it usually suffices to approximate the offending number with zero. This happens by default in Macintosh Pascal, and the programmer is given no indication. However, it is possible to arrange for an error-condition to occur, by the call:

```
SetHalt(underflow, true)
```

in which case underflow is treated in a similar manner to overflow. See Section D of the Technical Appendix for some sketchy details.

### 19.3.3 ROUNDOFF ERROR

*Almost all arithmetic operations on real values produce errors.* If the result of an arithmetic operation has more significant digits than can be stored in the fixed-length significand, the extra digits are discarded, and execution continues without warning. Some systems round the last retained digit, some just truncate without rounding. (The default in Macintosh Pascal is to round to the nearest representable number.) In any case, the resulting error is called **roundoff error**. Roundoff error occurs also when the significand of an **extended** value is reduced to assign the value to a variable of type **real** or **double**.

Roundoff error can most easily be appreciated by doing some calculations with a more manageable floating-point system. Let us postulate a machine called a Mad Mac, whose version of Pascal provides a single real type that uses a floating-point system with base $b = 10$, a two digit significand, and an exponent in the range –9..9. We shall write a number in this system as (*significand*, *exponent*). For example, $\pi = 3.141\,59 \ldots \times 10^0$ would be approximated by (3.1, 0).

Multiplication is done by multiplying the significands and adding the exponents, then normalizing if necessary. For example, consider computing **3.1 * 41**. This is $(3.1, 0) \times (4.1, 1)$. The exact answer is $(3.1 \times 4.1, 0 + 1) = (12.71, 1)$; it is rounded to (13, 1) and normalized to (1.3, 2). This exceeds the correct value by 2.9, so the rounding error is +2.9. This is not a large error relative to the correct result, and this desirable property is true even of a series of multiplications (and/or divisions).

Note that (1.3, 2) / (3.1, 0) represents 130/3.1, which equals 41.9..., and is therefore rounded to (4.2, 1). That is in real arithmetic in Mad Mac's Pascal, the algebraic law:

$$(x \times y)/x = y \text{ if } x \neq 0$$

does not always hold. The same goes for Macintosh Pascal. For example, execution of:

```
Write(1.7 * 5 / 5 = 1.7)
```

prints `False`.

Floating-point addition is slightly more complicated than multiplication, because the exponents must be made equal before the significands can be added. For example, consider computing (3.1, 0) + (4.1, 1), representing 3.1 + 41. The exact answer is (0.31, 1) + (4.1, 1) = (0.31 + 4.1, 1) = (4.41, 1); it is rounded to (4.4, 1), representing 44. The rounding error is −0.1. Again, this is not a large error relative to the correct result. But unlike the case with multiplication, the same is not necessarily true of a series of additions (and/or subtractions).

To see this, first consider computing (1.0, 1) + (4.9, −1), representing 10 + 0.49. The result is (1.0, 1), as it should be, since (1.0, 1) is the nearest floating-point number to the exact answer 10.49. It follows that the real variable **sum** contains (1.0, 1) after executing the following Mad Mac Pascal program segment, no matter what the value of **n**.

```
sum := 10.0;
for i := 1 to n do
  sum := sum + 0.49
```

So the relative error can be very large indeed! In fact, it is easy to construct examples where the absolute error is an arbitrarily large percentage of the correct answer; see Exercise 19.8.

There are two ways to avoid snowballing roundoff errors when computing sums of real numbers. The first is to add the numbers in increasing order of magnitude. This gives the smaller numbers a chance to contribute to the final result. When it is inconvenient to do this, the partial sums should be accumulated in a variable of a higher-precision real-type (if such a type is provided). In Macintosh Pascal, we should use type **extended**; the result can be converted to a variable of type **real** if desired. Note that in Macintosh Pascal, and any other system which does all arithmetic in extended precision, using variables of type **real** instead of **extended** saves space, not time.

### 19.3.4 CATASTROPHIC CANCELLATION

**Catastrophic cancellation** is a colorful term for the large loss of precision that can occur when a number is subtracted from another that is equal or almost equal. This is the single most important problem to be wary of when calculating with real numbers.

For example, consider evaluating the expression:

```
1 / x – 1 / (x + delta)
```

where real variables x and delta are non-zero, and delta is known to be small relative to x. Suppose x contains (1.2, 1), representing 12, and delta contains (2.5, –1), representing 0.25. Now (1.2, 1) + (2.5, –1) gives (1.2, 1), so the result in Mad Mac's Pascal is zero. But suppose the expression is reformulated in the algebraically identical form:

```
delta / (x * (x + delta))
```

This evaluates to (1.7, –3), representing 0.0017, the correct approximation to the exact answer 0.001 700 680....

## 19.4 Cautionary examples of numeric programming

### 19.4.1 EXAMPLE ONE

Suppose a, b, and c are real variables representing the lengths of the sides of a triangle, that their values satisfy $a \leqslant b \leqslant c$, and that the following action is to be refined:

```
var
  RightAngled : Boolean;
```

*Set* RightAngled *to* true *if the triangle is right-angled, otherwise* false

Mathematically, the triangle is right-angled if and only if:

$$a^2 + b^2 = c^2$$

But even if the values 0.3, 0.4, and 0.5 were read directly from the input data into a, b, and c respectively, representation roundoff error causes the Pascal expression:

```
sqr(a) + sqr(b) = sqr(c)
```

to give the value false (in Macintosh Pascal). Because of representation roundoff error and roundoff error from calculations, the following principle should be adhered to:

> **Principle** Avoid using the relational operators = and <> with real-valued expressions.

In our example, and in other situations where mathematical equality is a possibility, the best we can do is test for approximate equality:

```
const
  tolerance = 5E–4; { maximum acceptable relative error }

{ Set RightAngled to true if the triangle is right-angled, }
{ otherwise false }
  RightAngled := abs(sqr(a) + sqr(b) – sqr(c)) / sqr(c)
                  <= tolerance
```

The above test is said to check that sqr(a) + sqr(b) and sqr(c) are *equal to within 4 significant decimal digits*. Error tolerances are constrained by the accuracy of the data, the precision of the real types, and the accuracy of the calculations, that may influence the values to be compared.

Incidentally, if type extended were used for a, b, and c, the expression sqr(a) + sqr(b) = sqr(c) does give true for the above test values. But this is just luck: the same does not happen for the values 0.003, 0.004, and 0.005.

### 19.4.2 EXAMPLE TWO

A *quadratic equation* is an equation of the form:

$$ax^2 + bx + c = 0$$

A root of the equation is a value of $x$ that makes the equation true. A quadratic equation normally has two (possibly equal) roots, given by the well-known formula:

$$\frac{-b \pm \sqrt{b^2 - 4ac}}{2a}$$

The exceptions are if $a = 0$ and $b = 0$, when there are no roots, and if $a = 0$ and $b \neq 0$, when there is one root, namely $-c/b$. Also, if $b^2 - 4ac$, called the *discriminant*, is negative, then both roots are complex numbers.

Our task is to implement the following Standard Pascal procedure:

```
type
  RootsInfo = (None, OneReal, TwoReal, Complex);

procedure roots (a, b, c : real;
                 var root1, root2 : real;
                 var outcome : RootsInfo);
{ Sets root1 to the first real root, and root2 the second }
{ (if it exists), of the quadratic equation asqr(x) + bx + c = 0, }
{ and sets outcome accordingly. }
```

The task is complicated by the possibility that 4 * a * c may be very small relative to sqr(b). For then the discriminant will be almost sqr(b), and its square-root almost abs(b). Catastrophic cancellation will occur if this is added to –b if b is positive, or if added to b if b is negative.

Fortunately, one of the two roots can always be calculated without catastrophic cancellation, and since the product of the roots is c/a, the other can be calculated by dividing this product by the first root. The safe implementation is given below.

```
  var
    discriminant : real;
begin { roots }
  if a = 0 then
    if b = 0 then
      outcome := None
    else { b <> 0 }
      begin
        root1 := -c / b;
        outcome := OneReal
      end
  else { a <> 0 }
    begin
      discriminant := sqr(b) - 4 * a * c;
      if discriminant < 0 then
        outcome := Complex
      else { discriminant >= 0 }
        begin
          root1 := (-b - CopySign(b, sqrt(discriminant))) / (2 * a);
          root2 := c / a / root1;
          outcome := TwoReal
        end
    end
end; { roots }
```

CopySign is a function from the Standard Apple Numeric Environment, a library known to Macintosh Pascal as SANE. To make it available, the program-heading must be followed by the uses-clause:

```
uses
  SANE;
```

19.5

CopySign returns the absolute value of its second argument, multiplied by –1 if the first argument is negative.

SANE makes it possible to perform real arithmetic to a smaller precision than the default, and therefore test numeric subprograms which are designed to be portable. The procedure call:

```
SetPrecision(RealPrecision)
```

makes all real arithmetic produce results of type real. Using it, we execute the following test:

```
var
  a, b, c, x1, x2 : real;
  result : RootsInfo;

  SetPrecision(RealPrecision);
  a := 1.000E–4;
  b := 1.000;
  c := 1.000E–4;
  roots(a, b, c, x1, x2, result);
  Writeln('roots of (', a : 1 : 4, ')sqr(x) + (', b : 1 : 4, ')x + (',
          c : 1 : 4, ') are:');
  Writeln(x1 : 12, 'and ', x2 : 12)
```

The output is shown in the upper window in Figure 19.3. The roots are correct to the four significant figures displayed. The lower window shows the output produced by testing the naive implementation; i.e. by computing root2 with:

```
root2 := (–b + CopySign(b, sqrt(discriminant))) / (2 * a)
```

It demonstrates clearly the effect of catastrophic cancellation. The problem does not arise when using the normal extended precision.

### 19.4.3 EXAMPLE THREE

Once again, suppose we are working in real precision to develop portable software, and need to compute:

**Figure 19.3**
Text windows after tests of each version of roots

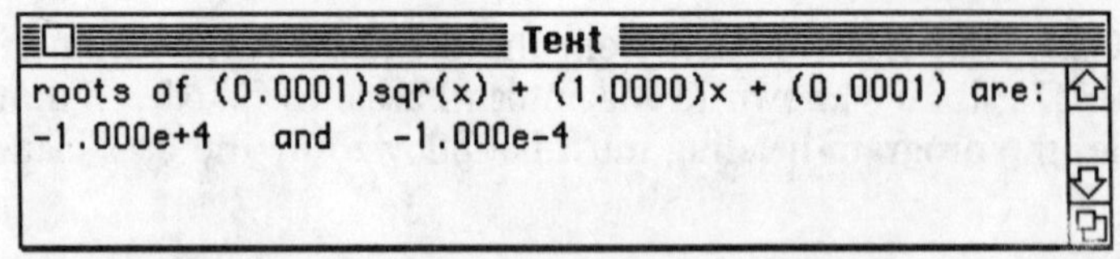


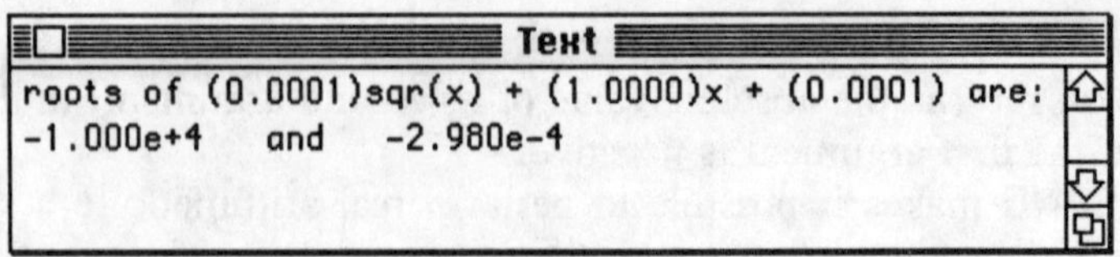


$$\sqrt{x^2+y^2}$$

where the magnitudes of x and y may both be very large or very small. The expression:

```
sqrt(sqr(x) + sqr(y))
```

could give rise to overflow or underflow, even though the result is well within range. This problem can be avoided by the following solution:

```
var
  min, max : real; { minimum and maximum of abs(x), abs(y) }

min := abs(x);
max := abs(y);
if min > max then
  begin
    min := max;
    max := abs(x)
  end;
...max * sqrt(1.0 + sqr(min / max))...
```

Exercise 19.11 invites you to verify the superior robustness of the second version.

### 19.4.4 EXAMPLE FOUR

The *mean* (average) and *variance* are perhaps the most commonly computed statistics. The mean μ and variance $\sigma^2$ of the values $x_1$, $x_2$, … , $x_n$ are defined as:

$$\mu = \frac{x_1 + x_2 + \cdots + x_n}{n}$$

$$\sigma^2 = \frac{(x_1 - \mu)^2 + (x_2 - \mu)^2 + \cdots + (x_n - \mu)^2}{n}$$

Using the definitions to compute the two statistics requires that the values $x_i$ be stored, because the computation of the variance uses both the mean and the values. However, the variance can be expressed as:

$$\sigma^2 = \frac{x_1{}^2 + x_2{}^2 + \cdots + x_n{}^2}{n} - \mu^2$$

and this permits both statistics to be computed with a single scan of the values.

Unfortunately, the single-scan approach is much more likely to suffer from catastrophic cancellation, as is demonstrated by the following program.

```
program stats (Input, Output);
{ Prompts for and reads real numbers followed by an end-of-line, }
{ and prints their mean and variance. }
  var
    n : 0..Maxint; { number of input values read }
    x, { last input value read }
    sumx, sumx2, { sums of input values read, and their squares }
    mean, variance { statistics for all input values read }
      : a real-type;
begin { stats }
  n := 0;
  sumx := 0.0;
  sumx2 := 0.0;
  Writeln('Enter real numbers (hit Return after last):');
  while not eoln do
    begin
      Read(x);
      n := n + 1;
      sumx := sumx + x;
      sumx2 := sumx2 + sqr(x)
    end;
  Readln;
  mean := sumx / n;
  variance := sumx2 / n – sqr(mean);
  Writeln('mean = ', mean : 1 : 5);
  Writeln('variance = ', variance : 14)
end. { stats }
```

The upper window in Figure 19.4 shows the result of a run of program **stats** with type **real** for *a real-type*. The value for the var-

**Figure 19.4**
The Text window after two runs of program **stats**.

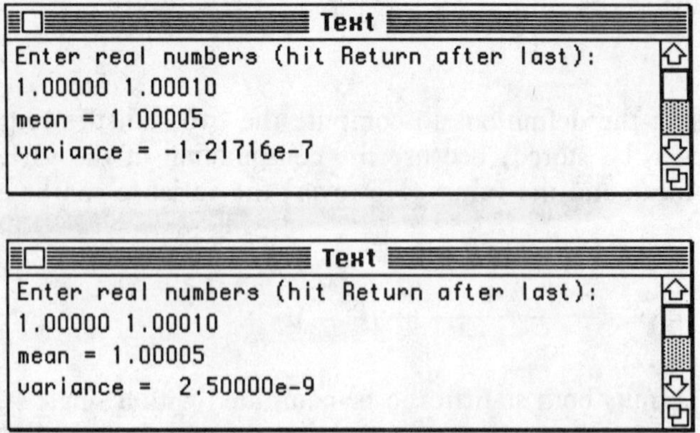


iance is meaningless — a variance cannot be negative! The lower window shows the result of a run with type **extended** chosen instead. The results are accurate. Exercise 19.12 invites the reader to check that there is no problem if the definition of the variance is used to calculate it.

### 19.4.5 SUMMARY

The examples and the preceding discussion demonstrate 2.999 999 9 facts:

- Computing with real numbers is fraught with danger.
- Inaccuracy can often be minimized by careful choice of algorithm.
- Inaccuracy can be reduced significantly by exploiting extended-precision arithmetic properly. Macintosh Pascal's use of **extended** precision overcomes many of the dangers inherent in expressions; for extensive calculations, it is safest to use **extended** variables.

The study of how to solve the special programming problems that arise when dealing with real numbers is called **numerical analysis**. It has a longer history than computer science, and many powerful and robust methods are known.

> **Principle** Numeric programming is no job for a novice. Fortunately, there are high-quality libraries which contain subprograms for most of the tasks you are likely to want to perform. Use them.

## 19.5 Macaveats

There is a very unfortunate consequence of out-of-range errors in longint arithmetic not causing error conditions, and that is that some out-of-range errors for integer assignments give spurious results. For example, execution of the following program segment prints 0!

```
var
  i : integer;

i := Maxint;
i := 4 * sqr(i + 1);
Writeln(i : 1)
```

19.6

The Reference advertises that if a variable of type computational is printed without an associated fraction-length, then it is treated as an integer value. This is not the case in Macintosh Pascal 2.0. The simplest way to print a variable of type computational without a decimal point is probably to use the required function round.

## 19.6 Further reading


(1) Atkinson, L. V. and Harley, P. J. (1983). *An Introduction to Numerical Methods with Pascal.* Reading, Mass: Addison-Wesley.
An introductory numerical analysis text, with programming examples in Pascal.


## EXERCISES

**19.1** What happens in Macintosh Pascal when the following statement is executed?

```
var
  i : integer;

i := (Maxint + Maxint) div 2
```

**19.2** Evaluate (9.9 + 9.9) / 2.0 in Mad Mac's Pascal.

**19.3** Suppose r and x are variables of types real and extended, respectively. Is there a value of x such that executing r := x gives overflow but executing r := 1 / x does not give underflow? Why? And what about vice versa?

**19.4** Suppose the values of a real-valued function f are to be summed at n + 1 equally spaced points from a to b, where n ⩾ 1. Two solutions are given below; they share the common context:

```
var
  sum : real; { sum of function values }
  delta : real; { = (b – a) / n }
  i : count; { in 0..n }

delta := (b – a) / n;
sum := 0.0;
```

Which solution is preferable? Why?

(I)

```
var
  x : real;

x := a;
for i := 0 to n do
 begin
  sum := sum + f(x);
  x := x + delta
 end
```

(II)

```
for i := 0 to n do
  sum := sum + f(a + i * delta)
```

**19.5** Trace the execution of the following Mad Mac's Pascal program. Before you do so, try to predict what happens.

```
var
  epsilon : real;

epsilon := 1.0;
while 1.0 + epsilon > 1.0 do
  epsilon := epsilon / 1.0E1
```

**19.6** What happens when the following Mad Mac's Pascal program is executed?

```
var
  x : real;

x := 1.0;
while true do
  x := x + 1.0
```

**19.7** Working with real variables, calculate the sum:

$$1 + \frac{1}{2^2} + \frac{1}{3^2} + \cdots + \frac{1}{1000^2}$$

by summing the values in both increasing and decreasing order. Repeat the process with **extended** variables. Explain the results.

**19.8** Show by example that it is possible for a sequence of additions or subtractions to produce a result with an arbitrarily large error relative to the exact answer.

*Hint*: Repeatedly subtract a relatively small number.

**19.9** The action:

> *Set* RightAngled *to* true *if the triangle is right-angled, otherwise* false

can be implemented with three applications of sqr, rather than the four given in the text. Do so.

**19.10** The quadratic equation:

$$x^2 + 150x + 2 = 0$$

has the following two roots:

$$x_1 = \frac{-150 + \sqrt{150^2 - 8}}{2} \quad \text{and}$$

$$x_2 = \frac{-150 - \sqrt{150^2 - 8}}{2}$$

Which root would procedure roots in the text calculate first?

**19.11** Consider the two versions given in the text of the calculation of

$$\sqrt{x^2 + y^2}$$

(a) Show by example that there are values of x and y such that the direct computation produces overflow in Mad Mac's Pascal, but the other does not.

(b) Ditto for underflow.

(c) Repeat (a) and (b) in Macintosh Pascal, but using real precision.

**19.12** Implement the following procedure in Standard Pascal. Since the values are stored, it would be folly to use the one-pass method.

```
const
  MaxIndex = ...;
type
  index = 1..MaxIndex;
  data = array[index] of real;

procedure MeanAndVar (var x : data;
                          n : index;
                          var mean, variance : real);
{ Computes the mean and variance of the values in x[1..n]. }
```

Test the procedure on the data used in Figure 19.4.

# 20 DYNAMIC DATA STRUCTURES

Everything in the universe goes by indirection.
— Ralph Waldo Emerson, *Society and Solitude*

## 20.1 Introduction

Pascal's structured types enable many common forms of information to be represented and manipulated. But there are many occasions where more flexibility is needed, to handle information of variable size, or which has interrelationships among its components that are more complex than those inherent in arrays, records, files, or Pascal's limited form of sets.

No programming language can hope directly to provide as many kinds of structured-types as programmers invent uses for. Pascal instead provides a low-level (and hence very general) device which can be used to construct a limitless variety of data structures, by permitting components to be dynamically created and linked during execution. The device is called the **pointer**.

A pointer is a value that points to a variable. In Pascal, each pointer is constrained to point to a variable of a fixed type; moreover, the variable must be created dynamically by the program, rather than declared in a block. This allows data structures to be created which have a lifetime unrelated to that of any instance of any particular block. Variables and data structures that are created and destroyed under direct control of the program are called **dynamic**; those used heretofore are called **static**.

## 20.2 Pointer types

Like all other values, a pointer has a fixed associated type, called a **pointer-type**. A pointer-type is created by placing the symbol ^ in front of the type of the dynamic variables to be pointed to, which is called

**Figure 20.1**
Initial values of two pointer-variables.

| p1 | p2 |
|---|---|
| ? | ? |

the **domain type** of the pointer-type. A pointer-type is not classed as either a simple-type or a structured-type:

type: *simple-type* | *structured-type* | *pointer-type* | *type-identifier*
pointer-type: ^ *type-identifier*

Like any other type, a pointer-type may be named and used to declare static variables. For example:

```
type
  CharPtr = ^char;
var
  p1, p2 : CharPtr;
```

They are initially undefined, as shown in Figure 20.1.

## 20.3 The fundamentals of pointers

### 20.3.1 THE SPECIAL VALUE **nil**

The value **nil** is a value of every pointer-type. (In this respect its role is like that of the empty set [] for set-types.) A pointer-variable that has the value **nil** is defined, but it does not point to anything. Continuing with our example, after execution of:

```
p1 := nil
```

we have the situation depicted in Figure 20.2. General pointer assignments are described in Subsection 20.3.3.

### 20.3.2 CREATING A DYNAMIC VARIABLE

A dynamic variable is created by calling the required procedure new. If *p* is a variable of a pointer-type with domain-type *T*, then the procedure call:

new(*p*)

creates an **anonymous** (i.e. unnamed) dynamic variable of type *T* with an undefined value, and assigns a pointer to this variable to *p*. Although the dynamic variable has no name, it can be accessed by the

| p1 | p2 |
| --- | --- |
| **nil** | ? |

**Figure 20.2**
After execution of
p1 := **nil**.

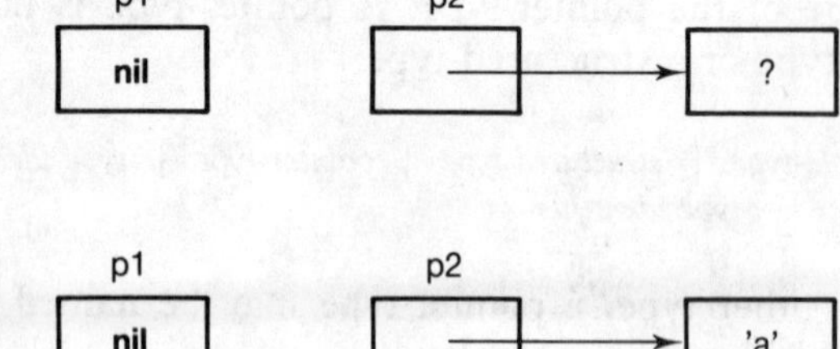


**Figure 20.3**
After execution of new(p2).

**Figure 20.4**
After execution of p2^ := 'a'.

**referenced-variable** *p*^ (as long as *p* points to it). The relevant syntax rules are:

> *variable: entire-variable* | *component-variable* | *referenced-variable*
> referenced-variable: *pointer-variable* ^
> pointer-variable: *variable*

For example, after execution of:

```
new(p2)
```

we have the situation depicted in Figure 20.3.

A referenced variable can be used like any other non-entire-variable of its type. (Not being an entire variable means, for instance, that it cannot be used as a control-variable of a for-loop.) For example, after execution of:

```
p2^ := 'a'
```

we have the situation depicted in Figure 20.4.

### 20.3.3 POINTER ASSIGNMENT

A pointer-variable may be assigned any value of the same type. To ensure that this stringent assignment-compatibility rule is met, obey the following principle:

> **Principle** Name each new pointer-type with a type-definition, and declare pointer-variables using the type-identifier.

We have seen already that the type of **nil** is determined by context, permitting it to be assigned to any pointer-variable. But the most common form of pointer assignment is to assign the value of one pointer-variable to another. After so doing, the pointer-variable on the left of the assignment symbol points to the same dynamic variable as does the pointer-variable on the right, or to nothing if the latter's value is **nil**. For example, after executing

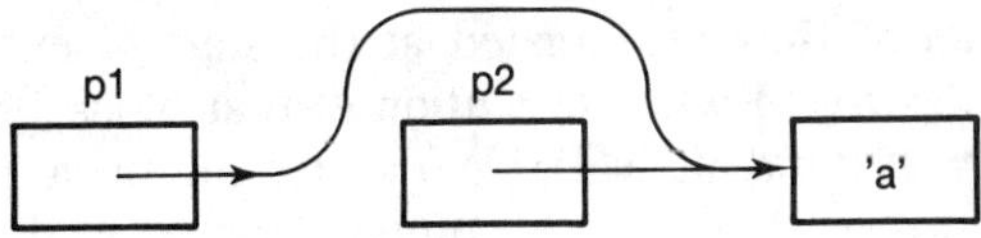


**Figure 20.5**
After execution of p1 := p2.

```
p1 := p2
```

we have the situation depicted in Figure 20.5.

There are no operators producing values of a pointer-type, but it is permitted for the result-type of a function to be a pointer-type. A pointer assignment may therefore have a function-designator on the right-hand side. The ability of Pascal functions to return pointers to arrays, records, and sets (but only dynamically created ones) can be exploited in the implementation of abstract data types in Pascal; refer to the 'Further reading' section of this chapter for details.

### 20.3.4 COMPARING POINTERS

The only operators that may be applied to pointers are the relational operators = and <>, which may be used to compare two pointers *p* and *q* of the same type. The expression:

$p = q$

gives **true** if both *p* and *q* point to the same dynamic variable, or are both **nil**; otherwise it gives **false**. The expression:

$p <> q$

gives the same result as does **not** (*p* = *q*). For example, in the situation depicted in Figure 20.5:

| | | |
|---|---|---|
| p1 = p2 | gives | true |
| p1 = **nil** | gives | false |

No other operators are applicable to pointers. Like values of enumerated types in Standard Pascal, pointers have no external representation, and therefore cannot be read from or written to text files.

### 20.3.5 DISPOSING OF DYNAMIC VARIABLES

The disposal of dynamic variables (as well as their creation) is under program control. The pointer variables p1 and p2 used in our examples above are static variables because they are introduced by a variable-declaration; they are created at the start of execution of their block, and are destroyed when execution of that block finishes.

However, a dynamic variable pointed to by a pointer-variable does not cease to exist when the pointer-variable is destroyed. There may, for instance, be another pointer-variable which points to it, and which outlives the original pointer-variable. A dynamic variable continues to exist until it is explicitly disposed of with the required procedure dispose. If *p* is a pointer-variable, then execution of:

```
dispose(p)
```

disposes of the dynamic variable pointed to by *p*, and makes *p* undefined. It is an error if *p* is undefined (before the call) or contains **nil**.

After execution of the above call, not only is *p* undefined, but so are all pointer-variables which were previously equal to *p* (i.e. pointed to the recently deceased dynamic variable). Many implementations will fail to record this fact by storing a suitable value in these other pointer-variables, in which case they are known as **dangling references**, and can give rise to catastrophic errors. Similar disasters can attend the disposal of a dynamic variable that is in use (as a variable parameter, or a record-variable of a with-statement); that, of course, is an error, but it too may go undetected.

> **Moral** Pointers are the least secure aspect of Pascal, and must be used with extreme caution.

## 20.4 Linear structures

The only reason to declare a type like CharPtr is pedagogical: it enables pointers to be discussed in the simplest possible context. The main use of pointers is to enable dynamic data structures to be created; the way to do so is to employ dynamic variables that have pointers as components.

The simplest kind of dynamic data structures represent sequences of values of some type *T*. They may be constructed by creating dynamic variables of a record-type with two fields, one containing a value of type *T*, the other containing a pointer to a dynamic variable of the same type.

For example, sequences of characters can be created by first defining the following types:

```
type
  ComponentPtr = ^component;
```

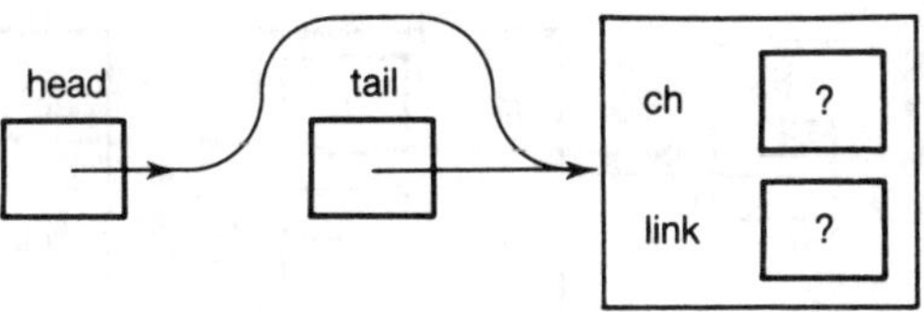


Figure 20.6

```
component = record
    ch : char;
    link : ComponentPtr
  end;
```

Notice that the type component is used in the definition of type ComponentPtr before it is defined. The use of an identifier as the domain-type of a pointer-type is permitted in a type-definition if the identifier is defined later in the same type-definition section. This is the only exception to Pascal's policy of definition before use.

Now suppose the following variables are declared:

```
var
  head, tail : ComponentPtr;
```

After execution of:

```
new(head);
tail := head
```

we have the situation depicted in Figure 20.6. We note that:

| | |
|---|---|
| tail^ | is a dynamic variable of type component |
| tail^.ch | is a component of type char of that dynamic variable |
| tail^.link | is a component of type ComponentPtr of that variable |

The variable tail^.ch can therefore be assigned a character, and the variable tail^.link made to point to a new dynamic variable of type component, by executing:

```
tail^.ch := 'c';
new(tail^.link)
```

We now have the situation depicted in Figure 20.7. By making tail point to the most recently created dynamic variable, and then repeating the above step, another component can be added to the dynamic data structure pointed to by head; and so on as long as desired. The data structure is called a (**singly-**) **linked list**.

Figure 20.7

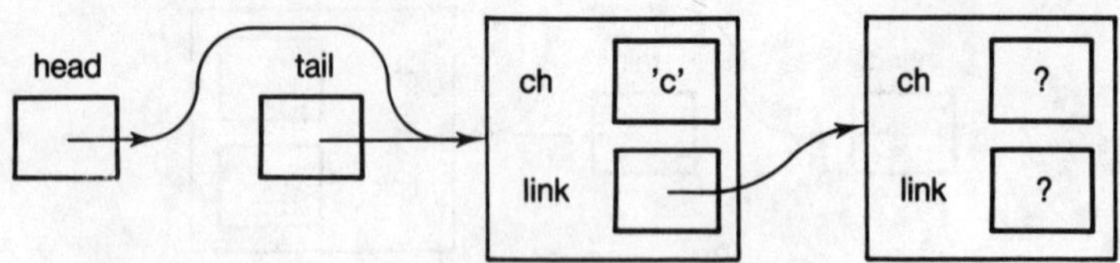


Here is a procedure that uses the techniques discussed above to create a linked list from the input data. It stores **nil** in the link field of the last component, enabling the end of the list to be recognized. As an exercise, desk-check a call of this procedure using diagrams like those above.

```
procedure ReadList (var head, tail : ComponentPtr);
{ Creates a linked list of dynamic variables containing the }
{ characters in the rest of the input line in order; sets head }
{ and tail to point to the first and last components. }
begin { ReadList }
  if eoln then
    begin
      head := nil;
      tail := nil
    end
  else
    begin
      new(head);
      tail := head;
      Read(tail^.ch);
      while not eoln do
        begin
          new(tail^.link);
          tail := tail^.link;
          Read(tail^.ch)
        end;
      tail^.link := nil
    end;
  Readln
end; { ReadList }
```

A sequence can be represented also by an array. The advantages are that extra space is not needed for pointers, and that the value in a given position can be found in constant time. The advantages of using a linked list are that the space needed is linear in the length of the sequence (whereas an array must be declared that is large enough for the maximum possible sequence), and that values may be inserted and deleted in constant time (provided the necessary pointer(s) are given).

For example, here is a procedure to insert into our sequence of characters:

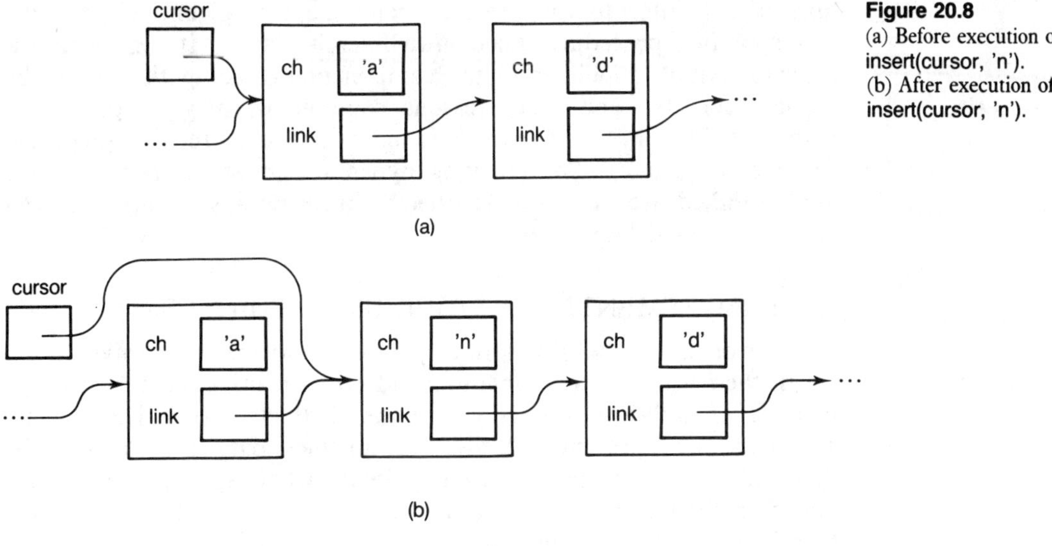


**Figure 20.8**
(a) Before execution of insert(cursor, 'n').
(b) After execution of insert(cursor, 'n').

```
procedure insert (ch : char;
                  var cursor : ComponentPtr);
{ Inserts a component containing ch after component cursor^, }
{ and updates cursor to point to the inserted component; }
{ assumes cursor is not nil. }
  var
    TempPtr : ComponentPtr;
begin { insert }
  TempPtr := cursor^.link;
  new(cursor^.link);
  cursor := cursor^.link;
  cursor^.ch := ch;
  cursor^.link := TempPtr
end; { insert }
```

The updating of cursor facilitates repeated insertion at the same point.

Figure 20.8 shows the situation before and after the following procedure-call:

```
var
  cursor : ComponentPtr; { points to a component of the linked }
                         { list with first component head^ }

insert(cursor, 'n')
```

Insertion into an empty linked list, and insertion before the first component, cannot be handled by procedure insert. For this reason linked lists are often equipped with a dummy first component, in which case procedure insert as written suffices in all situations.

A component can be deleted from a linked list in constant

time if a pointer to the previous component is given. Writing the corresponding procedure is left until Exercise 20.11. It can be unrealistic to require a pointer to the component preceding the one to be deleted; for that and other reasons components may be given two pointer fields, and the extra one used to point to the preceding component (if any). The resulting dynamic data structure is called a **doubly linked list**. It is still classified as linear because components can only be accessed sequentially.

### 20.4.1 IMPLEMENTING A STACK USING POINTERS

Because of the low-level nature of pointers, and the insecurities inherent in their use, it is advisable to avoid direct manipulation of pointers in favor of high-level operations on the abstract objects that pointers are used to represent. Ideally, an abstract data type should be designed, and implemented using pointers when appropriate. A programmer should avoid thinking in terms of pointers when engaged in high-level problem-solving.

One of the simplest and yet most common abstract data types is the **stack**. A stack is a possibly empty sequence in which both insertions and deletions take place at the front, called the **top**. It is also called a **LIFO list**, because the Last value In is the First value Out. Two examples are the stack of trays in a cafeteria, and the run-time stack used to allocate space for executing subprograms in Pascal. The abstract data type stack consists of a type, together with just four associated operations: creating an empty stack, adding a value to a stack (said to **push** *the value onto the top of the stack*), removing a value from a stack (said to **pop** *the top value*), and testing if the stack is empty.

A stack may be implemented as an array (as is usual for Pascal's run-time stack) or a singly linked list. We shall choose the latter implementation. We must provide a Pascal type stack, and a subprogram for each of the four abstract operations. Macintosh Pascal relaxes Pascal's strict order for definitions and declarations in a block, permit-
20.1 ting the following code to be retained as a unit. (A block may start with arbitrarily many sections of definitions or declarations, in any order, provided definition still precedes use.)

```
{ ADT stack: CreateEmpty, empty, push, pop. }
{ A stack is an initially empty sequence to which values may be }
{ added at the front, and from which values may be removed }
{ from the front. }
type
  StackItemPtr = ^StackItem;
  StackItem = record
```

```
      value : char;
      next : StackItemPtr
    end;
  stack = StackItemPtr;

procedure CreateEmpty (var s : stack);
{ Sets s to the empty stack. }
begin { CreateEmpty }
  s := nil
end; { CreateEmpty }

function empty (var s : stack) : Boolean;
{ Returns true if s is the empty stack, otherwise false. }
begin { empty }
  empty := s = nil
end; { empty }

procedure push (ch : char; var s : stack);
{ Adds ch to the top of s. }
  var
    top : StackItemPtr;
begin { push }
  new(top);
  top^.value := ch;
  top^.next := s;
  s := top
end; { push }

procedure pop (var s : stack;
               var ch : char);
{ Removes the top value from the stack, storing it in ch; }
{ assumes s is not empty. }
  var
    top : StackItemPtr;
begin { pop }
  top := s;
  ch := top^.value;
  s := top^.next;
  dispose(top)
end; { pop }

{ end of ADT stack }
```

The initial comment informs the programmer of the information available to the *user* of stacks (rather than the *implementor*): the type **stack**, and the subprograms **CreateEmpty**, **empty**, **push**, and **pop**. That comment, and the headings of each of the subprograms, are all the user should be concerned with.

After executing:

Figure 20.9

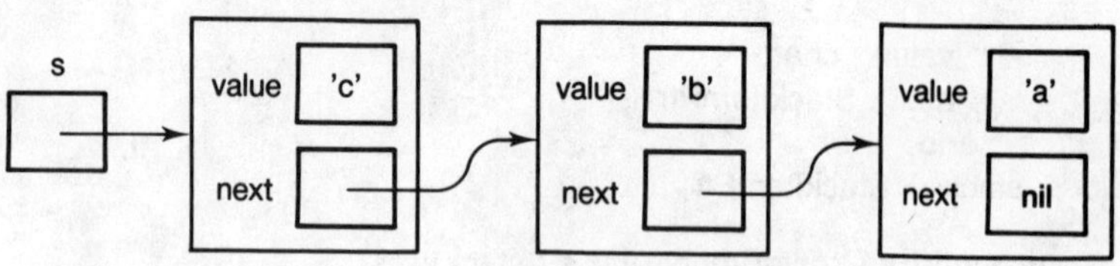


```
var
  s : stack;

CreateEmpty(s);
push('a', s);
push('b', s);
push('c', s)
```

we have the list depicted in Figure 20.9.

We have actually implemented a stack of characters. For a stack of values of some other type *T*, it is only necessary to replace each instance of char by *T*. Since the stack is a parameter of each subprogram, as many variables of type stack may be declared as desired, each representing an independent stack.

Here is an alternative implementation of procedure PrintReverseOfLine from Chapter 18, in which a stack is used rather than recursion:

```
  var
    s : stack; { of characters read before last }
    ch : char; { last character read }
begin { PrintReverseOfLine }
  CreateEmpty(s);
  while not eoln do
    begin
      Read(ch);
      push(ch, s)
    end;
  Readln;
  Write('Reverse of line: ');
  while not empty(s) do
    begin
      pop(s, ch);
      Write(ch)
    end;
  Writeln
end; { PrintReverseOfLine }
```

Figure 18.1 (not 20.1) shows the Text window after a test run. Note that there is no need to dispose of the dynamic variables at the end of the procedure, because each one created by calling push is disposed of by calling pop.

## 20.5 Non-linear structures

By equipping dynamic variables with two or more pointers, dynamic data structures may be created which have more complex interrelationships between their components than do the linear ones met previously. We shall examine one such **non-linear structure**, the **binary search tree**.

### 20.5.1 BINARY SEARCH TREES

A binary search tree is a restricted kind of binary tree. A **binary tree** is an arrangement of values of some type, which either contains no values, when it is called the **empty binary tree**, or consists of a distinguished value called the **root**, and two other binary trees, called the **left subtree** and the **right subtree**. This is a recursive definition that permits infinite binary trees; we are interested only in those that contain finitely many values.

Trees are traditionally drawn upside down in computer science. Figure 20.10 shows four binary trees of integers; tree (a) is the empty tree; each of the others contains the alphabetically preceding tree as its left subtree. The root of a tree is said to be at **level** 0, the roots of its left and right subtrees at level 1, and so on. The maximum level of a value in a tree is called its **depth**. Trees (b)–(d) in Figure 20.10 have depths 0, 1, and 2, respectively.

The empty binary tree is a binary search tree. A non-empty binary tree $t$ is a binary search tree if and only if it has the following properties:

(1) each value in the left subtree of $t <$ the root of $t$;

(2) each value in the right subtree of $t \geqslant$ the root of $t$;

(3) both subtrees of $t$ are binary search trees.

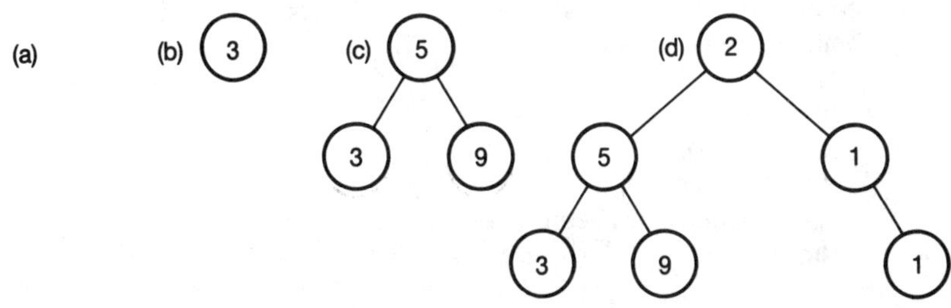


**Figure 20.10** Four binary trees of integers.

**Figure 20.11**
A binary search tree of integers.

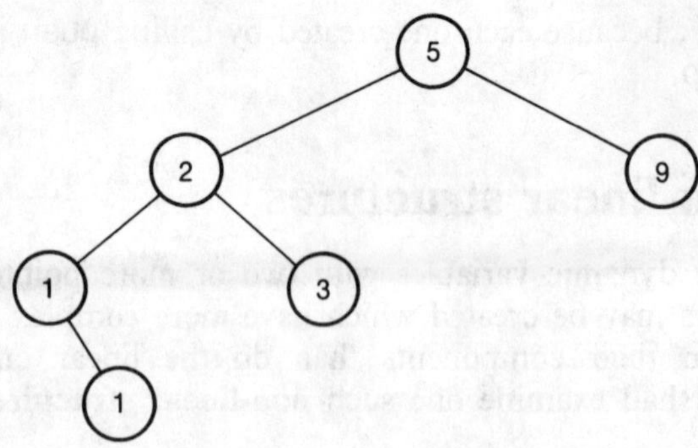


The type of values in the binary tree must have an ordering defined on its values.

In Figure 20.10, (a), (b), and (c) are binary search trees, but (d) is not. Figure 20.11 shows a larger example of the species which contains the same values as the tree in Figure 20.10(d).

Binary search trees have many uses in programming. Their main advantage over linked lists is that the time needed to insert or search for a particular value is order the depth of the tree. A binary search tree of depth $n$ can have as many as $2^{n+1} - 1$ values. (Trees (b) and (c) in Figure 20.10 are examples with $n = 0, 1$, respectively.) So the time-complexity to insert or search for a value in such a tree is logarithmic, as compared to the linear time needed for linked lists. It has been shown that the average-case complexity for random binary search trees is also logarithmic, but the worst case can be linear, because a tree can have the form of a list.

20.2

Below is a Pascal implementation of binary search trees as an abstract data type. Note that procedure **destroy** is provided to dispose of a tree when it is no longer needed. Note also that procedures **insert** and **destroy** are recursive, as is natural when processing a data structure that is recursively defined.

```
{ ADT BinarySearchTree: CreateEmpty, empty, insert, left, right, }
{                        root, destroy }
{ A BinarySearchTree t is a binary tree such that t is empty or }
{ each value in the left subtree of t < the root of t, and }
{ each value in the right subtree of t >= the root of t, and }
{ both subtrees of t are BinarySearchTrees. }
type
  BinarySearchTree = ^node;
  node = record
    value : integer;
    left, right: BinarySearchTree
  end;
```

```
procedure CreateEmpty (var t : BinarySearchTree);
{ Sets t to the empty binary search tree. }
begin { CreateEmpty }
 t := nil
end; { CreateEmpty }

function empty (t : BinarySearchTree) : Boolean;
{ Returns true if t is empty, otherwise false. }
begin { empty }
 empty := t = nil
end; { empty }

procedure insert (val : integer;
                  var t : BinarySearchTree);
{ Inserts val into t; assumes t is not a subtree of a BST. }
begin { insert }
  if t = nil then
    begin
      new(t);
      with t^ do
        begin
          value := val;
          left := nil;
          right := nil
        end
    end
  else if val < t^.value then
    insert(val, t^.left)
  else
    insert(val, t^.right)
end; { insert }

function left (t : BinarySearchTree) : BinarySearchTree;
{ Returns the left subtree of t; assumes t is not empty. }
begin { left }
 left := t^.left
end; { left }

function right (t : BinarySearchTree) : BinarySearchTree;
{ Returns the right subtree of t; assumes t is not empty. }
begin { right }
 right := t^.right
end; { right }

function root (t : BinarySearchTree) : integer;
{ Returns the root of t; assumes t is not empty. }
begin { root }
 root := t^.value
end; { root }
```

```
procedure destroy (var t : BinarySearchTree);
{ Disposes of t, leaving t undefined. }
begin { destroy }
  if t <> nil then
    begin
      destroy(t^.left);
      destroy(t^.right);
      dispose(t)
    end
end; { destroy }

{ end of ADT BinarySearchTree }
```

Program ShowTree in our final case-study shows how this abstract data type may be exploited. Exercise 20.20 gives a more practical example.

## 20.6 Case-study 12: Drawing a binary search tree

### 20.6.1 SETTING OF THE PROBLEM

We shall write a program that constructs and draws a binary search tree. Writing the program is an exercise in using the abstract data type BinarySearchTree, and is also our most challenging exercise in using recursion. The program can function as a experimental means of studying binary search trees.

### 20.6.2 SPECIFICATIONS

The program should prompt the user to type a sequence of integers and to hit the Return-key immediately after the last integer. It should construct a binary search tree by starting with an empty tree, and inserting each integer as it is read. The tree should be displayed in the Drawing window after the last integer has been read.

With one exception, the display should be a picture in the style of those in the text, i.e. the tree should be upside-down, values at the same level should be drawn at the same vertical level, and values in a left (right) subtree should appear to the left (right) of the root of that subtree. The exception is that values are to be centered in boxes rather than circles, with connecting lines drawn between the closest corners. (For a sneak preview of an acceptable style, see Figure 20.12.)

### 20.6.3 WRITING THE PROGRAM

The first refinement is very simple:

```
abstract data type BinarySearchTree as defined in the text

var
  t : BinarySearchTree; { built from input values read so far }

begin { ShowTree }
  CreateEmpty(t);
  Prompt for input, read each input value, and insert it into t;
  Draw t
end. { ShowTree }
```

The next refinement uses a familiar schema for processing input values followed by an end-of-line marker:

```
  type
    InputValue = a subrange of integer;
  var
    value : InputValue;  { last input value read }

{ Prompt for input, read each input value, and insert it into t }
  Prompt for input values followed by a Return;
  while not eoln do
    begin
      Read(value);
      insert(value, t)
    end
```

We leave the option of restricting the input values so that their representations in the drawing are not too large.

We are left with the action *Draw* t, and prepare to refine it by completely determining its specifications. We have some freedom in the horizontal placement of boxes. We could place them as in Figures 20.10 and 20.11, where space is left for each possible value at the last level. But we decide instead to draw boxes as close as possible (consistent with the specifications), to enable wider trees to be drawn with-

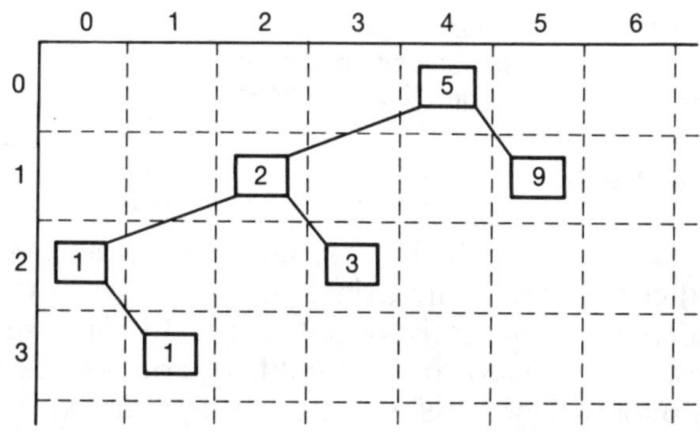


**Figure 20.12**
A picture of a binary search tree.

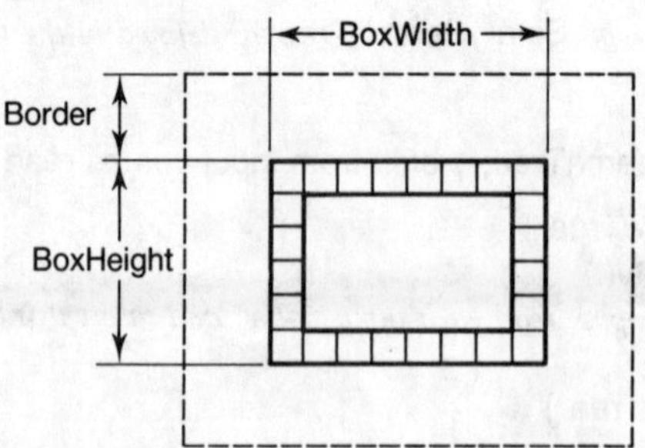


**Figure 20.13**
A blow-up of a box.

out clipping. The Drawing window is notionally regarded as a grid. As shown in Figure 20.12, which corresponds to the tree given earlier in Figure 20.11, one value appears in each successive column from the left, and values at successive levels appear in successive rows from the top. It is convenient for graphics calculations to number the rows and columns of the grid from zero onwards.

The details of the placement of boxes are fleshed out by Figure 20.13 and the accompanying definition of three constants:

```
const
  Border = ...; { width of border around each box }
  BoxWidth = ...;
  BoxHeight = ...;
```

An attractive property of the drawing scheme illustrated in Figure 20.12 is that a subtree has the same shape as a complete tree, with its placement depending only on the row of its root and the column of its leftmost value. This suggests that the complete tree may be drawn by calling a procedure which uses a recursive call to draw each subtree. So tentatively we refine the action *Draw* t with:

```
type
  count = 0..Maxint;

procedure DrawTree (t : BinarySearchTree;
        RootRow, { row for root of t }
        LeftCol : count); { column for leftmost value of t }
{ Draws t with given RootRow and LeftCol. }

DrawTree(t, 0, 0)
```

Let us now consider the implementation of DrawTree. We realize that left(t) can be drawn first, since the row of its root and its leftmost column are both known (RootRow + 1 and LeftCol respectively). The rightmost column used to draw left(t) determines the column for root(t). This information therefore needs to be returned by an output

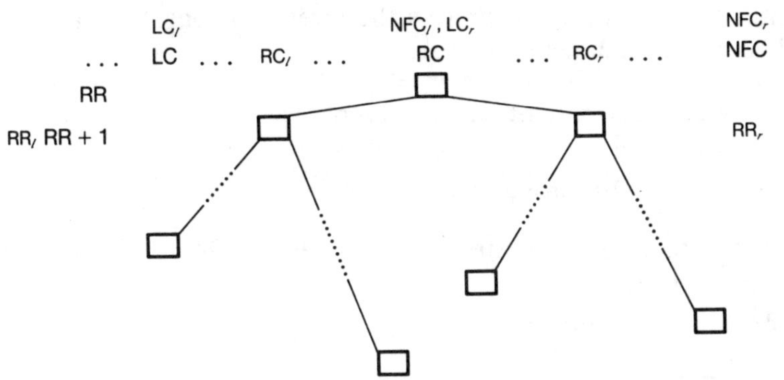


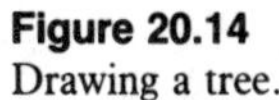
**Figure 20.14**
Drawing a tree.

parameter. Since left(t) may be empty, it is conceptually clearer for the first unused column to be returned. Let us call this output parameter NextFreeCol. So after drawing left(t), the position of the box for root(t) is known, as are the leftmost column and the row of the root for the drawing of right(t). But we have overlooked the links — for these to be drawn, the columns used for the roots of the two subtrees need to be returned. So we introduce another output parameter, RootCol.

DrawTree is now sufficiently general for it to be used recursively. The full heading is now:

```
procedure DrawTree (t : BinarySearchTree;
        RootRow, { row for root of t }
        LeftCol : count; { column for leftmost value of t }
        var NextFreeCol, { least unused column >= LeftCol }
        RootCol : count); { column of root of t (if t is not empty) }
    { Draws t with given RootRow and LeftCol, and returns }
    { NextFreeCol and RootCol (if t is not empty). }
```

The relevant parameters are shown in Figure 20.14 (abbreviated by omitting their lower-case letters). Also shown are the parameters for the recursive calls; they are in smaller type, and equipped with a subscript: *l* for left(t) and *r* for right(t). The broken links in the drawing represent the paths to the leftmost and rightmost values in the two subtrees; they may pass through intermediate values.

Implementing DrawTree is now straightforward; the obligation to define the two output parameters causes no difficulties. We stop the presentation of the development of the program at this point, because the remaining refinements concern the graphics and employ the usual techniques.

### 20.6.4 THE COMPLETE PROGRAM

The comment in the heading of DrawTree is extended to define the format of the drawing more precisely. The term **in-order** refers to a particular order in which to process the three components of a binary tree. Those most commonly used are:

**pre-order**: root, then left-subtree, then right-subtree;

**in-order**: left-subtree, root, right-subtree;

**post-order**: left-subtree, right-subtree, root.

Procedure destroy in the abstract data type BinarySearchTree processes values in post-order.

Here is the complete program:

```
program ShowTree (Input, Output);
{ Prompts user to input a number of non-negative integers, then }
{ constructs and draws a binary search tree containing them. }

  procedure DrawStringC (s : string);
  { Draws s with the center of its base line at the current pen }
  { position; leaves the pen position at the end of the string. }
  as given in Chapter 14

abstract data type BinarySearchTree as defined in the text

  const
    Limit = 999; { maximum input value }
    PointSize = 12; { size of text for drawing of tree }

  type
    InputValue = 0..Limit;
    count = 0..Maxint;

  var
    value : InputValue; { last input value read }
    t : BinarySearchTree; { built from input values read so far }
    dummy1, dummy2 : count;
      { dummy actual output parameters for DrawTree( ... ) }

  procedure DrawTree (t : BinarySearchTree;
          RootRow, { row for root of t }
          LeftCol : count; { column for leftmost value of t }
          var NextFreeCol, { least unused column >= LeftCol }
          RootCol : count); { column of root of t (if t is not empty) }
  { Draws t with given RootRow and LeftCol, and returns Next- }
  { FreeCol and RootCol (if t is not empty). The Drawing window }
  { is considered as a grid, with rows and columns numbered }
  { from 0 onwards. The values are disposed one per column in }
  { in-order. The row of a value is RootRow + its level. Each value }
  { is drawn in a box; if a value is a root (of a subtree), its box }
```

20.3

```
{ is linked to those for the roots of its subtrees. }
{ Global ADT: BinarySearchTree. }
 const
  Border = 5; { width of border around each box }
  BoxWidth = 25;
  BoxHeight = 15;

 var
  SubrootCol : count; { column of root of a subtree of t }

 procedure SetTopLeft (row, col : count;
                               var corner : Point);
 { Sets top-left corner of box for value in given row and col. }
 { Global consts: BoxHeight, BoxWidth, Border. }
 begin { SetTopLeft }
  SetPt(corner, Border + col * (BoxWidth + 2 * Border),
         Border + row * (BoxHeight + 2 * Border))
 end; { SetTopLeft }

 procedure DrawNode (row, col : count;
                              int : integer);
 { Draws a box containing int at (row, col) on grid. }
 { Global consts: BoxHeight, BoxWidth, PointSize. }
 { Global subprograms: SetTopLeft, DrawStringC. }
  var
   corner : Point; { top-left corner of box at (row, col) }
 begin { DrawNode }
  SetTopLeft(row, col, corner);
  FrameRect(corner.v, corner.h, corner.v + BoxHeight,
              corner.h + BoxWidth);
  MoveTo(corner.h + BoxWidth div 2, corner.v +
           (BoxHeight + PointSize) div 2);
  DrawStringC(StringOf(int : 1))
 end; { DrawNode }

 procedure DrawLink (row, FromCol, ToCol : count);
 { Draws a line between the closest corners of the boxes }
 { at (row, FromCol) and (row + 1, ToCol). }
 { Global consts: BoxHeight, BoxWidth. }
 { Global subprogram: SetTopLeft. }
  var
   FromTL, ToTL : Point; { top-left corners of the boxes }
 begin { DrawLink }
  SetTopLeft(row, FromCol, FromTL);
  SetTopLeft(row + 1, ToCol, ToTL);
  if ToCol > FromCol then
   begin
    MoveTo(FromTL.h + BoxWidth – 1, FromTL.v
```

```
                    + BoxHeight - 1);
        LineTo(ToTL.h, ToTL.v)
      end
    else
      begin
        MoveTo(FromTL.h, FromTL.v + BoxHeight - 1);
        LineTo(ToTL.h + BoxWidth - 1, ToTL.v)
      end
  end; { DrawLink }

begin { DrawTree }
  if empty(t) then
    NextFreeCol := LeftCol
  else
    begin
      DrawTree(left(t), RootRow + 1, LeftCol, RootCol, SubrootCol);
      DrawNode(RootRow, RootCol, root(t));
      if not empty(left(t)) then
        DrawLink(RootRow, RootCol, SubrootCol);
      DrawTree(right(t), RootRow + 1, RootCol + 1, NextFreeCol,
               SubrootCol);
      if not empty(right(t)) then
        DrawLink(RootRow, RootCol, SubrootCol)
    end
end; { DrawTree }

begin { ShowTree }
  TextSize(PointSize);

    CreateEmpty(t);
  { Read each input value and insert it into t }
    Writeln('Input integers in range 0..', Limit : 1, ', then hit Return.');
    while not eoln do
      begin
        Read(value);
        insert(value, t)
      end;

    DrawTree(t, 0, 0, dummy1, dummy2)
  end. { ShowTree }
```

Note that procedure TextSize is called in ShowTree rather than DrawTree, to avoid unnecessary repeated calls when DrawTree is called recursively.

Figure 20.15 shows the screen after a test run.

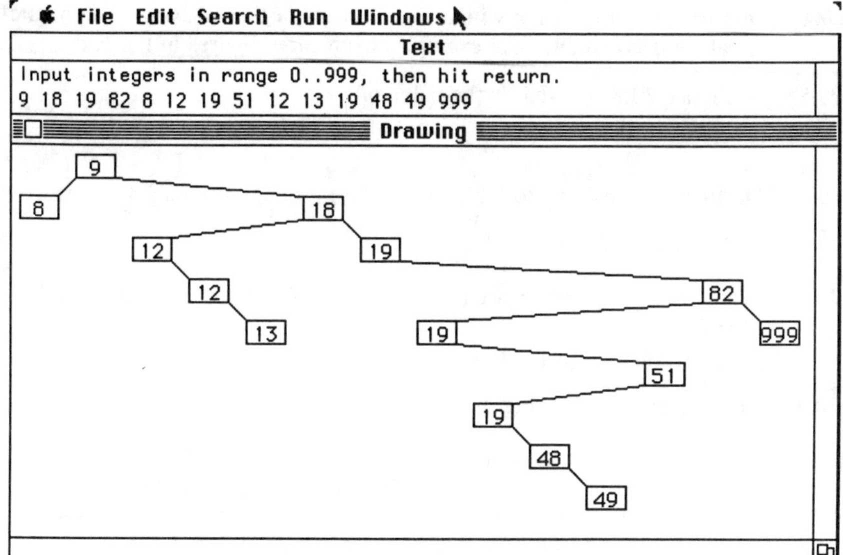


**Figure 20.15**
The screen after a run of program ShowTree.

# 20.7 Further reading

(1) Liskov, B. and Guttag, J. (1986). *Abstraction and Specification in Program Development*. Cambridge, Mass: MIT Press.
A second-level text illustrating a systematic high-level approach to program organization. Examples are in the programming-language CLU, a more modern and higher-level language than Pascal, but Chapter 7 shows how to adapt the techniques to Pascal. Not easy reading.

# EXERCISES

**20.1** Do Exercise 20.2.

**20.2** What does Exercise 20.1 contain?

**20.3** Given the following situation:

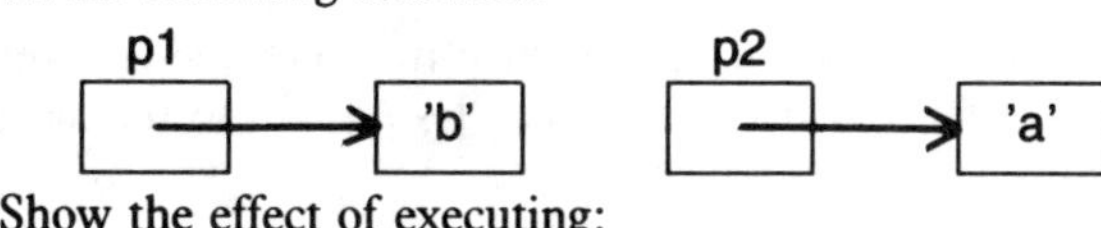


(a) Show the effect of executing:

p1^ := p2^

(b) What is the value of p1 = p2 afterwards?

(c) What is the value of p1^ = p2^ afterwards?

**20.4** One of the complications in using pointers is that aliasing of dynamic variables is common. Give examples from three figures in the text.

**20.5** In Figure 20.8(b), what is the value of:
(a) cursor^.ch? (b) cursor^.link^.ch?

**20.6** Desk-check a call of **ReadList** when the input stream is in the state:

. . . ↑dog□...

**20.7** What does the first procedure **insert** do if **cursor** is made a value-parameter?
*Hint*: Parameters of pointer-types follow the usual rules.

**20.8** Implement the following procedure:

```
function present (ch : char;
                  head : ComponentPtr) : Boolean;
{ Returns true if ch is present in a component of the chain }
{ pointed to by head; otherwise returns false. }
```

**20.9** Rewrite the first procedure **CreateEmpty** so that it creates a linked list with a dummy first component.

**20.10** Rewrite function **present** from Exercise 20.8 to apply to a linked list with a dummy first component.

**20.11** Write a procedure that is given a pointer to a component in a linked list with a dummy first component, and deletes the following component (which it may assume to exist).

**20.12** Rewrite the first procedure **CreateEmpty** so that it creates a doubly linked list from the input data. Both the forward pointer in the last component and the backward pointer in the first component should be set to **nil**.

**20.13** Add an operation to the abstract data type **stack** that destroys a given stack (i.e. disposes of its dynamic variables).

**20.14** Desk-check a call of **PrintReverseOfLine** when the input stream is in the state:

. . . ↑abc□...

Figure 20.9 should apply on termination of the first loop.

**20.15** A **queue** is a possibly empty sequence in which values are inserted at the end and removed from the front. Its social use has been perfected by the British.

(a) A queue is also called a **FIFO list**. Why?

(b) Implement a queue as an abstract data type. Provide operations **CreateEmpty**, **empty**, **enqueue** (to add a value), **dequeue** (to remove a value), and **destroy**.

*Hint*: Represent a queue by a record containing fields head and tail that point to the first and last components respectively in a singly linked list.

(c) *Using the ADT operations only*, write a procedure that queues the values in the input data in their order of appearance.

**20.16** Give an example of a binary tree of depth 3 with only 4 values.

**20.17** Procedure insert for the abstract data type BinarySearchTree has a specification that is violated by the recursive calls in its body. Explain this apparent contradiction.

**20.18** Give a non-recursive implementation of procedure insert for the abstract data type BinarySearchTree.

**20.19** Add an operation to the abstract data type BinarySearchTree that returns true if a given value appears in a given binary search tree, and false otherwise.

**20.20** Write a program to produce a *concordance*. It should read a text file, number the lines, and produce an alphabetical listing of each word (other than common words like 'a' and 'and') together with a list of the line-numbers of each occurrence, in non-decreasing order.

This is a substantial programming project. You should use the following data structures:

- a binary search tree for the set of common words which are to be ignored;
- a binary search tree containing all the words appearing in the text (so far) together with a queue of the line-numbers of their occurrences.

**20.21** Write a function that returns the depth of a binary search tree.

**20.22** Using your answer to the previous exercise, modify program ShowTree so that it draws a binary search tree in the style of the trees in Figures 20.10 and 20.11; i.e. it should reserve a column for each value of the largest possible tree with the same depth as the given one (a so-called **complete** tree, like trees (b) and (c) in Figure 20.10).

# APPENDIX

## A.1 The goto-statement

I became convinced that the **goto** statement should be abolished from all "higher-level" languages.
— E. W. Dijkstra, letter to *Communications of the ACM*, March 1968

Once upon a time, programming languages did not have adequate means for expressing conditional and repetitive execution. They relied instead on a very low-level statement called a **goto-statement**, which, in conjunction with some form of conditional statement, could be used to control the execution of a program. Pascal has a restricted form of goto-statement, an appendix left over from its evolution from these earlier languages. In this appendix we describe it for the sake of completeness of our description of Standard Pascal.

Pascal permits an arbitrary statement to be labeled with an unsigned number between 0 and 9999, called its **label**. Labels must be declared like identifiers; the label-definition-part comes at the very start of a block:

block: *label-declaration-part*
*constant-definition-part*
*type-definition-part*
*variable-declaration-part*
*procedure-and-function-declaration-part*
*statement-part*
label-declaration-part: **label** *label-list* ;
label-list: *label* ... , *label*
label: *unsigned-integer*
statement: *label*: *unlabeled-statement*
unlabeled-statement: *simple-statement* | *structured-statement*

Although a label has the same *syntax* as an unsigned-integer, it is not, and may not be used as, an integer.

Labels obey the same scope rules as identifiers. Additionally, each label may be used to label a statement only once in its scope, and that statement must be in the statement-part of the same block as the label-declaration-part (not an enclosed block). For example:

```
label
  13;
...
begin { of block }
  ...
  13: Writeln('ERROR: ... ');
  ...
end { of block }
```

A goto-statement is a new kind of simple-statement:

simple-statement: *empty-statement* | *assignment-statement* |
*procedure-statement* | *goto-statement*
goto-statement: **goto** *label*

The goto-statement must be in the scope of its label, though it may be in a block enclosed in that scope. Here is an example:

```
if UpTheCreek then
  goto 13
```

Informally, the effect of executing a goto-statement is to continue execution at the statement with the given label (as if execution had reached there by normal means). So in the given example, the statement:

```
13: Writeln('ERROR: ... ')
```

would be executed, and then the statement following it, and so on. Note that if execution reaches a labeled statement by normal means, it is still executed, so the above example is not very realistic.

The goto-statement does not sit well with structured statements, and restrictions are accordingly imposed:

- a goto-statement may not transfer control into a structured-statement, or into a component statement of a conditional-statement or while-statement, or into the component statement-sequence of a repeat-statement, from outside. For example:

```
...
... goto 2; { ILLEGAL }
...
```

```
if a > b then
  1: max := a { a useless label }
else
  begin
    ...
    2: ... ;
    ...
    ... goto 3; { permitted }
    ...
    ... goto 1; { ILLEGAL }
    ...
    ... goto 2; { permitted }
    ...
  end;
3: ...
```

- A goto-statement may have a non-local label only if the statement with that label is at the outermost level of statement-nesting in its block.

The effect of executing a goto-statement can be quite complicated, especially if its label is non-local, when it may cause premature termination of several calls of subprograms. Goto-statements also tend to undermine the programmer's firm ground; e.g. the number of executions of a for-statement may not be the usual function of its initial- and final-expression. For these and other reasons, goto-statements are best avoided. Not one is used in this book outside this appendix.

An arguably justifiable use of a goto-statement is to halt a program prematurely on discovering an error from which it is impossible to recover — perhaps when processing complex input data. For such occasions a single label and special procedure suffice:

```
label
  0; { end of program for premature halts }
...
procedure ErrorHalt (subprogram, ErrorMessage : string);
{ Prints an error message containing the parameters, then halts
  program. }
begin { ErrorHalt }
  Writeln('ERROR: program halted in subprogram ',
          subprogram, ':');
  Writeln(' ' : 7, ErrorMessage);
  goto 0
end; { ErrorHalt }
```

```
...
begin { program-identifier }
  ... ;
  0:
end. { program-identifier }
```

The label is attached to an empty-statement at the end of the program-block's statement-sequence.

Here is an example that uses this setup:

```
begin { ProcessInput }
  ... ;
  if (0 <= SSN) and (SSN <= 999999999) then
    accept(SSN)
  else
    ErrorHalt('ProcessInput', StringOf(SSN : 1,
              ' is an illegal social security number.'));
  ...
end; { ProcessInput }
```

If SSN has the value –31766, then the program will print:

```
ERROR: program halted in subprogram Process-Input:
                 -31766 is an illegal social security number.
```

and then halt.

## A.2 Syntax diagrams

Wirth originally presented the syntax of Pascal with **syntax diagrams**, and it has since become common to do so. Since the reader may come across this syntax notation in lectures or other books, we provide here a brief explanation.

A syntax diagram consists of a group of items with pairs of items connected by arrows; there are unique arrows called the *entrance* and the *exit*. Each item is a syntactic term (defined by its syntax diagram) or a symbol. A sequence of symbols is *generated by the diagram* if and only if it can be obtained by following arrows from the entrance to the exit, accepting the symbols encountered on the way in order. If a syntactic term is on the path, a sequence of symbols generated by its syntax diagram must be accepted in its place.

For example, Figures A.2.1 to A.2.4 are syntax diagrams defining a *movie-marathon* as done in our notation in Exercise 5.1.

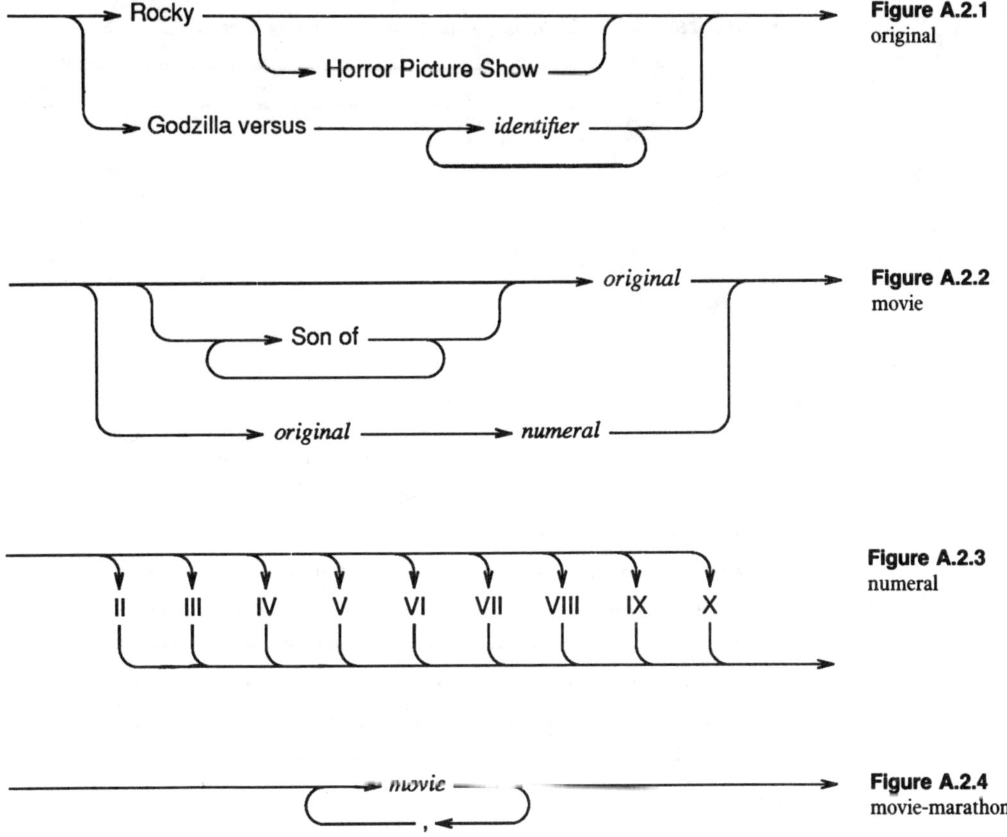


**Figure A.2.1**
original

**Figure A.2.2**
movie

**Figure A.2.3**
numeral

**Figure A.2.4**
movie-marathon

The term *identifier* is defined in Figure A.3.19. Note that the syntactic term *Son-of-sequence* is not used, and that no indication is given of the preferred layout.

## A.3 Syntax diagrams for Standard Pascal

Our path emerges for a **while**.
— Ernest Dowson, *Vitae Summa Brevis*

Figures A.3.1–A.3.22 constitute the complete syntax of Standard Pascal. The terms *letter* and *digit* denote the letters of the English alphabet and the decimal digits, respectively.

Figure A.3.1
program

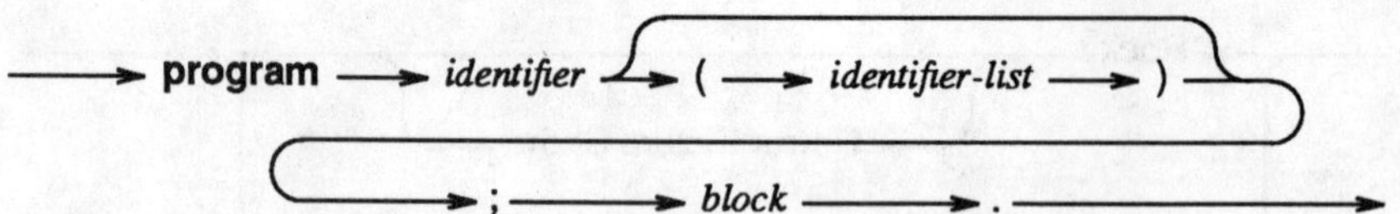


Figure A.3.2
block

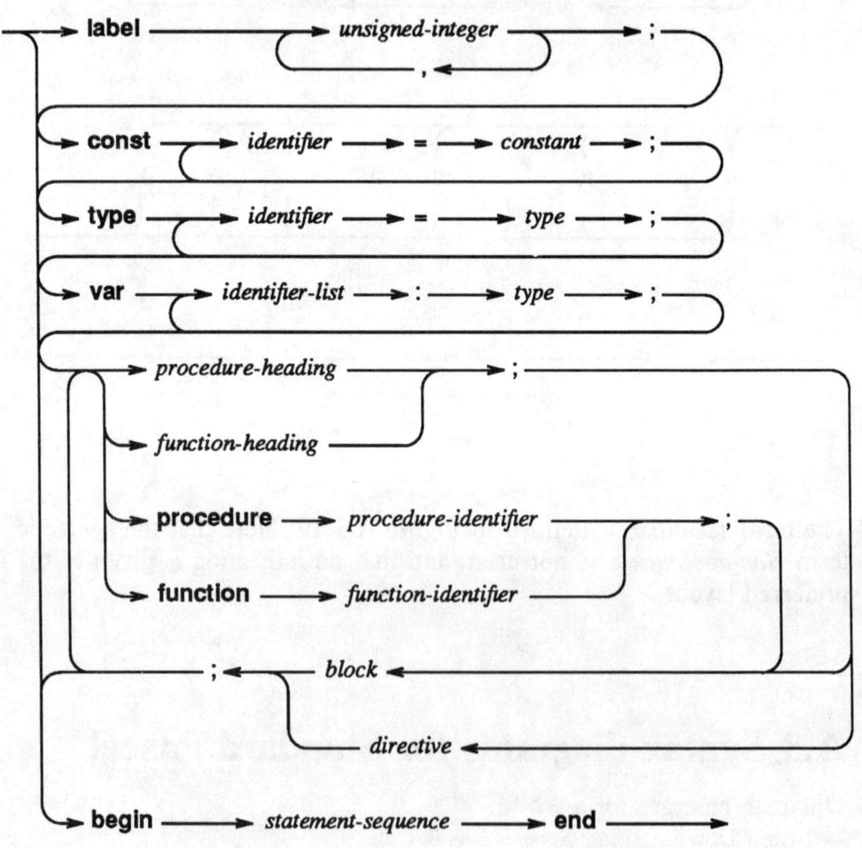

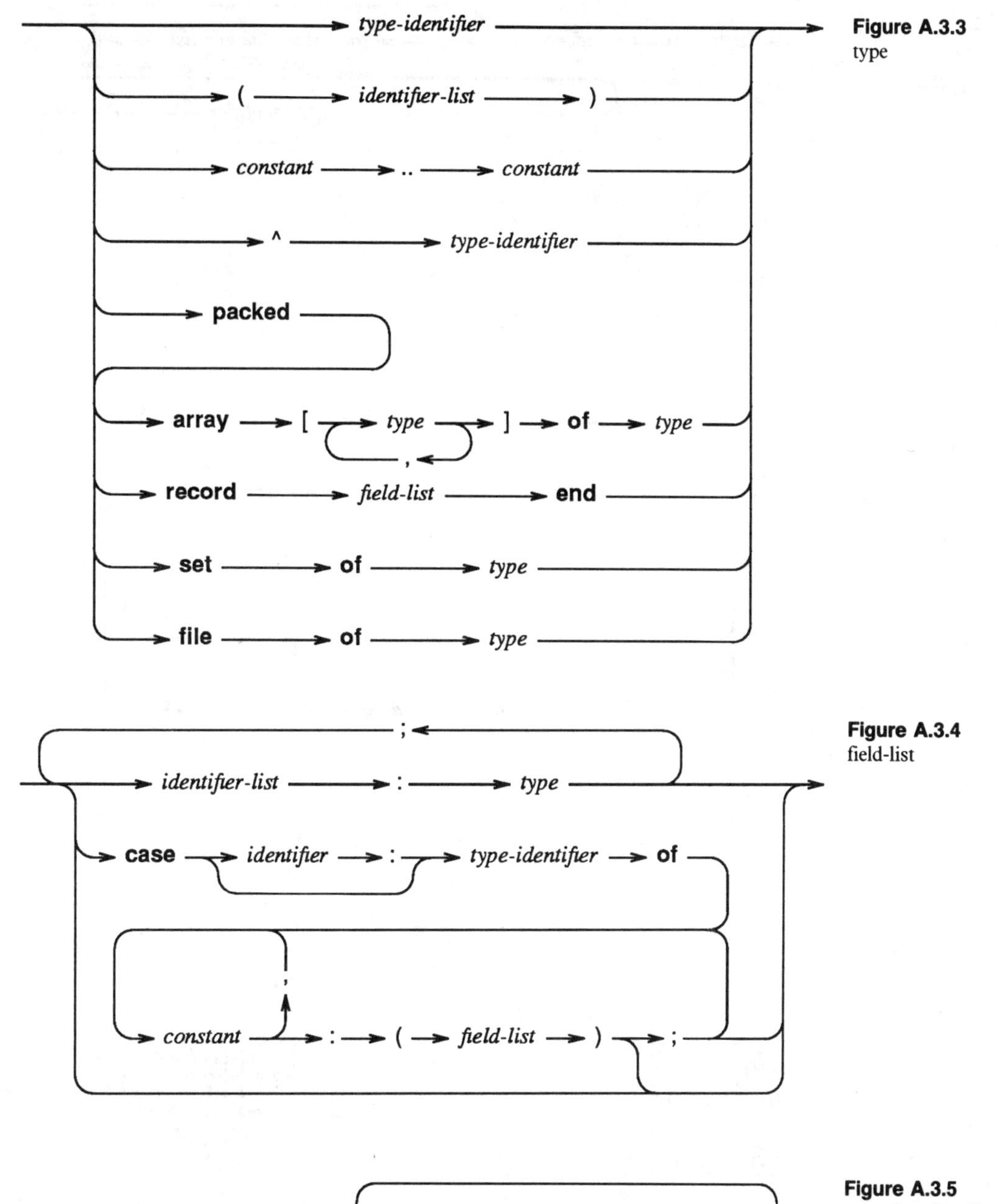


**Figure A.3.3**
type

**Figure A.3.4**
field-list

**Figure A.3.5**
procedure-heading

**Figure A.3.6**
function-heading

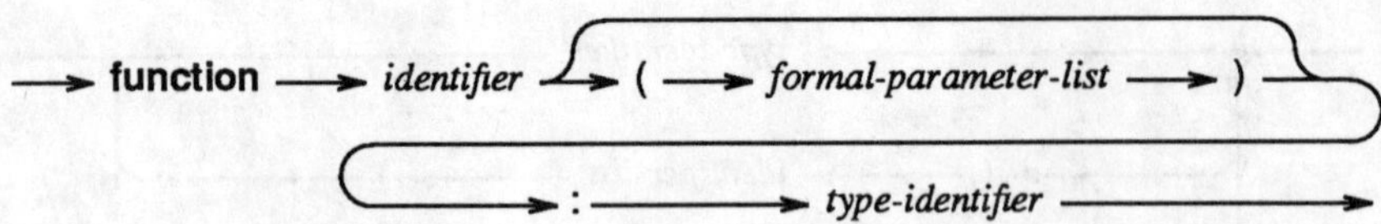


**Figure A.3.7**
formal-parameter-list

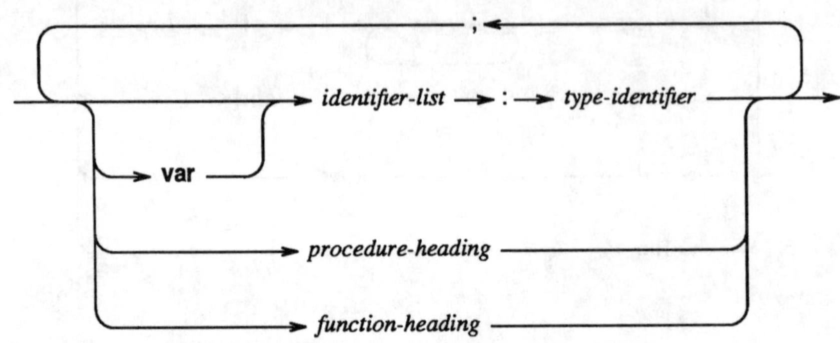


**Figure A.3.8**
statement-sequence

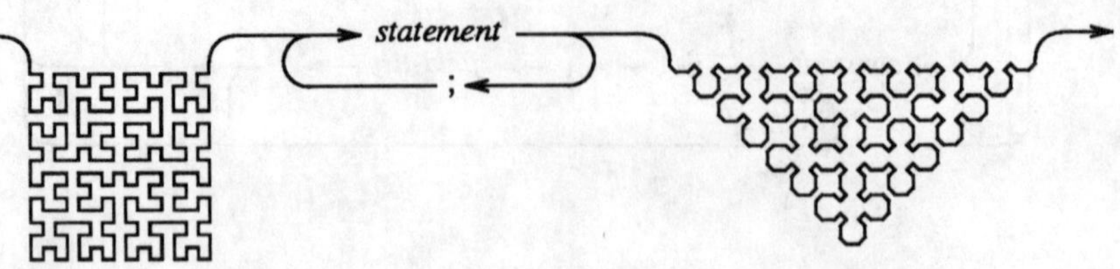

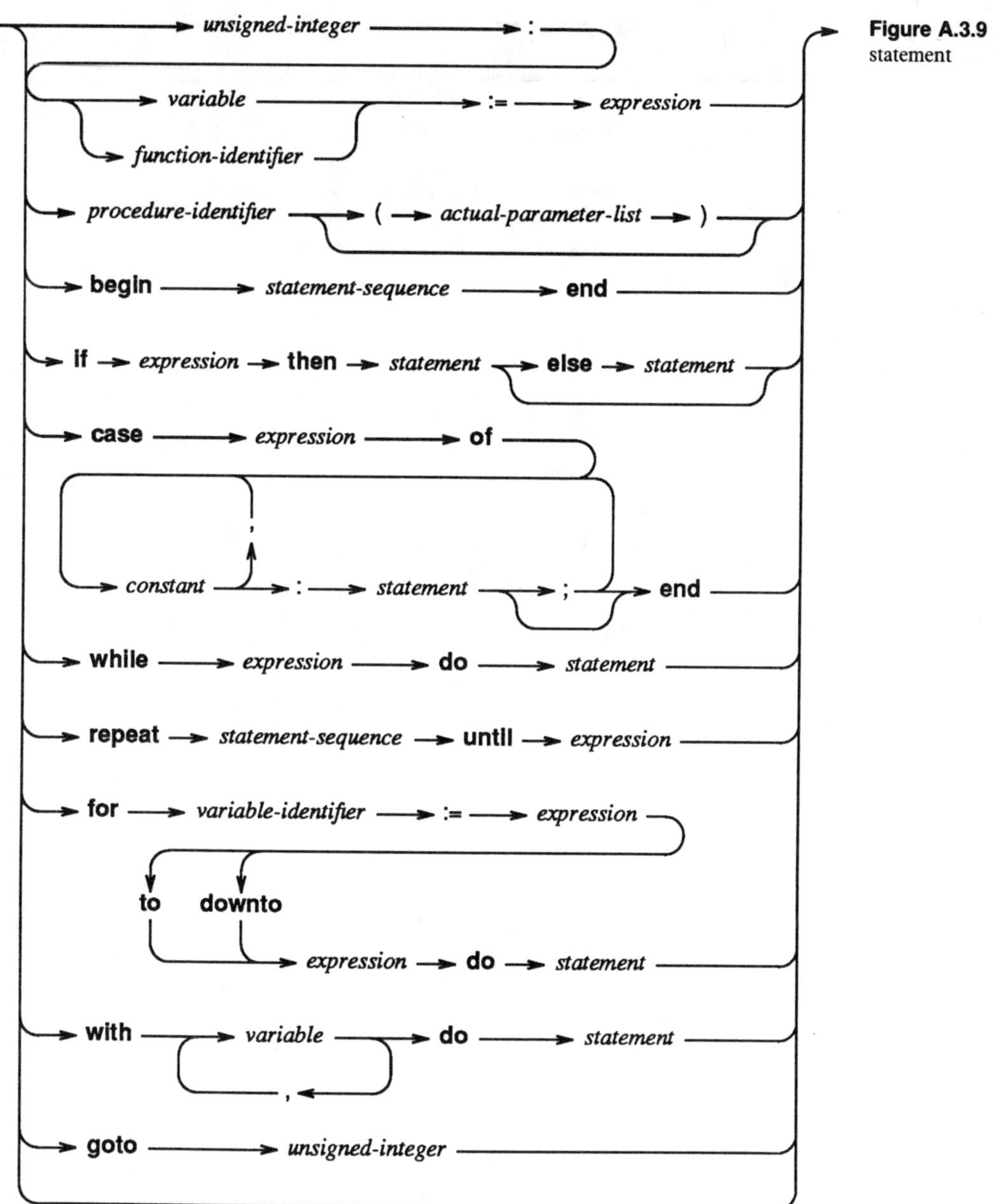


**Figure A.3.9**
statement

**Figure A.3.10**
actual-parameter-list

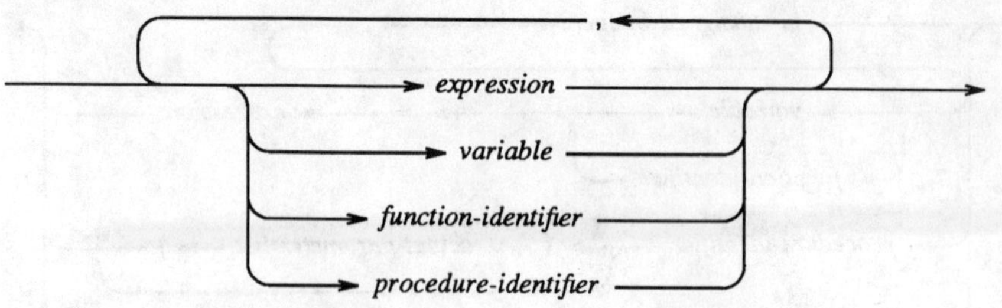


**Figure A.3.11**
expression

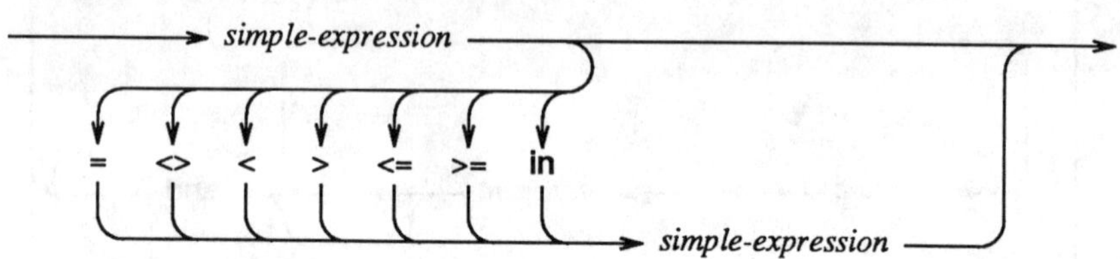


**Figure A.3.12**
simple-expression

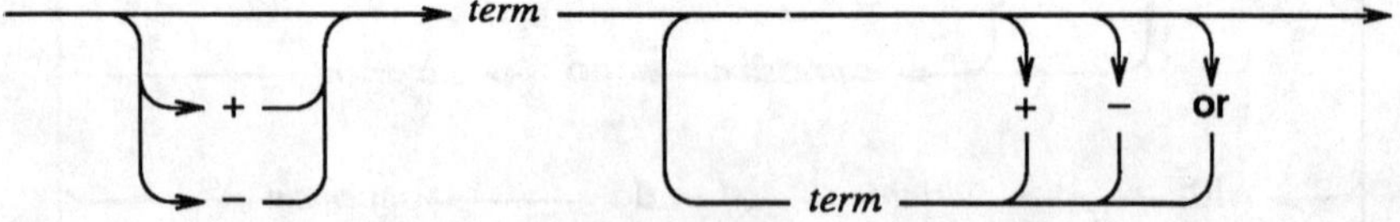


**Figure A.3.13**
term

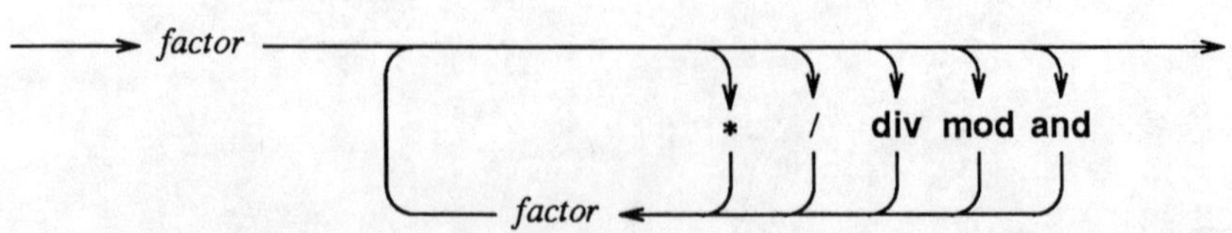

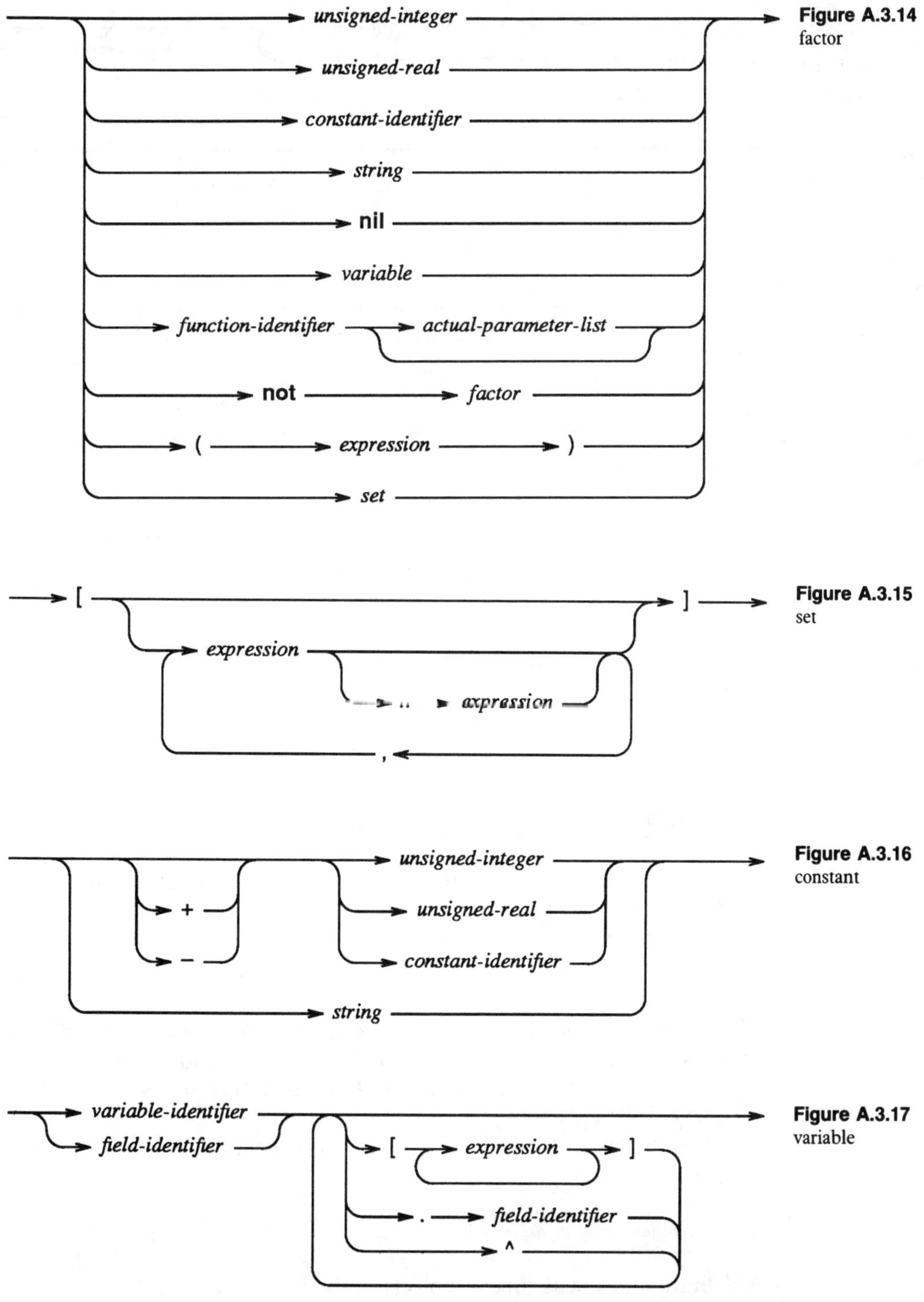


**Figure A.3.14**
factor

**Figure A.3.15**
set

**Figure A.3.16**
constant

**Figure A.3.17**
variable

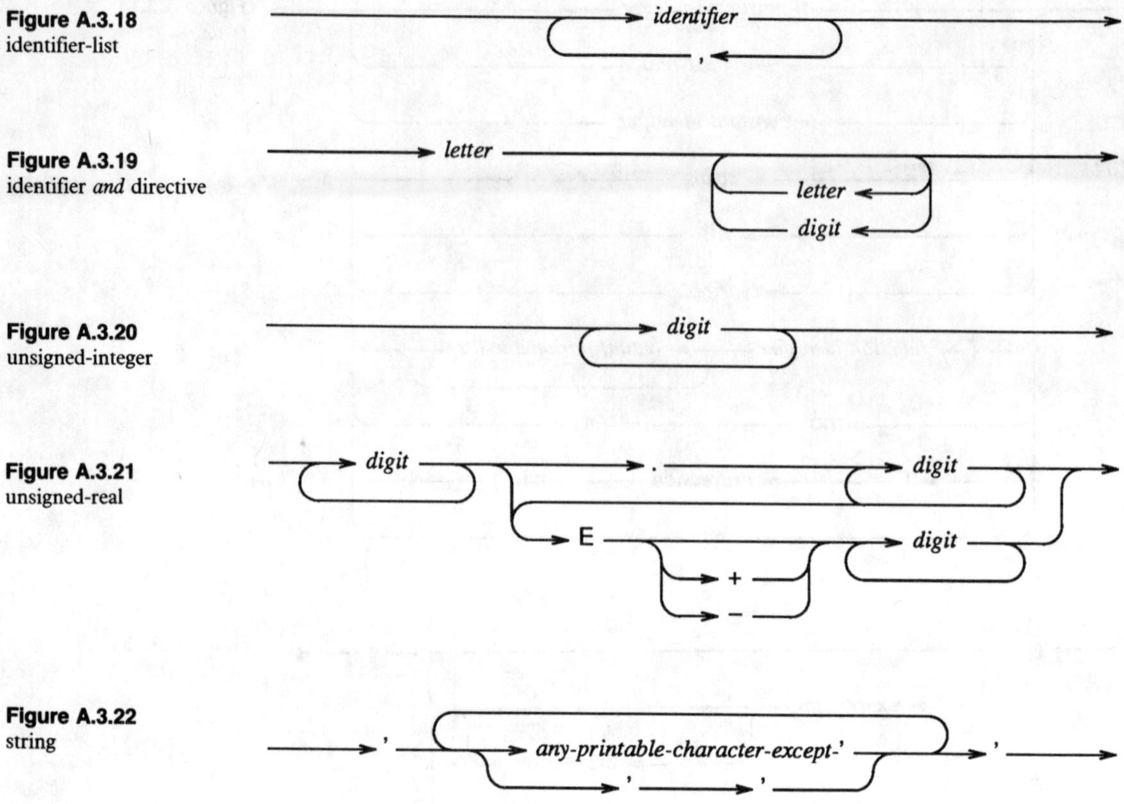


**Figure A.3.18**
identifier-list

**Figure A.3.19**
identifier *and* directive

**Figure A.3.20**
unsigned-integer

**Figure A.3.21**
unsigned-real

**Figure A.3.22**
string

# A.4 EBNF syntax notation

What can we do about the unnecessary diversity of notation for syntactic definitions?
— Niklaus Wirth, title of letter to *Communications of the ACM*, November 1977, proposing a new notation for syntactic definitions.

The Standard, Cooper's *Standard Pascal User Reference Manual*, the description of SANE in the Technical Appendix, and some books on Pascal, use a syntax notation called **Extended Backus Naur Formalism**, or **EBNF** for short.

A syntax rule in EBNF is called a **production**, and has the form:

*syntactic-term* = *definition*

A definition is a sequence of objects of the following forms.

| Syntactic object | Meaning |
|---|---|
| *" text "* | the literal sequence of symbols *text* |
| *syntactic-term* | a member of this syntactic class |
| $object_1$ \| $object_2$ | either $object_1$ or $object_2$ |
| [ *object* ] | either *object* or nothing |
| { *object* } | a sequence of zero or more copies of *object* |
| ( *object* ) | *object* (used only to bracket alternatives) |

A sequence of symbols is in the syntactic class denoted by a syntactic term if it can be obtained from the definition of the unique production with that term on the left-hand side. Here are EBNF definitions equivalent to the definitions in Exercise 5.1:

```
original = "Rocky" [ "Horror Picture Show" ] |
           "Godzilla versus" identifier { identifier } .
movie = Son-Of-Sequence original | original numeral .
Son-Of-Sequence = { "Son of" } .
numeral = "II" | "III" | "IV" | "V" | "VI" | "VII" | "VIII" | "IX" | "X" .
movie-marathon = movie { "," movie } .
```

## A.5 Notes on Lightspeed Pascal

You ain't heard nothin' yet, folks.
— Al Jolson, in *The Jazz Singer* (the first talking film), 1927

Lightspeed Pascal supports a slightly extended version of the Macintosh Pascal programming language, and a significantly enhanced programming environment. Since every feature of Macintosh Pascal has a counterpart in Lightspeed Pascal, what is said about the former applies, perhaps in a modified form, also to the latter.

Wherever Lightspeed Pascal usage is at variance with that of Macintosh Pascal as described in the text, or offers new possibilities, a numbered canned-L icon is found in the margin of the text. The identically numbered note in this appendix documents the Lightspeed Pascal usage.

### CHAPTER 1

1.1 The startup disk for Lightspeed Pascal is LP1.System.

1.2 Double-clicking on the LP1.System icon produces a window like that shown in Figure A.5.1. Note that neither scroll bar has a scroll box because all icons in the window are completely visible.

1.3 The Lightspeed Pascal programming environment is entered by selecting the Lightspeed Pascal icon, a Lightspeed Pascal program icon, or a Lightspeed Pascal project icon, and then opening it (or by just double-clicking on the icon).

## CHAPTER 2

2.1 If Lightspeed Pascal is entered by opening its icon, only its menu bar appears. To prepare to edit a new program, choose New from the File menu. A **Pascal editing window** appears which functions like Macintosh Pascal's Program window. Do likewise if entry was by opening a project icon. There is no need at this stage for the Text or Drawing window.

2.2 There is no Search menu in Lightspeed Pascal: the search commands are found in the Edit menu. Note that Find What... corresponds to What to find... in Macintosh Pascal.

Source Options

2.3 Although editing is possible at all times, the Lightspeed Pascal programming environment can only be controlled when a project is open — see Note 4.1. Choosing Source Options... from the Project menu opens a dialog box that displays a sample of the font in use in the editing, Instant, and Observe windows. It is possible to cycle through the available fonts by clicking on arrow buttons (one for each direction). The Indent and Tab Stops values may also be changed. In order to line up comments and statements, these two values should be the same; setting them to the size of the font works well. Note that files with Tabs will not be properly formatted if opened when no project is open.

The various options for the Text window can be controlled by choosing Run Options... from the Project menu.

2.4 Lightspeed Pascal's File menu additionally provides the command Save A Copy As..., which functions like Save As... except that the title in the active editing window does not change, because it is not associated with the copy that has been saved. This command is useful for making backup copies.

2.5 The information in an editing window may only be saved as Text Only or Entire Document. Only choose the latter when you wish to remember stop marks (see Section 4.3.3 of the text).

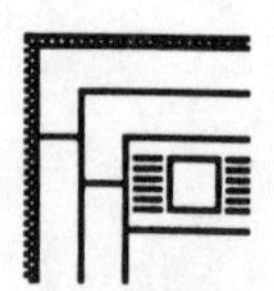

2.6 Several editing windows may be open at any time, although only one is active. Their titles are the names of the associated files, or

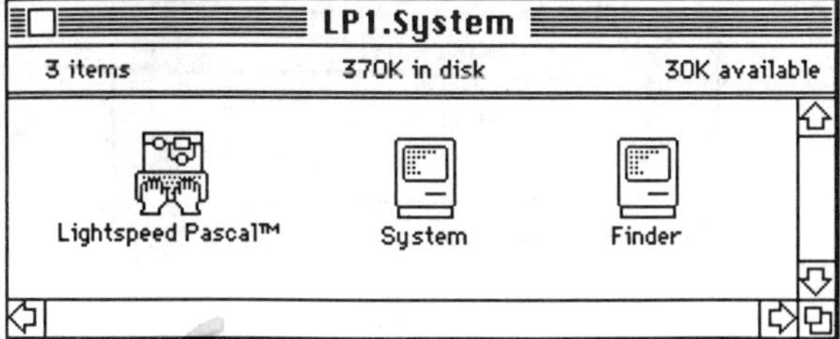


Figure A.5.1

have the form **Untitled** followed by a number if newly created and not yet saved. The editing windows are listed at the bottom of the Windows menu. A diamond mark at the left of a name signifies that the corresponding editing window has been changed since it was last saved.

◇Guess ⌘1

2.7 Copying between programs is easier in Lightspeed Pascal, because it permits multiple editing windows to be open. First ensure both the editing window containing the text to be copied, and the one to receive it, are open. Then make the former window active, and Copy (or Cut) the desired text from it. Finally, make the latter window active, and Paste into it. There is little need for the Note Pad or Scrapbook desk accessory.

2.8 The user's guide for Lightspeed Pascal is the first part (Chapters 1 through 15) of *the Manual:* Anon. (1986). *Lightspeed Pascal User's Guide and Reference Manual* Version 1, 1st edition., USA: THINK Technologies, Inc.

2.9 First open a new editing window.

2.10 Since new editing windows are empty, there is no need initially to type the Backspace-key.

2.11 The commands Find What... (corresponding to Macintosh Pascal's What to find...), Everywhere, Find, and Replace are chosen from the Edit menu.

2.12 Do the following instead. First choose New Project from the Project menu, and name the project 'temp'. Then you may choose Source Options... from the Project window to change the font and set Tab Stops and Indent Width. At the end of this step, choose Close Project from the Project window, then choose Delete... from the File menu to delete project 'temp'.

2.13 Open a different editing window, but do not close the current one (**YouGuess3**) beforehand.

2.14 Copy a section from the newly opened editing window into **YouGuess3**. Then close the newly opened editing window, and revert to the saved version of **YouGuess3**.

Figure A.5.2

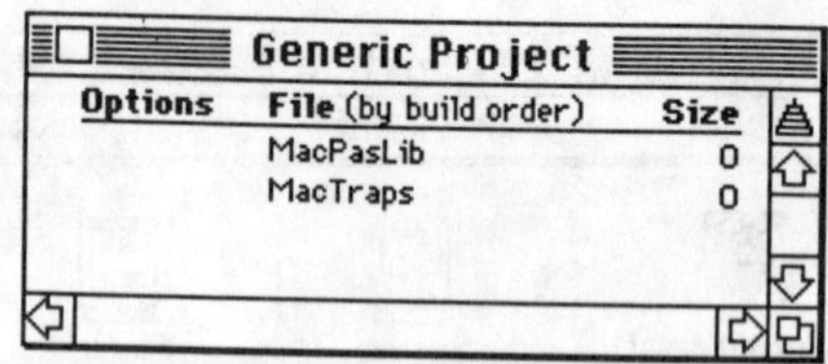


## CHAPTER 3

3.1 Running the program is not so simple in Lightspeed Pasca' Se Notes 4.1 and 4.2.

3.2 To rerun a program, you need only choose Go.

3.3 The language reference manual for Lightspeed Pascal is the second part of the Manual (Sections 1 through 10).

## CHAPTER 4

4.1 In Lightspeed Pascal, an executable program is constructed in the context of a single **project**, by compiling one or more editing files (one of which is the main program), and adding libraries of precompiled subprograms. All of the programs that we shall create use two libraries called MacPasLib and MacTraps. Accordingly, we can save work by first creating a generic project containing these two libraries. To do so, enter Lightspeed Pascal by double-clicking on its icon, and choose New Project from the Project menu. A dialog box appears. Name the project Generic Project, and associate it with the disk you will use to create and store programs, by using the Eject or Drive buttons (as described in Section 2.7 of the text) until that disk's name appears at the top right of the dialog box. Then click the Create button. The **Project window** appears (as shown in Figure A.5.2), and its title appears at the top of the Windows menu.

Now choose Build from the Run menu. If either library cannot be found, a dialog box appears asking if you want to search for the library. Click the OK button. A dialog box appears like that for Save As... shown in Figure 2.4. Insert the LP2.Libraries disk, and open the library. You will be asked a question about 'SUBSEQUENT (by build order) Project entries'. Click the Yes button. The libraries are copied into the file on your disk, and the Project window shows the size in bytes of each library. Now choose Close Project from the Project menu, and Quit from the File menu to leave Lightspeed Pascal.

Close Project

In future, whenever you want to create a new project (i.e. executable program), select the Generic Project icon by clicking on it *once*, choose Duplicate from the desktop's File menu, and name the copy appropriately. Then double-click on the new project's icon to enter Lightspeed Pascal with the Project window displayed.

4.2 A program cannot be run until it is compiled and linked to the libraries that it uses. To add the active editing window to a project, choose Add Window from the Project menu. The contents may then be compiled and added to the project file by choosing Build from the Project menu, after which the program may be executed by choosing Go from the Run menu. But it is sufficient just to choose Go — if the editing window has not been compiled, or has been changed since last compiled, Build will be automatically chosen. Also, if Confirm Saves in the Run menu is active (as indicated by a bullet to its left), you are given the opportunity to save the editing window before execution. Alternatively, you may activate either the Auto-Save or the Don't Save option.

Auto-Save
• Confirm Saves
Don't Save

4.3 To halt execution of a Lightspeed Pascal program, click on the bug spray can icon in the top right corner of the screen.

4.4 Note that the pointing hand will only enter procedures or functions when the Step Into Calls option in the Debug menu is enabled (signified by a check mark to its left). If the Auto Show Finger option is enabled, the editing window containing the hand is made active, to ensure the hand is always visible. Each of these options changes status when selected.

✓Step Into Calls
Auto-Show Finger

4.5 Step-Step is called Trace in Lightspeed Pascal.

4.6 Stops In is in the Debug menu.

4.7 The stop feature is switched off by rechoosing Stops In.

4.8 The Do It button is active only when execution of a program has commenced but has not yet finished (i.e. when the pointing hand is visible, or can be made so).

4.9 We assume that program **YouGuess3** is in the active editing window, and the project has been built (and can therefore be executed).

## CHAPTER 5

5.1 Lightspeed Pascal uses four additional reserved words:

**unit implementation interface inline**

## CHAPTER 9

9.1 QuickDraw is implicitly supported by Lightspeed Pascal. Besides SANE, other libraries provided are FixMath, for manipulating fractional numbers, Graf3D, for 3-dimensional graphics, Speech, for synthesized speech, and Profile, for gathering statistics concerning the execution of a program.

9.2 Since **unit** is a reserved word, change Unit to TimeUnit throughout.

9.3 QuickDraw is described in Appendix C of the Manual, and SANE in Appendix D.

## CHAPTER 10

10.1 This implementation of ran exploits the fact that integer arithmetic in Macintosh Pascal is carried out in type longint — see Section 19.1 of the text. This is not the case in Lightspeed Pascal (or Standard Pascal). Accordingly, change the expression determining the result to

```
lower + trunc((Random + 1.0 + Maxint) / (2 * (Maxint + 1.0)) *
        (upper – lower + 1)
```

## CHAPTER 11

11.1 Lightspeed Pascal version 1.0 does not permit an element of a packed array to appear in the variable-list of a Read or Readln statement, although this is permitted by the Standard.

11.2 Since **unit** is a reserved word, change Unit to TimeUnit throughout.

## CHAPTER 14

14.1 There is a bug concerning procedure delete in Lightspeed Pascal version 1.0. A call has no effect when the string to be deleted from is a variable formal parameter (of some subprogram).

## CHAPTER 15

15.1 An abstract data type should be represented in Lightspeed Pascal as a **unit**, which is a collection of strongly related definitions and declarations. In order to use a unit, either a main program or another unit must mention it in a **uses-clause**; see Section 16.4.4 of the text.

An abstract data type supporting variable-length strings is supplied by the following unit:

```
unit CharString;
interface
 const
  MaxStringLength = ...;
 type
  StringLength = 0..MaxStringLength;
  StringIndex = 1..MaxStringLength;
  CharString = record
    ch : packed array[StringIndex] of char;
    length : StringLength
   end;
   { represents the string ch[1], ch[2], ..., ch[length] }
 function length (var s : CharString) : StringLength;
 { Returns the length of s. }
 procedure concat (s1, s2 : CharString;
var result : CharString);
 { Sets result to s1 concatenated with s2; }
 { assumes length(s1) + length(s2) <= MaxStringLength. }
 headings of subprograms implementing other abstract operations
implementation
 function length;
 begin { length }
  length := s.length
 end; { length }
 procedure concat;
  var
   i : StringIndex;
 begin { concat }
  ...
 end; { concat }
 the remaining function and/or procedure declarations
end. { CharString }
```

Note that the type-identifier string has been changed to CharString because **string** is a reserved word in Lightspeed Pascal.

A unit has the following syntax:

**unit:**
*unit-heading* ;
*interface-part*
*implementation-part*
**end** .
unit-heading: **unit** *unit-identifier*
unit-identifier: *identifier*

The interface part declares those constants, types, variables, functions, and procedures which are to be made available when a uses-clause mentions the unit. Only the headings of procedures and functions are given. Also, any unit used by this unit must be named in a uses-clause; this goes for direct uses and indirect ones via the interface parts of other units (see Section 8.5 of the Manual).

interface-part:
**interface**
*uses-clause*
| *interface-declaration-part*
| ...
interface-declaration-part: *constant-definition-part* |
*type-definition-part* | *variable-declaration-part* |
*function-heading* | *procedure-heading*

The implementation part specifies the implementation of the subprograms in the interface part, omitting their formal parameter lists. To do so, further constants, types, variables, and subprograms may be declared (the latter in full), but they are not available to users of the unit.

implementation-part:
**implementation**
| implementation-declaration-part
| ...
implementation-declaration-part: *constant-definition-part* |
*type-definition-part* | *variable-declaration-part* |
*procedure-or-function-declaration*

Units have some attractive properties:

- They provide a simple form of **information hiding**; i.e. they give the programmer some control over which declarations are made available to users of a unit, and which are reserved for strictly internal use. This principle is fundamental to advanced programming, because it enables the different levels of abstraction in a program to be distinguished (and rules out many sources of error). Units are only partially successful in this respect. For example, because type CharString must be defined in the interface part, its implementation as a record cannot be hidden from the user of the unit, although it is very desirable to do so.

- They permit **modular programming**, in which a program is broken up into a collection of **modules** (groups of strongly related declarations), the interfaces between which are carefully controlled. This is a higher-level extension of the concept of subprograms, and offers similar, additional, and substantial advantages.
- They permit separate compilation. Only those modules which have been changed since last compiled need be recompiled.
- They permit the programmer to create his or her own libraries of precompiled subprograms. Only the interface parts of these libraries need be made available for use, just as the SANE unit on LP2.Libraries does for the SANELib library. See Chapter 9 of the Manual for the details.

Note that the order of the files in the Project Window is important. A unit file must appear before any file which uses it. The cursor changes into a hand when over the list of file names, permitting a file to be grabbed and moved elsewhere in the list. Note also that the order of unit-names in a uses-clause obeys a similar rule.

15.2 Lightspeed Pascal does support packed records.

## CHAPTER 16

16.1 The QuickDraw2 library is implicitly but not explicitly known to Lightspeed Pascal. Therefore the uses-clause must be deleted.

16.2 Lightspeed Pascal does support packed files.

16.3 This bug is not present in Lightspeed Pascal.

## CHAPTER 17

17.1 Lightspeed Pascal does support packed sets.

## CHAPTER 19

19.1 Integer arithmetic is carried out in type integer, unless a constant, variable, or function result of type longint is involved.

The philosophy is the same as that for mixed integer and real arithmetic. Note that the required functions **abs** and **sqr** give a result of the same type as the actual parameter. Thus, e.g., sqr(Maxint + 1) and sqr(600), for example, both give overflow (the former because its argument does), but sqr(32768) and sqr(long), where long is a longint variable with value 600, both evaluate correctly.

There are anomalies with abs in Lightspeed Pascal version 1.0; e.g. abs(Maxint + 1) and abs(Maxint) + 1 both give –32768.

19.2 If overflow checking is disabled, integer arithmetic also works this way in Lightspeed Pascal. But you are urged to leave overflow checking enabled, as signified by the V-option (to the left of the file name in the Project window) being boxed.

DNVR Guess

19.3 Provided the V-option is enabled, integer arithmetic in Lightspeed Pascal is secure.

19.4 This is not the case in Lightspeed Pascal version 1.0: `$19999.00` is printed.

19.5 Before adding roots to a project, add the SANE unit and the SANELib library (from LP2.Libraries).

19.6 Evaluation of i + 1 gives an error in Lightspeed Pascal. But note that zero would still be printed if i were declared to have type longint.

## CHAPTER 20

20.1 Not only should it be retained as a unit, but it should be implemented as a unit; see Note 15.1 above.

20.2 This abstract data type should also be implemented as a unit.

20.3 If the abstract data type BinarySearchTree is implemented as a unit, instead of incorporating the code in the text in the program, the program-heading should be followed by the following uses-clause:

```
uses
  BinarySearchTree;
```

## SOLUTIONS TO SELECTED EXERCISES

S.1 Since **unit** is a reserved word, change Unit to UnitLength throughout.

S.2 This gives an error in Lightspeed Pascal.

# SOLUTIONS TO SELECTED EXERCISES

So whoever thinks up all these problems is the biggest nonghead on the face of the earth.
— Jane Enright, letter to the Brisbane, Australia, *Courier-Mail*, 30 May 1986, complaining about high-school algebra.

## Chapter 1

**1.1** The effect of an algorithm may depend on input data.

**1.2** There is an algorithm for playing tic-tac-toe that cannot lose.

**1.4** Algorithm (a) is more abstract; algorithm (b) depends on a particular representation for numbers.

**1.5** 1 k.

**1.6** $2^{18} - 1 = 262\,143$.

**1.7** By following the sequence of instructions with an instruction that (conditionally) sets the PC to the address of the first instruction in the sequence.

## Chapter 3

**3.1** Yes; because $0 \leqslant x$ **mod** $y \leqslant y - 1$.

**3.2** Execution of the statement adds 1 to the current value of number.

**3.5**
```
program EvenOdd (Input, Output);
{ Reads a number and indicates whether it is even or odd. }
```

```
var
  num, rem : integer;
begin { EvenOdd }
  Readln(num);
  rem := num mod 2;
  if rem = 0 then
    Writeln('even')
  else
    Writeln ('odd')
end. { EvenOdd }
```

# Chapter 5

**5.1** (a) (i), (ii), (iv), and (vii) (since IV is an identifier).
(b) Rocky.
(d) Yes.

**5.2** (a) –2; (b) 0; (c) 32 767 (in Macintosh Pascal); (d) 9.

**5.4** See the solution to Exercise 5.11.

**5.5** (a) 0.001; (b) 0.333 3 ...; (c) 0.333 3 ...; (d) 4.0; (e) 1; (f) –1.0.

**5.6** (a) 'Q'; (b) 'O'; (c) 'x'; (d) 'Z'.
Only (c)'s value is guaranteed by the Standard.

**5.8** (a)
```
const
  Cost1 = 22; { cost in cents of first ounce }
  CostExtra1 = 17; { cost of each additional (part) ounce }
```
(b)
```
cost := Cost1 + trunc(weight) * CostExtra1;
if weight = trunc(weight) then
  cost := cost - CostExtra1
```

**5.10** (a) `abs(x) <= abs(y)`
(b) `(0 <= x) and (x <= 5)`
(c) `(x < 0) or (x > 5)`
(d) `(x >= 0) or (y >= 0)`

**5.11** (a)
```
NrBoxes := NrWanted div 20;
NrSingles := NrWanted mod 20;
NewBoxOpened := NrSingles > NrLoose;
NrLoose := (NrLoose - NrSingles) mod 20
```

(b)
```
NrBoxes := (NrWanted – NrLoose) div 20;
if NrWanted <= NrLoose then
  NrSingles := NrWanted
else
  NrSingles := NrLoose + (NrWanted – NrLoose) mod 20;
NewBoxOpened := NrSingles > NrLoose;
NrLoose := (NrLoose – NrSingles) mod 20
```

**5.12**
```
IsEven := not odd(n)
```

**5.14** We give only the new values of the variables.

(a) i = 215, r = –100.0, c = ' ';
(b) i = 215, r = –100.0, c = '–';
(c) i = 215, c = '–', r = 100.0;
(d) r = 215.0, i = –1, c = 'E';
(e) i = 215, r = –15.0, c = '5'.

**5.15**
```
Writeln('The speed of light is approximately ',
        LightSpeed : 1 : 2,' miles per second.')
```

**5.18**
```
Write('$', cost / 100 : 1 : 2)
```

**5.20** It means that the loop will execute forever (until the program is halted manually).

**5.21** Any integer > 16 384 (in Macintosh Pascal).

**5.24** There would be no way of telling the last statement in the statement-list.

**5.26**
```
begin
  S1;
  ...
  Sn;
  while not p do
    begin
      S1;
      ...
      Sn
    end
end
```

**5.28** (b) because an underscore (__) cannot appear in an identifier;
(c) because a hyphen (-) cannot appear in an identifier;
(f) because a period (.) cannot appear in an identifier;
(g) because a single-quote (') cannot appear in an identifier;

(h) because **downto** is a reserved word.

**5.29** Because the case of a letter is unimportant except in strings.

# Chapter 6

**6.2**

```
var
  hours12 : integer; { 12 hour clock's equivalent of hours }

{ Given time on 24-hour clock is hours:minutes, print time on }
{ 12 hour clock. E.g. for 0:00 print '12:00am', for 9:09 print }
{ '9:09am', for 12:00 print '12:00pm', for 23:59 print '11:59pm' }
{ Set hours12 = 12-hour version of hours }
if hours = 0 then
   hours12 := 12
 else if hours > 12 then
   hours12 := hours - 12
 else
   hours12 := hours;
{ Write time on 12-hour clock }
Write(hours12 : 1, ':', minutes div 10 : 1, minutes mod 10 : 1);
if hours < 12 then
  Writeln('am')
else
  Writeln('pm')
```

**6.3** (a) value <= limit

(b) value > limit

(c) (value < –2 * limit) **or** (value > limit)

(d) (value < –limit) **or** (value > limit)

**6.7** (a)

```
var
v := x0;
repeat
  Set v = the next member of the sequence (after v)
until v has property P
```

(b)

```
var
  m, { a number > n to be tested for primality }
  d : integer; { a candidate for a divisor of m }

{ Set NextPrime = the least prime > n }
m := n;

repeat
  m := m + 1;
```

```
  { Set d = least divisor >= 2 of m }
    d := 2;
    while m mod d <> 0 do
      d := d + 1
  until d = m;
  NextPrime := m
```

**6.8** Mult32 := ((x + 31) **div** 32) * 32

**6.12**
```
for OrdOfChar := 0 to 255 do
  Write(chr(OrdOfChar))
```

**6.17**
```
{ Set sum = 1 + 2 + 3 + ... + n, given n >= 0 }
  sum := n * (n + 1) div 2
```

**6.18**
```
var
  i : integer;

{ Set sum = 1 +1/2 + 1/3 + ... + 1/n, given  n >= 0 }
  sum := 0.0;
  for i := n downto 1 do
    sum := sum + 1.0 / i
```

**6.19**
```
var
  ch : char;

{ Set unused to number of characters in rest of line and skip to }
{ next line }
  unused := 0;
  while not eoln do
    begin
      Read(ch);
      unused := unused + 1
    end;
  Readln
```

**6.20**
```
var
  FibNr, NextFibNr, { two successive Fibonacci numbers }
  temp : integer;
```

(a)
```
{ Print the Fibonacci numbers <= limit }
  FibNr := 0;
  NextFibNr := 1;
  while FibNr <= limit do
    begin
      Write(FibNr);
      temp := NextFibNr;
      NextFibNr := NextFibNr + FibNr;
      FibNr := temp
    end
```

(b)
```
var
  i : integer;
{ Print the first n Fibonacci numbers, given n >= 0 }
 FibNr := 0;
 NextFibNr := 1;
 for i := 1 to n do
   begin
     Write(FibNr);
     temp := NextFibNr;
     NextFibNr := NextFibNr + FibNr;
     FibNr := temp
   end
```

More careful solutions are needed to avoid computing unnecessarily large numbers.

**6.21** (a) { d = least divisor >= 2 of m }

(b) { m >= 2 } (from context)

# Chapter 7

**7.1**

```
function IsLetter (ch : char) : Boolean;
{ Returns true if ch is a letter, otherwise false. }
{ N.B. Assumes both upper- & lower-case letters contiguous. }
begin { IsLetter }
  IsLetter := ('a' <= ch) and (ch <= 'z') or
              ('A' <= ch) and (ch <= 'Z')
end; { IsLetter }
```

**7.2** (a)

```
function even (i : integer) : Boolean;
{ Returns true if i is even, otherwise false. }
begin { even }
  even := not odd(i)
end; { even }
```

(b)

```
function even (i : integer) : Boolean;
{ Returns true if i is even, otherwise false. }
begin { even }
  even := i mod 2 = 0
end; { even }
```

**7.9**

```
function ForceUpper (ch : char;
                     upper : Boolean) : char;
{ If ch is a lower-case letter and upper is true, }
{ returns the upper-case version of ch, else returns ch. }
{ N.B. Assumes both upper- & lower-case letters contiguous. }
begin { ForceUpper }
  if upper and ('a' <= ch) and (ch <= 'z') then
```

```
        ForceUpper := chr(ord(ch) + ord('A') - ord('a'))
      else
        ForceUpper := ch
    end; { ForceUpper }
```

**7.12**
```
function lpf (n : integer) : integer;
{ Assumes n > 1; }
{ returns the least prime factor of n. }
  var
    d : integer; { candidate for a divisor of n }
begin { lpf }
  if not odd(n) then
    lpf := 2
  else
    begin
      d := 3;
      while (n mod d <> 0) and (sqr(d) < n) do
        d := d + 2;
      if n mod d = 0 then
        lpf := d
      else
        lpf := n
    end
end; { lpf }
```

The efficiency of the function can be further improved by precomputing the square root of n and thereby avoiding the repeated calls of **sqr**.

**7.13**
```
function product (x, y : integer) : integer;
{ Returns x * y. }
  var
    sum, { accumulates answer }
    temp : integer;
begin { product }
{ Arrange x, y such that abs(x) <= abs(y) }
  if abs(x) > abs(y) then
    begin
      temp := x;
      x := y;
      y := temp
    end;
{ Adjust signs if necessary to ensure x is non-negative }
  if x < 0 then
    begin
      x := -x;
      y := -y
    end;
```

```
{ Set product = x * y }
  if x = 0 then
    product := 0
  else
  begin
    sum := 0;
    while x <> 1 do
      begin
        if odd(x) then
          sum := sum + y;
        x := x div 2;
        y := y * 2
      end;
    product := sum + y
  end
end; { product }
```

**7.14** Our solution extends the function to negative integers.

```
function gcd (x, y : integer) : integer;
{ Returns the greatest common divisor of x and y; }
{ assumes x and y are not both 0. }
  var
    temp : integer;
begin { gcd }
  x := abs(x);
  y := abs(y);
  while x <> 0 do
    begin
      temp := x;
      x := y mod x;
      y := temp
    end;
  gcd := y
end; { gcd }
```

# Chapter 8

**8.3** The illegal calls are as follows:

(a) because '1' is not assignment-compatible with type integer;
(c) because sum is not an integer variable;
(d) because sum is not assignment-compatible with type integer
(e) because round(sum) is not an integer variable;
(f) because 0 is not an integer variable.

**8.4** (a)

```
1  2
2  0
1  2
```

(b)

```
1  2
2  0
2  0
```

**8.5**
(a) NrWanted, NrLoose.
(b) NrLoose, NrSingles, NrBoxes, NewBoxOpened.
(c) NrLoose.
(d) NrWanted.
(e) NrLoose, NrSingles, NrBoxes, NewBoxOpened.

**8.6**

```
procedure WriteStats (total1, total2, sum, jobs : integer);
{ Writes number of jobs (jobs); if jobs > 0, writes total time on }
{ each processor (total1, total2), and average time of job- }
{ completion (sum/jobs). }
  const
    start = 'The total time used on processor';
begin { WriteStats }
  Writeln;
  Writeln(jobs : 1, ' jobs processed.');
  if jobs > 0 then
    begin
      Writeln(start, ' 1 = ', total1 : 1);
      Writeln(start, ' 2 = ', total2 : 1);
      Writeln('The average time at which jobs complete = ',
               sum / jobs : 1 : 1)
    end;
end; { WriteStats }

WriteStats(TotalTimeOn1, TotalTimeOn2, SumOfCompletionTimes,
             JobCount)
```

**8.10** a and b should be value-parameters. Better — the procedure should be rewritten as a function.

**8.11** 1 is printed because b and max are aliased to big.

**8.13** The attempted definition of the constant pbase is in the scope of the declaration of the integer *variable* base.

# Chapter 9

**9.1** $(2 \times \text{Maxint} + 1)^2 = 4\,294\,836\,225$.

**9.2** Assuming all the pixels are visible: (a) 3; (b) 15.

**9.3** 22 (assuming all the pixels are visible).

**9.5**
```
procedure DrawDots (n, gap : integer);
{ Draws n dots in a horizontal line, separated by given gap; the }
{ pen is left at top-left corner of dot farthest from its initial }
{ position. }
 var
  i : integer;
begin { DrawDots }
 if n > 0 then
  begin
   Line(0, 0);
   for i := 2 to n do
    begin
     Move(gap, 0);
     Line(0, 0)
    end
  end
end; { DrawDots }
```

**9.6**
```
var
  MarkerAt, { horizontal coordinate of next marker }
  time : integer;

{ Draw and label markers for time axis }
 time := 0;
 MarkerAt := Left;
 while MarkerAt <= MaxWidth do
  begin
  { Draw and label next marker }
   MoveTo(MarkerAt, base);
   Line(0, Drop);
   Move(-PointSize div 2, PointSize);
   WriteDraw(time : 2);
  { Update time and MarkerAt }
   time := time + 2;
   MarkerAt := MarkerAt  + 2 * Unit
  end
```

**9.10** Dist ⩾ HeadWidth.

**9.11** A single empty statement.

# Chapter 10

**10.1** An enumerated type, *naturelment* .

**10.2** See the solution to Exercise 10.11.

**10.3**

```
const
  MaxSecret = 10;
var
  secret : 1..MaxSecret; { the number to be guessed }
  guess : integer;
```

**10.4**

```
type
  index = 0..15; { type of row or column of character set table }
```

**10.6**

```
procedure PrintMonth (m : Months);
{ Prints the string corresponding to the identifier of m. }
begin { PrintMonth }
  case m of
    January :
      Write('January');
    etc.
    December :
      Write('December')
  end { case }
end; { PrintMonth }
```

**10.7** (i) The answer to an exercise is not necessarily of type operand.
(ii) Incorrect answers may be input.

**10.9**

```
{ Set op to a random operation }
  case ran(0, OrdOfLastOp) of
    0 :
      op := plus;
    1 :
      op := minus;
    2 :
      op := times
  end { case }
```

**10.11**

```
program Calendar (Input);
{ Draws a month by month calendar for 1988. }
{ Run with Drawing window occupying the full screen; }
{ hit Return to draw each successive month. }
  type
    Years = 1753..9999;
    Months = (Jan, Feb, Mar, Apr, May, Jun, Jul, Aug, Sep, Oct,
              Nov, Dec);
    MonthLengths = 28..31;
    Days = (Su, Mo, Tu, We, Th, Fr, Sa);
  function NextDay (ThisDay : Days) : Days;
  { Returns day after ThisDay. }
```

```
begin { NextDay }
 if ThisDay = Sa then
   NextDay := Su
 else
   NextDay := succ(ThisDay)
end; { NextDay }

function LengthOfMonth (month : Months;
                        year : Years) : MonthLengths;
{ Returns number of days in given month for given year. }
as given in Chapter 10

procedure DrawStringC (s : string);
{ Draws s with the center of its base line at the current pen }
{ position; leaves the pen position at the end of the string. }
see Chapter 14

procedure DrawCal (year : Years;
                   Jan1 : Days);
{ Draws a month by month calendar for given year, with }
{ January 1st on day Jan1; waits for user to hit }
{ Return-key before printing new month. }
{ Global subprogram: LengthOfMonth. }
 var
   month : Months;
   FirstDay : Days; { first day in month }

  procedure DrawMonth (month : Months;
                       NrDays : MonthLengths;
                       var FirstDay : Days);
  { Draws calendar for given month having NrDays days and }
  { first day on FirstDay; updates FirstDay to first day }
  { of next month. }
  { Global subprogram: NextDay. }
   const
     Top = 32; { top left corner of rectangle for month's }
     Left = 40; { calendar is at (Left,Top). }
     BoxWidth = 40; { width of box for each day }
     CharSize = 12; { character size in points (default: 12) }
   var
     NrRows : 1..6; { number of rows in month's calendar }
     TopBox, LeftBox : integer; { top left corner of box for day
                                  is at (LeftBox,TopBox) }
     day : Days; { current day }
     DayNumber : 1..31; { number of current day }

   procedure DrawHeadings;
   { Draws month and day headings for month's calendar. }
   { Global consts: Top, Left, BoxWidth, CharSize. }
```

```
    { Global vars: month, year (parameters of DrawMonth). }
    { Global subprogram: DrawStringC. }
     var
       day : Days;
    begin { DrawHeadings }

  MoveTo(Left + 7 * BoxWidth div 2, Top – CharSize – 5);
  DrawStringC(StringOf(month, ' ', year : 1));
  for day := Su to Sa do
    begin
      MoveTo(Left + ord(day) * BoxWidth + BoxWidth div 2,
                Top – 3);
      DrawStringC(StringOf(day))
    end
 end; { DrawHeadings }

begin { DrawMonth }
 TextSize(CharSize);
 NrRows := (NrDays + ord(FirstDay) + 6) div 7;
{ Clear Drawing Window }
 EraseRect(0, 0, Maxint, Maxint);
{ Paint gray background for calendar }
 PenPat(gray);
 PaintRect(Top – 1, Left – 1, Top + NrRows * BoxWidth + 1,
            Left + 7 * BoxWidth + 1);
 PenPat(black);

 DrawHeadings;
{ Set coordinates of box for first day }
 TopBox := Top;
 LeftBox := Left + ord(FirstDay) * BoxWidth;

 day := FirstDay;
 for DayNumber := 1 to NrDays do
   begin
   { Erase box for day }
     EraseRect(TopBox + 1, LeftBox + 1, TopBox
                 + BoxWidth – 1, LeftBox + BoxWidth – 1);
   { Draw DayNumber in box }
     MoveTo(LeftBox + 2, TopBox + CharSize);
     WriteDraw(DayNumber : 1);
   { Advance day and set coordinates of its box }
     day := NextDay(day);
     if day = Su then
       begin
         TopBox := TopBox + BoxWidth;
         LeftBox := Left
       end
     else
```

```
        LeftBox := LeftBox + BoxWidth
      end;
    FirstDay := day
  end; { DrawMonth }

begin { DrawCal }
  FirstDay := Jan1;
  for month := Jan to Dec do
    begin
      DrawMonth(month, LengthOfMonth(month, year), FirstDay);
      Readln
    end
end; { DrawCal }

begin { Calendar }
  DrawCal(1988, Fr)
end. { Calendar }
```

# Chapter 11

**11.2** (a) 2; (b) error: 0 subscript is out of range; (c) 2; (d) 5.

**11.3**

```
var
  op : operation;
  i : 1..OrdOfLastOp; { = ord(op) }

{ Define OpWithOrd }
 OpWithOrd[0] := plus;
 op := plus;
 for i := 1 to OrdOfLastOp do
   begin
     op := succ(op);
     OpWithOrd[i] := op
   end
```

**11.4**

```
procedure PrintFrom (LowScore : ScoreRange;
                     var h : histogram);
{ Prints each score s and its frequency h[s], }
{ for s = LowScore, ... , MaxScore, in two headed columns. }
{ Global const: MaxScore. }
 var
   score : ScoreRange;
begin { PrintFrom }
 Writeln( 'score          frequency' );
 for score := LowScore to MaxScore do
   Writeln(score, h[score])
end; { PrintFrom }
```

**11.7** Count the examination scores, and take special action if there are none. This approach is best because it is simple, natural, and efficient.

**11.10** Yes.

**11.11** One way is to use schema Truncated Safe Linear Search:

```
function DifferAt (var m1, m2 : message) : ExtendedIndex;
{ Returns 0 if m1 and m2 are identical, otherwise the }
{ least index at which they differ. Global const: Length. }
  var
    i : index;
   begin { DifferAt }
     i := 1;
     while (i < Length) and (m1[i] = m2[i]) do
       i := i + 1;
     if m1[i] = m2[i] then
       DifferAt := 0
     else
       DifferAt := i
   end; { DifferAt }
```

Another is to use schema Boolean Safe Linear Search; we prefer the former as it avoids a Boolean variable.

**11.13** Because *all* elements in A[left..right] need to be examined.

**11.14** Yes, because NrLeft $\geqslant 2$ in the body of the for-loop.

**11.16**

```
function NumberOfInversions (var A : values;
                                 n : count) : count;
{ Returns the number of out-of-order pairs of elements in A[1..n]. }
  var
    i, j : index;
    answer : count;
begin { NumberOfInversions }
  answer := 0;
  for i := 1 to n - 1 do
    for j := i + 1 to n do
      if A[j] < A[i] then
        answer := answer + 1;
  NumberOfInversions := answer
end; { NumberOfInversions }
```

**11.18**

```
procedure reverse (var A : values;
                   left, right : index);
{ Reverses the order of the values in A[left..right]. }
{ Global subprogram: swap. }
```

```
  var
    d : 0..Maxint; { A[left + d], A[right – d] are to be swapped }
  begin { reverse }
   for d := 0 to (right – left – 1) div 2 do
     swap(A[left + d], A[right – d])
  end; { reverse }
```

Another solution may be given using a while-loop that increments **left** and decrements **right** in its body.

**11.19**
```
procedure ArraySwap (var V : values;
                             a, b, c : index);
{ Swaps the array sections V[a..b – 1] and V[b..c]. E.g. if }
{ a = 4, b = 7, c = 11, V[4..11] = (2, 4, 6, 8, 10, 12, 14, 16), }
{ after the swap V[4..11] =  (8, 10, 12, 14, 16, 2, 4, 6); }
{ assumes 1 <= a < b <= c <= MaxIndex. }
{ Global subprogram: reverse. }
begin { ArraySwap }
  reverse(V, a, b – 1);
  reverse(V, b, c);
  reverse(V, a, c);
end; { ArraySwap }
```

**11.20**
```
procedure PerfectShuffle (var OldDeck, NewDeck : deck);
{ Sets NewDeck by splitting OldDeck exactly in half and }
{ merging the cards, alternating between one half and the }
{ other; the first card should come from the second half. }
{ E.g. if NumberOfCards = 8 and OldDeck contains }
{ (c1, c2, c3, c4, c5, c6, c7, c8), then NewDeck should be }
{ set to (c5, c1, c6, c2, c7, c3, c8, c4). }
{ Global const: NumberOfCards. }
  var
    i : number;
begin { PerfectShuffle }
  for i := 1 to NumberOfCards div 2 do
    begin
      NewDeck[2 * i – 1] := OldDeck[NumberOfCards div 2 + i];
      NewDeck[2 * i] := OldDeck[i]
    end
end; { PerfectShuffle }
```

**11.22** The jobs are scheduled in input order. So the rest of the program can be tested before procedure **sort** is written.

# Chapter 12

**12.1** { Set total = sum of elements in A[1..n] }

```
total = 0.0;
{ Invariant: total = sum of elements in A[1..i – 1] }
for i := 1 to n do
  total := total + A[i]
```

The invariant applies just before the next value of i is compared to n.

**12.2** The invariant for Truncated Safe Linear Search is:

$a \leqslant v \leqslant b$, and $P(x)$ = false for $a \leqslant x < v$.

**12.3** Our version.

**12.4**

```
procedure split (var A : values;
                   n : index);
{ Rearranges A[1..n] so that the negative values precede the rest. }
{ Global subprogram: Swap. }
 var
  left, right : index;
begin { split }
 right := n;
 left := 1;
 { Invariant: A[1..left – 1] are negative, A[right + 1..n] are }
 { non-negative, 1 <= left, and  right <= n. }
 while right > left do
  if A[left] < 0 then
   left := left + 1
  else if A[right] >= 0 then
   right := right – 1
  else
   begin
    swap(A[left], A[right]);
    left := left + 1;
    right := right – 1
   end
end; { split }
```

**12.6** (a) A[$i$] $\leqslant$ A[$i$ + 1] for NrLeft $< i <$ n.

(b) A[$i$] $\leqslant$ A[$j$] if $1 \leqslant i \leqslant$ NrLeft $< j \leqslant$ n.

**12.8** Order logn, since a bounded number of operations is executed for each decimal digit, and n has order logn decimal digits.

**12.9** Order 1, i.e. constant.

**12.11** Let $n$ be the number of jobs in the input data.

(a) Order $n$, since each job is processed in a bounded number of operations.

(b) Order $n^2$ (in the worst-case), since the call of **sort** dominates the running time.

**12.12** Implement **sort** with a more efficient algorithm.

**12.13** Let $n$ be the number of elements in the array-section.
(a) Order $n$.
(b) Order $n^2$, since the elements may be shifted order $n$ places.

**12.14**
```
var
  increasing : Boolean;
{ Set k = maximum value such that A[1..k] are in non-
  decreasing order }
  k := 1;
  increasing := true;
  { Invariant: increasing = true iff A[1..k] are in non-decreasing
               order, and k <= n }
  while increasing and (k < n) do
    if A[k] <= A[k + 1] then
      k := k + 1
    else
      increasing := false
```

**12.17** (a) Yes.
(c) Order nlogn.

# Chapter 13

**13.1** (a)
```
if square[row, col] = Empty then
  square[row, col] := X
```

(b)
```
for row := 1 to 3 do
  for col := 1 to 3 do
    square[row, col] := Empty
```

**13.2** (a)
```
function CostOfStock (store : StoreNumber) : count;
{ Returns the total cost in cents of the stock held by the }
{ given store. Global var: cost. }
 var
  total : count;
  item : ItemType;
begin { CostOfStock }
 total := 0;
 for item := Barbie to Uzi do
  total := total + stock[item, store] * cost[item];
 CostOfStock := total
```

```
end; { CostOfStock }
```

(b)
```
{ Print the total cost of the stock held by each store }
  for store := 1 to NrStores do
    Writeln('Total cost of stock held by store ', store : 1,
            ' is $', CostOfStock(store) / 100.0 : 1 : 2)
```

**13.3** No, because temp and stock[cube] do not have the same type. The following changes permit it:

```
type
  ItemStock = array[StoreNumber] of count;
    inventory = array[ItemType] of ItemStock;
      var
        temp : ItemStock;
```

**13.4** $(b - a + 1) \times (d - c + 1)$ if $a \leqslant b$ and $c \leqslant d$; otherwise 0.

**13.6**
```
procedure transpose (var A : matrix; n : index);
{ Revolves A[1..n, 1..n] 180 degrees round its major diagonal; }
{ i.e. the i'th row becomes the i'th column, and vice versa. }
{ Global subprogram: swap. }
  var
    i, j : index; { A[i, j] and A[j, i] are to be swapped }
begin { transpose }
  for i := 2 to n do
    for j := 1 to i - 1 do
      swap(A[i, j], A[j, i])
end; { transpose }
```

**13.7**
```
function symmetric (var A : matrix;
                        n : index) : Boolean;
{ Returns true if A[1..n, 1..n] is symmetric, otherwise false. }
  var
    i : 1..Maxint;
    j : index; { in 1..i - 1 }
    OK : Boolean; { true iff all elements before A[i, j] (in row-major }
                  { order) are equal to their transposed images. }
begin { symmetric }
  i := 2;
  j := 1;
  OK := true;
  while OK and (i <= n) do
    if A[i, j] <> A[j, i] then
      OK := false
    else
      if j < i - 1 then
        j := j + 1
      else
```

```
      begin { Set (i, j) to first element in next row }
        i := i + 1;
        j := 1
      end;
  symmetric := OK
end; { symmetric }
```

**13.10**

```
procedure VFlip (var A : matrix;
                     rows : RowIndex;
                     cols : ColIndex);
{ Revolves A[1..rows, 1..cols] 180 degrees round its central }
{ vertical axis. I.e. A[r, 1] is swapped with A[r, cols], }
{ A[r, 2] is swapped with A[r, cols – 1], etc. }
{ Global subprogram: swap. }
  var
    row : RowIndex;
    col : ColIndex;
begin { VFlip }
  for row := 1 to rows do
    for col := 1 to cols div 2 do
      swap(A[row, col], A[row, cols + 1 – col])
end; { VFlip }
```

**13.11**

```
procedure ScreenToGrid (x, y : integer;
                        var row : ExtendedIndex1;
                        var col : ExtendedIndex2);
{ If screen position (x, y) is in grid, sets (row, col) to }
{ cell containing (x, y); otherwise sets row and col to 0. }
{ Global consts: Offset1, Offset2, MaxIndex1, MaxIndex2, Gap. }
begin { ScreenToGrid }
  if (Offset2 <= x) and (x < Offset2 + MaxIndex2 * Gap) and
     (Offset1 <= y) and (y < Offset1 + MaxIndex1 * Gap) then
    begin
      row := (y – Offset1) div Gap + 1;
      col := (x – Offset2) div Gap + 1
    end
  else
    begin
      row := 0;
      col := 0
    end
end; { ScreenToGrid }
```

**13.14** Simply increase NrShades to 5, change the comments for variable shade and procedure SetUp to remove the proviso about white being added, and change the body of procedure SetUp.

# Chapter 14

**14.1** (a) ' '; (b) 't'; (c) undefined.

**14.2** (a) '#'; (b) undefined.

**14.5** The rest of the current input line is stored in line[1], and the next two input lines are stored in line[2] and line[3] respectively.

**14.6**
```
procedure append (var extra, f : text);
{ Appends extra to f; assumes f is being written, extra has }
{ already been associated with an external file if necessary, }
{ and no line of extra contains more than 255 characters. }
  var
    line : string; { a line of extra }
begin { append }
  Reset(extra);
  while not eof(extra) do
    begin
      Readln(extra, line);
      Writeln(f, line)
    end
end; { append }
```

**14.7** Process Lines, hopefully.

**14.8** (a)
```
procedure PrintCycle (s : str100);
{ Prints each of the length(s) cyclic permutations of s, }
{ one per line. }
  var
    i : 0..100;
begin { PrintCycle }
  for i := 1 to length(s) do
    Writeln(copy(s, i, length(s)), copy(s, 1, i – 1))
end; { PrintCycle }
```

(b)
```
function CyclicPermutation (s1, s2 : str100) : Boolean;
{ Returns true iff s1 is a cyclic permutation of s2. }
begin { CyclicPermutation }
  CyclicPermutation := (length(s1) = length(s2)) and
                       (pos(s1, concat(s2, s2)) <> 0)
end; { CyclicPermutation }
```

**14.10**
```
function ShortForm (name : string) : string;
{ Assumes that name consists of 1 or more first names followed }
{ by a surname, with successive names separated by one }
{ space. Returns a name consisting of the initial letters of the }
{ first names, in order, each followed by a period, then a space }
```

```
{ and the surname; e.g. if name = 'Martin Luther King', then }
{ 'M.L. King' should be returned. }
 var
  initials : string; { initials of first names deleted from name }
  i : StringIndex; { = pos(' ', name) }
begin { ShortForm }
 initials := '';
 i := pos(' ', name);
 while i <> 0 do
  begin
   initials := concat(initials, copy(name, 1, 1), '.');
   delete(name, 1, i);
   i := pos(' ', name)
  end;
 ShortForm := concat(initials, ' ', name)
end; { ShortForm }
```

**14.13**

```
procedure compress (var s : string);
{ Assumes s is a string of words separated by 1 or }
{ more blanks; removes blanks so that successive words }
{ are separated by one space. }
 var
  t : string;
  i : StringIndex;
begin { compress }
 t := '';
 i := pos('  ', s); { N.B.: 2 spaces }
 { Invariant: as given }
 while i <> 0 do
  begin
   t := concat(t, copy(s, 1, i));
   while s[i] = ' ' do
    i := i + 1;
   delete(s, 1, i – 1);
   i := pos('  ', s) { NB: 2 spaces }
  end;
 s := concat(t, s)
end; { compress }
```

**14.17** Replace:

```
FindField('Path: ', PathToMe)
```

with:

```
GetPath(PathToMe)
```

where GetPath is declared as follows:

```
procedure GetPath (var path : string);
```

```
{ Reads lines from mailbox until one starting with 'Path' }
{ is found; if next character is ': ', sets path to rest of }
{ line; otherwise assumes '(n): ' follows, and path is }
{ assembled from rest of line and next n – 1 lines. }
{ Global var: mailbox. }
{ Global subprogram: FindField. }
 var
  PathInfo, { rest of line starting with 'Path' }
  line : str; { line of received message }
  LinesInPath, i : count;
  ch : char;
begin { GetPath }
FindField('Path', PathInfo);
if PathInfo[1] = ':' then
 path := copy(PathInfo, 3, length(PathInfo))
else
 begin { assume PathInfo = (n): first part of path }
  ReadString(PathInfo, ch, LinesInPath, ch, ch, ch, path);
  for i := 1 to LinesInPath – 1 do
   begin
    Read(mailbox, line);
    insert(line, path, length(path) + 1)
   end
 end
end; { GetPath }
```

# Chapter 15

**15.3** (a)

```
type
 time = record
  hour : 0..23;
  minute, second : 0..59
 end
```

(b)

```
procedure tick (var t : time);
{ Advances t by 1 second. }
begin { tick }
 with t do
  begin
   if second < 59 then
    second := second + 1
   else
    begin { advance to next minute }
     second := 0;
     if minute < 59 then
      minute := minute + 1
     else
      begin { advance to next hour }
       minute := 0;
       hour := (hour + 1) mod 24
```

```
          end
        end
      end { with t }
    end; { tick }
```

**15.5**

```
procedure GetMousePt (var pt : Point);
{ Sets pt to the position of the mouse. }
begin { GetMousePt }
 GetMouse(pt.h, pt.v)
end; { GetMousePt }
```

**15.6**

```
type
  bar = record
      b : array['a'..'z'] of integer;
      ...
    end;
  foo = array[1..10] of bar;
  T = record
      a : foo;
      c : 'a'..'z';
      d : 1..10;
    end;
var
  x, y : T;
```

**15.9**

```
function relationship (var s1, s2 : string) : relation;
{ If s1 and s2 are identical, returns Equal; otherwise returns }
{ LessThan if s1 precedes s2 in dictionary order, or }
{ GreaterThan if vice versa. }
  var
    MinLength : StringLength; { min of length(s1), length(s2) }
    i : 1..Maxint; { in 1..MaxStringLength + 1 }
    same : Boolean;
 begin { relationship }
 { Set MinLength }
  if s1.length <= s2.length then
    MinLength := s1. length
  else
    MinLength := s2. length;
 { Set i = first index at which s1 and s2 differ, or MinLength + 1 }
 { if all existing characters in matching positions are identical }
  same := true;
  i := 1;
  while same and (i <= MinLength) do
    if s1.ch[i] = s2.ch[i] then
      i := i + 1
    else
      same := false;
```

```
{ Return result }
  if i <= MinLength then
    if s1.ch[i] < s2.ch[i] then
      relationship := LessThan
    else
      relationship := GreaterThan
  else
    if s1.length < s2.length then
      relationship := LessThan
    else if s1.length > s2.length then
      relationship := GreaterThan
    else
      relationship := Equal
end; { relationship }
```

**15.10** See the definitions of the abstract data types stack and Binary-SearchTree in Chapter 20 for stylistic guidelines.

(a)
```
type
  complex = record
    re, im : real { real & imaginary parts }
  end;
```

**15.12**
```
procedure DragARect (DownAt : Point;
                     var r : Rect);
{ Assumes mouse button was pressed at location DownAt, and }
{ is still down; repeatedly draws and erases the frame of the }
{ rectangle with top-left corner at DownAt and bottom-right }
{ corner at current mouse position, until the mouse button is }
{ released. Only the last rectangle's frame remains; }
{ its coordinates are returned in r. }
begin { DragARect }
  with r do
    begin
      r.topLeft := DownAt;
      GetMouse(r.botRight.h, r.botRight.v);
      FrameRect(r);
      while button do
        begin
        { Erase frame of old rectangle }
          PenPat(white);
          FrameRect(r);
        { Define and draw frame of new rectangle }
          GetMouse(r.botRight.h, r.botRight.v);
          PenPat(black);
          FrameRect(r)
        end
    end { with r }
end; { DragARect }
```

# Chapter 16

**16.1** 1.

**16.2**
```
procedure CreateDiffFile (var ValuesFile : FileOfValues;
                          var GapsFile : FileOfGaps);
{ Sets i'th component of GapsFile to the difference between }
{ the (i + 1)'th and i'th components of ValuesFile; }
{ assumes values in ValuesFile are non-decreasing. }
  var
    old, new : 0..MaxValue; { successive components of }
                            { ValuesFile }
 begin { CreateDiffFile }
  Reset(ValuesFile);
  Rewrite(GapsFile);
  if not eof(ValuesFile) then
    Read(ValuesFile, old);
  while not eof(ValuesFile) do
    begin
      Read(ValuesFile, new);
      Write(GapsFile, new – old);
      old := new
    end
 end; { CreateDiffFile }
```

**16.5** We show the state of the file *after* execution of each statement.

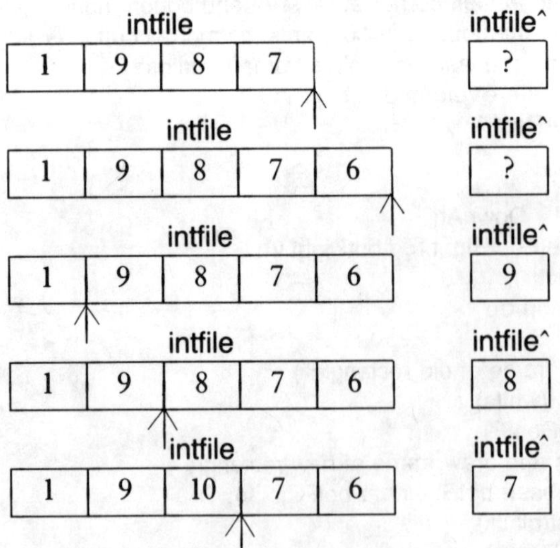


**16.6**
```
{ Add 1 to the n'th component of intfile }
seek(intfile, n – 1);
Write(intfile, intfile^ + 1)
```

**16.7** Maxint = 32767.

**16.8** (a) Because ErrorPosFile^ will be undefined for the last error message.

(b) Appending a component to ErrorPosFile giving the file-position at the *end* of the last error-message in ErrorFile.

# Chapter 17

**17.1** (a) $2^6 = 64$; (b) $2^5 = 32$; (c) $2^7 - 2^5 = 96$.

**17.2** (a) [2, 3, 4]; (b) []; (c) [–2, –1, 0, 1, 2]; (d) [2, 4, 6]; (e) ['0', '1', '2']; (f) ['i', 'j'].

**17.4** (a) [0, 2, 4, 5, 6, 8]; (b) [5]; (c) [0, 4, 6]; (d) [2, 8].

**17.5** (a) true; (b) true; (c) false; (d) false; (e) true; (f) true.

**17.6** (a) GetTextStyle(TypeFace)

(b)
```
{ Add underline to the current text style if it is not already }
{ present }
 GetTextStyle(TypeFace);
 TextFace(TypeFace + [underline])
```

(c)
```
{ Remove extend and condense from the current text style }
{ if both are present in it }
 GetTextStyle(TypeFace);
 if [extend, condense] <= TypeFace then
   TextFace(TypeFace – [extend, condense])
```

**17.7** IsPangram := letters = ['a'..'z']

**17.8** (a) ch **in** ['Y', 'y']
(b) ch **in** ['0'..'9']
(c) ch **in** ['0'..chr(ord('0') + b – 1)]
(d) ord(ch) **in** [0..31, 127]

**17.11**
```
const
  LastRow = ... ;
type
  RowNumber = 1..LastRow;
  RowAssignment = set of 'A'..'F';
  assignment = array[RowNumber] of RowAssignment;
var
```

```
assigned : assignment; { assigned[r] is set of assigned seats in }
                       { row r }
```

**17.13** 
```
type
  BinaryNumber = array[0..MaxExponent] of Boolean;
  { the i'th element is true iff bit i is 1 }
```

**17.14** Because the result-type of a Pascal function cannot be a set-type.

**17.16** First, because it is unlikely that the winning invariant is true initially.

**17.17** Yes. For example, suppose the non-empty piles have sizes 7, 4, and 5. Then taking 6 from the pile of 7, 2 from the pile of 4, or 2 from the pile of 5 makes the winning invariant true.

**17.18** Take 5 from the pile of 8.

# Chapter 18

**18.2** (a)
```
function factorial (n : count) : count;
{ Returns n! }
begin { factorial }
  if n = 0 then
    factorial := 1
  else
    factorial := n * factorial(n - 1)
end; { factorial }
```

(b)
```
function factorial (n : count) : count;
{ Returns n! }
  var
    i : 0..Maxint;
    product : 1..Maxint;
begin { factorial }
  product := 1;
  for i := 1 to n do
    product := i * product;
  factorial := product
end; { factorial }
```

(c) The time-complexity of each algorithm is order n. The space-complexity of the recursive algorithm is order n; that of the other is constant (order 1). These measures are not very meaningful in this situation, because the result of the function grows very rapidly.

**18.3**
```
function reverse (s : string) : string;
{ Returns the reverse of s. }
begin { reverse }
  if length(s) <= 1 then
    reverse := s
  else
    reverse := concat(reverse(omit(s, 1, 1)), copy(s, 1, 1))
end; { reverse }
```

**18.4**
```
function power (x : real;
                n : count) : real;
{ Returns x to the power n. }
begin { power }
  if n = 0 then
    power := 1
  else if odd(n) then
    power := x * power(x, n – 1)
  else
    power := sqr(power(x, n div 2))
end; { power }
```

**18.6**
```
function gcd (x, y : count) : count;
{ Returns the greatest common divisor of x and y; }
{ assumes x and y are not both 0. }
begin { gcd }
  if x = 0 then
    gcd := y
  else
    gcd := gcd(y mod x, x)
end; { gcd }
```

**18.9**
```
function surrounds (x, y : BoxNr) : Boolean;
{ Returns true iff box x contains box y, not necessarily }
{ directly; assumes x, y <= NrBoxes. }
{ Global vars: NrBoxes, around. }
begin { surrounds }
  if around[y] = 0 then
    surrounds := false
  else if around[y] = x then
    surrounds := true
  else
    surrounds := surrounds(x, around[y])
end; { surrounds }
```

**18.11** N.B. Procedure try directly references the parameter n and the local variables digit, number, and sum of procedure powers. Parameters could be added to avoid this, but there is little point because try is only meant to be used by powers.

```
const
  MaxNrDigits = ... ; { maximum number of decimal digits }
type
  size = 1..MaxNrDigits;
  count = 0..Maxint;
procedure powers (n : size);
{ Prints all non-negative numbers with n decimal digits that are }
{ equal to the sum of the n'th powers of their decimal digits. }
  var
  digit : array[0..MaxNrDigits] of 0..9;
   { digit[i] = chosen i'th digit (multiple of power(10, i), }
   { i = 0, 1, ... , n – 1 }
  number : count; { number corresponding to chosen digits }
                   { N.B. without zeros for unchosen digits }
  sum : count; { sum of n'th powers of chosen digits }

 procedure try (m : count); { m in 0..n – 1 }
 { Assumes digit[m + 1..n – 1] and corresponding number and }
 { sum defined; prints all numbers with these digits fixed that }
 { are equal to the sum of the n'th powers of their digits. }
 { Global vars: n, digit, number, sum. }
 { Global subprogram: power. }
  var
   d : 0..9; { m'th digit of trial number }
   dpower : count; { = d to the power n }
 begin { try }
  for d := 0 to 9 do
   begin
    digit[m] := d;
    number := 10 * number + d;
    dpower := power(d, n);
    sum := sum + dpower;
    if m = 0 then
     begin
      if sum = number then
       Writeln(number)
     end
    else
     try(m – 1);
    sum := sum – dpower;
    number := number div 10
   end
 end; { try }

begin { powers }
 sum := 0;
 number := 0;
 try(n – 1)
end; { powers }
```

**18.13** We give a complete program.

```
program HilbertCurve;
{ Draws a Hilbert curve of order Order. }
 const
  Order = 4; { of Hilbert curve }
  TopAt = 20; { Top-left point of curve ... }
  LeftAt = 20; { ... is at (LeftAt,TopAt) }
 type
  direction = (up, down, right, left); { relative to screen }

  UnitMoves = array[direction] of Point;
 var
  vector : UnitMoves; { vector[d] is change to position }
                      { to move 1 unit in direction d }
 procedure SetUp (var v : UnitMoves);
 { Sets v[d] = change to position to move 1 unit in direction d. }
  const
   Unit = 4; { length of unit move (unit vector) }
 begin { SetUp }
  SetPt(v[up], 0, –Unit);
  SetPt(v[down], 0, Unit);
  SetPt(v[right], Unit, 0);
  SetPt(v[left], –Unit, 0)
 end; { SetUp }

 procedure Hilbert (d1, d2, d3, dOther : direction;
                    i : integer);
 { Draws i'th order Hilbert curve starting at current position; }
 { leaves pen at end of curve; d1 is direction of 1st connecting }
 { move; sim. for d2, d3; dOther is direction other than d1-3; i.e. }
 { 1st order curve is drawn with: move d1, move d2, move d3. }

  procedure move (dir : direction);
  { Moves and draws line one unit in given direction. }
  { Global variable: vector. }
  begin { move }
   Line(vector[dir].h, vector[dir].v);
  end; { move }

 begin { Hilbert }
  if i > 0 then
   begin
    Hilbert(d2, d1, dOther, d3, i – 1);
    move(d1);
    Hilbert(d1, d2, d3, dOther, i – 1);
    move(d2);
    Hilbert(d1, d2, d3, dOther, i – 1);
    move(d3);
    Hilbert(dOther, d3, d2, d1, i – 1)
```

```
        end
      end; { Hilbert }

    begin { HilbertCurve }
      SetUp(vector);
      MoveTo(LeftAt, TopAt);
      Hilbert(right, down, left, up, Order)
    end. { HilbertCurve }
```

# Chapter 19

**19.1** The value Maxint is assigned to i.

**19.2** (9.9,0) + (9.9,0) / (2.0,0) = (2.0,1) / (2.0,0) = (1.0,1), so the result is 1.0E1 (ten).

**19.3** Yes, because underflow can be avoided by keeping an unnormalized representation. An example is x = 1E40. The phenomenon does not occur the other way around.

**19.4** Solution (II) is preferable because it avoids the accumulated roundoff errors occurring in (I).

**19.5** The successive values of epsilon are (1.0,0), (1.0,–1), (1.0,–2), whereupon the loop stops.

**19.6** The value of x eventually reaches (1.0,2), representing one hundred, and thereafter does not change.

**19.9**
```
{ Set RightAngled to true if the triangle is right-angled, }
{ otherwise false }
 RightAngled := abs((sqr(a) + sqr(b)) / sqr(c) – 1.0) <= tolerance
```

**19.10** $x_2$.

# Chapter 20

**20.1** See the solution to Exercise 20.2.

**20.2** A pointer to Exercise 20.2.

**20.3** (a)

p1 [ —→ ] → ['a']     p2 [ —→ ] → ['a']

(b) false.

(c) true.

**20.4** In Figure 20.5, p1^ amd p2^ are different names for the same dynamic variable. Similarly with **head^** and **tail^** in Figure 20.6, and head^.ch and tail^.ch also in Figure 20.6.

**20.5** (a) 'n'; (b) 'd'.

**20.7** It inserts the component correctly, but does not update the actual variable parameter corresponding to **cursor**.

**20.8**
```
function present (ch : char;
                  head : ComponentPtr) : Boolean;
{ Returns true if ch is present in a component of the chain }
{ pointed to by head; otherwise returns false. }
 var
  cursor : ComponentPtr;
  found : Boolean;
begin { present }
 cursor := head;
 found := false;
 while not found and (cursor <> nil) do
  if cursor^.ch = ch then
   found := true
  else
   cursor := cursor^.link;
 present := found
end; { present }
```

**20.11**
```
procedure DeleteNext (cursor : ComponentPtr);
{ Assumes cursor points to a component in a linked-list with a }
{ dummy first component; deletes the following component }
{ (which is assumed to exist). }
 var
  unwanted : ComponentPtr; { pointer to unwanted component }
begin { DeleteNext }
 unwanted := cursor^.link;
 cursor^.link := unwanted^.link;
 dispose(unwanted)
end; { DeleteNext }
```

**20.13** This implementation makes **s** undefined (unless it is initially **nil**).

```
procedure destroy (var s : stack);
{ Disposes of s, leaving s undefined. }
 var
  unwanted : StackItemPtr; { points to a component of s }
begin { destroy }
 if s <> nil then
  begin
```

```
    while s^.next <> nil do
      begin
        unwanted := s;
        s := s^.next;
        dispose(unwanted)
      end;
    dispose(s)
  end
end; { destroy }
```

**20.16** The tree consisting of only the leftmost branch of the tree in Figure 20.11.

**20.17** The comment is the specification for the user of the abstract data type, not the implementor.

**20.19**

```
function present (val : integer;
                  t : BinarySearchTree) : Boolean;
{ Returns true if val is present in t; otherwise returns false. }
begin { present }
  if t = nil then
    present := false
  else if t^.value = val then
    present := true
  else if val < t^.value then
    present := present(val, t^.left)
  else
    present := present(val, t^.right)
end; { present }
```

**20.21**

```
type
  DepthValue = -1..Maxint;
function depth (t : BinarySearchTree) : DepthValue;
{ Returns the depth of t if t is non-empty, otherwise -1. }
  var
    DepthLeft, DepthRight : DepthValue; { depths of subtrees of t }
begin { depth }
  if empty(t) then
    depth := -1
  else
    begin
      DepthLeft := depth(left(t));
      DepthRight := depth(right(t));
      if DepthLeft > DepthRight then
        depth := 1 + DepthLeft
      else
        depth := 1 + DepthRight
    end
end; { depth }
```

# INDEX

Syntactic terms are printed in *italics*; their associated page numbers refer to their definitions, the last of which is the final version; a page number in italics refers to a syntax diagram. Reserved words are printed in **boldface Helvetica**, and identifiers in Helvetica.